Money and Capital Markets

Third Edition

Money and Capital Markets

Third Edition

Miles Livingston
University of Florida

First published 1996

Blackwell Publishers, Inc.
238 Main Street
Cambridge, Massachusetts 02142

Blackwell Publishers Ltd.
108 Cowley Road
Oxford OX4 1JF
UK

Library of Congress Cataloging-in-Publication Data
  Money and capital markets / Miles Livingston – 3rd ed.
    p. cm.
  Includes bibliographical references and index.
  ISBN 1-55786-884-0 (pbk. : alk. paper)
  1. Money market. 2. Capital market. 3. Financial instruments. 4. Capital market—Problems, exercises, etc.—Computer programs. 5. Financial instruments—Problems, exercises, etc.— Computer programs. I. Title.
  HG226.L577   1996
  332'.0412—dc20   95-50937
                                                                                         CIP

British Library Cataloguing in Publication Data

A CIP catalogue record for this book is available from the British Library.
Typeset by AM Marketing

Typeset in Times Roman in 11 pt. by AM Marketing

Printed in the United States of America

This book is printed on acid-free paper

Dedication

To: Seymour
    Genie
    Vicki
    Valerie
    Wendy

Preface

This text presents a concise, but comprehensive coverage of money and capital markets. The first eight chapters of the book cover the major theories of the determinants of interest rates and the major public and private financial institutions in the economy, including the Federal Reserve, the U.S. Treasury, commercial banks, thrifts, security brokers and dealers, and investment bankers. Chapters nine through nineteen explain the workings of the major types of financial instruments, including government bonds, corporate bonds, mortgages, and equities. Chapters twenty through twenty-three focus upon derivative securities, namely, put and call options, futures contracts, and swaps.

Unique Features

There are two main differences which distinguish the Third Edition from other books on money and capital markets. In order to emphasize the factors determining the prices and risks of financial instruments, descriptive information about institutions is kept to a minimum in *Money & Capital Markets*. This allows instructors and students to develop a generalized framework for valuing particular types of securities and analyzing the operations of financial institutions. In *Money & Capital Markets* the links between different types of securities are shown through risk-free arbitrage. This provides a common framework for linking different types of bonds and for connecting futures markets with spot markets. Students will be able to apply this framework to other examples in their future employment and personal investments.

Using the Text

The prerequisites for *Money & Capital Markets* are an introductory finance course and some facility with algebra. These prerequisites combined with the text's comprehensive coverage allow the book to be used in three ways. First, it can be used as a primary textbook in courses covering the workings of money and capital markets. I have been using the book this way at the University of Florida. Next, the self-contained nature of most chapters makes the book an excellent candidate for a supplementary text in courses in investments and the management of financial institutions. Third, because the text incorporates a combination of theory and practice, it is particularly suitable for use in training programs at financial institutions.

Changes in the Third Edition

This third edition contains a number of improvements that have been suggested by my students at the University of Florida and by faculty using the earlier editions at other universities. In response to their comments, most institutional information has been updated, including the coverage of U.S. Treasury auctions, investment banking, brokers and dealers, bank regulation, and mortgage markets. The end of chapter problems and questions have been extensively revised to challenge the student to think critically about the material in the text by applying the analytical tools from the text to new situations. In order to make the chapters on spot and forward interest rates, coupon-bearing bonds, bond investment risks, and futures contracts more user-friendly, the text has been rewritten and some of the more technical material has been moved to the appendices.

Acknowledgements

Many people have provided comments which have improved the third edition. I would like to thank my students at the University of Florida for their helpful suggestions. Special thanks are due to the following faculty adopters of the earlier edition: Rick Le Compte, Joel Houston, Andy Naranjo, Stuart Williams. Finally, I would like to thank the production staff at Blackwell Publishers for their help.

Contents

1

Introduction

Overview

This book focuses on financial markets and instruments. These topics have increased in importance in recent years because of several major trends, including increased variability of interest rates, the growth of the amount of debt, the proliferation of debt instruments, and changing regulation of financial institutions. These trends are the focus of this chapter.

Increased Variability of Interest Rates

During the Korean War in the early 1950s, the Federal Reserve, the central bank of the United States, kept interest rates at a constant level to make it easier for the U.S. government to borrow money to finance the war. When the Korean War ended in 1953, the Federal Reserve began to allow market forces to set interest rates. Interest rates have risen considerably from the Korean War levels of 1.5 percent for short-term rates and 2.5 percent for long-term interest rates. Several factors have tended to push interest rates higher, including high inflation rates and large federal budget deficits. In addition, interest rates have become highly variable. The increase in interest rate levels and the great variability of rates are clearly evident in figure 1.1, which shows the behavior of short-term and long-term interest rates over time.

The high levels and the increased variability of interest rates have significantly increased the importance of debt financing decisions to both borrowers and lenders. For all the participants in the financial markets (i.e., households, businesses, government, and financial institutions), the stakes in the interest rate game have increased. In an environment of high and

Figure 1.1   Interest Rates Since 1947

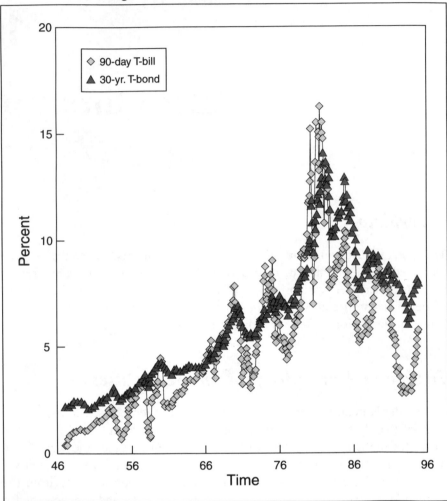

variable interest rates, two interrelated decisions have become important to borrowers and lenders: (1) When is the best time to issue debt? (2) Should short-term or long-term debt be used? The risk of making errors in these decisions has been called **interest rate risk**, a topic playing a central role in this book.

The best strategies for borrowers are shown in table 1.1. The cost of errors can be considerable. For example, suppose a borrower believes current interest rates are high and are likely to drop in the future. The best strategy is to borrow short term and roll over the loan in the future at a lower interest rate. However, if interest rates rise considerably, the loan must be refinanced

Table 1.1   Strategies of Borrowers

Borrower's Forecast	Best Strategy	What Can Go Wrong
High current interest rates	Borrow short term and roll over loan.	Interest rates may rise and new loan is at higher interest rate.
Low current interest rates	Borrow long term, locking-in the interest rate.	Interest rates may fall and the opportunity to borrow at lower rates is lost.

at much higher rates and the potential consequences for the borrower may be catastrophic.

The best strategies for lenders are shown in table 1.2. Suppose the lender thinks current interest rates are low and will rise in the future. The best strategy is to lend short term and roll over the loan at future higher interest rates. If the forecast is wrong and interest rates fall, the loan must be rolled over at a lower interest rate.

In an informationally efficient market, all current information is reflected in current interest rates, suggesting that changes in interest rates in the future are essentially random. In an efficient market, there is no way of consistently knowing whether today's rates are high or low relative to future interest rates. Since considerable evidence shows interest rates to be essentially random and unpredictable, there is no easy way to implement the timing strategies described here.

Table 1.2   Strategies of Lenders

Lender's Forecast	Best Strategy	What Can Go Wrong
High current interest rates	Lend long term and lock-in high interest rate.	Interest rates may rise and opportunity to lend at higher interest rate is lost.
Low current interest rates	Lend short term.	Interest rates may fall and the loan must be rolled over at a lower interest rate.

Growth of Debt

The debt obligations of households, businesses, and government are individually large and have been growing at rapid rates in recent years. Because of this increase in the size of the debt market, events in the debt market can have wide-ranging impacts upon the entire economic system.

To provide some indication of the size of the debt markets, figure 1.2 shows absolute levels of debt and debt as a percentage of Gross National Product (GNP). The categories of debt are federal government debt, tax-exempt debt issued by state and local governments, corporate bonds, mortgage debt, and consumer credit.

Several important things are revealed by figure 1.2. First, the absolute size of these debts is huge, especially U.S. government debt and mortgage debt. Second, since 1980, federal government debt and mortgage debt have not only been increasing in absolute size, but also as a percentage of GNP.

Growth in debt raises the public policy question about whether the amount of debt is too large for each individual sector or for the aggregate

Figure 1.2   Debt as a Percent of GNP (1966–93)

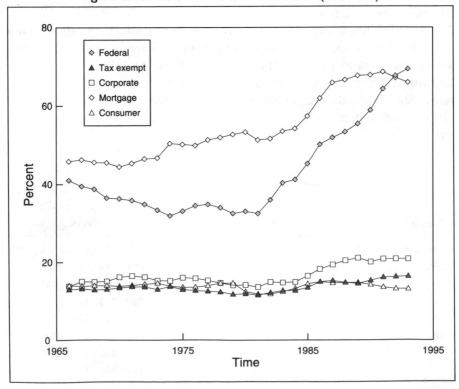

of all these economic sectors. Phrased differently, is the debt burden too large? The **debt burden** can be defined as the amount of debt relative to the ability to pay off that debt. There is a considerable debate about the size of debt burdens for consumers, businesses, financial institutions, and governments because the correct way of measuring debt burdens is not completely clear. Debt burdens might appear high using one measure, but considerably lower using another measure. The only foolproof test of debt burdens is "ex post." If the debt is actually paid, in perfect hindsight the burden was not too high.

Debt burdens typically are measured by a ratio, indicating the amount of debt relative to a measure of the ability to pay. The numerator can be the par value of debt or interest payments. The denominator can be income or assets. Thus, there are four basic measures of debt burdens:

1. (par value)/income
2. (par value)/assets
3. (interest payments)/income
4. (interest payments)/assets

To confound the measurement problem even more, there can be different ways of measuring income, and assets can be measured by book or market values.

It is a truism that the debts of one person or economic unit are the assets of another. If all the debts are added together, the total debt must equal total assets. From this point, it is tempting to argue that debt does not matter, since in the aggregate, debt and assets net to zero.

However, the total amount of debt may matter for three reasons. First, sizable numbers of defaults on debt obligations may have serious and widespread economic consequences. For example, if a major corporation defaults on its debt obligations and goes bankrupt, the repercussions might include a large increase in unemployment, both in some local areas and perhaps nationwide. Second, international debts may have a considerable impact upon currency exchange rates, with negative consequences for the production of goods and services. For example, large borrowing by the U.S. from other countries results in large purchases of U.S. dollars and an increase in the exchange rate. In turn, the higher exchange rate reduces the prices of imports and raises the prices of exports. The net result is a reduction in production and employment in the U.S. Third, the debt burdens of governmental units are also of concern. Historically, governments with huge debts have tended to resort to inflationary policies to pay off the debt with dollars of reduced real value. Thus, there is cause for concern over the debt burdens of economic units.

Proliferation of Debt Instruments

Since the mid-1970s, all security markets have been flooded with a deluge of new instruments that increase the choices available to borrowers and lenders. This trend is especially strong in the debt markets. Several examples of new debt instruments are given next. The driving force behind this growth in new instruments has been the increased variability of interest rates. The new instruments allow borrowers and lenders to shift some of the risk of changing interest rates to someone else.

Perhaps the most important variety of new instrument is the **variable rate loan**. These loans have interest rates that are tied to a short-term interest rate such as the prime interest rate or the Treasury bill rate. In the past, fixed-rate loans were the norm. With a fixed-rate loan, the interest rate is set over the entire life of the loan. The lending bank typically has to refinance this loan over its life. For example, if a 7 percent loan is for one year, the interest rate is fixed for one year to the borrower, but the bank may have to finance this loan with deposits whose rates vary as market conditions change. Initially, deposits may cost the bank 5.5 percent for a profit margin of 1.5 percent. But, if the interest rate on deposits jumps to 8 percent, the bank takes a loss on this position. Thus, with fixed-rate loans, the lender bears the risk that interest rates on deposits will increase.

In contrast, with a variable-rate loan, the borrower bears the interest rate risk. Thus, a commercial bank can shift interest rate risk to borrowers by making variable-rate loans. In an environment with highly variable interest rates, variable-rate loans allow commercial banks to reduce their exposure to changing interest rates. The bank can pass on the interest rate risk to its borrowers.

A second major innovation in the marketplace is the expansion of financial futures contracts for debt instruments. **Financial futures contracts** allow security holders, such as underwriters, to protect their net positions against rising interest rates. Underwriters, who market initial offerings of securities to the public, would find it much more difficult to operate in a world of highly variable interest rates without futures contracts.

A third innovation has been the expansion of markets for options contracts on underlying securities and on futures contracts. **Options** allow investors to protect themselves from unfavorable market price changes.

A fourth type of innovative instrument is the so-called **securitized loan**. In the past, commercial banks and thrifts made many mortgage loans, which the banks held for the duration of the mortgages. In recent years, many mortgage loans have been sold in the open market to investors as part of a pool of mortgages. The buyers get a **security**, which is a claim on the pool. This technique allows a bank to pass on the interest rate risk to the buyer of the security. The bank effectively takes on the role of intermediary by matching up the borrower with the lender or security buyer. After initiating the mortgage, the bank is essentially out of the picture, except for channeling the interest payments between the parties. Securitization has expanded to nonmortgage instruments as well.

A fifth type of innovative instrument is the original issue high yield or "junk" bond. **Junk bond** is a trade name for a low-quality bond with a high risk of default. In the past, most bonds were of relatively high quality when they were originally issued. If the firm fell upon hard times, the bond might become a junk bond. In recent years, a large number of bonds have been issued with very low credit ratings and high default risk. Many of the original issue bonds result from corporate takeovers. The growth of these original issue junk bonds has significantly altered the composition of the corporate bond market. On the one hand, the growth of the original issue junk bond market has opened up the capital market to a wider group of borrowers, who would have been cut out of the market under older standards. On the other hand, default risk is an increasingly real prospect for many corporate bonds today, requiring much greater care on the part of bond investors. In a serious recession, default rates on junk bonds can be expected to be high.

Swaps are a sixth type of financial innovation. A **swap** is an exchange of obligations by two parties. For interest rate swaps, one company with a fixed-rate debt exchanges this debt for another company's variable-rate debt. Each company improves its position. In general, swap dealers serve as intermediaries, exchanging variable-rate and fixed-rate debt for their own account.

Changing Regulation of Financial Institutions

Historically, financial institutions such as commercial banks, thrifts, pension funds, insurance companies, and security dealers have been important participants in the debt markets. These institutions play a valuable economic role in expediting the transfer of savings to ultimate investors in physical assets. There is a widely held view that financial intermediaries play a fiduciary role, meaning that financial intermediaries are perceived to be trustees of funds, not merely borrowers of funds. As an example, depositors in commercial banks are typically not perceived as creditors of the bank; the bank is usually viewed as a guardian of the depositors' funds. Because of their fiduciary role, financial intermediaries are regulated by the government.

For example, commercial banks have been regulated in several ways. Entry into banking is restricted to attain desirable levels of competition in the banking industry. Banks are examined by the regulatory authorities to ensure sound lending policies. Restrictions upon the amount of financial leverage are imposed on banks to control the risk of bank failure. Until recently, limits were placed on bank interest rates. To preserve confidence in the banking system, deposit insurance was instituted by the government. Restrictions have been placed upon nonbanking activities.

Beginning in the 1970s, the higher level and variability of interest rates caused many problems for commercial banks. Historically, the interest rates that banks were allowed to pay on deposits, their major source of funds, were closely regulated. As interest rates rose during the 1970s, market interest rates began to exceed the regulated interest rate ceilings. This meant that banks were unable to raise sufficient funds through deposits. As an example, if the deposit ceiling was 5 percent and the market interest rate was 6 percent, depositors with sizable amounts of money would find it to their advantage to shift their funds out of banks to earn an extra 1 percent.

During the 1970s, the view that financial intermediaries had been over-regulated became very popular. Many observers felt that banks would be better able to deal with higher and more variable interest rates if regulation were reduced. As a consequence, regulatory restraints on financial institutions were relaxed in the late 1970s and early 1980s in a process called **deregulation**. The resulting regulatory changes caused significant alterations in the operating procedures for financial intermediaries. These changes have made commercial banks increasingly capable of dealing with fluctuating interest rates. A major element of deregulation was the elimination of ceilings on deposits. Without interest rate ceilings on deposits, the rates paid by banks on deposits keeps pace with market rates; this means that banks do not suddenly suffer large deposit withdrawals as interest rates rise. In addition, there has been a shift toward variable rate loans, loans whose rate varies as the banks' cost of raising deposit funds changes. As discussed shortly, this allows banks to change their lending rates as their borrowing costs change.

Deregulation has contributed to the large number of failures of savings and loans and commercial banks in recent years. First, deregulation reduced the amount of bank examination, making bank fraud and embezzlement somewhat easier. Second, deregulation allowed savings and loans and banks to invest in some highly risky ventures, some of which failed. Third, weak banks and thrifts were allowed to operate and incur even larger losses eventually covered by the government insurance funds.

The response to the period of failures of banks and thrifts has been a tightening of regulation. Tighter regulation has taken the form of (1) an increase in the amount of bank equity capital required by regulators, (2) more careful bank examination, (3) closing of weak institutions sooner, before the insurance losses increase, (4) higher insurance premiums, and (5) encouragement of larger, more diversified institutions.

2

Determinants of Interest Rates

Overview

Many varieties of debt instruments exist in the market. Each type of instrument has a slightly different interest rate because of the particular characteristics of the debt instrument involved. Individual interest rates may be regarded as dependent upon an underlying interest rate factor plus an adjustment for the unique characteristics of the debt instrument. This chapter discusses economic factors determining the underlying interest rate, without regard to the important determinants unique to individual varieties of debt. These other factors, which are the focus of later chapters, include (1) taxation, (2) default risk, (3) call features, and (4) time preferences for consumption and investment. In addition, the first part of this chapter assumes no inflation. That is, it discusses inflation-free interest rates. Inflation is a process in which the general level of prices changes; it is the subject of the last part of the chapter. Thus, this chapter deals with a single-period, nontaxed, default-free, noncallable interest rate. This interest rate represents the pure time value of money.

Macroeconomics deals with the overall economy. It is concerned with several interconnected issues including the determinants of economic growth, inflation, unemployment, productivity, and foreign exchange rates, as well as government policies on taxation, spending, interest rates and monetary policy. This chapter and the next focus on several major macroeconomic theories of the determinants of the interest rate. Each of these theories provides some useful insights into the determinants of interest rates, but none offers a complete and satisfactory explanation.

In an economic system where money exists, the interest rate can never be negative if there are no transactions costs. Lenders would never lend at a negative interest rate since they have the alternative of holding money. For example, assume hypothetically an interest rate of negative 5 percent. A loan of $100 then results in a repayment of $95 one period later. No lenders would make this loan if they had the alternative of holding their $100 as cash. Therefore, zero is the lowest possible nominal interest rate if money exists.

Classical Theory

Until the 1930s, many economists believed in the classical theory of interest rates. According to the classical theory, the money supply does not affect interest rates. Two so-called real factors, business investment and savings by individuals, are judged to be the determinants of interest rates.

According to the classical theory, businesses compare the rate of return on their investments with the interest rate. If return on investment exceeds the interest rate, the firm earns something above the financing cost and a particular investment is undertaken. If the return on investment is below the interest rate, a particular investment is unprofitable after paying financing costs and is not undertaken.

For the economy as a whole, there is a schedule or list of all possible investments and their rates of return. For example, assume the five possible business investments shown in table 2.1. The most profitable investment has a return of 20 percent, the second most profitable has a return of 15 percent, the third most profitable has a return of 10 percent, and so on. If the first investment is undertaken, $10 m. is invested. If the first two projects are undertaken, then a cumulative total of $20 m. is invested, and so on.

The rate of return versus the cumulative amount invested is shown in figure 2.1 as the marginal efficiency of capital (MEI) curve. Figure 2.1

Table 2.1 Schedule of Investment Opportunities

Investment	Amount	Return(%)	Cumulative Amount
1	$10 m.	20%	$10 m.
2	$10 m.	15%	$20 m.
3	$10 m.	10%	$30 m.
4	$10 m.	8%	$40 m.
5	$10 m.	5%	$50 m.

Figure 2.1   MEI Curve

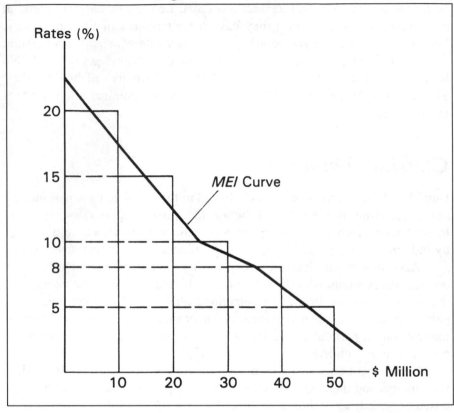

shows rates of return versus cumulative amount invested for all the possible investments ranked from the one with the highest rate of return to the one with the lowest rate of return.

In the classical theory, the cost of funds for business investment is the interest rate. This is equivalent to the assumption that all business investment is debt financed with no equity financing. In practice, equity financing is quite important.

The other factor determining interest rates in the classical theory is saving by individuals. According to the classical view, interest payments represent a compensation to savers for postponing consumption. For giving up consumption now, consumers want to be compensated by more consumption in the future. For example, consumers might be willing to trade $100 of consumption today for $110 of consumption in one year, implying an interest rate of 10 percent. If the interest rate is higher, individuals save more in the classical model. Savings as a function of the interest rate is represented in figure 2.2 as the curve labelled *S*. The upward slope shows greater savings by consumers at higher interest rates.

The point where the MEI curve intersects the *S* curve represents equilibrium. In equilibrium, the total amount borrowed by investors equals the total amount saved by consumers. In equilibrium, the interest rate is equal to the return on the marginal (or last) investment undertaken and also equal to the return required by the marginal saver.

If investment does not equal saving, a disequilibrium condition exists. Consider the case where the interest rate is above the equilibrium level in figure 2.3a. Because the amount saved is greater than the amount invested, the surplus savings drives down the interest rate as lenders compete with each other. If the interest rate is below the equilibrium level, as in figure 2.3b, the amount invested is greater than the amount saved. Borrowers compete with each other for funds, driving up interest rates and causing savers to save more.

Figure 2.2   MEI and Savings Curves and Equilibrium Interest Rate

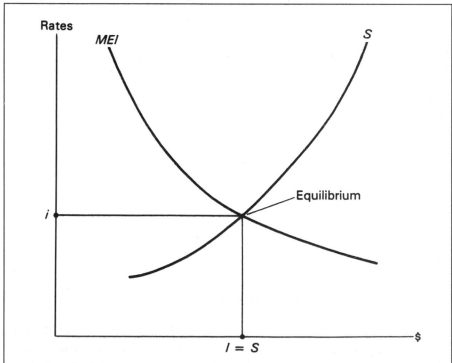

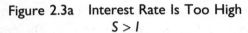

Figure 2.3a   Interest Rate Is Too High

$S > I$

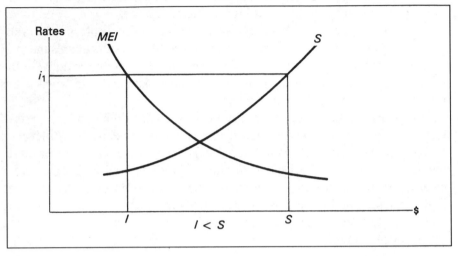

Figure 2.3b   Interest Rate Is Too Low

$S < I$

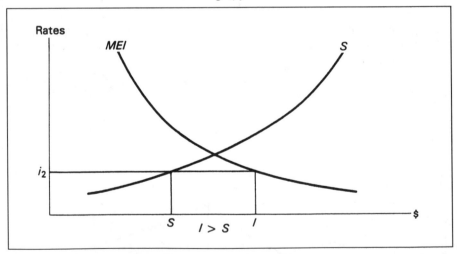

Loanable Funds Approach

According to the loanable funds approach, the interest rate is determined by the supply of and the demand for loanable funds. This approach is shown schematically in figure 2.4. The demand curve shows the relationship between the demand for funds and the interest rate. This curve is drawn with a

Figure 2.4 Loanable Funds Approach

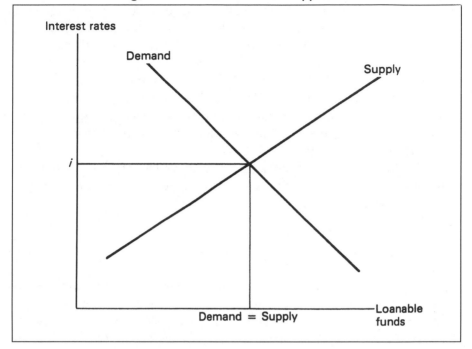

downward slope, indicating a greater demand for funds at lower interest rates. The supply curve shows the relationship between the supply of funds and the interest rate. The supply curve has an upward slope; at higher interest rates more funds are supplied to the market. The interest rate and the amount of funds changing hands are determined by the point where the two curves cross.

The loanable funds approach is similar to the classical approach. However, the loanable funds approach includes more entities as demanders and suppliers of funds. In the classical approach, the demand for funds comes only from business investment. The loanable funds approach adds consumers and the government as borrowers. Since consumer and government borrowings are huge, this addition is a move toward realism. Whereas the classical approach assumes that consumers are the only suppliers of savings, the loanable funds approach adds savings from businesses and increases in the money supply.

The Demand for Funds

The total demand for funds comprises consumer borrowing for consumption, business investment in plant and equipment, and governmental budget deficits. We have drawn the total demand curve as downward sloping, but considerable controversy exists about the demand curves for the components – consumer borrowing, business investment, and government deficits.

Consumer borrowing for "big ticket" items is interest rate sensitive. High interest rates cause reductions in consumer purchases of homes and automobiles, but purchases of relatively low-priced items may not be substantially affected by interest rates. Thus, the demand curve for expensive consumer goods is downward sloping. For other consumer goods, the slope is unclear. For the aggregate of all consumer goods, the demand curve is probably downward sloping.

The loanable funds approach also includes the demand for funds by business investors. This is the same as the marginal efficiency of capital curve discussed by the classical theory.

The Supply of Funds

The total amount of funds supplied to the market includes savings from individual consumers, business savings, and increases in the money supply. The supply curve has been drawn with an upward slope; higher interest rates lead to a larger supply of funds, but economists debate the slopes of the components of the supply curve.

Consumers save out of current income for future consumption. The amount of individual saving depends upon preferences, current income, wealth, and interest rates. The major determinants of savings are thought to be preferences, income, and wealth. Interest rates, however, may have only a secondary impact upon savings by consumers.

The direction of the effect of interest rates on savings is debatable. On the one hand, higher interest rates may attract funds from people who are willing to give up current consumption for a more attractive rate of return and resulting higher consumption in the future; this is called the **substitution effect** and implies an upward sloping supply curve. On the other hand, some savers have a target goal for total future income derived from savings. These individuals are able to reduce the amount saved and maintain the same future income level as interest rates rise. This is called the **income effect** and implies a downward sloping supply curve.[1] The net impact of these two effects upon total savings is not clear on purely deductive grounds.

---

[1] The classical approach did not include this income effect.

In addition, the market value of existing wealth is a function of interest rates. For example, as interest rates decline, the market value of debt instruments (and probably equity as well) increases. Thus, wealth and interest rates interact.

The impact of the interest rate on business savings is not entirely clear either. Business savings represent retained earnings and depreciation. Depreciation is a function of physical wear and tear on equipment and is probably not substantially affected by interest rates. The impact of the interest rate on retained earnings is ambiguous. Retained earnings equal earnings minus dividends. Thus, the impact of the interest rate on retained earnings can be decomposed into the impact of the interest rate on earnings and on dividends. Each of these impacts has an unclear direction. For example, the earnings of some firms, such as banks, may be very sensitive to interest rates, whereas other firms' earnings may be totally unaffected by interest rates. Most likely, interest rates are a minor determinant of retained earnings.

Although the level of interest rates affects the total amount of interest paid on the federal debt, it appears unlikely that interest rates materially affect federal government budget surpluses or deficits. However, state and local governments tend to postpone capital expenditures if interest rates are high.

As will be discussed in chapter 4 on the Federal Reserve, the money supply is largely determined by the Federal Reserve as it carries out monetary policy. Increases in the supply of money shift the supply curve of funds to the right, resulting in a lower interest rate (see figure 2.5).

In recent years, the foreign sector has become an increasingly important source of funds for the United States. The supply of these foreign funds is dependent upon many factors. First, expectations of exchange rate changes affect the sources of funds available in the United States. Those who feel that the U.S. dollar will appreciate can shift their funds into dollars in expectation of shifting out of dollars in the future at a more favorable exchange rate. For example, if $1 (U.S.) currently equals three francs (French), an investor holding francs and anticipating an appreciation in the U.S. dollar to $1 equals four francs can exchange three francs for $1. If the forecast is correct, the investor can then exchange the $1 for four francs, giving a profit of one franc. Investors expecting the dollar to decline would shift out of dollars and into the foreign currency, expecting to shift back into dollars after the dollar has declined. Second, interest rate differentials between countries affect the flow of funds, with funds tending to move from the countries with lower interest rates to those with higher interest rates. In spite of disagreements about the components of the supply curve, the aggregate supply curve is typically assumed to be upward sloping.

Figure 2.5   An Increase in The Money Supply

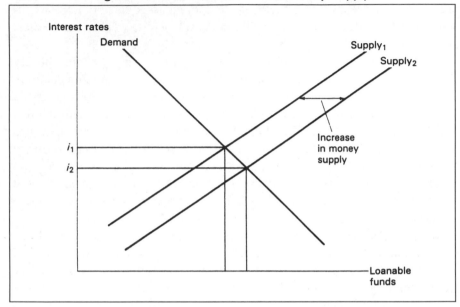

In the loanable funds framework, an increase in the government deficit (financed by additional borrowing) raises the total demand for funds, resulting in a shift to the right of the demand curve for funds. As shown in figure 2.6, the shift in the demand curve causes a rise in the interest rate. Unless the supply curve is perfectly flat, the total amount of funds supplied to the market does not increase as much as government borrowing. Some nongovernment borrowers are crowded out by the government borrowing. Consequently, increased government borrowing tends to make consumer and business borrowing more expensive, thus reducing consumer expenditures and business capital expenditures in the private economy. The added government borrowing shifts resources from the private sector to the government.

In the crowding-out view, large government deficits reduce business investment in plant and equipment below the level otherwise attainable. Since business investment is a primary ingredient for increasing productivity (output per man hour) and economic growth, large deficits and resulting higher interest rates slow the growth rate of the economy.

The Monetarist View of Interest Rates

The monetarist view of macroeconomics focuses upon the money supply as a major factor determining the course of the economy. The monetarist view

Figure 2.6   Increased Government Borrowing

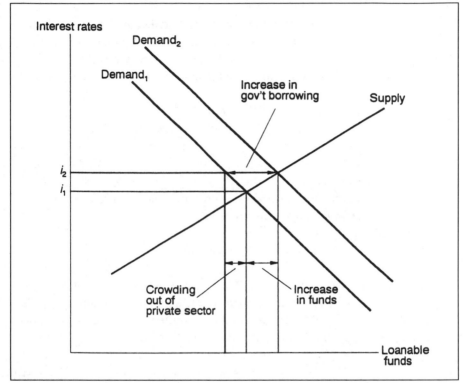

includes three eras: the old quantity theory, the classical quantity theory, and the modern quantity theory. We will discuss each of these in broad terms, noting that those economists calling themselves monetarists do not always agree.

The Old Quantity Theory

Several hundred years ago, money was in the form of coins made out of precious metals. As the supply of precious metals changed, so did the quantity of money. Observers noticed increased price levels when large increases in the supply of precious metals and resulting increases in the amount of money occurred. Essentially, more money was chasing the same amount of goods with a resultant increase in the price level. This argument came to be known as the **quantity theory of money**.

The Classical Quantity Theory

By the nineteenth century, financial systems had become more complex. Money was no longer restricted to coins but included paper currency and checking deposits. A more sophisticated quantity theory developed.

Let's begin with the equation of exchange, which is a truism:

$$MV \equiv PQ \tag{2.1}$$

where:

M = the money supply
V = the velocity of money, the number of times that an average
    dollar changes hands during a year
P = the price level
Q = the level of real (or physical) output

In equation 2.1, the total amount spent in a year is MV, the amount of money times the number of times money turns over. The total amount spent also equals PQ, the price level times the number of units purchased. The equation of exchange can be stated (approximately) in terms of rates of change as:

$$m + v = p + q \tag{2.2}$$

where:

m = the rate of growth in the money supply
v = the rate of growth of velocity
p = the rate of growth in prices, or the inflation rate
q = the rate of growth in real output

In equation 2.2, the rates of change in prices and real output are determined by the rates of growth in the money supply and velocity. According to the classical quantity theory, velocity is a constant (i.e., $v = 0$). This means that:

$$m = p + q \tag{2.3}$$

In other words, the rate of growth in the money supply must equal the rate of growth in prices plus the rate of growth in real output. Solving for the inflation rate, p:

$$p = m - q \qquad\qquad (2.4)$$

In order to have no inflation, the growth rate of the money supply must equal the growth rate of real output. If the money supply grows faster than real output, inflation occurs.

Besides assuming that velocity is constant, the classical quantity theory assumes full employment. Changes in the supply of money are assumed to have no impact upon GNP because the economy is always producing at maximum capacity and the growth rate of the economy is not affected by changes in the money supply. Changes in the money supply affect the price level exclusively.

Consider the following example. Velocity is constant with a growth rate of zero. The monetary authorities decide that the expected growth rate of real output is 3 percent. To ensure a zero inflation rate, p, the money supply should grow at 3 percent. If the money supply grows at a faster rate, inflation occurs. For example, if the money supply grows at 7 percent, the inflation rate is 4 percent (i.e., .07 − .03 = .04).

The Modern Quantity Theory

In the modern quantity theory, the money supply is the most important determinant of GNP. Modern monetarists believe that velocity is a relatively stable and predictable function of economic variables, rather than a never-changing constant as in the classical quantity theory.

Second, most modern monetarists believe in strict rules for government economic policy rather than wide discretion. According to this view, the government should estimate the long-run real growth rate of the economy. The money supply growth rate should be set equal to this real growth rate regardless of economic conditions. If the economy is temporarily weak, this rule injects money into the system. If the economy has a high inflation rate, the money supply rule chokes off the inflation. In the monetarist view, active tinkering with the money supply growth rate is counterproductive because the government has a tendency to do the wrong thing.

Third, modern monetarists feel that changes in the money supply have a wide-ranging impact upon the economy.[2] An increase in the money supply

---

[2] In the neo-Keynesian framework discussed in chapter 3, an increase in the money supply reduces interest rates on bonds, increases investment, and raises GNP.

affects holdings of all assets, not just bonds. For example, an increase in the money supply may stimulate purchases of common stocks and drive up stock prices, or it may directly increase purchases of consumer durables such as cars and appliances.

Fourth, modern monetarists take the position that fiscal policy (that is, government decisions on taxes and spending) has little impact upon the economy. Government policy should focus exclusively on monetary policy (i.e., controlling the supply of money).

Fifth, in the monetarist framework, increases in the money supply have three impacts, which may be offsetting. First, the added money tends to bid the prices of bonds up and interest rates down. Then the increase in the money supply tends to stimulate output, and this puts upward pressure on interest rates. Finally, changes in the money supply affect inflationary expectations. If bondholders fear a rapid growth in the money supply with resulting inflation, an inflationary premium is added onto the interest rate; the next section discusses the impact of inflation upon interest rates. In the modern monetarist view, the net impact of an increase in the money supply depends upon all of the three preceding factors (i.e., the initial increase in bond prices, the increase in output, and inflationary expectations). In the modern Monetarist view, an increase in the money supply may result in a net increase in interest rates if inflationary expectations are raised sufficiently.[3]

Inflation and Interest Rates

The term **inflation** means a process with a continual increase in the general price level. As prices go up, individuals try to protect their purchasing power and take actions which inadvertently perpetuate the inflation. For example, employees may try to protect themselves from inflation by having their wages tied to the cost of living. As prices rise, wages are forced up, which raises production costs, which raises selling prices, and so on, in a never-ending cycle. Throughout history, inflation has occurred frequently. Generally, inflation has a significant impact upon economic activity, including interest rates.

Precisely measuring the rate of inflation is a difficult task. The consumer inflation rate depends upon the price changes of individual consumer goods

---

[3] This contrasts with the neo-Keynesian view that interest rates decline if the money supply increases.

and the amounts consumed by actual consumers. Since consumer choices change as relative prices change, the basket of goods purchased by the average consumer changes over time. Finding the correct basket of goods is a major problem in measuring the inflation rate. Thus, considerable disagreement exists about the true inflation rate. Government statistics provide several price indexes – a consumer price index, a producer price index, and a GNP deflator. The rate of change in these indexes should each measure the inflation rate. But, these rates of change can differ considerably. We overlook these pragmatic problems in measuring the inflation rate and assume a hypothetical inflation rate.

Intelligent investors try to forecast important factors affecting their investments. Because investors are concerned with inflation-adjusted, or "real" returns, investors form anticipations of the future inflation rate, based upon all available current information. These anticipations of the future inflation rate are reflected immediately in security prices and interest rates. The actual realized inflation rate usually differs from the anticipated rate. The difference between the actual rate and the anticipated rate represents a forecasting error, or surprise, to the market. If the forecasted inflation rate is less than the realized rate, the difference represents unanticipated inflation.

Complete Certainty

The most clear-cut relationship between inflation and interest rates occurs when we have complete certainty about the future and there are no taxes. As will be explained shortly, lenders would add an inflation premium to the interest rate to compensate for declining purchasing power in this case.

The real rate of interest is defined as the rate that would prevail in an inflation-free world. Denote the real interest rate by r. Let the completely certain inflation rate be denoted by p. Let the observed, nominal (that is, money terms) interest rate be i.

In order to compensate lenders exactly for the declining purchasing power of money, the following condition must hold:

$$1 + i = (1 + r)(1 + p) = 1 + r + p + rp \qquad (2.5)$$

$$i = r + p + rp \qquad (2.6)$$

The following example illustrates this expression. The real interest rate is 5 percent and the inflation rate is 10 percent. Then the nominal rate, i, must equal the real rate, r (.05), plus the inflation rate, p (.10), plus the product of the two, rp (.05)(.10). Adding the inflation rate, p, compensates the lender for the declining value of the principal. Adding the term rp compensates the lender for the declining value of the real interest. This last term is frequently omitted, since the product of two rates has small absolute value. Thus, in the example, the nominal rate is frequently approximated by the first two terms as 15 percent.

 If interest income is taxable at the rate t, then the inflation rate must be increased to compensate the lender for taxes paid. That is, 1 plus the after-tax yield to maturity should equal $(1 + r)(1 + p)$. In equation form:

$$1 + i(1 - t) = (1 + r)(1 + p) \tag{2.7}$$

$$i = \frac{r + p + rp}{1 - t} \tag{2.8}$$

$$i = \frac{r}{1 - t} + \frac{p + rp}{1 - t} \tag{2.9}$$

$$\text{before-tax nominal} = \text{before-tax real} + \begin{array}{c}\text{before-tax} \\ \text{inflation premium}\end{array}$$

The before-tax nominal interest rate is represented by i. The term $r/(1 - t)$ is the before-tax real interest rate. The before-tax inflation premium is represented by $(p + rp)/(1 - t)$.

 With a tax rate of 50 percent, every 1 percent of inflation raises the nominal interest rate by $(p + rp)/(1 - .50)$, or by more than 2 percent. To illustrate, if the real interest rate, r, is 5 percent, the inflation rate is 10 percent, and the tax rate is 50 percent, the before-tax yield to maturity is $(.05 + .10 + .005)/(1 - .5)$, which equals 31 percent. Taxes increase the before-tax interest rate to 31 percent, so that the after-tax rate is 15.5 percent = $i(1 - t) = .31(1 - .50)$.

Uncertainty

If the inflation rate is uncertain, the impact of inflation upon interest rates is not as clear-cut. In a widely held view, the anticipated inflation rate is added to the real interest rate. In addition, a risk premium should be added, so that:

$$i = \frac{r + E(p) + h}{1 - t} \tag{2.10}$$

where $E(p)$ is the expected inflation rate and h is a **risk premium**. This premium compensates the lender for the possibility of a higher actual inflation rate than the expected rate. To illustrate, if the real interest rate is 5 percent, the expected inflation rate is 10 percent, the risk premium is 3 percent, and the tax rate is 50 percent, the nominal interest rate is $(.05 + .10 + .03)/(1 - .50)$, or 36 percent.

The previous discussion assumed that inflation does not affect the real interest rate. In practice, it is quite possible for inflationary expectations to alter real interest rates.

Empirical Tests

Empirically testing the relationship between inflation and interest rates is difficult because the anticipated inflation rate is not directly observable. Several ways of estimating anticipations have been suggested. First, surveys of anticipated inflation can be used as a proxy for the market's anticipation. The accuracy of this approach depends upon the individuals in the sample and the correspondence between the anticipations of the survey group and of the market. Second, econometric methods can be used to construct anticipations relating inflation anticipations to objectively observed current and past information. In order to use this approach, anticipations are assumed to be determined by a model using some observable information.

In another approach, some researchers have tried to see whether the nominal interest rate is a function of the recently observed inflation rate. Does the nominal interest rate change in unison with the observed inflation rate? If this simple model were true, nominal interest rates and inflation rates would closely correspond.

Empirically, the relationship between nominal interest rates and the recent actual inflation rates is weak. The reason is not entirely clear. A possible explanation is the divergence between anticipated and actual inflation. Theoretically, the anticipated inflation rate (not the actual inflation rate) determines the interest rate. In addition, the risk premium discussed earlier should be considered. Risk premiums may vary across time. Tests assuming a constant risk premium have a built-in bias.

Discussions of interest rates often subtract the most recently observed inflation rate from the interest rate to arrive at a number dubbed the "real rate." This reasoning assumes the most recent inflation rate is an unbiased forecast of the future inflation rate. The inflation rate in the recent past is probably a poor forecast of the inflation rate in the distant future. Therefore, investors should not base their behavior upon this so-called real rate.

Strategies for Behavior

In an inflationary environment, individuals try to protect themselves and even benefit from inflation. The first step is to compare a personal anticipated inflation rate with the rate anticipated by the market. If the personal antici-pated rate is considerably above the market's anticipation, borrowing money and buying real assets is beneficial. If the personal anticipated rate is consider-ably below the market's anticipation, selling real (overvalued) assets and lending money is profitable.

Table 2.2 illustrates the advantage of borrowing money if the actual inflation rate is above the rate anticipated by the market. Table 2.2 assumes that an investor borrows \$1 now, at time 0, and repays it one period later, at time 1. The rate of interest reflects the real rate, r, plus the market's anticipations of the inflation rate, p. The investor buys real assets with the funds borrowed and earns the nominal rate of return on them. The rate of return on real assets should reflect the real interest rate plus the actual inflation rate. If the actual inflation rate (p_{actual}) exceeds the rate anticipated by the market (p), the investor benefits.[4]

Consider the following example. The real interest rate, r, is 5 percent and the market anticipates a 2 percent inflation rate, p. You, as an astute investor, expect an actual inflation rate, i_{actual}, of 10 percent; you borrow and

Table 2.2   Profiting from Inflation

Action	Points in Time	
	0	1
Borrow	\$1	$-\$(1 + r + p + rp)$
Buy real assets	$-\$1$	$+\$(1 + r + p_{actual} + rp_{actual})$
Net	0	$(p_{actual} - p)(1 + r)$

---

[4] Some assets may have a convenience yield, a value from holding those assets. If the asset is a house, the convenience yield is the value received from living in the house. The convenience yield is subtracted from the returns. Thus, the return is $r + p_{actual} + rp_{actual} - conv$, where conv is the convenience yield. The net return from the strategy in table 2.2 is $(p_{actual} - p)(1 + r) - conv$.

invest in real assets. If correct in your forecast, your profits are 8.4 percent of the amount of real assets purchased, computed in table 2.3.

Because investors include anticipations of the future in current security prices, anticipated inflation rates should have an impact upon the current interest rate. In the case of complete certainty about future inflation, the inflation rate is added to the real interest rate to arrive at the observed nominal interest rate. If the future is uncertain, the nominal interest rate equals the real interest rate plus the anticipated inflation rate plus some risk premium.

Summary

In the classical theory of interest rates, the interest rate is determined by the demand for investment funds by businesses and by the supply of savings from individuals. The loanable funds framework includes individual and government borrowers in the demand for funds. Business savings and the money supply are included in the supply of funds.

In the monetarist view, interest rates are affected by the money supply in three ways: a liquidity effect, an output effect, and a price expectations effect.

Because investors include anticipations of the future in current security prices, anticipated inflation rates have an impact upon the current interest rate. In the case of complete certainty about future inflation, the inflation rate is added to the real interest rate to arrive at the observed nominal interest rate. If the future is uncertain, the nominal interest rate equals the real interest rate plus the anticipated inflation rate plus some risk premium.

Table 2.3   Example of Profiting from Inflation

Action	Points in Time	
	0	1
Borrow	$1	$-\$(1.05)(1.02) = -1.071$
Buy real assets	-$1	$+\$(1.05)(1.10) = 1.155$
Net	0	$(.10 - .02)(1.05) = .084$

Questions/Problems

1. Describe the differences between the classical and loanable funds approaches to the interest rate.

2. What are the major tenets of the classical quantity theory and the modern quantity theory of money? Is velocity a constant in each theory? In practice, what are the determinants of velocity?

3. Assume that the real rate of interest is 3 percent and that the inflation rate is 10 percent with complete certainty and no taxes. Determine the nominal interest rate.

4. Assume the same information as the preceding problem except that the tax rate is 28 percent. Determine the before-tax nominal interest rate and the before-tax real interest rate.

5. Assuming no taxes and complete certainty, you observe that the nominal interest rate is 15 percent and that the inflation rate is 5 percent. Determine the real interest rate.

6. Assume no taxes. The market anticipates an inflation rate of 8 percent. The real interest rate is known to be 4 percent. You anticipate an inflation rate of 15 percent. Explain how you might benefit from this information. If your inflation forecast is correct, what is the gain?

7. In a world of certainty with no taxes, the nominal interest rate is 10 percent and the real interest rate is 5 percent. What is the inflation rate?

8. Assume no taxes. The real interest rate is 5 percent and the market anticipates an inflation rate of 10 percent. You borrow money and repay it in one period. You use these borrowed funds to buy real assets and sell these assets at the end of one period. For what actual inflation rate will you make 15.75 percent of the amount borrowed?

9. Assume no taxes. The nominal interest rate is 10.25 percent and the real interest rate is 5 percent. You forecast deflation of 5 percent over the next year. Explain how you could try to profit from your forecast. What is your profit, if your forecast is correct?

10. Assume a world of complete certainty and no taxes. The nominal interest rate is 20 percent. The real interest rate is 8 percent. You forecast that the inflation rate is going to be 18 percent. You decide to borrow $1 and buy real assets. After one period, you liquidate the real assets and pay off the loan. At what inflation rate would you earn a profit of $.12?

11. Assume a world of no taxes. The market forecasts an inflation rate of 5 percent. You forecast an inflation rate of 15 percent. You decide to borrow $1 and invest in real assets for one period. Your forecast equals the actual inflation rate. When you sell the assets and repay the loan, you earn a profit of $.11. What is the real interest rate?

12. Assume no taxes. We observe that the nominal interest rate is 20 percent. What is the lowest possible value for the sum of the real interest rate and the inflation rate?

13. Assume no taxes. Suppose the real interest rate is 5 percent. The market forecasts a deflation rate of 15 percent. What is the nominal interest rate?

References

Andersen, L. C., "The State of the Monetarist Debate," *Federal Reserve Bank of St. Louis Review,* September 1973.

Chan, L. K. C., "Consumption, Inflation Risk, and Real Interest Rates: An Empirical Analyis," *Journal of Business,* 67, January 1994, pp. 69–96.

Darby, M. R., "The Financial Effects of Monetary Policy on Interest Rates," *Economic Inquiry,* 13, June 1975, pp. 269–82.

Feldstein, M. "Inflation, Income Taxes, and the Rate of Interest: A Theoretical Analysis," *American Economic Review,* 66, December 1976, pp. 809–20.

Fisher, I., *Appreciation and Interest,* New York: Macmillan, 1896.

Fisher, I., *The Theory of Interest,* New York: Macmillan, 1930.

Friedman, M., "The Quantity Theory of Money: A Restatement," in *Studies in the Quantity Theory of Money,* Chicago: University of Chicago Press, 1956.

Friedman, M., "Factors Affecting the Level of Interest Rates." *Conference on Savings and Residential Finance,* Chicago: U.S. Savings and Loan League, 1968.

Friedman, M., *A Theoretical Framework for Monetary Analysis,* Occasional Paper 112, New York: National Bureau of Economic Research, 1971.

Gibson, W. E., "Price Expectations Effects on Interest Rates," *Journal of Finance,* 25, March 1970, pp. 19–34.

Gibson, W. E., "Interest Rates and Inflationary Expectations: New Evidence," *American Economic Review,* 62, December 1972, pp. 854–65.

Kessel, R. A., "Inflation-Caused Wealth Redistribution: A Test of a Hypothesis," *American Economic Review,* 46, March 1956, pp. 43–66.

Keynes, J. M., *The General Theory of Employment, Interest and Money,* New York: Harcourt Brace Jovanovich, 1936.

Livingston, M., "Comment on Expectations, Taxes, and Interest: The Search for the Darby Effect," *American Economic Review,* 81, December 1991, pp. 1435–36.

Mishkin, F. S., *The Economics of Money, Banking, and Financial Markets,* 3rd ed., New York: HarperCollins, 1992.

Mundell, R., "Inflation and Real Interest," *Journal of Political Economy,* 71, June 1963, pp. 280–83.

Pennachi, George G., "Identifying the Dynamics of Real Interest Rates and Inflation: Evidence Using Survey Data," *Review of Financial Studies,* 4:1, 1991, pp. 53–86.

Ungar, M. and B. Zilberfarb, "Inflation and Its Unpredictability – Theory and Empirical Evidence," *Journal of Money, Credit, and Banking,* 25, November 1993, pp. 709–20.

3

Neo-Keynesian Model

Overview

Perhaps the most general approach to explaining interest rates is the neo-Keynesian approach. In the 1930s, John Maynard Keynes wrote a book that significantly changed macroeconomic thinking. Here we will discuss the neo-Keynesian model, which is a revised and improved version of the original. In the neo-Keynesian approach, several interrelated factors affect the interest rate: (1) decisions by investors to save or consume, (2) investment decisions by firms, (3) investors' preferences to hold money balances for speculative purposes, (4) demand for money balances for transactions purposes, (5) government spending and taxes, and (6) the total supply of money set by the monetary authorities. We discuss each of these factors and then show their interactions. The discussion assumes a domestic economy without international trade or international cash flows.

The Consumption Function

Consumption by individuals is affected by many factors, including the level of income, wealth, holdings of consumer durables, the population age distribution, attitudes and customs, and taxes. The neo-Keynesian model assumes that consumption is largely a function of income. Income can be divided into two parts: transitory and permanent. The consumption function depends upon permanent income. For example, if an employee receives a special cash bonus because of an unusual event, this bonus is viewed as a transitory event and probably does not affect consumption. On the other hand, an increase in base pay is a change in permanent income and affects consumption expenditures.

Consider figure 3.1. The upper part shows the circular flow between production and expenditures. Production of goods and services results in income to the workers. As it is spent, this income becomes expenditures. In turn, expenditures determine production, and so on.

The lower part of figure 3.1 shows the circular flow in a slightly different way. The horizontal axis is the Gross National Product (GNP), which is a measure of production and income. We use three terms to mean the same thing: **production**, **income**, and **GNP**. If output is produced in the economy, then someone must be paid for this production. The payment to employees is called income. Thus, total production is total income.

The vertical axis in figure 3.1 shows expenditures including consumer expenditures (C), business investment (I), and government spending (G). Total expenditures equal the total of consumer spending, business investment, and government spending. That is:

$$\text{Total Expenditures} = C + I + G \qquad (3.1)$$

Figure 3.1   Expenditures = Production or Income

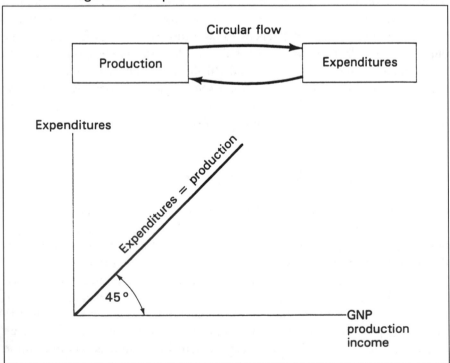

For the economy to be in equilibrium, total expenditures must equal total production or income. For example, if total expenditures were greater than total production, an insufficient quantity of goods would be produced to satisfy demand. Production would have to increase and/or expenditures decrease until the two were equal.

The equilibrium condition that total expenditures must equal total production is shown in figure 3.1 as a straight line making a 45° angle with the origin. The points along this line represent all the possible equilibriums where expenditures equal production. To find the actual equilibrium point, the consumption function (discussed shortly) is required.

Note that the following two facts must be true:

$$\text{Aggregate expenditures} = C + I + G \qquad (3.2)$$

$$\text{Aggregate Income} = C + S + T \qquad (3.3)$$

where:

S = total savings
T = total taxes
I = total investment
G = total government spending

In equilibrium, aggregate expenditures must equal aggregate income, meaning that:

$$C + I + G = C + S + T \qquad (3.4)$$

This simplifies to:

$$I + G = S + T \qquad (3.5)$$

Therefore, the equilibrium condition that expenditures must equal income is equivalent to the condition that investment plus government spending must equal personal savings plus taxes (i.e., $I + G = S + T$).

The **consumption function** is a straight line with the following form:

$$\text{Expenditures} = a + b[\text{GNP}] \qquad (3.6)$$

The consumption function represents the desired level of expenditures under the assumption that this desired level of expenditures is exclusively dependent upon the level of GNP or income. A consumption function is shown in figure 3.2. If GNP is zero, expenditures equal the intercept *a*. Since GNP represents income, if income is zero, the consumption function tells us that people would still like to consume the amount *a*. Since income is zero, intercept *a* represents consumption in excess of income, or dissavings.

The slope of the consumption function, *b*, equals the proportion of peoples' incremental income consumed. The slope of the consumption function is called the **marginal propensity to consume** (mpc). This slope is less than 1.0, because people consume less than 100 percent of an addition to income. Since the slope is less than 1.0, any drop in income results in a smaller fall in consumption. This results in the positive intercept *a* if income is zero.

Consider the following numerical example:

$$C = 75 + (.8)GNP \tag{3.7}$$

The income (GNP) is 0, consumption is 75, and the intercept is *a*. If income is 100, consumption equals $75 + (.8)100 = 75 + 80 = 155$. Out of the $100 increment in income, people spend only $80. The slope, or the marginal propensity to consume, is .80, or people consume 80 percent of any increases in income.

Figure 3.2   Consumption Function

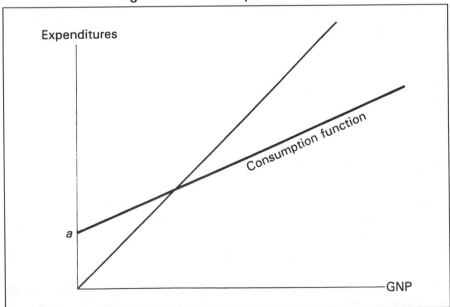

The **marginal propensity to save** (mps) is 1 minus the slope of the consumption function (i.e., $1 - b$). In the numerical example, the marginal propensity to save is .20, or 20 percent. People save 20 percent of any increments to income. As income increases from 0 to 100, people save 20 percent, or $20.

In the consumption function, the propensities to consume and to save are assumed to be stable and constant. They do not change much over time. These propensities are determined by social customs and attitudes, by the age distribution of the population, and by other factors that change very slowly over time.

Total expenditures equal consumption plus business investment plus government spending as shown in figure 3.3. In the figure, investment and government spending are added to consumption because they are determined by factors other than income. Investment is determined by the interest rate and the marginal efficiency of investment to be discussed shortly. Government spending is assumed to be an exogenous factor, i.e., something determined outside the economic system. It is determined by political considerations.

Equilibrium is determined by the intersection of the total expenditures function with the 45 degree line with the origin. At this intersection point,

Figure 3.3   Total Expenditures Equal $C + I + G$

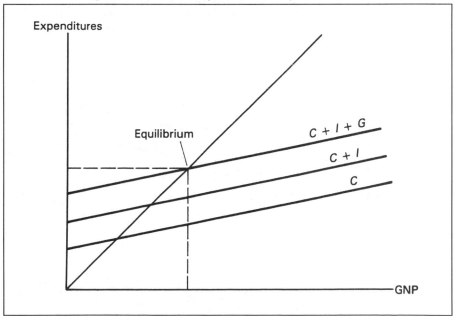

consumers have picked their desired level of consumption, and production equals expenditures.

If there is an outside shock, such as an increase in investment or government spending, the expenditures function shifts upward. This is shown in figure 3.4. From the geometry, the change in GNP (i.e., $GNP_2 - GNP_1$) is greater than the outside shock (i.e., $I_2 - I_1$). The change in equilibrium GNP equals the outside shock times $1/(1 - mpc)$, where mpc is the marginal propensity to consume or the slope of the consumption function. $1/(1 - mpc)$ is called the **multiplier**. Since mpc is less than 1.0, the multiplier must exceed 1.0. Table 3.1 shows the relationship between the marginal propensity to consume and the multiplier.

The multiplier increases as the marginal propensity to consume increases or as the consumption function gets steeper. If workers have a tendency to spend a larger proportion of their income, the multiplier is bigger. Table 3.1 also shows the marginal propensity to save, mps, which is equal to $1 - mpc$. As the marginal propensity to save decreases, the multiplier increases. Societies which have a smaller savings rate, and a higher propensity to consume, have a bigger multiplier. For these high multiplier societies, a change in investment or government spending has a big impact upon GNP. In practice, the multiplier is probably equal to 2.0 or less.

Figure 3.4   An Increase in Investment

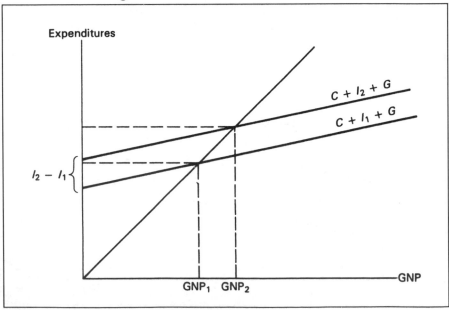

Table 3.1   The MPC and the Multiplier

mpc	Multiplier	mps
0.0	1.0	1.0
0.25	1.33	0.75
0.50	2.0	0.50
0.75	4.0	0.25
0.80	5.0	0.20
1.0	infinity	0.0

The earlier example had a marginal propensity to consume (i.e., slope of the consumption function) of .80. From table 3.1, the multiplier is 5. Every injection of $1 of investment or government spending causes a change of $5 in GNP.

To understand why an injection of $1 of investment spending causes a multiple expansion in GNP, note that the $1 of spending is income to some workers. Because the mpc is .80 in our example, these workers spend $.80 of this $1 and save $.20. This $.80 is income to another set of workers who spend 80 percent of it or $.64. In turn, this is income, 80 percent of which is spent, and so on. These respendings are shown in table 3.2. The total change in spending can be shown mathematically to equal the original injection of spending times $1/(1 - \text{mpc})$.

Marginal Efficiency of Investment

The second component of the neo-Keynesian framework is the **marginal efficiency of capital function** or **MEI**. This is also an important part of the

Table 3.2   GNP Multiplier

Incremental Income	Incremental Consumption	Cumulative Change in Consumption
$1.0	$.80	$.80
.80	.64	1.44
.64	.512	1.952
.512	.4096	2.3616
.	.	.
.	.	.
.	.	.
.00	.00	5.0

classical theory of interest rates discussed earlier. The MEI shows the amount of business investment for a given interest rate. In figure 3.5, a decrease in the interest rate from i_1 to a lower rate of i_2, increases business investment from I_1 to I_2. Interest rates and business investment are inversely related in the MEI function.

The slope of the MEI function is a subject of importance and debate. If the MEI curve is flat, then changes in interest rates cause large changes in business investment (see figure 3.6). The change in business investment shifts the consumption function upward and changes GNP, with the size of the change in GNP dependent upon the GNP multiplier discussed earlier. If the MEI is a steep function, then changes in interest rates bring about relatively small changes in business investment and a small shift in the consumption function.

For example, if the MEI is flat, a drop in the interest rate from 10 percent to 9 percent may cause business investment to increase by $30 b. If the MEI is steep, the same decline in interest rates may cause only a $10 b. increase in business investment.

Government policies can cause shifts in the MEI function. For example, a reduction in the business tax rate makes business investment more profitable. This shifts the MEI function upward and to the right, since each investment has a higher rate of return (see figure 3.7). If the interest rate is the same, the shift in the MEI increases the amount of business investment and this, in turn, increases GNP.

Figure 3.5   Marginal Efficiency of Investment
i = Interest Rate, I = Business Investment

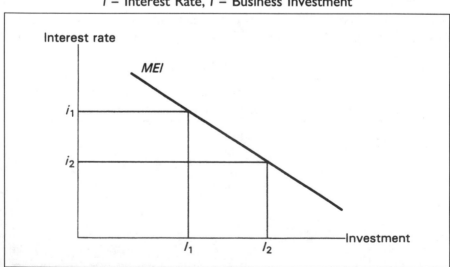

Figure 3.6   Flat versus Steep MEI

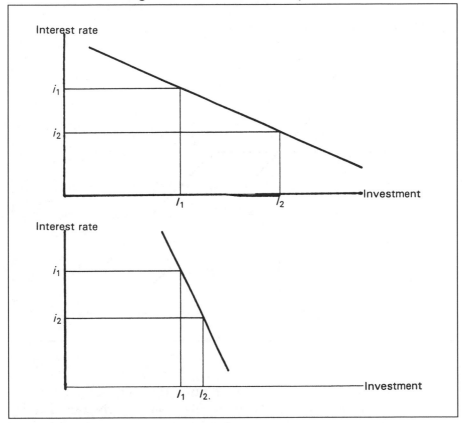

The Demand for Money

In the neo-Keynesian framework, two motives exist for holding money balances: the transactions motive and the speculative motive.[1] The transactions motive results in **transactions balances**. Transactions balances occur because the exact matching of cash inflows and outflows by businesses is usually not possible. Imagine a firm selling its output on Wednesday for $200 but not needing to pay its employees or suppliers until Friday. The

---

[1] Keynesians suggested a third motive – precautionary balances. These are cash balances kept as a precaution against transactions balances running short.

Figure 3.7   Shift in MEI

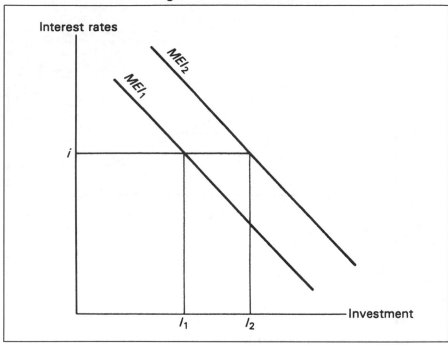

firm may consider investing this cash for the two days until Friday. However, a two-day investment involves brokerage fees, and search costs may be higher than the profits from investing for two days. Consequently, the best choice may be to hold cash for these two days as a transactions balance.

Transactions balances are dependent upon the level of production or income. As a firm's production increases, the amount of transactions balances increases because transactions balances are assumed to be some proportion of production. This is shown in figure 3.8. In the figure, transactions balances are assumed to be a percentage of GNP and are called M_T.

Speculative balances are cash balances held to buy securities, i.e., bonds, in the future at lower, more attractive prices. If people feel that prices will be lower in the future, speculative balances are high. In a later section of this book, bond prices and interest rates are shown to be inversely related. When bond prices are high, interest rates are low, and vice versa.

Now combine these two results. If investors believe current bond prices are high (i.e., current interest rates are low), speculative cash balances are increased in anticipation of a decline in future bond prices (that is, higher future interest rates). Consequently, the speculative demand for money is

Figure 3.8   Transactions Balances and Production

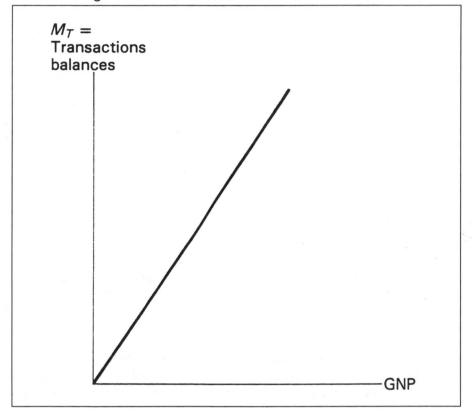

inversely related to the current interest rate. The shape of the function is shown in figure 3.9.

Chapter 8 of this book discusses the efficient market hypothesis – the idea that security markets react very rapidly to newly arrived information. If investors know that interest rates are going to change in the future, investors take action immediately, and the information is immediately reflected in interest rates. Consequently, changes in interest rates cannot be predicted. In an efficient market, interest rates are not high or low; they are appropriate given current information. The evidence is broadly consistent with markets being efficient.

The Keynesian view of the speculative demand for money contradicts market efficiency. The Keynesian view should be rejected. However, the interest rate and the money supply are inversely related for another reason. When interest rates are high, individuals and businesses have powerful incentives to move out of cash and into interest-bearing securities. They

Figure 3.9   Money Balances versus Interest Rates

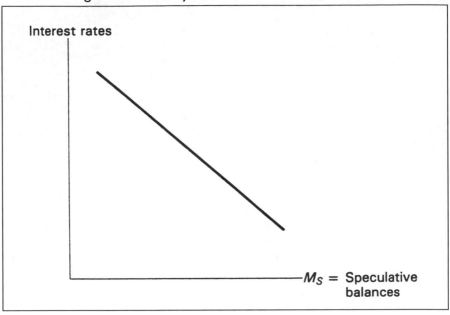

economize on their cash balances to earn interest. When interest rates are low, the incentives for economizing on cash balances are sharply reduced. Thus, the demand function for money is a function of both income and interest rates.

The line in figure 3.9 is called the **speculative demand for money**. Speculative money balances are inversely related to the level of interest rates – speculative balances are high (low) when interest rates are low (high). This speculative demand function for money exists because of speculative motives for holding money.

The total demand for money is the sum of the transactions demand and speculative demand. The total demand function is shown in figure 3.10. The demand function has two parts: (a) transactions balances (M_T) and (b) speculative balances (M_S). As income (GNP) increases, the transactions demand increases, and the demand function shifts to the right.

The supply of money is set by the monetary authorities. In the U.S., this is the Federal Reserve. The money supply is a vertical line in figure 3.11. The interest rate is given by the point where the demand curve for money crosses the supply curve. At this point, the amount of money demanded by people for transactions and speculative balances is exactly equal to the amount of money supplied by the monetary authorities.

Figure 3.10   Demand Function for Money

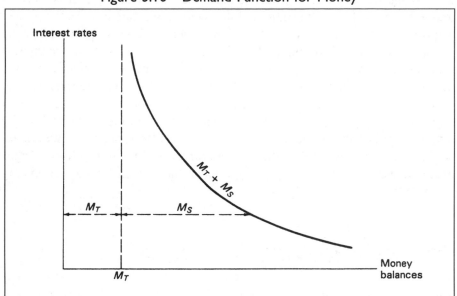

Figure 3.11   Demand and Supply for Money

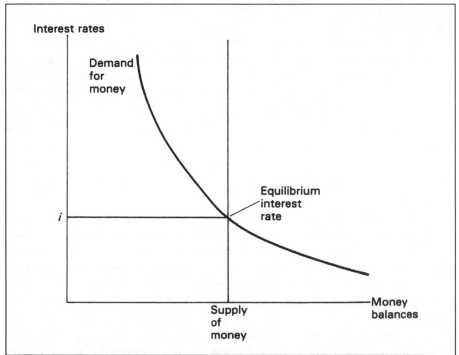

If the monetary authorities increase the money supply, the supply of money curve shifts to the right, and the interest rate declines. As the money supply increases, the extent of decline in interest rates depends upon the slope of the demand for money function. If the function is steep, the interest rate declines sharply (see figure 3.11). If the demand for money function is flat, an increase in the money supply has no impact upon the interest rate. The slope of this demand function clearly affects the impact of changes in the money supply upon the entire economy. Notice that a change in the money supply causes a change in the interest rate, affects business investment, and in turn changes GNP. If the demand for money function is flat, changes in the money supply have little impact upon the interest rate and ultimately upon GNP.

The Total Neo-Keynesian Model

Given the money supply and government spending and taxes, the neo-Keynesian approach has four components: the consumption function, the marginal efficiency of investment function (MEI), the transactions demand for money, and the speculative demand for money. These four functions are shown in figure 3.12.

All of the elements in the neo-Keynesian system are interrelated. To see this point more clearly, let's trace the impact of an increase in the money supply upon the whole system. In the lower left quadrant of figure 3.12, start with an initial money supply of M_1 as set by the Federal Reserve. The money supply and the total demand function for money imply an interest rate i_1. In the upper right quadrant, i_1 implies investment of I_1. In the lower right quadrant, the level of investment plus consumption and government spending determine GNP$_1$. In the upper left quadrant, GNP determines trans-actions balances M_{T1}. All of these elements in the system are simultaneously determined.

If the money supply increases to M_2, the demand function for money in the lower left quadrant tells us that the interest rate drops to i_2. The MEI function in the upper right quadrant indicates that the lower interest rate causes an increase in investment to I_2. The consumption function in the lower right quadrant implies that the increase in investment is followed by a bigger increase in GNP to GNP$_2$. The transactions demand function tells us that the larger GNP causes a bigger demand for transactions balances to M_{T2}, which tends to offset the original drop in interest rates because the demand function for money in the lower left quadrant shifts to the right.

Figure 3.12 Four Components of The Neo-Keynesian Model

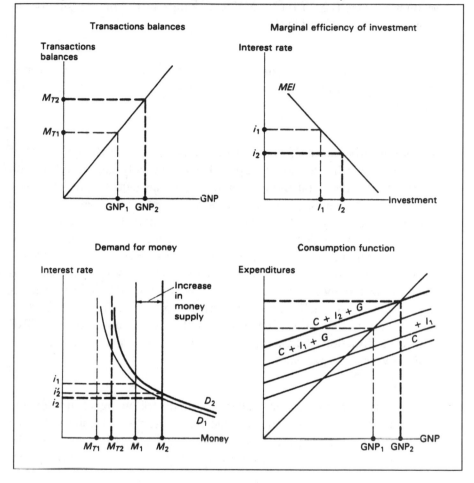

The net impact of an increase in the money supply is still a drop in interest rates, but to a slightly higher level than i_2.

The impact of a given change in the money supply upon interest rates and the other variables depends upon four factors:

1. The size of the multiplier. The bigger the multiplier, the bigger the impact upon GNP. Since the multiplier is directly related to the marginal propensity to consume, the impact of a change in the money supply is bigger for a larger marginal propensity to consume. A bigger multiplier implies a steeper consumption function.

2. The slope of the MEI function. If investment is more sensitive to changes in interest rates (i.e., a flatter MEI), a change in the money supply has a bigger impact upon GNP.

3. The slope of the demand function for money. If the demand function is steep, changes in the money supply cause large changes in interest rates and GNP.

4. Transactions balances. If transactions balances are a small percentage of GNP, a change in the money supply has a relatively large impact upon GNP. To see this point more clearly, assume an increase in the money supply. The initial response is a drop in interest rates, an increase in business investment, and an increase in GNP. Since GNP has increased, more money is needed for transactions balances, shifting the demand function for money to the right, boosting interest rates, and undoing some of the effect of the original change. The size of the shift in the demand function for money depends upon the proportion of GNP held as transactions balances. A small proportion causes a small shift in the demand for money and a small offsetting effect. With a small proportion of GNP held as transactions balances, an increase in the money supply has a relatively large impact upon GNP.

In summary, the interest rate depends upon the following: (1) the demand for speculative balances, (2) the demand for transactions balances, (3) the money supply, (4) the marginal efficiency of investment (MEI) curve, (5) the marginal propensity to consume (mpc) and the multiplier, and (6) government spending and taxes.

The following Appendix contains a geometric interpretation of the neo-Keynesian model in terms of so-called IS-LM curves.

Summary

In the neo-Keynesian approach, interest rates are dependent upon the transactions and speculative demand for money, the consumption function, the marginal efficiency of capital, the money supply, and government spending and taxes.

Questions/Problems

1. Explain the relationship between the marginal propensity to consume and the multiplier.

2. In the neo-Keynesian model, what determines the total demand for money?

3. If government spending increases in the neo-Keynesian approach, what is the impact upon interest rates?

4. If the money supply increases in the neo-Keynesian framework, explain the impact upon interest rates.

5. According to the modern monetarist approach, an increase in the money supply may increase inflationary expectations. Show how increased inflationary expectations may be incorporated into the neo-Keynesian model.

Appendix: IS-LM Curves

The IS Curve

The discussion of the neo-Keynesian model has a nice geometric interpretation in the form of IS-LM curves. An IS curve combines the MEI function, the consumption function, and equation 3.5 (i.e., $S + T = I + G$). See figure 3A.1.

To see how the IS curve is derived, start in the lower right quadrant of figure 3A.1 with the function MEI + G (i.e., marginal efficiency of investment plus government spending). For a given interest rate i_1, this function gives the total amount of investment plus government spending, $I_1 + G$.

Move to the upper right quadrant, which shows that $S + T = I + G$. The level of $I_1 + G$ from the previous quadrant equals the level of $S_1 + T$, that is, investment plus government spending equals savings plus taxes.

Move to the upper left quadrant, which shows a version of the consumption function. The vertical axis is total expenditures minus consumption (i.e., $[C + S + T] - C = S + T$), or savings plus taxes. Given $S_1 + T$ from the previous quadrant, the level of GNP is determined to be GNP_1.

Figure 3A.1   IS Curve

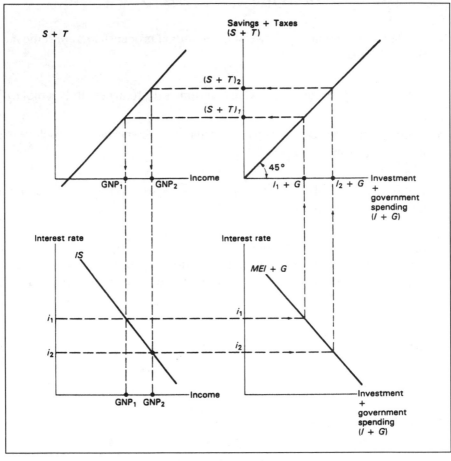

Move to the lower left quadrant. From the lower right quadrant, we know the interest rate i_1. From the upper left quadrant, we know the GNP level, GNP_1. This gives us one point on the IS function, GNP_1, i_1.

To obtain a second point on the IS function, the procedure is repeated by starting in the lower right quadrant with another interest rate i_2, giving another level of GNP, GNP_2, and so on.

The IS function shows a set of possible equilibriums in the economy, given the MEI and consumption function. As we have seen earlier, a lower interest rate induces more business investment which, in turn, changes GNP depending upon the size of the multiplier. Consequently, the IS function slopes down and to the right because higher GNP requires lower interest rates, given the MEI and consumption.

The LM Curve

Given the transactions demand for money, the speculative demand for money, and the total supply of money, the LM curve shows the possible equilibriums in the economy. The derivation of the LM curve is shown in figure 3A.2.

Start in the lower right quadrant of figure 3A.2 with the speculative demand curve. Given the interest rate i_1, the speculative demand curve tells us the level of speculative balances, M_{S1}.

Move to the upper right quadrant, which shows the total money supply and speculative and transactions balances. The total money supply, M, is equal to speculative balances, M_S, plus transactions balances, M_T:

Figure 3A.2   LM Curve

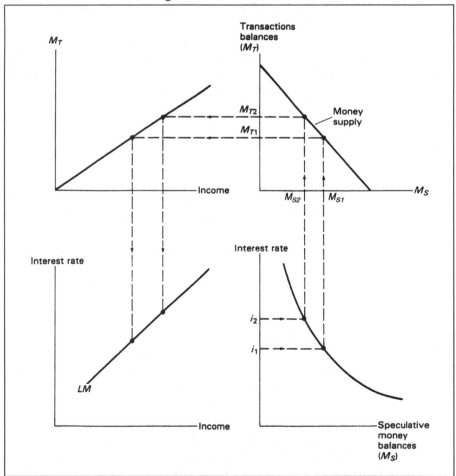

$$M = M_S + M_T \tag{3A.1}$$

In the upper right quadrant, if speculative balances are zero, the money supply is equal to transactions balances, giving us the vertical intercept. If transactions balances are zero, the money supply is all speculative balances, giving us the horizontal intercept. Given the level of speculative balances from the lower right quadrant and the total money supply M, the level of transactions balances is determined to be M_{T1}, i.e., $M_{T1} = M - M_{S1}$.

Move to the upper left quadrant, which shows GNP (income) versus transactions balances, or the transactions demand function. The level of transactions balances M_{T1} gives the level of GNP, GNP_1.

Given the interest rate i_1 from the speculative demand function and the GNP level GNP_1 from the transactions demand, we have one point on the LM function, shown in the lower left quadrant. Other points are derived by the same procedure.

The LM curve shows possible equilibrium levels of the interest rate and GNP given the transactions and speculative demand for money and the money supply. It slopes upward to the right because higher interest rates are necessary for higher GNP given the transactions and speculative demand for money.

Equilibrium of IS and LM Curves

Figure 3A.3 shows overall equilibrium. At the point where the IS and LM curves cross, the equilibrium interest rate and GNP are determined. This equilibrium is the point where the MEI function, consumption function, transactions demand, and speculative demand for money are all in equilibrium, given the total money supply and government spending and taxes. Clearly, the equilibrium interest rate depends upon all these factors.

A Change in the Money Supply

A change in the money supply can be analyzed through the IS-LM framework. Imagine that the monetary authorities increase the money supply, shifting the LM function to the right. The impact upon the interest rate depends upon the shapes of the IS and LM functions as shown in figure 3A.4.

Figure 3A.4 shows several scenarios. In case 1, an increase in the money supply shifts the LM curve to the right and causes a drop in interest rates and an increase in GNP. If this possibility describes the economy, recessions

Figure 3A.3   IS-LM Equilibrium

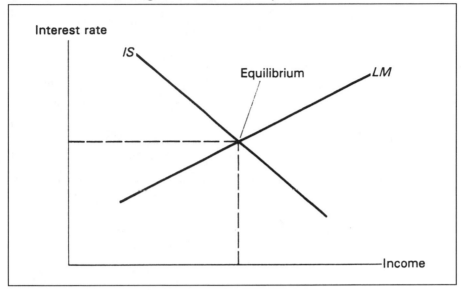

(i.e., low levels of GNP) can be cured by increases in the money supply, resulting in lower interest rates, greater production (GNP), and more employment.

Case 2 represents the so-called liquidity trap. In this unfortunate case, an increase in the money supply has no impact upon either interest rates or GNP. This case occurs if the demand curve for money is extremely flat. Then, increases in the money supply just cannot push interest rates any lower. Although Keynes was concerned about this case, it has not occurred in the U.S.

Case 3 is a situation in which an increase in the money supply has no impact upon interest rates but does increase GNP. This situation might occur if the MEI function is flat over some values.

In Case 4, an increase in the money supply reduces interest rates but does not change GNP. This case occurs if the MEI function is a vertical line over some values.

A Change in Government Spending

An increase in government spending can be analyzed through the IS-LM framework. As shown in figure 3A.5, an increase in government spending shifts the MEI function to the right, in turn shifting the IS curve to the right. The impact upon interest rates and GNP depends upon the shapes of the IS and LM curves. There are several interesting scenarios to consider.

Figure 3A.4   An Increase in the Money Supply

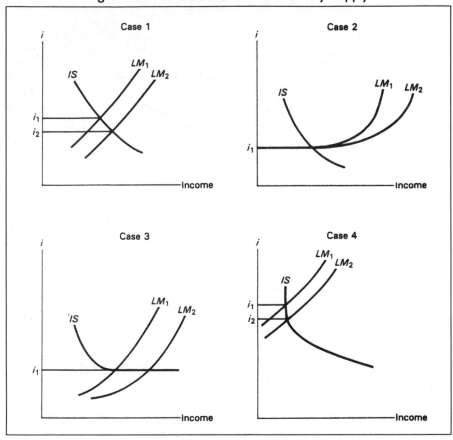

If the LM curve has a positive slope (case 1), an increase in government spending increases interest rates and GNP. Many Keynesian economists consider this situation very likely during a recession. Government spending increases output and employment and gets the economy out of the recession. However, because interest rates are pushed up, some business investment is crowded out of the market.

A second possibility (case 2) is a flat LM curve. Then an increase in government spending increases GNP but leaves interest rates unchanged. The increase in government spending does not crowd out any business investment. In this situation, we have a full multiplier effect from the increase in government spending. In this case an increase in government spending would have a very large impact upon GNP. Because interest rates are unchanged, no private business investment is crowded out.

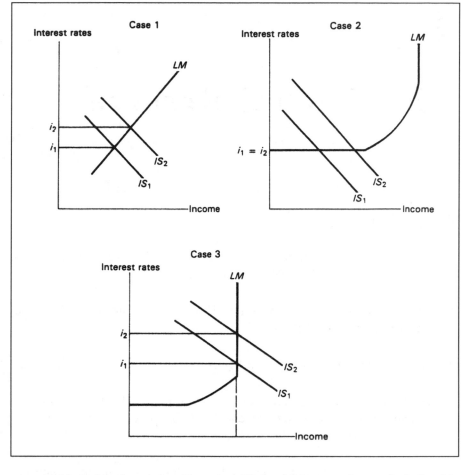

Figure 3A.5   An Increase in Government Spending

A third situation (case 3) occurs if the LM curve is vertical. In this case, the increase in government spending raises interest rates and crowds out enough investment to completely offset that increase in government spending.

References

Hansen, A. H., *A Guide to Keynes General Theory,* New York: McGraw-Hill, 1953.

Keynes, J. M., *The General Theory of Employment, Interest and Money,* New York: Harcourt, Brace, Jovanovich, 1936.

4

The Federal Reserve

Overview

The Federal Reserve System is the central bank of the United States. The major functions of the Federal Reserve are to:

1. Set and administer monetary policy. This involves controlling the money supply and/or interest rates.

2. Act as a lender of last resort to banks through the discount window.

3. Assist in the payments and collections systems. The Federal Reserve System plays a major role in the check clearing process and the electronic wire transfer of funds.

4. Regulate commercial banks. The Federal Reserve System, the Comptroller of the Currency, the Federal Deposit Insurance Corporation (FDIC), and state bank authorities all have some regulatory authority over commercial banks.

Federal Reserve Organization

The Federal Reserve system consists of two major parts: the Board of Governors and the 12 Federal Reserve District banks and branches. The Federal Reserve Board is composed of seven members appointed by the president for 14-year terms. The terms are staggered so that a new governor must be appointed every two years. One of the governors is appointed by the president as Chairman of the Board of Governors for a four-year term.

In practice, the chairman has considerable power in setting the course of monetary policy.

The Federal Reserve system is composed of 12 districts, each of which has a federal reserve district bank (and branches). See figure 4.1. These Federal Reserve banks are privately owned by the commercial banks that are Federal Reserve members in that district. The Federal Reserve pays dividends on the stock. Each district Federal Reserve bank has nine directors, six of which are selected by commercial banks that are members of that district and three selected by the Board of Governors. Each district bank has a president who participates in the Federal Open Market Committee.

The Federal Open Market Committee (FOMC) sets monetary policy. The voting members of the FOMC are the seven governors, the president of the federal reserve district bank of New York, and, on a rotating basis, four presidents of the other federal reserve district banks. The FOMC has eight regular meetings a year.

The primary task of these FOMC meetings is to draft a monetary policy directive, which sets guidelines for the growth rate of the money supply and the level of interest rates. This FOMC policy directive is kept secret for six weeks after the meeting. Many economists devote a great deal of time to monitoring monetary policy, trying to guess the contents of the secret directive. Therefore, any dramatic shift in monetary policy by the Federal Reserve is rapidly noted by the Federal Reserve watchers.

The Federal Reserve is technically independent for two reasons. First, the Federal Reserve earns more money from its operations than it needs to cover its operating expenses and, consequently, does not have to ask Congress for funds. The earnings of the Federal Reserve are largely interest earned on (U.S. Treasury) securities held in order to carry out monetary policy. The primary goals of monetary policy are to favorably influence employment, economic growth, and inflation. Earning interest is a side benefit to the Federal Reserve.

Second, the Federal Reserve system is not directly subject to control by the executive and legislative branches of the government because the members of the Board of Governors are appointed for 14-year terms and because the Federal Reserve banks are privately owned. That is, the Federal Reserve has the power to set monetary policy independent of the wishes of the president and both houses of Congress. However, since the Federal Reserve was established by an act of Congress and since Federal Reserve powers could be changed by further congressional action, the Federal Reserve is subject in the long run to pressure from Congress. Thus, the Federal Reserve's actions cannot be too far out of line with Congressional preferences.

Independence of the Federal Reserve has pros and cons. On the one hand, independence from the rest of the government allows the Federal

Figure 4.1   The Federal Reserve System

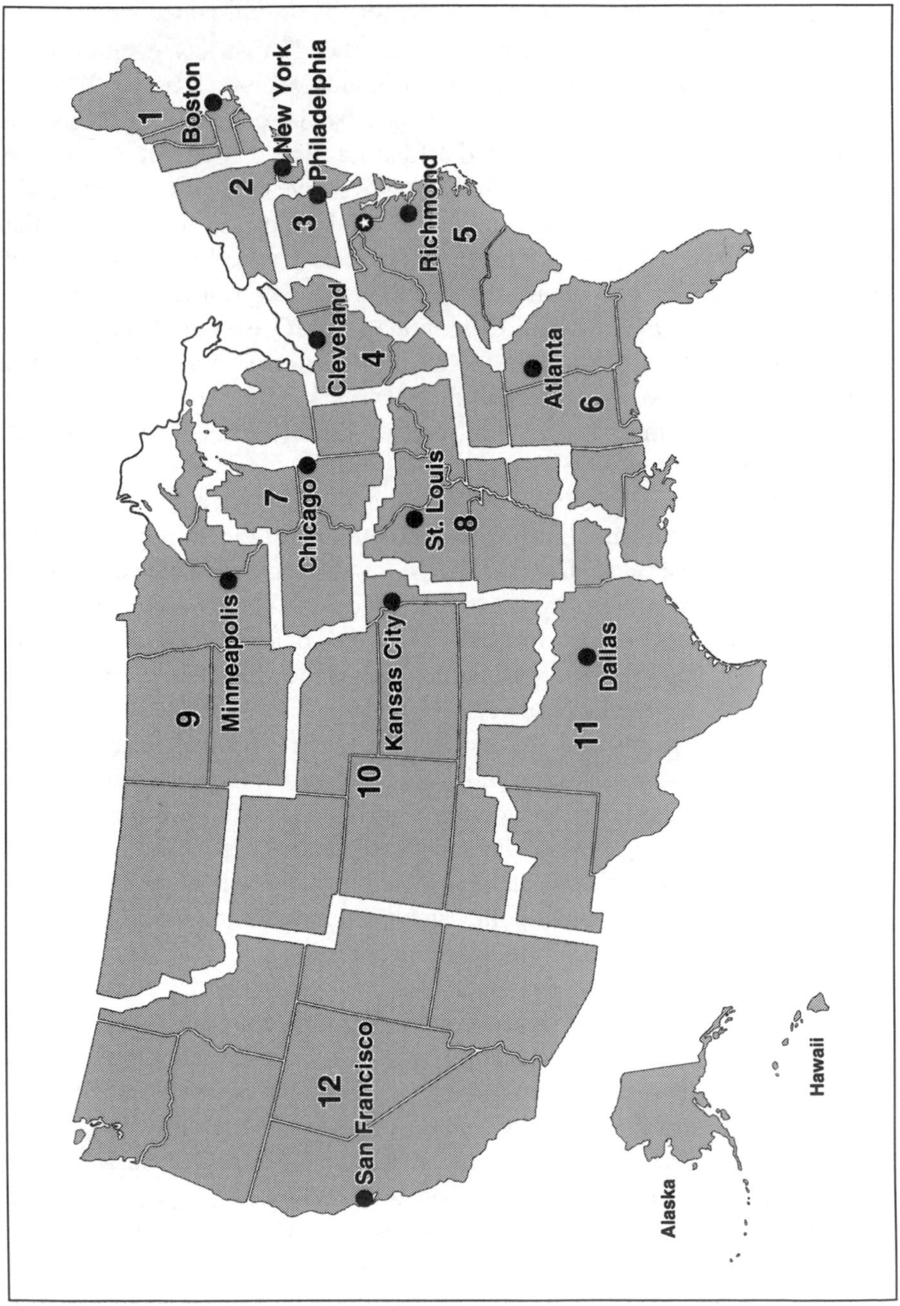

Reserve to look at policy from a long-run perspective. The Federal Reserve can follow a policy that should be good in the long run, as opposed to a short-sighted policy motivated by political expediency. On the other hand, too much independence may be undesirable if the policies of the Federal Reserve are in direct conflict with the rest of government economic policy.

Monetary Policy

The goals of monetary policy are to promote economic growth, full employment, and low inflation. **Economic growth** refers to increases in the wealth of the overall economy. On a per capita basis, wealth can be increased if the average worker produces more or if productivity increases. Productivity can be improved by increasing the amount of equipment available to workers and/or by making better use of that equipment.

Full employment refers to a situation in which all people who want to work are able to find work. In practice, full employment does not mean 100 percent employment and 0 percent unemployment. Because of so-called frictions, most economists feel that some people are always between jobs. Some unemployment is quite normal even though the economy is working at full capacity. Exactly what percentage of unemployment constitutes full employment is subject to some disagreement.

Inflation is an increase in the general price level. As discussed in chapter 2 on determinants of interest rates, measuring the inflation rate is a difficult process. There are several different price indexes, which are highly correlated but not identical.

Inflation is undesirable for two reasons. First, during inflationary periods, people try to stay ahead of inflation or even benefit in real terms. Strategies include trying to increase wages and prices and purchasing real assets. If some people are smarter or luckier than others, inflation may result in a redistribution of wealth, meaning that some people may be poorer and some people wealthier in real terms as a result of inflation. Second, people's efforts may be directed at keeping ahead of inflation and deflected from productive economic activity. The real wealth and the growth in that wealth may suffer. In effect, inflation may reduce real economic growth, curtailing the total wealth. Thus, inflation can reduce the total economic pie and alter its distribution.

In addition to the difficulties of measuring economic growth, employment, and inflation, these policy goals can be competing, forcing the Federal Reserve to make difficult policy choices. For example, it may be hard to achieve both full employment and low inflation. In order to keep the inflation rate relatively low, the Federal Reserve may have to follow a tight monetary policy, keeping the money supply growing at a slow rate and pushing up interest rates. As we know from the discussion of the neo-Keynesian (IS-LM) model, a small money supply (and high interest rates) reduces investment, income, and employment. The Federal Reserve typically adopts some compromise policy, which achieves neither full employment nor low inflation.

Another problem of conflicting policy goals concerns domestic and international policies. On the one hand, the Federal Reserve would like to follow a relatively expansionary domestic policy of adequate money growth and low interest rates. On the other hand, the Federal Reserve may want to control the rate of exchange between the U.S. dollar and foreign currencies by keeping interest rates high, stimulating inflows of foreign deposits. Again, the Federal Reserve must walk a tightrope.

The Money Supply

Although the Federal Reserve monitors the money supply, the exact meaning of the word *money* is subject to considerable controversy. Money has three characteristics: a medium of exchange, a unit of account, and a store of value. But exactly what constitutes money is not completely clear. Since no easy answer exists, the Federal Reserve has adopted several measures, called M1, M2, and M3. M1 includes currency and coins in circulation and travelers checks plus private bank deposits upon which checks can be written (see table 4.1). M2 includes M1 plus most types of personal savings accounts, including money market funds and money market deposit accounts at banks; M3 includes M2 plus large certificates of deposit and institutional money market funds.

The money supply measures are primarily intended to measure money as a medium of exchange. These are transactions balances, funds that can be used to make purchases of goods and services. The problem of measurement is that specific types of funds are not easy to categorize. There is unanimous agreement that currency, coins, and checking deposits held by the public are transactions balances, that is, funds that can be used at any time to make purchases. But, other varieties of funds may be partially held as transactions balances and partially for liquidity purposes as a store of value.

For example, M1 includes a category called ''other checkable deposits,'' which includes NOW, ATS, and share draft accounts. NOW (Negotiated Order of Withdrawal) accounts are deposits at commercial banks that allow checks to be written and which also pay interest. With ATS (Automatic

Table 4.1   The Money Supply

M1

Currency and coins held by the public
Checking deposits held by the public
Other checkable deposits
    NOW accounts
    ATS accounts
    Share draft accounts at credit unions

M2

M1
Savings accounts
Certificates of deposit for less than $100,000
Money market deposit accounts
Money market mutual funds held by individuals
Overnight repurchase agreements
Overnight Eurodollars

M3

M2
Certificates of deposit over $100,000
Repurchase agreements for longer than overnight
Eurodollars for longer than overnight
Institutional money market mutual funds

Transfer Service) accounts, funds are automatically transferred from an account that pays interest to a checking account paying no interest when checks come for collection. Share draft accounts at credit unions allow checks to be written. These accounts can, therefore, be used for making immediate payments. On the other hand, they may be used by some individuals as a store of value. While it is impossible to classify these accounts with complete certainty as transactions balances, they are counted as part of M1 because they are primarily held as transactions accounts.

    With each of the components of M2 and M3, some of the characteristics of transactions balances are apparent. An especially interesting example is money market deposit accounts at commercial banks (MMDA), which are deposits that pay interest and allow checks to be written. They are very similar to NOW accounts except that MMDAs have large minimum deposits and allow only a limited number of checks to be written. Because of these differences, MMDAs are counted in M2. However, the difference between a NOW account and an MMDA is a fine gradation, rather than a difference in kind. These types of differences make it very difficult to precisely pinpoint transactions balances.

Another interesting example is money market mutual fund deposits. A mutual fund is a pooling of funds by many investors. These funds are then managed for the investors for a fee. Money market mutual funds restrict their investments to short-term money market instruments with maturities of less than one year. Most money market mutual funds allow checks to be written on deposits with some restrictions. These deposits are quite similar to NOW accounts but, because of slight differences, they are classified as M2 for deposits held by individuals. The money market deposit accounts of institutions are classified as M3 because these are less likely to be used as transactions balances and more likely to be used as a store of value.

The amount of coins and paper currency held by the public is largely determined by the demand for these items. During some times of the year, the public desires to hold a large amount of cash. For example, during December the demand for currency goes up as a result of the Christmas buying season. One of the tasks of the Federal Reserve is to ensure that the public has enough cash available. Most of this cash is in the form of Federal Reserve notes (that is, paper currency), which the Federal Reserve produces as demand requires.

Repurchase agreements and Eurodollar deposits are short-term loans discussed extensively in chapter 16 on the money market. Overnight repurchase agreements and Eurodollar deposits are counted as part of M2, whereas long maturity loans are counted as M3.

Because of the difficulties in precisely measuring the money supply, the Federal Reserve monitors all of the measures of the money supply. The Federal Reserve monitors M2 and M3 more closely than M1 because the relationship between M1 and GNP has become less stable. In the IS-LM framework, the transactions demand for money is assumed to be a constant fraction of GNP. In recent years, M1 has not been a stable fraction of GNP. In other words, the velocity of M1 has been unstable. Recall that transactions balances, M_t, can be expressed as:

$$M_t = (k)\text{GNP} = \frac{\text{GNP}}{V_t} \qquad (4.1)$$

Transactions balances equal k percent of GNP or GNP divided by velocity. Solving for velocity V_t:

$$V_t = \frac{\text{GNP}}{M_t} = \frac{1}{k} \qquad (4.2)$$

That is, velocity is GNP divided by transactions balances.

M2 is more stable than M1 because M2 contains more items than M1. For example, consider funds being shifted from a NOW account to a money market deposit account. M1 changes but M2 does not change, because M2 includes both types of accounts and M1 includes only NOW accounts.

The stability of a particular velocity measure depends upon the stability of the particular money supply measure. Since M2 is more stable than M1, V2 velocity is more stable than V1 velocity.

Monetary Policy Tools

The primary task of the Federal Reserve is to establish and administer monetary policy guidelines for the money supply and interest rates. Technically, there are three possible tools of monetary policy available:

1. Changing reserve requirements.

2. Changing the interest rates on loans to banks through the Federal Reserve's discount window.

3. Open market operations.

In practice, the Federal Reserve concentrates on open market operations for several reasons. First, open market operations can be used effectively to make small adjustments in policy. In contrast, changing reserve requirements or changing the discount rate tends to result in large and inflexible changes in policy. Second, open market operations are easier to keep secret. In contrast, changes in the discount rate and reserve requirements involve public announcements. The Federal Reserve has a policy of keeping its policy secret in most circumstances. The advantages and disadvantages of secrecy are quite controversial.[1] Although secrecy is traditional with most central banks, many economists feel that policy would be more effective without secrecy. Next we will discuss each of the tools of the Federal Reserve.

---

[1] See Mayer (1987).

Reserve Requirements

Commercial banks are required to keep a proportion of their deposits as reserves. Required reserves may be kept as vault cash (coins and currency) and/or deposits with the Federal Reserve.

The Federal Reserve has the power to change reserve requirements on bank deposits within legislatively set bounds. For the first several million dollars of transactions balances, no reserves are required. For approximately the next $40 million of transactions, the reserve requirement is 3 percent. For higher levels of transactions balances, the reserve requirement may be varied by the Federal Reserve between 8 percent and 14 percent. For nonpersonal savings and time deposits, the reserve requirement may be varied by the Federal Reserve between 0 and 9 percent. Not all bank liabilities are considered deposits subject to reserve requirements. Three types of liabilities (federal funds, repurchase agreements, and foreign deposits) are exempt from reserve requirements. This makes the cost of these funds some-what lower for commercial banks, other things being equal.

Superficially, reserves are required for safety, to meet emergency cash needs. Since reserves continue to be required as long as deposits exist, required reserves can never be withdrawn. Safety is not the motivation for reserve requirements.

Required commercial bank reserves on deposit at the Federal Reserve allow the Federal Reserve to control the money supply and related monetary conditions by changing reserve requirements. For example, if the Federal Reserve were to reduce reserve requirements, excess reserves would be available to banks. These excess reserves would likely be lent out by the banks, tending to reduce interest rates, increase the supply of money, and stimulate the level of economic activity. If the Federal Reserve increased reserve requirements, banks would be forced to increase their deposits at the Federal Reserve. To obtain these required funds, banks would tend to reduce their lending, thereby raising interest rates, reducing the supply of money, and decreasing the level of economic activity.

In the past, the Federal Reserve has occasionally used the power to change reserve requirements to alter monetary conditions. In recent years, however, the Federal Reserve has focused upon open market operations. Recent reforms have extended Federal Reserve reserve requirements to most banks. Previously, national banks, chartered by the Comptroller of the Currency, as well as any state-chartered banks which chose to join the Federal Reserve, were subject to the Federal Reserve's reserve requirements. Many state-chartered banks chose not to join the Federal Reserve and instead were subject to lower reserve requirements set by state regulatory authorities. A lower reserve requirement allowed a bank to make more loans and earn higher profits. A countervailing factor was that Federal Reserve membership allowed a bank to use Federal Reserve services, including the discount window, funds transfer, and check clearing. Reforms in the 1980s have eliminated this two-tier system by making all depository institutions subject to the same reserve requirements and giving them the same access to the Federal Reserve.

Fractional Reserves and the Money Supply

Commercial banks are required to keep a fraction of deposits as reserves. Reserves may be in the form of deposits at the Federal Reserve or cash in the bank's vault. Assume for simplicity that the reserve requirement is 10 percent and deposits are $100. Then required reserves are $10. The bank may have $1 as vault cash and $9 on deposit with the Federal Reserve.

Banks may have an excess or a shortfall of reserves. In the preceding example in which required reserves are $10, if the bank has $2 in vault cash and $9 on deposit with the Federal Reserve, total reserves would be $11. There would be $1 of **excess reserves**. Excess reserves can be lent to make additional business loans.

A curious aspect of the fractional reserve banking system is that every dollar of excess reserves can create more than a $1 change in the money supply. Recall that the money supply includes currency in the hands of the public and checking deposits.[2] Assume that the bank takes the $1 of excess reserves and makes a $1 loan to a business customer. A new loan takes the form of a checking deposit. Total deposits increase by $1 to $101 and required reserves are $10.10. In effect, the money supply has increased by $1.

The new loan may be left on deposit. A more likely possibility is that the funds are spent by writing a check, which is then deposited in another bank. The additional $1 of deposits has become another bank's deposits. For the banking system as a whole, deposits have increased by $1. In the ensuing discussion, we consider all banks as a whole, as if they are one bank.

---

[2] Depending upon which definition of the money supply is used, other things are included as well.

For the banking system as a whole, the $1 of excess reserves results in a $1 increase in the money supply in the form of increased checking deposits. Required reserves increase by only $.10, meaning that excess reserves are $.90 (see table 4.2). The banking system can lend out another $.90, increasing checking deposits and the money supply by an additional $.90, for a total increase in the money supply of $1.90. Required reserves on the second loan are $.09, leaving $.81 as excess reserves, available to make loans that increase the money supply by a total of $2.71. This process continues until no excess reserves exist. The total increase in the money supply can be shown to be $1 divided by the 10 percent reserve requirement, or $10. Thus, a $1 increase in excess reserves has caused a $10 increase in the money supply.

In mathematical terms, the link between the money supply, the amount of reserves, and the reserve requirement is the following.

$$\text{Money Supply} = \left[\frac{\$ \text{ Reserves}}{\text{reserve } \%} \right] \qquad (4.3)$$

Table 4.2   Multiple Expansion of the Money Supply

Assumptions:
   10% Reserve requirement
   One bank for the entire economy
   All money is held as demand deposits
   Excess reserves are immediately lent

Excess Reserves	Additional Loans	Additional Required Reserves	Total Deposits
$1.0	$1.0	$.10	$1.0
$.90	$.90	$.09	$1.90
$.81	$.81	$.081	$2.71
$.729	$.729	$.0729	$3.439
.	.	.	.
.	.	.	.
.	.	.	.
$.00	$.00	$.00	$10.00
		Total required reserves = 1.00	

The preceding example must be adjusted for a number of important factors. Some individuals may prefer to hold their money balances in a form other than demand deposits. Perhaps individuals desire to withdraw funds in the form of currency. Others may deposit their funds into time deposit accounts, which have a different reserve requirement than checking deposits. In addition, some banks may not lend out excess reserves.

The point of the example is that any injection of reserves into the banking system has a multiple impact upon the money supply. The Federal Reserve must factor this multiple into its calculations when implementing monetary policy. Estimating this multiple is imprecise because of several unknowns: the percentage of checking deposits withdrawn as cash, the proportion of excess reserves sitting idle and not lent out, and so on. This imprecision adds to the difficulty of implementing a Federal Reserve policy. For example, if the Federal Reserve wants to increase the money supply by $100, estimating the amount of reserves to inject into the system involves some error.

In order to expedite the problem of keeping actual bank reserves in line with required reserves, the period for computing actual reserves lags behind the period for maintaining required reserves.[3] (See figure 4.2.) When a bank finds out its required reserves, it still has some time to adjust its actual reserves.

Discount Window

The Federal Reserve makes loans to banks through the **discount window**. The discount window allows the Federal Reserve to be a lender of last resort to banks in need. A bank that is short of funds has several courses of action to raise funds rapidly. The bank can borrow federal funds (that is, reserves of other banks on deposit with the Federal Reserve). The bank can also sell government securities in the market. The bank can issue certificates of deposit. Finally, loans from the Federal Reserve can be requested, if the other sources of funds are closed off.

At the time that the Federal Reserve was established in 1913, the discount window was the most important tool for the Federal Reserve. The prevailing view of monetary policy at the time was the so-called commercial

---

[3] For transactions balances, the lag is two days. For nonpersonal time deposits, the lag is four weeks.

Figure 4.2   Required Reserves versus Actual Reserves

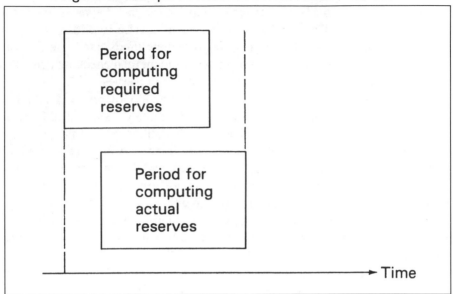

loan theory. According to this view, commercial banks should confine their loans to short-term loans to business. These loans were thought to be self-liquidating. An example is a loan to a retail firm to buy inventory. When the inventory is sold, funds are generated to pay off or liquidate the loan. Under the commercial loan theory, the central bank is supposed to control the economy by making loans to commercial banks backed by loans to business. By varying the discount rate on these loans, the Federal Reserve was supposed to able to control the economy. The commercial loan theory is now regarded as incorrect because it suffers from the basic flaw of overlooking economy-wide factors. For example, short-term business loans are not self-liquidating when an economy-wide recession or depression occurs and many firms are unable to sell their inventory.

The discount window still remains as a tool for the Federal Reserve to be lender of last resort, providing funds to individual banks or to the banking system as a whole at times when funds are short. Without the Federal Reserve serving as an injector of funds, a relatively small problem might become a large problem.

Three types of loans are available from the Federal Reserve. First, banks that are temporarily short of reserves to meet reserve requirements have access to loans from the Federal Reserve. The Federal Reserve is not required to make these loans. For example, if a bank tries to borrow too often, the Federal Reserve can refuse to make further loans. The discount rate on loans from the Federal Reserve may be lower than the federal funds rate, the rate at which a bank can lend to other banks. In this circumstance, a bank may be tempted to borrow from the Federal Reserve at the low discount rate and lend these funds at the higher federal funds rate – profiting from the difference. If the Federal Reserve feels that a bank is engaged in this type of arbitrage, it can refrain from making loans to the bank.

Second, the Federal Reserve makes seasonal loans to some banks. For example, banks serving agriculture communities may have a markedly seasonal demand for funds which the Federal Reserve may help to meet through seasonal loans.

Third, the Federal Reserve makes longer term extended credit loans to banks in serious financial trouble. An example is the large loans made to Continental Illinois Bank. These loans were intended to give the troubled bank some time to work out its problems. Before establishment of the Federal Reserve, bank failures sometimes precipitated runs on healthy banks and a generalized banking panic. A bank run occurs when depositors become concerned about the safety of their funds. Consequently, they "run" to the bank to withdraw their funds. Because most of a bank's assets are working assets, very little cash is available to pay depositors. Large withdrawal requests may force a bank to close its doors. The closing of one bank may provoke depositors in other banks to become nervous about the safety of their deposits, causing runs on these banks and more closings in an avalanche effect. Large-scale closings can easily precipitate a recession or depression in the overall economy. Federal Reserve loans to troubled institutions are one tool for trying to prevent such dire events.

Changes in the Federal Reserve's discount rate often receive great publicity in the press. Sometimes discount rate changes surprise the financial markets and contain some new information about Federal Reserve policy. More often, these changes are widely anticipated. Typically, changes in the discount rate tend to lag behind other interest rates (such as the federal funds rate), rather than set the trend. For example, when the Federal Reserve eases monetary conditions by buying Treasury bills, short-term interest rates (including the federal funds rate) decline. Somewhat later, the discount rate is lowered.

Some other examples of Federal Reserve action do not fit neatly into the preceding three cases. On October 19, 1987, the stock market crashed, with prices declining more than 20 percent in one day. This crash resulted in massive losses for securities dealers. On the following morning, many banks with outstanding loans to these dealers were hesitant to provide any more credit to them. If the dealers were denied credit, they would have been unable to operate as dealers and undoubtedly security prices would have taken a further dramatic plunge. The consequences for the economy might have been disastrous. To calm the situation, the Federal Reserve informed the banks that loans to dealers would be guaranteed by the Federal Reserve. The resulting injection of funds to dealers allowed them to continue to operate and gave the security markets some time to calm down. A worse crisis was avoided.

In another example, a major money center bank had both its main computer systems and backup systems fail. This meant that very large payments could not be settled at the end of the day. Payments by the institution with failed computers were necessary for many other banks to settle their accounts for the day. For example, suppose that the bank with failed computers owed $500 m. to a sound bank, which, without this $500 m., would have to default on payments to a third bank, which would have to default on payments to a fourth bank, and so on. Because of the effect of falling dominoes, default by one bank could bring the entire payments system to a close. To prevent this from occurring, the Federal Reserve immediately stepped in and made payment on the likely obligations of the bank with a guarantee that the Federal Reserve would pick up the tab if unresolved discrepancies occurred later. By acting quickly, the Federal Reserve was able to keep the payments systems moving smoothly.

Open Market Operations

Open market operations involve the purchase and sale by the Federal Reserve of U.S. Treasury securities in the open market. If the Federal Reserve buys bonds in the open market from an individual, the seller's commercial bank account is increased by the sale price. Since the money in this account can be spent, the money supply increases, and, other things equal, interest rates are reduced. If the Federal Reserve sells bonds to an individual, the buyer's bank account is reduced, the money supply goes down, and interest rates tend to go up.

When the Federal Reserve buys securities from a commercial bank, it pays for them by increasing the bank's balance at the Federal Reserve. Balances at the Federal Reserve in excess of required reserves can be withdrawn and used to make loans to bank customers, causing an increase in the money supply.

In practice, the Federal Reserve has unlimited buying power, because it can create balances in any amount with the stroke of a pen. In carrying out monetary policy, the Federal Reserve tends to accumulate a large portfolio of U.S. Treasury securities, upon which it earns interest. Part of this interest is used by the Federal Reserve to pay its operating expenses, and the rest is returned to the Treasury.

Funds Transfer and Check Clearing

There are three methods for making payments: (1) currency and coin, (2) checks, and (3) electronic transfer. The largest *number* of transactions is in the form of currency and coin, followed by checks and then electronic transfers. In terms of the *dollar* value of transactions, electronic transfers represent the largest amount, followed by checks, and then currency and coins. That is, there are a relatively small number of very large denomination wire transfers and a relatively large number of currency and coin transactions in small denominations.

The Federal Reserve plays an important role in the wire (electronic) transfer of funds over the Federal Reserve Wire. Banks can rapidly transfer funds over the Federal Reserve Wire for a fee. This allows transactions to be completed on the same day. For instance, a bank in New York can transfer funds to a bank in San Francisco over the Federal Reserve Wire. Without this capability, many types of transactions would be impossible. For example, federal funds and repurchase agreements involve overnight loans whereby the money is lent one day and repaid the next day. These transactions would be impossible without wire transfer. There are also a number of private wire transfer systems that supplement the Federal Reserve.

The Federal Reserve plays an important role in the clearing and collection of checks. Suppose Bob Buyer, located in Jacksonville, Florida, sends a check written against his account at the Barnett Bank of Florida to Dayton's Department Store in Minneapolis. In order to collect payment, Dayton's has to present the check to the Barnett Bank in Florida. While the check could be flown to Florida for collection at the Barnett Bank, the expense would be prohibitive.

Instead, the Federal Reserve provides a system to expedite check collection at moderate cost. Dayton's deposits the check in its local bank in Minneapolis. The check is transmitted to the regional Federal Reserve Bank in Minneapolis, which transmits it to the regional Federal Reserve Bank serving Jacksonville. Then the check is sent to the Barnett Bank for payment. The Federal Reserve then transmits the funds to the local bank in Minneapolis.[4] This entire procedure takes several days.

---

[4] The Federal Reserve has a predetermined time schedule for making payments on checks that are being collected. In this example, the Federal Reserve might make payment to Dayton's bank within two days, even if actual collection time is longer.

The Federal Reserve handles vast numbers of checks. Without this type of collection system, many payments by check would be essentially impossible. In recent years, the Federal Reserve has moved to a system in which users pay directly for services used. This pricing system has stimulated the use of private check clearing systems which supplement the Federal Reserve. We consider two varieties of private check collection systems: local and long distance.

For local check collection, the banks can have a private clearinghouse settle all the checks drawn on the participating banks. The clearinghouse cancels out some of the inter-bank transfers of funds, allowing the net shifts of funds between the banks to be made efficiently. Consider the following example of a three-bank clearinghouse to handle the checks of Barnett Bank, Sun Bank, and First Union Bank.

Table 4.3   Three-Bank Clearinghouse

Written on	Checks Deposited in Bank			Total Written
	Barnett	Sun	First Union	
Barnett	0	100	400	500
Sun	200	0	400	600
First Union	400	400	0	800
Total Deposits	600	500	800	1,900
Total Written	500	600	800	1,900
Net Deposits	100	−100	0	0

In the example, Barnett Bank has $600 of deposits and $500 of withdrawals, for a net of $100 deposits. Sun Bank has $500 in deposits and withdrawals of $600, for net withdrawal of $100. First Union Bank has $800 of checks written and $800 deposited, for a net of zero. The three banks can settle their accounts if Sun Bank pays $100 to Barnett Bank. This net transfer is shown in the bottom row as net deposits, that is, the change in reserves at the Fed. The clearinghouse has greatly simplified the transactions by netting them out.

Banks can circumvent the Federal Reserve collection system on long distance checks by using correspondent banks. A correspondent bank is a bank at which balances are maintained. Suppose both Bank A in Oregon and Bank B in Florida maintain correspondent balances with Bank C in Chicago. A check for $100 written on Bank A and deposited in Bank B can be settled by transferring the funds between the deposits at the correspondent bank. The advantage of using a correspondent bank is a slightly lower cost than using the Federal Reserve collection system.

Credit Regulation

The Federal Reserve has the power to regulate borrowing for the purchase of securities, a so-called margin purchase. For example, in recent years the Federal Reserve has required the buyer of common stock to put down at least 50 percent of the original purchase price. For other types of securities and transactions, the margin requirement has been different. Use of borrowed funds to buy securities is a form of financial leverage. The percentage changes in a levered (or margined) position are greater than the percentage changes in the underlying security.

The reason for giving the Federal Reserve power over security margin purchases is the concern that excessive use of security credit might contribute to boom and bust cycles in security prices and in the overall economy. An example of a boom-bust cycle is the period of the late 1920s and early 1930s. In the 1920s, security margin was not regulated. The typical margin for common stocks was 10 percent. The consequences of this margin requirement are illustrated in table 4.4. An investor putting down equity of $10 could borrow $90 and buy a stock worth $100. If the stock went up 10 percent to $110, the investor's equity would increase 100 percent to $20. Another $90 could be borrowed and more stock purchased. If many investors borrowed more as their profit increased, a snowballing effect would result. Rising prices would tend to bring about further rises.

In the examples in table 4.4, the equity of the margined position changes ten times as fast as the value of the underlying security. This is not a chance event. For the case where dividends, coupon payments, and interest on borrowed funds can be overlooked, the percentage change in the levered position equals the percentage change in the underlying security divided by the percent put down. That is:

$$\frac{\% \text{ change of levered}}{} = \frac{\% \text{ change underlying}}{\% \text{ put down}} \tag{4.4}$$

With a 10 percent margin, the levered positions change ten times as fast as the underlying; but with a 50 percent margin requirement, the levered position changes only twice as fast as the underlying.

The lower part of table 4.4 shows the magnification effect of leverage on the downside. If the underlying security decreases in price by 10 percent,

Table 4.4   Example of a 10% Margin Requirement

Assumptions:
  Overlook coupons or dividends on underlying security
  Overlook interest on borrowed funds

	Underlying Security Price	=	Borrowings	+	Equity
	100		90		10
	110		90		20
Percent Change	10%		0		100%
	Underlying Security Price	=	Borrowings	+	Equity
	100		90		10
	90		90		0
Percent Change	−10%		0		−100%

the equity of the levered position decreases by 100 percent and the equity is zero. Even before the equity went to zero, the investor would receive a margin call from the broker, who would request more collateral. If the investor is unable or unwilling to provide more collateral, the broker liquidates the position. By giving a margin call when the collateral is positive, the broker is able to protect the lender against losses. Otherwise, an investor with a negative equity position would be tempted to default, leaving the lender to absorb a loss equal to the amount borrowed minus the current market value of the securities.

A decline in security prices may set off a number of margin calls. Investors who are unable to put up more collateral are forced to sell out their positions, possibly aggravating the price declines. An avalanche effect may occur, with dropping prices causing further price drops. The avalanche effect is stronger if the margin requirement is lower.

The very low margin requirements of the 1920s apparently contributed to the sharp rises in security prices during the late 1920s and the subsequent precipitous decline from 1929 to 1932. Some authorities claim that the stock market boom-bust cycle contributed to a similar boom-bust in the economy. The effect of the stock market is two-fold. First, changes in stock prices can affect consumption spending, with higher stock prices causing greater spending. The reason appears to be that higher stock prices increase consumers' perceived wealth.[5] With higher perceived wealth, they tend to spend more. Second, a firm's cost of capital is affected by the level of stock prices, with the resulting impact upon the firm's investment spending. Fear of a repetition of the events of the 1930s and concern about the impact of security credit upon the entire economy has motivated Federal Reserve control of security credit.

Recently, the Federal Reserve has been concerned about the use of credit in so-called leveraged buyouts. These buyouts are mergers in which the acquiring firm has very little equity, with a great deal of the financing coming from high risk debt. The Federal Reserve's view has been that these leveraged buyouts are effectively margin purchases which are subject to the Federal Reserve's control.

Regulation of Banks

The Federal Reserve has important powers to regulate commercial banks, including the power to regulate the entry of banks into nonbanking activities. Many nonbanking activities are strictly prohibited. For example, banks are prohibited from engaging in commerce. But certain types of financial activities are allowed with the permission of the Federal Reserve.

The Federal Reserve regulates foreign banks that have opened offices in the United States. Regulation of foreign banks is a difficult problem. Ideally, all banks should be treated equally, but creating a set of regulations to achieve this goal is difficult. Banking regulations in foreign countries are different from, and typically more lenient than, those in the United States. Use of the same rules for all banks with offices in the United States may result in an inherent advantage for branches of foreign banks operating in the United States because of more favorable treatment in their non-U.S. operations.[6]

---

[5] The wealth is perceived rather than actual. Market values do not represent actual wealth because, if all holders of stock tried to "cash in" their holdings, market values would rapidly sink.

[6] For example, if the bank is required to keep a smaller percentage of non-U.S. deposits as reserves with the foreign central bank, the bank may be able to subsidize U.S. loans. In effect, the bank can make loans in the U.S. and finance these loans with relatively low-cost foreign sources of funds.

Foreign Exchange Rates

The balance of trade is the difference between exports and imports. Recently, the United States' balance of trade has become unfavorable since U.S. imports have greatly exceeded exports. In addition, the exchange rate of the U.S. dollar has fluctuated considerably. These two events have put some constraints upon the operation of monetary policy.

At times, the Federal Reserve has changed the level of interest rates to alter the exchange value of the dollar. For example, to keep the dollar from falling, the Federal Reserve has taken action to raise interest rates. Higher interest rates tend to attract foreign funds into the United States and keep the U.S. dollar at a higher level. Exchange rate goals and domestic policy goals may conflict. For example, a policy of high interest rates to keep up the exchange value of the dollar tends to reduce output and employment levels in the U.S. and may even bring on a recession. Policy makers have to weigh the relative importance of these competing goals.

Federal Reserve policy also has an impact upon the balance of trade. A more restrictive monetary policy dampens the level of economic activity and reduces the demand for imports, improving the balance of trade. The effect may only be short term. In the long run, the balance of trade is affected by major economic trends that are probably beyond the control of the Federal Reserve. The United States balance of trade has been adversely affected by the gradual depletion of cheap oil supplies in the United States, with the result being an increased reliance on oil imports. An increase of food production outside the United States has reduced United States food exports. A slow rate of improvement in productivity (output per manhour) in the United States has tended to make U.S. goods more expensive, stimulating imports and reducing exports.

The Money Supply versus Interest Rates

As chapters 2 and 3 on determinants of interest rates discussed, the neo-Keynesians and the monetarists disagree about the proper target of monetary policy. The neo-Keynesians have emphasized the importance of the level of interest rates. The monetarists have focused upon the growth rate of the money supply. During the 1950s and 1960s, the Federal Reserve tended to closely monitor the level of interest rates, following a largely neo-Keynesian approach. In the 1970s and early 1980s, the Federal Reserve's focus was on the growth rate of the money supply, tending to follow more of a monetarist approach, although not completely ignoring the level of interest rates. Recently, the Federal Reserve has returned to more of a focus on interest rates.

One frequently discussed area is the question of rules versus discretion. Should the Federal Reserve follow a set of predetermined rules in setting the growth rate of the money supply, or should the Federal Reserve exercise discretion and adapt policy to perceived current needs? Monetarists tend to feel that rules are better, arguing that the Federal Reserve has a tendency to make economic problems worse by their discretionary decisions. Neo-Keynesians tend to favor discretion.

Foreign Central Banks

Foreign central banks operate in much the same way as the Federal Reserve. A 1990 study by the International Monetary fund found similar operating procedures for the central banks of France, Germany, Japan, the United Kingdom, and the United States.[7]

Central banks differ in their degree of independence from the rest of the government. The central banks of Germany and Japan are more independent than the U.S. Federal Reserve. The central banks of the United Kingdom and France are more subject to politics than the U.S. Federal Reserve. The evidence shows countries with more independent central banks have lower inflation rates.[8]

Summary

The Federal Reserve is the central bank of the United States. Its primary functions are to set and administer monetary policy, be a lender of last resort, expedite payments and collections, and regulate commercial banks. The goal of monetary policy is to promote economic growth, stability, full employment, and low inflation. These goals can be competing, creating difficult policy choices for the Federal Reserve. In administering monetary policy, the Federal Reserve has attempted to control both the money supply and interest rates.

---

[7] See Batten et al. (1990).

[8] See Alesina and Summers (1993).

Questions/Problems

1. Describe the composition and role of the Federal Open Market Committee.

2. Why are there several measures of the money supply? What are the major differences among M1, M2, and M3?

3. Explain the impact of a reduction in required reserves on the money supply.

4. What are the functions of the Federal Reserve discount window?

5. Describe the relationship between the discount rate and other money market rates.

6. Why are open market operations the primary tool of monetary policy?

7. Explain the procedure for collecting a check drawn on a bank in one Federal Reserve district and deposited in another Federal Reserve district.

8. What is the advantage of having a local clearinghouse for check collection?

9. One of the functions of the Federal Reserve is to regulate security credit. What is the motivation behind this regulation?

10. Assume that reserve requirements on bank deposits are 5 percent and that there are no leakages such as cash withdrawals. Banks receive an injection of $1,000 in excess reserves. Determine the increase in the money supply if all excess reserves can be lent out.

11. Assume a single-bank economy with very strong loan demand and all money held as checking deposits. The money supply is initially $200,000. The Fed buys $10,000 of bonds from the bank. The money supply increases to $300,000. What is the reserve requirement?

12. Assume a single-bank economy with very strong loan demand and all money held as checking deposits. The money supply is initially $100,000. The Fed increases the reserve requirement by 2 percent and the money supply drops to $50,000. What percent is the new reserve requirement?

13. Assume that you purchase $5,000 worth of securities by putting down 25 percent margin. Compute the percentage gains and losses on the margined position if the underlying security increases by 10 percent and if it decreases by 20 percent. Assume that the broker has a rule to give a margin call when the equity in the levered position is worth 10 percent of the underlying security. At what point would a margin call occur?

14. Assume that you are required to put down 40 percent of the purchase price of a security. Overlooking any current interest or dividends, determine the percentage change in the underlying security if your equity changes by 25 percent.

15. The Federal Reserve regulates margin requirements for security purchases. Assume that the margin requirement (percent put down) is X percent. A speculator buys a security for $300 putting down X times $300. The security doubles in price. What is the rate of increase in the speculator's equity?

16. There are three banks in a city – Barnett Bank, Sun Bank, and First Union Bank. These banks establish a clearinghouse to handle all the interbank checks. Compute the net interbank transfers required to net out all these checks.

	Checks Deposited in Bank		
Written on	**Barnett**	**Sun**	**First Union**
Barnett	0	300	500
Sun	100	0	400
First Union	500	400	0

17. Three banks in Chicago established a clearinghouse for their checks written against each other.

	Checks Deposited in Bank		
Written on	**First**	**Second**	**Third**
First	0	100	800
Second	200	0	600
Third	300	700	0

What are the net transfers of funds to settle all these checks?

References

Alesina, A. and L. H. Summers, "Central Bank Independence and Macroeconomic Performance: Some Comparative Evidence," *Journal of Money, Credit, and Banking,* May 25, 1993, pp. 151–62.

Barger, H., *Money Banking and Public Policy,* Chicago: Rand McNally, 1962.

Batten, D. S., M. P. Blackwell, I. S. Kim, S. E. Nocera, and Y. Ozeki, "The Conduct of Monetary Policy in the Major Industrial Countries: Instruments and Operating Procedures," Washington, DC: International Monetary Fund, July 1990.

The Federal Reserve System, Purposes and Functions 7/e, Washington, DC: Government Printing Office, 1984.

Kasman, B., "A Comparison of Monetary Policy Operating Procedures in Six Industrial Countries," *Federal Reserve Bank of New York Quarterly Review,* 17, Summer 1992, pp. 5–24.

Mayer, T., "Disclosing Monetary Policy," New York University Salomon Brothers Center for the Study of Financial Institutions, *Monograph Series in Finance and Economics,* Monograph 1987–1.

Misback, A. E., "The Foreign Bank Supervision Enhancement Act of 1991," *Federal Reserve Bulletin,* 79, January 1993, pp. 1–10.

Stigum, M., *The Money Market,* Homewood, IL: Dow Jones Books, 1990.

5

Issuers of Securities

Overview

This chapter discusses the issuers of securities. In the United States, this list includes the U.S. Treasury, municipalities, corporations, U.S. government and government-sponsored agencies, and mortgage issuers. The security issuers in foreign countries are quite similar, although the existence of particular types of issuers depends upon the size and sophistication of financial markets. Countries such as Japan, Germany, the United Kingdom, and Canada are quite similar to the U.S. Other countries have fewer similarities.

The U.S. Treasury

The U.S. Treasury has the responsibility of paying U.S. federal government expenditures, collecting taxes, and borrowing to meet the deficit between expenditures and taxes. This borrowing is accomplished by selling debt securities of various types. The large federal deficits of recent years have greatly increased the total outstanding amount of U.S. Treasury debt. Since 1980, annual deficits of over $100 billion have been the norm. The total debt has ballooned to over $4 trillion in 1995.

Because of the enormous growth in the federal debt, the Treasury plays an increasingly important role in the debt markets. Treasury debt obligations are the dominant force in the bond market for two reasons. First, the total Treasury debt is enormous, over $4 trillion. Second, each Treasury issue is large compared to corporate and municipal debt. Treasury issues of $10 billion dollars or more are common. The average corporate bond issue is approximately $130 million. Thus, the typical Treasury bond issue is about 75 times as big as the typical corporate bond issue. Large size for each

Treasury debt issue implies a large volume of trading and a liquid market, i.e., a market in which dealers make active markets and in which buyers and sellers can trade without affecting prices.

The U.S. Treasury publishes the *Monthly Statement of the Public Debt.* This publication contains a wealth of information about Treasury debt, describing each debt issue and its terms. See Table 5.1 for an example.

Treasury securities are held by the Federal Reserve, by foreigners, by commercial banks, by nonbank financial institutions, and by individuals. The Federal Reserve buys and sells Treasury securities in the course of open market operations. In order to effectively control monetary conditions, the Federal Reserve must have sizable holdings of Treasury securities. Foreigners

Table 5.1   Monthly Statement of the Public Debt of the United States

MONTHLY STATEMENT OF THE PUBLIC DEBT OF THE UNITED STATES
APRIL 30, 1992
(Details, rounded in millions, may not add to totals)

TABLE I—SUMMARY OF PUBLIC DEBT OUTSTANDING, APRIL 30, 1992 AND COMPARATIVE FIGURES FOR APRIL 30, 1991

Title	APRIL 30, 1992		APRIL 30, 1991	
	Average Interest Rate	Amount Outstanding	Average Interest Rate	Amount Outstanding
Interest-bearing debt:				
Marketable:	Percent		Percent	
Bills:				
Treasury	¹4.473	$598.383	¹6.749	$504.404
Notes:				
Treasury	7.920	1,497.003	8.575	1,319.015
Bonds:				
Treasury	9.660	443.789	9.833	399.263
Other Securities:				
Federal Financing Bank²	8.917	15.000	8.917	15.000
Total Marketable	7.435	2,554.175	8.403	2,237.682
Nonmarketable:				
Depositary Series	2.000	1	2.000	1
Domestic Series	7.925	29.995	¹7.923	29.995
Foreign Series:				
Government Dollar Denominated	6.924	42.164	7.543	42.680
Government Account Series	8.734	961.491	9.140	842.527
R.E.A. Series	5.000	4	4.997	5
State and Local Government Series	¹7.883	159.633	8.234	159.945
United States Individual Retirement Bonds	6.548	17	6.501	18
United States Retirement Plan Bonds	6.147	73	6.125	77
United States Savings Bonds	6.906	141.320	6.973	129.145
United States Savings Notes	6.973	337	6.965	327
Total Nonmarketable	8.414	1,335.036	8.759	1,204.719
Total Interest-bearing debt	7.763	3,889.211	8.525	3,442.402
Non-interest-bearing debt:				
Matured Debt		1.970		1.896
Other		793		761
Total Non-interest-bearing debt		2.763		2.657
Total Public Debt Outstanding		3,891.974		3,445.059

TABLE II—STATUTORY DEBT LIMIT, APRIL 30, 1992

Public Debt subject to limit:	
Public Debt Outstanding	$3,891.974
Less amounts not subject to limit:	
Miscellaneous Debt	594
Unamortized Discount³	82.589
Federal Financing Bank	15.000
Total Public Debt subject to limit	3,793.791
Other debt subject to limit:	
Guaranteed Debt of Government agencies	419
Total debt subject to limit	3,794.210
Statutory Debt Limit⁴	4,145.000
Balance of Statutory Debt Limit	350.790

¹$500 thousand or less.
¹Computed on true discount basis.
²These marketable securities have been issued to the Civil Service Retirement Fund and are not currently traded in the market.

³Represents the unamortized discount on Treasury Bills, zero-coupon Treasury Bonds and Government Account Series zero-coupon bonds.
⁴Pursuant to 31 U.S.C. 3101. By Act of November 5, 1990, the Statutory Debt Limit was permanently increased to $4,145.000 million.

Source: Bureau of the Public Debt, Department of Treasury

hold Treasury securities because they are default-free and denominated in dollars, a relatively safe currency. Commercial banks hold Treasury securities as secondary reserves, i.e., assets that can readily be turned into cash as the need arises. Nonbank financial institutions include pension funds, insurance companies, and finance companies. These institutions are large holders of debt obligations. Debt obligations allow nonbank financial institutions to control their risk by matching the institutions' fixed obligations to pensioners or policyholders with fixed income investments in bonds. Individual investors hold Treasury securities because they are default-free, free of state income tax, and highly marketable. However, individuals hold a relatively small proportion of Treasury debt directly in their portfolios.

Deficits, Interest Rates, and Inflation

Interest Rates   The impact of Treasury borrowing upon interest rates can be analyzed by the loanable funds and neo-Keynesian frameworks. In the loanable funds framework, the demand curve for funds shifts to the right. The new equilibrium has a higher interest rate. (See chapter 2 on the determinants of interest rates.) Some non-Treasury borrowers are crowded out of the market by Treasury borrowing. In effect, the higher interest rate forces the rationing of the scarce resource, loanable funds.

In the neo-Keynesian framework, an increase in government borrowing shifts the marginal efficiency of capital (MEI) curve to the right. In turn, output increases and the demand for money function shifts to the right, raising interest rates. The higher interest rates crowd out some business investment.

Inflation   A very large public debt resulting from a series of large deficits may create a large repayment burden in the future. Apart from the problem of repaying the debt principal, the interest payments alone on a multi-trillion dollar debt may put a considerable strain on government finances in the future. For example, a debt of $4 trillion has an interest cost of about $250–300 billion per year. Instead of raising taxes and/or cutting government expenditures to make the contractual payments on the debt, the government may be tempted to reduce the debt burden through inflation. For example, a doubling of the price level reduces the real cost of the debt by 50 percent. Political expediency may make this inflationary course of action easier than other options. After all, most politicians are not anxious to raise taxes or reduce current expenditures.

The earlier discussion of determinants of interest rates suggests that inflationary expectations tend to be incorporated into current interest rates. Huge current federal budget deficits tend to create expectations that the government will follow an inflationary policy in the future. In turn, the anticipated inflation is reflected in current interest rates because the expected inflation rate is added to the real interest rate to obtain the nominal interest rate. The bottom line is that current budget deficits can raise interest rates by creating inflationary expectations.

Types of Treasury Securities

The Treasury issues nonmarketable and marketable debt.

Nonmarketable Debt   About one quarter of the Treasury debt is nonmarketable. The original buyer cannot resell it. Nonmarketable is primarily of two types – savings bonds and bonds sold to government agencies. The U.S. Treasury sells some nonmarketable bonds in the form of savings bonds. Savings bonds have a fixed interest rate, cannot be resold (although they can be redeemed early with penalty), and generally are held until maturity. Only a small part of Treasury borrowing is in the form of savings bonds. A large part of the nonmarketable debt is securities sold to government retirement funds for civil service employees and the military.

Marketable Debt   The Treasury sells three major types of marketable debt: (1) bills, (2) notes, and (3) bonds. Treasury bills (T-bills) are discussed in more detail in the chapter on money market instruments. In brief, they have maturities up to one year. They are issued on a discount basis, meaning no coupon payments. The buyer pays the purchase price and receives the par value at maturity. The difference is interest.

Treasury notes and bonds are originally issued with maturities exceeding one year. Notes and bonds pay semiannual coupon interest to the owners. The distinction between notes and bonds is largely semantic. Notes have original maturities of up to ten years. Bonds have original maturities of between ten and 30 years.

There are some legal restrictions on the Treasury's ability to issue debt. First, Congress has put a ceiling on the national debt. As the total debt has grown, Congress has been forced to raise the debt ceiling. Secondly, there have been Congressional restrictions on the amount of Treasury bonds outstanding. Again, these limits have been raised as the debt has grown.

Treasury Debt Management Issues

Issue Pattern   Every year the Treasury needs to sell about $1.5 trillion of debt. Part of the sales result from the current deficit (recently about $.25 trillion). The rest is from refinancing of maturing issues.

Because of the enormous sums to be raised, the Treasury spreads its issues out over the course of the year. In addition, the Treasury regularizes its pattern for issuing securities so that the market is not surprised by a particular issue. The Treasury feels that a regular pattern results in lower yields on average. To illustrate, the Treasury might announce the following issue pattern: 13-week and 26-week bills every week, 52-week bills every fourth week, two-year notes every month, etc.

Debt Maturity   The maturity of its debt is an important issue for the Treasury for two reasons. First, since short-term interest rates usually are lower than long-term interest rates, issuing short-term debt results in lower interest costs on average.[1] Figure 5.1 shows an upward sloping yield curve that has been typical in recent years. The long-term interest rates has recently been 2–4 percent higher than the short-term interest rate. Short-term securities have an immediate cost saving with a rising yield curve.

Second, short-term debt has to be refinanced more frequently than long-term debt. Since short-term interest rates fluctuate considerably, the rollover of short maturity debt may take place at very high interest rates. A policy of issuing short maturities exclusively has lower total interest cost on average – but greater variability of total interest cost – than issuing long maturities.

Since a considerable part of the current deficit is interest on outstanding debt, the question of debt maturity affects the level and variability of deficits themselves. If the Treasury followed a policy of issuing only short-term debt, the average interest cost of the debt would be relatively low compared to issuing exclusively long-term debt. However, the interest cost of the debt would be closely tied to the level of interest rates. When rates were high, the interest cost of the debt would be very high. The political consequences might be considerable, if the interest on the debt increased at the same time that the other components of the federal deficit were high. A policy of issuing

---

[1] However, a policy of issuing Treasury bills only would dramatically increase the supply of bills, driving their prices down and pushing up short-term interest rates. This increase in interest rates would at least partially offset the lower short-term interest rates.

Figure 5.1   Upward Sloping Yield Curve

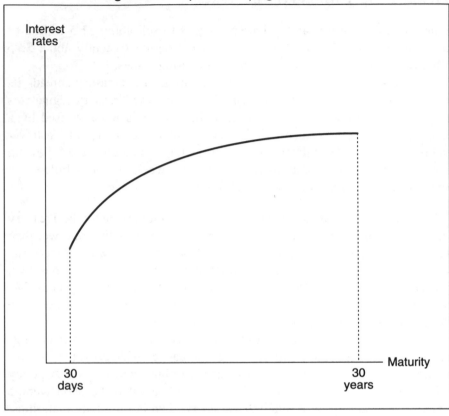

long-term debt exclusively would stabilize interest costs but make them relatively high on the average. In practice, the Treasury issues debt with many different maturities. The maturity composition is about 25 percent bills, 50 percent notes, and 25 percent bonds.

Procedures for Issuing Treasury Securities

Because of the enormous amounts of money involved, the procedures for issuing Treasury securities are quite important. The Treasury sells bills, notes, and bonds at weekly auctions. Prospective buyers must submit sealed bids by a specified time. Bids may be competitive or noncompetitive.

Noncompetitive Bids   Noncompetitive bids must not exceed $1 million par value for bills and $5 million for notes and bonds. The noncompetitive bidder does not specify a price, but merely specifies the par value of the securities desired. Noncompetitive bidders agree to accept the average price of the accepted competitive bids. All noncompetitive bids are accepted by the Treasury.

Competitive Bids For competitive bids, the bidder specifies the price. The Treasury accepts the competitive bids with highest prices (and lowest interest rates) and rejects the others (see figure 5.2). To illustrate the acceptance procedure, suppose the Treasury announces a sale of $5 billion par value of 52-week Treasury bills. One billion dollars of noncompetitive bids and $8 billion of competitive bids are received. The $1 billion of noncompetitive bids are accepted and the $4 billion of competitive bids with the highest prices (lowest yields) are accepted. The weighted average price of the accepted competitive bids determines the price for the noncompetitive bids.

Discriminatory Auctions In determining the prices paid by competitive bidders, the Treasury has used two procedures. Historically, all accepted competitive bidders have paid the price bid. This type of auction has been called a **discriminatory auction** because each bidder can pay a different

Figure 5.2   Prices Paid in a Sealed-Bid Auction

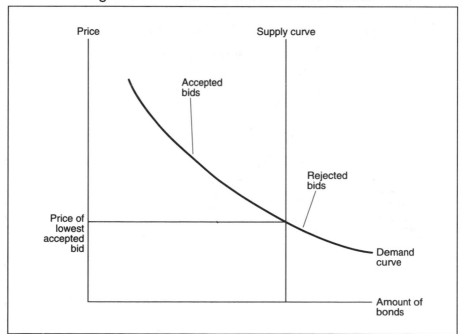

price. The noncompetitive bidders pay the average of these accepted competitive bid prices.

In practical terms, the difference between the highest and lowest accepted competitive bids tends to be small. In technical terms, the demand curve tends to be relatively flat, since new issues must be competitively priced relative to traded old issues. For example, every week the Treasury issues a new 13-week Treasury bill. The bidders for a new 13-week bill can observe yields on the 12-week bill, issued the previous week. These 12-week bill yields provide a good estimate of the fair prices for 13-week bills.

Single-Price or Dutch Auctions   Recently, the Treasury has used a single-price or Dutch auction in some offers. With a single-price auction, each accepted bid pays the price of the lowest accepted bid. A single-price auction has two impacts. First, for a given set of bids, the Treasury receives lower revenue, since everyone pays the lowest accepted price.

Second, in a single-price auction the average bidder may bid a higher price, shifting the demand curve to the right, offsetting and perhaps overwhelming the first effect (see figure 5.3). The reason for the demand curve shift is the problem of the **winner's curse** in a discriminatory auction. Imagine yourself as a bidder in a discriminatory auction. If you bid a high

Figure 5.3   Impact of Single-Price Auction upon Demand Curve

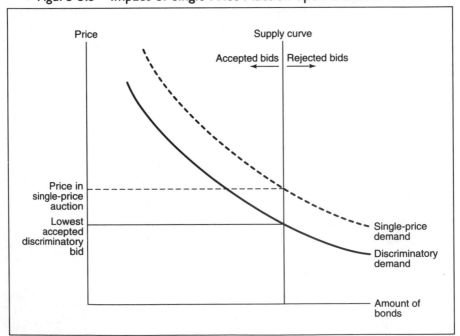

price, your bid wins but you are cursed with a high price. If you bid a low price, the probability of rejection is higher, but an accepted bid receives a low price. Risk averse bidders may elect to place low bids to avoid the winner's curse. The average bid is lower. A discriminatory auction shifts the demand curve to the left.

When-Issued Trading   Between the time a Treasury auction is announced and the time the securities are actually sold, trading in unissued, or when-issued, securities occurs. In the when-issued market, the buyers and sellers agree on a price to be paid in the future after the securities are sold at the auction. Since when-issued trading occurs before auction bids are submitted to the Treasury, auction bidders have a good idea of market prices for the new securities.

Issuing Notes and Bonds   Issuing coupon-bearing Treasury notes and bonds presents a special problem. Notes and bonds repay a stated par value to the owner at maturity. If these securities were originally issued at nonpar prices, the tax law provides that they would have special tax liabilities that many investors would like to avoid. To ensure issue prices of par, a special bidding procedure is necessary. Bids are solicited in terms of yields. The Treasury selects the winning bids, i.e., the ones with the lowest yields. The coupon on the bond issue is set equal to the yield on the average winning bid. If the coupon rate equals the yield, the bonds and notes must sell at par.

Limits on Bidders   The competitive bidders in Treasury auctions are typically dealers who intend to resell the securities in the secondary market. If one dealer was able to purchase an entire new issue, that dealer might bc able to charge unfairly high prices in the secondary market. To prevent dealer monopolies, the Treasury limits the percentage of a particular issue purchased by a single bidder. Recently, Salomon Brothers, a large dealer, violated Treasury restrictions and purchased a large proportion of an issue. Salomon Brothers was penalized severely for this transgression.

Municipalities

Municipalities are state and local governments. These governmental units are sizable issuers of debt instruments. There are many varieties of municipal debt. Some municipal bonds are general obligation (GO) bonds, which are backed by the full taxing power of the municipality. Other municipal bonds are revenue bonds, which are sold to finance a specific project. Only the revenues from that project are used to repay the revenue bonds. An example would be a toll highway; the revenues from the tolls are used to repay the bondholders. Revenue bonds are higher risk and carry higher yields than general obligation bonds.

The interest paid on municipal bonds is exempt from federal income taxes. Consequently, the (before-tax) yields on municipal bonds are relatively low. In effect, the federal government provides a tax subsidy to state and local governments. These tax aspects are discussed in chapter 18 on taxes.

Corporations

Corporations are large issuers of debt and equity. Since 1980, issues of corporate debt have skyrocketed. Part of this increase in corporate debt is explained by merger activity in which many corporate mergers were heavily financed by debt. The use of very small amounts of equity and large amounts of debt makes the debt very risky. Bonds with high default risk are called **junk bonds**. Junk bond financing has increased markedly.

Corporate debt obligates the issuing firm to make fixed payments to debtholders. A fixed payment obligation may be advantageous or disadvantageous to stockholders depending upon the fortunes of the firm. If a corporation does extremely well, all incremental returns above the payments to the bondholders go to the stockholders, who earn high returns. If the corporation does poorly, there may be little or nothing left for stockholders after paying the fixed obligations to bondholders. The stockholders may lose everything invested. Consequently, use of debt financing tends to magnify the returns to stockholders. If the firm does well, stockholders do *very* well; if the firm does poorly, stockholders do *very* poorly.

Textbooks on corporate finance devote considerable attention to the question of the optimal, or best, amount of debt financing for a firm. These texts do not provide any simple solution to the problem. Besides the question of the increased risk from magnification of stockholders' returns, a major controversy concerns the so-called tax advantage of debt. Because interest payments on corporate debt are deductible in computing corporate income taxes, there are possible tax advantages of debt. But expert opinions vary on measuring this possible benefit.

For some firms, the managers of the firms may have better information about the firm's prospects than the market. The decision to issue bonds or stock is affected by this difference in information, known as **asymmetric information**. For example, if *only* the management knows of extremely attractive investment opportunities, the stock price of the firm does not reflect the profits from these opportunities and is relatively low. Sale of stock at this depressed price is a mistake; issuing debt is a better idea.

In large corporations, the stockholders typically hire managers to act as agents on behalf of the stockholders. The gain to the agent from a particular corporate strategy may differ from the gain to the stockholders. Rational agents can be expected to act in their own personal interest, not in the stockholders interest, creating an **agency problem**. This conflict of interest may affect the decision to issue stock or bonds.

Government Agencies

Several agencies of the federal government issue debt obligations. These include the Government National Mortgage Association (GNMA), the Export-Import Bank, and the Tennessee Valley Authority.

There are several agencies which are privately owned but sponsored and backed by the federal government. Several of these are large borrowers in the debt markets, including the Federal Home Loan Banks, the Federal National Mortgage Association (FNMA), the Federal Home Loan Mortgage Corporation (FHLMC), and the Farm Credit Bank. The first three were set up to promote the inflow of credit to the housing market and the last one to promote the flow of funds into the farming industry.

The securities of government agencies are the direct obligations of private agencies. They are not the direct obligations of the federal government and, therefore, are not default-free in the same sense as Treasury securities. But in practical terms, the chance for default is very tiny. The federal government would not allow any of these agencies to fail. Consequently, agency securities are almost interchangeable with Treasury securities. Agency securities are usually smaller size issues than Treasury securities and are somewhat less marketable. The securities of the government-sponsored agencies have a slightly higher default risk than the government agencies (e.g., GNMA). In practical terms, default risk on the government-sponsored agencies is minimal because of the high probability of a government bailout.

Mortgages

Mortgages are loans backed by real estate as collateral. The total amount of real estate loans outstanding is enormous. Historically, thrift institutions were the major financial institutions in the mortgage market. Thrifts traditionally made real estate loans and then held these loans as assets until the mortgage matured. In recent years, thrifts have begun to sell mortgages in the secondary market. The usual procedure is for a sizable number of mortgages to be put together into a pool, which is then sold to investors. Claims on this mortgage pool are typically marketable and can be exchanged between investors. The thrift institution which originates the securities in the pool no longer holds the mortgage but continues to process the collection of mortgage payments for the pool.

This process of selling mortgages is called **securitization** because the mortgages are effectively changed into securities that can be bought and sold in the resale market. Securitization has several important consequences. First, the originating thrift no longer bears the risk of default on the mortgage or the risk that interest rates might change adversely in the future; these risks are borne by the buyers of the mortgages. Second, securitization opens up the market for mortgages to many more lenders, increasing the availability of funds to the mortgage market and reducing interest costs to borrowers. In effect, the efficiency of the borrowing and lending process has been improved.

Government agencies have played a major role in the development of a national mortgage market. Government guarantees have eliminated the default risk of mortgages and greatly increased their marketability.

In recent years, so-called derivative mortgage products have expanded dramatically. Derivatives are securities based upon mortgages. However, the cash flows from the underlying mortgages are broken into separate packages. Some derivatives are low risk. Some derivatives are extremely high risk; their prices can change dramatically as interest rates change. Some buyers of mortgage derivatives have incurred huge losses after interest rates changed.

Summary

The United States Treasury issues debt to finance federal budget deficits. Given the large cumulative total of the deficits over time, the total amount of debt is large. The Treasury has a serious task to issue debt to cover new deficits and rollover the maturing debt from previous deficits. Given the magnitude of Treasury operations, the impacts upon interest rates can be considerable.

Other large issuers of securities include government agencies, government-sponsored agencies, municipalities, corporations, and mortgage issuers.

Questions/Problems

1. Since 1980, the market for Treasury debt has become increasingly important. Why?

2. What types of entities are the major holders of Treasury securities and why?

3. Explain the procedure by which the Treasury auctions securities. What are the pros and cons for using this type of auction?

4. The Treasury announces an auction of $10 billion par value of 52-week Treasury bills. Two billion dollars of noncompetitive bids are received. The competitive bids are as follows:

Price per $1 of Par	Par Value
.9200	$3 billion
.9194	$3 billion
.9188	$4 billion
.9180	$2 billion
.9178	$6 billion

Compute the price per dollar of par paid by noncompetitive bidders with (a) a discriminatory auction and (b) with a single-price (Dutch) auction.

5. The Treasury auctions $12 billion of 52-week Treasury bills. Three billion dollars of noncompetitive bids are received. The competitive bids are:

Price per $1 of Par	Par Value
.9200	$5 billion
.9180	$4 billion
.9170	$3 billion
.9160	$2 billion

What is the price paid of per dollar of par (to 4 decimals) by noncompetitor's bidders with (a) a discriminatory auction and (b) a single-price (Dutch) auction?

6. What are the advantages and disadvantages for a corporation to issue bonds as opposed to selling equity or retaining earnings?

7. What does the term *securitization* mean?

References

Bikhchandani, S., and C. Huang, "Auctions with Resale Markets: A Model of Treasury Bill Markets," *The Review of Financial Studies,* 2, 1989, pp. 311–39.

Bikhchandani, S., and C. Huang, "The Economics of Treasury Security Markets," *Economic Perspectives,* 7, Summer 1993, pp. 117–34.

Boudoukh, J., and R. F. Whitelaw, "Liquidity as a Choice Variable: A Lesson from the Japanese Government Bond Market," *Review of Financial Studies,* 6, 1993, pp. 265–92.

Cammack, E., "Evidence on Bidding Strategies and the Information in Treasury Bill Auctions," *Journal of Political Economy,* 99, February 1991, pp. 100–30.

Kamara, A., "Liquidity, Taxes, and Short-Term Treasury Yields," *Journal of Financial and Quantitative Analysis,* 29, September 1994, pp. 403–17.

Simon, D. P., "Markups, Quantity Risk, and Bidding Strategies at Treasury Coupon Auctions," *Journal of Financial Economics,* 35, February 1994, pp. 43–62.

Stigum, M., "*The Money Market,*" Homewood, IL: Dow Jones Books, 1990.

Umlauf, S. R., "An Empirical Study of the Mexican Treasury Bill Auction," *Journal of Financial Economics,* 33, 1993, pp. 313–40.

U.S. Government Printing Office, *Monthly Statement of the Public Debt.*

U.S. Government Printing Office, *Treasury Bulletin.*

6

Financial
Intermediaries

Overview

Financial intermediaries expedite the flow of funds from sectors with surpluses to sectors with deficits. Types of financial intermediaries include banks, thrifts, insurance companies, pension funds, mutual funds, investment bankers, security dealers, and brokers. The total assets of financial intermediaries are huge, and they play an important role in the economy.

Many of these intermediaries (e.g., banks, thrifts, insurance companies, etc.) expedite the flow of savings from savers to investors in capital equipment. Individuals or economic units with savings in excess of their own investment opportunities have several avenues available. First, savings can be invested directly in financial claims, such as stocks and bonds. This is illustrated in figure 6.1. Second, surplus funds can be invested with financial intermediaries, who then reinvest the funds, as shown in figure 6.2. Financial intermediaries expedite the flow of savings from savers to ultimate investors in cases where direct investment is inefficient, undesirable, or impossible. Because of these financial intermediaries, the economy has more capital

Figure 6.1   Economy with Direct Investment

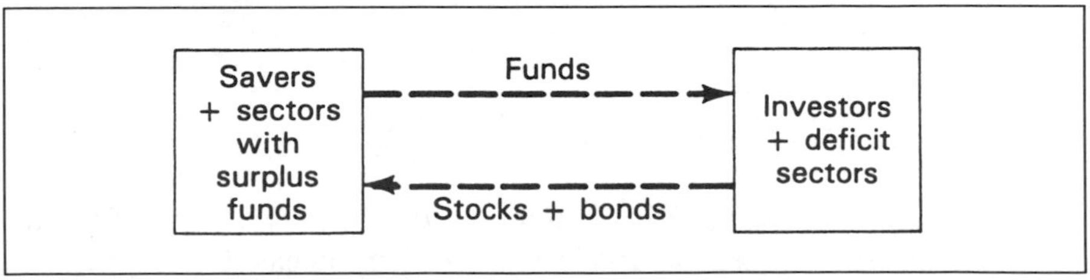

Figure 6.2 Economy with Financial Intermediaries

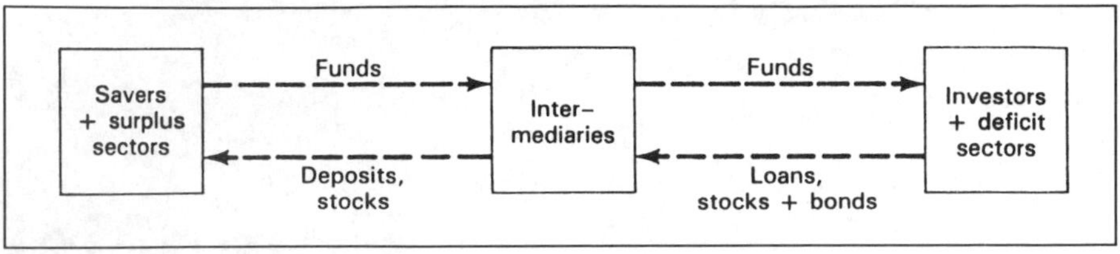

equipment, higher productivity, and higher living standards. From the viewpoint of individual savers, financial intermediaries offer the advantages of higher returns and/or lower risks.

Financial intermediaries provide a number of advantages including the following:

1. pooling of small savings
2. diversification of risks
3. economies of scale in monitoring information and evaluating investment risks
4. lower transactions costs

Deregulation

Historically, financial institutions have been heavily regulated, and these regulations have limited the activities of individual financial institutions. In the late 1970s and the early 1980s, a strong movement to deregulate financial institutions developed. A major motivation was to allow financial institutions to better cope with highly variable interest rates. The net result has been a blurring of the distinctions between the types of institutions. For example, commercial banks formerly had the exclusive right to offer checking deposits. Now thrift institutions, mutual funds, and brokerage houses offer these accounts. Formerly, banks were largely excluded from the securities business, but now they are allowed to engage in some brokerage and investment banking.

Commercial Banks and Thrifts

Commercial banks and thrift institutions are the largest variety of financial intermediary. A **commercial bank** is an institution that has checking deposits and makes commercial loans. A **thrift** institution offers savings deposits. The term *thrift* includes savings institutions of various types, such as savings and loans, mutual savings banks, and credit unions.

The thrift industry is composed of three types of savings institutions: savings and loan associations, mutual savings banks, and credit unions. Savings and loan associations (S&Ls) and mutual savings banks take deposits and primarily make real estate loans. Mutual savings banks are owned by the depositors. S&Ls and mutual savings banks were created to funnel more funds into home mortgages. During the era of deregulation in the 1980s, riskier types of loans were allowed for things other than home mortgages. Losses on these risky loans contributed significantly to the many failures since 1980. Since 1970, more than half of the S&Ls have failed.

Credit unions are depository institutions for some group with a common bond. They take deposits from these individuals and make consumer loans to them. As an example, educators in a particular town might establish a credit union. All educators would be allowed to make deposits and borrow from this credit union. Noneducators would not have access.

By taking deposits and making loans, commercial banks and thrift institutions expedite the flow of funds from savers (depositors) to investors (borrowers). Banks offer several advantages compared to direct transfers of funds between savers and final investors. First, banks allow the pooling of small amounts of funds. Second, because of the large size of a bank relative to an individual saver, banks provide the advantage of loan diversification. Diversification is a process by which risks are spread among many investments. The bank is able to make a large number of loans. Although the bank may lose money on some of these loans because of default by the borrower, on the entire portfolio of bank loans, the bank will probably realize a nice profit. In contrast, a small saver making a single loan might suffer devastating losses if there is a default. The bank is able to spread this risk of default over many loans. The small lender cannot spread the risk.

Third, banks have the advantage of low costs resulting from economies of scale. Because of its large size, a bank is able to spread fixed costs over many units. Besides operating economies, banks have the advantage of economies of information production about prospective loan applicants. On a per unit basis, investigating many loan applicants is cheaper than investigating one or two applicants. By dealing in large volumes of funds, banks can achieve lower transactions costs.

A major reason for the existence of commercial banks is the banks' ability to offer a special service – namely, checking deposits. For depositors, the ability to write checks against checking deposits is extremely desirable for mail payments and for large transactions since payment with currency is ponderous and poses a theft risk. From the viewpoint of the overall economy, checking deposits perform a valuable function. They allow otherwise idle transactions balances to be pooled together by the banks and then used to finance loans.

Since commercial banks are one of the major means by which the Federal Reserve controls the money supply and interest rates, commercial banks perform a valuable function for the entire economy. Partly because of this role in monetary policy, commercial banks are very heavily regulated, as discussed in chapter 7.

Besides pure banking activities, commercial banks engage in some of the activities of other nonbank financial intermediaries. For example, a number of banks engage in investment banking for municipal bonds. Some banks engage in discount brokerage. Over time, banks have tried to enter more and more nonbanking activities. The allowable activities of banks are regulated by the Federal Reserve.

Mutual Funds

Mutual funds provide a clear example of the diversification role played by financial intermediaries. A mutual fund is a pooling of the funds of many small savers. Each investor has a proportional claim on the assets of the fund. These funds are then invested by the managers of the mutual fund in stocks, bonds, and other financial claims, as allowed by the fund's prospectus. The management charges a fee which varies with the investment objective of the fund. Funds requiring a great deal of managerial effort charge higher fees.

Closed-end mutual funds have an initial offering of shares, and no additional shares are sold. Existing shares cannot be redeemed. Thus, a closed-end fund has no new cash inflows or redemptions. Shares of closed-end funds trade on the open market at prices that may differ from their net asset value. The net asset value (NAV) of a mutual fund is the liquidating value, or the amount available to distribute if all the fund's assets were sold off. Typically, closed-end fund shares trade at a discount from their net asset value, although sometimes they may trade at premiums. Closed-end fund discounts from net asset value cannot get too large, since very large discounts would provide a profit opportunity to a large investor, who would buy all the shares of the fund at a discount and then liquidate the fund for a profit.

Korea Fund is an interesting example of a closed-end fund. An offering of Korea Fund shares was made in the U.S. The proceeds were invested in Korean stocks with the special permission of the Korean government. Since ownership of Korean stocks is generally restricted to Korean residents, Korea Fund was given special access to the Korean markets. Consequently, the shares of Korea Fund typically trade at a premium above the net asset value. The net asset value is determined by the prices of the stocks as traded in Korea, that is, the value of Korean stocks to Koreans. The shares of the Korea fund sell in the U.S. at their value to U.S. residents; this value is higher than the value to Koreans.

Most mutual funds are **open-end** funds; the fund continuously stands ready to sell new shares and redeem old shares. For open-end funds, additional shares can be sold, or existing shares can be redeemed by investors.

Many open-end mutual funds have front-end loads. Front-end loads are sales commissions that are deducted from the money invested. For example, a $10,000 investment with an 8.5 percent commission would result in a net investment of $9,150. A sizable number of mutual funds are no-load funds. These funds charge no sales commissions. Other things being equal, an investor should clearly prefer a no-load fund to one with a load. Someone investing in a no-load fund has to investigate the fund himself, since a security salesperson has a strong incentive to suggest a load fund. No-load mutual funds are typically purchased through the mail. Three especially informative sources about mutual funds are Morningstar *Mutual Fund Sourcebook, Investment Companies* by Arthur Weisenberger and *The Handbook for No-Load Investors.*

The investment objectives of mutual funds vary. There are stock funds, bond funds, and funds investing in both stocks and bonds. Within each of these categories, many different objectives are available. In the area of bond funds, specialties include U.S. Treasury securities, corporate bonds, high-risk corporate bonds, municipal (tax-free) bonds, foreign bonds, and money market funds. For many people, money market mutual funds have provided an attractive alternative to bank savings and time deposit accounts. Money market mutual fund accounts typically provide a number of attractive services, including limited check-writing privileges and the ability to transfer funds by telephone between mutual funds or between the mutual fund and a bank. For stock mutual funds, specialized objectives include small company funds, growth funds, value funds, foreign funds, and global funds. Index funds try to duplicate the returns on a broad stock index.

Mutual funds provide several advantages over direct investment by savers. First, the mutual fund is large enough to be able to invest in a number of different securities and thus diversify away some of the risk. Using direct purchase of securities, individual investors might be too small to buy enough securities to diversify, since probably ten or more different securities are required to achieve most of the benefits of diversification. Secondly, mutual funds provide economies of scale, including efficient record keeping and, more importantly, economies in information search. For small portfolios, the amount of time required to monitor an efficient portfolio can be large relative to the absolute benefits of monitoring, implying significant advantages of having a mutual fund manager carry out the task. For example, an investor with $10,000 to invest might have to spend 10 hours per week, or over 500 hours per year, to monitor a portfolio of direct investments. Even if the rate of return were 20 percent, the total return of $2,000 may be too small to justify spending 500 hours per year monitoring the investments. A mutual fund can spend the same 500 hours and pro-rate the cost.

Because mutual funds can trade securities in large quantities, transactions costs are significantly lower than for individual small investors.

Insurance Companies

Insurance companies are another type of financial intermediary providing the important function of risk diversification. An insurance company agrees to make a financial payment to insured individuals if a particular event occurs.

The insurance company charges a fee, called a **premium**. An insurance company insures a large number of individuals. On the basis of statistical evidence, the insurance company can predict with a high degree of accuracy the likelihood of a particular event occurring to the entire group of insured individuals. The insurance premium is set at a level high enough to cover the expected payments to the insured individuals, plus a profit margin. By spreading the risk over a large number of insured individuals, insurance companies can protect people against the financial consequences of disastrous events. The insurance premium is the cost of this protection for the individual.

Life and casualty are the major types of insurance. Life insurance is of two varieties. Permanent life insurance (whole life or universal life) has a constant premium; term insurance has a premium that varies as the risks change. A 25-year-old person pays a lower initial premium for term insurance than for permanent life insurance. As time elapses and the risk of death increases, the premium on the term insurance rises and eventually surpasses the level premium on permanent life insurance. For permanent life insurance, the insurance company invests the extra premium in the early years to earn enough to cover the added risks in later years. Permanent life incorporates an element of saving, whereas term insurance is pure insurance.

Property and casualty insurance companies insure against losses from fire, theft, flood, automobile accidents, and many unexpected events. Because property and casualty insurance risks are harder to predict than life insurance risks, these companies make lower risk investments than life insurance companies.

For example, consider an insurance company selling flood insurance exclusively. The insurance company sells insurance policies in widely diverse geographical areas. On the basis of historical evidence, the company can predict with great accuracy the number of areas likely to flood in any one year. The insurance company can also forecast the probability of flooding in a particular area and can estimate the likely losses. The historical evidence can be used to set insurance premiums at a high enough level to cover the predicted losses. The insured entities then pay a premium reflecting the average expected losses.

The advantage of insurance to the insured is the payment of a relatively small, periodic, and stable amount. The insured prefers this small loss from paying an insurance premium to a possibly large (and potentially catastrophic) loss if there is no insurance. An uninsured entity can expect to occasionally suffer severe and catastrophic losses. For risk averters, protection against a devastating loss makes insurance very attractive. The insured accepts a regular small loss (the insurance premium) in order to avoid a major loss.

Insurance companies invest insurance premiums, using the proceeds from investments to pay off claims. Because insurance companies are large investors, insurance companies in the aggregate channel a large flow of savings into investment.

Life insurance companies provide a large inflow of funds for savings. Life insurance typically involves a long-term contract. The insured individual pays a premium for an agreed time period. If the individual dies, the insurance company pays the principal. For permanent life insurance, the premium in the initial years exceeds the expected payouts by the insurance company. The excess is invested to provide sufficient funds in the later years of the contract to pay the expected claims. This investment of premiums provides a large flow of funds.

Regulation of insurance companies is left to the states. Regulators curtail unfair sales practices, require liquid assets to meet loss payments, and limit investment in risky assets.

Insurance companies face the problem of adverse selection. That is, individuals with the greatest risk to the insurance company are most likely to seek insurance. For example, someone with a known medical condition is most likely to buy life insurance. In addition, insurance may induce riskier behavior for the insured (the moral hazard problem). A car driver with insurance may be less careful than the uninsured (self-insured) driver.

Insurance companies do several things to reduce the company's risk. The extremely high-risk insurance applicants may be denied insurance. The premium may be adjusted for the individual's risk. Restrictive covenants may be included in the insurance contract. Thus, life insurance may not apply when the insured operates an airplane. Coinsurance can be used to require the insured to bear some percentage of the losses. The insurance policy may have a maximum total payment.

Pension Funds

Pension funds represent savings for payment of employee retirement benefits. Pension funds differ in the vesting period. An employee who leaves employment before the required vesting period loses all retirement benefits. Some plans are immediately vested. Some require a period of five or ten years before vesting occurs.

For some pension funds (defined contribution plans), the employer contribution is specified. The actual payment received by the employee at retirement depends upon the actual investment performance of the funds. If the investment returns are high, the employee retirement benefit is high; if the returns are low, the payment is low.

Other pension funds (defined benefit plans) specify the amount to be paid to employees at retirement. For example, a pension fund for state employees might specify the benefit to be 1.8 percent times the number of years employed times the average salary for the last five years employed. Someone employed for 20 years, earning $40,000 average salary for the last five years, would receive $14,400 (.018 × 20 × 40,000).

Determining the appropriate amount of pension fund contributions is difficult with defined benefit plans. The employer must estimate the probable payments to employees at retirement. The current contributions necessary to achieve this goal depend upon the rate of return until the retirement date. Consequently, employers have some discretion to determine the current contributions to the pension fund. For example, if interest rates are assumed to be high, lower current contributions are necessary.

Many employers fully fund their defined benefit plans. That is, current pension fund contributions are sufficient to meet all contingencies. Other employers have underfunded their plans by contributing insufficient funds. Since pension fund contributions are a business expense reducing reported income, some firms with low earnings have reduced pension fund contributions to boost reported earnings. In some cases, firms with underfunded pension funds have gone bankrupt, leaving insufficient funds to make payments to retirees.

The Employee Retirement Income Security Act (ERISA) of 1974 sets minimum standards for corporate disclosure of pension fund information, contains rules for vesting and restrictions on underfunding, and controls pension fund investments. The Act established the Pension Benefit Guarantee Corporation to insure pension funds against underfunding. In the view of some experts, the Pension Benefit Guarantee Corporation has insufficient funds to cover expected underfunding from future corporate bankruptcies. Inadequate auditing of covered pension funds has contributed to the problem. Careful auditing by the Guarantee Corporation should allow underfunded pension funds to be detected early and funding adjustments made before the insurance company incurs losses.

The Primary Market

The market for the original sale of securities is sometimes called the **primary** or **new issue market**. The resale market is frequently called the **secondary market** and is discussed shortly.

Original issues of securities are classified as public or private offerings. The exact meaning of the term *public* is a technical legal question. In practical terms, a **public offering** has a sufficiently large size and has a sufficiently large number of buyers. Issues failing to meet the conditions for public offerings are considered **private offerings**. Public offerings of securities have to be registered with the Securities and Exchange Commission (SEC) before the securities can be sold, whereas private offerings are not registered. The purpose of SEC registration is to have the SEC verify the factual accuracy of the information about the securities to reduce the chance of fraud by issuers of securities. SEC endorsement does not indicate desirable investments but rather represents a confirmation of informational accuracy.

Original issues of securities occur in two major forms: competitive bidding (that is, auctions) and negotiated offerings.[1] By law, several types of securities must be sold by competitive bidding, e.g., U.S. Treasury securities and municipal securities. These requirements are motivated by the belief that competitive bidding brings out the highest bids and reduces costs to the issuer. Nongovernmental (that is, corporate) issues are typically sold by negotiation with an investment banker or syndicate of investment bankers. Negotiated offerings are of several varieties, including underwritings and best efforts selling.

---

[1] An extensive literature discusses whether competitive bidding or negotiated offerings are better for the issuer. See Smith (1987).

Investment Banking

Investment banking firms are engaged in the marketing of securities when they are originally sold. Investment bankers expedite the sale.

Investment bankers typically use syndicates to sell securities. A syndicate is a group of investment bankers who combine their efforts to market an issue. A particular investment banker organizes the syndicate and is called the lead underwriter. A larger syndicate gives access to a larger group of potential buyers. Syndicates are usually employed for issues of common stock since the stock is sold to many small buyers, who are more easily reached with more syndicate members. Syndicates are smaller, or nonexistent, for debt issues since bonds tend to be purchased by a small number of large financial institutions.

Firm Commitments   **Firm commitments (underwriting)** involve the outright purchase of an entire security issue by an investment banker (or syndicate), which takes on the risks of reselling the issue to the public. The underwriter purchases the issue and tries to resell it publicly at a higher price, earning the difference as an underwriting fee or spread. Since the resale price is not guaranteed, the underwriter runs the risk of being forced to sell the issue below the purchase price. Part of the underwriting fee is compensation for this risk.

The underwriter pays SEC registration expenses. A public registration may take several weeks or more. During this period, market conditions may change, and the underwriter may be exposed to considerable risks from a declining market. In order to speed up the issuing process, a procedure called a shelf registration is now permitted. With a **shelf registration**, securities are effectively preregistered with the SEC for the following two years. Once the registration is approved, the issue can be brought to market on very short notice. This allows an issuer to try to time an issue as market conditions change.[2] For example, a firm issuing bonds would like to reduce its financing costs by selling the bonds when interest rates are low. With a shelf registered issue, the firm can rapidly bring the bonds to market if conditions become very favorable.

Best Efforts   Public offerings may involve **best-efforts** selling. In this case, an investment banking firm tries to sell as much of an issue as possible.

---

[2] See Thatcher and Thatcher (1988).

Any unsold amount reverts back to the issuer. The investment banking firm does not bear much risk with best-efforts selling. Best-efforts selling appears to be concentrated among the low risk and the high risk offerings. For high risk offerings, the issuer does not need an underwriter to absorb the risk, since the risk is small. For high risk offerings, underwriters are unwilling to absorb the risk. Moderate risk offerings tend to be underwritten.

Stock Offerings

Initial Public Offerings (IPO)   The first public offering of a common stock involves special problems for an underwriter. With a first public offering, the common stock has never before been publicly traded. In making a bid for a new stock issue, the underwriter has to try to estimate the fair market value of the stock. Firms with long and successful operating histories are easier to value. In fact, a typical IPO has been operating as a private company for seven years or more.

When similar firms with publicly traded stocks exist, the underwriter can approximate the new company's market value by estimating its earnings and valuing these earnings in the same way as the earnings of existing firms. For example, if a privately owned automobile company decides to go public, an underwriter can get a fairly good estimate of the market value by looking at the valuation of the other auto companies: General Motors, Ford, and Chrysler. These other companies may be selling for eight times their current earnings, suggesting that the new company might also be worth eight times earnings.

For an original public offering with no publicly traded firms in the same field and limited or no operating history, the problem of the underwriter is more difficult. An example was the original public offering of the firm Genentech, involved in genetic engineering. There was no simple way to deduce the fair value of this company, since it was the first of its kind to be publicly traded. Compounding the problem was the lack of a history of operating profits at the time that Genentech went public. Genentech was a firm with high-tech skills of unproved market value.

The incentives of the underwriter may conflict with the incentives of the issuing firm. The firm would prefer a high bid from the underwriter. Underwriters have an incentive to underprice original public offerings. If the underwriter's bid is too high, the underwriter has to absorb large losses to sell the issue. If the underwriter's bid is below the fair market value, then the underwriter can rapidly sell the issue and make a nice profit. However, underwriters who consistently underprice securities will lose future underwriting business to underwriters pricing issues closer to the true market value. In the case of Genentech, the stock rose considerably after issue, suggesting underpricing by the underwriter.

In practice, the average initial public offering has a rising stock price on the first day of trading.[3] Over the subsequent three years, the average initial public offering has poor returns on a risk-adjusted basis. These empirical findings are paradoxical. The average initial public offering seems underpriced in the short run immediately after issue and overpriced in the long run. One explanation is the bunching of IPOs at times when stock prices are booming. Excessive investor enthusiasm boosts the price immediately after issue. Because IPOs typically appear at peaks in stock prices, the long-run performance is poor.

Secondary Offerings   Firms with existing publicly traded stock may choose to sell additional stock to the public. One procedure is to sell the stock directly to existing stockholders in a rights offering. Existing stockholders get *n* rights per share currently held. Each right represents the option to buy shares at a price slightly below the current market price. Those desiring to exercise their options can buy additional shares. Stockholders not wanting additional shares can sell their rights in the market.

Firms with existing publicly traded stock may also sell a block of additional stock to the public in a secondary offering. These shares are sold at a slight discount to the current market price to allow the market to absorb a large block of stock. Typically, the shares are purchased by an underwriting syndicate and resold to the public.

Debt Issues

Every year, the sale of debt instruments in the primary market is enormous. These debt issues include the U.S. Treasury, mortgages, state and local government (municipalities), and corporations. Treasury debt and municipal debt is sold at auction. Corporate debt can be sold in several ways: (1) to investment bankers through negotiated offerings, and (2) through private placements.

---

[3] There is a large literature on original public offerings and underpricing. See Tinic (1988), Johnson and Miller (1988), and Ritter (1991).

Private Placements   Some corporate securities are sold directly to buyers in what is called a **private offering**. An example would be the direct sale of a corporate bond issue to an insurance company. Insurance companies are large buyers of private offerings of bonds.

Private offerings may have advantages. First, the issuer does not have to bear the cost of registration of a public offering. Second, the issue can be tailor-made to the needs of the issuer and buyer. An insurance company may find a particular privately offered bond attractive because of its specific maturity, perhaps 13 years, which is not easily found in the market.

Private offerings have disadvantages as well. First, private offerings cannot be widely traded. The resale market is limited. Private offerings are relatively illiquid. Second, the interest rate on a private placement is higher than an otherwise identical public issue. The higher interest rate is a disadvantage to the issuer, although an advantage to the buyer.

Rule 144a Offerings   A rule 144a offering is a sale of securities to qualified institutional buyers, typically insurance companies, mutual funds, or pension funds. Because these institutional buyers are assumed to be informed investors, these securities are not registered with the SEC. Rule 144a securities can be resold to other institutional buyers. Thus, they have somewhat more liquidity and somewhat lower yields than private placements. Rule 144a offerings are largely debt obligations.

Corporate Debt Issues: Comparison of Public, Rule 144a, and Private Debt Offerings with Bank Loans

Corporate debt includes the following four types.

1. Public offerings of debt are made by large, established firms that are relatively easy to monitor. Public offerings have long maturities, have relatively few restrictive covenants, and are callable. The size of the issue is large, typically over $100 million. Large size is necessary to spread the sizable cost of a public offering and registration with the SEC over many bonds. Of the four types of debt, public offerings have the lowest interest rates.

2. Bank loans are the major source of debt financing for small firms and firms with relatively poor credit quality. They have short maturities. The interest rate is adjustable. The bank places many restrictive covenants on the actions of the borrower and closely monitors the firm.

3. Private placements of debt are made by medium size firms with a credit history that is too weak to justify public offerings of debt, but strong enough to justify private placement. The maturities are intermediate. The debt has many restrictive covenants and typically cannot be refinanced. The typical purchaser of the bonds is a life insurance company, which monitors the firm closely and holds the bonds until final maturity. Private placements are typically less than $50 million in size. The interest rate on private placements is between the rates on public offerings and the rates on bank loans.

4. Rule 144a offerings fall somewhere between public offerings and private offerings. The debt is purchased by qualified financial institutions and can be resold to other qualified financial institutions. Thus, it is partially marketable. It is typically sold by more established firms that don't want to go through the expense of a public offering.

Separation of Investment Banking from Banking

The term **investment banking** is a misnomer, since investment banking firms are marketers of securities and are not banks. A bank is generally defined as an institution that takes checking deposits and makes commercial loans. The term *investment banking* developed in earlier days, when commercial banks engaged in marketing of securities in addition to lending activities.

Since 1933, the Glass-Steagall Act has restricted banks engaging in investment banking (that is, security marketing) activities and stock brokerage. There are several reasons for this restriction. First, it is conceivable that banks might be able to use bank funds to manipulate security prices. Second, if banks are heavily involved in the stock market, it is possible that ups and downs in stock market prices might adversely affect the stability of the banking system.

Third, banks are regulated and therefore receive some protection from competition by restrictions on branching as well as protection from the consequences of failure by deposit insurance. Consequently, banks might have an unfair advantage over nonregulated, or nonprotected, investment bankers, brokers, or dealers. A counterargument is that a financial services firm can separate banking and investment banking activities within the same firm. According to this view, the banking activities would be regulated, and the rest would not be regulated. According to supporters of Glass-Steagall, such separation of activities within a firm is unlikely in practice; banks will probably use their competitive advantage against nonbanking firms.

According to opponents of the separation of banking from investment banking, nonbanks have been increasingly allowed to engage in banking activities, without the burdens of regulation suffered by the banks. Consequently, in the interest of fairness, banks should be allowed to compete with nonbanks engaging in banking activities. A particularly lucrative part of the investment banking business is mergers. Investment bankers can earn very large fees for arranging mergers. Commercial banks would like to share some of these fees.

The Federal Reserve is charged with the task of determining which nonbanking activities banks are allowed. The trend over time has been to allow banks to engage in additional investment banking and some brokerage and dealer activities. Thus, the Glass-Steagall restrictions have slowly been reduced.

In the U.S., banks have limited ability to engage in underwriting and security dealing and brokerage; U.S. banks are not allowed to write insurance or to have ownership interests in commercial businesses. Compared to the U.S., other industrialized nations have less separation of banking from other financial intermediaries.[4] In the United Kingdom and in former British commonwealth countries, banks are allowed to engage in investment banking. In the German system (also in the systems of the Netherlands and Switzerland), banks are effectively financial supermarkets. German banks also engage in underwriting, security dealing, insurance, and even have direct ownership in commercial businesses.

The Secondary Market: Dealers and Brokers

Resale markets for securities have an important function. The opportunity for investors to buy or sell securities rapidly without affecting the price makes securities more liquid and the ownership of securities more desirable. Increased liquidity reduces the returns required by investors, making the cost of funds lower for business and governmental borrowers. Trading securities in the resale market in the United States usually takes the form of a continuous **double auction** market. In a double auction, buyers and sellers submit bids

---

[4] The Japanese system is very similar to the U.S.

simultaneously and all participants are aware of everyone else's bids. In a continuous double auction, buyers and sellers continuously submit bids. Recall that original issues of Treasury and municipal securities are sold in sealed-bid auctions in which securities are sold only at one point in time and bidders are not aware of each others' bids. Antiques and artwork are usually sold through an English auction. An English auction is an open, oral auction in which the price is raised until only one bidder remains. The bidders are able to observe each other during the bidding process in an English auction.

Organized Exchanges

For common stocks, a large proportion of security trading takes place on organized exchanges. Access to trading on organized exchanges is restricted to exchange members. Nonmembers pay members a commission to brokers to execute orders on the floor of the exchange.

The New York Stock Exchange (NYSE) is the largest organized stock exchange in the United States by volume of trading, and it dominates common stock trading. The American Stock Exchange (AMEX) is the second largest organized stock exchange in the United States. Members of an exchange are described as having a **seat**. This is not a place to sit but instead represents the right to trade on the floor of the exchange. Exchange seats are traded and their market value fluctuates as market conditions change. To trade on the floor of the exchange, one must purchase a seat and pass other standards set by the exchange. Members of the exchange may have more than one seat, if they have a great deal of business on the floor of the exchange.

There are several types of stock exchange members. The largest group is **commission brokers** who execute buy and sell orders for the public for a fee. Some members are **odd-lot brokers**. An **odd-lot** is defined as a transaction of fewer than 100 shares. A **round lot** is 100 shares or a multiple of 100 shares. Transactions for fewer than 100 shares have to go through odd-lot brokers who charge a fee. Odd-lot brokers break round lots into odd-lots and vice versa. Another type of member is a **registered trader**, who trades for his or her own account. Because the cost of a seat is quite high, registered traders must be individuals who do enough trading to cover the large investment required to own a seat. Registered traders probably feel that proximity to the action on the exchange floor gives then the advantage of speedy execution.

Specialist firms are the final type of exchange members. **Specialists** are designated market makers for individual securities listed on the NYSE.

Every listed security has one, and only one, specialist who has a monopoly position as market maker. Specialist firms are typically market makers for several different securities. To be a specialist, a firm has to have enough capital to maintain an inventory of the traded securities.

The stated purpose of the specialist system is to reduce the variability of security prices. When too many sellers exist, the specialist is supposed to be a buyer to keep prices from falling temporarily. When too many buyers exist, the specialist is supposed to be a seller to prevent prices from rising temporarily.

Proponents of the specialist system claim that a monopoly position for a market maker is desirable. However, the Chicago Board Options Exchange operates very effectively with several market makers. In addition, over-the-counter markets typically have several market makers for any one security.

Two facts reflect very negatively on the specialist system. First, Securities and Exchange Commission evidence indicates very high profits for specialist firms. Second, specialist firms have the right to request a suspension in trading, when buy and sell orders are allegedly imbalanced. The specialist is supposed to alleviate these imbalances. The profit incentives of the specialist conflict with his role as stabilizer of prices. When many sell orders are entering the market and prices are dropping, the specialist has a profit incentive to postpone buying until prices have dropped. In contrast, the specialist's mandate is to buy as prices are going down. The NYSE has suspended trading in a particular security at the request of the specialist because of alleged order imbalances, and, at the same time, market makers off the exchange have continued to trade the very same security. The non-NYSE dealers did not seem to notice these order imbalances.

There are several ways of placing orders. A **market order** allows the commission broker to execute the order at the most favorable price at the time that the order hits the exchange floor. The advantage of a market order is that the order will definitely be carried out. The disadvantage is that the price might change adversely. For example, an investor may place a market order to buy at 2:00 PM when the price is $40. By the time that the order is executed at 2:02, prices may have changed. The best purchase price available at the time may be $41. The order will be executed by the broker at this price.

Another type of order is a **limit order**. This represents an order with some constraints. The order will be executed only if the constraints are met. For example, at 2:00 PM a limit buy order may be placed to purchase at $40 or less. If the best purchase price exceeds $40 when the order reaches the exchange floor, the order will not be executed. The limit order can specify if it is to be canceled if not executed immediately (called **fill-or-kill**). A limit order can also be left outstanding indefinitely. The order would then be executed if the price reaches $40.

In some situations, investors may want to place a **stop order**, which is an order to close out an existing position. For example, an investor may purchase a stock at $40 but with great fear that the price might decline sharply. To provide downside protection, the investor might place a stop order at $37 to sell this stock. If the price declines to $37, the stop order will be executed.

If an investor feels that the price of a security is going to decline, the investor can try to benefit through a **shortsale**. In a shortsale, a security is borrowed and sold in expectation of buying this security back later at a lower price. In effect, the investor tries to sell high and buy low, profiting by the difference. For example, if an investor feels that IBM stock is overpriced at $135, the investor can shortsell, hoping to purchase IBM at $120 for a $15 profit.

In general, the proceeds from a shortsale cannot be used by the shortseller but must be left on deposit with the broker. The shortseller must pay any cash dividends to the lender of the securities. This rule results from the fact that a stock usually goes down by approximately the after-tax amount of a cash dividend on the ex-dividend (dividend payment) date.

In addition, the NYSE has a rule that shortsales cannot take place following a downtick in prices. The NYSE keeps a record of every transaction price for every security and every shortsale must be designated as such. The downtick rule says that if prices have dropped, the next transaction cannot be a shortsale. In technical terms, the downtick rule says that a shortsale is prohibited if the last, previous, different price was higher. For example, if the price sequence is 40, 41, 41 or 40, 41, the next sale can be a shortsale. If the past price sequence was 41, 40, a downtick has occurred and the next transaction cannot be a shortsale.

The motivation for the downtick restriction on shortsales is to preclude a deluge of shortsales from driving prices sharply lower. In the past, unscrupulous traders have been able to create panic selling in a particular security by shortselling large quantities of the stock. After the panic has driven prices to extremely low levels, the shortsellers can then buy back the stock for huge gains. To prevent this type of price manipulation, the downtick rule has been instituted.

The organized exchanges have a set of requirements for a security to be traded, or, as it is usually called, **listed**. These requirements deal with a minimum size, a minimum number of shareholders, and a minimum period of existence. In the past, being listed on an exchange was considered an advantage. Some investigators believed that listing by itself raised the stock price. Currently, listing is regarded as less desirable. Many large and well-known firms are not traded on the NYSE or AMEX but over-the-counter (discussed shortly).

Over time, transactions on the NYSE are becoming increasingly automated. Thus, small buy and sell orders are matched by computer. In addition, the stock exchange and the futures exchanges are linked by computer so that transactions on both exchanges can be executed simultaneously.

For many years, the NYSE had a fixed set of commission rates charged by all member firms. Because these commissions were quite high for large transactions, a market developed for over-the-counter trading of stocks listing on the NYSE. This market has been called the **Third Market**.[5] The competition from the Third Market forced the NYSE and AMEX to move to a negotiated commission schedule, with lower fees for large transactions.

Trading of options and futures takes place on organized exchanges. Since participants in the options and futures markets may have possible financial liabilities exceeding their original cash commitments, a special organization called a **clearinghouse** is required to guarantee performance. Clearinghouses are discussed more fully in chapters 20 and 21 on options on futures contracts.

Trading of securities on organized exchanges in the United States is conducted by continuous auction. For a number of hours during the day, the exchange remains open and trading can occur continuously, as often as buyers and sellers enter the market. On some other exchanges, trading occurs for only a short period during the day. All the buyers and sellers get together at the designated time and agree to one price at which all purchases and sales are executed. Examples of this type of trading include the London Gold Market and the Israeli Stock Exchange.

Over-the-Counter

Over-the-counter (OTC) trading involves a network of dealers who make markets in individual securities. OTC dealers stand ready to buy at the bid price and sell at the (higher) asked price, hoping to profit on average by the difference. A sizable amount of stock trading is done over-the-counter. Virtually all bond trading is carried out over-the-counter.

---

[5] The NYSE is considered the first market and the AMEX is considered the second market.

Apart from New York Stock Exchange corporate bond trading, the resale market for debt instruments is essentially an OTC market composed of dealers and brokers. Dealers make markets in securities, that is, dealers maintain inventories and risk their own funds. Dealers stand ready to buy at the bid price and sell at the asked price, hoping on the average to make this difference or spread.

In contrast to dealers who risk their own funds, brokers do not own securities; instead they try to match buyers and sellers for a fee. Frequently, brokers will serve as a middleman expediting trades between dealers.

A dealer hopes to make the bid-asked spread on average. However, on an individual transaction, a dealer may buy at the current bid price of $100 and a few hours later sell at the then-current asked price of $99. This inventory loss is the primary risk of being a dealer. Hopefully, gains on profitable trades at least offset losses on unprofitable trades, but there is no guarantee of profit.

Dealers can try to make money by gambling on the direction of price movements – so called **positioning**. For example, if a bond dealer feels that interest rates are going to fall, the dealer can buy bonds in expectation of selling the bonds back at future higher prices. If the dealer's forecast is wrong, the dealer must close the position at unfavorable prices and absorb a loss.

Security dealers are heavily levered. That is, the dealer's equity is a small percentage of the market value of his inventory. Most dealer financing is in the form of debt. For U.S. Treasury bond dealers, a small proportion of debt financing is in the form of bank loans. The majority of dealer (debt) financing is in the form of repurchase agreements (repos).

A **repurchase agreement** involves the sale of a U.S. Treasury security with an agreement to repurchase the same security the next day at the sale price plus overnight interest. Some repurchase agreements may be for longer than overnight; these are called **term repos**. Repurchase agreements are discussed in more detail in Chapter 16 on money market instruments.

Because dealers are so highly levered, the risk of dealer bankruptcy cannot be neglected. Several dealers have gone bankrupt in recent years. Some dealer losses have exceeded dealer equity, meaning that someone besides the dealer has had to absorb part of the dealer losses.

Until recently, regulation of government bond dealers has been minimal. Entry into the dealer market has been free, with minimal official restrictions on dealer behavior. Because of recent bankruptcies, new legislation requires the U.S. Treasury to regulate dealers.

A considerable amount of stock trading occurs over the counter. The National Association of Security Dealers Automated Quotation (NASDAQ) system serves two functions. First, information about bid-asked prices is exchanged over NASDAQ. An investor wishing to transact in a particular OTC stock can see the prices quotes of market-making dealers. The most favorable price can be found. Second, small trades are matched and consummated by computer.

Several computerized trading systems have been developed for large blocks of stock. The buyers and sellers place their orders anonymously. Other investors are able to search the posted quotes for desirable prices and consummate transactions. The transactions costs for these large block computerized systems are extremely low.

Determinants of Bid-Asked Spreads

Dealers quote a bid price (at which they are willing to buy) and an asked price (at which they are willing to sell). The bid-asked spread represents the price of dealer services. Since spreads differ for particular securities, an interesting and important question is the determination of these spreads.

Spreads have been found to be related to the risks borne by dealers. First, spreads are inversely related to the volume of trading. For example, spreads tend to be large if trading is infrequent (a so-called **thin market**). An inactive resale market implies a longer holding period for dealer inventory. The longer the holding period, the greater the chance of price change. The likelihood of an unfavorable event increases for longer holding periods and the bid-asked spread increases.

In the bond market, U.S. Treasury securities have active markets. In contrast, the majority of corporate and municipal bonds are infrequently traded and have large bid-asked spreads. To a considerable extent, this difference between Treasury securities and corporate and municipal bonds results from the size of each issue. Individual Treasury issues have total par values in the billions of dollars, whereas corporate and municipal bond issues have total par values in the millions of dollars.

Second, spreads are positively related to the inherent price risk of individual securities. Some securities can be expected to have a bigger percentage price change over a particular time interval compared to other securities. For example, short-term (30-day) U.S. Treasury bills tend to have smaller percentage price changes than long-term (30-year) U.S. Treasury bonds.[6] As a consequence, the bid-asked spreads on bills will be much smaller than the bid-asked spreads on bonds.

---

[6] The relationship between maturity and price volatility is discussed in chapter 11 on bond price and reinvestment risks. In general, longer maturity implies greater price volatility for fixed income securities.

Third, the bid-asked spread should be a function of dealer financing costs. When interest rates are high, bid-asked spreads should, other things equal, be relatively high to compensate the dealer for the high cost of financing inventory. Since most of a bond dealer's inventory is financed with bank loans and repurchase agreements, changes in these interest rates would tend to be reflected in bid-asked spreads.

Fourth, the bid-asked spread may depend upon the possibility that the dealer is trading against an informed investor who knows more than the dealer.[7] In such circumstances, the dealer has an incentive to increase the size of the bid-asked spread. For example, if a dealer believes that a sell order is from an informed trader, the dealer has an incentive to drop the bid price and widen the spread.

The Flow of Information

In an over-the-counter market, transactions typically occur over the telephone. Maintaining up-to-date information on prices is critical in this type of market. As a consequence, electronic quotation systems have developed. These systems allow dealers to feed the latest bid-asked quotations into the system. They also allow dealers, brokers, buyers, and sellers to see the price quotes of competing dealers.

In OTC stock trading, the NASDAQ system was developed. This is an automated system for quoting the bid and asked prices of dealers in the OTC market. In the bond market, three competing services provide quotations. Inactively traded securities do not have prices quoted electronically. Price information for inactive securities is disseminated in the old fashioned way – by paper quote sheets.

Every transaction on the New York Stock Exchange is recorded and a highly accurate record of prices is available. In contrast, the bond market is an OTC market with no centralized record of actual transaction prices.

The available price quotations on bonds observed in business newspapers are really bid-asked quotes rather than actual transactions prices. For example, *The Wall Street Journal* provides price quotes for U.S. Treasury bills, notes, and bonds. These are average bid-asked quotes based upon a survey of several bond dealers at midafternoon. Actual transaction prices might be significantly different. Active bond market participants subscribe

---

[7] See Glosten and Milgrom (1985) and Seyhun (1986).

to a quotation service providing up-to-the-minute bid-asked quotes on debt instruments.

The Flow of Funds

The U.S. government (that is, the Federal Reserve) monitors the flow of funds between various parts of the economy through a Flow of Funds Statement. The economy is divided into sectors: households, nonfinancial business, government, banks, nonbank finance, and foreign. The Flow of Funds shows transfer *between* sectors and can be a useful tool for understanding money flows from one sector to another. For example, the Flow of Funds for recent years shows the government to be a large net borrower of funds. These government borrowings are financed by domestic households and foreign sources. In the Flow of Funds, financial intermediaries show up as (essentially) neither a net saver nor investor; the intermediaries are conduits of funds.

Summary

Financial intermediaries expedite the flow of savings from savers to ultimate investors in physical assets. Compared to direct investment, financial intermediaries offer some advantages, including pooling of savings, diversification of investment risks, economies of scale in monitoring information and evaluating investment risks, and lower transactions costs. In addition, individual types of intermediaries provide specialized services.

Investment bankers are engaged in the original sale of securities to the public. Dealers make markets in individual securities, trying on the average to make a profit by buying at the bid price and selling at the asked price. Brokers match buyers and sellers of securities for a fee.

Questions/Problems

1. Describe the reasons why financial intermediaries exist.

2. Explain the meaning of the term **diversification**. Under what circumstances is there a benefit from diversifying?

3. What role do investment bankers play in the financial system? What are the economic benefits of investment bankers?

4. Why has investment banking been separated from banking? Are there any disadvantages of separating the two?

5. Describe the various types of orders for securities, including market order, limit order, stop order, and a shortsale.

6. What are the pros and cons of a having the specialist system of market making?

7. Explain the economic reasons for the existence of bid-asked spreads.

References

Allen, D. S., R. E. Lamy, and G. R. Thompson, "The Shelf Registration of Debt and Self-Selection Bias," *Journal of Finance,* 45, March 1990, pp. 275–88.

Benston, G. J. and C. W. Smith, Jr., "A Transactions Cost Approach to the Theory of the Financial Intermediation," *Journal of Finance,* 31 May 1976, pp. 215–32.

Cantor, R., and F. Packer, "The Credit Rating Industry," *Quarterly Review,* Federal Reserve Bank of New York, 19, Summer-Fall 1994, pp. 1–26.

Carey, M. S., S. D. Prowse, J. Rea, and G. Udell, "Recent Developments in the Market for Privately Place Debt," *Federal Reserve Bulletin,* 79, February 1993, pp. 77–92.

Cohen, K. J., S. F. Maier, R. A. Schwartz, and D. K. Whitcomb, *The Microstructure of Securities Markets,* Englewood Cliffs, NJ: Prentice Hall, 1986.

Demsetz, H., "The Cost of Transacting," *Quarterly Journal of Economics,* 82, February 1968, pp. 33–53.

Garbade, K. D. and W. L. Silber, "Price Dispersion in the Government Securities Market," *Journal of Political Economy,* 84, August 1976, pp. 721–40.

Glosten, L. and P. Milgrom, ''Bid, Ask and Transaction Prices in a Specialist Market with Heterogeneously Informed Traders,'' *Journal of Financial Economics,* 14, March 1985, pp. 71–100.

Grant, D. and R. Whaley, ''Transactions Costs on Government Bonds: A Respecification,'' *Journal of Business,* 51, January 1978, pp. 57–64.

Huang, R. D. and H. R. Stoll, ''Major World Equity Markets: Current Structure and Prospects for Change,'' New York University Salomon Center, *Monograph Series in Finance and Economics,* Monograph 1991–3.

Johnson, J. M. and R. E. Miller, ''Investment Banker Prestige and the Underpricing of Initial Public Offerings,'' *Financial Management,* 17, Summer 1988, pp. 19–29.

Laux, P. A., ''Trade Sizes and Theories of the Bid-Asked Spread,'' *Journal of Financial Research,* 16, Fall 1993, pp. 237–49.

Morningstar Mutual Fund Sourcebook, Chicago, Illinois, 1994.

No-Load Investor, *Handbook for No-Load Investors,* Hastings-on-Hudson, NY: The No-Load Fund Investor, 1992.

Pyle, D. H., ''On the Theory of Financial Intermediation,'' *Journal of Finance,* 26, June 1971, pp. 737–47.

Ritter, J., ''The Long-Run Performance of Initial Public Offers,'' *Journal of Finance,* 46, March 1991, pp. 3–27.

Seyhun, H. N., ''Insiders' Profits, Costs of Trading, and Market Efficiency,'' *Journal of Financial Economics,* 16, 1986, pp. 189–212.

Skousen, K. F., *An Introduction to the SEC,* Cincinnati, OH: South-Western Publishing, 1991.

Smith, R. L. ''The Choice of Issuance Procedure and the Cost of Competitive and Negotiated Underwriting: An Examination of the Impact of Rule 50,'' *Journal of Finance,* 42, July 1987, pp. 703–20.

Solnik, Bruno, *International Investments,* 2e, Reading, MA: Addison-Wesley, 1991.

Stigum, M., *The Money Market,* Homewood, IL: Dow Jones Books, 1990.

Tanner, J. E. and L. A. Kochin, ''The Determinants of the Difference Between Bid and Ask Prices on Government Bonds,'' *Journal of Business,* 44, October 1971, pp. 375–79.

Thatcher, J. S. and J. G. Thatcher, ''Timing Performance and the Flotation of Shelf-Registered Bonds,'' *Financial Management,* 17, Spring 1988, pp. 16–26.

Tinic, S. M., ''Anatomy of Initial Public Offerings of Common Stock,'' *Journal of Finance,* 43, September 1988, pp. 789–822.

Urich, T. J., ''U.K., German and Japanese Government Bond Markets,'' New York University Salomon Center, *Monograph Series in Finance and Economics,* Monograph 1991–2.

Van Horne, J. C., *Financial Market Rates and Flows,* 4e, Englewood Cliffs, NJ: Prentice Hall, 1994.

Weisenberger, A., *Investment Companies,* New York: Warren, Gorham, and Lamont, 1994.

7

Bank Regulation and Management

Overview

Commercial banks and thrift institutions[1] have a sizable impact upon the economic system; they are the largest components of the financial services industry. Commercial banks and thrifts are also important participants in the money and debt markets, both as borrowers of funds and as lenders.

Commercial banks and thrift institutions are regulated by a number of regulatory agencies. One purpose of this chapter is to describe the basic regulatory framework. This includes the reasons for regulation as well as some of the major regulations and their consequences. A second purpose of this chapter is to describe the major managerial issues faced by depository institutions. In recent years, increased variability of interest rates has altered the regulation and management of banks and thrifts.

A commercial bank is an institution which offers checking deposits and makes commercial loans. There used to be a sharp distinction between commercial banks and thrift institutions. Formerly, thrift institutions were not allowed to have checking deposits and were primarily restricted to real estate loans. Now this distinction is blurred because thrift institutions are allowed to offer checking deposits and to make more nonreal estate loans. Most of this chapter focuses upon commercial banks. The regulation and management of thrift institutions are quite similar.

---

[1] The term thrift means savings and loan, savings bank, or credit union.

There are over 11,000 commercial banks in the United States. These are generally divided into three types: (1) money center banks, (2) regional banks, and (3) local banks. Money center banks are very large banks; they make loans nationwide and raise a sizable portion of their funds in the money market, especially in the form of large-denomination certificates of deposit. Although the number of money center banks is relatively small, these banks hold a large proportion of total bank assets because of the huge size of individual money center banks. The total assets of the banking system are very heavily concentrated among a relatively small number of these large money center banks. Regional banks are smaller in size than money center banks, tend to concentrate more of their loans in their own region, and have a smaller dependence upon money market sources of funds. The large majority of banks are small local banks, serving a small geographical area and raising a large proportion of funds through deposits.

Motivations for Bank Regulation

Banks are heavily regulated, and an understanding of the basics of regulation is important. There are several motivations for regulating banks.

Bank Safety

First, bank safety is considered essential. Bank depositors are not regarded as bank creditors, who should bear the risk of bank default. Instead, banks are typically viewed as trustees for depositors' funds. This trustee view suggests the desirability of government insurance for depositors. Once insured, the government has an incentive to regulate bank activities to prevent fraud, embezzlement, and excessive risk taking.

Impact upon Economy

Another motivation for regulation is fear of bank failures seriously damaging local economies, and perhaps the overall economy, by worsening recessions and depressions. From historical evidence, banking panics (with widespread bank failures) have possibly precipitated and definitely worsened economic downturns.

Competition in Banking

In another view, regulation is essential to maintaining competition. Competitive markets have many competing banks, charging low interest rates on loans and paying high rates on deposits. Regulators are concerned about the extremes of too few banks or too many banks.

An insufficient number of banks results in a monopoly or oligopoly situation. The term **monopoly** means only one firm in the market. With an **oligopoly**, a small number of firms compose the market. The oligopolistic firms have incentives to act in concert. In effect, an oligopolistic industry is very much like a monopoly. Because monopolists or oligopolists have very strong market positions, they charge very high prices and make abnormally high profits. In the case of monopoly or oligopoly banks, the bank pays low interest rates to depositors and charges high interest rates on loans. The banks make high profits at the expense of the bank customers.

In a competitive market, individual firms, acting in their own interest, have incentives to compete with the other firms by cutting prices. Price competition tends to reduce monopoly and oligopoly profits to a level that represents a fair return for the risk taken. The beneficiary of this competition is the customers, who enjoy lower prices. In the case of banks, the bank customers enjoy high interest rates on deposits and low interest rates on loans.

The other extreme is too many firms in an industry, resulting in cut-throat competition. With cut-throat competition, the many competing firms bid aggressively against each other for market share, driving prices to extremely low levels and reducing profits to very low and even negative levels. Under such circumstances, a number of firms will fail. These business failures tend to be disruptive to the economy as many individuals become unemployed. Another possibility is for weak firms to merge into a larger firm which is in a stronger and more profitable position. After the so-called shakeout of the weak firms, the industry may become heavily concentrated. In other words, cut-throat competition may ultimately create a monopoly or oligopoly. In addition, the disruption associated with cut-throat competition may be harmful to parts of the economy.

An important problem in regulating competition is defining the trade area, which is frequently done by defining the market geographically and by product. For example, a narrow definition of the geographic market might result in a large number of small, high-cost banks. An important issue in banking should be diversification. A bank that serves a small local community dependent upon one industry is typically in a high-risk position. If that industry falls upon hard times, the nondiversified bank runs a high risk of failure. In the United States, diversification has been of lesser importance to regulators than in many foreign countries. The result has been a large number of small, nondiversified banks in the United States compared to many other countries.

Bank Costs

In trying to determine the number of banks necessary to serve a particular community, the relationship between a bank's operating cost and its size is important. This relationship is called a **cost function** and is shown in figure 7.1. The horizontal axis shows bank size as measured by total assets. The vertical axis shows cost per dollar of assets. As the bank size gets bigger, cost per dollar of assets tends to decline because of economies of scale. Economies of scale occur as fixed costs are spread over more units as size increases.[2]

Figure 7.1   Operating Costs of Banks

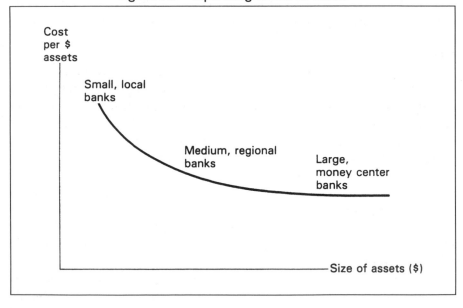

---

[2] See Kolari (1987) and Le Compte and Smith (1990) for a discussion of bank costs.

In the diagram, small, local banks tend to have high costs. In effect, their size of operation is too small to realize economies of scale. Medium size, regional banks tend to realize considerable economies of scale. Very large, money center banks are roughly as efficient as medium size banks.

Regulators facing the practical issue of desirable bank size should try to determine the bank size for which the cost function becomes relatively flat. At this relatively flat part of the curve, the added benefits of additional size are small. While very small banks operate at high cost, the point at which the cost curve flattens is not completely clear. Thus, there is no simple answer about desirable bank size.

Forms of Regulation

Regulation of banks takes several forms: (1) chartering, (2) branching restrictions, (3) examination, (4) capital adequacy, (5) insurance (6) restrictions on entry into nonbanking activities.

Chartering

A bank charter constitutes the right to operate as a bank. National charters are granted by the Comptroller of the Currency for commercial banks.[3] State charters are issued by state regulatory authorities. The difference between a national and state charter has blurred in recent years. In deciding upon a charter, the issuing authority considers whether the new bank has a market, adequate capital, and proper management.

Branching

A branch is an additional office of a bank. Historically, bank branching has been regulated in two ways. First, federal law prevented interstate (between state) branching. Second, state laws restricted branching within states. These two sets of laws have had serious consequences for the banking system including the following: (1) The U.S. has a very large number of banks –

---

[3] Similarly, savings and loans and credit unions may have national or state charters. This will be discussed later.

over 11,000. (2) Many banks are small and have high operating costs. (3) Many banks are not diversified geographically or across industries. As a consequence, the U.S. has had the highest bank failure rate among industrialized countries.

Recent legislation has lifted the ban on interstate branching. Most likely, consolidation of many smaller banks into larger banks with multiple branches will result. The larger banks will have lower operation costs, will be more diversified geographically and across industries, and will have a lower failure rate.

A major motivation for restrictions on bank branching has been the feeling that local needs are better met with a small local bank. This reasoning is a leftover from a time when transportation was much slower. With cars, telephones, electronic transfer of funds, and automated teller machines (ATMs), the need for a local bank is dramatically reduced.

The existence of restrictions on bank branching has contributed to the large number of banks in the United States. Countries with unrestricted branching have fewer banks per capita, each of which typically has many branches. As an example, Canada has a handful of banks with nationwide branches.

The branching restrictions have also contributed to a high rate of bank failure in the United States compared to other developed countries. Small banks serving local areas are unable to achieve economies of scale and to diversify loans across different regions and industries. Many U.S. banks have failed because of too close a tie to a one-product local economy.

Bank Examination

Banks are examined to maintain good loan quality and to prevent fraud and embezzlement. Examiners give banks so-called CAMEL ratings from 1 (highest quality) to 5 (lowest quality). Banks with ratings of 5 are called problem banks and are monitored more closely. The relevant regulatory authorities are the Federal Reserve, Comptroller of the Currency, FDIC, and state authorities. These agencies share oversight responsibilities to prevent duplication of effort.

The term CAMEL is an acronym, standing for Capital adequacy, Asset quality, Management, Earnings, and Liquidity. The definitions of the five CAMEL ratings are as follows.

1. An institution that is basically sound in every aspect.
2. An institution that is fundamentally sound, but with modest weaknesses.

3. An institution with financial, operational, or compliance weaknesses that give cause for supervisor concern.
4. An institution with serious financial weaknesses that could impair future viability.
5. An institution with critical financial weaknesses that render the probability of failure extremely high in the near term.

Capital Adequacy

Regulators try to determine the appropriate level of owners' equity as a percentage of total assets. The lower the level of equity, the greater is the bank's risk but the higher is the bank owners' expected rate of return. A lower level of bank capital results in greater average bank profits and a higher rate of bank failure. In recent years, bank capital requirements have been raised to reduce the risk of bank failure.

Capital adequacy is measured by the ratio of capital to risk-adjusted assets (i.e., capital/assets). Regulators use two measures of capital – core capital and total capital. Core capital is the sum of paid-in capital, surplus, retained earnings, and minority interests in consolidated subsidiaries. Total capital is core capital plus several types of long-term debt.

In computing risk-adjusted assets, each type of asset is weighted by a risk weighting from 0 for the lowest risk to 1 for the highest risk assets (see table 7.1). Thus, cash, deposits with the Federal Reserve, and short-term Treasury securities have a weighting of 0 percent. Commercial loans have a weighting of 100 percent. Since the weight is in the denominator of the capital ratio, a weight of 0 percent for low-risk assets reduces the denominator and raises the ratio. Thus, lower risk assets increase the capital ratio.

Table 7.1   Risk-adjusted Asset Weights

Weight	Types of Assets*
0% no risk	cash, deposits with Fed, short-term Treasury securities
20% low risk	cash in collection, short-term claims on U.S. depository institutions, general obligation municipal bonds
50% moderate risk	one- to four-family residential mortgages, municipal revenue bonds
100% standard risk	commercial loans

*These are examples of the assets in each category, not an exhaustive list.

A bank is considered adequately capitalized if the core capital ratio exceeds 4 percent and the total capital ratio exceeds 8 percent. Banks with lower ratios are inadequately capitalized and are more closely monitored. If the ratios are sufficiently low, the bank is closed.

Deposit Insurance and Bank Failures

The Federal Deposit Insurance Corporation (FDIC) insures commercial bank and savings and loan deposits up to $100,000. The FDIC administers two insurance funds. The Bank Insurance Fund (BIF) provides insurance for commercial banks. The Savings Association Insurance Fund (SAIF) provides insurance to savings and loans.

Deposit insurance guarantees most depositors against the risk of bankruptcy of the bank. The purpose is to create confidence in the banking system and to prevent runs on banks and resulting panics. Rumors of serious financial problems about an uninsured bank could easily induce depositors to withdraw their funds. Even for basically sound banks, a sudden large cash withdrawal is devastating since banks typically retain only a small percentage of their deposits as currency; the majority of deposits are lent to earn interest. Deposit insurance reduces the incentive to withdraw funds, which reduces the chance of a bank run.

Insurance Premiums   In the past, deposit insurance premiums were the same rate for all banks regardless of the riskiness of their loan portfolio. Constant premiums encouraged some banks to take on excessively risky loans and contributed to the high rate of failure for commercial banks and savings and loans in the 1980s.

Under current regulations, insurance premiums are risk adjusted. Higher risk banks pay higher premiums. The premiums are shown in table 7.2. The premium depends upon two risk factors – the CAMEL rating from the bank examiners and the total (risk-adjusted) capital ratio. The CAMEL rating is

Table 7.2   FDIC Insurance Premiums

Total Capital Ratio	CAMEL Ratings		
	1 or 2	3	4 or 5
Greater than 10%	.23%	.26%	.29%
Between 8 and 10%	.26%	.29%	.30%
Less than 8%	.29%	.30%	.31%

a measure of the quality of the assets, i.e., the default probability of the loans. The capital ratio is a measure of financial leverage. Banks with poor loan quality (CAMEL of 4 or 5) and high leverage (capital ratio of less than 8 percent) have higher risk and pay higher premiums.

Bank Failures   The FDIC, which insures deposits, has administrative responsibility for **bank failures**. Theoretically, a bank is bankrupt when the market value of equity is zero or negative, basically when the market value of loans is less than the amount owed to depositors. Since the market value of loans is not directly observable, determining the point when a bank should be closed is difficult.

If the value of the bank's assets (primarily loans) is less than the amount owed to depositors, the FDIC insurance fund is responsible for the shortfall.[4] There are three alternatives for dealing with a failed bank. One alternative is for the FDIC to arrange a merger with a sounder financial institution. The FDIC, as the insurer, compensates the acquiring bank to make the merger financially feasible. A second alternative is for the FDIC to pay off insured depositors and then liquidate assets, using any residual proceeds to pay off uninsured depositors. A third alternative is for the FDIC to take over the failed institution and operate it.

Regulatory Response to Bank Failures

In the 1980s, the number of bank failures increased considerably for several reasons.

1. Rising interest rates hurt many banks with a large proportion of fixed-rate loans. The failure rate for savings and loans has been especially high because of long-term fixed-rate mortgage loans. If a savings and loan makes a long-term loan at a fixed rate and interest rates subsequently rise, the cost of funds can rise above the fixed rate earned on the loan. A sustained period of high interest rates will result in failures.

2. Poor economic conditions in some regions have caused bank failures, since smaller banks typically do not geographically diversify their loans.

---

[4] Technically, the FDIC is responsible for insured deposits only. In practice, other deposits may be covered.

The clearest examples have been in the farming and oil regions. Poor economic conditions in these industries have caused many loan defaults and resulting bank failures. To some extent, these failures were caused by restrictions on branching, resulting in many small, nondiversified banks serving small geographic areas, often with a one-product economy. If the local product falls upon hard times, the failure of local banks is more likely than the failure of geographically diversified banks.

3. Deregulation allowed some banks to make risky or unwise loans.

In response to the many failures in the 1980s, the government has taken a number of remedial actions. (1) Bank examination has become stricter. (2) Failing banks are closed sooner. (3) Risk-adjusted insurance premiums were introduced. (4) Capital requirements were raised and risk-adjusted capital measures were utilized. (5) Consolidation of the banking industry is being encouraged with relaxation of branching restrictions. Larger, more diversified and cost-efficient banks should result.

Entry into Nonbanking Activities

Entry by banks into nonbanking activities has been restricted for several reasons.[5] First, the safety of banks might be reduced if they engage in other lines of business. Second, banks might be able to use the advantages of regulation to compete unfairly with other businesses. Third, bank funds might be used to manipulate markets. The Federal Reserve is in charge of determining what nonbanking activities banks may enter.

Thrift Institutions

Thrift institutions include savings and loan associations, mutual savings banks, and credit unions. Savings and loan associations are the largest group of thrift institutions. Savings and loan were set up to promote the flow of funds into real estate mortgages. They can be federally chartered or state

---

[5] For a more detailed discussion, see chapter 6 on financial intermediaries.

chartered, with more than half being state chartered. Nationally chartered savings and loans are regulated by the Office of Thrift Supervision. S&L's are insured by SAIF.

Mutual savings banks are owned by the depositors, although some are now owned by stockholders. Mutual savings banks were set up to promote savings. Effectively, they are hard to distinguish from savings and loans because the majority of loans are for real estate. The majority of mutual savings banks are insured by the FDIC.

Credit unions are associations of some people with a common bond for the purpose of collecting savings. The common bond may be a common employer, religion, labor union, or others. The credit union makes consumer loans to the members. Federally chartered credit unions are regulated by the National Credit Union Administration. All federally chartered credit unions must belong to the National Credit Union Insurance Fund; state chartered credit unions can elect to join. This insurance fund operates in the same way as the FDIC.

A Bank Balance Sheet

To provide a framework for discussing bank managerial issues, a brief discussion of a typical bank balance sheet is helpful (see table 7.3).

Bank Assets

Cash Balances   Cash consists of coins and currency, balances at correspondent banks, and reserve balances at the Federal Reserve. Coins and currency are kept to meet the needs of bank customers. Banks keep correspondent balances at other banks in order to expedite a number of transactions such

Table 7.3   A Bank Balance Sheet

Assets		Liabilities and Owners' Equity	
Currency and coins	3%	Checkable deposits	18%
Correspondent deposits	2%	Savings deposits	17%
Deposits at Fed	2%	Time deposits	34%
Securities	19%	Borrowings	16%
Loans	67%	Other liabilities	8%
Other assets	7%	Capital	7%

as check clearing. Balances at the Federal Reserve are necessary to meet reserve requirements set by the Federal Reserve and cannot be withdrawn.

Securities   Banks hold marketable short-term fixed income securities (largely Treasury securities) as secondary reserves, that is, highly liquid assets available to sell rapidly if the bank needs to raise cash. These secondary reserves tend to earn relatively lower returns. In addition, many banks hold municipal bonds issued by municipalities served by the bank. The municipality is typically a customer of the bank. The coupon interest payments for municipal bonds are exempt from federal income taxes, making the after-tax return quite attractive.

Loans   The major earning asset of a bank is its loans. The lion's share of bank revenues tend to come from interest on loans. Banks make a variety of loans, including commercial and industrial loans, mortgage loans, and consumer loans.

Other Assets   Other assets include bank buildings, usually a small percentage of a bank's assets. Another type of asset is repurchase agreements. Banks with excess funds may find it profitable to lend these funds to security dealers as part of a repurchase agreement or to other banks in the form of federal funds. As will be discussed in chapter 16 on money market instruments, bond dealers finance a sizable portion of their inventory of securities by selling them one day with a contract to repurchase them with interest the next day. The lender (e.g., a bank) initially buys the securities with a contract to sell them back with overnight interest to the bond dealer the next day. From the viewpoint of the lender, the transaction is called a **reverse**.

A third type of asset is federal funds lent to other banks. Federal funds are loans of reserves on deposit at the Federal Reserve. A bank with excess reserves may find it attractive to loan those funds in the federal funds market. Small banks tend to be lenders of federal funds and big money center banks tend to be borrowers of federal funds.

Liabilities and Owners' Equity

Checkable Deposits   A sizable proportion of bank funds is raised by deposits on which checks can be written. Checking deposits have been offered by commercial banks for many years and pay no interest. Other types of deposits, such as money market deposit accounts, allow check writing and pay interest.

Savings Deposits Savings deposits have no check-writing privileges and pay interest to the depositor.

Time Deposits There are many kinds of time deposits. Small-denomination certificates of deposit (CD) are nonmarketable, interest-earning deposits of less than $100,000 for a fixed period of time. There are typically penalties for early withdrawal. Large-denomination certificates of deposit are marketable, interest-earning deposits of $100,000 and above for a fixed period of time. Money center banks raise a sizable proportion of their funds in the form of large-denomination certificates of deposit.

Borrowings Borrowings include foreign deposits and federal funds purchased. Foreign deposits are so-called Eurodollar deposits in foreign subsidiaries of U.S. banks. Money center banks tend to raise a large proportion of their funds from Eurodollar deposits.

Money center banks tend to be net buyers of federal funds and small banks tend to be net sellers. The term **purchased funds** is used to describe large certificates of deposit, Eurodollar deposits, and federal funds. Money center banks are heavy users of purchased funds.

Equity Bank equity represents owners' contributions to funds. Regulators set a lower bound on equity and monitor it carefully.

Bank Managerial Issues

In trying to earn returns for its owners, a commercial bank is faced with the following management issues: (1) credit risk, (2) asset and liability maturities, (3) liquidity risk, and (4) financial leverage or capital adequacy.

Credit Risk

The bank must decide which loan applicants are acceptable credit risks. There is no simple procedure for making these decisions. For consumer loans with many loan applicants, numerical credit scoring techniques can be used. Based upon the repayment history of past loans, statisticians can develop a model able to predict the likelihood of default with considerable accuracy. But these statistical techniques do not apply for loan applicants with unique situations. For evaluating these applicants, the banker's judgment is essential.

The interest rate charged on a loan should reflect two elements: a pure time value of money component and a premium to compensate the bank for default risk. Loans made to borrowers with high risk of default should be made at higher interest rates. The rate on the loan should be set high enough to allow for the expected losses from default.[6] If the bank makes a large number of loans, on average it should make a profit if the interest rates charged individual customers reflect the default risks of those customers.

Bank loans are typically secured by the assets of the borrower. If there is a default on the loan, the bank has first claim on these assets. For a loan, the marketability of the assets is an important risk element to the lending bank. If the assets backing a loan have a stable market value and can be sold quickly, the risk of losses to the lender is obviously low. Consequently, the marketability of the collateral for a loan has an important impact upon the interest rate charged. Highly marketable collateral implies a lower interest rate because the risk to the lender is lower.

An important aspect of credit risk is proper diversification of a bank's loan portfolio. A bank making most of its loans to one industry is not sufficiently diversified, since many of the loans may default if that industry does poorly. Widespread defaults in one industry can easily cause a poorly diversified bank to fail. A number of bank failures have occurred in nondiversified banks with loans heavily concentrated in the oil industry, the farming industry, or in local real estate.

Asset and Liability Maturities

A major bank decision involves the maturity of assets and liabilities. Typically, longer term interest rates are higher than shorter term interest rates. To take advantage of this, banks frequently raise a large proportion of their funds from short-term deposits at low interest rates and lend out these funds for longer maturities at high rates. The bank profits by the difference in rates.

Unfortunately, shorter term interest rates tend to fluctuate more than longer term rates.[7] Consequently, longer term bank loans financed by the

---

[6] Chapter 13 on default risk shows the impact of default risk upon the interest rate.

[7] This is discussed extensively in chapter 11 on bond price volatility.

bank with short-term funds are refinanced in the future at a highly uncertain interest rate. While the average refinancing is at relatively low short-term rates, sometimes the refinancing is at high rates, perhaps at rates exceeding the original bank loan. For example, consider a bank that makes a one-year loan at 8 percent. This loan is financed with a three-month certificate of deposit at 6 percent, implying that the bank makes a 2 percent profit spread apart from its overhead costs. After three months, the bank has to refinance by selling another certificate of deposit. The interest rate on this new certificate of deposit may be above 8 percent, with the bank absorbing a loss.

Refinancing risks can be considerable. A major cause of failure of thrift institutions in recent years has been refinancing risks. Typically, thrift institutions have made long-term fixed-rate mortgage loans and financed these by deposits – a very short-term source of funds. As interest rates rose in the 1970s, many fixed-rate mortgage loans previously made at low rates had to be financed at very high interest rates, causing large losses for the thrift institutions.

Commercial banks hold a more diversified loan portfolio than thrift institutions; banks make many relatively short-term business and consumer (nonmortgage) loans. Consequently, commercial banks have not been as badly affected by rising interest rates as the thrift organizations.

In recent years, interest rates have been quite variable by historical standards. To reduce the risk of changing interest rates, many banks match the maturities of loans (assets) and financing (liabilities). For example, consider a commercial bank making a six-month loan to a construction company at 12 percent. If the bank finances this with six-month certificates of deposit at 9 percent, the bank locks in the borrowing and lending rates and does not bear the risk of fluctuating interest rates. On the other hand, the bank loses a potential source of bank profit (that is, the spread between longer term and shorter term rates). In the preceding example, the bank might be able to sell one-month certificates of deposit at 7 percent. At the end of this month, the bank has to refinance. If the refinancing rate is 7 percent or less over the remaining five months, the bank earns an extra 2 percent profit. On the other hand, if interest rates rise, the refinancing rate is higher. Profits are reduced and perhaps losses occur.

Many banks (and thrift institutions) make a sizable proportion of variable-rate loans, for which the interest rate adjusts periodically. The new rate is tied to some market rate. For example, assume a six-month loan to a construction company with the loan rate tied to the rate on 30-day maturity United States Treasury bills. The loan rate is the 30-day bill rate plus 4 percent. If the current 30-day bill rate is 7 percent, the loan to the construction company carries an initial interest rate of 11 percent. Every month, the loan rate is revised. The bank expects to raise funds at a rate varying with the bill rate, perhaps the bill rate plus 1.5 percent. The bank earns 2.5 percent on this loan minus operating costs and expected default losses. These variable-rate loans are effectively short-term loans. Thus, banks can effectively transform longer maturity loans into short-term loans by making the interest rate variable.

With variable-rate loans, the borrower pays short-term interest rates. The interest rate risk (that is, the risk of fluctuating short-term rates) is borne by the borrower. By the same token, the borrower has the reward of paying lower average rates than on longer maturity loans. The bank shifts the risks and rewards to the borrower. This risk shifting reduces bank risk, but also reduces bank profitability.

Another strategy for reducing interest rate risk of a bank is to sell loans in the market.[8] Selling of mortgages is discussed extensively in Chapter 15 on mortgages. The sale of mortgages in the secondary market reduces the role of a bank to that of a middleman who originates the loan and then funnels the mortgage payments to the buyer of the mortgages. This strategy reduces the bank's risk but also some of the bank's expected profit. The risk is passed on to the buyer of the mortgages, who also has higher expected profits.

Banks try to control the risk of fluctuating interest rates for the bank as a whole through a process called GAP management. The procedure is to classify assets and liabilities by maturity, comparing the differences or gaps in maturity. Consider the example in table 7.4 which classifies banks assets (loans) and liabilities (financing) by maturity.

Table 7.4　GAP Management

Maturity	Assets	Liabilities
0– 6 months	40%	50%
7–12 months	30%	20%
13–24 months	20%	20%
25– months	10%	10%
	100%	100%

---

[8] This process has been called **securitization**, since now loans can trade in the resale market in the same way as securities.

For this bank, asset and liability maturities match for maturities of 13 months and longer. There is a mismatch of the shorter term assets and liabilities. For 0 to 6 months, there are 10 percent more liabilities than assets. For 7 to 12 months, there are 10 percent more assets (loans) than liabilities. For 10 percent of its total balance sheet, this bank is financing with maturities of less than six months and using these funds to make loans with maturities of 7 to 12 months. Since the 0 to 6 month borrowing rate averages less than the 7 to 12, the bank increases its average profits through this mismatch of maturities. However, the bank bears some risk of higher short-term interest rates. When rates are high, the bank's profits are low or negative. Each bank has to decide what mismatch, if any, is desirable by comparing the potential extra profit from the mismatch with the possible losses if short-term rates rise sharply.

Liquidity Risk

The term **liquidity** refers to nearness to money. The most liquid asset is money. Banks bear several interrelated liquidity risks: (1) inability to pay depositors on demand, (2) inability to raise funds in the market at reasonable rates, and (3) insufficient funds to make attractive loans.

Banks keep only a small proportion of their assets in the form of cash available to meet deposit withdrawals, because banks earn no return on cash holdings. Therefore, the ability to meet deposit withdrawals depends upon the ability to raise funds in the market. Similarly, the availability of funds to meet loan demand depends upon the bank's access to the market.

Market perceptions of a bank's financial position heavily affect liquidity. If the market's view of the bank is very negative, the bank is unable to raise funds and, consequently, is unable to meet deposit withdrawals or loan demand. Thus, liquidity management reduces to running the bank in a way that maintains confidence in its financial position.

Financial Leverage or Capital Adequacy

Given regulatory restrictions, banks must decide on the extent of financial leverage. A smaller percentage of equity financing (and, therefore, a bigger percentage of debt financing) results in higher average returns to stockholders but greater variability in those returns and, therefore, greater risk. Each bank must decide on the appropriate level of leverage, given regulatory restraints. In general, larger money center banks have greater leverage than small local banks.

As part of the financing decision, banks must decide on the mix of debt. The forms of debt financing available to a bank include deposits on which checks may be written, savings deposits, time deposits, large denomination certificates of deposit, federal funds, and repurchase agreements. Banks typically do not issue long-term bonds. Large money center banks make extensive use of foreign deposits and of money market funds, that is, large CDs, fed funds, and repos (see chapter 16 on money market instruments). Smaller banks rely more heavily on local sources of funds, including demand deposits and savings and time deposits.

Summary

Commercial banks and thrift institutions are a major component of the financial services industry. Because these institutions are viewed as playing a fiduciary role, they are regulated. Regulation of banks takes several forms: (1) chartering, (2) branching restrictions, (3) examination, (4) capital adequacy, and (5) deposit insurance. The major managerial issues faced by bank management are determining the appropriate level of credit risk, deciding on desirable asset and liability maturities, managing liquidity risk, and determining the best level of financial leverage, given regulatory constraints.

Questions/Problems

1. What is the difference between a commercial bank and a savings and loan?

2. What are the motivations for regulating banks?

3. What are the practical differences if a bank has a national as opposed to a state charter?

4. How would fixed-rate insurance deposit premiums affect the risk taking attitudes of bank management?

5. What are the purposes of bank examination? If a problem bank does not improve its performance, what courses of action are available to regulators?

6. If a bank fails, how can the FDIC handle the situation?

7. Why do banks hold cash and marketable securities?

8. Explain why default risk raises the interest rate on a loan.

9. Why is diversification of a loan portfolio important to a bank?

10. What risk reduction alternatives are available to a bank faced with variable interest rates on its sources of funds?

11. Why has the failure rate of thrift institutions been high?

12. What steps have regulators taken to reduce the likelihood of bank and thrift failures in the future?

References

Becketti, S., "Are Derivatives Too Risky for Banks," *Economic Review,* Federal Reserve Bank of Kansas City, Third Quarter 1993, pp. 27–42.

Benston, G., G. Hanweck and D. Humphrey, "Operating Costs in Commercial Banking," Federal Reserve Bank of Atlanta, *Economic Review,* November 1982, pp. 6–21.

Benston, G. J. and G. G. Kaufman, "Risk and Solvency Regulation of Depository Institutions: Past Policies and Current Options," Salomon Brothers Center for the Study of Financial Institutions, Graduate School of Business Administration New York University, *Monograph Series in Finance and Economics,* Monograph 1988–1.

Berger, A., G. Hanweck and D. Humphrey, "Competitive Viability in Banking: Scale, Scope, and Product Mix Economies," *Research Papers in Banking and Financial Economics,* Board of Governors of the Federal Reserve System, January 1986.

Calem, P. S., "The Proconsumer Argument for Interstate Branching," *Business Review,* Federal Reserve Bank of Philadelphia, May/June 1993, pp. 15–29.

Calem, P. S., "The Impact of Geographic Deregulation on Small Banks," *Business Review,* Federal Reserve Bank of Philadelphia, November/ December 1994, pp. 17–31.

Federal Reserve, *FIMS: A New Monitoring System for Banking Institutions,* Federal Reserve Bulletin, 81, January 1995, pp. 1–15.

Gilbert, R. A., C. C. Stone, and M. E. Trebing, "The New Capital Adequacy Standards," *Federal Reserve Bank of St. Louis Review,* May, 1985.

Gilligan, T. and M. Smirlock, "An Empirical Study of Joint Production and Scale Economies in Commercial Banking," *Journal of Banking and Finance,* 8, 1984, pp. 67–77.

Gilligan, T., M. Smirlock, and W. Marshall, "Scale and Scope Economies in the Multi-Product Banking Firm," *Journal of Monetary Economics,* 13, 1984, pp. 393–405.

Kolari, J., *Bank Costs, Structure, and Performance,* Lexington, MA: Lexington Books, D.C. Heath, 1987.

Le Compte, R. L. B. and S. D. Smith, "Changes in the Cost of Intermediation: The Case of Savings and Loans," *Journal of Finance,* December 1990, pp. 1337–46.

Mester, L. J., "Efficient Production of Financial Services: Scale and Scope Economies," *Business Review,* Federal Reserve Bank of Philadelphia, January/February 1987, pp. 15–25.

Mester, L. J., "A Multiproduct Cost Study of Savings and Loans," *Journal of Finance,* 42, June 1987, pp. 433–45.

Murray, J. and R. White, "Economies of Scale and Economies of Scope in Multiproduct Financial Institutions: A Study of British Columbia Credit Unions," *Journal of Finance,* 38, June 1983, pp. 887–902.

Wheelock, D. C., "Is the Banking Industry in Decline? Recent Trends and Future Prospects from a Historical Perspective," *Federal Reserve Bank of St. Louis Review,* 75, September/October 1993, pp. 3–22.

8

Efficient Markets

Overview

A security market is said to be **informationally efficient** if all currently available public information is very rapidly reflected in security prices. A market is efficient if a number of investors try to utilize information for their own benefit. If a security is underpriced given current public information, these investors buy the security in anticipation of the price rising to its equilibrium price. Consequently, the price should rise immediately to its equilibrium value if investors monitor the flow of information. Competition for profits is the driving force behind informational efficiency.

The concept of an informationally efficient market is illustrated in figure 8.1. Before new information becomes public, the security has an old value. Then new information hits the market. In an efficient market, the price instantly adjusts to its new equilibrium level. If the market is inefficient, the market may underreact or overreact to new information. If there is underreaction, the price adjustment is too gradual, as shown in figure 8.1. If there is overreaction, the market price overshoots the new equilibrium before it eventually reverts to the new equilibrium value. Between the time of the news revelation and the adjustment to the new equilibrium value, astute investors would be able to profit at the expense of less sophisticated investors, if the market is inefficient.

According to the efficient market hypothesis, the market rapidly incorporates any and all information affecting the value of a security. Tests of market efficiency require a definition of the relevant information and a model showing the impact of this information upon prices. Therefore, most tests of efficiency are joint tests of a particular pricing model and of efficiency.

Figure 8.1   Market Reaction to New Information

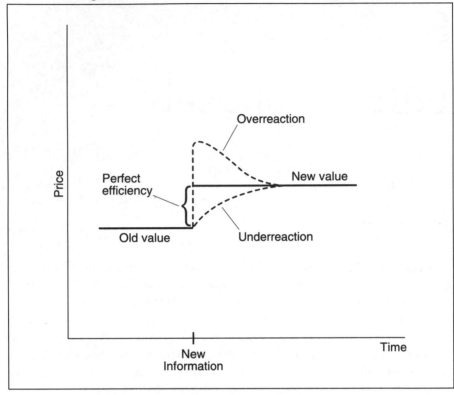

The efficient market hypothesis can be broken down into three sub-hypotheses, which differ according to the type of information.[1]

Weak-Form Efficiency

According to the weak form of market efficiency, past price and volume of trading information are instantaneously incorporated into current prices. Therefore, knowledge of past price and volume information does not allow prediction of future price changes.

Assume the following time line:

---

[1] See Fama (1970) for a careful discussion of market efficiency.

Points in Time

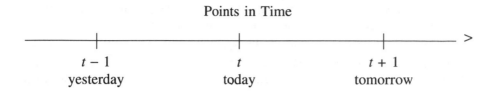

$t - 1$ t $t + 1$
yesterday   today   tomorrow

Let E_t equal the expectation given the information available at time t; P_t is today's price; and P_{t+1} is tomorrow's price.

If the market is weak-form efficient, the expectation of tomorrow's price is today's price. In other words, today's price is the best predictor of tomorrow's price.

$$E_t(P_{t+1}) = P_t \qquad (8.1)$$

Equation 8.1 can be rewritten as:

$$E_t(P_{t+1} - P_t) = 0 \qquad (8.2)$$

In other words, the expected change in price is zero in an efficient market. For this reason, price changes in an efficient market cannot be predicted given past information. Recent changes in price should convey no information about future changes in price. In an efficient market, the knowledge of a price rise yesterday conveys no information about future price changes; rising prices yesterday do not imply rising or falling prices tomorrow.

Strictly speaking, equations 8.1 and 8.2 are valid only for very short periods such as days or possibly weeks. Over longer periods of time, prices of some securities have an upward price trend. For example, in order for investors to hold risky common stocks, expected returns increase as risk increases. Part of the expected return of holding common stocks is the expected capital appreciation, that is, an expected upward trend in stock price. Equations 8.1 and 8.2 can be adjusted for the long term by adding in a term for the long-term uptrend for risk. When equation 8.1 is adjusted for risk, the expected price for next period equals the current price plus an expected increase because of the upward trend. Prices fluctuate randomly around this uptrend.

The viewpoint that price changes cannot be predicted has been called the **random walk hypothesis**, named after the following problem in statistics. Imagine a very large room whose floor is composed of many squares. If an extremely intoxicated person is put onto the square in the middle of the room and then proceeds to take steps from one square to another (without any predictable pattern), what is the best predictor of his location after *n* steps? The answer is the square where he began.

According to the random walk hypothesis, price changes are drawn from a probability distribution which does not change over time. This constant distribution assumption is a subset of weak-form efficiency. Weak-form efficiency can hold, even though the distribution of prices shifts over time.

Weak-form efficiency in equation 8.1 is a short-run hypothesis covering periods such as days or perhaps weeks. Over long time intervals such as years, security price changes can have an uptrend, representing a return for the time value of money and for risk bearing. Over shorter intervals, such as days, this uptrend can be ignored for practical purposes.

With regard to bonds and interest rates, the random walk hypothesis suggests essentially random or unpredictable bond price changes. If bond price changes are random, then changes in interest rates are approximately random also.

There have been extensive empirical tests of weak-form market efficiency or the random walk hypothesis for common stocks, bonds, and futures contracts. Overall, the evidence is consistent with price changes of these different types of securities being random. With regard to interest rates, the evidence is consistent with interest rates following a random walk.

Two approaches have been used to test weak-form market efficiency. One approach looks for statistically significant patterns in security price changes and essentially finds no meaningful patterns. A second approach searches out profitable short-term trading rules. After brokerage commissions costs, these trading rules have been found to be unprofitable. This evidence indicates no simple and stable relationship between price changes at different points in time.

Semistrong-Form Efficiency

In the semistrong market efficiency hypothesis, the impact of nonprice information upon security prices is practically instantaneous. For common stocks, information about earnings and dividends is rapidly reflected in security prices. For bonds, information about determinants of interest rates is instantaneously incorporated into prices. The majority of the evidence supports semistrong efficiency.

Testing semistrong efficiency raises two serious problems. First, a model of the determinants of security prices must be chosen. Second, tests of the model must distinguish between anticipated and unanticipated information.

Fully anticipated information should already be incorporated into security prices. Only unanticipated information or surprises have an impact upon security prices.

For example, money supply announcements by the Federal Reserve have been suggested as a determinant of interest rates. To test the impact of money supply announcements upon interest rates, the actual announcement must be decomposed into the anticipated and unanticipated amount, or surprise. In a semistrong-efficient market, the anticipated amount should be incorporated into prices before the announcement. Surprise deviations of the actual prices from the anticipated prices result in rapid price adjustments in a semistrong-efficient market. The accuracy of tests for efficiency is affected by the procedure for separating announcements into anticipated amounts and surprises. The existing evidence is consistent with the market's adjusting rapidly to surprises.

Strong-Form Efficiency

In a strong-form efficient market, information available to special groups of investors is already incorporated into security prices and, therefore, is of no real value to these investors.

Professional money managers are one special group that has been investigated. The average mutual fund earns fair rates of return given the risk levels. This finding is consistent with efficiency. But in some studies of experts' interest rate forecasts, the experts do not beat the simple strategy of extrapolating the current interest rate. The current interest rate is a better forecast of the next period's interest rate than the experts' forecasts.

Another special group is investment advisory services. Several hundred of these "market letters" are currently available. Following the investment advice of these services produces no more than a fair return.[2] This evidence is consistent with market efficiency.

Corporate insiders are an additional special group. A corporate insider is a director, officer, or large stockholder. These people are involved in management and have access to nonpublic information. Profit from insider information through short-term trading gains is illegal. However, corporate insiders are allowed to buy and sell the securities of their employing firm

---

[2] See Granger and Morgenstern (1970).

for long-term investment purposes.[3] These transactions are called **insider trading** and must be reported to the Securities and Exchange Commission (SEC), which, in turn, releases this information to the public.

Corporate insiders have done quite well. When insiders are buying (or selling) heavily, the stock subsequently does relatively well (or poorly). Consequently, monitoring SEC insider reports has become a source of investor information. Several market letters acquire insider information from the SEC and report this information to the letters' subscribers.

Merger and takeover activity is an active aspect of security markets. Although insider profits from mergers and takeovers are illegal, the price of an acquired firm's stock tends to rise significantly prior to the public announcement of a tender offer. Apparently, some insiders are profiting from nonpublic information.

The exact meaning of the term *insider* is subject to judicial interpretation. In one interpretation an insider is anyone who receives inside information. For example, if an insider tells you nonpublic information, your profiting from this information is illegal. People who receive inside information may be considered constructive insiders by the law and treated as if they were insiders. According to the law, both the insider and the constructive insider are supposed to sit quietly on the sidelines and not buy or sell securities on the basis of nonpublic information. In addition, those who acquire insider information from overhearing a conversation or from a rumor are supposed to ignore this "insider information." These individuals are also subject to prosecution by the SEC.

Enforcement of insider trading laws is a difficult job for the SEC. There are many thousands of insiders and even larger numbers of (potential) constructive insiders. Monitoring all these people is not feasible. The SEC has computer programs which follow stock trading to try to uncover investors who are likely to have illegally used insider information.

Efficient Market Anomalies

Although most of the evidence is consistent with security markets being efficient, a number of anomalies have been found. Generally, the deviations

---

[3] What constitutes a short-term (as opposed to long-term) gain is a difficult question which must be determined in each case. A clear-cut case would occur if a corporate insider were to buy the company's stock two days before an earnings increase is announced and sell the stock for a large profit one week later.

from efficiency are small and the opportunities for profiting from the anomalies appear to be minimal after accounting for transactions costs. The overwhelming body of evidence remains consistent with markets being reasonably efficient.

Weekend Effect

There is a small, unexplained – but statistically significant – tendency for stock prices to decline over the weekend and on Monday mornings. The name **weekend effect** has been coined to describe this phenomenon since most of the effect occurs in Monday's opening price.[4] The reason for the weekend effect is not clear, but one explanation is the possibility of bad news arriving over the weekend. After paying transactions costs, profiting from the weekend effect is difficult since the decline in prices averages one tenth of one percent. One strategy would be to hold securities from Monday afternoon until Friday afternoon. At this point, the portfolio is liquidated and the funds are invested in money market instruments over the weekend. The costs of buying and selling every week would reduce and probably eliminate any profit from this strategy. Nevertheless, the weekend effect is a statistically significant and interesting phenomenon.

January Effect

Stock returns are relatively high for the month of January, the so-called **January effect**.[5] The explanation of this January effect is not clear. One hypothesis is that investors take tax losses by selling stocks in December, depressing December prices, and making for high returns in January.

Small Firm Effect

Small firms have been found to have relatively high returns after adjusting for risk; this has been dubbed the **small firm effect**. According to the

---

[4] See French (1980), Gibbons and Hess (1981), and Harris (1986). Jacobs and Levy (1988) present a summary of the literature on so-called calendar anomalies.

[5] See Rozeff and Kinney (1976), Keim (1983), Rogalski and Tinic (1986), Ariel (1987), and Seyhun (1988).

evidence, the small firm effect and the January effect are interrelated because most of the January excess returns appear to be among small firms.[6] Another explanation is the lack of careful monitoring of small firms by security analysts, resulting in a tendency for good news about small firms to be hidden from the market.[7] Skewness of returns may be an additional reason. If small firms have larger skewness of returns than big firms and if investors are averse to skewness, higher returns will be required on stocks of small firms as compensation for bearing the risk.

Individual Investor's Performance

Some individual investors have been found to have abnormally good performance over time. An example is the Value Investment Advisory Service. This service rates a large population of stocks from 1 to 5 for performance in the future. Stocks rated 1 are predicted to be above average performers; stocks rated 5, below average performers. Value Line uses a secret mathematical equation to determine the ratings. The inputs for the equation are current and past financial data of the firms. In a perfectly efficient market, this publicly available information should not generate superior performance. Many Value Line firms rated 1 have done extremely well during some periods of time; during other time periods, firms rated 1 have not done so well. Thus, the evidence is mixed.[8]

Overshooting

Security prices for both stocks and bonds have been shown to fluctuate more than the probable underlying determinants of prices.[9] In the view of several investigators, this greater volatility is an indicator of inefficiency. Some observers have described this effect as **overshooting**, meaning a psychological tendency for markets to put too much weight upon relatively recent news.

---

[6] See Ritter (1988).

[7] See Arbel and Strebel (1982); Arbel, Carvell, and Strebel (1983); and Arbel (1984–85).

[8] See Copeland and Mayers (1982) and Stickel (1985).

[9] See West (1988) for a literature review.

For example, stock prices have been found to fluctuate more than actual earnings, which are frequently said to be a determinant of prices, possibly because earnings forecasts tend to overshoot actual earnings. Overshooting is illustrated in figure 8.2. The swings in stock prices are much larger than the swings in earnings, the underlying determinants of stock prices.

Overshooting has been called mean reversion in returns. If high (low) returns in one period are followed by relatively low (high) returns in subsequent periods, returns are called **mean reverting**. In effect, the security catches up with its long-run mean return. Astute investors might be able to profit from mean reverting returns by buying (shortselling) securities with relatively low (high) returns in the recent past in anticipation of the security catching up with its long-run mean return in the future.

One of the early statements of this overshooting viewpoint is by John Maynard Keynes.[10] Keynes compared the stock market to a beauty contest

Figure 8.2   Price Is More Volatile than Earnings

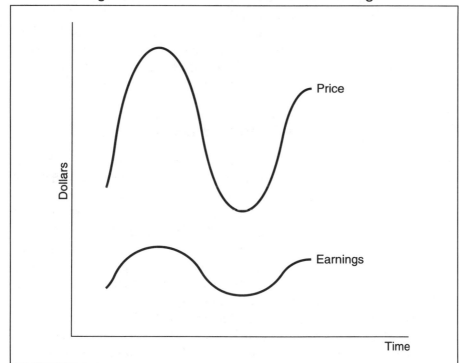

in which the public chooses the winner. Prizes are awarded to those individuals whose choice most closely conforms to the choice of the public. Winning a prize does not require picking the most beautiful contestant, but rather the one that everyone thinks everyone else will chose, given that everyone knows that the majority view determines the most beautiful. Oscar Morgenstern has suggested almost the same viewpoint, namely that security prices are determined by whatever people will pay for them.[11] This view has sometimes been called the **bigger fool theory**.

A similar view has been presented by Burton Malkiel, who has suggested that security prices are often affected by speculative bubbles.[12] During these bubbles, security price levels are not justified by objective determinants of value. An example is the tulip bulb craze in Holland several hundred years ago. Tulip bulb prices went through a boom and bust cycle. The tulip bulb craze is especially interesting, since tulip bulbs have no objective value. Their value is their beauty. Even though the beauty of the bulbs was essentially constant, market prices fluctuated wildly. Malkiel describes a number of other bubbles of more recent vintage.

In the view of all of these authors, psychological factors can, and do, affect security prices. According to this viewpoint, no solely objective models of security price determination exist. Consequently, tests of market efficiency should somehow incorporate these subjective psychological factors.

Behavior in an Efficient Market

An important question is, "How should investors behave in an efficient market, since earning more than a fair rate of return is extremely difficult?" First, investors should decide upon their preferences about levels of expected returns and risk and select a portfolio accordingly. Investors desiring to be worry-free should choose low risk portfolios; bolder investors should have higher risk portfolios. Second, an investor should try to minimize transactions costs. A strategy involving frequent trading involves large transactions costs. The added costs are not offset by trading gains in an efficient market. Third, the investor should try to minimize taxes paid.

In an efficient market, most securities are fairly priced most of the time. The competitive nature of security markets makes it very hard to earn more than a fair return on a risk-adjusted basis. But not all investors should

---

[11] Malkiel (1981) discusses Morgenstern's argument.

[12] See Malkiel (1981).

abandon the search for inefficiency in the form of mispriced securities. If all investors assumed a perfectly efficient market, then, paradoxically, the market would be inefficient. For the market to be efficient, some investors must believe the market to be inefficient; these investors seek out profit opportunities and force the market toward efficiency. The actions of these "nonbelievers" are essential to driving the market toward efficiency.

Efficiency has important implications for issuers of securities. Issuers would like to sell stock when prices are high and issue bonds when interest rates are low. In an efficient market, prices are definitely known to be high and interest rates definitely known to be low only after the fact. Consistently accurate prediction of price and interest rate changes in the future is not possible in an efficient market. Consequently, long-term success in timing issues is very unlikely. In an efficient market, issuers should not try to time their new issues.

Fundamental Analysis

One approach to investing is to estimate the fundamental value of securities and then compare this fundamental value to market price. If the estimated fundamental value exceeds the market price, the security is underpriced and should be purchased. If the estimated fundamental value exceeds the market price, the security is overvalued and should be sold.

There are various methods for estimating the fundamental value. One approach is, first, to estimate expected earnings and then multiply by an expected price/earnings multiple. A second approach is to estimate the value of the assets of the firm.

In a perfectly efficient market, all securities are always correctly priced; the market price equals the fundamental value of the security. In a market that is partially inefficient, the market price deviates from the fundamental value. Analysts able to discover the fundamental value ahead of the rest of the market can reap substantial profits as market prices approach the fundamental value. The actions of these profit-seeking investors push the market toward efficiency.

Technical Analysis

Technical analysts try to develop predictors of security price changes.[13] One strategy is uncovering time series providing an early warning signal. This

---

[13] In the academic literature, people who trade on the basis of technical analysis are called **noise traders**.

predictive series will peak (turn down) before security prices peak and turn up before security prices turn up (see figure 8.3).

In an efficient market, a simple predictive rule using past information should not work. Any successful rule attracts the attention of profit-seeking investors. These market watchers act as soon as the predictor gives a signal, causing prices to adjust almost instantaneously. To get a jump on the market watchers, an investor has to find a predictor that predicts the predictor and has to keep this information secret. Any simple rules allowing investors to predict future price changes consistently are quickly uncovered by the market watchers.

Another strategy is the contrarian approach – find some consistently wrong predictor and do the opposite. One contrarian approach is the odd-lot theory. Purchases and sales of stock for 100 shares or more are called round lots; transactions for fewer than 100 shares are called odd lots, which are transactions by small investors. In the odd-lot theory, the small investors who deal in odd lots are poorly informed, and perhaps even stupid, and consistently wrong in their stock picks. The sure way to make money is to do the opposite of the odd-lotters. According to the theory, when odd-lotters are buying heavily in anticipation of prices going up, prices will surely go down. When odd-lotters are selling heavily, anticipating falling prices, prices will assuredly rise.

Figure 8.3   A Leading Indicator of Stock Prices

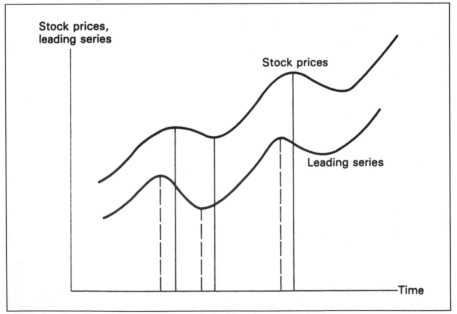

The empirical evidence shows odd-lotters to actually be right some of the time. When odd-lotters are buying, prices sometimes rise. Sometimes the stupid people are smart! On occasion, the odd-lot theory gives no signals. That is, the odd-lotter transaction pattern sometimes does not change at price peaks or troughs. This evidence is consistent with market efficiency. Following the odd-lotters does not lead to consistently high returns.

Many technical analysts believe in the forecasting power of statistics on volume of trading. High (low) volume of trading on days when prices rise and low (high) volume on declining days is considered to be bullish (bearish), a sign of rising (falling) future prices. According to this line of thinking, high volume on rising prices indicates the existence of many investors who are monitoring the market watching for price increases. When price increases occur, these market watchers jump on the bandwagon, implying large volume. Advocates of volume believe price declines combined with high volume to be bearish, that is, a predictor of future price declines. The student of volume is always warned that extremely large volume and huge price declines are indicators of a "selling climax." According to many technical analysts, a bear market must end with a selling climax, a day when all the nervous holders of stocks cathartically relieve their anxieties and sell out all their stocks. The market is left with stocks being held in strong hands, that is, held by investors who will not sell, and the bear market ends.

But the plot does not end here. The volume experts warn us about the sinister possibility of multiple selling climaxes. Wave after wave of frenzied selling may occur during a bear market. A series of cathartic releases may be required to put the wild bear to rest. Some even believe that three selling climaxes are necessary before a bear market ends.

There is no evidence to support the relationship between prices and volume. Evidence does exist relating the absolute size of price change and volume. On days when heavy trading occurs, large price changes tend to occur, although the direction of price change can be up or down. Critics of technical analysis believe the preceding story about volume to be little more than saying that prices rise when they go up and decline when they go down.

There are many other approaches to technical analysis, which readers can investigate on their own. From the evidence, these approaches cannot consistently give abnormally high rates of return.

Summary

A security market is said to be efficient if all currently available public information is very rapidly reflected in security prices. A market is weakly efficient if past price information does not allow prediction of future price changes. Then, the best predictor of tomorrow's price is today's price. Semistrong efficiency deals with nonprice information, and strong-form efficiency deals with special groups. The empirical evidence is basically consistent with efficiency, although some relatively small deviations from efficiency are reported. The evidence indicates that earning more than a fair rate of return is difficult.

In an efficient market, investors should decide upon their risk preferences and try to minimize transactions costs and taxes. Similarly, corporations should not try to time issues of stocks and bonds.

Questions / Problems

1. What is an informationally efficient market?

2. Describe the economic forces that tend to make financial markets informationally efficient.

3. Efficiency has sometimes been broken down into weak-form, semistrong-form, and strong-form efficiency. What are the differences among these forms of efficiency?

4. Describe the empirical evidence concerning the three forms of the efficient market hypothesis.

5. How should investors behave in a market that is informationally efficient? How does this differ from behavior in a market that is not informationally efficient?

6. What is technical analysis? Why is there a conflict between technical analysis and efficient markets?

References

Arbel, A., "Generic Stocks: The Key to Market Anomalies," *Journal of Portfolio Management,* 11, 1984–85, pp. 4–13.

Arbel, A. and P. Strebel, "The Neglected and Small Firm Effects," *Financial Review,* 17, 1982, pp. 201–18.

Arbel, A., S. Carvell, and P. Strebel, "Giraffes, Institutions, and Neglected Firms," *Financial Analysts Journal,* 39, 1983, pp. 57–63.

Ariel, R., "A Monthly Effect in Stock Returns," *Journal of Financial Economics,* 18, March 1987, pp. 161–74.

Brick, J. R. and H. E. Thompson, "Time Series Analysis of Interest Rates: Some Additional Evidence," *Journal of Finance,* 33, March 1978, pp. 93–104.

Chang, E. C., J. M. Pinegar, and R. Ravichandran, "International Evidence on the Robustness of the Day-of-the-Week Effect," *Journal of Financial and Quantitative Analysis,* 28, December 1993, pp. 497–513.

Copeland, T. E. and D. Mayers, "The Value Line Enigma (1965–1978): A Case Study of Performance Evaluative Issues," *Journal of Financial Economics,* November 1982, pp. 289–322.

Datta, S. and U. S. Dhillon, "Bond and Stock Market Response to Unexpected Earnings Announcements," *Journal of Financial and Quantitative Analysis,* 28, December 1993, pp. 565–577.

DeBondt, W. F. M. and R. Thaler, "Does the Stock Market Overreact?" *Journal of Finance,* 40, July 1985, pp. 793–805.

DeBondt, W. F. M. and R. Thaler. "A Mean-Reverting Walk Down Wall Street," *Journal of Economic Perspectives,* 3, Winter 1989, pp. 189–202.

Domain, D. L., "Money Market Mutual Fund Maturity and Interest Rates," *Journal of Money Credit and Banking,* 24, November 1992, pp. 519–27.

Eysell, T. H. and J. P. Reyburn, "The Effects of the Insider Trading Sanctions Act of 1984: The Case of Seasoned Equity Offerings," *Journal of Financial Research,* 16, Summer 1993, pp. 161–170.

Fama, E. F., "Efficient Capital Markets: A Review of Theory and Empirical Work," *Journal of Finance,* 25, May 1970, pp. 383–417.

French, K. K., "Stock Returns and the Weekend Effect," *Journal of Financial Economics,* 8, November 1980, pp. 55–69.

Gibbons, M. R. and P. Hess, "Day of the Week Effects and Asset Returns," *Journal of Business,* 54, October 1981, pp. 579–96.

Granger, C. W. J., and O. Morgenstern, *Predictability of Stock Market Prices,* Lexington, MA: Heath Lexington Books, 1970.

Harris, L., "A Transaction Data Study of Weekly and Intradaily Patterns in Stock Returns," *Journal of Financial Economics,* 16, May, 1986, pp. 99–118.

Ippolito, Richard A., "On Studies of Mutual Fund Performance, 1962–1991," *Financial Analysts Journal,* January/February 1993, pp. 42–51.

Jacobs, B. I. and K. N. Levy, "Calendar Anomalies: Abnormal Returns at Calendar Turning Points," *Financial Analysts Journal,* 44, November/December 1988, pp. 28–39.

Keim, D., "Size Related Anomalies and Stock Return Seasonality," *Journal of Financial Economics,* 12, June 1983, pp. 13–32.

Keynes, J. M., *The General Theory of Employment Interest and Money,* New York: Harcourt, Brace & World, 1964.

Lakonishok, J., A. Shleifer, And R. W. Vishny, "Contrarian Investment, Extrapolation, and Risk," *Journal of Finance,* 49, December 1994, pp. 1541–78.

Malkiel, B. G., *A Random Walk Down Wall Street,* 2e, New York: W. W. Norton, 1981.

Pesando, J. E., "On the Efficiency of the Bond Market: Some Canadian Evidence," *Journal of Political Economy,* 86, December 1978, pp. 1057–76.

Ritter, J. R., "The Buying and Selling Behavior of Individual Investors at the Turn of the Year," *Journal of Finance,* 43, July 1988, pp. 701–19.

Rogalski, R. and S. M. Tinic, "The January Size Effect: Anomaly or Risk Measurement?" *Financial Analysts Journal,* 42, 1986, pp. 63–70.

Rozeff, M. S. and W. R. Kinney, "Capital Market Seasonability: The Case of Stock Market Returns," *Journal of Financial Economics,* 3, October 1976, pp. 379–402.

Seyhun, H. N., "The January Effect and Aggregate Insider Trading," *Journal of Finance,* 43, March 1988, pp. 129–41.

Stickel, S. E., "The Effect of Value Line Investment Survey Rank Changes on Common Stock Prices," *Journal of Financial Economics,* 14, May 1985, pp. 121–43.

West, K. D., "Bubbles, Fads, and Stock Volatility Tests: A Partial Evaluation," *Journal of Finance,* 43, July 1988, pp. 639–60.

9

Spot and Forward Interest Rates

Overview

This chapter covers present value and future value calculations and concepts when the interest rate varies by maturity. The discussion of present value and interest rates assumes an abstract world of **frictionless** (or **perfect**) **financial markets**. In a world of frictionless financial markets, the following assumptions will hold: (1) no taxes, (2) no default risk, (3) noncallable securities, (4) no transactions costs, and (5) unrestricted shortselling (defined below) is allowed. In practice, markets are not frictionless. However, frictionless markets are a necessary starting point.

Shortsales

In a **shortsale**, an investor sells a security that is not owned. The intent of a shortsale is to sell the security at current prices, expecting to buy the security back at a lower price in the future. To carry out the shortsale, the shortseller borrows certificates of ownership from another investor who owns the security (see figure 9.1). The shortseller must pay the lender of the certificates any dividends due on the securities. When the shortseller closes out the shortsale by buying the security in the market, the new certificates are returned to the individual who lent the securities to the shortseller. The shortseller makes a profit (loss) if the securities are repurchased at a lower (higher) price. A shortsale has no time limit. Short positions can remain in effect indefinitely as long as collateral requirements are met.

Figure 9.1   Shortsales

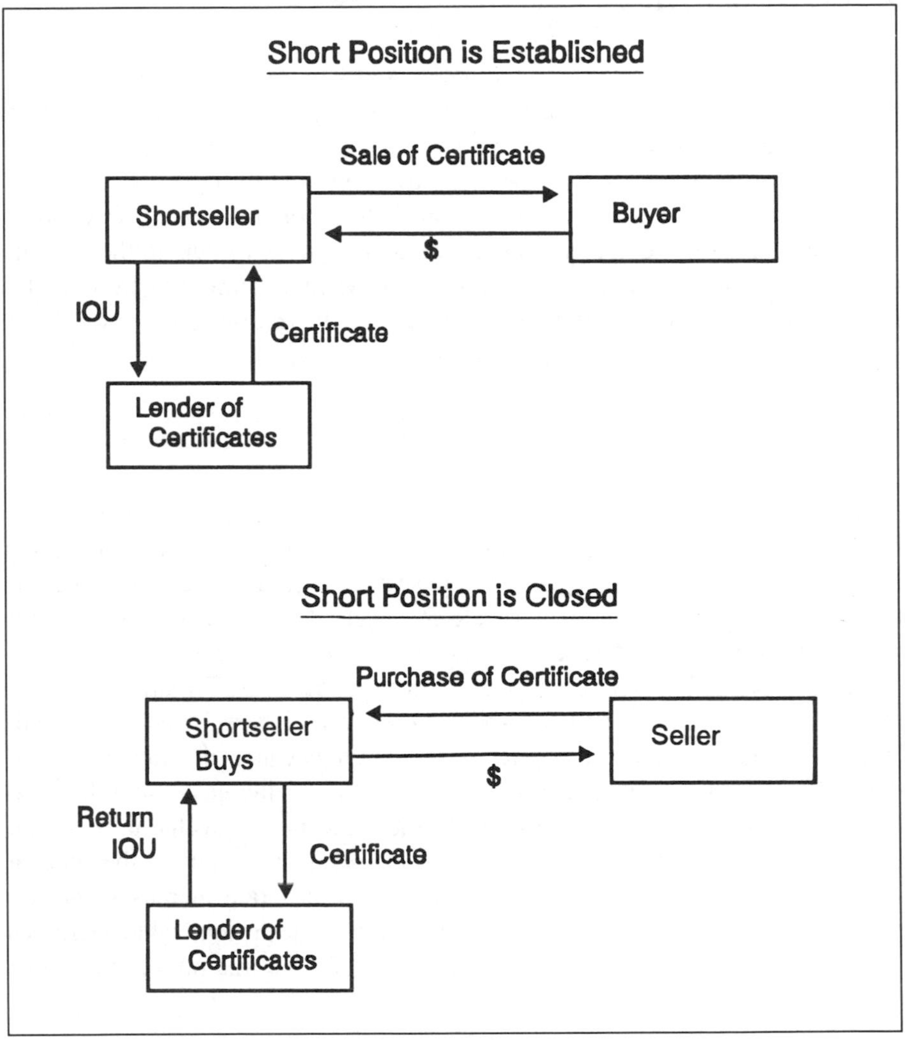

Short Position is Established

Sale of Certificate

Shortseller → Buyer

$ (arrow from Buyer to Shortseller)

IOU

Certificate

Lender of Certificates

Short Position is Closed

Purchase of Certificate

Shortseller Buys ← Seller

$

Return IOU

Certificate

Lender of Certificates

In an **unrestricted shortsale**, the shortseller can use the proceeds from the sale. In practice, most shortsellers are not able to use the proceeds because of the possibility of a shortseller absconding with the funds. In addition, shortsellers usually have to post **collateral** to guarantee against default. For example, if someone shortsold a security at $100 and the price moved up to $120, the shortseller has an unrealized loss of $20. Unless collateral of at least $20 has been posted, the shortseller might be tempted to default by simply walking away from the transaction. The lender of the securities has legal recourse, but at considerable expense.

Present Values

Figure 9.2 shows the distinction between points in time and periods of time. Point in time 0 is now; point in time 1 is one period from now; point in time 2 is two periods from now; and so on. All cash flows occur at points in time (that is, at the ends of periods) as illustrated by figure 9.2.

Because of the time value of money, one dollar received at a future date has a present value of less than one dollar. We will denote the present (that is, the time 0) value of $1 received n periods from now by D_n. The interest rate is the discount rate (denoted by R_n) that solves equation 9.1.

$$D_n = \frac{1}{(1 + R_n)^n} \tag{9.1}$$

D_n represents both the **present value** of $1 received in n period and the **spot price** of a zero coupon bond with a par value of $1. The purchaser of this zero coupon bond pays the purchase price D_n at time zero and receives the par value of $1 at time n. The rate R_n is called the zero coupon discount rate or the **spot interest rate**. The spot market is the market for immediate delivery. Some observers call the spot market the "cash" market.

The spot price D_n and the spot interest rate R_n are inversely related. When the rate goes up, the price goes down because the rate is in the denominator. As the rate increases, the denominator increases, and the ratio (that is, the price) decreases. Figure 9.3 and the present value table at the end of this book illustrate this point. Look across any row of the present value table. As you move to the right, the interest rate increases and the present value decreases. In the present value table, the present value decreases as maturity increases for a given interest rate. To see this point, look down

Figure 9.2   Time Line

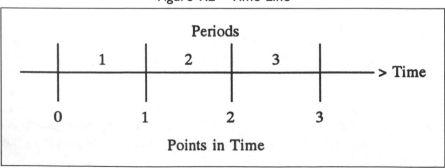

Figure 9.3   Price versus Spot Rate

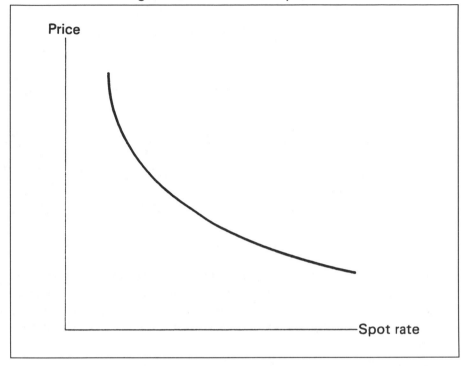

any column of the table. The lowest present values are in the lower right corner of the table for long maturities and high interest rates.

Consider the examples in figure 9.4. The spot rate is 4 percent for one period, 6 percent for two periods, 8 percent for three periods. D_1 equals .9615, meaning that the present value of $1 received one period from now is $.9615. D_2 is .8900, indicating that the present value of $1 received two periods from now is $.8900. The present value of $1 received three periods from now is D_3, $.7938.

The future value is the inverse of the present value. If one dollar is received today and invested at the interest rate R_n for n periods, the future value is $(1 + R_n)^n$, which equals $1/D_n$.

The Term Structure of Interest Rates

The pattern of spot interest rates for different maturities is called the **term structure of interest rates**. One possible term structure pattern is for all spot interest rates to be the same; this is called a **flat** term structure and is

Figure 9.4   Present Values

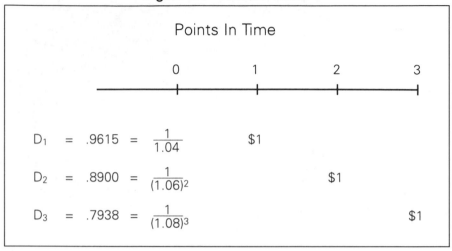

$$D_1 \ = \ .9615 \ = \ \frac{1}{1.04} \qquad \$1$$

$$D_2 \ = \ .8900 \ = \ \frac{1}{(1.06)^2} \qquad\qquad \$1$$

$$D_3 \ = \ .7938 \ = \ \frac{1}{(1.08)^3} \qquad\qquad\qquad \$1$$

illustrated in the figure 9.5. Although a flat term structure rarely occurs in practice, flat term structures are widely discussed, since they are easier to handle mathematically. If the spot interest rates increase with maturity, the term structure is **rising** (see the example in the figure 9.5). Rising term

Figure 9.5   Term Structure

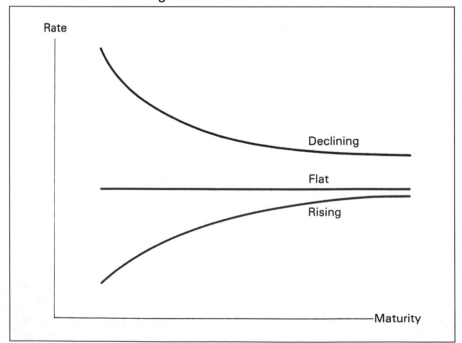

structures are the most common pattern in practice; longer maturity interest rates are typically higher than short maturity interest rates. Spot interest rates decreasing with maturity are called a **declining** (or **inverted**) term structure.

Zero Coupon Bonds

In practice, most bonds are coupon-bearing, paying coupons every six months until maturity, when the par value is repaid. However, there are a sizable number of zero coupon bonds which have only one payment, the par value, at maturity. One example is U.S. Treasury bills, which are issued in huge volume with maturities running up to one year. Treasury bills are discussed extensively in the chapter on money market instruments. A second example is zero coupon bonds issued by corporations. Since these corporate zero coupons have default risk (and thus do not fit the frictionless market assumption), they are discussed under default risk.

A third example are zero coupon securities, created from the "stripping" of U.S. Treasury securities.[1] In recent years, the market for stripped securities has grown enormously. Over $100 billion of the par value of U.S. Treasury bonds has been stripped.

When the stripping process began in 1982, a financial institution purchased a block of U.S. Treasury securities, put the original securities in trust, and then sold claims on the parts, which traded separately. For example, if a five-year bond with ten semiannual coupons was stripped, it was decomposed into 11 parts (that is, ten coupons and the par value). Each of the 11 parts traded separately. The stripped securities were given various names. Salomon Brothers called their zeros CATS. Merrill Lynch called their zeros TIGRS.

In 1985, the U.S. Treasury began to allow Treasury bonds to be stripped through the Federal Reserve's book entry accounting system. Book entry is an electronic ownership system. Stripping by book entry is much cheaper than the previous trust arrangements. Consequently, these Treasury strips now dominate the market. These securities are called STRIPS, which stands for *separate trading of registered interest and principal securities.*

---

[1] See Livingston and Gregory (1989) for a detailed analysis of coupon stripping.

Table 9.1 and figure 9.6 show hypothetical prices of STRIPS and the computed term structure.[2] As with most bonds, the STRIPS prices are quoted per hundred dollars of par. The reader should look up actual STRIPS prices in *The Wall Street Journal.*

Arbitrage

One of the most important concepts in finance is the concept of **arbitrage**, also called the **law of one price**. In frictionless markets, the same asset must have one price at a particular instant in time, no matter where it is traded. As a simple example, consider a common stock traded on both the New York Stock Exchange and the Pacific Stock Exchange. If the stock has a price of $50 in New York and $53 on the Pacific Exchange, an arbitrager can simultaneously buy the stock at $50 and sell (shortsell) it at $53, for an immediate and risk-free profit of $3. The purchase at $50 and the sale at $53 drive the prices together. An arbitrager does not need any capital to make arbitrage profits. Therefore, one small arbitrager who repeatedly and rationally exploits price differences is able to drive the prices together.

Arbitrage and Interest Rates

Arbitrage has many important implications in financial markets. In the following example, arbitrage is shown to constrain present values. A dollar

Table 9.1   STRIPS Example

Maturity (Years)	Price per $100 of Par	Spot Rate
1	$96.15	.04
2	$89.00	.06
3	$79.38	.08
4	$68.30	.10

[2] Stripped securities carry tax liabilities for the buyer as discussed in Chapter 18 on taxes. With tax liabilities, the frictionless market assumption of no taxes is not met. Therefore, the term structure shown in the example is not the term structure for a frictionless market, except if bond buyers have a zero tax rate.

Figure 9.6   STRIPS Term Structure

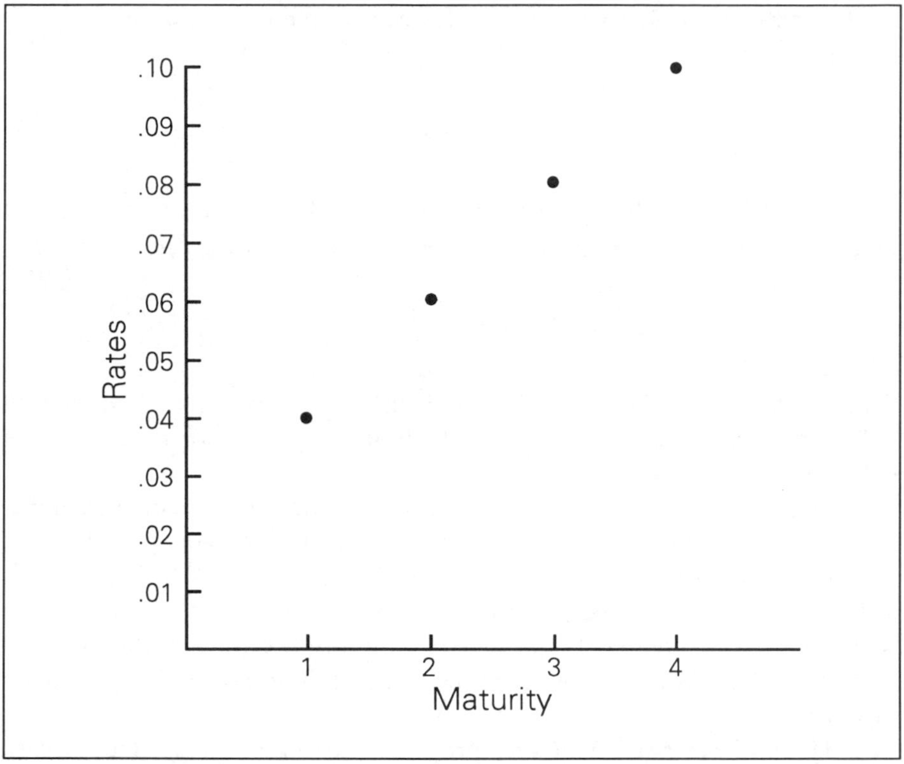

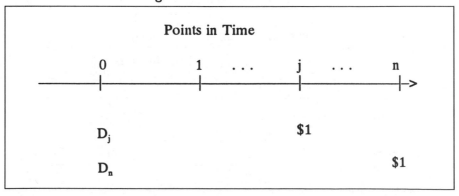

received in the more distant future cannot have a higher present value than a dollar received sooner. Arbitrage guarantees this result.

Consider $1 received j periods from now and $1 received n periods from now, where j is sooner (see figure 9.7). Intuitively, the present value

Figure 9.7   Present Values

Points in Time

| 0 | 1 | . . . | j | . . . | n |

D_j

D_n

$1 (at j)

$1 (at n)

of the $1 received in period j is larger because it is received sooner. Between time j and n, the dollar can be used for consumption or investment.

If maturity n is more distant then maturity j, then:

$$D_j \geq D_n \tag{9.2}$$

Equation 9.2 states that the present value of $1 received at time j has a greater (or equal) present value than $1 received at time n. In general:

$$D_1 \geq D_2 \geq D_3 \geq \ldots \geq D_n \tag{9.3}$$

Equation 9.3 states that $1 received at time 1 has a greater (or equal) present value than $1 received at time 2, which has a greater (or equal) present value than $1 at time 3, and so on.

To prove this result by arbitrage, consider the following counterexample. Assume D_1 is $.70 and D_2 is $.80. That is, the present value of a dollar in one period is $.70 and the present value of a dollar in two periods is $.80. A bond paying $1 at time 1 costs $.70; $.80 is the price of a bond paying $1 at time 2. The following arbitrage opportunity is available. Buy the one-period bond and shortsell the two-period bond. The cash flows are shown in table 9.2.

The arbitrager makes a sure profit of $.10 immediately; the $1 cash inflow at time 1 can be used to pay off the cash outflow of $1 at time 2; conceivably, interest might be earned from time 1 to time 2. This sure profit is immediate and requires no collateral. Therefore, one arbitrager without any collateral can repeatedly engage in this arbitrage transaction until the profits from arbitrage disappear.

The arbitrage operations drive prices toward their equilibrium values. That is, purchase of the one-period bond by the arbitrager drives its price

Table 9.2   Arbitrage if $D_1 < D_2$

Action	Points in Time		
	0	1	2
	Cash Flows		
Buy one period	−$.70	+$1.00	
Sell two period	+$.80		−$1.00
Net	+$.10	+$1.00	−$1.00

up; sale of the two-period bond forces its price down. Arbitrage profits cease to exist when D_1 is greater than or equal to D_2, or when the present value of $1 received in one period is greater than or equal to the present value of $1 received in two periods.

Conditions for Arbitrage

In the case where a security sells for different prices in two markets, the arbitrage is straightforward. Buy in the underpriced market and simultaneously sell in the overpriced market. In cases of multi-period cash flows, the existence of a profitable arbitrage is not as clearcut. The following rule identifies an arbitrage opportunity.

Arbitrage Rule: If the cumulative cash flows from a position are never negative and are positive in at least one period, an arbitrage opportunity exists.

Suppose that the present value of a dollar received at time 2 is $.89 (i.e., $D_2 = .8900$) and the present value of a dollar received at time 1 is $.9615 (i.e., $D_1 = .9615$). An individual decides to buy one two-period bond and short a one-period bond. The transaction, the net cash flows, and the cumulative net cash flows are shown in table 9.3. The cumulative net cash flows simply add the cash flows starting at time zero without adjusting for time value. The cumulative net cash flows are positive at time zero, negative at time 1, and positive at time 2. This is not an arbitrage opportunity.

In contrast, the cumulative net cash flows in table 9.2 are always positive. Table 9.2 shows an arbitrage opportunity.

Table 9.3   Cash Flows From a Portfolio Position

Action	Points in Time		
	0	1	2
Buy two period	−.8900		+1.0
Short one period	+.9615	−1.0	
Net cash flows	+.0715	−1.0	+1.0
Cumulative net cash flows	+.0715	−.9285	+.0715

Forward Interest Rates

In financial markets, most transactions are in the spot market, the market for immediate purchase.[3] A person buying a bond in the spot market pays for the bond immediately and starts earning interest immediately. Whereas spot transactions are carried out immediately, forward transactions involve a contract signed in the present to do something in the future. For example, a student might sign a forward contract with a car dealer to purchase a car at the end of the school year (see figure 9.8). The contract price is set at time zero but the transaction does not occur until the stipulated delivery date. Money changes hands and the car is delivered only at this future date.

Some financial transactions are forward transactions. In these transactions, the parties agree right now to exchange securities in the future at a price agreed upon right now. If securities are exchanged in the forward market, the buyer (called the **long**) contracts right now to purchase the bond at some future date (called the **delivery date**) at a specified price. The long investor agrees to *lend* funds beginning on the delivery date of the forward contract. The other party to the transaction is the seller, or shortseller (called the **short**) of the bond; the short agrees to *borrow* funds as of the delivery date. In effect, the buyer of a bond lends money and the shortseller borrows the funds.

The **forward interest rate** for period n is denoted by f_n. This represents the interest rate set at time zero for funds loaned from time $n - 1$ to time n. Also, f_2 is the forward interest rate on funds loaned from time 1 until time 2; f_2 is agreed upon as of time zero. Figure 9.9 shows the relationship between forward and spot interest rates.

Figure 9.8   Forward Contracts

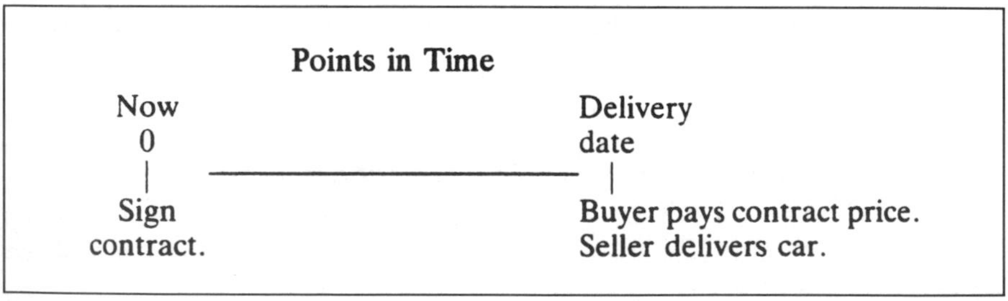

Points in Time	
Now	Delivery
0	date
|	|
Sign	Buyer pays contract price.
contract.	Seller delivers car.

---

[3] In practice, many transactions in the spot market are for regular settlement, which occurs on a subsequent day. In frictionless markets, this delay in settlement would not occur.

Figure 9.9   Spot and Forward Interest Rates

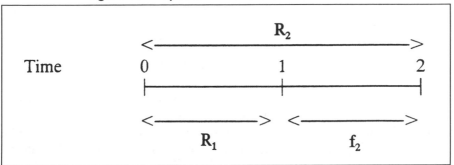

Consider the example in figure 9.10 in which the one-period spot rate is 4 percent, the forward rate is 8.04 percent, and the two-period spot rate is 6 percent. The forward rates are single-period interest rates. For example, f_2 is the interest rate from time 1 until time 2; interest is earned for period 2. The forward rate f_3 is the rate of interest from time 2 until time 3; interest is earned for period 3.

The spot interest rates generally involve interest earned over a number of periods. The interest is earned beginning at time zero and extending over n periods into the future. R_1 is the interest rate from time zero to time 1; it is a single-period rate. R_2 is the interest rate from time zero until time 2; it is the rate over two periods. R_3 is the interest rate from time zero until time 3; it is a three-period rate.

The Link Between Spot and Forward Interest Rates

Arbitrage forces a precise relationship to hold between forward and spot interest rates. For two periods, the relationship is:

Figure 9.10   Example of Spot and Forward Interest Rates

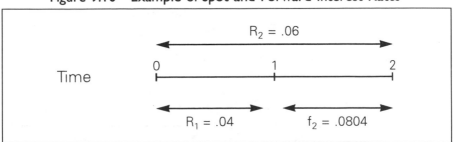

$$[1 + R_2]^2 = [1 + R_1][1 + f_2] \qquad (9.4)$$

In our numerical example:

$$[1.06]^2 = [1.04][1.0804]$$

In other words, the two-period spot rate is the geometric mean of the one-period spot rate and the forward rate for period 2. This is approximately the same as saying that the two-period spot interest rate is the arithmetic mean of the one-period spot rate and the forward rate for period 2. In other words, the approximate link between spot and forward interest rates is:

$$R_2 = \frac{R_1 + f_2}{2} \qquad (9.5)$$

In our numerical example,

$$.0602 = \frac{.04 + .0804}{2}$$

The arithmetic mean is 6.02 percent, whereas the geometric mean is 6 percent, a close approximation.

To see the economic rationale behind equations 9.4 and 9.5, imagine an investor who has \$1 to invest at time zero. The investor has two investment choices: (1) invest for one period and then reinvest for another period at the forward rate, or (2) invest for two periods. These choices are shown in table 9.4.

Option (1): Investing in the one-period spot rate, $1 + R_1$ dollars are accumulated as of time 1. As of time 0, the investor can contract to reinvest this total amount in the forward market at the rate f_2. After two periods, the amount accumulated is $[1 + R_1][1 + f_2]$. Option (2): A two-period loan

Table 9.4   Investment Choices

Investment Action	Points in Time		
	0	1	2
One period, reinvest forward	\$1	\$1 + R_1	\$(1 + R_1)(1 + f_2)
Two periods	\$1		\$(1 + R_2)^2

accumulates to $[1 + R_2]^2$. Since both the sequence of a one-period spot plus a forward and a two-period loan can lock-in terminal values at time 2, the terminal values should be the same. This is what equation 9.4 says; equation 9.5 says the same thing, overlooking compound interest.

The previous analysis can be clarified by our example in which the one-period spot rate (R_1) is .04 and the forward rate for period 2 (f_2) is .0804 (see table 9.5). A $1 investment at the one-period spot interest rate followed by reinvestment at the forward interest rate will result in $(1.04)(1.0804) = 1.1236 at time 2. Investing $1 for two periods at the two-period spot rate should also result in $1.1236 at time 2. Since 6 percent is the rate R_2, the present value of $1.1236 equals $1.00.

In general, the relationship between forward and spot interest rates may be written as follows:

$$[1 + R_n]^n = [1 + R_{n-1}]^{n-1}[1 + f_n] \qquad (9.6)$$

In the three-period case:

$$[1 + R_3]^3 = [1 + R_2]^2[1 + f_3]$$

Since R_{n-1} may be expressed in terms of forward interest rates:

$$[1 + R_n]^n = [1 + R_1][1 + f_2][1 + f_3] \ldots [1 + f_n] \qquad (9.7)$$

In other words, the n-period spot rate R_n is the geometric mean of R_1 and the forward rates. Equation 9.7 is approximately the same as R_n being the arithmetic mean of R_1 and the forward rates. Namely:

$$R_n = [R_1 + f_2 + f_3 + \ldots + f_n]/n \qquad (9.8)$$

Table 9.5   Investment Choices

Investment Action	Points in Time		
	0	1	2
One period, reinvest forward	$1	$1.04	$(1.04)(1.0804)
Two periods	$1		$(1.06)^2 $1.1236

Creating Forward Contracts from Spot Securities

The development of financial futures markets has had a dramatic impact upon spot financial markets. An understanding of the relationships between the two types of markets is essential. Futures markets are very similar to forward markets.[4] This section discusses the link between spot and forward markets, laying the groundwork for the link between spot and futures markets. The primary lesson of this section is: **arbitrage provides the fundamental link between the spot and forward markets**.

An investor can create a forward position from spot securities in a frictionless market. The two-period case provides the basic insight. A long forward position has a zero cash flow at time 0, an outflow at time 1, and an inflow at time 2 (see table 9.6).

Assume one-period funds are trading at the spot rate R_1 (spot price of D_1) and two-period funds trade at the spot rate R_2 (spot price of D_2). Creating a forward position requires finding some combination of one- and two-period spot securities having the same cash flows as a forward position in table 9.6. The necessary positions are shown in table 9.7. Go long (buy) a single two-period bond and simultaneously shortsell x percent of a one-period bond, with the constraint that the net cash flows at time 0 are zero. Algebraically, find a value of x such that $xD_1 = D_2$, implying that x must equal D_2/D_1. The time 0 net cash flows have a sum of zero; the time 1 net cash flows are an outflow equal to D_2/D_1, which is the forward price; at time 2 there is a cash inflow of $1. This set of cash flows is defined as a long forward position, that is, a loan of funds in the forward market.

The amount D_2/D_1 is a forward price; it represents the time 1 value of $1 received at time 2. Denoting this forward price as F_2, the definitions of forward price, forward rate, and of D_1 and D_2 imply that:

Table 9.6   Long Forward Position

	Points in Time		
	0	1	2
Long forward	0	−Forward price	+$1

---

[4] Chapter 21 on futures markets discusses the differences.

Table 9.7   Creating a Long Forward Position

Actions	Points in Time		
(at time 0)	0	1	2
Long 1 two-period bond	$-D_2$		$+\$1$
Short D_2/D_1 one-period bonds	$+D_1 \left[\dfrac{D_2}{D_1}\right]$	$-1 \left[\dfrac{D_2}{D_1}\right]$	
Net = long forward	0	$-\left[\dfrac{D_2}{D_1}\right]$	$+\$1$

$$\text{Forward Price} = F_2 = \frac{1}{1 + f_2} \qquad (9.9)$$

$$= \frac{D_2}{D_1} = \frac{\dfrac{1}{[1 + R_2]^2}}{\dfrac{1}{1 + R_1}}$$

This equation leads to exactly the same relationship between forward and spot rates presented earlier in equation 9.4. The same analysis can be repeated for period n, with the result that the forward price equals D_n/D_{n-1}.

To illustrate the relationship between spot and forward interest rates, consider the following example. Assume:

$R_1 = .04 \qquad D_1 = .9615$
$R_2 = .06 \qquad D_2 = .8900$

Then, the operations shown in table 9.8 create a forward position from a spot position.

The forward interest rate is the discount rate for which \$1 at time 2 has a value of \$.9256 at time 1. That is, the forward rate f_2 satisfies the following equation: $.9256 = 1/(1 + f_2)$. The resulting forward interest rate is 8.04 percent. The two-period spot interest rate of 6 percent is the geometric average of the one-period interest rate of 4 percent and the forward rate of 8.04 percent, that is, $(1.06)^2 = (1.04)(1.0804)$.

Arbitrage forces a precise relationship between forward and spot rates of interest. Consider the case where the one-period interest rate R_1 is .04

Table 9.8   Example of Creating a Long Forward Position

Actions (at time 0)	Points in Time		
	0	I	2
Long I two-period bond	−.8900		+$I
Short .89/.9615 one-period bonds	+.8900	−.9256	
Net = long forward	0	−.9256	+$I

and the two-period interest rate R_2 is .06. Then, the forward interest rate f_2 from equation 9.4 is also .0804. What happens if the market for forward loans has a rate of .15? Arbitragers are able to profit and, by their exploitation of profit opportunities, drive all interest rates toward equilibrium values. The arbitrage operation to profit from the price disparity is to borrow at a rate of .0804, which is the forward rate implicit in R_1 and R_2, and lend at .15.

To borrow at the forward rate of .0804 implicit in the one-period and two-period spot rates, a short forward position is created as table 9.9 shows. By shorting 1 two-period bond and going long .9256 one-period bonds, the investor creates a net short forward position in which the investor borrows $.9256 at time 1 and repays $1 at time 2 for an 8.04 percent forward rate. Shorting a bond is the same as borrowing; buying a bond (or going long) is the same as lending.

Table 9.10 shows the arbitrage to profit from the disparity between the 15 percent forward rate and the 8.04 percent rate implicit in the one-period

Table 9.9   Creating a Short Forward Position

Actions (at time 0)	Points in Time		
	0	I	2
Short I two-period bond	+.8900		−$I
Long .89/.9615 one-period bonds	−.8900	+.9256	
Net = short forward	0	+.9256	−$I

Table 9.10   Arbitrage

Actions	Points in Time		
(at time 0)	0	1	2
Go short forward implicit in R_1 and R_2 (borrow forward)		+.9256	−1.00
Go long forward (lend forward)		$\frac{-1}{(1.15)} = -.87$	+1.00
Net	0.0	+.0556	0.0
Cumulative Net	0.0	+.0556	+.0556

and two-period bonds. The arbitrage is to borrow (go short) forward at 8.04 percent and lend (go long) forward at 15 percent. The arbitrage results in a positive cash flow of about $.0556 per dollar of par value at time 1 and zero cash flows at time 0 and time 2.

This arbitrage is completely risk-free, since the investor taking this position has a certain profit at time 1. The arbitrage operations force the interest rates toward their equilibrium values. That is, lending at the 15 percent rate forces this rate down; borrowing at 8.04 percent forces this rate up. Arbitrage ceases to be profitable when the two rates are identical.

Forward Rates versus Forward Prices

The n-period **forward price** is defined as $1/(1 + f_n)$. This represents the value at time $n - 1$ of $1 received at time n. Figure 9.11 illustrates the forward rate and forward price.

As shown in figure 9.12, if R_1 is 4 percent and R_2 is 6 percent, then f_2 is 8.04 percent, and the forward price is $.9256. One dollar received at time 2 would have a value of $.9256 as of time 1. Alternatively, if $.9256 is loaned forward at time 1, the time 2 loan repayment plus interest of $.0744 will equal $1. An investor who has a long forward position makes a commitment at time 0 to lend the principal amount $1/(1 + f_n)$ at time $n - 1$ and to receive $1 at time n, representing repayment of principal plus interest. The forward price is a type of discounted value factor for period n. One dollar received at time n is worth $1/(1 + f_n)$ as of time $n - 1$.

Figure 9.11   Forward Rates and Forward Prices

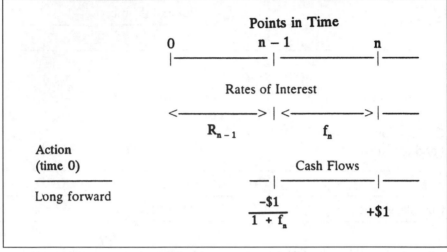

Figure 9.12   An Example of Forward Rates and Forward Prices

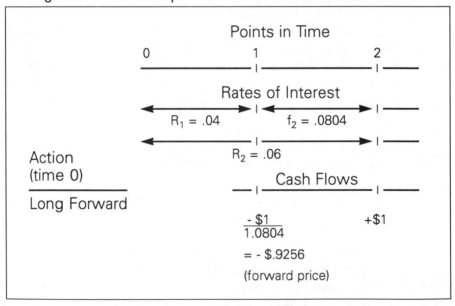

Forward and spot prices can be applied to solving the following practical example. You are given a choice between $100 one period from now or $108.04 two periods from now. Which is better? The problem is shown in figure 9.13.

Figure 9.13   Comparing Cash Flows at Different Points in Time

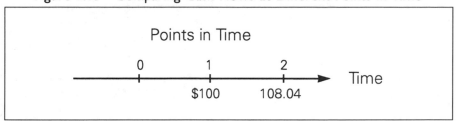

The problem can be solved by expressing the time 2 cash flow in terms of its time 1 value, that is, $108.04/(1 + f_2)$. Algebraically, the problem reduces to finding when:

$$100 \gtrless 108.04/(1 + f_2)$$

$$100/108.04 \gtrless 1/(1 + f_2)$$

$100 at time 2 has a greater (lesser) value than $108.04 at time 2 when the forward price is less (greater) than 100/108.04. Solving for the forward rate, $100 at time 2 has a greater (lesser) value than $108.04 at time 2 when the forward rate is greater (less) than 8.04 percent.

Denote the forward price for period n as F_n. That is, F_n is equal to $1/(1 + f_n)$. Then, it must be true that:

$$D_n = D_1 F_2 F_3 \ldots F_n \tag{9.10}$$

Substitute the definitions of forward price:

$$\frac{1}{(1 + R_n)^n} = \frac{1}{(1 + R_1)(1 + f_2)(1 + f_3) \ldots (1 + f_n)} \tag{9.11}$$

That is, the present value of a dollar received n periods from now is equal to the product of the forward prices. The reason is that the forward prices are single-period present value factors. F_n discounts $1 received at time n to its time $n - 1$ value; F_{n-1} discounts this value back one more period to its time $t - 2$ value, and so on. D_n is the product of these present value factors.

Consider a three-period example, shown in the figure 9.14. Assume that F_3 equals .8919, F_2 equals .9256, and D_1 equals .9615. Then D_3 must

Figure 9.14   Three-Period Example of Forward Prices and Spot Prices

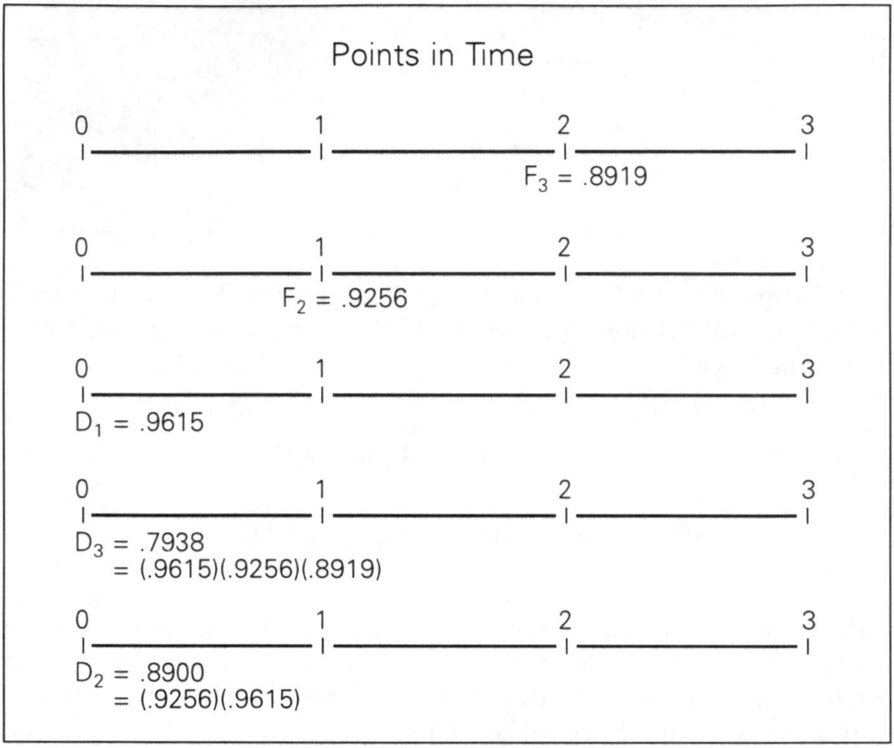

equal $(.8919)(.9256)(.9615)$, or $.7938$. That is, the present value of $1 received three periods from now is $.7938. D_2 is the present value of $1 received in two periods and must equal D_1F_2, or $(.9256)(.9615) = \$.8900$. D_3 must equal D_2F_3 or $(.8900)(.8919) = \$.7938$.

D_n may also be expressed in the following way:

$$D_n = D_{n-1}F_n \qquad (9.12)$$

In terms of interest rates:

$$\frac{1}{(1 + R_n)^n} = \frac{1}{(1 + R_{n-1})^{n-1}(1 + f_n)} \qquad (9.13)$$

In other words, the forward price F_n is equal to the ratio of the spot prices D_n/D_{n-1}. Alternatively, $1 + f_n$ must equal $(1 + R_n)^n/(1 + R_{n-1})^{n-1}$.

Forward Rates and the Shape of the Term Structure

The spot rate is an average of the forward rates. This implies that spot rate yield curves will be smoother than forward rate curves as illustrated in figures 9.15 and 9.16.

The following relationship exists between the spot rates and the forward rates.[5]

$$R_n \gtrless R_{n-1} \text{ as } f_n \gtrless R_n \tag{9.14}$$

To elucidate this relationship, consider three special cases that are shown in figure 9.15.

Figure 9.15   Rising and Declining Forward Rates

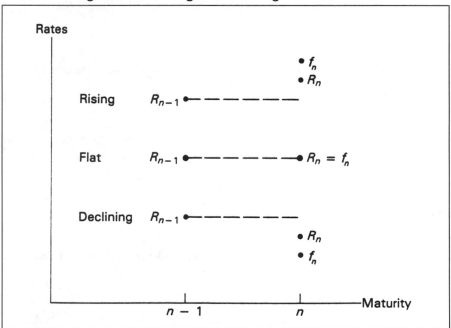

---

[5] This result is proved in this chapter's Appendix A.

Figure 9.16   Spot and Forward Rates

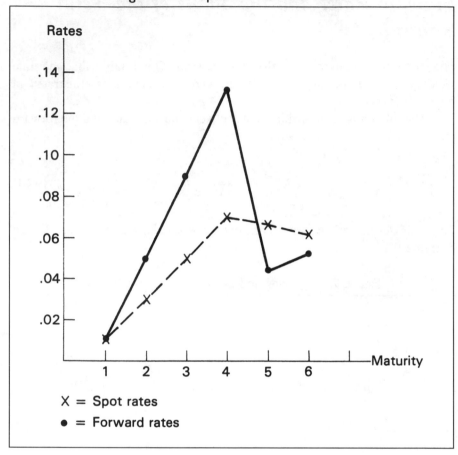

Flat Term Structure

If the term structure is flat, then all the spot and forward interest rates are equal, meaning that:

$$R_n = R_{n-1} \text{ and } f_n = R_n \qquad (9.15)$$

Consider the following example. Suppose that the one-period and two-period spot rates are 4 percent. Since $1 + f_n = (1 + R_n)^n/(1 + R_{n-1})^{n-1}$, the forward rate must be 4 percent also (see figure 9.15).

Rising Term Structure

If the term structure is rising, the longer term rates are greater than the shorter term rates, meaning that:

$$R_n > R_{n-1} \text{ and } f_n > R_n \tag{9.16}$$

In this case, the forward rate for maturity n must exceed the spot rate for maturity $n - 1$ (see figure 9.15). Consider the following example. Suppose that the one-period spot rate is 4 percent and the two-period spot rate is 6 percent. Since $1 + f_n = (1 + R_n)^n/(1 + R_{n-1})^{n-1}$, the forward rate must be greater than 6 percent. In fact, the forward rate equals 8.04 percent.

Falling Term Structure

If the spot interest rates decline as maturity increases:

$$R_n < R_{n-1} \text{ as } f_n < R_n \tag{9.17}$$

For the spot rates to decline, the forward rate for maturity n must be less than the spot rate for maturity $n - 1$ (see figure 9.15). If the one-period spot rate is 4 percent and the two-period spot rate is 3 percent, the forward rate must be less than 3 percent. Since $1 + f_n = (1 + R_n)^n/(1 + R_{n-1})^{n-1}$, the forward rate equals 2.01 percent.

The spot rate curve can be falling even though the forward rates are rising. This is illustrated by the example in table 9.11, shown graphically in figure 9.16.

Curiously, the six-period spot rate (.0625) is lower than the five-period spot rate (.065), even though the forward rate for the sixth period (.0501)

Table 9.11   Example of Forward and Spot Rates

Maturity (Periods)	Spot Rate	Forward Rate
1	.01	.01
2	.03	.0504
3	.05	.0912
4	.07	.1323
5	.065	.0452
6	.0625	.0501

is higher than the forward rate for the fifth period (.0452). Thus, spot rates can decline while forward rates are rising.

A Lower Bound on Forward Rates

The present value of $1 received n periods from now must have a present value less than or equal to the present value of $1 received $n - 1$ periods from now. In formal terms, $D_{n-1} \geq D_n$. Footnote 6 proves that:[6]

$$D_{n-1} \geq D_n \text{ as } f_n \geq 0 \qquad (9.18)$$

In other words, D_{n-1} being greater than or equal to D_n is equivalent to the forward interest rate being greater than or equal to zero. If the forward rate equals zero, then $D_{n-1} = D_n$. If the forward rate is positive, then $D_{n-1} > D_n$. If the forward rate is negative, then $D_{n-1} < D_n$; therefore, the forward rate cannot be negative. Thus, the conditions in equations 9.3 and 9.18 that a more distant cash flow cannot have a higher present value than a nearer cash flow are equivalent to saying that forward interest rates cannot be negative.[7] Consider the following examples.

Case of $D_1 < D_2$.   Assume that D_1 is .9615 (implying that R_1 is .04) and D_2 is .97 (implying that R_2 is .0153). Since $1 + f_2 = [1 + R_2]^2/[1 + R_1]$, f_2 should equal $-.0088$. The forward price is .97/.9615, which equals $1.0088. Thus, the negative forward interest means that someone would lend $1.0088,

---

[6] Substitute the definition that:

$$D_n = D_{n-1}/(1 + f_n)$$

$$D_{n-1} \geq \frac{D_{n-1}}{1 + f_n}$$

Simplifying:

$$f_n \geq 0$$

[7] Appendix B presents the implications of this result for the shape of the term structure.

agreeing to receive $1 in repayment. No investor with the alternative of merely holding cash would engage in this unfavorable loan.

Case of $D_1 = D_2$. If $D_1 = D_2 = .9615$, then $R_1 = .04$, $R_2 = .0198$, $f_2 = 0.0$, and $1/(1 + f_2) = 1$. Thus, $1 is lent at time 1 and $1 is repaid at time 2 for a zero forward interest rate.

The Chicken and the Egg

The preceding discussion of spot and forward interest rates shows the relationships between the various rates. Given a set of forward rates, the spot rates can be determined; similarly, given a set of spot rates, the forward rates can be derived. In effect, forward and spot rates are two sides of the same coin. The ultimate determinants of all the rates are discussed in Chapter 12 on term structure theories. Some theories focus on forward rates and some concentrate on spot rates.

Summary

Spot interest rates involve loans that start earning interest immediately. Forward interest rates involve loans that start earning interest at some future date. The interest rate on forward loans is contractually set at the current time, although the loan does not begin until some future date. The set of spot interest rates is called the term structure of interest rates. Term structures can take on many patterns, including flat, rising, and declining.

Spot or forward interest rates cannot be negative in a world where investors can hold money balances. The n-period spot interest rate is the geometric mean of the one-period spot rate and the forward rates up until maturity n.

Questions/Problems

1. Suppose the spot rates of interest for periods one through four are 3 percent, 4 percent, 5 percent, and 6 percent, respectively. Compute D_1, D_2, D_3, and D_4. Determine spot prices for Treasury STRIPS per $100 of par. Compute forward interest rates for periods 2, 3, and 4.

2. Assume the following interest rates: $R_1 = .08, f_2 = .01, f_3 = .12, f_4 = .03$. Compute spot interest rates for periods 2, 3, and 4. Compute the prices of STRIPS per $100 of par.

3. You are told the following information about the prices of STRIPS with $100 par values.

Price	Maturity (Years)
$94.34	1
$88.17	2
$81.64	3
$74.22	4

Compute the spot interest rates, the forward interest rates, and forward prices for these STRIPS. Graph the spot and forward rates. (Assume that investors pay no taxes.)

Next compare the following three investment possibilities using the preceding information about STRIPS. Explain which choices are better than others. Can you rank the choices from the best to the worst?
A. Invest in two-period STRIPS.
B. Invest in the bank for one period at 7 percent and then reinvest for the second year at the prevailing interest rate in one year.
C. Invest in the bank for one period at 7 percent and then reinvest for the second year at the forward interest rate.

4. You are given the choice of $100 one year from now or $115 two years from now. Which is better? What does the choice depend upon? What would the answer be using the interest rates in problem 1?

5. You are given a choice of $100 at time 1, $110 at time 2, $130 at time 3, and $140 at time 4. Compute the time 0, 1, 2, 3, and 4 values of each of these cash flows using the information from problem 1. Which is the best? Are the answers the same? Why or why not?

6. Assume STRIPS with $100 par values and prices of $85 for a two-period bond and $80 for a one-period bond. Show the arbitrage opportunities available to investors.

7. Use the one-period and two-period STRIPS in problem 3. Show how a long forward contract can be created from these two securities and

determine the price and yield of the forward contract. Show how a short forward position can be created.

8. Assume that $D_1 = .85$ and $D_2 = .80$. You decide to short a one-period zero coupon bond and go long one two-period zero coupon bond. Is the resulting position a forward position or an arbitrage opportunity? Be sure to compute the cumulative cash flows.

9. Assume that the one-period spot interest rate is 10 percent, the two-period spot interest rate is 8 percent, and the forward rate f_2 is 0 percent. Compute D_1 and D_2 and the prices of one-period and two-period STRIPS per $100 of par. Is this information consistent with equilibrium? What arbitrage opportunities are available to investors?

10. Assume that $R_1 = .12$, $R_2 = .10$, and $R_3 = .03$. Compute the prices of one-period, two-period, and three-period STRIPS. Are these interest rates consistent with equilibrium? Explain why or why not.

11. Assume that the one-period spot interest rate is 6 percent. What value for the forward rate would make the two-period spot rate be double the one-period spot rate? Repeat for the three-period spot rate being double the value of the two-period spot rate? Can you draw any conclusions about the general pattern?

12. Look in *The Wall Street Journal* for prices and yields of U.S. Treasury STRIPS. Plot the yields to maturity versus maturity at yearly intervals for the first four years. Then plot the forward interest rates.

13. Given the following information about forward interest rates, what is the smallest possible value of the four-period spot interest rate and what will the forward interest rate be? What is the largest possible value for the four-period spot interest rate and what will the forward rate be? See Appendix B.

Maturity (Periods)	Interest Rates
1	$R_1 = .12$
2	$f_2 = .10$
3	$f_3 = .08$

Appendix A: Forward and Spot Rates

This Appendix examines the link between forward interest rates and the term structure of spot interest rates. The basic result: a rising term structure (i.e., $R_n > R_{n-1}$) occurs when the n-period forward rates exceeds the n-period spot rate. A flat term structure occurs when the forward rate equals the spot rate. A falling term structure occurs when the forward rate is less than the spot rate.

Proof that:

$$R_n \gtreqless R_{n-1} \text{ as } f_n \gtreqless R_n \tag{9A.1}$$

Start with:

$$R_n \gtreqless R_{n-1} \tag{9A.2}$$

Add 1 to both sides and raise to the $n - 1$ power. Then multiply both sides by $1 + f_n$.

$$(1 + R_n)^{n-1}(1 + f_n) \gtreqless (1 + R_{n-1})^{n-1}(1 + f_n) \tag{9A.3}$$

The right side equals $(1 + R_n)^n$. Substitute and simplify to:

$$f_n \gtreqless R_n \tag{9A.4}$$

Appendix B: The Maximum Decline in Spot Rates

This Appendix places a bound on the decline in spot interest rates. As maturity gets larger, the bound gets tighter and the decline in spot interest rates must be relatively small.

The fact that D_{n-1} must be greater than or equal to D_n puts a restriction on the relationship between R_{n-1} and R_n. Start with the following restriction on spot prices:

$$D_{n-1} \geq D_n \tag{9B.1}$$

Express prices in terms of rates:

$$\frac{1}{(1 + R_{n-1})^{n-1}} \geq \frac{1}{(1 + R_n)^n} \tag{9B.2}$$

Rearrange:

$$(1 + R_n)^n \geq (1 + R_{n-1})^{n-1} \tag{9B.3}$$

Take the $n - 1$ root of both sides:

$$(1 + R_n)^{n/(n-1)} \geq 1 + R_{n-1} \tag{9B.4}$$

Take the natural logs of both sides of the preceding expression. Note that the log of $1 + R_n$ is approximately equal to R_n. Then rearrange the expression:

$$R_n \geq \left[\frac{n - 1}{n}\right] R_{n-1} \tag{9B.5}$$

As n gets large, the ratio $(n - 1)/n$ approaches 1.0, implying that R_n cannot be very much smaller than R_{n-1}. Declines in the yield curve are going to be small for long maturities.

The maximum decline in the term structure occurs when the forward rate is equal to zero. If f_n equals zero, then $D_n = D_{n-1}$. For example, if R_3 is equal to 10 percent, then D_3 is equal to $1/(1 + .10)^3 = .7513$. If the forward rate equals its lowest value of zero, the maximum decline in the term structure occurs and D_4 equals .7513, implying R_4 equals 7.41 percent. This is illustrated in figure 9B.1. In equations 9B.4 and 9B.5, the difference between R_n and R_{n+1} must get smaller as maturity n gets larger. For example, if R_7 is 10 percent, $D_7 = .5132$. If the forward rate f_8 is zero, then $D_8 = .5132$, and R_8 must equal 8.70 percent. Clearly, the decline in the spot rate is smaller for the more distant maturity.

References

Lim, K. and M. Livingston, ''Stripping of Treasury Securities and Segmentation in the Treasury Securities Market,'' *The Journal of Fixed Income*, 4, March 1995, pp. 88–94.

Figure 9B.1 Maximum Decline in Spot Rate When Forward Rate Is Zero

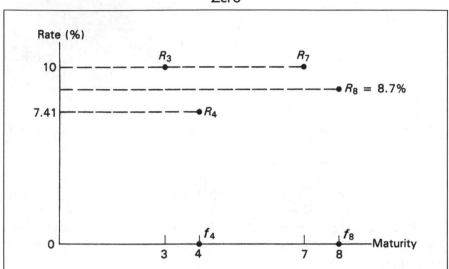

Livingston, M. and D. W. Gregory, "The Stripping of U.S. Treasury Securities," New York University Salomon Brothers Center for the Study of Financial Institutions, *Monograph Series in Finance and Economics,* Monograph 1989–1.

Livingston, M. and D. W. Gregory, "Development of the Market for U. S. Treasury STRIPS," *Financial Analysts Journal,* 48, March/April 1992, pp. 68–74.

Malkiel, B. G., *The Term Structure of Interest Rates,* Princeton, NJ: Princeton University Press, 1966.

Nelson, C. R., *The Term Structure of Interest Rates,* New York: Basic Books, 1970.

10

Coupon-Bearing Bonds

Overview

Most bonds are coupon-bearing, paying semiannual coupons plus the par value at maturity. In effect, a coupon-bearing bond is a portfolio of zero coupon bonds. However, coupon-bearing bonds have their own important characteristics, which are the focus of this chapter.

Price Quotations

Bond prices are quoted in *The Wall Street Journal* and other newspapers. Since the bond market is an over-the-counter market, no central record of actual trades exists. The newspaper price listings for U.S. Treasury securities are representative bid and asked prices. Dealers are willing to buy at the bid price and sell at the asked price.

Assume the same term structure as used in chapter 9. The one-period spot rate of interest is 4 percent (R_1) and the two-period spot rate is 6 percent (R_2). The present value of $1 received in one period is .9615 [$D_1 = 1/(1 + R_1)$]; the present value of $1 received in two periods is .89 [$D_2 = 1/(1 + R_2)^2$]. The forward interest rate is 8.04%. Table 10.1 shows some typical bond quotations based upon this term structure.[1]

---

[1] The yield is calculated based upon the actual price. The calculation is:

$$Price = \frac{c}{1 + R_1} + \frac{c + PAR}{(1 + R_2)^2}$$

The actual prices are $96.41 for the $4 coupon; $100.11 for the $6 coupon; and $103.81 for the $8 coupon.

Table 10.1   Bond Price Quotes

Coupon	Maturity		Bid Price	Asked Price	Yield to Maturity
4's	2006 Feb	...	96–12	96–14	.0596
6's	2006 Feb	...	100–02	100–04	.0594
8's	2006 Feb	...	103–25	103–27	.0592

The Wall Street Journal prices for U.S. Treasury securities are quoted per $100 of par value in 32nds. Thus, a price of 96–12 means $96.375 (that is, 96 plus 12/32). In practice, actual par values are $1,000, $5,000, or even larger units.

U.S. Treasury securities come closest to our frictionless market assumptions. These bonds are differentiated by their maturity and coupon. The actual maturity is a particular day in a particular month in a particular year. The newspaper listings show the maturity month and the last two digits of the maturity year. For example, a bond that matures on February 15, 2006, is shown as 06 Feb. The investor must verify from another source the actual day of the month, although U.S. Treasury notes and bonds tend to mature on the fifteenth of the month.[2] The day in the maturity month is important because coupons are paid at six-month intervals ending at maturity. Thus, a February 15 maturity implies coupon payments on February 15 and August 15 until maturity.

The annual bond coupon is quoted in terms of dollars per $100 of par value. A coupon quotation of 8's is an $8 annual coupon per $100 of par value. The "'s" after the 8 represents a type of punctuation mark. Actual coupons are paid semiannually and are equal to the annual coupon divided by two.

The Wall Street Journal also provides information on two bond yields – the current yield and the yield to maturity. This chapter describes these yields in detail. Very briefly, the current yield is the ratio of coupon divided by price. The yield to maturity is the internal rate of return on the bond.

This example contains three bonds with the same maturity but with different coupon levels. Notice that the three bonds have different prices

---

[2] The *Monthly Statement of the Public Debt of the United States* is an authoritative source of information on U.S. Treasury securities.

and different yields to maturity.[3] For bonds of the same maturity, the impact of coupon level upon price and upon yield to maturity is the focus of this chapter.

Annuities

An **annuity** has the same cash flow per period; they are quite common in finance. For example, coupon-bearing bonds pay an annuity of the coupon payment, and a grasp of annuities is essential for understanding coupon-bearing bonds. We will consider an annuity that pays $1 per period for n periods starting at time 1. Any other annuity can be expressed as this $1 annuity times a constant. The cash flows from the $1 annuity are shown in table 10.2.

The present value of the first dollar is D_1. The present value of the second dollar is D_2, and so on. We can express the value of the entire annuity as A_n, the present value of a dollar received for each of the next n periods:

$$A_n = D_1 + D_2 + \ldots + D_n \tag{10.1}$$

To illustrate, let's return to the example at the beginning of this chapter. The values of the spot prices, D_js, are shown in table 10.3. A two-period annuity would pay $1 at time 1 and at time 2 and would have a present value of $A_2 = D_1 + D_2$ (see table 10.4). Since $A_2 = \$1.75$, every dollar of annuity adds $1.75 to the present value. Similarly, a three-period annuity would pay $1 per period for three periods and have a present value of $A_3 = D_1 + D_2 + D_3$.

The present value of an annuity is a number between zero and n. If all of the spot rates (R_j, $j = 1, \ldots, n$) are infinity, each of the spot prices (D_j)

Table 10.2 Cash Flows from an Annuity

	Points in Time			
	0	1	2 ...	n
Cash flows		$1	$1 ...	$1

---

[3] The yield to maturity in this example is computed from the average of the bid and asked prices.

Table 10.3   A Two-Period Example

Points in Time		
0	1	2
$D_1 = .9615$	$1	
$D_2 = .8900$		$1

Table 10.4   Two-Period Annuity Example

Points in Time		
0	1	2
$1.8515 = .9615$	$1	$1
$+ .89$		
$A_2 = D_1 + D_2$		

is equal to zero and the present value of the annuity is zero, its minimum value. If each of the spot rates is equal to zero, the spot prices take on their maximum value of 1.0. The sum of n of these spot prices equals n, the maximum value of the annuity.

In the case where the R_js are all equal, we have a **flat term structure**. In this case:

$$A_n = \frac{1}{(1 + R)} + \frac{1}{(1 + R)^2} + \frac{1}{(1 + R)^3} + \ldots + \frac{1}{(1 + R)^n} \qquad (10.2)$$

$$= (1/R)[1 - (1 + R)^{-n}]$$

where R is the interest rate for all maturities. In the case of a perpetual annuity, n in equation 10.2 is infinity. The present value of a perpetual annuity is $1/R$.

The present value of an annuity is shown in a table at the end of this text for a wide range of interest rates and maturities. As an example, if the discount rate for all maturities is 10 percent and the present value of an annuity of $1 per period for four periods is $3.1699, then:

$$A_4 = (1/.1)[1 - (1.1)^{-4}] = 3.1699$$

For any row in the present value of an annuity table, the interest rate increases and the present value of an annuity decreases; because the interest rate is in the denominator of equation 10.2, a higher interest rate causes a lower present value. For any column of the annuity table, the present value of an annuity increases as maturity increases; increasing maturity adds more terms to the summation in equation 10.2.

The annuity table can be used to find the interest rate for any given present value and maturity. For example, assume the present value of a $1 annuity for 10 periods is $6.1446. Look across the ten-period row in the annuity table; the interest rate is 10 percent.

The Impact of Coupon upon Price for a Given Maturity

Although bonds pay semiannual coupons, most of this chapter deals with annual coupons. This annual coupon assumption greatly simplifies the presentation without changing the nature of the results. A later part of the chapter presents some details on semiannual coupons.

Consider an n-period bond paying annual coupons of c dollars and having a price of P and a par value of PAR at maturity. The cash flows from purchasing this bond are shown in table 10.5.

Higher Coupon Bonds Have Higher Prices

A bond with a higher coupon (and the same maturity) must have a higher price; otherwise arbitrage opportunities exist. Consider the example in table 10.6. Bonds G and H are two-period bonds with par values of $100 and

Table 10.5   Cash Flows from a Coupon-Bearing Bond

	\multicolumn{4}{c}{Points in Time}			
	0	1	2 ...	n
Cash flows	−P	+c	+c	+(c + PAR)

Table 10.6   Cash Flows from Two-Period Bonds

	\multicolumn{3}{c}{Points in Time}		
	0	1	2
Bond G	−100	+6	+106
Bond H	−100	+8	+108

prices of $100. Bond G has a coupon of $6 and bond H has a coupon of $8. The higher coupon bond has the same price as the lower coupon bond. These prices present an arbitrage opportunity: shortsell G and buy bond H. The cash flows are shown in table 10.7.

At time zero, the net cash flow is zero; the net cash flows at time 1 and 2 are +$2. The cumulative net cash flow is always zero or positive, resulting in a risk-free arbitrage profit. The actions of arbitragers push the price of bond H higher relative to bond G.

The arbitrage no longer results in a risk-free profit when the price of the higher coupon bond exceeds the price of the lower coupon bond. For example, if bond H has a price of $102, the cash flows from shortselling bond G and buying bond H are shown in table 10.8. There is a cash outflow of $2 at time zero and cash inflows of $2 at times 1 and 2. This position is not a risk-free arbitrage, since the cumulative net cash flows are negative in one period.

The discussion can be generalized. Let the prices of bonds G and H be P_G and P_H and their coupons be c_G and c_H. As long as c_H exceeds c_G and

Table 10.7   Cash Flows from Arbitrage: $P_G = P_H = 100$

	Points in Time		
	0	1	2
Shortsell Bond G	+100	−6	−106
Buy Bond H	−100	+8	+108
Net Cash Flow	0	+2	+2
Cumulative Net Cash Flow	0	+2	+4

Table 10.8   Cash Flows from Shorting G and Buying H: $P_G = 100$, $P_H = 102$

	Points in Time		
	0	1	2
Shortsell Bond G	+100	−6	−106
Buy Bond H	−102	+8	+108
Net Cash Flow	−2	+2	+2
Cumulative Net Cash Flow	−2	+0	+2

P_H is less than or equal to P_G, an arbitrage opportunity exists.[4] Consequently, a bond with a higher coupon (and the same maturity) must have a higher price.

Bond Price Is the Present Value of Future Cash Flows

The price of an n-period bond with coupon c and par value of PAR is the present value of the individual cash flows. That is:

$$P = cD_1 + cD_2 + \ldots + (c + \text{PAR})D_n \tag{10.3}$$

Rewriting this in terms of an annuity:

$$P = cA_n + (\text{PAR})D_n \tag{10.4}$$

For bonds identical in every way except coupon level, equation 10.4 indicates a linear relationship between bond price and coupon level. The slope of this equation is A_n, the price of an annuity. If the coupon increases by \$1, the price increases by A_n dollars. $(\text{PAR})D_n$ is the vertical intercept and represents the present value of a zero coupon bond with a face value of PAR.

The earlier example of three two-period bonds illustrates this result. The example assumed R_1 of 5 percent ($D_1 = .9615$) and R_2 of 6 percent ($D_2 = .8900$) and $A_2 = 1.8515 = D_1 + D_2$. If the actual price is the average of the bid-asked prices, the slope of equation 10.4 is 1.8515 (A_n) and the intercept is 89 (D_2 times a PAR value of 100). Thus:

$$P = cA_2 + (\text{PAR})D_2 \tag{10.5}$$
$$= c(1.8515) + (\text{PAR})(.89)$$

The bond prices in table 10.1 were computed using this formula.

The linear relationship between coupon level and price is illustrated in figure 10.1. Appendix A presents a formal arbitrage proof of a linear relationship between bond price and coupon for a given maturity.

---

[4] All the tables in the text can be repeated with these symbols in lieu of the numerical example.

Figure 10.1   Bond Price as a Function of Coupon

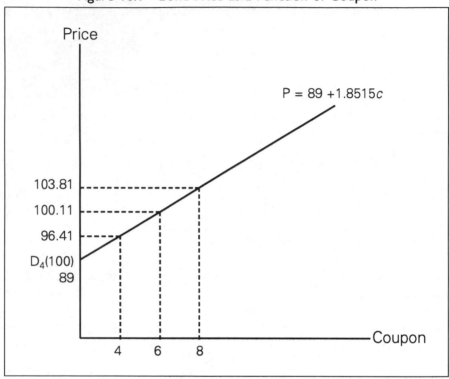

Bond Yield to Maturity

A bond's yield to maturity, denoted by y, is that constant discount rate for all maturities making the present value of the coupons and face value equal to the bond's price. In mathematical terms, y is the rate satisfying equation 10.6:

$$P = \frac{c}{(1 + y)^1} + \frac{c}{(1 + y)^2} + \ldots + \frac{c + PAR}{(1 + y)^n} \qquad (10.6)$$

Equation 10.6 indicates that a bond's price and yield are inversely related. As the yield increases, the price declines. The inverse relationship results from yield to maturity, y, being in the denominator of equation 10.6.[5] Equation 10.6 can also be expressed as:

---

[5] To see that a larger denominator results in a smaller fraction, ask yourself, "Which is bigger, 1/2 or 1/3?"

$$P = c\left(\frac{1}{(1 + y)^1} + \frac{1}{(1 + y)^2} + \cdots + \frac{1}{(1 + y)^n}\right) + \frac{PAR}{(1 + y)^n} \qquad (10.7)$$

$$P = c\left(\frac{1 - (1 + y)^{-n}}{y}\right) + \frac{PAR}{(1 + y)^n} \qquad (10.8)$$

$$P = c\left(\begin{array}{c}\text{Present Value} \\ \text{of an Annuity}\end{array}\right) + PAR\left(\begin{array}{c}\text{Present Value} \\ \text{of \$1}\end{array}\right) \qquad (10.9)$$

The term $[1 - (1 + y)^{-n}]/y$ is the present value of an annuity of \$1 per period for n periods discounted at the rate y. $c[1 - (1 + y)^{-n}]/y$ represents the present value of the coupons. $1/(1 + y)^n$ is the present value of \$1 received n periods into the future. $PAR/(1 + y)^n$ is the present value of par.

Consider the following example. Assume a ten-year bond with annual coupon of \$10, par value of \$100, and yield to maturity of 10 percent. Then equation 10.7 becomes:

$$100 = 10[6.1446] + 100[.3855]$$

The present value of a \$1 annuity for ten periods at a 10 percent discount rate is \$6.1446. The present value of \$1 received in ten years is .3855. The present value of the coupons is \$61.446 and the present value of par is \$38.55. This actually totals \$99.996, but if the present value factors are not rounded to four digits, the price equals \$100.00 exactly.

Given a bond's price, the yield to maturity is found by trial and error. To illustrate, assume price and par values of \$100, coupon of \$9, and maturity of ten periods. To find the yield to maturity by trial and error, a starting trial rate is needed. A procedure for finding a good trial rate is described in detail in the next section.

For now, assume an initial trial rate of 7 percent. Then find the present value of the coupons and par value at 7 percent using the present value tables (see table 10.9). The present value of a \$1 annuity for ten periods at 7 percent is 7.0236. The present value of \$1 received ten periods in the future is .5083. The present value at 7 percent of the coupons plus par value

Table 10.9 Finding Yield to Maturity by Trial and Error

Interest Rate	Present Value Calculation
7%	\$114.04 = 9[7.0236] + 100[.5083]
8%	\$106.71 = 9[6.7101] + 100[.4632]
9%	\$99.999 = 9[6.4177] + 100[.4224]

is $114.04, which is higher than the actual price of $100. Because yield to maturity is in the denominator of the present value calculations, present value is inversely related to yield. To make the present value smaller (that is, closer to $100, the actual price), a higher rate of discount must be used. To reduce the present value, try a higher interest rate, 8 percent (see table 10.9). Using 8 percent, present value is $106.71, which is closer to the price of $100, but still too high. Next, try 9 percent. This gives a present value of $99.999, which would be exactly $100 if the present value tables had more digits. The yield to maturity on this bond is 9 percent.

Comparing the Current Yield, Stated Yield, and Yield to Maturity

In addition to yield to maturity, two other types of bond yields are important. The current yield is defined as the coupon divided by the bond's price. The stated yield is defined as the bond's coupon divided by its par value. Table 10.10 shows the relationship between these various yields for discount, par, and premium bonds. A discount bond sells below par. A premium bond sells above par in the market.

In table 10.10, bonds selling at a discount below par have relatively low coupons. The lowest coupon and the biggest discount from par is a zero coupon bond. The yield to maturity for an n-period zero coupon bond is R_n. Bonds selling at premiums above par will have relatively high coupons compared to discount bonds.

Relating these results to the example in table 10.1 at the beginning of the chapter, we have:

Table 10.10   Yield to Maturity (y), Current Yield (c/P), and Stated Yield (c/PAR)

Discount bond $P <$ PAR	$y > \dfrac{c}{P} > \dfrac{c}{\text{PAR}}$
Par bond $P =$ PAR	$y = \dfrac{c}{P} = \dfrac{c}{\text{PAR}}$
Premium bond $P >$ PAR	$y < \dfrac{c}{P} < \dfrac{c}{\text{PAR}}$

Discount bond
$$P = 96.41 \ (y = .0596) > (c/P = 4/96.41 = .0415) > (c/PAR = .04)$$

The yield to maturity is equal to the current yield plus some return because of the \$3.59 (that is, \$100 − \$96.41) capital gain at maturity. Consequently, the yield to maturity must exceed the current yield.

Premium bond
$$P = 103.81 \ (y = .0592) < (c/P = 8/103.81 = .0771) < (c/PAR = .08)$$

The yield to maturity on the premium bond is equal to the current yield minus some return because of the \$3.81 (that is, \$103.81 − \$100) capital loss at maturity.

   The calculation involved in finding the yield to maturity assumes a bond held to maturity. If the bond is sold before maturity, the realized rate of return over a particular horizon does not have to equal the yield to maturity. The realized holding period return for a bond sold before maturity equals the yield to maturity if all original forward interest rates equal the actual future interest rates.

   In general, bonds are originally issued at par. Issuing at par occurs largely for tax reasons, since bonds originally issued at nonpar prices may have some unfavorable tax consequences for the purchaser (as discussed in chapter 18 on taxes). If interest rates rise after a bond is originally issued at par, the bond becomes a discount bond. Similarly, if rates fall after a bond is originally issued at par, the bond sells at a premium above par. To generalize, bonds with high coupons (premium bonds) were issued when interest rates were higher; bonds with low coupons (discount bonds) were issued when interest rates were lower.

Perpetual Bonds

A perpetual bond pays a coupon indefinitely and its price is the present value of the coupons discounted at the yield to maturity, y. Using the formula for an infinite sum, the bond price can be:

$$P = \frac{c}{(1 + y)} + \frac{c}{(1 + y)^2} + \frac{c}{(1 + y)^3} + \ldots \qquad (10.10)$$

$$= \frac{c}{y}$$

Solving this expression for yield to maturity, y:

$$y = \frac{c}{P} \qquad (10.11)$$

Yield to maturity for a perpetual bond equals coupon divided by price, which is the current yield.[6] For example, assume a perpetual bond with a price of $100 and a coupon of $8. Then the yield to maturity and the current yield are 8/100, or 12.5 percent.

For long-term coupon-bearing bonds with maturities of 25 years or more, the present value of par is relatively small compared to the present value of the coupons. Consequently, these long-term coupon-bearing bonds are quite similar to perpetual bonds, implying that the yield to maturity on a long-term coupon-bearing bond is very close to the yield on a perpetual bond, namely, coupon divided by the price, or the current yield.

In practice, perpetual bonds are rarely issued in the United States, although there have been some corporate perpetual bonds. In the United Kingdom, the British government has issued perpetual bonds called **consols**.

Approximations of Yield to Maturity

The yield to maturity is the rate y that satisfies equation 10.6. In equation 10.6, yield to maturity is a complicated function of the bond price, P, the maturity, n, the coupon, c, and the par value, PAR. For this reason several approximations for yield to maturity have been developed.[7] These approximations were of great practical importance before calculators made the yield to maturity easily available.

For bonds with maturities of less than 15 years, the following expression has been found to give a close approximation of yield to maturity.

$$\text{Approximate yield to maturity} = \frac{c + \dfrac{(\text{PAR} - P)}{n}}{\dfrac{(\text{PAR} + P)}{2}} \qquad (10.12)$$

---

[6] For both par bonds and perpetual bonds, the current yield equals the yield to maturity.

[7] See Hawawini and Vora (1982).

For bonds with maturities in excess of 15 years, the current yield, c/P, gives a fairly close approximation of yield to maturity because such bonds are priced in very much the same way as perpetual bonds. Recall that $y = c/P$ for perpetual bonds. These two approximations imply a rule for getting a reasonable initial trial value when computing yield to maturity. If maturity is less than 15 years, use the approximation in equation 10.12. If maturity is more than 15 years use c/P, the current yield.

Electronic calculators tend to use the following procedure to find the yield to maturity. First, upper and lower bounds are determined for the yield to maturity. Then, a trial rate is set halfway between these upper and lower bounds. The calculator tests whether the actual rate is higher or lower than the trial value. If the actual rate is above (below) the trial rate, the bounds are reset so that the trial rate is the new lower (upper) bound. A new trial rate is established halfway between the bounds and the procedure is repeated. This procedure keeps cutting the feasible solution interval in half, until the interval between the upper and lower bounds is sufficiently small.

Semiannual Compounding and Accrued Interest

In practice, bond coupons are paid semiannually, that is, every six months. The semiannual coupon is equal to the annual coupon divided by two. If n is the number of years until maturity and i is the semiannual yield to maturity, then:[8]

$$P = \frac{c/2}{(1 + i/2)} + \frac{c/2}{(1 + i/2)^2} + \ldots + \frac{c/2 + \text{PAR}}{(1 + i/2)^{2n}} \qquad (10.13)$$

The price can also be expressed in terms of the yield to maturity, y:

$$P = \frac{c/2}{(1 + y)^5} + \frac{c/2}{(1 + y)} + \ldots + \frac{c/2 + \text{PAR}}{(1 + y)^n} \qquad (10.14)$$

In equation 10.14, the exponents are the number of years until the payment is received. The first coupon of $c/2$ is received in .5 years and the

---

[8] Technically, this is the annualized semiannually compounded yield to maturity – for short, the semiannual yield.

exponent is .5. In contrast, the exponents in equation 10.13 are the number of six-month periods. The first coupon of $c/2$ is received in one period and the exponent is 1.

The relationship between the annual yield to maturity, y, and the semiannual yield to maturity, i, is found by setting equation 10.14 equal to equation 10.13. The result is $1 + y = (1 + i/2)^2$, implying that $y = i + i^2/4$. The annual yield is higher than the semiannual yield by $i^2/4$, a relatively small difference. The U.S. market uses the semiannual yield.

In practice, bonds are usually not purchased exactly one period before the first coupon payment of $c/2$. Two complications result. First, the number of periods discounted is affected. For example, if the first coupon is received in 90 days (roughly 1/2 of a six-month period), the first coupon payment is discounted for 1/2 of a period. The second coupon is discounted for 1.5 periods, and so on.

Second, bonds accrue interest to the holder of record on a daily basis. If a semiannual period is 180 days, the bondholder accrues (earns) 1/180 of the next coupon ($c/2$) every day.[9] The purchaser of a bond is required to pay the agreed price as well as accrued interest. The accrued interest is computed by multiplying the semiannual coupon payment by the proportion of a semiannual payment period elapsed since the last coupon was paid. For example, if there are 180 days in half a year and the next semiannual coupon will be paid in 90 days, the bond purchaser pays accrued interest equal to $(90/180)(c/2)$.[10]

Unless accrued interest is paid, bond prices would fall by the amount of the semiannual interest payment right after the coupon is paid on the ex-coupon date. In contrast, common stocks are traded without accruing dividends. Consequently, stock prices drop by approximately the amount of the dividend right after the dividend is paid.[11]

---

[9] In contrast, dividends on stocks do not accrue. The stockholder of record on a particular date receives the entire dividend.

[10] If accrued interest is AI and j is the proportion of a period remaining until the next coupon, then:

$$P + AI = \frac{c/2}{(1 + i/2)^j} + \frac{c/2}{(1 + i/2)^{j+1}} + \cdots + \frac{c/2 + \text{PAR}}{(1 + i/2)^{2n-1+j}}$$

[11] Technically, the prices drop by the after-tax amount of the dividend.

The Term Structure and the Yield to Maturity

The example in table 10.1 at the beginning of this chapter presents a hypothetical case with three two-year bonds maturing on the same date, but with different coupons of \$4, \$8, and \$12. The three bonds in table 10.1 are all fairly priced given the term structure. Each cash flow is discounted at the fair market rate (R_j) for that maturity.

The yields to maturity of these three bonds are different. This difference in yields to maturity is called the **coupon effect upon yield to maturity**, or **coupon effect** for short.[12] The yield to maturity is merely some average of these spot discount rates. For this reason, some observers have suggested that the computed yield to maturity is a meaningless number. *Higher yield to maturity does not represent a better bond to buy.*

The coupon effect depends upon the term structure of interest rates, that is, the pattern of the R's, and upon the mathematics of computing yield to maturity. To see this relationship explicitly for an n-period bond, express bond price in terms of spot interest rates as in equation 10.3 and in terms of yield to maturity as in equation 10.6. That is:

$$P = cD_1 + cD_2 + \ldots + (c + \text{PAR})D_n$$

$$= \frac{c}{(1 + R_1)^1} + \frac{c}{(1 + R_2)^2} + \ldots + \frac{c + \text{PAR}}{(1 + R_n)^n} \qquad (10.15)$$

$$= \frac{c}{(1 + y)^1} + \frac{c}{(1 + y)^2} + \ldots + \frac{c + \text{PAR}}{(1 + y)^n}$$

Equation 10.15 shows the yield to maturity to be some complicated polynomial average of the spot interest rates $R_1, \ldots, R_n$. The yield to maturity must lie somewhere between the lowest spot interest rate and the highest. However, the averaging process depends upon the coupon, maturity, and the term structure. If higher (lower) yields to maturity occur for higher coupon bonds, there is a **positive coupon effect (negative coupon effect)**. The same yield for all coupon levels is a **neutral coupon effect**.

In general, there is no way to explicitly solve for the yield to maturity in terms of the spot interest rate. Yield to maturity is found by trial and

---

[12] Brooks, Levy, and Livingston (1989) present empirical evidence for the existence of a measurable coupon effect when comparing coupon-bearing Treasury notes with otherwise identical (noncoupon-bearing) Treasury bills.

error. The case of par bonds provides one interesting exception and is discussed shortly.

Special Cases: Yield to Maturity Equals the Spot Interest Rate

In general, the yield to maturity depends upon the term structure of interest rates. In three special cases, the yield to maturity equals the spot interest rate.

Flat Term Structure   In the case of a flat term structure, all the spot interest rates are the same, namely $R_1 = R_2 = \ldots R_n = R$. If all the spot interest rates in equation 10.15 are equal, the yield to maturity equals the spot interest rate for all bonds, regardless of coupon and maturity. There is no coupon effect (or a neutral effect).

One–Period Bonds   In the case of one-period bonds, the yield to maturity equals the spot interest rate, regardless of the bond's coupon level. To see this point, write bond price in terms of both the yield to maturity and the spot rate:

$$P = \frac{c + \text{PAR}}{1 + y} = \frac{c + \text{PAR}}{1 + R_1} \tag{10.16}$$

Equation 10.16 holds only if the yield to maturity, y, equals the spot interest rate, R_1.

Zero Coupon Bonds   For zero coupon bonds, the yield to maturity equals the spot interest rate. Write the price of an n-period zero coupon bond in terms of both its yield and the spot interest rate:

$$P = \frac{\text{PAR}}{(1 + y)^n} = \frac{\text{PAR}}{(1 + R_n)^n} \tag{10.17}$$

Equation 10.17 holds only if the yield to maturity, y, equals the spot interest rate, R_n.

Special Case: Par Bonds

The yield to maturity for a par bond can be explicitly expressed in terms of the term structure for par bonds. Letting par equal the yield to maturity on a par bond, we have:[13]

$$\text{ypar} = \frac{1 - D_n}{A_n} = \frac{1 - D_n}{D_1 + D_2 + \ldots + D_n} \tag{10.18}$$

$$= \frac{1 - \dfrac{1}{(1 + R_n)^n}}{\dfrac{1}{(1 + R_1)} + \dfrac{1}{(1 + R_2)^2} + \ldots + \dfrac{1}{(1 + R_n)^n}}$$

To illustrate this formula, consider the example from table 10.1 in the beginning of the chapter. The one-period spot rate, R_1, is 4 percent and the forward rate, f_2, is 8.04 percent. The two-period spot rate, R_2, is the geometric mean of these two rates,[14] that is, 6 percent. The yield on a two-period par bond is:

$$\text{ypar} = \frac{1 - \dfrac{1}{(1 + R_1)(1 + f_2)}}{\dfrac{1}{(1 + R_1)} + \dfrac{1}{(1 + R_1)(1 + f_2)}} \tag{10.19}$$

$$\text{ypar} = \frac{1 - \dfrac{1}{(1 + .04)(1 + .0804)}}{\dfrac{1}{(1 + .04)} + \dfrac{1}{(1 + .04)(1 + .0804)}} = 5.94\%$$

---

[13] To prove this, set price equal to par value:

$$\text{PAR} = cA_n + (\text{PAR})D_n$$
$$\text{PAR}[1 - D_n] = cA_n$$
$$c/\text{PAR} = (1 - D_n)/A_n$$

Since for par bonds c/PAR equals the yield to maturity y, the proof is complete.

[14] $(1 + R_2)^2 = (1 + R_1)(1 + f_2)$.

The yield on this two-period par bond is 5.94 percent, which is also the stated yield or the coupon as a percent of par.[15] The yield on this par bond is an average of the one-period spot rate, 4 percent, and the two-period spot rate, 6 percent. The par bond yield is relatively close to the two-period spot rate because most of the cash flows on this bond are the par value and coupons received at time 2.

The relationship between the spot interest rates and the yield on a par bond is shown in figure 10.2. Notice that the yield to maturity on a two-period zero coupon bond is 6 percent, R_2. This means that a coupon-bearing discount bond (with a price below par) must have a yield to maturity somewhere between 6 percent and 5.94 percent, the par bond yield. Premium bonds (with prices above par) have yields below 5.94 percent. This is an

Figure 10.2   Relationship Between Spot Rates
and Yields on a Par Bond

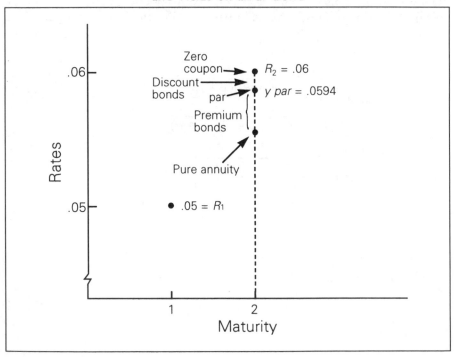

---

[15] In practice, coupons are in increments of eighths of a percent.

example where higher coupon bonds have lower yields, a so-called negative coupon effect.

Appendix B contains a careful discussion of the term structure conditions resulting in positive or negative coupon effects. A positive (negative) coupon effect occurs for declining (rising) term structures. Detailed examples of each case are included.

In practice, the coupon effect is significantly affected by taxes. In a world with taxes, a positive coupon effect tends to occur for discount bonds for the majority of term structures; negative coupon effects frequently occur for premium bonds. The cause is favorable tax treatment for low and high coupon bonds. Frequently, the highest yields are for par bonds.[16]

Creating Treasury STRIPS from Coupon-Bearing Treasury Bonds

Beginning in 1985, the U.S. Treasury began to allow designated Treasury securities to be decomposed by dealers into STRIPS.[17] STRIPS are zero coupon securities paying par value at maturity, but with no coupons on intervening dates. Some investors, such as pension funds, may find STRIPS attractive investments, since the cash inflow at a particular horizon date is guaranteed. Arbitrage should link the prices of STRIPS and the prices of the underlying strippable bonds. For example, suppose that pension funds have a very strong demand for STRIPS, driving their prices up and their yields down. Unless the price of the underlying strippable bonds adjust upward, arbitragers can make a profit from buying the underlying bond, stripping it, and selling the STRIPS.

The following example illustrates the arbitrage link between STRIPS and coupon-bearing bonds. Suppose there is a two-period bond with an 8 percent coupon selling for $102. One-period and two-period STRIPS with the prices shown are in table 10.11.

There is an arbitrage opportunity from buying the two-period 8 percent coupon bond and stripping it. The prices of the two STRIPS imply that

---

[16] These issues are discussed fully in chapter 18 on taxes.

[17] The Monthly Statement of the Public Debt contains a list of strippable Treasury securities.

Table 10.11   STRIPS vs. Coupon-Bearing Bonds

Maturity	Coupon	Price per $100 Par
1	0	$96.15
2	0	$89.00
2	8%	$102.00

$D_1 = .9612$ and $D_2 = .89$. Thus, the value of the coupon-bearing bond as STRIPS is:

$$
\begin{aligned}
Value &= (c)(D_1) + (c)(D_2) + (PAR)(D_2) \\
&= (8)(.9615) + (8)(.89) + (100)(.89) \qquad (10.20) \\
&= 103.81
\end{aligned}
$$

The arbitrager buys the coupon-bearing par bond for $102 and sells the parts as STRIPS for $103.81. The arbitrage profit is $1.81. The repeated actions of arbitragers force the prices of the STRIPS and strippable coupon-bearing bonds to converge. If the value of STRIPS is too low relative to underlying bonds, the arbitrager buys a portfolio of STRIPS and rebundles them into coupon-bearing bonds.

Several factors may impede the arbitrage in practice. First, bid-asked spreads may create slight differences in STRIPS prices and underlying bond prices. Second, the Treasury distinguishes between a *coupon strip,* made a coupon, and a *par strip,* made from a par value. Coupon STRIPS and par STRIPS with the same maturity date are not interchangeable. When rebundling STRIPS into underlying bonds, the par component of the bond must come from par STRIPS. But coupon STRIPS with the same maturity date are interchangeable, even if they originally came from different bonds. Consequently, for a particular maturity, there are both par STRIPS and coupon STRIPS, and they may have slightly different prices because there is no simple arbitrage between the two varieties of STRIPS.[18]

---

[18] The arbitrage links between STRIPS and underlying bonds is discussed in Lim and Livingston (1995), Livingston and Gregory (1989, 1992), and Daves and Ehrhardt (1993).

Estimating Spot Interest Rates from Observable Bond Yields

To compare investments with different cash flows, investors should find the present value by discounting the cash flows in each period by the appropriate spot interest rate for that period. In general the spot interest rates are not directly observable, but must be estimated.

U.S. Treasury STRIPS provide possible estimates of spot interest rates. In practice, STRIPS are subject to complicated tax rules which can create a difference between the yields on STRIPS and after-tax spot rates.[19]

Yields to maturity on coupon-bearing bonds have frequently been used to estimate spot interest rates. However, yield to maturity on a coupon-bearing bond can be substantially different from the spot rate R_n in many cases. This difference has been called **coupon-bias**. The next section on Flattening of Yield Curves presents numerical examples showing large coupon biases.

To estimate the spot interest rates, the investigator usually selects a set of very similar bonds but with different maturities and coupons. Two frequently used data sets have been U.S. Treasury debt instruments and British government bonds. Some type of mathematical function is fitted to the yields on these bonds for a particular point in time. This function allows the estimation of spot rates for various maturities. The chance for coupon bias is substantial.

Theoretically, two methods lead to precise estimates of the true spot rates. First, if two bonds with different coupon levels exist for the same maturity, the spot interest rate can be determined from this pair of bonds. See Appendix C for a proof. In practice, this approach has a number of difficulties. With bid-asked spreads, a range for the spot rate can be established as opposed to a point estimate. If the bonds in the pair have different tax status, the method cannot be used. Most importantly, pairs of bonds are available for a limited number of maturities; thus, spot rates can be derived for only a few selected maturities.

Second, if at least one bond exists for each maturity, the spot rates can be found recursively. This method is discussed in Appendix D. The recursive method is not very practical, since the method does not work with missing maturities.

---

[19] Chapter 18 on taxes discusses these complications.

Flattening of Yield Curves

Yield curves have been observed to flatten out for long maturities. Burton Malkiel and Friedrich Lutz have argued that flattening is an empirical regularity that should be explained by a term structure theory.[20] In fact, flattening is going to occur regardless of the pattern of forward interest rates. There are two reasons for this. First, spot interest rates are an average of the forward rates. This average weights the shorter term forward rates heavily; the longer term forward rates have a very small weight in the average. Consequently, long-term spot rates are essentially an average of the shorter term forward rates.

The second reason for flattening is that yield to maturity on coupon-bearing bonds is an average of the spot interest rates. As maturity lengthens, the longer term spot interest rates contribute very little to this average. Thus, yield curves for coupon-bearing bonds tend to become even flatter than yield curves for zero coupon bonds. Flattening of yield curves for par bonds is illustrated by table 10.11, which is shown graphically in figure 10.3.

In this example, the one-period forward rate is 1 percent; forward rates increase by 1 percent per year. In table 10.11, the spot interest rates do not increase as fast as the forward rates. As maturity gets longer, the increase in the spot rates gets smaller and smaller; the spot rate is the geometric average of the forward rates.[21]

In table 10.12, the par bond yields increase by even smaller amounts than the spot interest rates since the par bond yields are an average of the spot interest rates. By a maturity of 25 years, the increase in par bond yields is very small, even though the forward rates continue to increase by 1 percent per year.

The last column in the table is coupon bias, representing the difference between the spot rate and the par bond yield. This coupon bias increases for longer maturities. The discrepancy between the spot rates and the par

---

[20] Malkiel (1966) argued that liquidity premiums would stop increasing for long maturities (i.e., flatten out) and this would explain the flattening of yield curves. Lutz (1940) suggested that flattening would result from expectations of distant future interest rates being a constant.

[21] Recall that the spot rate for period n is:

$$R_n = [(1 + R_1)(1 + f_2) \ldots (1 + f_n)]^{1/n} - 1$$

Figure 10.3   Flattening of Yield Curve

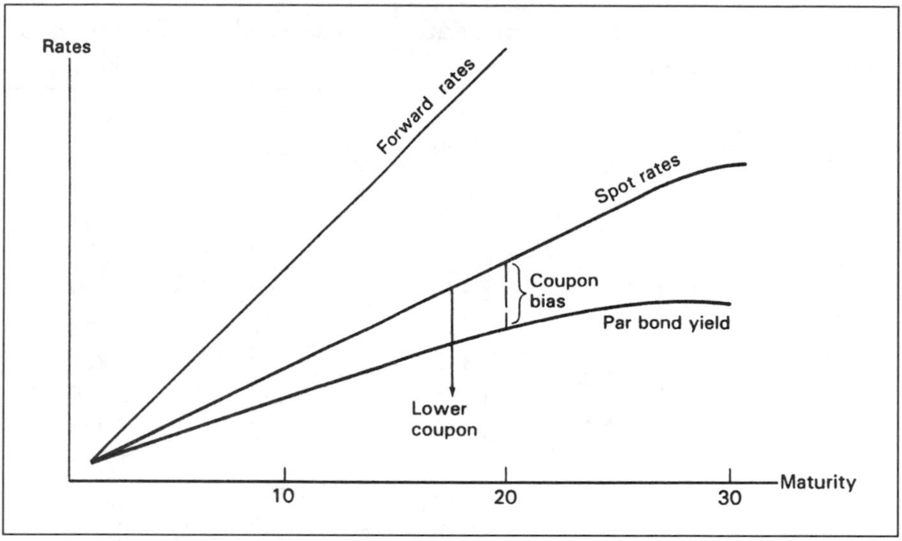

yields increases for longer maturities because par bond yields are an average of more and more spot rates. Appendix E presents some theorems about flattening of yield curves for par bonds.

Summary

This chapter examines coupon-bearing bonds. For bonds of the same maturity but different coupons, higher coupon bonds must have higher prices. For bonds of the same maturity, the relationship between coupon and yield to maturity can be positive, neutral, or negative. This coupon effect depends upon the term structure of interest rates. The coupon effect is positive for a declining term structure, neutral for a flat term structure, and negative for a rising term structure.

For bonds selling at a discount from par, the yield to maturity exceeds the current yield (coupon/price), because the buyer of a discount bond earns the current yield plus a capital gain at maturity equal to the discount from par. For bonds selling at par, the yield to maturity and the current yield are identical. For premium bonds, the yield to maturity is less than the current yield, since the buyer of a premium bond sustains a loss equal to the premium.

Table 10.12   Example of Flattening of the Yield Curve

Maturity	Forward Rate in %	Spot Rate in %	Par Yield in %	Coupon Bias in %
1	1	1.0	1.0	0.0
2	2	1.499	1.495	0.004
3	3	1.997	1.984	0.013
4	4	2.494	2.463	0.031
5	5	2.99	2.932	0.058
6	6	3.486	3.387	0.099
7	7	3.981	3.827	0.154
8	8	4.475	4.25	0.225
9	9	4.968	4.654	0.314
10	10	5.461	5.038	0.423
11	11	5.953	5.4	0.553
12	12	6.444	5.739	0.705
13	13	6.935	6.056	0.879
14	14	7.424	6.348	1.076
15	15	7.913	6.616	1.297
16	16	8.402	6.86	1.542
17	17	8.89	7.081	1.809
18	18	9.377	7.279	2.098
19	19	9.863	7.454	2.409
20	20	10.349	7.609	2.74
21	21	10.835	7.744	3.09
22	22	11.319	7.861	3.458
23	23	11.803	7.962	3.841
24	24	12.287	8.047	4.24
25	25	12.769	8.119	4.651
26	26	13.251	8.179	5.073
27	27	13.733	8.228	5.505
28	28	14.214	8.269	5.946
29	29	14.685	8.302	6.393
30	30	15.174	8.328	6.846

Questions/Problems

1. Compute the present value of a two-period annuity of $1 per period if the discount rate is 10 percent.

2. A two-period annuity of $1 per period has a present value of $1.808. Find the discount rate from the present value table.

3. An annuity of $1 per period runs from time 9 through time 13. Find the present value of this annuity if the interest rate is 6 percent. (Hint: Subtract an eight-period annuity from a 13-period annuity.)

4. An annuity of $1 period runs from time 9 through time 13. The annuity has a present value of $2.3864. Find the yield to maturity on this annuity.

5. The one-period spot interest rate is 4 percent and the two-period spot interest rate is 10 percent.
   (a) Compute the price of a two-period bond with $100 par value and coupon of $7.
   (b) Estimate the yield to maturity, the current yield, and the stated yield.
   (c) Compute the approximate yield to maturity in equation 10.12.
   (d) Compute the yield to maturity for a par bond. What is its annual coupon, current yield, and stated yield?

6. Suppose there are two-period bonds with $100 par values. The $4 coupon sells for $92. The $8 coupon sells for $99.
   (a) Compute the price of a two-period annuity of $1 per period.
   (b) What is the price of two-period $10 coupon bond?
   (c) What is the price of a zero coupon bond and the two-period spot interest rate?
   (d) Given your answer to (c), compute the one-period spot interest rate.
   (e) Compute the yield on a two-period par bond.

7. Suppose that one-period and two-period STRIPS sell for $95 and $87 per $100 of par. Compute the price of a two-period 5 percent coupon bond. Then compute its yield to maturity.

8. The current yield of a two-period bond is 6 percent. Its price is $90 per $100 of par. Compute the bond's yield to maturity.

9. A perpetual bond has a coupon of $8, par value of $100, and price of $80. Compute its yield to maturity, current yield, and stated yield.

10. Bonds K and M are each two-period bonds with $100 par values. Bond K has a coupon of $9 and Bond M has a coupon of $11. Bond K sells for $98 and Bond M sells for $98. Explain the arbitrage available to

investors. Is there an arbitrage opportunity if the price of Bond M is $99? Explain.

11. Assume a bond paying a coupon of $4 semiannually and having a $100 par value and price. Determine the semiannual and annual yields to maturity. Compare the two.

12. The yield to maturity on a one-period par bond is 6 percent. The yield on a two-period par bond is 8 percent. Compute the forward interest rate for period 2.

13. Suppose Treasury STRIPS per $100 of par are $90 for a one-period and $85 for a two-period. A two-period bond with an $8 annual coupon and $100 par sells for $97. What arbitrage opportunities are available? What arbitrage opportunities would be available if the coupon-bearing bond sold for $101?

14. Suppose par is $100. A two-period bond has a coupon of $3 and price of $90. Another two-period bond has a $7 coupon and price of $99. Are these prices possible in equilibrium? Are there any arbitrage opportunities?

15. A four-year bond has a coupon of $4, a par value of $100, and a price of $100. A two-year bond has an annual coupon of $10, a par value of $100, and a price of $100. Which bond is a better buy? Does your answer depend upon individual investor preferences? Are there any arbitrage opportunities?

16. In *The Wall Street Journal,* find the prices and yields of Treasury notes, bonds, and bills. For the longest maturity bill, longest maturity note, and longest maturity bond, compute the yield to maturity. Compare your answer with the yield in the newspaper.

17. In *The Wall Street Journal,* find three or more securities with the same maturity, but different coupons. Plot price (bid and asked) versus coupon (horizontal axis). Also plot yield to maturity versus coupon.

Appendix A: Arbitrage Proof of Linear Relationship Between Bond Price and Coupon

In frictionless markets,[22] arbitrage guarantees a linear relationship between bond coupon level and bond price for bonds with the same maturity, i.e., $P = cA_n + (PAR)D_n$. To prove this, consider a case where a linear relationship does not exist. Consider three bonds with coupons and prices such that:

$$c_1 < c_2 < c_3 \qquad (10A.1)$$
$$P_1 < P_2 < P_3 \qquad (10A.2)$$

There are two nonequilibrium cases to examine. In the first case, the price of a bond with coupon c_2 lies above the straight line joining P_1 and P_3. We call this price P_2^{high}. (See figure 10A.1.) An investor can then create a portfolio of bonds 1 and 3 with the same coupon and face value as bond 2. Assume that the arbitrager invests w percent in bond 1 and $1 - w$ percent in bond 3, with the constraint that the total coupon is equal to c_2. That is:

$$c_2 = (w)(c_1) + (1 - w)(c_3) \qquad (10A.3)$$

Solving for w leads to:

$$w = \frac{c_3 - c_2}{c_3 - c_1} \qquad (10A.4)$$

An arbitrager can shortsell bond 2 for P_2^{high} and buy w percent of bond 1 and $1 - w$ percent of bond 3. From equation 10A.3, the portfolio of bonds 1 and 3 will have a coupon equal to c_2, a face value of PAR [that is, wPAR $+ (1 - w)$PAR = PAR], and a portfolio price of $wP_1 + (1 - w)P_3$. From the geometry of the figure, the portfolio price must be less than P_2^{high}. The arbitrager profits by the difference. This is illustrated by the example in figure 10A.1.

---

[22] If bond investors are subject to lower taxation on capital gains than on coupon income, then investors would probably prefer low coupon bonds, creating a convex relationship between coupon and price. This argument is discussed extensively in chapter 18 on taxation.

Figure 10A.1   Equilibrium Prices

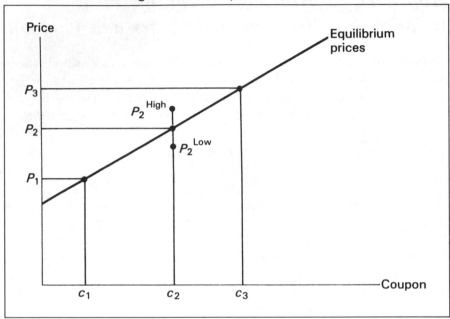

Second, if the bond price P_2^{low} is below the straight line joining bonds 1 and 3, the investor can buy bond 2 and shortsell a combination of bonds 1 and 3 with a higher present value but identical coupon and face value as bond 2. The arbitrager makes a profit from this difference.

In frictionless markets, if two bonds with different coupon levels exist for a particular maturity, an investor can use the original two bonds to create other bonds with any desired coupon level. The procedure is to create an annuity and a zero coupon bond from the two existing bonds and from these create a bond of the desired coupon level. This procedure is shown in detail in the Appendix C.

Appendix B: Coupon Effect

Bonds with the same maturity, but different coupon levels, have different yields to maturity. The impact of coupon level upon the yield to maturity depends upon the term structure of interest rates and the maturity. The relationship between the term structure of interest rates and the coupon effect can be seen by the following reasoning. First, write bond price in two ways:

$$P = \frac{c}{1 + y} + \ldots + \frac{c + \text{PAR}}{(1 + y)^n} = cA_n + (\text{PAR})D_n \qquad (10\text{B}.1)$$

By implicit differentiation, the derivative of yield to maturity with respect to coupon is:

$$\frac{dy}{dc} = \frac{\left(\dfrac{1}{1 + y} + \ldots + \dfrac{1}{(1 + y)^n}\right) - A_n}{\dfrac{c}{(1 + y)^2} + \dfrac{2c}{(1 + y)^3} + \ldots + \dfrac{n(c + \text{PAR})}{(1 + y)^{n+1}}} \qquad (10\text{B}.2)$$

Since the denominator is always positive, the sign of the derivative will depend exclusively on the sign of the numerator. The first term in the numerator is the present value of an annuity at the rate y. Let's call the present value of this annuity Y_c. The second term in the numerator, A_n, is the present value of an annuity at the rates implicit in the term structure of interest rates. Call the yield to maturity on this second annuity r_a.

Because the price of a bond is composed of the annuity A_n and a zero coupon bond D_n, the yield to maturity on the bond must lie between the yields to maturity on these two components. If we have a rising term structure,[23] then r_a must be less than R_n. With a declining term structure, r_a is greater than R_n. For a flat term structure, r_a equals R_n. Table 10B.1 summarizes these results.

A negative coupon effect is illustrated by the following term structure: $R_1 = .05263$, $R_2 = .08465$, $R_3 = .10064$, and $R_4 = .09327$. In this term structure, the yield to maturity on a four-period annuity is less than R_4. We describe this as a rising term structure. Given this term structure, the coupons, prices, and yields to maturity are shown for four-period bonds in table 10B.2. This

Table 10B.1   Term Structure Conditions for Coupon Effect

Term Structure	Yields	Annuities	Coupon Effect
Rising	$r_a < y < R_n$	$A_n > Y_c$	Negative
Flat	$r_a = y = R_n$	$A_n = Y_c$	Neutral
Declining	$r_a > y > R_n$	$A_n < Y_c$	Positive

[23] The term *rising* does not mean monotonically rising; it is not necessary to have $R_1 < R_2 < \ldots < R_n$.

Table 10B.2 Prices and Yields of Four-Period
Bonds for Rising Term Structure

Coupon	Price	Yield to Maturity
$0.0	$70.0	.0933
2.0	76.50	.0930
4.0	83.00	.0928
6.0	89.50	.0926
8.0	96.00	.0924
10.00	102.50	.0922
12.00	109.00	.0921
14.00	115.50	.0919
16.00	122.00	.0918
18.00	128.50	.0917

term structure implies that A_4 is 3.25 and D_4 is .70. Price[24] is equal to $(c)(3.25)$ + $(100)(.70)$. Given the price for a particular coupon level, the yield to maturity is calculated and shown in table 10B.2.

Table 10B.2 illustrates two results quite clearly. First, the relationship between price and coupon is linear.[25] Second, the yield to maturity decreases as coupon increases. This is a negative coupon effect and it occurs for a rising term structure.

If the term structure is declining,[26] there is a positive coupon effect, meaning that higher coupon bonds of a given maturity have higher yields to maturity. The example in table 10B.3 illustrates a positive coupon effect. The example is based upon the following term structure: $R_1 = .09$, $R_2 = .08$, $R_3 = .07$, and $R_4 = .06$. Given the term structure, the price is computed for each coupon level. Then the yields to maturity are calculated.

---

[24] These are prices in frictionless markets, meaning that the prices are decimals. In practice, prices are quoted in increments of 32nds.

[25] To see this, make a graph or note that the change in price divided by the change in coupon is a constant.

[26] A declining term structure is one in which the yield to maturity on an n period annuity is greater than the n period spot rate R_n.

Table 10B.3   Prices and Yields of Four-Period
Bonds for a Declining Term Structure

Coupon	Price	Yield to Maturity
$0.0	$79.21	.06
2.0	85.98	.0605
4.0	92.74	.0610
6.0	99.51	.0614
8.0	106.27	.0618
10.00	113.04	.0622
12.00	119.81	.0625
14.00	126.57	.0628
16.00	133.34	.0631
18.00	140.11	.0634

Appendix C: Computing the Prices of Zero Coupon Bonds and Annuities

If there are two bonds with the same maturity but different coupon levels, the price of a zero coupon bond (and the spot interest rate) and the price of an annuity can be simply computed using the following formulas. This method can be used to estimate the spot interest rate for a particular maturity.

In frictionless markets, if two bonds with different coupon levels exist for a particular maturity, an investor can use the original two bonds to create other bonds with any desired coupon level. The procedure is to create an annuity and a zero coupon bond from the two existing bonds, and then from these create a bond of the desired coupon level.

Assume two bonds with the same maturity but with different coupons, c_1 and c_2 ($c_1 < c_2$), and prices of P_1 and P_2 ($P_1 < P_2$). Table 10C.1 shows the correct combination of these two bonds to create an annuity A_n and a zero coupon bond D_n:

$$A_n = \frac{P_2 - P_1}{c_2 - c_1} \tag{10C.1}$$

$$D_n = \frac{c_2 P_1 - c_1 P_2}{c_2 - c_1} \tag{10C.2}$$

Table 10C.1   Creating a Zero Coupon Bond and an Annuity

Creating a Zero Coupon Bond

Action	Time 0	1 ...	n
Shortsell $c_1/(c_2 - c_1)$ units of bond 2	$\dfrac{+c_1 P_2}{c_2 - c_1}$	$\dfrac{-c_1 c_2}{c_2 - c_1}$	$\dfrac{-c_1(c_2 + PAR)}{c_2 - c_1}$
Buy $c_2/(c_2 - c_1)$ units of bond 1	$\dfrac{-c_1 P_1}{c_2 - c_1}$	$\dfrac{+c_2 c_1}{c_2 - c_1}$	$\dfrac{+c_2(c_1 + PAR)}{c_2 - c_1}$
Net	$\dfrac{-(c_2 P_1 - c_1 P_2)}{c_2 - c_1}$	0 ...	PAR

Creating an Annuity from Two Bonds

Action	Time 0	1 ...	n
Buy $1/(c_2 - c_1)$ units of bond 2	$\dfrac{-P_2}{c_2 - c_1}$	$\dfrac{+c_2}{c_2 - c_1}$	$\dfrac{+(c_2 + PAR)}{c_2 - c_1}$
Shortsell $1/(c_2 - c_1)$ units of bond 1	$\dfrac{+P_1}{c_2 - c_1}$	$\dfrac{-c_1}{c_2 - c_1}$	$\dfrac{-(c_1 + PAR)}{c_2 - c_1}$
Net	$\dfrac{-(P_2 - P_1)}{c_2 - c_1}$	1 ...	1

Appendix D: Recursive Method for Estimating Term Structure

If a coupon-bearing bond exists for each maturity, the following method can be used to compute the spot interest rates for each maturity. The basic approach is to first estimate the one-period interest rate, then use this rate to estimate the two-period spot rate. Use these two to estimate the three-period spot rate, and so on.

Assume a bond exists for each maturity. Bond price for maturity j is P_j, and coupon for maturity j is c_j. Algebraically:

Maturity

1

$$P_1 = \frac{c_1 + \text{PAR}}{1 + R_1} \tag{10D.1}$$

2

$$P_2 = \frac{c_2}{1 + R_1} + \frac{c_2 + \text{PAR}}{(1 + R_2)^2} \tag{10D.2}$$

3

$$P_3 = \frac{c_3}{1 + R_1} + \frac{c_3}{(1 + R_2)^2} + \frac{c_3 + \text{PAR}}{(1 + R_3)^3} \tag{10D.3}$$

Given the price and coupon of a one-period bond, we can compute the one-period spot rate R_1 from the first equation. Then, given R_1 and the price and coupon of a two-period bond in the second equation, we can determine R_2. Given R_1 and R_2 and the price and coupon in the third equation, we can compute R_3, and so on.

Appendix E: Flattening of Yield Curves

Yield curves for coupon-bearing bonds have been shown empirically to flatten out for long maturities. The following bounds show flattening of yield curves to be a mathematical result of the way that yield to maturity is computed. Yield curves for coupon-bearing bonds will flatten out whether or not forward and spot rates flatten out.

For par bonds, the following bounds upon changes in yield to maturity show in a more precise way that yield curves will flatten out for long maturities.

Bound 1:[27]   Increases in yield to maturity from maturity n to maturity $n + k$ must be less than $1/n$. If $y(n)$ and $y(n + k)$ are the yields to maturity on n and $n + k$ maturity par bonds, then:

$$y_{n+k} - y_n - 1/n \tag{10E.1}$$

As n gets large, this bound becomes very tight, since $1/n$ becomes small. The bound is illustrated by the example in figure 10E.1. Consider a

---

[27] See Livingston and Jain (1982) for a proof.

Figure 10E.1   Illustration of Bound 1

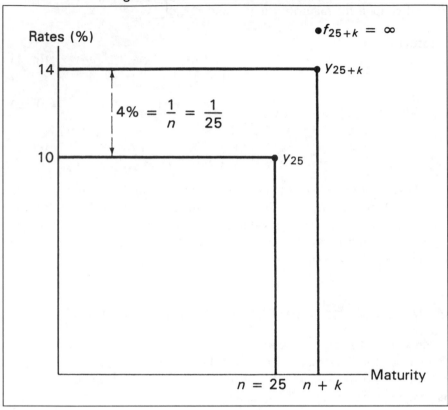

25-year par bond with a yield to maturity of 10 percent. According to the bound, yields can never increase by more than 1/25, or 4 percent. Bonds with maturities greater than 25 years must have yields less than 14 percent independent of the term structure of interest rates. Thus, even if forward rates for maturities beyond 25 years were infinity, the yields on par bonds could never exceed 14 percent. Intuitively, a high forward rate implies a low present value. This particular rate does not contribute much to the price, and, therefore, does not have much impact upon the yield to maturity.

Bound 2:[28]   If the term structure is flat or rising until maturity n, the increase in yields from maturity n to $n + k$ can never exceed 1 divided by the future value of an n-period annuity of $1 per period. That is:

---

[28] See Livingston and Jain (1982) for a proof.

$$y_{n+k} - y_n \leq \frac{1}{\dfrac{[(1+ y_n)^n - 1]}{y_n}} \tag{10E.2}$$

This bound is much tighter than bound 1, since the future value of an annuity must be greater than (and usually substantially bigger than) n. Thus, if yield curves are rising for shorter maturities, a positive slope is harder to achieve for longer maturities. Bound 2 gets tighter as the level of interest rates, y_n, gets larger. In other words, for higher interest rates, yield curves tend to become flatter for shorter maturities.

Bound 3:[29]   For declining yields, the yield on a par bond can never decline from maturity n to maturity $n + 1$ by more than y_n/n. In formal terms:

$$y_n - y_{n+1} \leq \frac{y_n}{n} \tag{10E.3}$$

This bound will be quite tight as n gets bigger, since y_n is a small number. See figure 10E.2 for an illustration.

References

Brooks, R., H. Levy, and M. Livingston, "Bond Coupon Effects and Term Premiums," *Journal of Financial Research,* March 1989, pp. 15–22.

Caks, J., "The Coupon Effect on Yield to Maturity," *Journal of Finance,* 32, March 1977, pp. 103–16.

Cramer, R. H. and S. L. Hawk, "The Consideration of Coupon Levels, Taxes, Reinvestment Rates and Maturity in the Investment Management of Financial Institutions," *Journal of Financial and Quantitative Analysis,* 10, March 1975, pp. 67–84.

Daves, P. R., and M. C. Ehrhardt, "Liquidity, Reconstitution, and the Value of U.S. Treasury Strips," *Journal of Finance,* 48, March 1993, pp. 315–329.

---

[29] See Livingston and Jain (1982) for a proof.

Figure 10E.2   Illustration of Bound 2

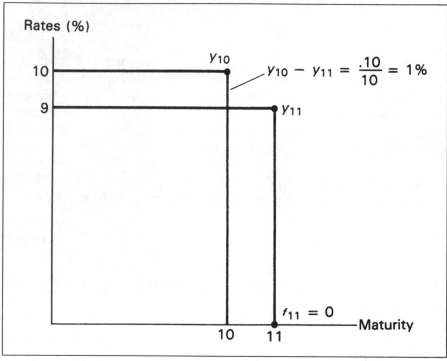

Hawawini, G. A. and A. Vora, "Yield Approximations: A Historical Perspective," *Journal of Finance,* 37, March 1982, pp. 145–56.

Lim, K. and M. Livingston, "Stripping of Treasury Securities and Segmentation in the Treasury Securities Market," *The Journal of Fixed Income,* 4, March 1995, pp. 88–94.

Livingston, M., "Taxation and Bond Market Equilibrium in a World of Uncertain Future Interest Rates," *Journal of Financial and Quantitative Analysis,* 14, March 1979, pp. 11–27.

Livingston, M., "The Pricing of Premium Bonds," *Journal of Financial and Quantitative Analysis,* 14, September 1979, pp. 517–27.

Livingston, M., "Flattening of Bond Yield Curves," *Journal of Financial Research,* 10, Summer 1987, pp. 17–24.

Livingston, M. and D. W. Gregory, ''The Stripping of U.S. Treasury Securities,'' New York University Salomon Brothers Center for the Study of Financial Institutions, *Monograph Series in Finance and Economics*, Monograph 1989–1.

Livingston, M. and D. W. Gregory, ''Development of the Market for U.S. Treasury STRIPS,'' *Financial Analysts Journal*, 48, March/April 1992, pp. 68–74.

Livingston, M. and S. Jain, ''Flattening of Bond Yield Curves for Long Maturities,'' *Journal of Finance*, 37, March 1982, pp. 157–67.

Lutz, F., ''The Structure of Interest Rates,'' *The Quarterly Journal of Economics*, 55, November 1940, pp. 36–63.

Malkiel, B. G., *The Term Structure of Interest Rates: Expectations and Behavior Patterns*, Princeton, NJ: Princeton University Press, 1966.

Schaefer, S. M., ''The Problem with Redemption Yields,'' *Financial Analysts Journal*, 33, July/August, 1977, pp. 59–67.

Weingartner, H., ''The Generalized Rate of Return,'' *Journal of Financial and Quantitative Analysis*, 1, September 1966, pp. 1–29.

11

Price and Reinvestment Risks of Bonds

Overview

Risk-averse investors in fixed income securities are concerned with four primary types of risk: (1) the risk of declining security prices if interest rates rise, (2) uncertainty about the reinvestment rate on coupons, (3) the risk of default by the issuer, and (4) the risk of prepayment following a drop in interest rates. This chapter deals with the first two of these risks – price risk and reinvestment risk.

Bond Price Volatility

Risk-averse investors are very concerned about the possibility of bond prices going down as interest rates rise. The sensitivity of bond prices to changes in interest rates depends upon the coupon and maturity in a complicated way. Therefore, a simple measure of the bond price sensitivity to changing interest rates is valuable to investors. Two measures of the interest rate sensitivity of bonds are discussed in the literature: Macaulay's duration[1] and elasticity. In practical terms, they are virtually identical. Duration is discussed in the following section, and elasticity is covered in the Appendix.

---

[1] The literature also examines the relationship between duration and the risk of common stocks. See Boquist, Racette, and Schlarbaum (1975) and Livingston (1978).

There are two basic conclusions. First, the prices of low coupon bonds are more sensitive to changes in interest rates than the prices of high coupon bonds. Second, longer maturity bonds are generally more sensitive to changing interest rates than shorter maturity bonds. The most risky bonds to hold are generally long maturity and low coupon bonds. The least risky bonds are short maturity and high coupon bonds.

Duration

The most common measure of volatility is the percentage change in bond price for a change in interest rates, assuming a flat yield curve. This measure is called (Macaulay's[2]) **duration**, which we denote by DUR.

$$\text{DUR} = \frac{\text{percentage change in price}}{\text{change in yield}} \qquad (11.1)$$

$$\text{DUR} = \frac{\dfrac{1c}{(1 + y)^1} + \dfrac{2c}{(1 + y)^2} + \cdots + \dfrac{n(c + \text{PAR})}{(1 + y)^n}}{\text{price}} \qquad (11.2)$$

The numerator of duration is (minus) the derivative of bond price with respect to yield to maturity times $(1 + y)$. The derivative divided by the price is equal to the instantaneous percentage change in price as interest rates change. Each term in the numerator is the present value of the cash flows in a particular period times the number of periods until those cash flows are received. This represents a weighted average maturity of the cash flows.

Computing DUR using the preceding formula can be time consuming, especially if n is large. To make the computations faster, it is convenient to take the sum in the numerator analytically,[3] resulting in:

---

[2] See Macaulay (1938).

[3] The easiest way to derive the simplified formula is to first express bond price in the following way:

$$P = (c/y)[1 - (1 + y)^{-n}] + \text{PAR}/(1 + y)^n$$

Then take the derivative of price with respect to yield to maturity, multiply by $-(1 + y)$, and divide by price.

$$DUR = \frac{\left[\dfrac{c(1+y)}{y}\right]\left[\dfrac{1-(1+y)^{-n}}{y}\right] + \left[\dfrac{n(PAR - c/y)}{(1+y)^n}\right]}{price} \qquad (11.3)$$

Since $[1 - (1 + y)^{-n}]/y$ represents the present value of an n-period annuity discounted at the rate y, DUR can easily be computed using the preceding formula and a hand-held calculator.

The duration calculations can be illustrated by the following example. Assume a ten-year bond with $6 annual coupon, $100 par value, and yield to maturity of 8 percent. The price of this bond is $86.58. Table 11.1 shows the computations of the numerator using equation 11.2.

Adding these ten numbers results in a numerator of 659.31. Dividing the numerator by the price results in 659.31/86.58 or a duration of 7.62. The number 7.62 represents a weighted average maturity of the cash flows. Using the duration formula in equation 11.3 gives the same result but with far fewer calculations:

$$7.62 = \frac{\dfrac{6(1.08)}{.08}\left[\dfrac{1-(1.08)^{-10}}{.08}\right] + 10\left[\dfrac{100 - 6/.08}{(1.08)^{10}}\right]}{86.58} \qquad (11.4)$$

47.12   *24.84*

Durations for Zero Coupon, Par, and Perpetual Bonds, and Mortgages

Durations for several types of debt instruments are of special interest.

Zero Coupon Bonds   For a zero coupon bond, set coupon equal to zero in equation 11.3. The duration is equal to maturity, n. Formally:

Table 11.1   Duration Calculations

Maturity	$jc/(1 + y)^j$	$n(c + PAR)/(1 + y)^n$
1	5.56	
2	10.29	
3	14.29	
4	17.64	
5	20.42	
6	22.69	
7	24.51	
8	25.93	
9	27.01	
10		490.98

$$\text{DUR}_0 = n \qquad (11.5)$$

Par Bonds   For a par bond, equation 11.3 simplifies since price equals PAR and PAR equals c/y. The duration for a par bond is:

$$\text{DUR}_{PAR} = (1 + y)\left[\frac{1 - (1 + y)^{-n}}{y}\right] \qquad (11.6)$$

The duration of a PAR bond equals $(1 + y)$ times the present value of an annuity for n periods, i.e., $[1 - (1 + y)^{-n}]/y$. The Duration of a par bond must be less than n, the duration of a zero coupon bond.[4]

Perpetual Bonds   The duration of a perpetual bond is found by setting n equal to infinity in equation 11.3. We have:

$$\text{DUR}_\infty = \frac{1 + y}{y} = \frac{1}{y} + 1 \qquad (11.7)$$

Mortgages   A mortgage is an annuity. The duration of n-period mortgage is found by setting the PAR value in equation 11.3 equal to zero:

---

[4] The present value of annuity for n periods at the rate y is:

$$\frac{1 - (1 + y)^{-n}}{y} = \frac{1}{(1 + y)} + \frac{1}{(1 + y)^2} + \cdots + \frac{1}{(1 + y)^n}$$

The right side of this expression is the sum of n terms. If y is positive, each of the n terms must be less than 1. Therefore, the sum of the n terms must be less than n.

The duration of a par bond is $(1 + y)$ times the present value of an annuity or:

$$\frac{(1 + y)[1 - (1 + y)^{-n}]}{y} = \frac{(1 + y)}{(1 + y)} + \frac{(1 + y)}{(1 + y)^2} + \cdots + \frac{(1 + y)}{(1 + y)^n}$$

$$= 1 + \frac{1}{(1 + y)} + \frac{1}{(1 + y)^2} + \cdots + \frac{1}{(1 + y)^{n-1}}$$

This sum is 1 plus $n - 1$ terms, each of which must be less than 1.0 for $y > 0$. Therefore, the sum must be less than n for positive values of y.

$$DUR_{MOR} = \frac{1 + y}{y} - \frac{n}{(1 + y)^n - 1} \qquad (11.8)$$

In this equation, the duration of a mortgage has two components. The first term is the duration of perpetual bond. The second term is subtracted because of the finite life of the mortgage.

Properties of Duration

Duration has three important properties, which we will call propositions.[5]

Proposition 11.1: Duration and Coupon   For a given maturity, duration is a decreasing function of coupon for maturities greater than one period except for perpetual bonds. This means that higher coupon bonds have lower price sensitivity to changes in interest rates. Zero coupon bonds have the biggest price sensitivity (of n) for bonds of a particular maturity. Consequently, zero coupon bonds have the greatest price risk for bonds of a given maturity. For all one-period bonds, duration equals 1.

The link between coupon level and duration can be seen by the following reasoning. The duration can be expressed as:

$$DUR = n - [n - DUR_{PAR}]\left[\frac{c/P}{y}\right] \qquad (11.9)$$

where c/P is the coupon divided by the price or current yield.[6] For a zero coupon bond, the last term drops out and the duration is n. As the coupon

---

[5] See Hawawini (1984), Hopewell and Kaufman (1973), Homer and Liebowitz (1972), and Malkiel (1966). Malkiel presents five theorems that are widely quoted. The first theorem states that interest rates and bond prices are inversely related. The other theorems are less general than the three following propositions. Malkiel focuses upon par bonds, whereas the propositions deal with bonds of all coupon levels. In addition, Malkiel uses both duration and elasticity. Homer and Liebowitz explicitly discuss elasticity and argue that it is a better measure of volatility.

[6] See Caks et al. (1985) for a derivation.

increases, the last term increases. Since the last term is subtracted, the duration gets smaller as coupon increases.

Proposition 11.2: Duration and Maturity   For a given coupon level, duration is an increasing function of maturity for all par bonds, for all premium bonds, and for most discount bonds (with the exception of very long maturities). For practically all bonds, longer maturity bonds have greater sensitivity to changes in interest rates. That is, long-term bonds have the biggest price changes as interest rates change. Long maturity bonds are the riskiest bonds.

Combining the two propositions, the riskiest bonds are long maturity, deep discount (i.e., low coupon) bonds, with zero coupon bonds having the greatest price volatilities. High coupon, short maturity bonds have low volatilities.

The greater price sensitivity of long maturity bonds has important implications for term structure theories. In the liquidity preference theory,[7] the greater price volatility of long term bonds causes investors to require higher yields as maturity increases to compensate for higher risk.

The relationship between duration, maturity, and coupon level is illustrated by table 11.2, and the relationship between duration and maturity is

Table 11.2   Duration for Various Coupons and Maturities
Yield to Maturity of 8%

| Maturity | Coupon | | | | | |
	0	.04	.06	.08	.10	.12
1	1	1	1	1	1	1
5	5	4.59	4.44	4.31	4.20	4.11
10	10	8.12	7.62	7.25	6.97	6.74
15	15	10.62	9.79	9.24	8.86	8.57
20	20	12.26	11.23	10.60	10.18	9.88
25	25	13.25	12.15	11.53	11.12	10.84
30	30	13.77	12.73	12.16	11.80	11.55

Perpetual bond has duration of $1.08/.08 = 13.50$.

---

[7] See Chapter 12 on term structure theories for a more complete discussion.

shown in figure 11.1, which assumes the same yield, y, for all bonds. The duration for premium and par bonds[8] increases as maturity gets larger, eventually reaching the duration of a perpetual bond of $(1 + y)/y$. For discount bonds, the duration increases as maturity gets larger until, at a long maturity,[9]

Figure 11.1   Duration versus Maturity

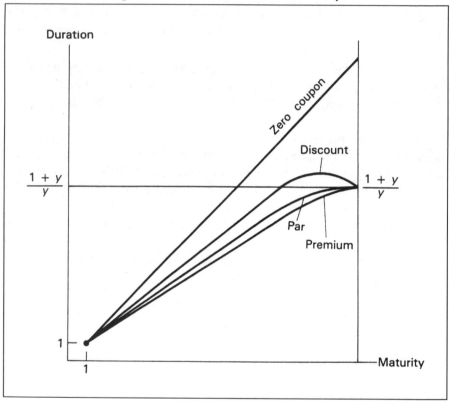

---

[8] The curves for premium, par, and discount bonds each have a constant coupon. The coupon for the premium bond is greater than the coupon for the par bond, which is greater than the coupon for the discount bond.

[9] Duration reaches its maximum for a maturity of:

$$\frac{1 + y}{y - c/\text{PAR}} + \frac{1}{\ln(1 + y)} + \frac{y[\text{PAR}/c - 1/y]}{(1 + y)^n \ln(1 + y)}$$

it reaches a maximum value;[10] then, the duration declines until it reaches the duration of a perpetual bond.

Some authorities suggest restating yield curves (which show yield to maturity versus maturity) in terms of yield versus duration.[11] Restatement in terms of duration leads to illogical conclusions.[12] Yield to maturity is a function of coupon and maturity and not just one single variable.

Proposition 11.3: Duration and Yield to Maturity   For one-period and zero coupon bonds, duration is independent of yield to maturity. For coupon-bearing bonds with maturities exceeding one period, duration decreases as the level of interest rates increases. In general, higher levels of yields imply lower duration. The proposition implies an interesting converse.

Converse   Except for one-period and zero coupon bonds, a given proportional change in bond prices results in a larger basis point change in yield to maturity for higher interest rates.

In recent years, the level and volatility of interest rates has been relatively high. The converse of proposition 11.3 provides at least a partial explanation. When interest rates are high, the absolute changes in yield are larger even if the percentage changes in price remain constant. Thus, the increase in the absolute volatility of interest rates in recent years is mathematically inevitable if the underlying price volatility is constant.

Duration of Portfolios

The duration of a portfolio of bonds is the price-weighted average of the durations of the bonds in the portfolio.[13] To illustrate the calculation of the

---

[10] This maximum value is:

$$\frac{1 + y}{y} + \frac{y[\text{PAR}/c - 1/y]}{(1 + y)^{n^*}(1 + y)}$$

where n^* is the maturity where duration has attained a maximum. Notice that this maximum value is only slightly larger than the duration of a perpetual bond. The first term is the duration of a perpetual bond; for large values of n^*, the second term is close to zero.

[11] See Hopewell and Kaufman (1973).

[12] See Livingston and Caks (1977).

[13] See Bierwag (1987).

duration of a portfolio, suppose there are two bonds with prices P_1 and P_2 and durations DUR_1 and DUR_2. Then the portfolio duration is:[14]

$$DURATION_{portfolio} = \frac{(P_1)(DUR_1) + (P_2)(DUR_2)}{P_1 + P_2} \qquad (11.10)$$

As example, consider the duration of a portfolio composed of two ten-year bonds: a 6 percent coupon bond with a price of $86.58 per $100 of par and an 8 percent coupon bond with a price of par. The portfolio duration is calculated as follows.

$$DURATION_{portfolio} = \frac{(86.58)(7.62) + (100)(7.25)}{86.58 + 100} \qquad (11.11)$$

$$= 7.42$$

An Intuitive Interpretation of Duration

Since duration represents the percentage change in bond prices as interest rates change, the change in bond price must be approximately equal[15] to the duration of a bond times the change in interest rates:

$$Price\ Change \approx [price][Duration][change\ in\ yield] \qquad (11.12)$$

where the symbol $\approx$ indicates *approximately equal to*. Dividing both sides by price results in:

$$Percent\ Price\ Change \approx [Duration][change\ in\ yield] \qquad (11.13)$$

---

[14] This formula assumes a flat term structure. The bonds can have different maturities or coupons. If the bonds have the same price, the portfolio duration is simply the average of the individual durations. Par bonds are a case where the portfolio duration is the simple average of the individual durations.

[15] For a discussion of the accuracy of this approximation, see Livingston (1979).

Consider the following example, shown in figure 11.2. The yield to maturity, y, is 10 percent and the interest rate changes from 10 percent to 11 percent. A perpetual bond's duration equals $(1 + y)/y = 1.10/.10 = 11$. If the perpetual bond initially has a yield of 10 percent and a coupon of $10, the price is $100.

$$P_0 = \frac{c}{y} = \frac{10}{.10} = 100 \tag{11.14}$$

If the interest rate increases to 11 percent, the bond's price declines to $90.91:

$$P_1 = \frac{c}{y} = \frac{10}{.11} = 90.91 \tag{11.15}$$

Figure 11.2   Duration as an Approximation of Price Change

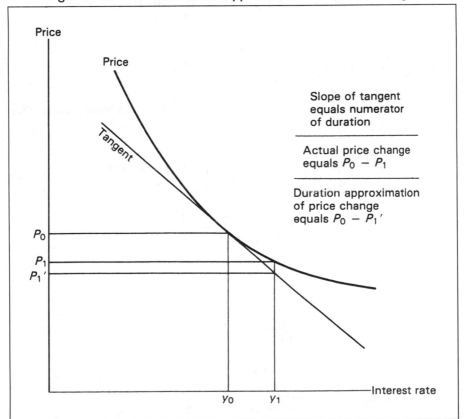

The percentage change in price is:

$$\%\Delta P = \frac{P_1 - P_0}{P_0} = \frac{90.91 - 100}{100} = -9.09\% \tag{11.16}$$

where Δ indicates the change in a variable. The duration approximation is:

$$\%\Delta P \approx (\text{Duration})(\Delta y) \tag{11.17}$$
$$\approx (11)(.01) = .11$$

The duration approximation suggests a price decline by approximately 11 percent (i.e., [11][.01]) to \$89. Thus, the duration approximation has an error of about 2 percent. If the changes in interest rates are smaller, the duration approximation is more accurate. In fact, for infinitesimal changes in interest rates, the duration approximation is highly accurate.

More Accurate Approximations

Using a Taylor expansion, the total percentage change in bond price as yield changes can be expressed in terms of all the derivatives:

$$\frac{\%\Delta P}{P} = \left[\frac{dP}{dy}\right]\left[\frac{1}{P}\right]\Delta y + \left[\frac{d^2P}{dy^2}\right]\left[\frac{1}{P}\right]\left[\frac{(\Delta y)^2}{2!}\right] \tag{11.18}$$
$$+ \left[\frac{d^3P}{dy^3}\right]\left[\frac{1}{P}\right]\left[\frac{(\Delta y)^3}{3!}\right] + \cdots$$

where:

$$\frac{dP}{dy} = \text{first derivative}$$

$$\frac{d^2P}{dy^2} = \text{second derivative}$$

$$\frac{d^3P}{dy^3} = \text{third derivative}$$

The Taylor expansion expresses the percentage change in bond price ($\Delta P/P$) in terms of the first, second, and higher derivatives. The first derivative term incorporates minus duration divided by $1 + y$.[16] That is,

$$\frac{-\text{duration}}{(1 + y)} = \left[\frac{dP}{dy}\right]\left[\frac{1}{P}\right] \tag{11.19}$$

The second derivative term incorporates what has been called **convexity**.

$$\text{Convexity} = \left[\frac{d^2P}{dy^2}\right]\left[\frac{1}{P}\right]\left[\frac{1}{2}\right] \tag{11.20}$$

In the Taylor expansion, the convexity is multiplied by the change in the change in yield squared [i.e., $(\Delta y)^2$]. The impact of the second derivative or convexity term is shown in figure 11.3 as the dotted line.

The second derivative makes the approximation more accurate. For increases in interest rates to y_2, the duration plus convexity approximation gives a high estimate of the bond price. For decreases in interest rates to y_3, the duration and convexity approximation give a low estimate of the price.[17]

---

[16] Duration divided by $1 + y$ is called **modified duration** and is a better measure of price sensitivity than duration by itself.

[17] To see why an increase in yields gives high estimates, note that the odd-numbered derivatives (i.e., dP/dy) are negative. If the interest rate increases (decreases), then the odd-numbered derivatives are multiplied by a positive (negative) Δy, implying that the odd-numbered derivative terms are negative (positive). The second derivative is positive and multiplied by Δy squared, which is always positive. Consequently, the second derivative term is always positive.

As each derivative is added to the Taylor expansion, the approximation converges to the true value. When interest rates increase, the signs of the terms in the Taylor expansion are negative, positive, negative, and so on. The only way for the approximation to converge to the true value is for the approximation with the first term to lie below the true value, with the second term included to lie above, with the third term included to lie below, and so on. When interest rates decline, all the terms in the Taylor expansion are positive. The first term gives a low estimate and as additional terms are added, the approximation gets closer, but never higher than the true value.

Figure 11.3   Duration and Convexity

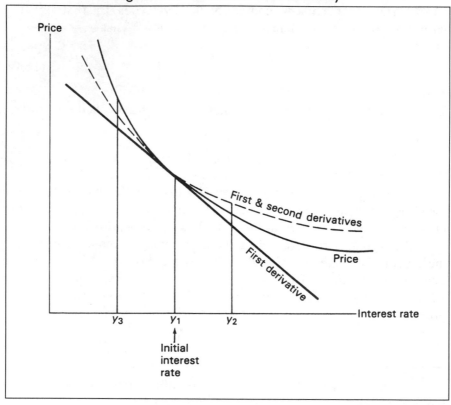

In the case of a perpetual bond, the Taylor expansion is:[18]

$$\frac{\%\Delta P}{P} = \frac{-\Delta y}{y} + \frac{(\Delta y)^2}{y^2} - \frac{(\Delta y)^3}{y^3} + \ldots = \frac{-\Delta y}{y + \Delta y} \qquad (11.21)$$

In this equation, the first derivative term is $-\Delta y/y$, which is duration divided by $(1 + y)(\Delta y)$. The second derivative term is $(\Delta y)^2/y^2$, which is the convexity (i.e., $1/y^2$) times $(\Delta y)^2$. The Taylor series has a simple sum for perpetual bonds, namely $-\Delta y/(y + \Delta y)$.

From the Taylor series, each term equals the previous term times $\Delta y/y$. As long as Δy is small relative to y, the additional derivatives add

---

[18] See Livingston (1979) for a derivation.

progressively smaller amounts to the total change. The example in table 11.3 illustrates the importance of the terms in the Taylor expansion.

Assume a perpetual bond with an $8 annual coupon and an interest rate of 8 percent, implying a price of $100 (i.e., 8/.08 = 100). If the interest rate increases to 9 percent, the price becomes $88.89 (i.e., 8/.09 = 88.89). The decline in price is $11.11, or 11.11 percent. Compare this actual change with the individual terms in the Taylor expansion.

The errors in table 11.3 get closer to zero as more terms are added. The estimated change from the first term is too large by .0139, or 1.39 percent. The estimated change from the sum of the first two terms is too small by .0017, or .17 percent, but the absolute size of the error is reduced. Using the sum of the first three terms, the estimated change is again too large, although the absolute value of the error has become even smaller.

For perpetual bonds, the higher derivative terms are less important as the change in yield becomes smaller because each term in the Taylor expansion equals the previous term times $\Delta y/y$. The higher derivatives are also less important as the yield increases because the yield is in the denominator of each term of the Taylor expansion.

The percent error for perpetual bonds is:

$$\%_e = \frac{\dfrac{-\Delta y}{y + \Delta y} - \dfrac{-\Delta y}{y}}{\dfrac{-\Delta y}{y + \Delta y}} \quad\quad (11.22)$$

$$= \frac{-\Delta y}{y}$$

Table 11.3   Taylor Expansion for a Perpetual Bond

First derivative $-\Delta y/y$	Second derivative $(\Delta y/y)^2$	Third derivative $-(\Delta y/y)^3$	Total change $-\Delta y/(y + \Delta y)$
$-.01/.08$ $= -.125$	$(.01/.08)^2$ $= +.0156$	$-(.01/.08)^3$ $= -.0020$	$-.01/(.08 + .01)$ $= -.1111$

First term	Sum of first two terms	Sum of first three terms	Total change
$-.125$	$-.1094$	$-.1114$	$-.1111$

Errors =	Approximation	− Total Change	
.0139	$-.0017$	.0003	

If the absolute value of the change in yield is small relative to the level of yield, the percent error from the duration (i.e., first derivative) approximation is close to zero. Adding the higher derivatives does not add much accuracy.

The preceding discussion of the Taylor expansion has been for perpetual bonds. Similar results apply for shorter maturity bonds. In addition, for shorter maturities, the higher derivative terms are less important.[19] Thus, for shorter maturities the duration approximation is quite accurate.

Immunization

Some investors are faced with a very specialized type of problem. The investor has X dollars today to invest and must achieve an investment goal of H dollars $(H > X)$ n years from now. Severe penalties are incurred if the investment goal of H dollars is not attained; a value of more than H dollars results in no rewards. This type of investor is called an immunizer, because such investors would like to protect themselves against the chance of attaining less than the goal of H dollars. Pension funds and life insurance companies are investors with this type of problem. Using actuarial tables, the pension fund can predict with considerable accuracy its obligations to the pensioners in defined benefit plan. The pension fund manager has no direct incentive to attain more than the contractually bound retirement benefits and a big incentive to avoid defaulting on these obligations.[20] Several strategies have been advocated for immunizers. We will discuss the pros and cons of each.

Zero Coupon Strategy

One simple strategy to lock in a target of H dollars is to buy zero coupon bonds. Since these bonds have no coupons, the risk of uncertain returns from investing the coupons is solved. The only cash flows occur at time 0 and time n as shown in figure 11.4.

Until recently, relatively few long-term zero coupon bonds have existed for investors to buy. Treasury bills with maturities of less than one year

---

[19] See Brooks and Livingston (1992) for a more detailed discussion of the value of the higher derivatives.

[20] If the pension fund does well, the employer may be able to put smaller amounts into the pension fund in the future.

Figure 11.4   The Zero Coupon Strategy

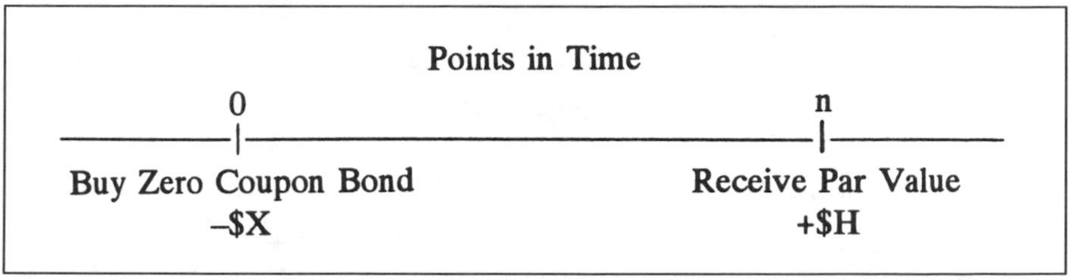

Points in Time	
0	n
—————|————————————————|————	
Buy Zero Coupon Bond	Receive Par Value
–$X	+$H

have been widely available. Since the horizons of immunizers have been much longer than one year, Treasury bills have not been useful for immunizers. In the late 1970s, corporations began to issue zero coupon bonds. Corporate zero coupon bonds do have some value to immunizers, but they also have default risk, an undesirable characteristic from the immunizer's viewpoint.

The U.S. Treasury allows a number of Treasury securities to be stripped of their coupons. That is, the individual coupons and par value are sold separately. The resulting securities are called STRIPS and are actively traded.[21]

As an example, if a three-year Treasury bond with annual coupons is stripped, its three annual coupons and one par value are resold as four separate securities. In equilibrium, the price (P) of the underlying bond must equal the total price of the STRIPS (see figure 11.5). STRIPS represent default-free zero coupon bonds, which are ideal immunizing vehicles. Demand for stripped bonds has been strong. A significant proportion of U.S. Treasury securities have been stripped to satisfy this demand.

With the growth of the market for STRIPS, the need for more complicated strategies to immunize has been reduced. Nevertheless, an extensive literature has developed on procedures for immunizing with coupon-bearing bonds. In effect, these strategies try to create the equivalent of a zero coupon bond position from a portfolio of coupon-bearing bonds.

Maturity Strategy

Some investigators use the so-called maturity strategy as a benchmark. In this strategy, an investor purchases a coupon-bearing bond with maturity equal to the investor's horizon. The cash flows are shown in figure 11.6.

---

[21] See Livingston and Gregory (1989, 1992) for a detailed discussion of STRIPS.

Figure 11.5   An Example of Stripping of U.S. Treasury Securities

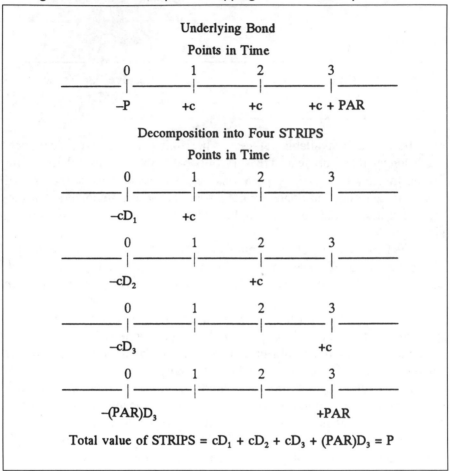

Underlying Bond

Points in Time

0	1	2	3
−P	+c	+c	+c + PAR

Decomposition into Four STRIPS

Points in Time

0	1	2	3
$-cD_1$	+c		

0	1	2	3
$-cD_2$		+c	

0	1	2	3
$-cD_3$			+c

0	1	2	3
$-(PAR)D_3$			+PAR

Total value of STRIPS = $cD_1 + cD_2 + cD_3 + (PAR)D_3 = P$

Figure 11.6   Maturity Strategy

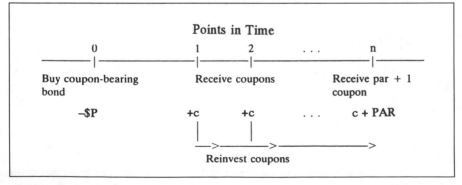

Points in Time

0	1	2	. . .	n
Buy coupon-bearing bond	Receive coupons			Receive par + 1 coupon
−$P	+c	+c	. . .	c + PAR

Reinvest coupons

An investor following this strategy is faced with the problem of reinvesting the coupons received in the future. For example, the coupon received at time 1 must be invested. If this coupon is invested in coupon-bearing bonds, then subsequent coupons must be reinvested. Since the reinvestment rates are not known at time 0, the total value of the bond portfolio is not known for certain. If interest rates at times 1 through $n - 1$ are lower than the initial interest rate at time 0, the total portfolio value is less than the amount required.

Duration Strategy

Another investment strategy is to invest in coupon-bearing bonds with maturity greater than the horizon date. This is shown in figure 11.7. The value of the bond portfolio using this strategy is uncertain for two reasons. First, the coupons from time 1 until time $n - 1$ have to be reinvested at uncertain future interest rates. Second, the bond portfolio is sold at the horizon date n. Since the bonds will have $m - n$ periods left until maturity, the market value of the portfolio at this horizon date is uncertain.

Two different adverse events could upset this strategy and make the liquidating value of the portfolio less than the required goal. First, interest rates might decline. Then, the reinvestment rate on the coupons is low, but the market value of the bonds at the horizon date is high; these two factors affect the liquidating value of the portfolio at the horizon date in opposite directions. A second possibility is a rise in interest rates. This would raise

Figure 11.7 Duration Strategy

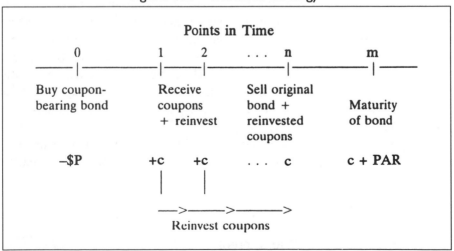

the reinvestment rate on coupons but lower the market value of the bonds on the horizon date. The higher reinvestment rate and the lower market value have opposite impacts upon the liquidating value of the portfolio. The net impact is not clear.

Investors can lock-in the liquidating value of their portfolio on the horizon date by setting the duration of the portfolio equal to the number of periods until the horizon date.[22] This duration strategy is completely effective if two assumptions are met: (1) yield curves are flat and (2) only one small change in interest rates occurs immediately after the portfolio is chosen.

Under the duration immunization strategy, if interest rates rise and the market value of the bonds in the portfolio goes down, the bond coupons are reinvested at high rates of interest, exactly offsetting the decline in the bond's market value. If interest rates decline, offsetting effects occur in the opposite direction. The market value of the bond portfolio rises and the coupons are reinvested at lower rates of interest. The immunizer would be certain of the value of the portfolio at the horizon date for increases and decreases in interest rates.

Table 11.4 illustrates the workings of the duration strategy. An investor has an 11-year horizon, and the interest rate is 10 percent. Perpetual bonds are used to immunize. Their duration is $(1 + y)/y$ or $1.10/.10 = 11$, the horizon of this investor. Perpetual bonds have a par value and price of $100 and coupon of $10 [i.e., $c = yP = (.10)(100)$].

With a zero coupon bond with a maturity of 11 years, the immunizer locks in a terminal value of $(100)(1.10)^{11} = \$285$ for $100 invested at time 0. Will an investor be able to duplicate this result by following a duration strategy?

Consider a case where the interest rate rises from 10 percent to 11 percent immediately after the investment is made. The rate is assumed to remain at 11 percent until year 11. The immunizer buys a perpetual bond for $100 at time zero and then reinvests all of the coupons by buying additional perpetual bonds at 11 percent. The price of a perpetual bond with a $10 coupon is $90.9090 for an interest rate of 11 percent (i.e., $P = c/y = 10/.11 = 90.9090$). Each additional bond, or part of a bond, is purchased at this new price.

The details of the coupons received and bonds purchased are shown in table 11.4. At time 0, the investor purchases 1 bond for $100. At time 0′,

---

[22] See Bierwag (1977) for a proof.

Table 11.4   Duration Immunization Example

Time	Price	Coupon Received	Bonds Purchased	Total # Bonds	Total Value
0	100.00	0	1	1	100.00
0′	90.90	0	0	1	90.90
1	90.90	10	$\frac{10}{90.90}$	1.11	90.90(1.11)
2	90.90	10(1.11)	$\frac{10(1.11)}{90.90}$	$(1.11)^2$	$90.90(1.11)^2$
3	90.90	$10(1.11)^2$	$\frac{10(1.11)^2}{90.90}$	$(1.11)^3$	$90.90(1.11)^3$
4	90.90	$10(1.11)^3$	$\frac{10(1.11)^3}{90.90}$	$(1.11)^4$	$90.90(1.11)^4$
5	90.90	$10(1.11)^4$	$\frac{10(1.11)^4}{90.90}$	$(1.11)^5$	$90.90(1.11)^5$
6	90.90	$10(1.11)^5$	$\frac{10(1.11)^5}{90.90}$	$(1.11)^6$	$90.90(1.11)^6$
7	90.90	$10(1.11)^6$	$\frac{10(1.11)^6}{90.90}$	$(1.11)^7$	$90.90(1.11)^7$
8	90.90	$10(1.11)^7$	$\frac{10(1.11)^7}{90.90}$	$(1.11)^8$	$90.90(1.11)^8$
9	90.90	$10(1.11)^8$	$\frac{10(1.11)^8}{90.90}$	$(1.11)^9$	$90.90(1.11)^9$
10	90.90	$10(1.11)^9$	$\frac{10(1.11)^9}{90.90}$	$(1.11)^{10}$	$90.90(1.11)^{10}$
11	90.90	$10(1.11)^{10}$	$\frac{10(1.11)^{10}}{90.90}$	$(1.11)^{11}$	$90.90(1.11)^{11}$

one instant after the original purchase is made at time 0, the interest rate rises from 10 percent to 11 percent and the bond price drops from $100 to $90.90. At time 1, the investor receives a $10 coupon from his 1 bond and reinvests this coupon at the prevailing bond price of $90.90. The additional bonds purchased are 10/90.90 or .11 bonds, leaving a total of 1.11 bonds worth 90.90(1.11). At time 2, the investor receives a coupon payment of $10 per bond or a total of $10(1.11) that is invested at the price of $90.90. The total number of bonds is $(1.11)^2$ with a market value of $90.90(1.11)^2$. The procedure for later periods is similar.

At time 11, the investor's bonds are worth $90.90(1.11)^{11}$ or $286.49. Had the investor purchased zero coupon bonds at 10 percent at time 0, the value of those bonds would be $285 at time 11. Thus, the duration strategy almost matches the zero coupon strategy. The difference between the two terminal values is small and arises because the change in interest rates (i.e., 1 percent) is relatively large. If the change in interest rates is infinitesimal, the duration strategy gives the same results as the strategy of buying zero coupon bonds.

The duration strategy assumes one change in interest rates and a flat term structure. Now, consider immunization strategies if these two assumptions are relaxed. If multiple changes in interest rates occur, the portfolio can be approximately immunized if portfolio rebalancing occurs after each small change in interest rates. After each change, the duration is set equal to the number of periods until the horizon date. If yield curves are not flat, the duration strategy works approximately if the portfolio is rebalanced each time a small change in interest rates occurs.

In practice, two major drawbacks limit the use of duration immunization strategies employing coupon-bearing bonds. First, the need to rebalance the portfolio frequently results in expensive transactions costs. Second, the biggest advantage of immunization occurs for long horizons. Since the maturity of a bond is larger than its duration, a portfolio with a long duration has a much longer maturity. The lack of long-term bonds limits the use of the strategy. For example, a portfolio with a 20-year duration might require bonds with maturities of 40 years, depending upon the level of interest rates. Since bonds with maturities of more than 30 years are rare, immunization is not practical in this case.

Forward Market Strategy

If there were forward markets for all possible future maturities, an investor could immunize by using forward markets. To illustrate, consider the example in figure 11.8. Suppose an investor wants to immunize, or lock-in, terminal wealth over a ten-year horizon by buying a ten-year coupon-bearing bond. The terminal wealth at year 10 can be locked-in by reinvesting coupons in the forward market. Consider the coupon, c, received at time 1. The investor can contract to reinvest this at the forward rate f_2; then, to reinvest this amount at the forward rate f_3; and so on. The coupon received at time 1 consequently results in a terminal wealth at time 10 of $c(1 + f_2)(1 + f_3) \ldots$ $(1 + f_{10})$. Similarly, the coupon received at time 3 can be reinvested forward with a time 10 value of $c(1 + f_3)(1 + f_4) \ldots (1 + f_{10})$.

Figure 11.8 Forward Market Strategy

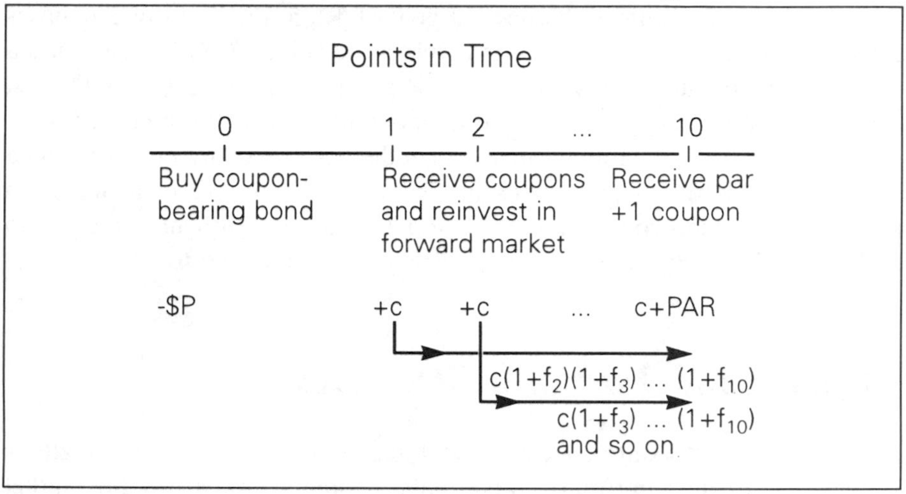

Points in Time

```
      0                   1     2      ...         10
 ──────┃──────────────────┃─────┃─────────────────┃────
  Buy coupon-            Receive coupons   Receive par
  bearing bond          and reinvest in    +1 coupon
                        forward market

  -$P                    +c    +c      ...      c+PAR
                          ┗━━━━━━┓
                                 ┗━━━━━━▶
                              c(1+f₂)(1+f₃) ... (1+f₁₀)
                                ┗━━━━━━▶
                                 c(1+f₃) ... (1+f₁₀)
                                 and so on
```

With the development of futures markets, which are quite similar to forward markets,[23] the need for duration immunization strategies is reduced. However, futures contracts are available only for relatively short maturities; long-horizon investors cannot protect themselves through futures positions.

Dedicated Portfolio Strategy

Another strategy used by bond investors to lock-in a terminal value at their horizon date is called a dedicated portfolio strategy. This strategy assumes a very low reinvestment rate on coupons. In order to achieve the same terminal value with a lower reinvestment rate, the investor must initially invest more money. This will guarantee the minimum goal even under the worst case scenario. However, the initial cost of the dedicated strategy is higher than a duration strategy. With a duration strategy, there are costs for rebalancing after the initial investment. If the strategy falls short of its goals, additional funds will have to be contributed.

One example of a dedicated portfolio would be to assume that the reinvestment rate on coupons is 0. Consider our 11-period duration example and assume a dedicated portfolio strategy. An 11-period par bond is purchased at 10 percent. For a $100 bond, 11 annual coupons of $10 and a par value

---

[23] See Chapter 21 on futures markets.

of $100 at maturity are received for a total cash inflow of $210 [i.e., (11)(10) + 100 = 210]. To achieve the desired goal of $285, the investor purchases 285/210 (or 1.36) bonds with a total purchase price of $136. This initial cost of $136 for the dedicated strategy is greater than the initial $100 cost of the duration strategy. With the assumption of a positive but conservative reinvestment rate, the amount invested in the dedicated strategy is reduced below $136. Zero coupon bonds are extremely desirable in a dedicated strategy. With zero coupon bonds, which have a reinvestment rate equal to the yield to maturity, the total amount invested is reduced to $100.

Other Bond Portfolio Strategies

Some bond investors are concerned with the risk of short-term fluctuations in the value of their portfolio. In particular, if interest rates rise, the market value of the portfolio falls.

Several strategies are available for these investors. The simplest strategy is to invest in very short-term securities. Then, the value of the portfolio is very stable. The disadvantage is the relatively low returns available on short-term bonds.

Two riskier strategies (with higher expected returns) are available. The so-called ladder strategy invests approximately equal proportions of the portfolio in a wide variety of maturities. If interest rates rise, the shorter maturity part of the portfolio has only small price declines. When the shortest maturity bond matures, the proceeds can be reinvested at the higher prevailing interest rate. The total portfolio risk is much lower than investing in a long-term bond exclusively.

The barbell strategy invests equal proportions of the portfolio in short-term and long-term bonds. A rise in interest rates causes the prices of long-term bonds to drop considerably, but those of short-term bonds to remain relatively stable. When the short-term bond matures, reinvestment at the new higher interest rate is available. The barbell strategy is higher risk than the ladder strategy, but much lower risk than 100 percent investment in long-term bonds.

Summary

Bond investors are interested in the sensitivity of their bond holdings to changes in interest rates. Two measures of interest rate sensitivity have been used – duration and elasticity. Holding maturity constant, interest rate sensitivity declines as bond coupon gets larger. Holding coupon constant, interest rate sensitivity increases as maturity increases, except for some very long maturity discount bonds. Shorter maturity, higher coupon bonds are low risk; and longer maturity, lower coupon bonds are high risk.

Duration measures the percentage change in price for an absolute change in bond yields, and elasticity measures the percentage change in price for a proportional change in yields. In most ways, these volatility measures are the same. Elasticity gives a better measure of volatility when comparing bonds with different interest rates.

Some investors are immunizers who want to lock in a terminal value at a particular horizon date. These investors can select from the zero coupon bond, maturity, duration, and dedicated strategies. Buying zero coupon bonds (STRIPS) is the best strategy, if available.

Questions/Problems

1. Assume a yield to maturity of 8 percent. Compute the duration for the following bonds. Assume $100 par values. For the 12 percent coupon bond, compute the duration using three formulas: Equations 11.1, 11.2, and 11.9. Which formula is easier to compute?
   (a) 10 years, zero coupon
   (b) 10 years, 8 percent coupon
   (c) 10 years, 12 percent coupon

2. In problem 1, assume that yields change from 8 to 9 percent. Work out the exact change in price and compare it with the change in price predicted by duration. Explain the difference. Assume $100 par values.

3. Compute the duration of a portfolio composed of equal proportions of a ten-year, zero coupon bond and a ten-year, 8 percent coupon bond, assuming 89% yields to maturity.

4. A perpetual bond has a coupon of $6 and a yield to maturity of 6 percent. Work out the actual percentage change in price and the duration approximation in the following three cases.
   (a) The yield decreases by 1 percent.
   (b) The yield increases by 1 percent.
   (c) The yield increases by 8 percent.

5. For an investor who desires to immunize a portfolio, compare the advantages and disadvantages of a duration strategy versus a dedicated strategy in a real-world situation. How does the zero coupon bond strategy compare with each of these other strategies?

6. Compute the duration of the longest maturity Treasury bond and longest maturity Treasury note listed in *The Wall Street Journal.*

Appendix: Elasticity – Another Volatility Measure

While the sensitivity of bond prices to changes in interest rates has frequently been measured by duration, the **elasticity** of bond price to changes in interest rates is another measure of volatility.[24] Elasticity is equal to (minus) the percentage change in bond price for a percentage change in interest rates. In contrast, duration measures the percentage change in bond price for an absolute change in interest rates. Let elasticity be denoted by E. Then:

$$E = \frac{(-dP)(y)}{(dy)(P)} \tag{11A.1}$$

$$E = \frac{\dfrac{1cy}{(1+y)^2} + \dfrac{2cy}{(1+y)^3} + \cdots + \dfrac{ny(c+\text{PAR})}{(1+y)^{n+1}}}{\text{price}} \tag{11A.2}$$

$$E = \frac{c\left[\dfrac{1-(1+y)^{-n}}{y}\right] + \dfrac{ny(\text{PAR}-c/y)}{(1+y)^{n+1}}}{\text{price}} \tag{11A.3}$$

Elasticity is equal to duration times $y/(1+y)$. That is, elasticity is equivalent to a bond's duration divided by the duration of a perpetual bond, $(1+y)/y$. Consequently, elasticity is a type of relative duration measure.

The earlier propositions about the impact of coupon and maturity upon duration also hold for elasticity. That is, for a given maturity, higher coupon bonds will have lower elasticity. For a given coupon level, longer maturity bonds will have higher elasticity for premium and par bonds; for discount

---

[24] Homer and Liebowitz (1972) explicitly discuss elasticity.

bonds, elasticity increases with maturity until it reaches a maximum at a very large maturity and then declines.

If elasticity is equal to 1, a proportional change in interest rates will bring about the same proportional change in bond prices. If elasticity is less (greater) than 1, a proportional change in interest rates will result in a smaller (greater) proportional change in bond prices. For example, if the interest rate were originally 10 percent and then rose to 12 percent, the proportional change in interest rates would be 20 percent. The estimated change in bond prices would depend upon the elasticity. If elasticity were equal to 1, then the estimated change in bond prices would be 20 percent. If elasticity were 1/2, then the estimated change in bond prices would be (.5)(.2), or 10 percent.

Several properties of elasticity are interesting. First, elasticity must be positive, since bond prices and yields move in opposite directions.[25] Second, elasticity must be less than 1 for premium and par bonds,[26] indicating that a proportional change in yields brings about a smaller proportional change in bond prices. For discount bonds:

$$E \underset{<}{\overset{>}{=}} 1 \text{ as } n \underset{<}{\overset{>}{=}} \frac{1+y}{y - c/\text{PAR}} \qquad (11\text{A}.4)$$

In this equation, bond price volatility becomes quite large for long maturities [i.e., for n greater than $(1 + y)/(y - c/\text{PAR})$], since elasticity is greater than 1. For these long maturities for discount bonds, a proportional change in interest rates brings about a greater proportional change in bond

------

[25] Elasticity is defined as $-(dP/dy)(y/P)$. Since dP/dy is negative, minus dP/dy is positive and elasticity is positive.

[26] To derive these results, set elasticity in equation 11A.3 greater than, equal to, and less than 1. This simplifies to comparing the numerator of equation 11A.3 to price. The coupon terms cancel on both sides, resulting in:

$$\frac{ny(\text{PAR} - c/y)}{(1 + y)^{n+1}} \underset{<}{\overset{>}{=}} \frac{\text{PAR}}{(1 + y)^n}$$

For premium bonds, the left side is negative and for par bonds it is zero, implying elasticity is less than 1.0. For discount bonds, the condition in equation 11A.4 applies.

prices. In general, elasticity is less than 1 and bond prices change by a smaller proportion than the proportional change in interest rates. To compare duration with elasticity, consider the four special types of bonds in table 11.A.1.[27]

Elasticity and the Level of Interest Rates

The relationship between bond price volatility and the level of interest rates is interesting. As interest rates increase, elasticity increases for zero coupon, par, and premium bonds. For discount bonds, elasticity increases except for very long maturities.

This result has an interesting converse. For higher interest rates, a given proportional change in bond price results in a smaller proportional change in yield to maturity for all bonds except very long maturity discount bonds. There are a number of practical implications. First, when rates of interest increase as they have in recent years, the elasticity decreases if the underlying price volatility of the bonds remains constant merely because of the mathematics. Recall from the earlier discussion of duration, higher interest rates result in greater duration for constant price volatility. Second, when compar-

Table 11A.1   Bond Price Volatilities for Special Types of Bonds

Type of Bond	Duration	Elasticity
Zero coupon	n	$\dfrac{ny}{1+y}$
Par	$\dfrac{(1+y)[1-(1+y)^{-n}]}{y}$	$1-(1+y)^{-n}$
Perpetual	$(1+y)y$	1.0
Annuity	$\dfrac{1+y}{y}-\dfrac{n}{(1+y)^n-1}$	$1-\dfrac{ny}{(1+y)[(1+y)^n-1]}$

[27] The results are derived as follows from the duration and elasticity formulas. For zero coupon bonds, set c equal to zero and simplify. For par bonds, set price equal to par. For perpetual bonds, set n equal to infinity. For an annuity, set PAR equal to zero.

ing two bonds with different levels of interest rates (perhaps because of different tax status), the bond with the higher interest rate has lower elasticity in the case where the underlying price volatility is the same. For duration, the volatility as measured by duration increases for the bond with higher interest rates.

These contradictory results raise the question whether the relative yield change (i.e., elasticity) is a better measure of volatility than the absolute yield change (i.e., duration). When interest rates are constant, the two measures are equivalent. But if the level of interest rates changes over time or if two securities with different interest rates are being compared, the two volatility measures give different results. An ideal measure of volatility would remain constant if the underlying volatility remained constant. Since neither measure meets this criterion, the better volatility measure is not clear.

References

Bierwag, G. O., "Immunization, Duration and the Term Structure of Interest Rates," *Journal of Financial and Quantitative Analysis,* 9, December 1977, pp. 725–41.

Bierwag, G. O., *Duration Analysis: Managing Interest Rate Risk,* Cambridge, MA: Ballinger, 1987.

Bierwag, G. O., and G. G. Kaufman, "Coping with the Risk of Interest Rate Fluctuation: A Note," *Journal of Business,* 50, July 1977, pp. 364–70.

Boquist, J. A., G. A. Racette, and G. G. Schlarbaum, "Duration and Risk Assessment for Bonds and Common Stocks: A Note," *Journal of Finance,* 30, 1975, pp. 1360–5.

Brooks, R. and M. Livingston, "Relative Impact of Duration and Convexity on Bond Price Changes," *Financial Practice and Education,* 1992.

Caks, J., W. R. Lane, R. W. Greenleaf, R. G. Joules, "A Simple Formula for Duration," *Journal of Financial Research,* 8, 1985, pp. 245–9.

Fisher, L., and R. L. Weil, "Coping with the Risk of Interest-Rate Fluctuations: Return to Bondholders from Naive and Optimal Strategies," *Journal of Business,* 44, October 1971, pp. 408–31.

Hawawini, G., "On the Relationship Between Macaulay's Bond Duration and the Term to Maturity," *Economic Letters,* 16, 1984, pp. 331–7.

Homer, S. and M. L. Liebowitz, *Inside the Yield Book,* Englewood Cliffs, NJ: Prentice Hall, 1972.

Hopewell, M. H. and G. G. Kaufman, "Bond Price Volatility and Term to Maturity: A General Respecification," *American Economic Review,* 63, September 1973, pp. 749–53.

Livingston, M., "Duration and Risk Assessment for Bonds and Common Stocks: A Note," *Journal of Finance,* 33, March 1978, pp. 293–5.

Livingston, M., "Measuring Bond Price Volatility," *Journal of Financial and Quantitative Analysis,* 14, June 1979, pp. 343–9.

Livingston, M. and J. Caks, "A 'Duration' Fallacy," *Journal of Finance,* 32, March 1977, pp. 185–7.

Livingston, M. and D. Gregory, "The Stripping of U.S. Treasury Securities," New York University Salomon Brothers Center for the Study of Financial Institutions, Monograph 1989–1.

Livingston, M. and D. Gregory, "Development of the Market for U.S. Treasury STRIPS," *Financial Analysts Journal,* 48, March/April 1992, pp. 68–74.

Macaulay, F. R., *Some Theoretical Problems Suggested by the Movements of Interest Rates, Bond Yields, and Stock Prices in the United States since 1856,* New York: National Bureau of Economic Research, 1938.

Malkiel, B. G., *The Term Structure of Interest Rates,* Princeton, NJ: Princeton University Press, 1966.

12

The Term Structure of Interest Rates

Overview

Interest rates differ by maturity, or **term**. This chapter focuses on the reasons why. A schedule of spot interest rates by maturity is called the **term structure of interest rates**. The term structure can be rising, flat, declining, or humped.

The term structure is not directly observable, since no tax-free, default-free zero coupon bonds exist. Analysts generally try to estimate the term structure from the yields for coupon-bearing bonds. A **yield curve** shows the relationship between interest rates and maturity for coupon-bearing bonds. Every quarter, the *Treasury Bulletin* constructs yield curves from U.S. Treasury bills, notes, and bonds, differing in coupon level, call features, and some other characteristics. *The Wall Street Journal* also constructs yield curves from bonds with a wide variety of characteristics.

Figures 12.1 through 12.4 show several common shapes of the yield curve and the dates when these shapes occurred. Figure 12.4 shows a recent yield curve with a very steep slope.

Historical Patterns in Yield Curves

According to Malkiel, the most frequent shape for yield curves is upward sloping.[1] Downward sloping yield curves have occurred at the end of the

---

[1] See Malkiel (1966).

Figure 12.1   Yields on Treasury Securities on June 29, 1979

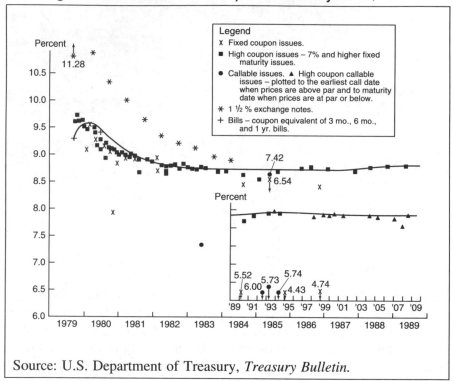

Source: U.S. Department of Treasury, *Treasury Bulletin.*

expansion phase of business cycles. At these business cycle peaks, heavy demand for credit, inflationary pressures, and tight money tend to push all interest rates to high levels. This business cycle pattern for the term structure is illustrated in figure 12.5.

This business cycle pattern implies the following three empirical regularities for term structures:[2]

1. Short-term interest rates are more variable than long-term interest rates.[3]

---

[2] See Malkiel (1966).

[3] While short-term interest rates are more variable than long-term interest rates, the prices of short-term bonds are less variable than the prices of long-term bonds. Thus, long-term bonds are riskier because their prices are more variable.

Figure 12.2   Yields on Treasury Securities on December 31, 1980

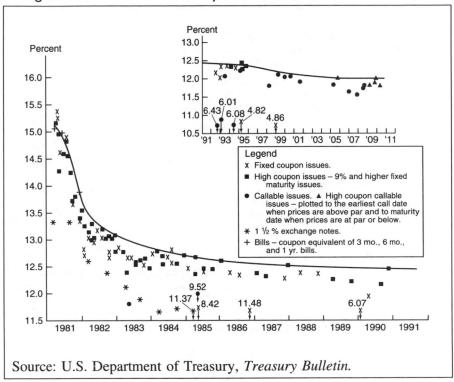

Source: U.S. Department of Treasury, *Treasury Bulletin.*

2. Declining yield curves occur when interest rates are historically high.
3. The most common yield curve shape is upward sloping. On average, yield curves are upward sloping.

The evidence of Reuben Kessel indicates a fourth term structure regularity, independent of the business cycle.[4]

4. For maturities of six months and less, the yield curve has an upward slope most of the time.

The evidence of Ibbotson and Sinquefield (1982) indicates a fifth empirical regularity.

---

[4] See Kessel (1965).

Figure 12.3   Yields on Treasury Securities on September 28, 1984

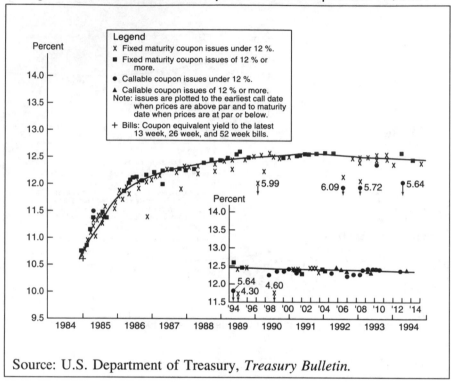

Source: U.S. Department of Treasury, *Treasury Bulletin.*

5. The prices of long-term bonds are more variable than the prices of short-term bonds.

Although the prices of long-term bonds are more variable than the prices of short-term bonds (in regularity 5), the yields on short-term bonds are more variable (in regularity 3). These are not contradictory statements as shown by the following simple example. Consider a one-year bond and a 30-year bond, each with a price and par value of $100 and coupons of $8, implying yields to maturity of 8 percent on each of the bonds. Suppose the yield on the one-year bond increases by 2 percent to 10 percent and the yield on the 30-year bond increases by 1 percent to 9 percent. Then, the new prices are:

$$\text{1-year: } P = \frac{108}{(1.10)} = \$98.18 \tag{12.1}$$

$$\text{30-year: } P = 8\left[\frac{1 - (1.09)^{-30}}{.09}\right] + \frac{100}{(1.09)^{30}} = 89.69 \tag{12.2}$$

Figure 12.4   Yields on Treasury Securities on September 30, 1991

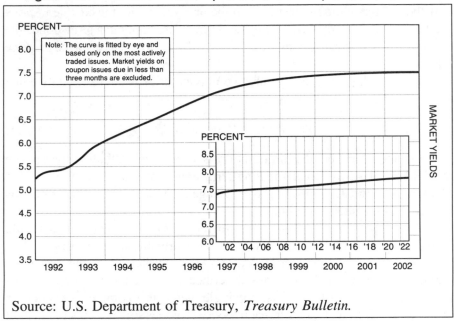

Note: The curve is fitted by eye and based only on the most actively traded issues. Market yields on coupon issues due in less than three months are excluded.

Source: U.S. Department of Treasury, *Treasury Bulletin.*

Figure 12.5   Business Cycle Patterns for the Term Structure

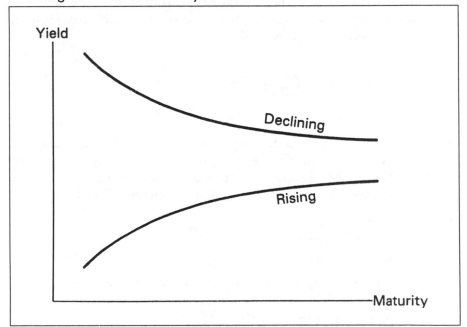

Although the change in the interest rate on the 30-year bond is one half the change in the interest rate on the one-year bond, the change in price for the 30-year bond is five times as large. For the longer term bond, the change in interest rates compounded over 30 periods causes a large price reaction.

In general, the percentage change in bond price is approximately equal to the duration times the change in yield. Formally:

$$\%\Delta\text{Price} = [\text{Duration}][\Delta y] \qquad (12.3)$$

For long-term bonds, the duration is very large. Although the change in yield is relatively small for long-term bonds, the duration effect is big enough to dominate. Thus, the total change in price for long-term bonds is bigger than for short-term bonds.

A theory inconsistent with any of these empirical regularities should be rejected as a valid explanation of the term structure of interest rates. Any complete theory of the term structure should predict all of the preceding regularities. None of the theories described in this chapter predicts all of the empirical regularities. Thus, no single theory is a complete explanation of the term structure. However, each theory provides some interesting insight into the term structure.

Empirically, yield curves become flat for long maturities.[5] Flattening of yield curves occurs for coupon-bearing bonds because of the nature of the yield to maturity computation.[6] Thus, yield curves become flat whatever term structure theory describes reality.

Term Structure Theories

Segmented Markets

In the segmented markets theory, a separate market exists for each maturity.[7] Interest rates for each maturity are set by demand and supply for funds for that maturity. In other theories, investors shift between maturities. In the segmented markets theory, investors do not shift between different maturities.

---

[5] See Malkiel (1966).

[6] Chapter 10 on coupon-bearing bonds presented formal analysis of this point.

[7] See Culbertson (1957).

According to the segmented markets theory, some investors – for example, commercial banks – confine their bond holdings to short maturities, whereas other investors – such as life insurance companies – purchase long-term bonds exclusively and hold these to maturity. Thus, short-term and long-term markets exist independent of the other market.

To illustrate the segmented markets hypothesis, consider commercial banks. Commercial banks typically confine their bond holdings to short maturity bonds, because the prices of these bonds do not change much as interest rates change. These low risk short-term bonds earn modest rates of return and appeal to low risk investors. Consequently, short-term bond holdings serve banks as low risk, low return, highly liquid reserves, available to meet sudden and unexpected needs for immediate funds.

A proponent of the segmented markets hypothesis might argue as follows. When demand for bank loans is low, banks have excess funds, which they invest in short-term bonds. The increased demand by banks drives bond prices up and interest rates down. When demand for bank loans is high, banks reduce their holdings of short-term bonds and use the proceeds to make commercial loans. Sales of bonds lower bond prices and increase short-term interest rates. Thus, the actions of commercial banks affect short-term interest rates, but longer maturity interest rates are not affected.

The segmented markets theory is consistent with any shape of yield curve, but it does not predict any of the empirical regularities of the term structure. In the segmented markets theory, bonds with different maturities are not perfect substitutes for investors. According to Culbertson, perfect substitutes should have the same holding period returns.[8] If bonds with different maturities have different holding period returns, they are imperfect substitutes and markets are segmented by maturity. Empirically, holding period returns differ by maturity, consistent with segmented markets. Elliott and Echols found the supply of bonds of different maturities affects the yields for those maturities – a bigger supply tends to lower prices and increase interest rates.[9]

Increasing Liquidity Premiums

In the theory of increasing liquidity premiums, yields increase as maturity increases for two reasons. First, bond investors are risk averse (that is, they

---

[8] This position has been described as the local expectations hypothesis and is described in detail later.

[9] See Elliott and Echols (February 1976 and March 1976).

prefer lower variability of return). Second, bond prices for longer term bonds are more variable.[10] Bond investors require higher yields to maturity on longer term bonds to compensate for the higher risk.

The concept of risk aversion deserves some discussion.[11] There are two ways to describe risk aversion – through utility functions and through certainty equivalents.

A **utility function** shows the relationship between utility (or subjective value) and the terminal wealth resulting from an investment. All rational investors prefer more wealth to less; their utility functions have a positive slope. For risk-averse investors, additional dollars of wealth add smaller amounts of utility (or subjective value). That is, if the first dollar of wealth adds one unit of utility, the second dollar adds less than one unit of utility, and so on. The resulting utility function is concave (see figure 12.6). For risk-neutral investors, every additional dollar of wealth adds the same amount to utility, indicating a straight line utility function. For risk-seeking investors, additional dollars of wealth add increasing amounts of utility, implying a convex utility function. These utility functions are shown in figure 12.6.

Utility functions with risk-averse, risk-neutral, or risk-seeking sections are quite plausible.[12] An example is shown in figure 12.7, where the investor is risk averse for small amounts of wealth, but becomes a risk seeker for large amounts of wealth.

In a world where all investors are risk neutral, expected return for all investments equals the risk-free interest rate. For risk neutrality, if the risk-free interest rate is 5 percent, all investments – stocks and bonds – have an expected rate of return of 5 percent.

Risk aversion can be analyzed in terms of certainty equivalents. A **certainty equivalent** of a gamble with risky outcomes is defined as an amount of money with certainty making an investor indifferent between the certain cash and the gamble. The following example illustrates certainty equivalents.

At one time there was a television program called "Let's Make a Deal" in which enthusiastic contestants answered straightforward questions for

---

[10] See Hicks (1946).

[11] See Levy and Sarnat (1984) for a thorough and clear discussion of risk aversion and utility functions.

[12] See Levy and Sarnat (1984) for a detailed discussion of this point.

Figure 12.6   Utility Functions

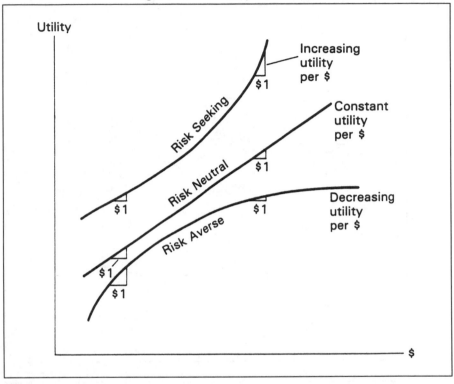

large prizes. After accumulating prizes worth *X* dollars, the contestant was given a choice of leaving with the prizes or giving up these prizes in exchange for an opportunity to undertake a gamble. The gamble involved picking one of three doors. Behind two of the doors were two desirable prizes and behind the third door was a booby prize. Without knowing the location of the booby prize, the contestant had to make a decision – leave with the existing *X* dollars worth of prizes or take the gamble.

Imagine yourself making this important decision to leave with *X* dollars or to take a gamble. Logically, there must be some amount of money (that is, the certainty equivalent) creating indifference between the risky gamble and the certain cash. Suppose you compute the expected value of the gamble by weighting each outcome of the gamble by its probability. In our example each door has a one-third chance of occurring. Therefore, the expected value of the gamble is one-third times the value of the first prize plus one-third times the value of the second prize plus one-third times the value of the

Figure 12.7   A Complicated Utility Function

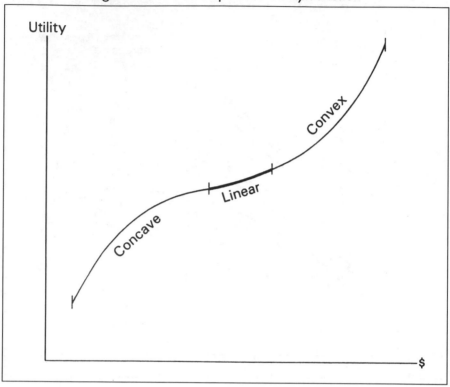

third prize. If the prizes were $20,000, $10,000, and $0, the expected value would be $(1/3)(20,000) + (1/3)(10,000) + (1/3)(0) = \$10,000$.

If a decision maker's certainty equivalent equals the expected value of the gamble, the decision maker is risk neutral. If the certainty equivalent is less (more) than the expected value, the decision maker is risk averse (a risk seeker). In effect, this risk averse decision maker is willing to give up some money (relative to the expected value) to avoid taking the gamble, because one of the outcomes of the gamble is very unfavorable.

Returning to our contestant, suppose the expected value of the gamble is $10,000 and the contestant is risk averse with a certainty equivalent of $8,000. Our contestant should be indifferent between the gamble and the $8,000 with certainty. If the contestant must choose between $6,000 and the gamble, the contestant should prefer the gamble, since the certainty equivalent of the gamble exceeds the $6,000. If the choice is between $9,000 or the gamble, $9,000 is preferable because it exceeds the certainty equivalent.

If all investors are risk neutral, the expected rate of return on all invest-ments equals the risk-free interest rate, implying a flat term structure.[13] If investors are risk averse, the higher risk securities have higher expected returns.

The theory of increasing liquidity premiums assumes two things: (1) risk-averse investors, and (2) greater risk for longer term bonds. To illustrate the basic idea, assume an initially flat term structure, a 10 percent interest rate, a one-year bond and a perpetual bond with annual coupons of $10 and selling at par of $100. If interest rates increase to 11 percent, the price of the one-year bond becomes 110/1.11 = $99.099, a small percentage change of 0.9 percent. The price of the perpetual bond becomes 10/.11 = 90.909, a large percentage change of approximately 9.1 percent. In the liquidity preference theory, the larger price declines for longer maturity bonds causes buyers of long-term bonds to require higher interest rates as compensation for the greater risk of declining prices. Therefore, the initial yields on the one-period and the perpetual bonds cannot be 10 percent. The perpetual bond sells at a higher yield to compensate for the larger risk of price declines.

The liquidity preference theory overlooks bond issuers. Some bond issuers prefer long-term funds, locking in a fixed interest rate. Other bond issuers prefer short-term or intermediate-term funds. A complete term struc-ture theory should account for the maturity needs of all borrowers.

The theory of increasing liquidity premiums implies yield curves that are always rising.[14] The empirical evidence contradicts this implication. Yield curves usually slope upward, but sometimes they slope downward. Declining yield curves and humped yield curves contradict the theory.

Preferred Habitat

In the **preferred habitat theory**, investors prefer to purchase bonds of particular maturities – not necessarily short- or long-term – and require

---

[13] This statement assumes that investors' expectations of future interest rates are the same for all future dates. See the following discussion of the unbiased expectations hypothesis.

[14] This statement is correct if the increasing liquidity premium theory, by itself, describes the world.

higher yields to buy bonds of other maturities.[15] The preferred habitat theory is effectively a combination of the segmentation theory and the liquidity preference theory. Instead of always preferring short maturities, as in the liquidity preference theory, investors may prefer other maturities, depending upon their individual investment objectives. Instead of being totally unwilling to shift from the preferred maturity as in the segmentation theory, the preferred habitat theory suggests a willingness to purchase nearby maturities, but only at higher interest rates. For a maturity farther from the preferred habitat, the required interest rate is higher to compensate the buyer for the risks involved.

In the liquidity preference theory, longer maturity implies greater risk to the buyer of a bond. The preferred habitat theory allows for the possibility that shorter maturity bonds might be riskier.[16] For example, assume an investor who wants to invest for ten periods and is concerned exclusively with the value of the portfolio at the end of the ten-year period and not with the value on intervening dates. For this individual, investing in one-year securities and then reinvesting repeatedly in other one-year securities is riskier than locking-in a fixed return by buying a ten-year zero coupon bond. If such investors are common in the market, short-term interest rates are higher than longer term rates because of risk aversion.

The preferred habitat theory is consistent with any shape of the term structure. But the theory does not, by itself, predict any of the five empirical regularities.

Money Substitute

In the money substitute theory of Reuben Kessel, very short-term bonds are close substitutes for holding cash.[17] According to this view, many investors restrict their purchases to short-term money market instruments because the risks associated with these are very small. Consequently, the prices of money market instruments are driven up and their rates down relative to longer maturity rates.

---

[15] See Modigliani and Sutch (1966), Modigliani (1967), and Woodward (1983).

[16] Woodward (1983) has presented a rigorous theoretical analysis of the relationship between maturity preferences and risk.

[17] See Kessel (1965).

The money substitute theory assumes a large number of investors in short-term bonds relative to the supply. That is, buyers of bonds have a stronger preference for very short maturities than issuers. This drives bond prices up and interest rates down.

The main justification for this belief is the restricted options available to these short-term investors. A corporation with temporarily excess funds does not want to take on much risk of loss. This constraint eliminates most other investments from consideration. For example, corporations with temporarily excess cash for two weeks want no risk of loss and minimal transactions costs. A two-week money market instrument is a very attractive investment.

An additional justification for the money substitute theory is the preference of issuers for somewhat longer maturities. In order to minimize the costs of issuing securities, issuers attempt to reduce the frequency of issue by issuing longer maturity instruments less frequently.

The money substitute theory predicts the tendency of the yield curve to have upward slopes for very short maturities. The money substitute theory does not, by itself, predict any of the other empirical regularities.

Expectations Hypothesis

The most widely discussed theory of the term structure of interest rates is the expectations hypothesis. This theory is composed of several similar, but different theories.[18] All of the expectations theories have the common thread that market participants are indifferent about holding bonds of different maturities. We discuss two of these theories.

In the **local expectations hypothesis**, the expected rate of return over the next period for bonds of all maturities is the risk-free interest rate, that is, the return on the shortest maturity bond. The local expectations theory does not provide any insights about the shape of the yield curve or the empirical regularities. Several empirical studies have examined holding period returns on bonds of different maturities and found a difference in

---

[18] See Cox, Ingersoll, and Ross (1981).

average returns.[19] Thus, the local expectations hypothesis is not empirically true.

Several papers have shown the local expectations hypothesis to be approximately the same as the unbiased expectations hypothesis (discussed next) both theoretically and empirically.[20] Since the unbiased hypothesis is much more intuitively appealing, further discussion of the local hypothesis is unnecessary.

The **unbiased expectations hypothesis** is the most widely discussed of the expectations theories. In the unbiased expectations hypothesis, the current forward interest rates are determined by the market's anticipations of future interest rates. For the two-period case, the forward rate for period 2 is an unbiased predictor of the one-period spot rate observed one-period later. In mathematical terms:

$$_0f_2 = E[_1R_1] \tag{12.4}$$

In other words, the forward interest rate is determined by people's anticipation of the average spot interest rate next period. If the market believes the spot interest rate next period will be high relative to the current spot rate, then the forward interest rate is higher than the current spot rate; the current yield curve is rising. Thus, the shape of the current yield curve is linked to anticipations of interest rates in the future. Some concrete examples are presented shortly.

In the general case:

$$_0f_j = E[_{j-1}R_1] \tag{12.5}$$

where:

---

[19] The holding period return over the next period is computed as follows:

$$\frac{\text{ending price} - \text{beginning price} + \text{coupon}}{\text{beginning price}}$$

[20] See Brooks and Livingston (1992a and 1992b) and Campbell (1986). Brooks and Livingston (1992b) show that with continuously compounded interest rates in discrete time, the local and unbiased expectations hypotheses are identical. Since discretely compounded interest rates are very close to continuously compounded rates, the local and unbiased expectations hypotheses are virtually indistinguishable in practice.

E = the expectation

$_0f_j$ = the forward rate observed at time zero (presubscript) for period j (postsubscript).

$_{j-1}R_1$ = the spot rate observed at time $j - 1$ (presubscript) and lasting one period (postsubscript)

This notation is illustrated in figure 12.8.

According to the unbiased expectations hypothesis, the forward interest, $_0f_2$, is an unbiased predictor of the spot rate, $_1R_1$, observed one period later; on average, the forward rate equals the subsequent spot rate. The forward rate $_0f_3$ is an unbiased predictor of the spot rate $_2R_1$ observed two periods later, and so on (see figure 12.9).

The unbiased expectations hypothesis links the forward rates observed today to expectations of future spot interest rates. Since today's spot rates are the geometric mean of today's forward rates,[21] the unbiased expectations hypothesis ties today's spot interest rates to spot interest rates expected to prevail in the future.

The unbiased expectations hypothesis is consistent with any yield curve shape. Under this hypothesis, a flat yield curve occurs if the market expects all future interest rates to equal the current one-period spot rate. For example, if the current spot rate is 6 percent and all expected future spot rates are 6 percent, all current forward and spot rates are 6 percent (see figure 12.10).

Figure 12.8 Elapsed Time and Spot and Forward Interest Rates

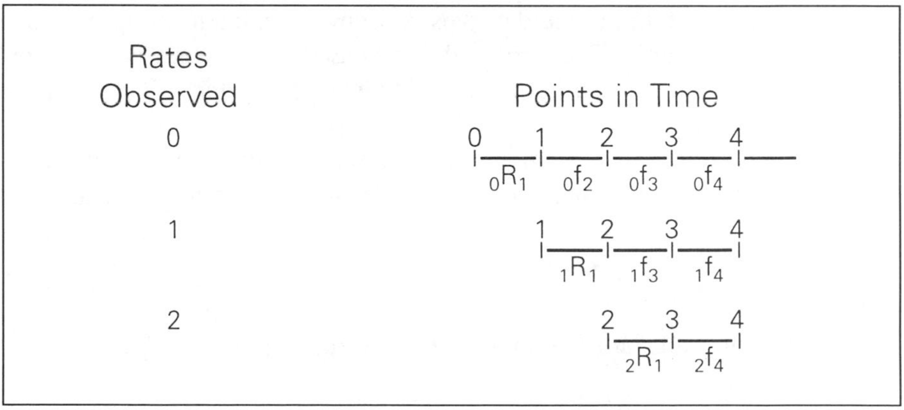

[21] See Chapter 9 on spot and forward interest rates.

Figure 12.9   Unbiased Expectations Hypothesis: Forward Rates Predict
Future Spot Interest Rates

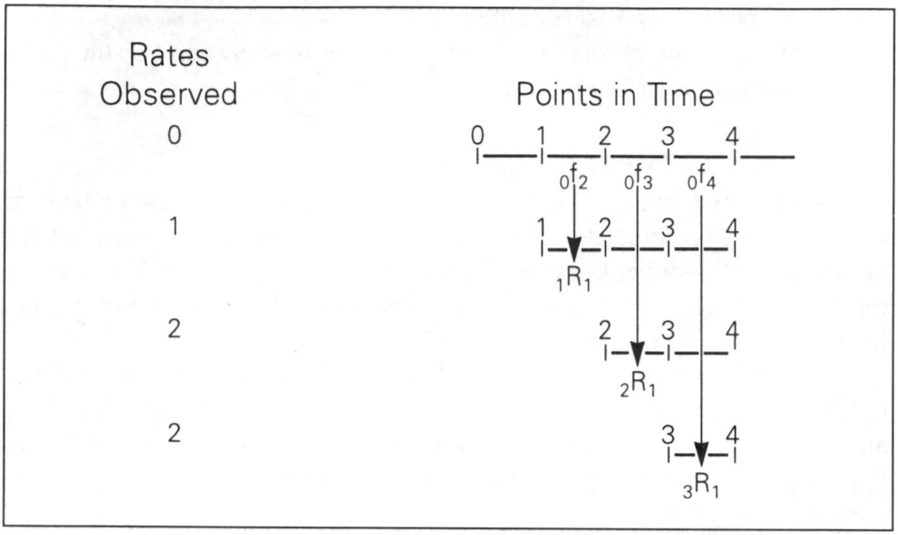

If the market anticipates higher future interest rates, the yield curve rises. In figure 12.11, the market expects rising future interest rates, and the current spot rates also rise.[22] If the forward interest rates decline monotonically, the spot rates decline also. Figure 12.12 illustrates how a declining yield curve can occur.

One of the empirical regularities mentioned earlier in this chapter is the tendency for declining yield curves to occur when interest rates are high by historical standards. The unbiased expectations hypothesis is consistent with this pattern if the market is forecasting interest rates to decline from their current levels.

An unusual and interesting yield curve shape is the humped (or humpbacked) yield curve. Humped yield curves occur when interest rates are high

---

[22] The spot rates are computed from the following formula:

$$(1 + {_0R_n})^n = (1 + {_0R_1})(1 + {_0f_2}) \ldots (1 + {_0f_n})$$

For example, for the four-period case:

$$(1 + {_0R_4})^4 = (1 + {_0R_1})(1 + {_0f_2})(1 + {_0f_3})(1 + {_0f_4})$$

Figure 12.10   Example of a Flat Term Structure

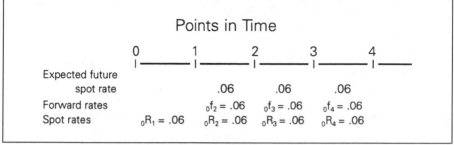

Figure 12.11   Example of a Rising Term Structure

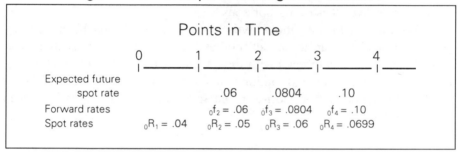

Figure 12.12   Example of a Declining Term Structure

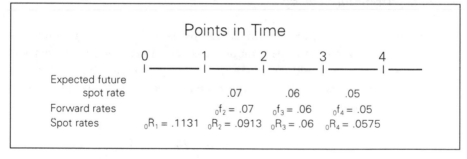

by historical standards. Under the unbiased expectations hypothesis, humped yield curves occur if the market expects interest rates to rise for a while and then to decline. Figure 12.13 presents an example where the current spot rate is 5.01 percent, and the forward rate rises to 7 percent and then declines to 6 percent and 5 percent.

The unbiased expectations hypothesis has been faulted by some observers for making the unrealistic behavioral assumption that investors can forecast very distant future interest rates. These distant forecasts are essential for setting the forward interest rates. How can investors forecast interest

Figure 12.13   Humped Term Structure

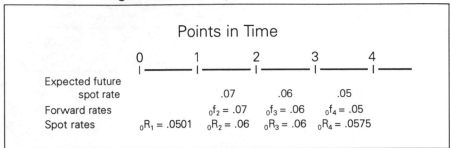

rates 10, 15, 20, or 25 years into the future when there is so much uncertainty about events over these long horizons?

The unbiased expectations hypothesis does not, by itself, predict any of the empirical regularities of yield curves. However, if the unbiased expectations hypothesis is combined with the additional hypothesis of greater variability of nearer term expectations of future rates, the combined theory predicts the tendency for short-term interest rates to be more variable than long-term rates.

Combining the Unbiased Expectations Hypothesis with the Increasing Liquidity Premium Theory

Combining the unbiased expectations hypothesis with the liquidity premium theory results in a more powerful theory. This combined theory is consistent with any shape of the yield curve and predicts upward sloping yield curves most of the time. In the combined theory, the forward rate equals the expected future spot rate plus a liquidity premium:

$$_0f_j = E[_{j-1}R_1] + L_j \qquad\qquad (12.6)$$

where L_j is the liquidity premium for maturity j. Liquidity premiums may increase with maturity (that is, L_j is greater than or equal to L_{j-1}). For example, suppose an expected future spot interest rate of 5 percent, and a liquidity premium of 1 percent for period 2, 1.5 percent for period 3, and 2.0 percent for period 4. Then, the forward and spot rates are as shown in figure 12.14. The spot interest rates increase with maturity, although the market expects future spot rates to be unchanged from the current one-period spot rate.

With the combined theory, a declining term structure is possible even though liquidity premiums increase with maturity. For example, suppose

Figure 12.14 Rising Term Structure and Constant Expected Future Interest Rates

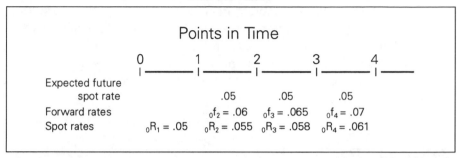

there is a liquidity premium of 1 percent for period 2, 1.5 percent for period 3, and 2.0 percent for period 4, but with the declining expected future spot interest rates shown in figure 12.15. The spot rates decline because the fall in the expected future spot rate is greater than the increase in the liquidity premium.

Humpbacked Curves

The most unusual yield curve is the hump(back)ed curve. This curve occurs when interest rates are high by historical standards. An actual example of a humped yield curve from the *Treasury Bulletin* was presented earlier.

There are several explanations of humped curves.[23] First, according to the unbiased expectations hypothesis, a humped curve occurs if interest rates

Figure 12.15 Rising Liquidity Premiums and a Declining Term Structure

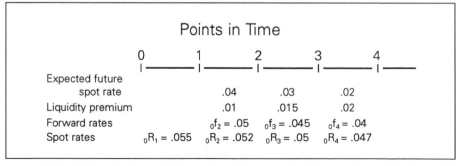

---

[23] See Livingston (1977).

are expected to rise over the next several periods and then decline. An example was given earlier in the chapter. Second, humped curves can result from skewed expectations of future interest rates. That is, the market may believe constant future interest rates are likely, but a small probability exists for considerably lower interest rates in the future; then the yield curve is humped. Humped yield curves might also occur in a segmented market, with a particular segment of the yield curve having higher rates than shorter and longer maturities.

Holding Period Returns

The holding period return (or realized return) depends upon the current spot interest rate and changes in forward rates over time. Let:

$_0P_n$ = the price observed at time 0 of a zero coupon bond maturing at time n

$_1P_n$ = the price observed at time 1 of a zero coupon bond maturing at time n

HPR = holding period return

The holding period return on this bond is:

$$\text{HPR} = \frac{_1P_n}{_0P_n} \tag{12.7}$$

The prices of the two bonds can be expressed in terms of spot and forward interest rates.

$$_0P_n = \frac{1}{(1 + {_0R_1})(1 + {_0f_2})(1 + {_0f_3}) \ldots (1 + {_0f_n})} \tag{12.8}$$

$$_1P_n = \frac{1}{(1 + {_1R_1})(1 + {_1f_3}) \ldots (1 + {_1f_n})} \tag{12.9}$$

Substitute the definitions of prices into the holding period return, equation 12.7.

$$\text{HPR} = \frac{(1 + {_0R_1})(1 + {_0f_2})(1 + {_0f_3}) \ldots (1 + {_0f_n})}{(1 + {_1R_1})(1 + {_1f_3}) \ldots (1 + {_1f_n})} - 1 \tag{12.10}$$

Equation 12.10 is approximately the same as:

$$\text{HPR} = {}_0R_1 + [{}_0f_2 - {}_1R_1] + [{}_0f_3 - {}_1f_3] + \ldots + [{}_0f_n - {}_1f_n] \quad (12.11)$$

From equation 12.11, the holding period return is approximately the current spot rate $({}_0R_1)$ plus the difference between the second period forward rate and next period's spot rate $({}_0f_2 - {}_1R_1)$ plus the sum of the changes in the forward rates $([{}_0f_3 - {}_1f_3] + \ldots + [{}_0f_n - {}_1f_n])$. Thus, the holding period return depends upon the forward rates and various future rates. Consider the expected holding period return:

$$E(\text{HPR}) = {}_0R_1 + [{}_0f_2 - E({}_1R_1)] + [{}_0f_3 - E({}_1f_3)] + \ldots + [{}_0f_n - E({}_1f_n)]$$
$$(12.12)$$

In equation 12.12, the expected holding period return equals the current spot interest rate $({}_0R_1)$ if the forward rate for period two $({}_0f_2)$ equals the expected spot rate next period $[E({}_1R_1)]$ and the more distant forward rates $({}_0f_3)$ equal the expected forward rates next period $[E({}_1f_3)]$. The terms with the differences between the forward rates and the expected future rates represent risk premiums. If these terms are positive, there are risk premiums and the expected holding period return is higher than the current spot rate. In the expectations hypothesis, the forward rates equal the expected future rates, the expected holding period return equals the spot interest rate for all bonds, and there are no risk premiums.[24] In contrast, in the increasing liquidity premium theory, longer term bonds have forward rates higher than the expected future rates, and the expected return exceeds the current spot interest rate.

In the case of two periods, the holding period return is approximately:

$$\text{HPR} = {}_0R_1 + [{}_0f_2 - {}_1R_1] \quad (12.13)$$

The holding period return is the one-period spot rate plus the difference between the forward rate and the spot rate next period. This difference is often called the forecast error.

---

[24] Cox, Ingersoll, and Ross (1981) distinguish among various forms of the expectations hypothesis. Brooks and Livingston (1992a and b) show the local and unbiased expectations hypotheses to be essentially indistinguishable for practical purposes.

The expected holding period return is:

$$E(\text{HPR}) = {}_0R_1 + [{}_0f_2 - E({}_1R_1)] \tag{12.14}$$

The expected holding period return is the one-period spot rate plus the difference between the forward rate and the expected future spot rate. This difference is called the liquidity premium, L_2. If the expectations hypothesis holds, the forward rate equals the expected future spot rate and the liquidity premium is zero. If the combined theory applies, the forward rate equals the expected future spot rate plus a liquidity premium.

Summary

Yield curves exhibit five empirical regularities: (1) Short-term interest rates are more variable than long-term interest rates; (2) declining yield curves occur when interest rates are historically high; (3) the most common yield curve shape is upward sloping; (4) for maturities of six months and less, the yield curve has an upward slope most of the time; (5) long-term bond prices are more variable than short-term bond prices.

Three types of theories of the term structure are the segmented markets theory, liquidity theories, and expectations theories. Each of these theories provides some insights, but none provides a complete explanation of yield curves and their empirical regularities. Table 12.1 summarizes the predictive value of the various theories.

Table 12.1 Predictions of the Theories

	Consistent with:	
Theory	Yield Curve Shapes	Empirical Regularity Number
Segmented markets	Any	
Increasing liquidity premiums	Rising	3,5
Preferred habitat	Any	
Money substitute	Rising	4,5
Local expectations		
Unbiased expectations	Any	
Combined	Any	3,5

Questions/Problems

1. Describe the major empirical regularities of the term structure of interest rates.

2. Explain each of the major term structure theories.

3. To what extent are the theories consistent with the empirical regularities?

4. Which of the term structure theories are consistent with rising, flat, declining, or humped yield curves?

5. Assume an initially flat term structure with all interest rates equal to 6 percent. Compute the price change for a one-year par bond if the interest rate increases by 2 percent. Then compute the price change on a perpetual par bond if the interest rate on this bond increases by 1 percent. Compute the durations of each bond. Which bond has a greater percentage price change and why?

6. Explain the concepts of risk neutrality, risk aversion, and risk seeking in terms of marginal utility and certainty equivalents.

7. Michelle is indifferent between $100 and the following gamble. Is she risk averse, risk neutral, or a risk seeker?

	Gamble		
Outcomes	$0	$100	$200
Probabilities	.2	.6	.2

8. How does your answer to question 7 change if Michelle is indifferent between $80 and the gamble? What if she is indifferent between $110 and the gamble?

9. What additional assumptions would make the unbiased expectations hypothesis consistent with the empirical regularities?

10. You observe the following term structure. What term structure theories are consistent with it?

Maturity (years)	Spot Rate
1	.12
2	.14
3	.05
4	.04

11. Assume the combined theory explains the term structure. The one-period spot rate is 5 percent, the expected spot rate next period is 7 percent, and the liquidity premium is 2 percent. What is the two-period spot interest rate?

12. Assume the following term structure: $_0R_1 = .04$ and $_0f_2 = .08$. Compute the holding period return over the next period for a two-period zero coupon bond for each of the following values for next period's spot interest rate: $5, 8 percent, 12 percent.

13. You observe the following interest rates for the current and next periods. Compute the exact holding period return for a four-period zero coupon bond. Also compute the approximate return using the approximation in the text.

$$_0R_1 = .05, \ _0f_2 = .06, \ _0f_3 = .07, \ _0f_4 = .08$$
$$_1R_1 = .055, \ _1f_3 = .065, \ _1f_4 = .078$$

Appendix: Testing the Unbiased Expectations Hypothesis

Several empirical studies have tested whether forward interest rates are unbiased predictors of subsequent spot interest rates.[25] If the unbiased expectations hypothesis is true, then the forward rate $_0f_2$ should predict the spot interest rate in the next period. That is, the mean of $_0f_2$ should equal the mean of $_1R_1$. Empirically, forward interest rates are upwardly biased estimates of future spot rates, that is, forward interest rates are high relative to actually realized rates. For example, the mean of $_0f_2$ is higher than the mean of $_1R_1$.

---

[25] See Kessel (1965) and Fama (1976).

Furthermore, for more distant forward interest rates, the bias tends to increase. This finding is consistent with liquidity premiums.

Another procedure for testing the unbiased expectations hypothesis is to test whether the following condition holds:

$$_1R_1 = a + b[_0f_2]$$ (12A.1)

If the unbiased expectations hypothesis is true, then coefficient a should equal zero and coefficient b should equal one. There is some evidence that this relationship is true for three-month Treasury bills.[26]

Another approach[27] is to subtract the current spot interest rate from both sides of equation 12A.1 and test whether:

$$_1R_1 - {_0R_1} = a + b[_0f_2 - {_0R_1}]$$ (12A.2)

If the unbiased expectations hypothesis is true, then coefficient a should equal 0 and coefficient b should equal 1. The reason is that $_0f_2 - {_0R_1}$ represents the predicted change in the spot interest rate if the unbiased expectations hypothesis is true. The term $_1R_1 - {_0R_1}$ is the actual change in the spot interest rate. The equation merely says that the actual change in the spot interest rate should equal the change predicted by the unbiased expectations hypothesis. The empirical evidence indicates that coefficient b is a positive number less than 1. This is inconsistent with the unbiased expectations hypothesis. But the evidence does support the view that changes predicted by the forward interest rates are related to actual changes. If forward rates are a function of the market's anticipations of future rates, then the evidence is consistent with some type of expectations hypothesis, although not unbiased expectations.

A widely discussed procedure for testing the unbiased expectations hypothesis is the error-learning model of D. Meiselman.[28] Meiselman theorized that if the unbiased expectations hypothesis is true, forward rates are not perfect predictors of the subsequent spot rates. Then unanticipated forecast errors, or surprises, for the shortest term forward rate (that is, $_0f_2 - {_1R_1}$)

---

[26] See Hamburger and Platt (1975).

[27] See Fama (December 1984a).

[28] See Meiselman (1962).

should be highly related to revisions in more distant forward rates (that is, the revision $_1f_n - _0f_n$, where $n > 2$). Meiselman hypothesized that:

$$_1f_n - _0f_n = a + b[_1R_1 - _0f_2] \qquad (12A.3)$$

According to Meiselman, coefficient a should be zero and coefficient b should be positive if the unbiased expectations hypothesis is true. In equation 12A.3, the change in the distant forward rate $(_1f_n - _0f_n)$ is related to the change in the shortest maturity forward rate $(_1R_1 - _0f_2)$. If the actual rate, $_1R_1$, is greater than the forecasted rate, $_0f_2$, equation 12A.3 indicates that the distant forward rates should be revised upward. Since error learning merely indicates a positive correlation between forward interest rates, error learning can exist even if the unbiased expectations hypothesis does not hold. A positive correlation coefficient between forward rates shows forward rates are affected by some of the same factors. The unbiased expectations hypothesis makes a much more restrictive assumption.

To summarize, anticipations of future interest rates incorporated in forward interest rates are related to subsequent spot rates, that is, forward rates incorporate forecasts of the future. But the anticipations incorporated in forward rates are biased predictors rather than unbiased predictors. The evidence is consistent with an expectations hypothesis, but not an unbiased one.

Linking Theory with Empirical Tests

Theoretically, the term structure of interest rates is concerned with spot (or zero-coupon) interest rates, $R_1, R_2, \ldots, R_n$. Recall that R_1 is the discount rate for funds received 1 period into the future, R_2 is the discount rate for funds received 2 periods into the future, and so on.

Although term structure theories are couched in terms of spot interest rates, most empirical evidence is based upon yields to maturity from coupon-bearing bonds. Some investigators try to deduce spot rates from yields on coupon-bearing bonds, but the validity of these approximations has never been established.[29] Some empirical research uses Treasury bill data. Since

---

[29] See McCulloch (1975) and Echols and Elliott (1976). Some recent papers have used models that asymptotically flatten out for long maturities. See Barrett (1988) and Siegel and Nelson (1988).

Treasury bills are zero coupon securities, use of Treasury bill data solves the problem of coupon effects. Treasury bills are restricted to maturities of one year or less, limiting study of the term structure to these short maturities.

In recent years, the availability of Treasury STRIPS provides a tempting data source for studying the term structure. Because STRIPS are zero coupon bonds, adjustments for coupon are unnecessary. However, STRIPS have a complicated method of taxation, resulting in the buyer of STRIPS having tax liabilities over the life of the bond.[30] Because of these tax liabilities, STRIPS are not truly zero coupon securities to taxable buyers.

References

Barrett, W. B., "Term Structure Modeling for Pension Liability Discounting," *Financial Analysts Journal,* 44, November/December 1988, pp. 63–7.

Brooks, R. and M. Livingston, "The Difference between the Local and Unbiased Expectations Hypotheses," *Review of Quantitative Finance and Accounting,* 1, 1992a, pp. 377–90.

Brooks, R. and M. Livingston, "The Local versus Unbiased Expectations Hypotheses with Discrete Compounding," *Journal of Business Finance and Accounting,* 19, 1992b, pp. 877–88.

Campbell, J. Y., "A Defense of Traditional Hypotheses about the Term Structure," *Journal of Finance,* 41, March 1986, pp. 183–93.

Cox, J., J. E. Ingersoll, Jr., and S. A. Ross, "A Reexamination of Traditional Hypothesis about the Term Structure of Interest Rates," *Journal of Finance,* 36, September 1981, pp. 769–99.

Culbertson, J. M., "The Term Structure of Interest Rates," *Quarterly Journal of Economics,* 71, November 1957, pp. 485–517.

---

[30] See Chapter 18 on taxation for a discussion of the tax treatment of STRIPS.

Dobson, S. W., R. C. Sutch, and D. E. Vanderford, "An Evaluation of Alternative Empirical Model of the Term Structure of Interest Rates," *Journal of Finance,* 31, September 1976, pp. 1035–65.

Echols, M. and J. W. Elliott, "A Quantitative Yield Curve Model for Estimating the Term Structure of Interest Rates," *Journal of Financial and Quantitative Analysis,* 11, 1976, pp. 87–114.

Elliott, J. W., and M. E. Echols, "Market Segmentation, Speculative Behavior and the Term Structure of Interest Rates," *Review of Economics and Statistics,* 59, February 1976, pp. 40–9.

Elliott, J. W., and M. E. Echols, "Rational Expectations in a Disequilibrium Model of the Term Structure," *American Economic Review,* 66, March 1976, pp. 28–44.

Fama, E. F., "Forward Rates as Predictors of Future Spot Rates," *Journal of Financial Economics,* 3, October 1976, pp. 361–77.

Fama, E. F., "The Information in the Term Structure," *Journal of Financial Economics,* 13, December 1984a, pp. 509–28.

Fama, E. F., "Term Premiums in Bond Returns," *Journal of Financial Economics,* 13, December 1984b, pp. 529–46.

Fisher, I., *Appreciation and Interest,* New York: Macmillan, 1896.

Fisher, I., *The Theory of Interest,* New York: Macmillan, 1930.

Hamburger, M. J., and E. N. Platt, "The Expectations Hypothesis and the Efficiency of the Treasury Bill Market," *Review of Economics and Statistics,* 57, May 1975, pp. 190–9.

Heath, D., R. Jarrow, and A. Morton, "Bond Pricing and the Term Structure of Interest Rates: A Discrete Time Approximation," *Journal of Financial and Quantitative Analysis,* 25, 1990, pp. 419–40.

Hicks, J. R., *Value and Capital,* 2e, London: Oxford University Press, 1946.

Ibbotson, R. G. and R. A. Sinquefield, *Stocks, Bonds, Bills and Inflation: The Past and the Future,* Charlottesville, VA: The Financial Analysts Research Federation, 1982.

Kessel, R. A., "The Cyclical Behavior of the Term Structure of Interest Rates," in *Essays in Applied Price Theory,* Chicago: The University of Chicago Press, 1965.

Levy, H. and M. Sarnat, *Portfolio and Investment Selection: Theory and Practice,* Englewood Cliffs, NJ: Prentice Hall, 1984.

Livingston, M., "A Theory of Humpbacked Bond Yield Curves," *Journal of Finance,* 32, December 1977, pp. 1747–51.

Longstaff, F. A., "Time Varying Term Premia and Traditional Hypotheses About the Term Structure," *Journal of Finance,* 45, 1990, pp. 1307–14.

Malkiel, B. G., *The Term Structure of Interest Rates,* Princeton, NJ: Princeton University Press, 1966.

McCulloch, J. H., "An Estimate of the Liquidity Premium," *Journal of Political Economy,* 83, January/February 1975, pp. 95–119.

Meiselman, D., *The Term Structure of Interest Rates,* Englewood Cliffs, NJ: Prentice Hall, 1962.

Modigliani, F., "Debt Management and The Term Structure of Interest Rates: An Empirical Analysis of Recent Experience," *Journal of Political Economy,* 75, Supplementary August 1967, pp. 569–89.

Modigliani, F. and R. Sutch, "Innovations in Interest Rate Policy," *American Economic Review,* 56, May 1966, pp. 178–97.

Nelson, C. R., *The Term Structure of Interest Rates,* New York: Basic Books, 1972.

Roll, R., *The Behavior of Interest Rates: An Application of the Efficient Market Model to U.S. Treasury Bills,* New York: Basic Books, 1970.

Sarig, O. and A. Warga, "Bond Price Data and Bond Market Liquidity," *Journal of Financial and Quantitative Analysis,* 24, 1989, pp. 367–78.

Siegel, A. F. and C. R. Nelson, "Long-term Behavior of Yield Curves," *Journal of Financial and Quantitative Analysis,* 23, March 1988, pp. 105–10.

Woodward, S., "The Liquidity Premium and the Solidity Premium," *American Economic Review,* 73, June 1983, pp. 348–61.

13

Default Risk

Overview

For corporate bonds, default by the bond issuer is always a possibility. The evidence indicates an increasing rate of corporate default in recent years as well as an increase in the size of failed firms.[1]

Every corporate bond issue has an **indenture** – a formalized contract between the issuing firm, the bondholders, and a trustee. The indenture specifies the obligations of the firm to the bondholders, including the coupon payments, the maturity, the call feature, call prices, and sinking fund requirements. The bond trustee is appointed to act on behalf of the bondholders, who might otherwise find it difficult to protect their own interests. Consequently, the trustee must be independent of the issuing firm. Typically, the trustee will be the trust department of a large bank. The firm pays the trustee a fee as stated in the bond indenture.

A bond indenture contains protective covenants, which are prohibitions on the actions of the firm. The basic idea of protective covenants is to protect the bondholders from possible firm or stockholder actions that might be harmful to the bondholder.[2] As a simple example, suppose a firm issues a mortgage bond which has specific assets pledged as collateral. To protect this pledged collateral, the indenture includes protective covenants, prohibiting the sale of the pledged asset or the use of this collateral for some other

---

[1] See Altman (1983).

[2] For further information on covenants, see Smith and Warner (1979) and Malitz (1986).

loan, and requiring proper upkeep. Protective covenants restricting dividend payments to stockholders are common. A dividend restriction prevents the firm from liquidating assets and paying the proceeds to stockholders or from underinvesting in new assets. Many other protective covenants are included in bond indentures as standard practice.

The term **default** means a violation of any part of the bond indenture including nonpayment of interest and/or violation of a protective covenant. For example, if a protective covenant in the indenture requires the firm's current ratio (i.e., current assets divided by current liabilities) to be above 2.0, the firm is in default if the ratio falls below 2.0. A default requires the trustee to act on behalf of the bondholders. After default, one possibility is a renegotiation of the contact; this is likely to occur if the default is a minor violation of the indenture. A second possibility is to file for bankruptcy (see figure 13.1).

A bankruptcy is a legal proceeding administered by special bankruptcy courts. The firm itself or the creditors can file to begin a bankruptcy proceeding. During the bankruptcy proceeding, the court protects the firm's assets and appoints someone to run the firm's operations to avoid poor management practices and/or disappearance of the firm's assets.

Bankruptcy courts perform a special and important function for the legal system.[3] To see the value of the bankruptcy courts, consider a situation

Figure 13.1   Financial Distress, Default, and Bankruptcy

Time Sequence of Alternatives			
——————>——————>——————>——————			
Financial Distress	1. Default	1. Bankruptcy	1. Reorganize
	2. Sell assets	2. Renegotiate	2. Liquidate
	3. Sell equity		
	4. Merge		
	5. Borrow more		
	6. Use depreciation		
	7. Government assistance		

[3] See Jackson (1986) for an excellent discussion of the reasons for bankruptcy courts.

of default without any bankruptcy courts. Imagine a firm that has defaulted on its financial obligations to its ten creditors. Without bankruptcy courts, the ten creditors of the firm seek legal redress by suing the defaulting firm individually. Legally, the priorities of creditors are determined by the time when suits are begun. The creditor who initiates legal action first has first claim; the second one has second claim; and so on. This type of competitive priority system forces the creditors to act in their own interest at the expense of the other creditors. The problem with this system is that the total amount available to creditors may be reduced by their acting in their self interest. This has been called the **common pool problem**.

The common pool problem is illustrated by the following example. Imagine a lake that has a fish population worth $100,000 if caught and sold immediately to consumers. If 1/3 of the fish are caught each year, reproduction is sufficient to maintain the fish population at a constant level, and a constant fish harvest of $33,000 can occur year after year. If there is only one fisherman, that fisherman is faced with the following choice: harvest $100,000 of fish in the current year or harvest $33,000 of fish indefinitely. If the discount rate for finding the present value of the perpetual harvest is less than 33.33 percent, then the present value of the perpetual harvest exceeds $100,000, the amount available from the single big harvest. For example, if the discount rate is 10 percent, the present value of the harvest is $330,000, and the single fisherman chooses to have a small annual harvest.

If there are many fishermen in this one lake, individual fishermen can maximize the present value of their own income by fishing as much as possible, as quickly as possible. The fishermen have incentives to catch all the fish immediately. The total amount received by all the fishermen is $100,000. If the fishermen could design a system for them to harvest fish in concert, they would increase the present value of their catch.

The purpose of bankruptcy courts is to solve the common pool problem. Without bankruptcy courts, individual creditors have incentives to sue a defaulting firm and try to rapidly seize as many assets for themselves as possible. The actions of these competing creditors can easily destroy a sizable part of the value of a firm. Bankruptcy courts are a system for settling creditors' claims jointly so that the creditors can act in concert for their mutual benefit. Instead of individual creditors acting in ways to harm each other, the bankruptcy courts allow the settlement of their claims jointly.

There are two possible resolutions of bankruptcy. First, a firm may be liquidated by the court. In a liquidation, the individual assets of the firm are sold. Second, and most frequently, the firm may be reorganized by the court (see figure 13.1). In a reorganization, the claimants against the firm agree to surrender their old claims in exchange for a new set of scaled down claims. The reorganized firm continues to operate during and after the bankruptcy. Firms are reorganized because a going concern may have more value than a liquidation of individual assets. A reorganization and liquidation do not have to be mutually exclusive, since a reorganization can involve liquidation of some assets.

From a theoretical financial viewpoint, bankruptcy should occur when the value of equity is zero, or, equivalently, when the firm's fixed obligations exceed the value of the firm. This implies that stockholders should receive nothing from the resolution of bankruptcy. In practice, stockholders frequently receive positive payoffs from bankruptcy. The explanation of this phenomenon is not entirely clear. Possibly, bankruptcy proceedings themselves are biased in favor of equity holders. The bankruptcy procedure involves negotiations among the claimants. Stockholders may be able to out-negotiate the others.

A bankruptcy proceeding involves costs, the most obvious of which are payments to the courts and to attorneys. Court costs are a small percentage of assets for large bankrupt firms.[4] The largest costs of bankruptcy are probably lost profit opportunities. Because opportunity costs are hard to measure, the size of total bankruptcy costs is difficult to estimate. Firms in bankruptcy may be unable to undertake profitable investment opportunities for two reasons. First, the court (which has the responsibility for running the firm) has protection of creditors' interest as its primary goal. Secondly, raising funds by issuing stocks and bonds is constrained during bankruptcy. In addition, sales from existing product lines may falter because customers may hesitate to buy from a bankrupt firm. Imagine the second thoughts of an individual considering the purchase of a car from a firm in bankruptcy. What value is a warrantee from a firm in bankruptcy? Will replacement parts be available? What will the future trade-in value be?

Financial Distress

Failure to make interest payments constitutes default. If a firm's operating income (or earnings before interest and taxes) is less than interest payments (fixed charges), the firm is in imminent danger of default and is in financial distress. However, financial distress does not inevitably lead to default and

---

[4] See Warner (1977).

subsequently to bankruptcy. Firms have a number of possible courses of action prior to defaulting on interest payments. These actions allow the firm to "buy time" to recover. Figure 13.1 shows the time sequence of possible events.

One possible course of action is to sell assets and use the proceeds to pay interest. The assets of a firm in financial distress typically have a low market price, since the assets' profit potential is questionable. The reduced price is a clear-cut cost of this strategy. A second course of action is to raise more equity capital. Since financial distress often results in a relatively low current stock price, sale of equity to outside investors at depressed prices is costly to existing stockholders.

A third alternative is to merge with another firm, which would use its resources to cover the shortfall in operating income. As in the case of selling more equity, the poor status of the firm's profits may create unfavorable merger terms. An offsetting factor is that firms in financial distress may have large losses, which can reduce the tax liabilities of the acquiring firm.

A fourth alternative is to borrow more money, with either new loans or renegotiation (or rescheduling) of the old loans. New loans have the drawback that the new lender, aware of the firm's difficulties, may require a premium interest rate and highly restrictive protective covenants. Renegotiation of old loans often offers some bargaining power to the firm in financial distress. In some circumstances, lenders may find renegotiation beneficial to them. By extending more credit or by postponing due dates, the lender may recover more money than by forcing the troubled firm to retrench. As a footnote, renegotiation of loans to countries is not uncommon. Generally, a country in financial distress has more renegotiating power than a company. A company is subject to an independent set of laws, whereas a country does not have this constraint.

A fifth course of action for a company in financial distress is to pay interest with funds needed to replace depreciating equipment. This strategy allows the physical plant to deteriorate. In the short run, this strategy allows the firm to continue to exist; the strategy buys time for the firm to recover. In the long run, this strategy destroys the firm's physical plant.

A sixth course of action is to obtain government assistance. The availability of government assistance depends upon the current political climate and the economic importance of the firm. A large firm, such as Chrysler Corporation, might have a greater chance of government aid because of Chrysler's large absolute size and the small number of domestic firms in the automobile industry.

Financial distress may have considerable costs to firms. First, each of the preceding strategies for avoiding default has a cost. Second, firms in financial distress may well suffer lost sales. As an example, imagine a retail store, Junk-Mart, which carries a large variety of low-quality consumer goods. Much of the merchandise sold by Junk-Mart is financed by trade credit, meaning that the manufacturer sends the goods to Junk-Mart but does not require payment for 30 days. If Junk-Mart gets into a state of financial distress, most manufacturers will stop extending trade credit and require cash payment when merchandise is delivered. Since Junk-Mart's problem is a lack of cash, merchandise may be hard to acquire. Without merchandise, sales suffer, and the firm's financial condition deteriorates.

Types of Corporate Debt

Mortgage bonds are backed by specific assets. If there is default on mortgage bonds, the mortgage bondholders have the first claim on the pledged asset.

Corporate debentures are unsecured debt. Unsecured debt has a general claim on the assets of the firm rather than a claim on specific assets. A firm may sell several different issues of debentures. These may be ordered in terms of priority of claims. Senior (or unsubordinated) debt has prior claim compared to junior (or subordinated) debt.

Income bonds arise out of a bankruptcy proceeding; they pay interest only if sufficient income is earned. The exact conditions when interest must be paid are specified in the bond indenture. Any interest not paid is owed for future payment.

Income bonds give a firm that has gone through bankruptcy more "breathing room" compared to a straight bond. Nonpayment of interest on straight bonds constitutes default and most likely will precipitate bankruptcy. An income bond is similar to a preferred stock, except that interest is a tax-deductible expense and preferred dividends are not.

Protective Covenants

The management of a corporation is the agent for the stockholders and is supposed to act in the best interest of the stockholders. In this agent role, the management can be expected to seek out ways to benefit the stockholders at the expense of the bondholders. Consequently, there is a natural conflict between the stockholders and the bondholders. One way for the bondholders to protect themselves against the stockholders is to require the inclusion of protective covenants in the bond indenture. Protective covenants make it difficult for the stockholders to expropriate the wealth of bondholders.

The American Bar Association has prepared a document entitled *Commentaries on Model Debenture Indenture Provisions.* This book lists standard bond indenture provisions. These protective covenants are written by legal experts and are based upon previous case law, i.e., cases in which bondholders sued firms that had acted against the interests of the bondholders. These model indentures are specifically designed to prevent repetition of these actions. The indenture provisions in the *Commentaries on Model Debenture Indenture Provisions* are widely used by corporation bonds and are often called **boilerplate**.

Four types of protective covenants are quite common: restrictions on (1) the issuance of additional debt, (2) dividend payments, (3) mergers, and (4) disposition of assets. Clearly, the stockholders benefit at the expense of the bondholders if the firm sells additional debt with a higher priority than existing debt, if the firm pays large cash dividends or repurchases large amounts of its stock in the market, if the firm merges and bondholders receive a riskier post-merger claim, or if the working assets of the firm are not properly maintained. Protective covenants try to prevent the stockholders from reducing the value of bonds.

Default Risk and Bond Yields

In the event of default and bankruptcy, bondholders can expect to take losses. Expectations of possible future losses should be reflected in current bond yields. To clarify this point, consider a very simplified world with one period and risk-neutral investors.[5] For bonds with $1 par values, the contractual yield on the bonds is y. The percentage of contractual payments actually recovered by the bondholders in the event of default is r, p equals the probability of default, and $1 - p$ is the probability that contractual payments are made. The contractual and expected cash flows are shown in figure 13.2.

Set the current price of $1 equal to the present value of expected payments:

$$1 = \frac{(1 + y)rp}{1 + R_1} + \frac{(1 + y)(1 - p)}{1 + R_1} \tag{13.1}$$

---

[5] Recall that risk-neutral investors base decisions upon expected (mean) values.

Figure 13.2   Cash Flows in a One-Period Bond

Points in Time

0	1

Purchase price
$1

Contractual payments
$1 + y

Payments in the
event of default
$(1 + y)r

	In the event of default	In the event of full payment
Expected payments =	$(1 + y)rp$	+ $(1 + y)(1 - p)$

$$\text{Present value of expected payments} = \frac{(1 + y)rp}{1 + R_1} + \frac{(1 + y)(1 - p)}{1 + R_1}$$

Solve for the contractual rate y:

$$y = \frac{R_1 + p - rp}{1 - p + rp} \tag{13.2}$$

To illustrate this result, consider three cases. First, if the recovery rate, r, is 100 percent, the contractual rate simply becomes the default-free rate, R_1. Second, if the recovery rate is 0 percent, the contractual rate becomes:

$$y = \frac{R_1 + p}{1 - p} = \frac{R_1}{1 - p} + \frac{p}{1 - p} \tag{13.3}$$

The first term $(R_1/1 - p)$ represents the default-free rate plus a premium to compensate for the expected loss of interest. The second term $(p/1 - p)$ is compensation for the loss in principal in the event of default. If the default-free interest rate is 8 percent and the probability of default is 10 percent, then:

$$y = \frac{.08}{1 - .10} + \frac{.10}{1 - .10} \tag{13.4}$$

$$y = .0889 + .1111 = .20 \tag{13.5}$$

The contractual rate equals 8 percent for default-free interest, .89 percent to compensate for the risk of default on the interest payment, and 11.11 percent as compensation for the risk of default on the principal payment.

In the third case, the recovery rate r lies between 0 and 1. Then, the contractual rate may be expressed as:

$$y = \frac{R_1}{1 - p + rp} + \frac{p - rp}{1 - p + rp} \tag{13.6}$$

The first term is the default-free interest rate plus a default premium for possible loss of interest. The second term is a compensation for possible loss of principal. To illustrate, assume a default-free interest rate of 8 percent, a probability of default of 10 percent, and a recovery rate of 80 percent. Then:

$$y = \frac{.08}{1 - .1 + (.8)(.1)} + \frac{.1 - (.8)(.1)}{1 - .1 + (.8)(.1)} \tag{13.7}$$

$$y = .0816 + .0204 = 10.2\% \tag{13.8}$$

The contractual rate is the default-free rate of 8 percent plus .16 percent as compensation for default on interest payments plus 2.04 percent as compensation for the risk of default on principal payments. The contractual interest rate of 10.2 percent with an 80 percent recovery rate in the event of default is considerably lower than the earlier example of a 20 percent contractual interest rate when bondholders recover nothing in the event of default.

If investors are risk averse, then a risk premium of h percent must be added. The contractual interest rate is:

$$y = \frac{R_1}{1 - p + rp} + \frac{p - rp}{1 - p + rp} + h \tag{13.9}$$

This approach can be extended to more than one period with similar, but more complicated, results.

Bond Ratings

The chance of default is an important consideration to all buyers of corporate bonds. Since there are many thousands of different bond issues, gathering information to assess the chances of default is a difficult process. Bond rating agencies have been developed to help provide this information to the market. Moody's and Standard & Poor's (S&P) are the two primary rating agencies. Their ratings categories are shown in table 13.1.

Ratings are good relative predictors of default.[6] The highest rating category (AAA) has the smallest frequency of default. The second highest rating category (AA) has a slightly larger frequency of default, and so on. Since the ratings are good predictors of default frequency, the next logical question is what determines the ratings. The ratings agencies do not reveal the exact procedure used to derive ratings, but the ratings are related to debt levels, profitability, and firm risk levels. A bond will tend to have a higher rating if the following are true:

1. The firm has lower debt ratios (debt/assets, debt/equity).
2. The firm has higher interest coverage ratios (earnings before interest and taxes divided by interest).

Table 13.1   Bond Ratings for Moody's and S&P

Ratings	Ratings		Default Risk	Yield
	Moody's	S&P		
Highest	Aaa	AAA	Low	Low
	Aa	AA		
	A	A		
	Baa	BBB		
Junk	Ba	BB		
	B	B		
	Caa	CCC		
Low	Ca	CC		
	C	C	High	High
		DDD	Default	
		DD		
		D		

---

[6] See Hickman (1958).

3. The firm has higher rates of return of assets (profit/assets, profit/equity).
4. The firm has lower relative variation in earnings over time.
5. The firm is of larger size.
6. The bond issue is unsubordinated.

Default rates have a life cycle. Immediately following the issue, the default rate is relatively low. The default rate increases until the issue has been outstanding for eight or nine years. Then, the default rate decreases. Bonds with higher default risk should have higher yields. Several studies have examined the determinants of corporate bond yields and have found that the preceding six factors (which explain bond ratings) also explain the yields to maturity.[7]

Predictors of bankruptcy have considerable interest to bondholders, corporate management, and stockholders.[8] The same financial ratios that determine ratings tend to deteriorate before bankruptcy occurs. Several years before actual bankruptcy, deterioration of these ratios is an early warning sign.

In an informationally efficient market, ratings changes by Moody's and Standard & Poor's should not have any incremental informational value. That is, prices should not adjust after a rating change because the market has already reacted to the same information as the rating agency. Overall, the evidence seems to be consistent with efficiency, although in some circumstances a rating change may affect prices.[9]

In a small percentage of circumstances, a particular bond issue may have a split rating, namely, different ratings by Standard & Poor's and by Moody's. Standard & Poor's might rate an issue at its highest rating, AAA. At exactly the same time, Moody's might rate the same issue at its second-highest rating, Aa. The reasons for split ratings are not entirely clear.[10]

Moody's has recently introduced subratings. For example, A-rated bonds are broken down into the categories of A-1, A-2, and A-3. The subratings are finer gradations, and they allow for gradual changes in ratings.

---

[7] See Fisher (1959).

[8] See Altman (1983).

[9] See Katz (1973) and Weinstein (1977).

[10] See Ederington (1986).

High-Yield (Junk) Bonds

Bonds with lower ratings (i.e., BB and below) are called high-yield (junk) bonds. There are two types of high-yield bonds; **fallen angels** and **original-issue**. Fallen angels are bonds originally issued with higher ratings, which have declined as the firm has fallen on hard times. Until recently, most high-yield bonds were fallen angels.

Since 1977, many original-issue high-yield bonds appeared. Original-issue high-yield bonds are of two varieties. Some are issued by firms with very high business (operating) risk. Others are issued by highly levered firms.[11] Some highly levered mergers have been financed with high-yield bonds. Because these mergers had a very small proportion of equity financing, the bonds carried a high risk of default and high yields.

The role of original issue high-yield bonds has been controversial. Traditionally, the market for investment-grade public debt has been restricted to larger firms. Smaller firms have been forced to finance with bank debt, or possibly private placements of debt with insurance companies. Original issue high-yield debt has opened up a new source of funds to many smaller and high risk firms. In one view, high-yield debt has been a stimulus to economic expansion because firms were removed from the straightjacket of highly restrictive bank loans.[12] In the opposing view, high-yield debt issuers escaped the important monitoring function provided by commercial banks and consequently suffered from unwise financing and investment decisions.

Several authors have argued that the junk bond market was monoplized by the underwriter firm of Drexel, Burnham, Lambert under the direction of Michael Milken.[13] In this view, Milken was able to sell junk bonds at unfair yields and at high underwriter fees. The evidence of Livingston, Pratt, and Mann (1995) shows the bond yields and underwriter fees on Drexel's junk bonds were in line with those of other issuers.

A sizable number of corporate bond issues now contain covenants to protect the bondholders against possible bondholder losses from mergers. One such covenant is a due-on-sale clause or **poison put**, requiring existing

---

[11] See Altman (1989), Blume and Keim (1991), and Fons (1987).

[12] See Yago (1991).

[13] See Bruck (1988), Stein (1992), and Stewart (1992).

bonds to be repaid before a merger can occur.[14] Corporate bonds without such protective covenants may have a premium added to the yield to compensate the bondholders for the possibility of merger.[15]

The securities of firms actually in bankruptcy continue to trade in the market at depressed prices.[16] Investing in the bonds of a bankrupt firm is a high-risk, potentially high-return strategy. The majority of the bonds of bankrupt firms are not very good performers, but some of the bonds of bankrupt firms will turn out to be very lucrative investments, if the fortunes of the firm turn around sharply.

Investing in high-yield bonds is a specialized field. It requires a detailed knowledge of bankruptcy law as well as knowledge about individual firms. A number of high-yield bond mutual funds have been established. Besides allowing investors to diversify, these mutual funds allow investment in high-yield bonds by those who do not have the knowledge and time to evaluate each particular high-yield bond issued.

Default rates increase as bond rating decreases. High-yield bonds (rated Ba, B, Caa) have much higher default rates than investment-grade bonds (Aaa, Aa, A, Baa).

Yield Spreads

A **yield spread** is generally defined as the difference between the yield to maturity on a bond with default risk minus the yield on the otherwise identical default-free bond. The yield spread is a measure of the default premium. For example, if a AAA-rated corporate bond has a yield of 11 percent, and a U.S. Treasury bond with the same maturity has a yield of 9 percent, the yield spread (or default premium) is 2 percent.

---

[14] Such due-on-sale clauses are often used in mortgage debt. If the home is sold, the entire mortgage principal must be repaid. Some mortgages are assumable by the new owner.

[15] Crabbe (1991) found evidence that poison put clauses reduce bond yields. Pratt and Livingston (1993) find evidence that poison puts have no impact upon bond yields for industrial debt. Cook and Easterwood (1994) find that firms issuing poison put bonds have negative stock price reactions.

[16] See Morse and Shaw (1988).

Yield spreads are affected by a number of factors. First, the bond rating has a significant impact upon yield spreads. Yield spreads increase (at an increasing rate) as the rating decreases, since the probability of default increases for lower rated bonds.[17]

Second, yield spreads are affected by maturity.[18] Typically, spreads increase with maturity because the chance of default is perceived to be greater for larger maturities. However, under "crisis" situations, yield spreads have been found to decrease with maturity.[19] In some years during the difficult period of the 1930s, yield spreads on short-term corporate bonds were larger than yield spreads on long-term corporate bonds. Firms with short-term debt were faced with a crisis of repaying or refinancing their debt under very adverse conditions. Firms with longer maturity debt were able to postpone debt repayment until a distant date when, it was hoped, economic conditions would be much more favorable.

Third, the business cycle appears to affect yield spreads in a complicated fashion. Over the course of a business cycle, default risks tend to change. Actual bankruptcy rates tend to lag behind the business cycle. That is, bankruptcy rates tend to increase during recessions and continue to increase for a while after an upswing has begun. Since yield spreads in an efficient market would anticipate future bankruptcy, the relationship between the business cycle and yield spreads is very complex.

Summary

A corporate bond represents a contractual agreement between a firm, bondholders, and a trustee. The obligations of the parties are spelled out in the bond indenture, which contains protective covenants. Violation of this contractual agreement constitutes default. Bankruptcy is a legal proceeding, administered by special bankruptcy courts. In a bankruptcy, the assets of the firm are liquidated or the firm is reorganized.

---

[17] Livingston, Pratt, and Mann (1995) document this relationship for a sample of over 2,700 bonds.

[18] Rodriguez (1988) suggests that there is a complex relationship between yield spreads and maturity.

[19] See Johnson (1967).

Financial distress occurs when the firm's operating income is insufficient to meet interest payments. Before defaulting, the firm can consider the following actions: sell assets, sell equity, merge, borrow more, use depreciation funds, or seek government assistance.

Both financial distress and bankruptcy are costly, especially in terms of lost sales and investment opportunities. Predicting chances of default are important. Ratings of corporate bonds provide valuable information about default probabilities. Ratings are a function of debt levels, firm profitability, the riskiness of the firm's assets, and firm size.

Questions/Problems

1. Describe the functions of a corporate bond indenture. What role does the bond trustee play?

2. Why do bond indentures include protective covenants? Give some examples of protective covenants and the reasons why they might be included.

3. Why do special bankruptcy courts exist?

4. Define financial distress. What alternatives are available to firms in financial distress instead of defaulting? Describe the pros and cons of each alternative.

5. Describe the costs associated with financial distress and bankruptcy.

6. What does the term secured debt mean?

7. Describe the financial characteristics that determine bond ratings.

8. Are high-yield bonds good investments? Why or why not?

9. Assume a one-period world with risk-neutral investors. The default-free interest rate is 5 percent. XYZ Corporation issues one-year bonds. The probability that XYZ will not default on these bonds is 85 percent. If there is a default, the bondholders will recover 70 cents on the dollar. What is the contractual interest rate under these assumptions?

10. Assume the same information as the preceding example except that the recovery rate is zero. Determine the contractual interest rate. Compare your answer to the previous problem and explain the reasons for the difference.

References

Altman, E. I., *Corporate Financial Distress,* New York: Wiley, 1983.

Altman, E. I., "Measuring Corporate Bond Mortality and Performance." *Journal of Finance,* September 1989, pp. 909–22.

American Bar Association, *Commentaries on Model Debenture Indenture Provisions,* Chicago, 1971.

Asquith, P., D. W. Mullins, Jr., and E. D. Wolff, "Original Issue High Yield Bonds: Aging Analysis of Defaults, Exchanges, and Calls," *Journal of Finance,* 44, 1989, pp. 923–52.

Asquith, P. and T. A. Wizman, "Event Risk, Covenants, and Bondholder Returns in Leveraged Buyouts," *Journal of Financial Economics,* 27, 1990, pp. 195–214.

Bae, S. C., D. P. Klein, and R. Padmaraj, "Event Risk Bond Covenants, Agency Costs of Debt and Equity, and Stockholder Wealth," *Financial Management,* 23, Winter 1994, pp. 28–41.

Billingsley, R. S., R. E. Lamy, M. W. Marr, and G. R. Thompson, "Split Ratings and Bond Reoffering Yields," *Financial Management,* 14, Summer 1985, pp. 59–65.

Blume, M. E., D. B. Keim and S. A. Patel, "Returns and Volatility of Low-Grade Bonds 1977–1989," *Journal of Finance,* March 1991, pp. 49–74.

Boardman, C. M. and R. W. McNally, "Factors Affecting Seasoned Corporate Bond Prices," *Journal of Financial and Quantitative Analysis,* 16, June 1981, pp. 207–26.

Bruck, Connie, *The Predators' Ball: The Junk-Bond Raiders and the Man Who Staked Them,* New York: American Lawyer: Simon and Schuster, 1988.

Cantor, R. and F. Packer, "The Credit Rating Industry," Quarterly Review, Federal Reserve Bank of New York, 19, Summer–Fall 1994, pp. 1–26.

Chatfield, R. E. and R. C. Moyer, "Putting Away Bond Risk: An Empirical Examination of the Value of the Put Option on Bonds," *Financial Management,* 15:2, 1986, pp. 26–33.

Cohan, A. B., *Yields on Corporate Debt Directly Placed,* New York: National Bureau of Economic Research, 1967.

Cook, D. O. and J. C. Easterwood, "Poison Put Bonds: An Analysis of Their Economic Role," *Journal of Finance,* 49, December 1994, pp. 1905–20.

Cornell, B. and K. Green, "The Investment Performance of Low-Grade Bond Funds 1977–1989," *Journal of Finance,* 46, March 1991, pp. 29–48.

Crabbe, L., "Event Risk: An Analysis of Losses to Bondholders and 'Super-Poison-Put' Bond Covenants," *Journal of Finance,* 46, 1991, pp. 689–706.

Ederington, L. H. "Why Split Ratings Occur," *Financial Management,* 15, Spring 1986, pp. 37–47.

Fisher, L., "Determinants of Risk Premiums on Corporate Bonds," *Journal of Political Economy,* 67, June 1959, pp. 217–37.

Fitzpatrick, J. D., and J. T. Severiens, "Hickman Revisited: The Case for Junk Bonds." *The Journal of Portfolio Management,* Summer 1978, 53–7.

Fridson, M. A., "The State of the High Yield Bond Market: Overshooting or Return to Normalcy?" *Journal of Applied Corporate Finance,* Spring 1994, pp. 85–97.

Fridson, M. S., and M. A. Cherry. "Initial Pricing as a Predictor of Subsequent Performance of High Yield Bonds," *Financial Analysts Journal,* July/August 1990, pp. 61–67.

Fridson, M. A., "Fraine's Neglected Findings: Was Hickman Wrong?" *Financial Analysts Journal,* September/October 1994, pp. 43–53.

Fons, J. S., "The Default Premium and Corporate Bond Experience," *Journal of Finance,* 42, March 1987, pp. 81–97.

Hand, J. R. M., R. W. Holthausen, and R. W. Leftwich, "The Effect of Bond Rating Agency Announcements on Bond and Stock Prices," *Journal of Finance,* 47, June 1992, pp. 733–52.

Hickman, W. B., *Corporate Bond Quality and Investor Experience,* New York: National Bureau of Economic Research, 1958.

Hradsky, G. T., and R. D. Long. "High Yield Losses and the Return Performance of Bankrupt Debt," *Financial Analysts Journal,* July–August 1989, pp. 38–49.

Jackson, T. H., *The Logic and Limits of Bankruptcy Law,* Cambridge, MA: Harvard University Press, 1986.

Joehnk, M. D., and J. F. Nielsen, "Return and Risk Characteristics of Speculative Grade Bonds," *Quarterly Review of Economics and Business,* 15, Spring 1975, pp. 27–46.

Johnson, R. E., "Term Structure of Corporate Bond Yields as a Function of Risk of Default," *Journal of Finance,* 22, May 1967, pp. 313–45.

Kalay, A., "Stockholder-Bondholder Conflict and Dividend Constraints," *Journal of Financial Economics,* 10, 1982, pp. 211–33.

Katz, S., "The Price Adjustment Process of Bonds to Reclassifications: A Test of Bond Market Efficiency," *Journal of Finance,* 29, May 1971, pp. 551–59.

Laber, G., "Bond Covenants and Managerial Flexibility," *Financial Management,* 19, Spring 1990, pp. 82–9.

Lamy, R. E. and G. R. Thompson, "Risk Premia and the Pricing of Primary Issue Bonds," *Journal of Banking and Finance,* 12, 1988, pp. 585–601.

Liu, P. and W. T. Moore, "The Impact of Split Ratings on Risk Premia," *Financial Review,* 22, 1987, pp. 71–86.

Livingston, M., H. Pratt, and C. Mann, "Drexel, Burnham, Lambert's Debt Issues," *Journal of Fixed Income,* March 1995.

Malitz, I., "On Financial Contracting: The Determinants of Bond Covenants," *Financial Management,* 15, Summer 1986, pp. 18–25.

Michel, A. and I. Shaked, "The LBO Nightmare: Fraudulent Conveyance Risk," *Financial Analysts Journal,* 46, 1990, pp. 41–50.

Morse, D. and W. Shaw, "Investing in Bankrupt Firms," *Journal of Finance,* 43, December 1988, pp. 1193–206.

Platt, H. D., "Underwriter Effects and the Riskiness of Original-Issue High Yield Bonds," *Journal of Applied Corporate Finance,* 6, Spring 1993, pp 89–94.

Pratt, H. M. and M. Livingston, "Effects of Super Poison-Put Clauses on Industrial Debt," *The Journal of Fixed Income,* 3, December 1993, pp. 33–45.

Roberts, G. S. and J. A. Viscione, "The Impact of Seniority and Security Covenants on Bond Yields: A Note," *Journal of Finance,* 35, 1984, pp. 1597–602.

Rodriguez, R. J., "Default Risk, Yield Spreads, and Time to Maturity," *Journal of Financial and Quantitative Analysis,* 23, March 1988, pp. 111–17.

Sarig, O. and A. Warga, "Some Empirical Estimates of the Risk Structure of Interest Rates," *Journal of Finance,* 44, December 1989, pp. 1351–60.

Shyam-Sunder, L., "The Stock Price Effect of Risky versus Safe Debt," *Journal of Financial and Quantitative Analysis,* 26, December 1991, pp. 549–58.

Smith, C. and J. B. Warner. "On Financial Contracting: An Analysis of Bond Covenants," *Journal of Financial Economics,* 7, 1979, pp. 117–62.

Soldofsky, R. M. and D. F. Max, *Holding Period Yields and Risk-Premium Curves for Long-Term Marketable Securities: 1910–1976,* New York: New York University Salomon Brothers Center for the Study of Financial Institutions, 1978.

Stein, B. J., *A License to Steal,* New York: Simon & Schuster, 1992.

Stewart, J. B., *Den of Thieves,* New York: Touchstone, Simon & Schuster, 1992.

Summers, M. S., *Bankruptcy Explained,* New York: John Wiley, 1989.

Van Horne, J. C., "Optimal Initiation of Bankruptcy Proceedings by Debt Holders," *Journal of Finance,* 31, June 1976, pp. 897–910.

Van Horne, J. C., "Behavior of Default-Free Premiums for Corporate Bonds and Commercial Paper," *Journal of Business Research,* 7, December 1979, pp. 301–13.

Warner, J. B., "Bankruptcy Costs: Some Evidence," *Journal of Finance,* 32, 1977, pp. 337–47.

Weinstein, M. I., "The Effect of a Rating Change Announcement on Bond Price," *Journal of Financial Economics,* 5, 1977, pp. 329–50.

Yago, G., *Junk Bonds: How High Yield Securities Restructured Corporate America,* Oxford: Oxford University Press, 1991.

14

Call Features on Bonds

Overview

The call feature on a bond gives the bond's issuer the right to force the bondholders to turn in their bonds for the call price. Call features are widely used for corporate and municipal government bonds.[1]

The call price is the price paid to bondholders when the bond is called. It is par or above. Frequently, the call price starts out at par plus one year's interest. As the bond ages, the call price declines toward par (see figure 14.1). The exact terms and dates are stated in the bond indenture.

In recent years, callable corporate bonds have had a period of call protection after the bond is originally issued. During the call-protected period, the bond cannot be called and replaced by another bond. However, most bonds can be called for reasons other than replacement with another lower cost bond – so-called **redemptions**. Thus, bonds can be redeemed and replaced by stock even during the period of call protection.

A firm might exercise a bond's call option for one of several reasons. First, calling a bond allows a firm to retire a debt issue to remove an undesirable protective covenant in the bond indenture. Second, if a firm has improved its credit rating, a higher coupon bond can be called and replaced with a lower coupon bond.[2]

---

[1] Although most authorities claim that corporate bonds are virtually all callable, Kish (1988) found that 20 percent of corporate bond issues were noncallable for the period 1977–1986.

[2] This higher coupon bond would have been issued in the past when the firm had a poorer credit rating.

Figure 14.1 Callable Bonds

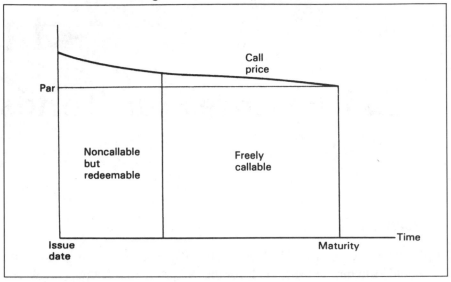

The third reason for calling a bond is refunding. In a **refunding**, a bond with a high coupon is called and replaced by a lower coupon bond following a decline in interest rates. The firm gains the present value of the coupons saved. This saving has to be balanced against the costs of refunding, which include paying the call premium, flotation costs for the replacement bond issue, and loss of the opportunity to call the bond in the future if interest rates were to drop even farther.

Refunding is a zero sum game. That is, the gains to the firm from a refunding are losses to the bondholders. If a high coupon bond is called after a decline in interest rates, the bondholders are able to reinvest the call price at a lower interest rate. The bondholders' coupon interest is lower. This loss to the bondholders' is the firm's gain.

When a callable bond is issued, the bondholders are aware of the *possibility* of a future call. To compensate for the risk of possible future calls, the bondholders require a higher coupon (on a callable as opposed to noncallable bond), a call premium, and, typically, a period of call protection during which the original coupon is locked in (see figure 14.1).

In an efficient market, the bondholders have the same information about prospects for future exercise of the call option as the firm. The compensation for call risks (i.e., the higher coupon, call premium, and period of call protection) should be fair at the issue date. This conclusion has the following interesting implication. In a perfectly efficient market, there is no net advantage for a firm to issue callable versus noncallable bonds. That is, the higher cost of the callable bond should exactly offset the anticipated gains from future refunding. To illustrate, in an efficient market, a firm and the bondholders might be indifferent between a noncallable 25 year par bond with an 8 percent coupon and a callable par bond with a 9 percent coupon and 10 years of call protection.

Refunding

In a bond refunding, an existing bond is called and replaced by a lower coupon bond. There are three interrelated issues in evaluating a corporate refunding.

1. What is the appropriate replacement bond?
2. What is the net benefit of an immediate refunding?
3. What is the optimal time to refund?

We answer the first two questions and then address the third question of timing. In addition, we begin by assuming no taxes and later address tax issues.

At time zero a firm issues a callable par bond with call premium above par of Q and with annual coupon of c. At time of issue, the yield to maturity on this callable par bond is c/par. The yield on a noncallable par bond is lower.

At a later point in time, t, interest rates are assumed to fall enough so that the firm is considering refunding the existing callable bonds. The bond matures at time $t + n$, so that at time t the bond has n periods left until maturity (see figure 14.2).

The first question to consider is the nature of the replacement bond. Suppose the replacement bond is noncallable with the same par value, coupon, and maturity date as the old callable bond. This assumption constrains the fixed payments on the old and new bonds to be identical. Since interest rates have fallen, this replacement noncallable bond sells above par for a price

Figure 14.2   The Sequence of Events

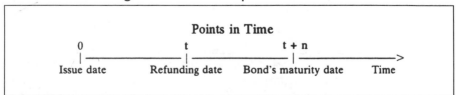

Points in Time

0	t	t + n	
Issue date	Refunding date	Bond's maturity date	Time

of PNEW. The cash flows from this refunding are shown in table 14.1. FL are flotation costs.

Since the coupons and par values from the old and new bonds in the first and second rows are equal, the net cash flow is the market value of the new noncallable bond (PNEW) minus the call price of the old bond minus the cost of floating the new bond.

Table 14.2 contains the following numerical example. The old callable bond has a $100 par value, a $10 coupon, a call premium of $10, and a remaining maturity of 14 years. Flotation costs for the new replacement bond issue are $3. Interest rates have dropped so that noncallable bonds with a $10 coupon and $100 par value sell for market prices of $150.

The future coupons and par values exactly cancel for the old callable bond and the new noncallable bond. At time t there is a net cash inflow of $37 equal to the market value of the new bond (150) minus the flotation costs for the new bond (3) minus the call price (110).

The Timing of Refunding

In addition to cash flows resulting from an immediate refunding, firms must consider the possibility of waiting to refund on possibly better terms. To

Table 14.1   Refunding Cash Flows

	Points in Time			
	t	$t + 1$	...	$t + n$
Cash flows old bond		$-c$	...	$-(c + \text{PAR})$
Cash flows new bond		$-c$	...	$-(c + \text{PAR})$
Call old bond	$-(\text{Par} + \text{PREM})$			
Sell new noncallable bond	$+\text{PNEW} - \text{FL}$			
Net	PNEW − (Par + PREM + FL)	0		0

Table 14.2   A Refunding Example

	Points in Time			
	t	$t + 1$	. . .	$t + 20$
Cash flows old bond		−10	. . .	−(10 + 100)
Cash flows new bond		−10	. . .	−(10 + 100)
Call old bond	−(100 + 10)			
Sell new noncallable bond	+150 − 3			
Net	+37	0		0

clarify this point, consider the courses of action to the firm at time t as shown in figure 14.3. At time t, the firm can either refund and realize a net refunding benefit of B_t or wait. If the firm refunds at time t, it cannot refund this same bond again. If the choice at time t is to wait, then at time $t + 1$ the choices are to wait or to refund for a benefit of B_{t+1}, which may be greater than, equal to, or less than B_t. Thus, waiting may result in an additional benefit, no change, or a reduced benefit. The same scenario applies for waiting and refunding at later points in time. Because waiting and refunding in the future may result in a greater refunding benefit, the call option may have some value beyond the current intrinsic value of refunding immediately.

To illustrate the possible advantage of waiting to call the bond, consider the preceding numerical example in which the immediate benefit from refunding is $37. If the firm decides not to refund immediately, there are three possible levels of interest rates in the next period as shown in figure 14.4. The first possibility is that interest rates rise and refunding becomes unprofitable. In this case, the firm loses any gain from refunding. Second, interest rates remain the same resulting in a refunding benefit of $37 next period. Third, if interest rates fall in the future so that the noncallable bond would sell at $200, the future cash inflow from refunding would be $87. For simplicity, we ignore any refunding possibilities after next period.

In deciding whether to refund now or to wait, the firm must compare the present value of possible future incremental gains from refunding against

Figure 14.3 Refunding Choices

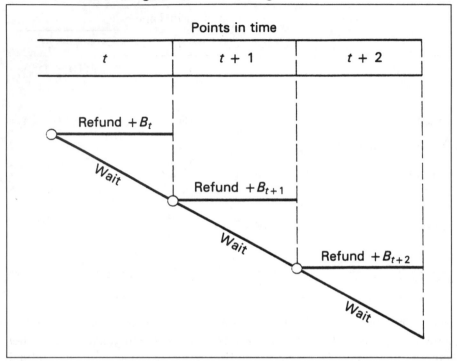

the immediate benefit. If each of the three possibilities next period has a 1/3 probability of occurring and if the one-period interest rate is 8 percent, then the expected present value of waiting is shown in equation 14.1:

$$\frac{0(1/3) + 37(1/3) + 87(1/3)}{1.08} = \frac{41.33}{1.08} = 38.27 \qquad (14.1)$$

$41.33 is the expected future value of waiting. Dividing by 1.08 gives a present value of $38.27. Since the expected present value of waiting is $38.27 and the immediate benefit of refunding is $37, there is an expected advantage in waiting. This advantage depends critically upon the future levels of interest rates and their probabilities.

The Call Option

The value of a call option on a bond is composed of two parts: (1) the intrinsic value, and (2) the excess value. The intrinsic value is the value

Figure 14.4   Two-Period Example of Bond Refunding

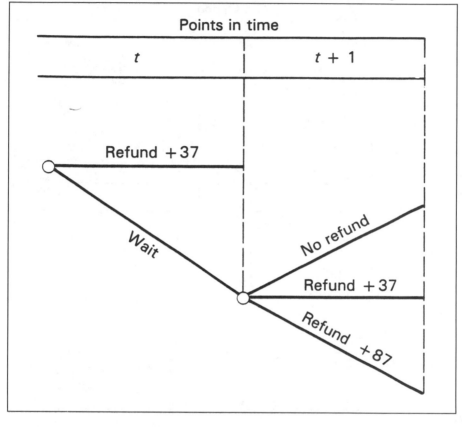

realized if the option is exercised immediately and is equal to the value of the noncallable bond minus the call price, PNEW − (PAR + PREM).

The excess value represents the value of the option beyond what is received if the option is immediately exercised. The excess value is the current value from possible *future* exercise of the call option at more favorable terms; it represents the incremental value from waiting to exercise the call option. The excess value represents the present value of additional refunding benefits in the future.

Figure 14.5 clarifies the relationship between the values of the call option, the noncallable bond, and the callable bond. On the horizontal axis, figure 14.5 shows the value of a noncallable bond. As interest rates get lower, the value of the noncallable bond increases.

The left vertical axis shows the value of a call option for a callable bond with the same coupon, par value, and maturity as the noncallable bond. The origin for the left axis is the point where the thick black lines cross.

Figure 14.5   The Values of Callable Bonds, Noncallable Bonds, and the
Call Option

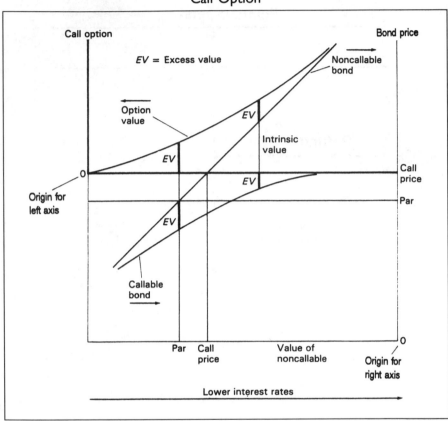

As interest rates go down, the market value of a noncallable bond increases and, looking at the figure, the value of the call option also increases.

The right vertical axis shows the price of noncallable and callable bonds with the same coupons, maturity, and call price. The origin for the right axis is the lower right corner of the figure. The value of a callable bond is equal to the value of the noncallable bond minus the call option value. As interest rates fall, the value of the callable bond approaches the call price.

Look at the right axis in figure 14.5; if the value of the noncallable bond is below the call price, the market price of the callable bond is equal to the noncallable price minus the excess option value. If the noncallable bond has a market value above the call price, the price of the callable bond equals the call price minus the excess option value. Consequently, the price of the callable bond approaches the price of the noncallable bond for high interest rates and approaches the call price for low interest rates.

Optimal Refunding Rules

If a firm exercises the nonmarketable call option on its bond, the firm loses the excess value of the option, since the call option cannot be resold and can be exercised only by the issuing firm. Because the call option is nonmarketable, the excess option value, which represents the incremental value from possible future exercise, can be realized only by waiting.

The loss of the excess option value is a cost of refunding and is subtracted from the cash inflows from refunding. If EV is the option's excess value and FL represents flotation costs, the net refunding benefit is:

$$\text{PNEW} - (\text{PAR} + \text{PREM} + \text{FL}) - \text{EV} \qquad (14.2)$$

Refunding is desirable (overlooking flotation costs) when:

$$\text{EV} < \text{NEW} - (\text{PAR} + \text{PREM}) \qquad (14.3)$$

$$\begin{matrix} \text{Excess} \\ \text{option} \\ \text{value} \end{matrix} < \begin{matrix} \text{Value of} \\ \text{noncallable} \\ \text{bond} \end{matrix} - \begin{matrix} \text{Call} \\ \text{price} \end{matrix} \qquad (14.4)$$

Look at figure 14.6; the excess value of the call option is shown for several levels of interest rates. If the interest rate is r_0, such that the noncallable bond sells at the call price (implying that the intrinsic value of the call option is zero), then the net refunding benefit is negative. That is:

$$\text{Net Benefit} = \text{PNEW} - (\text{PAR} + \text{PREM}) - \text{EV} \qquad (14.5)$$
$$= \text{PAR} + \text{PREM} - (\text{PAR} + \text{PREM}) - \text{EV}$$

If interest rates fall even more to the level r_1, so that the excess value of the option equals its intrinsic value ($\text{EV}_1 = \text{IV}_1$, implying that $\text{PN}_1 = \text{PAR} + \text{PREM} + \text{IV}_1$), the net refunding benefit is zero. That is:

$$\text{Net Benefit} = \text{PAR} + \text{PREM} + \text{IV}_1 - (\text{PAR} + \text{PREM}) - \text{EV}_1 = 0 \qquad (14.6)$$

For interest rates at or above the level r_1, refunding does not pay. Refunding is beneficial only if interest rates drop below r_1 to a level such as r_2, where the excess option value EV_2 is less than the option's intrinsic value IV_2. At the rate r_2, $\text{PN}_2 = \text{PAR} + \text{PREM} + \text{IV}_2$ and:

Figure 14.6 The Excess Value of the Call Option at Various Interest Rates

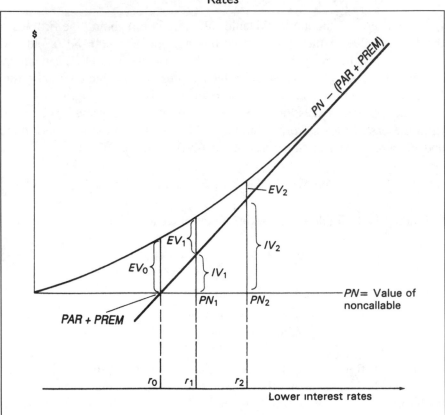

$$\text{Net Benefit} = (\text{PAR} + \text{PREM} + \text{IV}_2) - (\text{PAR} + \text{PREM}) - \text{EV}_2 \quad (14.7)$$
$$= \text{IV}_2 - \text{EV}_2 > 0$$

Refunding becomes attractive at interest rates below r_1 because the possibility of additional gains from waiting for even lower interest rates is outweighed by the possibility of higher interest rates and loss of the existing refunding benefit. For example, if the interest rate equals r_2, the firm can lock in cash inflows from refunding. If the firm waits, it may lose some of the existing benefit if rates go higher, or it may get a larger benefit if rates go lower. If the existing benefit is large enough relative to possible future incremental benefits, immediate refunding pays.

Since refunding is advantageous if the value of the noncallable bond rises sufficiently above the call price, a strategy of calling the bond when the noncallable bond sells at the call price is suboptimal. Too much option value is given up for an insufficient immediate cash inflow. Empirically, refundings occur after the value of the noncallable bond has risen well above the call price. Most newly issued callable corporate bonds contain a period of call protection. Call protection reduces the coupon compared to an immediately callable bond.

Refunding is clearly best when the excess value of the call option is zero, implying absolutely no chance of refunding on more favorable terms in the future. Then the callable bond sells at the call price. Using this reasoning, some authors suggest that the optimal time to refund occurs when the callable bond sells at its call price.[3] There is a circularity in this reasoning. A rule that says to refund if the market price of the callable bond equals the call price bases the decision to call the bond upon the bondholders' estimate that immediate call is best. In turn, the bondholders base the market price upon an estimate of the firm's optimal decision since the bondholders have the same information as the firm. Thus, the rule is based upon the bondholders' belief of the firm's belief of the bondholders' belief of . . . and so on. The rule reduces to the following: call the bond if calling is optimal. This is a truism that provides no operational guidelines.

Taxes and Refunding

Introduction of corporate taxes doesn't change the nature of the analysis. With taxes, the bond coupon, call premium, and flotation costs are tax deductible. The net refunding benefit is the present value of the after-tax cash flows.

Issuing Callables versus Noncallables in a Perfect Market

In a market in which the same information is available to both bondholders and the issuing firm, the features (i.e., coupon, call premium, and period of call protection) on a callable bond should be set so that the marginal bondholder and the marginal firm are indifferent between callable and noncallable bonds. If this indifference did not exist, bondholders and firms would have

---

[3] See Brennan and Schwartz (1977).

incentives to switch their positions. To highlight the relationship between callable and noncallable bonds, table 14.3 shows a simplified two-period example. The firm has a choice of issuing two-period noncallable bonds with annual coupon of c_{non} or issuing two-period callables with annual coupon of c_{call}. If interest rates drop at time 1, the firm with callable bonds can refund at a call price of par with a new one-period bond with coupon c_1.

Consider the numerical example in table 14.4 in which a firm can issue a callable bond with an 8 percent coupon or a noncallable bond with a 7 percent coupon. At time 1, the one-period rate on a new noncallable bond is either 5 percent or 10 percent.

Issuing callable bonds results in an extra coupon of $c_{call} - c_{non}$ (i.e., 1 percent) at time 1 and at time 2 if refunding does not occur. If refunding occurs at time 2, the callable bond saves $c_1 - c_{non}$ (i.e., 2 percent) in interest costs compared to a noncallable bond. The market sets the coupon on the callable bond to compensate the bondholders for the risk of a call at time 1.

Although firms should be indifferent between issuing callable and noncallable bonds in a perfect market, the decision to refund or not refund after a change in interest rates is not a matter of indifference. If interest rates drop sufficiently, a firm has an opportunity to call its bond and make a gain at the expense of the bondholders. To realize this refunding gain, the firm must exercise its call option.

Table 14.3   Comparing the Coupon Payments on
Noncallable and Callable Bonds

Type of Issue	Points in Time			
	0	1	2	
			Refund at Time 1	Not Refund
Two-period noncallable		c_{non}	c_{non}	c_{non}
Two-period callable		c_{call}	c_1	c_{call}
Incremental coupons: callable – noncallable		$c_{call} - c_{non}$	$c_1 - c_{non}$	$c_{call} - c_{non}$

Table 14.4 Comparing the Coupon Payments on
Noncallable and Callable Bonds

Type of Issue	Points in Time		
	0	1	2
			Refund at Time 1	Not Refund
One-period noncallable		7%	7%	7%
Two-period callable		8%	5%	8%
Incremental coupons: callable − noncallable		8%–7%	5%–7%	8%–7%

The Existence of Call Provisions

Call provisions are included in about 80 percent of corporate debt issues in recent years.[4] Noncallable bonds are often issued with short and intermediate maturities by firms with high ratings. In a perfectly efficient market, the added coupon on a callable bond, the call premium, and the period of call protection should reflect the fair value of the prospect of exercise of the call option. There should be no net advantage to issue debt with call features. Consequently, the inclusion of call features in the majority of corporate bonds is puzzling. Several possible explanations have been suggested. None of these is a very satisfactory explanation.

One possible explanation of the frequency of call features is superior knowledge on the part of corporate management about the future course of interest rates. If management had special information about a future decline in interest rates, the call feature could be included at a relatively small cost. This explanation is of questionable validity since it seems unlikely that corporate managements have special skill in forecasting future interest rates.

---

[4] See Kish (1988) for an extensive study of the inclusion of call provisions in corporate debt. Kish and Livingston (1992) analyze the factors determining the inclusion of a call feature.

A considerable proportion of corporate bonds are purchased by professional money managers for financial institutions. There seems to be very little chance for professional money managers to have consistently inferior forecasting ability compared to corporate managers.

A second possible explanation of call features is risk aversion on the part of both borrowers and lenders. According to this argument, borrowers are averse to the risk of being locked-in to paying high interest rates and, therefore, desire a call feature; lenders are averse to bond price declines and do not value the call feature very highly. This view of lenders' risk preferences is unsatisfactory, since many institutional lenders may have the preferences of an immunizer, wanting to lock-in total return over a bond's entire life.

A third possible explanation of call features centers on corporate management's superior knowledge of a firm's individual prospects – asymmetric information. According to this scenario, the management of a firm issuing callable bonds has a more favorable view of the firm's prospects than the bondholders' perceptions. The bondholders believe that the firm has a relatively high probability of default and, therefore, they require a high coupon on debt. By issuing callable debt now, the corporate management expects to refinance at a future date on more favorable terms when the firm's performance has improved.

This scenario suffers from several drawbacks. Those firms with positive information would issue callable bonds and those with negative information would issue noncallables. If callable bonds are issued by 80 percent of firms, why should positive asymmetric information be available to such a large proportion of firms? A priori, about half of the firms should have positive asymmetric information and about half negative unless the security markets are biased against positive information – an assumption that has no apparent justification. In addition, some firms issue both callable and noncallable bonds. How can asymmetry of information explain this?

Finally, if there is a difference between private corporate information and public information, the firm can reduce its current financing costs by immediately divulging favorable information to the market. For the asymmetric information explanation of call features to be viable, firms need a strong reason not to release favorable information immediately. By not releasing information, the firm must pay higher financing costs. The advantage of withholding information must outweigh the immediate costs.

A fourth possible explanation for the existence of call options on bonds concerns growth opportunities.[5] In some circumstances, a firm which has

---

[5] See Aivazian and Callen (1980) and Bodie and Taggart (1978 and 1980).

issued noncallable bonds and has favorable investment opportunities may have incentives not to undertake these investments because of the possibility that the bondholders may get a large share of the rewards if the investments are successful. This line of reasoning is as follows. Debtholders typically bear a large proportion of bankruptcy costs. Profitable investments reduce the likelihood of bankruptcy costs. Thus, the benefits of the investments may accrue largely to the bondholders. If the firm has issued callable bonds, the firm can call these bonds if investment returns are favorable, limiting the returns to the bondholders and capturing most of the returns for the stockholders.

Callable Debt versus Short Maturity Debt

An alternative to issuing long maturity callable bonds is issuing short maturity debt. The plan would be to refinance the shorter maturity debt at maturity at (hopefully) lower interest rates. In comparing long maturity callable bonds versus short-term debt, several factors are important. First, with short-term debt, several refinancings may be necessary. Each refinancing involves flotation costs. The total flotation costs may be higher with short-term debt.

Second, use of short-term debt in anticipation of refinancing at lower interest rates runs the risk of an incorrect forecast. If interest rates rise, the refinancing of short-term debt *must* take place at higher interest rates. In contrast, issuing long-term callable debt provides protection against interest rate increases by locking-in the borrowing costs.

To see more clearly how callable bonds may be a substitute for short-term debt, consider the following simplified two-period scenario shown in table 14.5. At time 0, the firm issues either a one-period noncallable debt with coupon $c_{non,0}$ that must be refinanced at time 1 with another one-period bond with coupon $c_{non,1}$ or it issues a two-period callable bond with coupon $c_{call,0}$ that may be called at time 1 and replaced with a one-period bond with coupon $c_{non,1}$. Next consider the numerical example in table 14.6 in which a firm can issue a callable bond with an 8 percent coupon or a noncallable bond with a 6 percent coupon. At time 1, the one-period rate is either 5 percent or 10 percent.

The amount $c_{call,0} - c_{non,0}$ (i.e., 2 percent in the numerical example) is positive since it represents the higher coupon on a two-period callable bond minus the coupon on a one-period noncallable bond. The firm issuing callable bonds pays this higher coupon at time 1. If refunding occurs, the firm issuing a callable bond pays the same coupon in period 2 as a new one-period bond. If refunding does not occur, the firm issuing a callable bond enjoys a lower

Table 14.5 Callable Bonds versus Short-Term Debt

Type of Issue	Points in Time		
	0	1	2
			Refund at Time 1 / Not Refund
One-period noncallable		$c_{non,0}$	$c_{non,1}$ / $c_{non,1}$
Two-period callable		$c_{call,0}$	$c_{non,1}$ / $c_{call,0}$
Incremental coupons: callable – noncallable		$c_{call,0} - c_{non,0}$	0 / $c_{call,0} - c_{non,1}$

Table 14.6 Example of Callable versus Short-Term Debt

Type of Issue	Points in Time		
	0	1	2
			Refund at Time 1 / Not Refund
One-period noncallable		6%	5% / 10%
Two-period callable		8%	5% / 8%
Incremental coupons: callable – noncallable		8%–6%	0 / 8%–10%

coupon $c_{call,0}$ (i.e., 8 percent) compared to the firm refinancing with a new one-period bond at $c_{non,1}$ (i.e., 10 percent).

In a perfectly efficient market, the coupons on the various bonds are determined by the market so that the marginal firm and investor are satisfied. Some firms or individuals prefer one position to another. For some firms, paying the added coupon on a callable bond is worth avoiding the prospect of having to pay a high coupon on refinancing of short-term bonds. Other firms would prefer the risk of using short-term debt.

Advance Refundings

Typically, callable bonds are issued with a period of call protection. If interest rates drop considerably before the period of call protection ends, the firm might consider an advance refunding. In advance refunding, the firm offers to purchase call-protected debt at a price above the call price. Bondholders are *not* required to sell their bonds back to the firm. However, the offer can be made attractive enough for most bondholders to sell their bonds and for the firm to reap a refunding benefit as well.

To illustrate, assume that a bond has two years of call protection remaining, a call price of $112 per $100 of par value, and an annual coupon of $12. If current interest rates are 6 percent, the firm has an incentive to refund. Instead of waiting two years and refunding at possibly higher or lower rates, the firm can offer to retire the issue right now and refund.

The first step is to estimate a price sufficient to induce the bondholders to sell but not eliminate too much of the firm's refunding benefit. If current interest rates are low enough, refunding when the bond becomes freely callable in two years seems almost inevitable. From the bondholders' viewpoint, the bond's value is the present value of the $12 coupon for the next two years plus the present value of the call price two years from now. If d is the appropriate discount rate, then:

$$\text{Value} = \frac{12}{1 + d} + \frac{12 + 112}{(1 + d)^2} \qquad (14.8)$$

If d is 6 percent, the value is $121.68. By offering slightly more, the firm should be able to induce the bondholders to sell their bonds.

An advance refunding allows a firm to realize some refunding benefits immediately. This must be weighed against the added cost of open market purchase.

Refunding Discounted Debt

Refunding usually occurs after interest rates have dropped. Some authors claim that refundings may be profitable after interest rates have gone up.

The argument is that open-market repurchase of an existing bond below par value and replacement with a higher coupon par bond is beneficial. This argument is incorrect if there are no taxes. Under some special tax rules, these refundings might have advantages.

In order to refund discounted debt, a firm must repurchase the bonds in the open market.[6] If there is some advantage to the firm to refund this debt and if the bondholders are aware of this advantage, rational bondholders would require a premium price. In effect, the bondholders would share the refunding gain with the firm. This sharing would reduce the firm's gain from the refunding.

Sinking Funds

Many corporate bonds contain a sinking fund provision, which requires the issuing firm to retire part of the bond issue at intervals stated in the bond indenture. Figure 14.7 presents an example in which a firm issues 25-year bonds with annual sinking fund payments of 2 percent of principal beginning in the tenth year. This means 15 annual sinking fund payments of 2 percent, leaving 70 percent of par value to be repaid at final maturity.

At the indicated sinking fund dates, the firm has the option to purchase the required number of bonds in the open market or to call these bonds.

Figure 14.7   Sinking Fund Payments

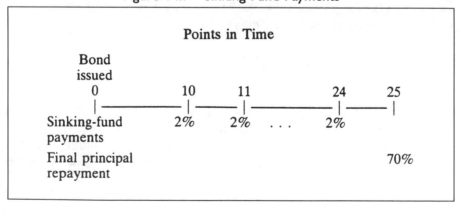

---

[6] In contrast, in a refunding after a decline in interest rates, the firm can force the bondholders to sell their bonds at the call price.

Every sinking fund bond issue has a special call provision allowing the firm to call bonds at random on the required sinking fund dates. At each sinking fund date, the firm chooses the cheaper option.

The rationale for including a sinking fund is not entirely clear. First, a sinking fund provision may signal lower default risk. Firms raise funds for making sinking fund payments internally or externally. The availability of sufficient internal funds from current operations to meet sinking fund payments is a signal of high profitability. The availability of sufficient external funds to meet sinking fund payments is a signal that new lenders have confidence in the firm. Thus, sinking funds signal the favorable future prospects of the firm, implying lower default risk and reduced yields on the bonds.

Second, some bonds are scheduled to be called under the terms of the sinking fund. As we have seen, the call feature tends to raise the coupon rate on bonds. The net impact of these two offsetting effects – favorable signals and the call feature – is not apparent a priori.

Refunding Municipal Bonds

Municipal bonds are issued by state and local governments. Interest income is exempt from federal income taxes, although subject to state income taxes. Because of this tax exemption, the yields on municipal bonds are lower than those on otherwise identical taxable bonds.

Municipal bonds typically have a call option. After declines in interest rates, municipalities refund with lower coupon debt. The analysis of the benefit of a municipal refunding is essentially the same as for a corporate refunding. The biggest difference is that municipalities do not pay income taxes.

In addition, many municipal bonds have serial maturities, i.e., the maturities are staggered over a number of years. This pattern of maturities is very similar to a sinking fund. Under either alternative, a proportion of the bond principal is repaid over a number of years.

Summary

Corporate and municipal bonds usually allow the issuer to call the bonds at a stated call price. This call feature allows the issuer to refund the issue at a later date after a decline in interest rates. A refunding allows the firm to replace a high coupon debt with a lower coupon debt, saving interest costs over the remaining life of the bond.

In an informationally efficient market in which the bondholders and the firm have the same information, the market sets the features (i.e., coupon, call price, and period of call protection) on a callable bond to make the marginal bondholder and issuing firm indifferent between callable and non-callable bonds. Similarly, the marginal market participant is indifferent between long-term callable bonds and short-term bonds. In imperfect markets, firms may have incentives to issue callable bonds.

Questions/Problems

1. In a perfectly efficient market, what does a firm gain if it issues callable bonds instead of noncallable bonds?

2. Explain the impact of call deferment and call premiums on the coupon of a callable bond.

3. A firm has decided to immediately refund an existing callable bond issue. Under what circumstances is there an immediate benefit to refunding? What does that benefit depend upon?

4. Instead of refunding a callable bond issue immediately, a firm has the choice of waiting to refund until some future date. Explain the possible advantages and disadvantages of waiting to refund.

5. Some have argued that market imperfections provide an incentive to issue callable bonds. Explain the pros and cons of these market imperfections arguments.

6. How can callable bonds be a substitute for short-term bonds?

7. Sinking fund provisions are widely used. What is a sinking fund? How are bonds retired under the sinking fund provisions? Explain the advantages and disadvantages of a sinking fund to the bond issuer and to the bondholder. What are the impacts of sinking funds on yields? Municipal bonds have serial maturities. Compare a serial maturity with a sinking fund.

8. A firm has a perpetual callable bond outstanding with a par value of $100 and an annual coupon of $14. The firm can refund this with a new noncallable perpetual bond having an 8 percent coupon. The call price on the old bond is $114. Flotation costs for a new issue are 2 percent of par. What is the myopic benefit of refunding?

9. In problem 8, how would your answer change if the new bond was callable and had a coupon of 10 percent?

10. If there is a corporate income tax rate of 30 percent, how does your answer to problem 8 change?

11. A firm has a perpetual callable bond with a 12 percent coupon. The bond has a call premium of 12 percent. Flotation costs are 2 percent and there are no taxes. The firm can refund immediately with a 9 percent noncallable perpetual bond. If it decides to postpone refunding until next period, interest rates on noncallable bonds will be 6 percent, 9 percent, or 12 percent, each with probability of 1/3. Should the firm refund immediately or wait? Initially, consider the case where the firm is risk neutral. Then, introduce risk aversion.

References

Aivazian, V. and J. L. Callen, "Future Investment Opportunities and the Call Provision on a Bond: Comment," *Journal of Finance,* 35, 1980, pp. 1051–54.

Allen, D. S., R. E. Lamy, and G. R. Thompson, "Agency Costs and Alternative Call Provisions: An Empirical Investigation," *Financial Management,* 16, Winter 1987, pp. 37–44.

Bodie, Z. and R. A. Taggart, "Future Investment Opportunities and the Value of the Call Provision on a Bond," *Journal of Finance,* 33, 1978, pp. 1187–200.

Bodie, Z. and R. A. Taggart, "Future Investment Opportunities and the Call Provision on a Bond: Reply," *Journal of Finance,* 35, 1980, pp. 1055–56.

Bowlin, O. D., "The Bond Refunding Decision: Another Special Case in Capital Budgeting," *Journal of Finance,* 21, March 1966, pp. 55–68.

Brennan, M. J. and E. S. Schwartz, "Savings Bonds, Retractable Bonds, and Callable Bonds," *Journal of Financial Economics,* 5, August 1977, pp. 67–88.

Crabbe, L. E., and J. Helwege, "Alternative Tests of Agency Theories of Callable Corporate Bonds," *Financial Management,* 23, Winter 1994, pp. 3–20.

Kish, R. J., "Noncallable Debt: Evidence and Effect," unpublished Ph.D. dissertation, University of Florida, 1988.

Kish, R. J. and M. Livingston, "The Determinants of the Call Feature on Corporate Bonds," *Journal of Banking and Finance,* 16, 1992, pp. 687–703.

Kraus, A., "The Bond Refunding Decision in an Efficient Market," *Journal of Financial and Quantitative Analysis,* 8, December 1973, pp. 793–806.

Lewellen, W. G. and D. R. Emery, "On the Matter of Parity Among Financial Obligations," *Journal of Finance,* 35, March 1980, pp. 97–111.

Livingston, M., "Bond Refunding Reconsidered," *Journal of Finance,* 35, March 1980, pp. 191–5.

Livingston, M., "Measuring the Benefit of Bond Refunding: The Problem of Nonmarketable Call Options," *Financial Management,* 16, Spring 1987, pp. 38–40.

Longstaff, F. A., "Are Negative Option Prices Possible? The Callable U.S. Treasury Bond Puzzle," *Journal of Business,* 65, October 1992, pp. 571–92.

Longstaff, F. A., and B. A. Tuckman, "Calling Nonconvertible Debt and the Problem of Related Wealth Transfer Effects," *Financial Management,* 23, Winter 1994, pp. 21–7.

Mauer, D. C., A. Barnea, and C. S. Kim, "Valuation of Callable Bonds Under Progressive Personal Taxes and Interest Rate Uncertainty," *Financial Management,* 20, Summer 1991, pp. 50–9.

Mitchell, K., "The Call, Sinking Fund, and Term-to-Maturity Features of Corporate Bonds: An Empirical Investigation," *Journal of Financial and Quantitative Analysis,* 26, June 1991, pp. 201–22.

Narayanan, M. P. and S. P. Lim, "On the Call Provision on Corporate Zero Coupon Bonds," *Journal of Financial and Quantitative Analysis,* 24, March 1989, pp. 91–103.

Ofer, R. A. and R. A. Taggart, "Bond Refunding: A Clarifying Analysis," *Journal of Finance,* 32, March 1977, pp. 21–30.

Pye, G., "The Value of the Call Option on a Bond," *Journal of Political Economy,* 74, April 1966, pp. 200–5.

Van Horne, J. C., *Financial Management and Policy,* 7e, Englewood Cliffs, NJ: Prentice Hall, 1986.

Vu, J. D., "An Empirical Investigation of Calls of Non-callable Bonds," *Journal of Financial Economics,* 16, June 1986, pp. 235–65.

Wingler, T. R. and G. D. Jud, "Premium Debt Tenders: Analysis and Evidence," *Financial Management,* 19, Winter 1990, pp. 58–67.

15

Mortgages

Overview

A mortgage is a loan with property as collateral. Mortgages are an extremely important component of the debt markets. The amount of mortgage credit outstanding is huge, amounting to more than 50 percent of GNP in the United States.[1]

In the event of default by the borrower, the property is sold to satisfy the obligations to the lender. The legal arrangements used to guarantee the rights of the lender vary by state. In some states, the lender has title to the property. In other states, the borrower owns the property and the lender has a claim upon it in the event of default. In practice, there is little difference between these legal arrangements, especially for residential mortgages.

Usually, the amount of the loan is less than the collateral, i.e., the market value of the property, implying some protection to the lender. However, since real estate values sometimes decline, a loan for 80 percent of the market value of the property in good economic times might exceed the market value of the property in bad economic times.

Sometimes borrowers obtain loans from thrifts or banks holding the mortgages until they are paid off.[2] In other cases, borrowers initiate loans with institutions selling the loans in the market to a final lender. An institution initiating loans with borrowers and then selling them in the secondary market is called a **loan originator**. The originator usually processes the monthly

---

[1] See the evidence in chapter 1.

[2] Many mortgages are prepaid before the final maturity.

payments and earns a fee for this service. Originators of mortgages include thrifts, banks, and mortgage companies. Mortgage companies are firms that match borrowers with ultimate lenders (that is, investors) and that consequently sell most of their mortgages in the secondary market. Mortgage companies originate and administer mortgage loans but sell them rather than hold them as investments.

Mortgage loans are frequently categorized as one- to four-family homes (residential property) and income property (office space and apartment buildings). The three biggest originators of funds for one- to four-family homes are commercial banks, thrifts, and mortgage companies. About half of the originations by thrifts and banks are sold in the secondary market in the form of mortgage pools. For income properties, commercial banks, thrifts, and insurance companies are large originators of loans.[3] These institutions tend to hold mortgages on income properties, rather than sell them in the secondary market.

Mortgages can be divided into two types: (1) **fixed-rate, constant payment mortgages** and (2) **variable payment mortgages**. Through the 1960s, mortgages in the U.S. were almost universally fixed-rate. In the 1970s, mortgages with variable payments were introduced as interest rates rose dramatically. Since 1980, the practice of selling fixed-rate mortgages to investors in the secondary market became important and has continued to expand.

The biggest lenders in the residential mortgage market have been thrift institutions and commercial banks. Until the 1960s, these institutions tended to make long-term fixed-rate mortgages with constant periodic payments. Banks and thrifts financed these mortgages with short-term borrowings in the form of savings and time deposits. In the 1970s, as interest rates rose and became highly variable, many existing fixed-rate loans earned less interest than the cost of financing them. Lending institutions suffered large losses. Since thrift institutions concentrated most of their lending in mortgages, thrifts were especially hurt. By 1985, more than one quarter of all thrifts had failed.

To adapt to high and variable interest rates, banks and thrifts began to make more variable interest mortgage loans. With a variable interest rate mortgage, the interest rate charged on the mortgage goes up and down with

---

[3] Many of the larger income property loans originate through correspondent mortgage companies.

the level of interest rates. If rates rise, the borrower pays more; if rates fall, the borrower pays less. With variable-rate loans, the borrower bears the risks (and possible rewards) of changing interest rates; the bank or thrift no longer bears these risks.

With marketable or so-called securitized mortgages, a group of residential mortgages are put into a pool and marketable claims on the pool are sold to ultimate investors. For marketable mortgages, the mortgage originator is distinct from the final lender or investor. Banks and thrifts formerly originated and held most of their residential mortgages until maturity. Now, a sizable proportion of mortgages are sold in the secondary market. Selling of mortgages allows banks and thrifts to pass on the risk of changing interest rates to final lenders. The originators still earn fees for processing the mortgages.[4] The processing fees are much smaller than the possible profits from holding the loans to maturity. Also, the risks of an originator are much lower than the risks of holding the mortgage until maturity.

With marketable mortgages, the mortgage market has become a national market where borrowers raise funds in the large, impersonal national market for funds. A national market is undoubtedly more efficient since borrowers and lenders can be matched more easily. The result is a reduction in interest costs to borrowers and an increase in interest rates earned by lenders. These gains are earned at the expense of thrifts and banks who increasingly act as originators of residential mortgage loans.

In the 1960s, the mortgage market was much more of a localized market. Individuals made deposits in local banks and thrifts, which made mortgage loans locally. With these localized markets, disparities in interest rates occurred. Mortgage borrowers in some areas paid higher rates than in other areas. With a national mortgage market, borrowing rates are much more uniform.

Active primary and secondary national markets in mortgages require homogeneous mortgages. The biggest obstacle to homogeneous marketable mortgages is default risk. If a borrower defaults, the lender has the messy problem of seeking legal redress. This default problem has been overcome by mortgages being guaranteed by government agencies and by private insurance companies. Once a mortgage has been guaranteed, the guaranteeing

---

[4] For residential mortgages, the originators usually suffer losses even after loan initiation fees. They try to make up the losses through loan service fees.

agency bears the default risk and the ultimate mortgage buyer is not concerned with default. The resulting guaranteed mortgage is a highly attractive investment to many investors.

Standard Fixed-Rate Mortgages

Until the 1970s, banks and thrifts in the U.S. offered almost all of their mortgages with fixed interest rates. A borrower would take out a mortgage loan for a principal amount, P, and repay it in equal monthly installments of M. The interest rate would be fixed at y. To simplify the discussion, we assume n annual installment payments.

The present value of the installment payments must equal the mortgage principal, P, that is:

$$P = \frac{M}{(1 + y)} + \frac{M}{(1 + y)^2} + \ldots + \frac{M}{(1 + y)^n} \qquad (15.1)$$

This may be expressed as:

$$P = M\left[\frac{1}{y}\right]\left[1 - \frac{1}{(1 + y)^n}\right] \qquad (15.2)$$

$$P = M[\text{present value of annuity}] = M[\text{PVA}_n] \qquad (15.3)$$

PVA_n denotes the present value of an n period annuity at the interest rate y. Given the maturity, n, the interest rate, y, and the amount of the principal, P, the preceding equation can be solved for the installment payment, M:

$$M = \frac{P}{\text{PVA}_n} \qquad (15.4)$$

Consider a numerical example with a principal of $1,000, an interest rate of 10 percent, and a 20-year repayment period. Then the annual installment payment is:

$$M = \frac{1,000}{8.514} = 117.45 \qquad (15.5)$$

Since there are 20 annual mortgage payments of $117.45, the total amount paid over the entire life of the mortgage is $2,349. One thousand dollars of this total is repayment of the original loan. The remaining $1,349 is interest. Even though the total amount of interest is quite large, these payments represent a fair price for an interest rate of 10 percent.

Each mortgage payment, M, includes a payment for interest and repayment of part of the principal, sometimes called amortization of principal. As the principal is reduced, the total interest on the principal is reduced, and more of the mortgage payment is repayment of principal.

The interest and principal repayment may be computed recursively. The interest payment is the previous period's principal times the interest rates. The repayment of principal is the mortgage payment minus the interest. The computations are illustrated in table 15.1.

In general, for an n period loan with mortgage payment of M and interest rate y, the principal repayment and interest for period j are:

$$\text{Principal repayment} = M\left(\frac{1}{1 + y}\right)^{n-j+1} \tag{15.6}$$

Table 15.1   Computation of Interest and Principal Repayment
Principal = $1,000; Interest Rate = 10%;
Maturity = 20 years; Mortgage Payment = $117.45

Point in Time	Principal	Interest	Repayment of Principal
0	1,000.00		
1	982.55	100.00	17.45
	= 1,000 − 17.45	= .1(1,000)	= 117.45 − 100
2	963.36	98.26	19.19
	= 982.55 − 19.19	= .1(982.55)	= 117.45 − 98.26
3		96.34	
		= .1(953.36)	

$$\frac{\text{Interest}}{\text{payment}} = M\left[1 - \left(\frac{1}{1+y}\right)^{n-j+1}\right] \tag{15.7}$$

The loan balance remaining after j payments is equal to:

$$\frac{\text{Remaining}}{\text{principal}} = M\sum_{i=1}^{n-j}(1+y)^{-i} \tag{15.8}$$

$$= M[\text{PVA}_{n-j}]$$

where PVA_{n-j} is the present value of an $n - j$ period annuity. This formula says that the remaining principal is merely the present value of the remaining mortgage payments of M dollars per period discounted at the interest rate y. The percent of the original principal reamining after j periods is the remaining principal divided by the original principal. That is,

$$\frac{\text{\% of original}}{\text{principal}} = \frac{M[\text{PVA}_{n-j}]}{P} \tag{15.9}$$
$$\text{remaining}$$

$$= \frac{M[\text{PVA}_{n-j}]}{M[\text{PVA}_n]} = \frac{\text{PVA}_{n-j}}{\text{PVA}_n}$$

This formula implies that the percentage of an n-period mortgage repaid after j periods is:

$$\frac{\text{\% of principal}}{\text{repaid}} = \frac{[\text{PVA}_n - PVA_{n-j}]}{\text{PVA}_n} \tag{15.10}$$
$$\text{after } j \text{ periods}$$

Variable-Rate Mortgages

With fluctuating interest rates, lenders have incentives to pass on interest rate risk in the form of variable-rate loans. The interest rate charged to borrowers can be tied to the rate on a widely quoted money market rate, perhaps the one-year Treasury bill rate plus 2 percent. The lender's cost of raising funds varies with this rate, possibly equalling the one-year bill rate plus .5 percent. By setting the loan rate at the one-year bill rate plus 2 percent, the lender can lock in a profit of 1.5 percent minus operating costs and default risk.

On the other side of the coin, the borrower bears the risks and possible returns of changing interest rates. In the long run, the benefits from borrowing short-term may be considerable because long-term interest rates are typically higher than short-term rates. A bank borrowing short and lending long-term earns this term premium on average. By making variable-rate loans, banks pass on these potential profits to borrowers. With variable-rate loans, the bank avoids possible catastrophic losses when short-term interest rates exceed long-term rates; in addition, the bank loses possible large profits if short-term interest rates drop.

A practical alternative to variable-rate loans is fixed-rate mortgage loans with the borrower having prepayment options. These fixed-rate loans are a two-edged sword to lenders. If interest rates rise, the lender loses because the cost of short-term funds increases. If rates decline, the lender loses because mortgages are prepaid and the lender has to reinvest at lower interest rates. The only scenario where fixed-rate mortgages with prepayment options are really profitable to the lender occurs when interest rates are stable. Then, the lender makes the difference between the long-term lending rate and the short-term borrowing rate. As we know from term structure theory, the spread between the long-term rate and the short-term rate is a risk premium reflecting the possibility of interest rates changing in the future. Although lenders can expect to earn some average return as a reward for risk bearing, lenders can expect to sometimes suffer sizable losses from this strategy. Lenders have to be prepared to bear the risks involved. If not, a prudent strategy is to pass on the risks by offering variable-rate loans. Alternatively, the fixed-rate mortgage can be sold to investors.

Assumable Mortgages

When a real estate property is sold, some mortgages allow the new owner to take over (or assume) the existing mortgage. From the buyer's viewpoint, an assumable mortgage has the advantage of avoiding loan initiation fees on a new mortgage. From the seller's view, the assumable mortgage avoids possible prepayment penalties. These advantages of an assumable mortgage should be reflected in a higher selling price for the property in a perfect market.

An assumable mortgage may be at a lower interest rate than the interest rate on a new mortgage. The selling price should reflect this advantage. For example, suppose a house with an assumable 25-year mortgage with $50,000 principal and 6 percent interest rate is sold when interest rates on new mortgages are 10 percent. The interest payments on the mortgage are $3,911 (that is, $50,000/12.873). A 10 percent mortgage with principal of $50,000 has annual payments of $5,508. The difference in interest has a present value of $14,496 (that is, [5,508 − 3,911][9.077]) that should be reflected in a higher selling price.

Nonassumable mortgages have a due on sale clause making the principal amount of the mortgage due if the property is sold. In addition, the seller must pay any prepayment penalties.

Mortgage Prepayments

Most conventional mortgages allow the borrower to prepay the remaining principal of the loan before final maturity.[5] Prepayments occur for two major reasons: (1) The homeowner moves and the mortgage is not assumable by the new owner. (2) Interest rates fall and the mortgage can be refinanced at a lower interest cost.

Following a drop in interest rates, a borrower can save interest costs by replacing an existing high interest rate mortgage with a low rate mortgage.[6] To evaluate the advisability of prepayment, the present value of interest saved has to be balanced against any prepayment fees and costs of initiating a new mortgage. Typically, lenders charge substantial loan initiation fees (sometimes called points) for making a new mortgage loan. In addition, the borrower must decide whether waiting to replace the mortgage may be better. The prepayer has to weigh the present value of interest savings versus costs of replacement plus the present value of possible additional benefits from waiting.[7]

To illustrate, consider a borrower taking out a 25-year mortgage at 12 percent with a principal of $10,000. After five years have elapsed, interest rates on new mortgages are 10 percent. Should the mortgage be replaced

---

[5] Some mortgages contain prepayment penalties. The mortgage covenant may allow 20 percent of the mortgage to be prepaid in each of the first five years of the mortgage without penalty and the entire mortgage to be paid after five years.

[6] The mortgage prepayment decision is the same problem as refunding of a corporate bond after a drop in interest rates.

[7] Chapter 14 on bond call features discusses the refunding issue in detail.

with a new 20-year mortgage assuming no prepayment penalties and a loan initiation fee of 3 percent?

To solve this problem, first compute the mortgage payment, M, on the original loan:

$$M = \frac{\text{principal}}{\text{PVA}} = \frac{10,000}{7,843} = 1,275 \qquad (15.11)$$

The remaining mortgage principal after five years is:

$$\frac{\text{Remaining}}{\text{principal}} = M\sum_{i=1}^{n-j}(1 + y)^{-i} \qquad (15.12)$$

$$\frac{\text{Remaining}}{\text{principal}} = 1,275\sum_{i=1}^{20}(1.12)^{-i} = 9,523 \qquad (15.13)$$

The summation term in this equation is merely the present value of a 20-year annuity at the rate of 12 percent. The new mortgage is assumed to have the same principal of $9,523 as the old mortgage. At 10 percent, the mortgage payments on the new mortgage are 9,523/8.514 or $1,119. The immediate benefit from refinancing now is:

$$\begin{aligned}\frac{\text{Immediate}}{\text{refinancing}}_{\text{benefit}} &= (1,275 - 1,119)(8.514) - (9,523)(.03)\\[4pt] &= (156)(8.514) - 286 \qquad (15.14)\\[4pt] &= 1,328 - 286 = 1,042\end{aligned}$$

The savings for each of the next 20 years is $156 (that is, 1,275 − 1,119). The present value of these savings is $156 times the present value of an annuity at 10 percent or $1,328 (that is, 156 × 8.514). The cost of refinancing the mortgage is 3 percent of the principal or $286 (that is, 9523 × .03). The net present value of the savings is $1,042. An additional cost of refinancing immediately is the present value of the possible incremental benefits from waiting to finance at future lower interest rates. The borrower must estimate whether the additional value of waiting might exceed the immediate benefit of $1,042.

If interest rates drop substantially, borrowers are able to refinance at lower interest rates. On the other side of the coin, lenders must reinvest prepaid mortgages at lower interest rates. Consequently, the option for the borrower to prepay a mortgage is undesirable from the lender's viewpoint.

To protect themselves, lenders can include prepayment penalties, charge a somewhat higher interest rate to reflect the refinancing risk, and charge loan initiation fees on new mortgages to discourage frequent refinancings. In a perfectly efficient market, the risks of future refinancings should be built into the pricing of mortgages.

Government Agencies

Government agencies and government-sponsored agencies have played an important role in transforming the mortgage market. There are two major functions performed by these agencies: guaranteeing mortgages against default and selling claims on pools of residential mortgages. As a result of government activity, the market for mortgage-backed securities has developed. The growth of mortgage-backed securities has made the mortgage market increasingly like the bond market, with funds being raised very competitively in the national market. The result is more uniform interest rates (instead of geographical differences), somewhat lower rates available for buyers, and somewhat higher rates available to lenders. Also, the supply of mortgage funds is not as subject to abrupt stoppages.

Two government agencies guarantee mortgages: the Federal Housing Administration (FHA) and the Veterans Administration (VA). The operations of both are quite similar except that the FHA insures mortgages to qualified borrowers, whereas the VA guarantees mortgages for veterans only. Each agency sets standards for approving loan applications and the loans have standard terms with respect to maturity, assumability, prepayment, and so on.

There are a number of private insurance companies for mortgages. The private companies developed for several reasons. First, FHA and VA loans have caps on the maximum amount of the loan. Private insurers do not have these caps and serve a special segment of the market. Second, FHA and VA loan applications take a long time to process, perhaps as much as two months. Private insurers can process loan applications much faster. Third, government guarantors have very rigid requirements on loans, whereas private insurers can be more flexible. An appraiser examines homes applying for coverage. FHA and VA guarantees require rigid specifications. Homes failing to meet these specifications may still be perfectly safe and sound. Private insurers have the flexibility to account for these differences. For example, the FHA may require certain types of gutters. A home with different gutters would not qualify for FHA insurance, although private insurers would have no problem insuring the home.

Private mortgage insurance has the advantage of flexibility over the FHA and VA. However, private insurance has a disadvantage; the private insurance company itself can go bankrupt and default on its insurance obligations. If a severe recession or depression occurs, a large number of mortgage defaults would undoubtedly occur. If the total obligations of the insurance company to pay defaulted mortgages exceeds the reserves available, the insurer may be forced to default on the insurance. Whereas the risks of default by individual borrowers can be diversified away in a large portfolio of mortgages, the risk of a major downturn in the economy cannot be diversified away. In effect, private mortgage insurance represents only partial protection against mortgage default.

Three government agencies are involved in the creation of marketable mortgage claims: the Government National Mortgage Association (GNMA or Ginnie Mae), the Federal National Mortgage Association (FNMA or Fannie Mae), and the Federal Home Loan Mortgage Corporation (FHLMC or Freddie Mac). FNMA and FHLMC actually purchase mortgages to put into pools; GNMA does not purchase the mortgages but guarantees mortgages in a pool created by a mortgage originator. All three agencies guarantee the payment of interest and principal. FNMA also purchases mortgages which they hold as investments, using bonds as financing.

GNMA is a government agency, that is, a part of the United States government. The other two, FNMA and FHLMC, are government-sponsored agencies, that is, private entities which have the backing of the federal government. Because of the view that the government will come to the rescue of a sponsored agency, the security markets probably perceive little difference between a government agency and a government-sponsored agency.

There are two other government-sponsored agencies that play a role in the mortgage market. The Farmers Home Administration makes mortgage loans to farmers. The Federal Home Loan Banks sell bonds and lend the funds to thrift institutions.

Marketable Mortgages[8]

Figure 15.1 illustrates several alternatives for mortgage financing. The traditional approach for mortgage financing is for a borrower to receive a mortgage

---

[8] Marketable mortgages are also called **mortgage backed securities** (MBS) or **securitized mortgages**.

Figure 15.1   Methods of Mortgage Financing

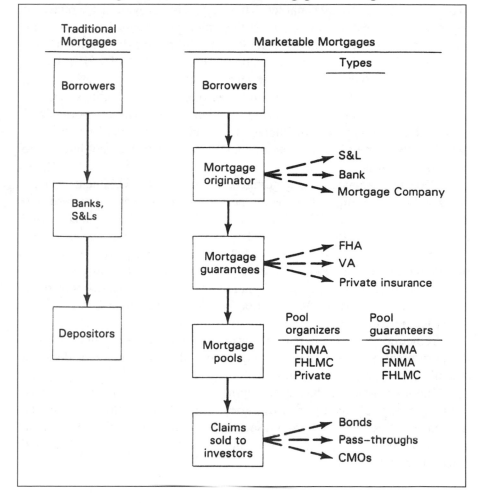

loan directly from a commercial bank or a thrift institution, which finances the loan with deposits. Since these deposits can be withdrawn on short notice, the bank or thrift is financing a long-term mortgage with short-term funds and bearing the risk of rising interest rates.

In the second type of mortgage loan, the borrower approaches a mortgage originator (that is, a commercial bank, thrift, or mortgage company), who submits the loan application to a guarantor. As discussed shortly, there are private mortgage guarantors and government agencies (that is, the FHA and VA) that guarantee payments if the borrower defaults. If the guarantor accepts a mortgage, the mortgage is included in a mortgage pool. Mortgage pools can be organized by private firms. However, the majority are organized by government agencies created to promote the flow of funds from the bond market into the mortgage market. These agencies provide a guarantee of payment of interest and principal on their mortgage pools. Thus, there are two layers of protection against default by the borrower: the insurers (FHA, VA, or private insurer) and the pool organizers[9] (GNMA, FNMA, or FHLMC). This double layer of insurance is necessary for two reasons. First, the insurers (FHA, VA) put limits on the amount of their liabilities. Second, long legal delays can occur in trying to collect funds. The pool organizers guarantee timely payment of interest and principal and thus bear the risks of delays. Because of these dual guarantees, the buyer does not have to be concerned with default risk.[10]

Pools of guaranteed mortgages are put together by government agencies or by private institutions. Claims on the pool of mortgages are then sold to investors. Since these claims have no default risk and have standardized features, they are highly marketable. Highly marketable securities are attractive to investors, implying relatively low interest rates. This process of putting mortgages into pools and selling claims on the pools has been called securitization of mortgages. Securitization of mortgages benefits homeowners since at least part of the reduction in interest rates is passed on to the mortgage borrower.

Some mortgage pools may be formed through a sale of mortgages to the pool organizer.[11] In other mortgage pools, the pool guarantor does not actually purchase the mortgages.[12]

The pool organizer has three alternatives for selling claims to finance the mortgage pool (see figure 15.1). First, bonds can be sold to finance the mortgages.[13] Second, pass-through securities (discussed shortly) can be sold; this the most common procedure. Third, derivative securities (discussed shortly) can be issued.

---

[9] GNMA pools have FHA and VA insurance. FHLMC and FNMA pools have private insurance.

[10] It is possible that the mortgage guarantor may go bankrupt. This point is discussed shortly.

[11] FHLMC and FNMA pools are formed in this way.

[12] GNMA pools are formed in this way. GNMA does not actually purchase mortgages.

[13] This procedure is used by FNMA on some of its mortgages.

Prepayments

Mortgages are frequently prepaid before final maturity. Even though a typical long-term mortgage might have a 30-year maturity, a large proportion of the mortgages are prepaid by 10-12 years, for two primary reasons. First, mortgages are typically repaid when homeowners move. Second, mortgages are refinanced after interest rates drop.

The resulting pattern of prepayments is shown in figure 15.2. The vertical axis shows the annual prepayment rate. The horizontal axis shows the change in interest rates from the original mortgage rate. In figure 15.2, some prepayments occur because some homeowners move and repay their mortgages. These moving prepayments are largely independent of changes in interest rates.[14]

When interest rates increase above the original mortgage yield, refinancing does not pay; prepayments are largely moving prepayments. When interest rates fall sufficiently, homeowners refinance to take advantage of lower interest rates on new mortgages. The decline in interest rates has to be large enough to cover refinancing costs to trigger a refinancing. A small decline in interest rates does not cause refinancings. For larger drops in interest rates, more homeowners find refinancing attractive. Thus, for declining interest rates, prepayments have a moving component and a refinancing component.

Prepayment Assumptions

When figuring the value of a mortgage, the possibility of prepayment should be included. Typically, analysts assume a particular pattern of prepayments and then figure the value of the mortgage given these prepayments. Several types of prepayment assumptions are used.

The Public Securities Association (PSA) approach assumes low prepayments in the beginning since new home buyers are unlikely to move immediately after buying a home. As time goes by, homeowners are more

---

[14] As the pace of economic activity increases in an economic expansion, interest rates increase at the same time that demand for labor increases. More job opportunities cause greater labor mobility, more home sales, and more mortgage prepayments. Thus, interest rate increases may be associated with some increase in moving prepayments.

Figure 15.2   Annual Refinancings versus the Change in the Interest Rate

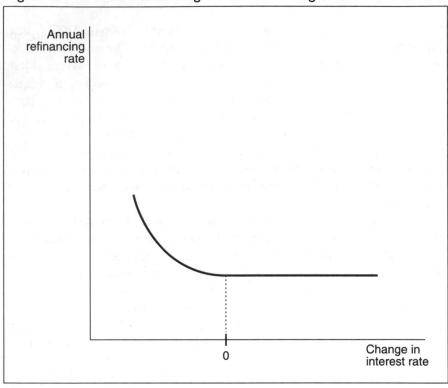

likely to move, and interest rates are more likely to change. The annualized prepayment rate increases until month 30. Thereafter, the prepayment rate is 6 percent per year.

The **constant prepayment rate** (CPR) assumes that a constant percent of the remaining principal is prepaid annually over the life of the mortgage. The advantage of this approach is its simplicity.

When mortgages are valued, some assumption is made about the prepayment pattern. The value of the mortgage or the derivative securities can be dramatically affected by the payment assumption. A prepayment assumption of 100 percent of PSA gives markedly different cash flows from 300 percent of PSA.

Derivative Mortgage Products

If mortgages are put into a pool, there are a number of ways of handling prepayments. First, a claim on a mortgage pool may entitle the holder to a prorated share of all payments. These claims are called **pass-through securities** because the mortgage payments are merely passed through the pool to the final investor.[15] In this case, each claimant shares in the prepayments. Sharing in prepayments means that each claim gets a percentage of the principal repaid. When the principal is reduced, future interest payments are reduced. Pass-through securities are generally standardized contracts, which makes them highly liquid, with an active resale market. Investors who purchase or sell pass-throughs are able to change their market holdings rapidly without affecting prices.

A second possibility is to partition prepayments. Some investors want to avoid prepayments and others do not. To accommodate these investment needs, pool organizers have developed many ways of partitioning the prepayments. The resulting securities are called **derivative mortgage products**, **collateralized mortgage obligations** (CMO), or **real estate investment mortgage conduits** (REMIC). The major varieties include sequential pay securities, Z bonds, planned amortization classes, and principal only or interest only derivatives.

Partitioning of prepayment cash flows is a two-edged sword. The prepayment risk to some investors is reduced, and they receive a lower risk position and lower expected returns. But the prepayment risk to other investors is increased; they have a higher risk position and higher expected returns. For high risk investors, the gains and losses from interest rate movements can be considerable. Sometimes interest rates will move in favor of the high risk investors and sometimes against them. The realized returns may be very favorable or very poor.

The partitioning of mortgage cash flows produces a net benefit to mortgage borrowers. Each class is purchased by investors who want to hold a mortgage with a particular expected prepayment pattern. The buyers of individual classes can be expected to accept somewhat lower yields for separate classes than buyers of a claim on the entire pool. In effect, dividing a mortgage pool into parts increases the value of the mortgages and reduces their yields. The yield reduction is at least partially passed on to borrowers. Part of the yield reduction is realized as (arbitrage) profit by the pool organizer.

The primary disadvantage of partitioning is reduced marketability because of the large variety of different securities. The terms of REMICs,

---

[15] The term **participation certificate** (PC) is also used.

especially the number of classes, are not standardized. The number of classes has varied from three to ten. A three-class REMIC is quite different from a ten-class REMIC. This situation may easily change if some set of terms with large market appeal becomes standard. In spite of the lack of marketability, issues of REMICSs have increased dramatically. The reduction in the uncertainty surrounding prepayment is apparently very important to many REMIC buyers.

Sequential Pay or Plain Vanilla Derivatives

A sequential pay REMIC divides the prepayments into classes (or tranches). The most common pattern is for all principal payments to be used to pay down the nearest remaining class.[16]

Imagine principal payments broken into four classes. The first 25 percent of payments are used to pay off the principal of class 1. As part of the principal is repaid in class 1, future interest payments to class 1 are reduced as well. When all of the principal of class 1 is paid, this class ceases to exist. The next 25 percent of principal payments goes to class 2. When all of these principal payments are made, class 2 ceases to exist, and so on.

Z Bonds

A Z bond is the lowest priority class. It accrues interest until all other classes are repaid their principal. Then the Z bond receives interest and principal.

Z bonds are extremely high risk for two reasons. First, they have long effective maturities. As interest rates change, the present value of the cash flows fluctuates sharply because each cash flow is discounted for many periods. Second, uncertainty about the timing of prepayments is very large for this class with a residual claim on the cash flows. Z bonds should have high yields because of the high risk; however, the realized returns will have great variability.

---

[16] The principal payments can be handled in two ways. First, all payments of principal, including both scheduled amortization and prepayments, are made to the nearest remaining class. This procedure is the most common one. Second, all remaining classes can share in the scheduled amortization of principal, but prepayments go to the nearest remaining class.

Figure 15.3 shows the cash flows for a four class sequential pay REMIC. Class A receives interest until all of its principal is repaid. Class B receives interest until all of class A's principal is repaid; then class B begins to receive principal and interest. Class C receives interest until class B's principal is completely repaid; then C receives principal and interest. The last class is a Z bond. Notice that the Z bond gets no cash flows until all of the principal for the first three classes is completely paid off.

Planned Amortization Class (PAC)

A planned amortization class or PAC has a fixed principal payment schedule that must be met before other classes receive principal payments. The PAC payments are made from scheduled amortization and prepayments. The pool organizer estimates the probable prepayments, then part of the pool is sold as PACs. The PAC class is small enough so that the PAC payments are made under most interest rate scenarios.

Figure 15.4 shows the cash flows from a mortgage pool with four classes of PACs and companion classes, which receive the residual cash flows after PACs are paid. The cash flows are shown for several scenarios of PSA. Expected prepayments are 100 percent of PSA. The top segment shows 80 percent of PSA, close to the expected prepayments. The four PAC classes get paid as scheduled, but the companion classes get paid at the end. In the lowest segment, the prepayments are fast, 250 percent of PSA. Then the companion classes get repaid rapidly.

The buyers of the companion classes face considerable uncertainty about the timing of their cash inflows. If interest rates rise, the companion classes are paid in the distant future, and the present value is low because of the higher interest rate used to discount the cash flows. If interest rates drop, the companion classes are paid rapidly, and the low interest rate contributes to a relatively high present value. Obviously, the value of the companion classes fluctuates dramatically as interest rates change.

Principal Only and Interest Only Derivatives

Some mortgage pools are divided into separate segments receiving **principal only** (PO) and **interest only** (IO). As unscheduled prepayments occur, the holders of POs receive the added cash flows. Since the remaining principal is reduced, holders of IOs receive reduced interest payments.

Figure 15.3   Sequential Pay Classes

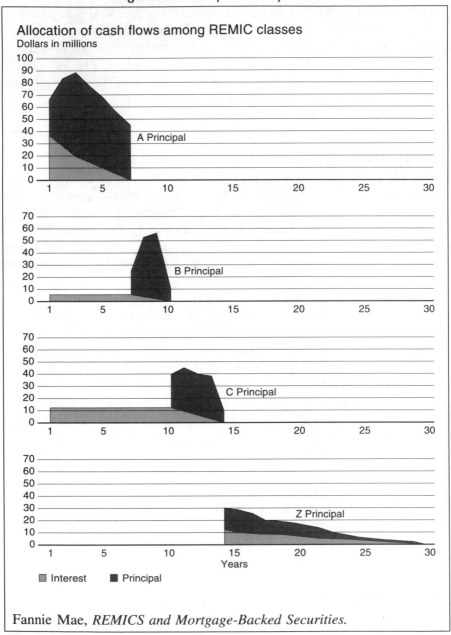

Allocation of cash flows among REMIC classes
Dollars in millions

Fannie Mae, *REMICS and Mortgage-Backed Securities.*

Figure 15.4   Planned Amortization Classes

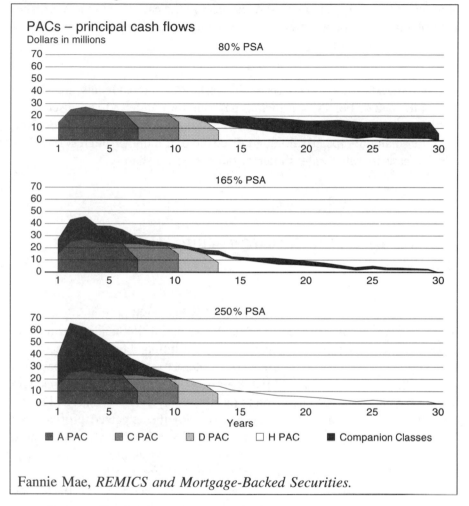

Fannie Mae, *REMICS and Mortgage-Backed Securities.*

Buyers of IOs and POs assume some pattern of prepayments in valuing their securities. If the actual prepayments differ, values are significantly affected.

Falling Interest Rates   If prepayments are faster than anticipated because of falling interest rates, principal payments are received sooner and discounted at a lower interest rate; the value of POs rises. Earlier principal payments reduce interest payments to IOs. These interest payments are discounted at a lower interest rate, partially offsetting the decline in payments. For small declines in interest rates, IOs might actually increase in value. For larger declines in interest rates, prepayments are substantial and IOs decline sharply in value. If large drops in interest rates occur in the early life of the mortgage, IO holders may actually receive less money than they invested – for a negative rate of return.

Rising Interest Rates   With rising interest rates, prepayments are slower than anticipated. For POs, principal payments are deferred and discounted at higher interest rates; the value of POs drops. For IOs, interest received is higher than anticipated, although discounted at a higher interest rate. IOs can increase in value unless interest rates increase sharply.

Impact of Securitization upon Banks and Thrifts

The securitization of the mortgage market has had an important impact upon banks and thrifts. Before securitization, banks and thrifts made considerable profits from residential mortgages. These institutions held mortgages until maturity and were bearers of credit risk, interest rate risk, and prepayment risk. With securitization, credit risk is passed on to insurers and interest rate and prepayment risk are passed on to mortgage buyers. The banks and thrifts do not bear these risks, but they also forego the expected profits from bearing these risks. Securitization has made banks and thrifts much more like mortgage bankers, that is, originators and processors of loans. Banks and thrifts have become less profitable, but they are also less risky.

Frequently, the buyers of mortgage backed securities are banks and thrifts. Quite conceivably, the same institutions are also sellers of mortgages. By both selling and buying mortgages, lenders can reconstitute the risks of their mortgage portfolio. For example, a thrift might sell all the mortgages that it originates and then buy pass-throughs with the proceeds. The thrift holds government insured, geographically diversified mortgages. The gain to the thrift is the elimination of default risk. In a simplified theoretical world in which banks and thrifts sold all their mortgages into pools to create pass-throughs and then repurchased the same dollar amount of pass-throughs, the thrifts would be able to transfer all risk of default to insurers. Conceivably, the thrift might purchase CMOs, eliminating some prepayment risk in addition to default risk.

Summary

A mortgage is a loan with real estate as collateral. For income properties (such as office buildings and apartment complexes), commercial banks, thrifts, and insurance companies are large originators and holders of mortgages. For residential mortgages, banks, thrifts, and mortgage companies are originators of loans. Before 1970, banks and thrifts held residential mortgages until maturity. Since 1970, groups of residential mortgages have been increasingly insured by government or private insurers against default, packaged together and sold to investors.

The majority of mortgages tend to be prepaid before final maturity. There are two major reasons for prepayment: the sale of the property or a decline in interest rates, which allows the borrower to refinance at a lower interest rate. The buyer of a pass-through security has a proportional claim on the pool of mortgages. When some of the mortgages in the pool are prepaid, all holders of pass-throughs share in the prepayments. Mortgage derivatives break the prepayments into classes.

Government agencies have played an important role in the securitization of mortgage debt. First, government agencies have acted as insurers against default by the borrower. Second, government agencies have pooled together individual mortgages and sold claims (that is, pass-throughs) on the pool.

Securitization of mortgages has provided desirable investment vehicles for some investors. In addition, securitization has changed the operations of commercial banks and thrifts in the residential mortgage market. Increasingly, banks and thrifts have acted as originators and processors of mortgages and have held fewer mortgages in their portfolios. This has tended to reduce risk and expected returns for banks and thrifts.

Questions/Problems

1. For a standard fixed-rate mortgage, compute the annual mortgage payment for a five-year annual mortgage loan with principal of $50,000 and interest rate of 10 percent.

2. In the preceding problem, break each mortgage payment into interest on remaining principal and amortization. Also compute the remaining balance on the mortgage at each point in time. What is the total amount of interest paid over the mortgage's life? Does this seem high or low, fair or unfair?

3. Assume that you take out a 15-year mortgage at a 10 percent interest rate and $100 principal. Compute the amortization in year 13. Compute the percentage of the mortgage principal repaid by year 13. How many years does it take for half of the original principal to be repaid?

4. Suppose Susan has a 15-year mortgage with $100 principal. In year 8, the amortization of the principal is $6.23. Use the present value tables to compute the interest rate on the mortgage.

5. Assume that you take out a 15-year mortgage at a 10 percent interest rate and $100 principal. After one year, the interest rate on new loans is 7 percent. If you refinance, there is a loan initiation fee of 3 percent. Compute the immediate gain from refinancing.

6. Suppose Justin inherits a house from his grandfather. When the house was originally purchased by Grandpa 20 years ago, the mortgage was for 30 years. The original mortgage principal was $100. The remaining is now $62.47. The current interest rate is 6 percent and refinancing costs are 3 percent. Does it pay to refinance? (Hint: First find the interest rate on the existing loan.)

7. Explain what it means to originate a mortgage loan. Who are the originators?

8. A bank has a choice of making a two-year loan at 10 percent or a variable-rate loan at the one-year Treasury bill rate plus 2 percent. Currently, the Treasury bill rate is 7 percent. Under what circumstances is the two-year loan better than the variable-rate loan and vice versa?

9. An investor buys a claim on a pool of 15-year mortgages at 10 percent and $100 principal. Compute the interest and principal repayments for the first three years assuming no prepayments. Next, assume that 6 percent of the original principal is prepaid every year. Compute the interest and the scheduled principal payments and the prepayments for the first two years.

10. A thrift institution decides to sell all its mortgages and use the proceeds to purchase pass-through securities. What is the gain to the thrift institution? Whatever the thrift gains, someone else loses. Who takes the other side of this transaction and what are the consequences for this party? Is there any net gain to the system from shifting risks in this way?

11. What are the consequences of pass-throughs and mortgage-backed for commercial bank and thrift institution risks and profits?

12. Explain the differences between a mortgage guarantee from FHA or VA versus insurance from a private insurance company.

13. Look in your local newspaper for interest rates on a long-term fixed-rate and a variable-rate mortgage. Report the loan initiation costs. How is the interest rate adjusted on the variable-rate mortgage?

References

Breeden, D. T., "Complexities of Hedging Mortgages," *Journal of Fixed Income,* 4, December 1994, pp. 6–41.

Carron, A. S., "Understanding CMOs, REMICs, and Other Mortgage Derivatives," *Journal of Fixed Income,* 2, June 1992, pp. 25–43.

Dunn, K. B., and J. J. McConnell, "Valuation of GNMA Mortgage-Backed Securities," *Journal of Finance,* 36, 1981, pp. 599–617.

Fabozzi, F. J., ed., *Mortgage-Backed Securities: New Strategies, Applications, and Research,* Chicago: Probus Publishing, 1987.

Fannie Mae, "REMICs and Mortgage-Backed Securities," Washington, D.C., 1994.

Maisel, S. J., *Real Estate Finance,* San Diego, CA: Harcourt Brace Jovanovich, 1987.

Patruno, G. N., "Mortgage Prepayments: A New Model for a New Era," *Journal of Fixed Income,* 4, December 1994, pp. 42–56.

Sellon, G. H., Jr., and D. VanNahmen, "The Securitization of Housing Finance," *Economic Review,* Federal Reserve Bank of Kansas City, 73, July/August 1988, pp. 3–20.

Simpson, T. M. and Z. M. Pirenian, *Mathematics of Finance,* 3e, Englewood Cliffs, NJ: Prentice Hall, 1951.

Smith, H. C. and J. B. Corgel, *Real Estate Perspectives: An Introduction to Real Estate,* Homewood, IL: Irwin, 1992.

Stanton, R., "Rational Prepayment and the Value of Mortgage-Backed Securities," *Review of Financial Studies,* 1995.

Stone, C. A., and A. Zissu, "The Risks of Mortgage-Backed Securities and their Derivatives," *The Journal of Applied Corporate Finance,* 7, Fall 1994, pp. 99–111.

16

Money Market Instruments and Rates

Overview

The most active market for securities as measured by daily volume of trading is the **money market**,[1] which is defined as the market for securities with less than one year to maturity at the original issue date. Money market instruments include the following: Treasury bills, federal funds, repurchase agreements, certificates of deposit, commercial paper, and bankers' acceptances. Each of these instruments has slightly different characteristics, and thus each has a slightly different interest rate. Since many investors regard the individual money market instruments as close substitutes, changes in all the money market interest rates are highly correlated.

Money market instruments allow some issuers to raise funds for short periods of time at relatively low interest rates. These issuers include the U.S. Treasury which issues Treasury bills; corporations that sell commercial paper; banks which issue certificates of deposit; and security dealers who finance their holdings in the money market. Simultaneously, many investors find money market instruments to be highly liquid investments with relatively low default risk. An investment is liquid if it can be bought or sold rapidly

---

[1] The most thorough treatments of money market instruments are Marcia Stigum's book, *The Money Market,* and *Instruments of the Money Market* edited by Timothy Q. Cook and Timothy D. Rowe. The reader should consult these books for more details.

without affecting the market price and if the risk of price fluctuation is small. These money market investors include individuals, corporations, banks, and other institutions with temporary excess funds, and money market mutual funds. The money market is largely a wholesale (as opposed to retail) market, with the denominations of most transactions in the millions of dollars. The primary participants are financial institutions and large nonfinancial businesses. Consumers play a limited role in the money market; they buy some money market securities and invest in money market mutual funds.

U.S. Treasury Bills

Treasury bills (T-bills) are issued by the U.S. Treasury to finance government expenditures. For practical purposes, Treasury bills are default-free, since the Federal Reserve effectively has the power to provide sufficient funds to meet Treasury obligations.

Treasury bills are highly liquid assets. They can be bought or sold rapidly without affecting the price, and the risk of price fluctuation is small. Consequently, Treasury bills have small bid-asked spreads.

Every Monday in its weekly auction, the Treasury issues large amounts of 13-week (91-day) and 26-week (182-day) Treasury bills. Every fourth week, the Treasury issues 52-week bills as well. Consequently, there are large numbers of Treasury bills outstanding. This large supply of securities increases trading volume and substantially enhances Treasury bill liquidity. Because Treasury bills are short-term securities, their price fluctuations are small when interest rates change.[2] Thus, the risk of price decline is small for Treasury bills, as it is with the typical money market investment.

The interest earned on Treasury securities, including Treasury bills, is not subject to state and local income taxes. For this reason, Treasury bills may have a slightly lower interest than other money market instruments subject to these taxes. The default-free status of Treasury bills makes their yields lower than yields on otherwise identical money market instruments having some chance for default.

Federal Funds

Commercial banks are required to keep reserves on deposit at the Federal Reserve. Banks with reserves in excess of required reserves can lend these

---

[2] See chapter 11.

funds to other banks. These interbank loans are called **federal funds** (abbreviated as **fed funds**) and are usually overnight loans. Through the fed funds market, commercial banks with excess funds are able to lend those funds to banks that are short of reserves. Large money center banks tend to be net buyers of fed funds, and small local banks tend to be net sellers.

Fed funds transactions are in large denominations, since otherwise the overnight interest would be insufficient to justify the transaction. The rate on these transactions is called the **federal funds rate**. This interest rate is the most volatile interest rate in the entire market. Daily fluctuations in the federal funds rate have sometimes been 4 or 5 percent. One reason for this rate volatility is that some banks may be suddenly forced to meet Federal Reserve requirements by borrowing fed funds. At the end of each quarter of the year, the federal funds rate has sometimes fluctuated dramatically. Annualized interest rates of 100 percent have been observed.[3]

During the 1970s, the Federal Reserve Board monitored the federal funds rate very closely in implementing monetary policy. Until October 1979, the Federal Open Market Committee set fairly precise bands for the level of the federal funds rate. When market conditions pushed the rate outside of these bounds, the Federal Reserve took action to push the rate back within the bounds.

Since October 1979, the directives of the FOMC have put wider bounds upon the federal funds rate. The federal funds rate has experienced increased variability since October 1979. Most other money market interest rates are highly correlated with the federal funds rate and have had significantly greater variability since October 1979.

Repurchase Agreements

Repurchase agreements (called repos, or RPs) are generally overnight sales of U.S. government securities with an agreement to repurchase on the next business day. The volume of transactions in overnight repos is huge.

To illustrate repos, imagine a bond dealer closing operations for January 15 with an inventory of $450 million of Treasury securities. These securities

---

[3] An interest rate of 100 percent seems impossible. But since the interest rate is an annualized rate and federal funds are overnight loans, the actual interest paid for one day is approximately 100/365 or about .33 percent.

are held by the dealer in its role as a market, with the dealer hoping to profit by the average bid-asked spread. The equity of the dealer is $50 million. An additional $400 million is required to pay for these securities since the terms of purchase require same-day payment. One possible source of dealer financing is a bank loan with the securities used as collateral for the loan. A second (and slightly less expensive) method of financing is a repo. That is, the dealer sells the securities to a lender for $400 (plus accrued interest) on the afternoon of January 15, agreeing to repurchase them the following morning of January 16 for $400 million plus one day's interest. Table 16.1 illustrates this sequence of events.

The price for the repurchase agreement is the current price plus interest.[4] Since the loan is overnight, the interest rate on repos is typically slightly below the federal funds rate. Thus, repos allow nonbanks, which do not hold reserves at the Federal Reserve and consequently are unable to lend at the federal funds rate, to lend at a rate slightly below the fed funds rate. Repos are confined to large dollar amounts per transaction. Otherwise, the cost of carrying out the transaction would outweigh the overnight interest. Repos for longer than overnight (called term repos) are possible, although they are not as common as overnight repos.

Repurchase agreements are extensively used as a means of short-term financing by government security dealers and by banks. In recent years, other money market securities (i.e., certificates of deposit, prime bankers' acceptances, and commercial paper) have been repoed. Dealers in these securities can now use repos as a source of financing.

Table 16.1   Financing Needs of a Bond Dealer

Points in Time		
2:00 PM January 15	5:00 PM January 15	9:00 AM January 16
Dealer buys $450,000,000 of bonds	Dealer sells $400,000,000 of bonds as repo	Dealer repurchases $400,000,000 and pays overnight interest

---

[4] Note that the current price includes accrued interest for coupon-bearing securities.

From the viewpoint of the lender of funds, a repo is called a **reverse**. Reverses are quite attractive to a number of lenders, including nonfinancial corporations, banks, municipalities, and thrift institutions. These lenders can invest their temporarily excess funds in reverses for very short periods of time with minimal risk. Municipalities are typically restricted in their investments to federal government securities; reverses provide an attractive investment in these securities. Some reverses are used as a means of borrowing securities; that is, the lender of funds is also a borrower of securities. These borrowed securities may be used in a shortsale.

In general, the amount lent in a repo is slightly less than the market value of the bonds. This discount from market value is called a **haircut** and provides some protection to the lender if the dealer goes bankrupt and the securities are liquidated at the prevailing market price. The size of the haircut depends upon the underlying price risk of the security, with riskier securities having bigger haircuts.

The risk of a repo depends upon its legal status. Depending upon the wording, a repo may constitute a sale or a collateralized loan. If the repo is a sale, the lender owns the securities; in the event of borrower default, the lender can sell the securities and use the proceeds if the lender has physical possession of the securities. If a repo is a collateralized loan, the borrower owns the securities; in the event of borrower default, the lender merely has a general claim upon the borrower. With this latter type of arrangement, the lender is at greater risk, and the interest rate is higher.

Commercial Paper

Commercial paper is a promissory note issued by large firms with high credit ratings as a source of short-term funds. The commercial paper market has existed because commercial paper can be a cheaper source of funds for financially sound firms than commercial bank loans. During recent years of high interest rates, the number of firms issuing commercial paper has increased significantly because the interest costs saved have increased substantially.

The majority of commercial paper is issued by financial companies, including bank holding companies, finance companies, and insurance companies. Financial companies tend to use commercial paper as a regular source of funds. Nonfinancial firms tend to issue commercial paper on an irregular basis to meet special financing needs.

Commercial paper is not secured by specific assets of the issuing firm. In a secured loan, specific assets are pledged as collateral behind the loan.

In the event of default, the secured lender has first claim upon the pledged asset. If this specific asset is insufficient to pay off the lender's claim, the lender then has a general claim upon the other assets of the borrower. An "unsecured" loan does not have specific assets pledged as collateral. However, the lender has a general claim upon the assets of the borrower rather than on a specific asset. Thus, the term **unsecured** is a type of misnomer.

Although commercial paper is unsecured, it is typically backed by lines of credit at commercial banks. A line of credit is essentially a prearrangement between a commercial bank and a borrowing firm that allows the firm to borrow up to some prearranged limit during a stated time interval. Lines of credit are not legally binding on the bank. Except during periods of extremely tight money, banks honor these lines of credit. In order to obtain a line of credit, a firm may be required to maintain compensating deposit balances at the bank of perhaps 10 percent or to pay explicit fees to the bank for the line of credit. These costs are clearly part of the cost of issuing commercial paper.

Most commercial paper is issued with original maturities of less than 45 days. Commercial paper with maturities of less than nine months does not have to be registered with the Securities and Exchange Commission (SEC) as a public offering. This saves the considerable expense of SEC registration and may also avoid delays involved in the registration process.

Commercial paper may be sold directly by the issuer or may be sold to dealers who charge a placement fee of perhaps 1/8 percent. Firms regularly issuing commercial paper find it more economical to set up a department to issue commercial paper rather than use outside dealers. Since issues of commercial paper are heterogeneous, having many different issuers and many different maturity dates, there is no active secondary market for commercial paper. However, dealers may repurchase commercial paper for a fee.

Prime Rate

The **prime interest rate** is often said to represent the rate at which commercial banks lend to their most creditworthy (and, therefore, lowest risk) customers. In practice, many loans are made at rates below the prime; the prime rate is not the rate for the most creditworthy firms. Nevertheless, the prime interest rate is a benchmark indicator of the level of interest rates. Since the market for bank loans is highly competitive, all commercial banks quote a single prime rate. The prime rate changes for all banks simultaneously.

Bankers' Acceptances

Bankers' acceptances (BAs) are short-term debt obligations guaranteed by large commercial banks. Prime bankers' acceptances of the ten largest banks trade anonymously. They are highly liquid, low risk, and low return investments.

Bankers' acceptances typically arise out of international trade. Consider the following example illustrated in figure 16.1. Assume an importer located in the U.S. and an exporter in Japan. The exporter would like to send goods to the U.S. and receive payment in 90 days. In domestic transactions, trade credit is widely used to finance this transaction. With trade credit, the goods producer sends the merchandise and allows the purchaser some time before payment is made. During this period of time, the purchaser attempts to sell the merchandise and generate the cash to make payment. In international transactions, the parties are located in different countries, implying that suppliers may not know the financial status of buyers. Legal remedies are more difficult and expensive in international transactions. To reduce the risk of collecting payment in 90 days, a bankers' acceptance can be used.

In a bankers' acceptance, the importer obtains a commercial letter of credit from her bank in the U.S. Through this commercial letter of credit, the U.S. bank guarantees payment for the imported goods in 90 days. The letter of credit is sent to the exporter's bank in Japan. The exporter ships the goods and endorses the shipping documents. The documents and a time draft for the amount to be paid are presented to the exporter's bank. The Japanese bank then sends the draft and documents to the U.S. bank, which "accepts" them. We now have a bankers' acceptance.

Frequently, the U.S. bank pays the exporter's bank the present value of the purchase price and in turn these funds are paid to the exporter. The U.S. bank can hold on to the bankers' acceptance and earn interest or sell it in the market. If the acceptance is sold in the market, the U.S. bank has not lent any net funds. However, the U.S. bank does guarantee payment. If the importer is unable to make payment on the due date, the U.S. bank guarantees payment. In addition to any interest earned, the U.S. bank also receives a fee from the importer.

The Federal Reserve has a set of standards for designating BAs as collateral for loans from the Fed. A bank with eligible BAs can obtain loans from the Federal Reserve at the discount rate. Eligible BAs are much more liquid than noneligible BAs.

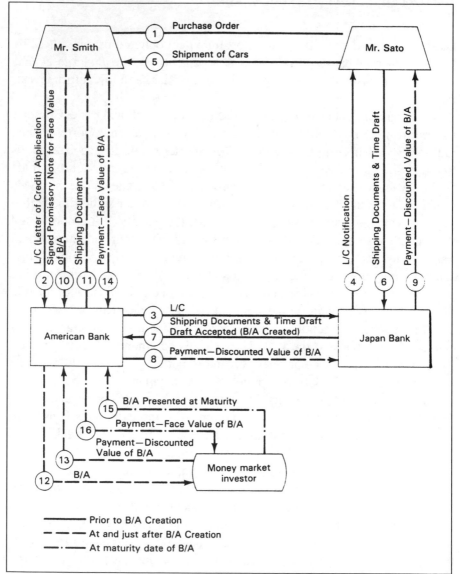

Figure 16.1   Bankers' Acceptances

Bank Certificates of Deposit

Large **certificates of deposit** (CDs) at commercial banks represent a major source of funds for commercial banks. These large certificates (with face values of over $100,000) are a significant source of funds for money center and large regional commercial banks. There are four basic types of large certificates of deposit: domestic CDs, Eurodollar CDs, Yankee CDs, and thrift CDs.

Large domestic CDs were first issued by the First National City Bank of New York in 1961 in order to regain deposits lost during a period of rising interest rates because of restrictions on the interest rates allowed on deposits. With some interruptions, the domestic CD market continued to grow until the early 1980s when banks were allowed to issue Money Market Deposit Accounts (MMDAs) and Super Now accounts. These new accounts allow banks to pay interest on checking accounts, thus eliminating some of the advantage of domestic CDs.

Negotiable domestic CDs of major banks are highly liquid investments. An active resale market exists for these CDs. A number of foreign banks have branches in the United States. Dollar-denominated CDs of these foreign banks are called Yankee CDs. A small number of thrift institutions sell large-denomination thrift CDs.

Eurocurrency Certificates of Deposit

A **Eurocurrency deposit** is defined as a deposit denominated in terms of a foreign currency. Thus, a deposit in U.S. dollar terms made in London, England, is considered a Eurodollar deposit. A deposit of Japanese yen in London is also called a Eurodollar deposit, although technically it is a "Euroyen" deposit. Large U.S. banks frequently raise funds through Eurodeposits in branches of the banks located outside the United States. The interest rate on Eurodeposits is typically slightly higher than the rate on domestic U.S. deposits, making these rates attractive to depositors. These subsidiaries are typically free of regulatory restrictions, thus reducing the net cost of deposits to the bank. Freedom from regulation tends to benefit both the depositors and the banks.

Eurodollar CDs are dollar-denominated certificates of deposit issued by banks located outside the U.S., with London being the most common location. The most common issuers of Eurodollar CDs are branches of U.S., Canadian, Japanese, and European banks. A U.S. bank may decide to issue Eurodollar CDs through its London branch if the interest rate on a Eurodollar CD compares favorably with the rate on a domestic CD. However, non-negotiable Eurodollar time deposits are a more important source of funds for U.S. banks than Eurodollar CDs.

The interest rates on Eurocurrency CDs are quoted as LIBOR plus some markup. **LIBOR** is the **London Interbank Offered Rate**, which is the interest rate at which Eurobanks in London offer to lend to one another. Eurocurrency CDs have higher interest rates than U.S. domestic CDs, partially because the foreign countries involved may impose exchange controls, possibly forbidding repayment of the CD. This risk is called **sovereign risk**.

Money Market Funds

As interest rates rose markedly during the 1970s, many small investors found themselves cut off from high money market rates of return. Because most money market instruments are in large denominations, small investors were typically restricted to savings deposits at commercial banks and savings banks. These savings deposits paid rates several percent less than the rates available on money market instruments.

To fill this gap and provide access for small investors to the money market, money market mutual funds developed. These funds pooled the resources of small investors and invested those resources at attractive money market rates. Consequently, there were large outflows of funds from savings accounts into the money market. Many depository institutions lost funds in a process called **disintermediation**. In effect, money market funds bypassed banks and let investors put their money directly into the money market. To permit banks to compete with money market mutual funds, banks are now allowed to offer depository accounts with rates competitive with money market rates. These new accounts are called Money Market Deposit accounts and Super Now accounts.

The typical money market fund holds a portfolio of Treasury bills, bank certificates of deposit, commercial paper, and bankers' acceptances. Some money market funds specialize in particular instruments such as Treasury bills (for very low risk investors) or municipal notes, which are exempt from federal income taxes. Money market funds typically allow investors to write checks on their accounts with some restrictions. Thus, in many ways, large money market funds are like banks, although money market funds are not insured by the FDIC.

Money Market Rates

The Wall Street Journal publishes a daily table entitled Money Rates. An example is shown in figure 16.2. For example, the table shows the previous day's federal funds rates – the high, the low, and the close.

One of the peculiarities of the money market is its way of quoting interest rates. Some money market instruments (Treasury bills, commercial

Figure 16.2   Money Rates

MONEY RATES

Monday, April 17, 1995
The key U.S. and foreign annual interest rates below are a
guide to general levels but don't always represent actual transactions.
PRIME RATE: 9%. The base rate on corporate loans posted
by at least 75% of the nation's 30 largest banks.
FEDERAL FUNDS: 6 3/16% high, 6 1/16% low, 6 1/16% near
closing bid, 6 1/8% offered. Reserves traded among commercial
banks for overnight use in amounts of $1 million or more. Source:
Prebon Yamane (U.S.A.) Inc.
DISCOUNT RATE: 5 1/4%. The charge on loans to depository
institutions by the Federal Reserve Banks.
CALL MONEY: 7 3/4%. The charge on loans to brokers on
stock exchange collateral. Source: Dow Jones Telerate Inc.
COMMERCIAL PAPER placed directly by General Electric
Capital Corp.: 5.96% 30 to 59 days; 5.98% 60 to 89 days; 5.99%
90 to 119 days; 6% 120 to 149 days; 6.02% 150 to 179 days;
6.04% 180 to 270 days.
COMMERCIAL PAPER: High-grade unsecured notes sold
through dealers by major corporations; 6.06% 30 days; 6.08%
60 days; 6.10% 90 days.
CERTIFICATES OF DEPOSIT: 5.34% one month; 5.43% two
months; 5.51% three months; 5.76% six months; 5.97% one
year. Average of top rates paid by major New York banks on
primary new issues of negotiable C.D.s, usually on amounts of
$1 million and more. The minimum unit is $100,000. Typical
rates in the secondary market: 6.06% one month; 6.13% three
months; 6.27% six months.
BANKERS ACCEPTANCES: 5.95% 30 days; 5.96% 60 days;
5.97% 90 days; 5.98% 120 days; 6% 150 days; 6.01% 180
days. Offered rates of negotiable, bank-backed business credit
instruments typically financing an import order.
FOREIGN PRIME RATES: Canada 9.75%; Germany 4.67%;
Japan 3%; Switzerland 5.25%; Britain 6.75%. These rate indica-
tions aren't directly comparable; lending practices vary widely
by location.
TREASURY BILLS: Results of the Monday, April 17, 1995,
auction of short-term U.S. government bills, sold at a discount
from face value in units of $10,000 to $1 million: 5.56%, 13
weeks; 5.69%, 26 weeks.
FEDERAL HOME LOAN MORTGAGE CORP. (Freddie Mac):
Posted yields on 30-year mortgage commitments. Delivery within
30 days 8.33%, 60 days 8.38%, standard conventional fixed-
rate mortgages; 6.125%, 2% rate capped one-year adjustable
rate mortgages. Source: Dow Jones Telerate Inc.
FEDERAL NATIONAL MORTGAGE ASSOCIATION (Fannie
Mae): Posted yields on 30 year mortgage commitments (priced at
par) for delivery within 30 days 8.41%, 60 days 8.47%, standard
conventional fixed rate-mortgages; 7.350, 6/2 rate capped one-
year adjustable rate mortgages. Source: Dow Jones Telerate
Inc.
MERRILL LYNCH READY ASSETS TRUST: 5.58%. Annualized average rate of return after expenses for the past 30 days;
not a forecast of future returns.

Source: The Wall Street Journal, April 18, 1995.

paper, and bankers' acceptances) are quoted on a discount basis. Other rates
(fed funds, Federal Reserve discount rate, and repo rates) are quoted on an
add-on basis. Each of these rates is different from the yield to maturity, the
rate generally used for comparing coupon-bearing bonds. The following
discussion explains discount rates, add-on rates, and bond equivalent yields.

Quoting Rates on a Discount Basis

To understand the meaning of a money market rate quoted on a discount
basis, consider the relationship between the discount rate, denoted by d, and

the price, denoted by P. Let the number of days until maturity be denoted by t. Then:

$$P = PAR\left[1 - \frac{dt}{360}\right] = PAR[1 - \text{interest}] \qquad (16.1)$$

Let's consider a simple example. A 90-day Treasury bill with a $1,000,000 par value has a discount rate of 8 percent. Its price is:

$$P = 1,000,000\left[1 - \frac{(.08)(90)}{360}\right] = \$980,000$$

The buyer of this Treasury bill pays $980,000 and, in 90 days, receives $1,000,000. The interest received is $20,000, which is 2 percent of the par value. Two percent for 90 days corresponds to an annualized rate of 8 percent for 360 days.

Several aspects of equation 16.1 are noteworthy. The denominator uses 360 and, therefore, implicitly assumes a 360-day year. The term $dt/360$ represents the interest earned from investing P dollars. The interest is deducted from the par value because the discount rate d is a percent of par. In contrast, most other interest rates are expressed as a percentage of the amount lent or of the price.

The apparent reason for this unusual way of quoting rates is the development of this market before hand-held calculators. Imagine trying to compute the semiannual yield to maturity, i, without an electronic calculator. The semiannual yield to maturity is the rate-solving equation 16.2.

$$P = \frac{PAR}{(1 + i/2)^{2t/365}} \qquad (16.2)$$

Solving for i:

$$i = 2\left[\frac{PAR}{P}\right]^{(365/2t)} - 2 \qquad (16.3)$$

Because rapid calculations of this type are essentially impossible without an electronic calculator, market participants decided to adopt the convention of quoting prices in terms of discount rates. There is nothing wrong with this practice, since the market participants are actually thinking in terms of price. For example, every trader in the market knows that a change of one basis point (i.e., .01 percent) in the discount rate for 90-day Treasury bills results in a $25 change in price for a $1,000,000 par value. That is, $1,000,000(.0001)(90/360) = $25.

Add-On Rate Calculations

Federal funds, the Federal Reserve discount rate, and repos are quoted in terms of a rate called the add-on interest rate. Add-on interest rates are quoted on the basis of an assumed 360-day year. Denoting the add-on rate by a, the amount of the loan by P, the number of days to maturity by t, and the amount of the loan plus interest to be repaid by PAR, then:

$$\text{PAR} = P\left[1 + \frac{at}{360}\right] \tag{16.4}$$

As an example, assume that $980,000 is lent for 90 days at the add-on rate. The par value is $1,000,000. The discount rate is 8 percent. To find the add-on rate, solve equation 16.4 for a:

$$a = \frac{360}{t}\left[\frac{\text{PAR}}{P} - 1\right] \tag{16.5}$$

Substitute t = 90 days, PAR = $1,000,000, and P = $980,000. The add-on rate is 8.16 percent.

Comparing the Discount Rate with the Add-On Rate

To see the relationship between the discount rate and the add-on interest rate, assume a loan of P dollars for t days with a repayment of PAR. Solve equations 16.1 and 16.4 for P/PAR:

$$\frac{P}{\text{PAR}} = 1 - \frac{dt}{360} \tag{16.6}$$

$$\frac{\text{PAR}}{P} = 1 + \frac{at}{360} \tag{16.7}$$

Solving these equations for a, the add-on interest rate, results in:

$$a = \frac{d}{1 - \dfrac{dt}{360}} \tag{16.8}$$

The denominator of equation 16.8 is the price per dollar of par. Since $1 - dt/360$ is less than \$1, a is greater than d.

Bond Equivalent Yields

The bond equivalent yield is another money market rate. Denote the bond equivalent yield as r. The bond equivalent yield is the rate-satisfying equation 16.9.

$$P = \frac{\text{PAR}}{1 + \dfrac{rt}{365}} \tag{16.9}$$

Then solve for r:

$$r = \left[\frac{365}{360}\right]\left[\frac{d}{1 - \dfrac{dt}{360}}\right] = \left[\frac{365}{360}\right][a] \tag{16.10}$$

The first term in equation 16.10 corrects the discount rate for a 365-day year. The second term divides the discount rate by the price per dollar of par and is equivalent to the add-on rate, a. This term restates the discount rate as a percent of the purchase price. Since 365/360 is always bigger than 1.0, the bond equivalent yield is always greater than the add-on rate. Since $a > d$ and $r > a$, $r > a > d$.

As an example of the bond equivalent yield, assume a 90-day Treasury bill with a discount rate of 8 percent. The bond equivalent yield, r, is computed as follows:

$$r = \left[\frac{365}{360}\right]\left[\frac{.08}{1 - \dfrac{(.08)(90)}{360}}\right] = 8.28\% \tag{16.11}$$

The bond equivalent yield is 28 basis points higher than the discount rate of 8 percent. The difference between the bond equivalent yield and the discount rate is bigger for longer maturities and for higher levels of d. Thus, the error in using d as a measure of return increases for longer maturities and for higher rates.

The bond equivalent yield is widely used by market participants for comparing rates of return on Treasury bills with the yields to maturity available on coupon-bearing Treasury notes and bonds. The daily listings of *The Wall Street Journal* give bond equivalent yields for Treasury bills.

The bond equivalent yield, r, is an approximation of the yield to maturity for a bond. Although the two are fairly close, they are not identical. For short maturities, the difference can be considerable. As maturity approaches 182.5 days, the two converge.

Yield to Maturity

The semiannual and annual yield to maturity can also be computed for a money market instrument. The semiannual yield to maturity is the rate solving equation 16.12.

$$P = \frac{\text{PAR}}{[1 + i/2]^{(2t/365)}} \tag{16.12}$$

Then solve for i:

$$i = 2[\text{PAR}/P]^{(365/2t)} - 2 \tag{16.13}$$

Annual yield to maturity, y, is the rate-solving equation 16.14.

$$P = \frac{\text{PAR}}{[1 + y]^{(t/365)}} \tag{16.14}$$

Then solve for y:

$$y = [\text{PAR}/P]^{(365/t)} - 1 \tag{16.15}$$

Comparing Money Market Rates

There are at least five different money market rates:[5] the discount rate, the add-on rate, the bond equivalent yield, and the semiannual and annual yields to maturity. Table 16.2 summarizes the previous results. The semiannual yield compounds every six months; the annual yield compounds every 12 months. The annual yield is bigger than the semiannual yield.[6] Table 16.2

Table 16.2   Comparing Money Market Rates

Discount rate (d):

$$P = PAR\left[1 - \frac{dt}{360}\right] \qquad d = \left[\frac{360}{t}\right]\left[1 - \frac{P}{PAR}\right]$$

Add-on rate (a):

$$P = \frac{PAR}{1 + \dfrac{at}{360}} \qquad a = \left[\frac{360}{t}\right]\left[\frac{PAR}{P} - 1\right]$$

Bond equivalent yield (r):

$$P = \frac{PAR}{1 + \dfrac{rt}{365}} \qquad r = \left[\frac{365}{t}\right]\left[\frac{PAR}{P} - 1\right]$$

Semiannual yield to maturity (i):

$$P = \frac{PAR}{[1 + i/2]^{(2t/365)}} \qquad i = 2[PAR/P]^{(365/2t)} - 2$$

Annual yield to maturity (y):

$$P = \frac{PAR}{[1 + y]^{(t/365)}} \qquad y = [PAR/P]^{(365/t)} - 1$$

---

[5] Academic research sometimes uses the continuously compounded discount rate. See also footnote 7.

[6] $(1 + y) = (1 + i/2)^2$, where y is the annual yield and i is the semiannual yield. This implies that $y = i + (i^2)/4$. To prove these results, set the prices in table 16.2 equal and simplify.

expresses price in terms of the five different rates and shows the five rates as a function of price.

To illustrate the relationships between the five rates, consider a case in which the discount rate, d, is 8 percent and the number of days, t, is 91.25. Since 91.25 days is one quarter of a year, the calculation of the semiannual and annual yields is simple. First, compute the price, given these values of d and t and an assumed par value of $1:

$$P = \text{PAR}\left[1 - \frac{dt}{360}\right] = 1\left[1 - \frac{(.08)(91.25)}{360}\right] = .979722 \quad (16.16)$$

The price per dollar of par is $.979722. In table 16.3, the formulas are used to compute the four remaining money market yields.

These money market yields for 91.25 days are shown graphically in figure 16.3. The relationship between the five money market rates is shown

Table 16.3   Money Market Yields for 91.25 Day Instruments, $d = .08$

Add-on rate (a):

$$a = \left[\frac{360}{t}\right]\left[\frac{\text{PAR}}{P} - 1\right]$$

$$a = \left[\frac{360}{91.25}\right]\left[\frac{1}{.979722} - 1\right] = 8.17\%$$

Bond equivalent to yield (r):

$$r = \left[\frac{365}{t}\right]\left[\frac{\text{PAR}}{P} - 1\right]$$

$$r = \left[\frac{365}{91.25}\right]\left[\frac{1}{.979722} - 1\right] = 8.28\%$$

Semiannual yield to maturity (i):

$$i = 2[\text{PAR}/P]^{(365/2t)} - 2$$

$$i = 2[1/.979722]^{(365/182.5)} - 2 = 8.36\%$$

Annual yield to maturity (y):

$$y = [\text{PAR}/P]^{(365/t)} - 1$$

$$y = [1/.979722]^{(365/91.25)} - 1 = 8.54\%$$

Figure 16.3   Money Market Rates

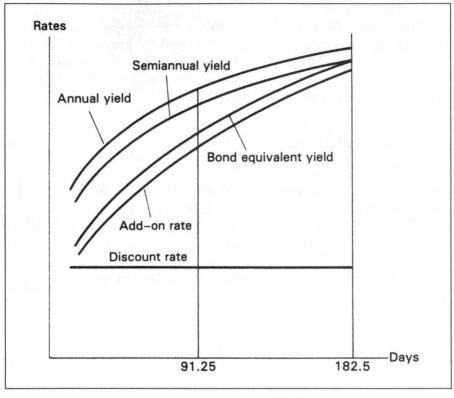

in figure 16.3 for maturities up to one-half year, i.e., 182.5 days. Several tendencies are apparent from figure 16.3. First, the biggest rate is the annual yield, followed by the semiannual yield, the bond equivalent yield, the add-on rate, and the discount rate. Second, the bond equivalent yield approaches the semiannual yield to maturity as maturity approaches one-half year. Third, the differences between the bond equivalent yield and the semiannual yield are sizable for shorter maturities. Bond equivalent yield is a poor approximation of semiannual yield for the shorter maturities. Fourth, the differences between the discount rate and the other rates increase for longer maturities, suggesting that the discount rate is quite misleading for maturities close to one-half year.

Figure 16.3 has a lesson for investors in the money market. Express all money market investments in terms of the same type of rate before selecting investments. Choosing among investments quoted in terms of different rates could lead to poor investment choices.

A more important implication of figure 16.3 and the discussion of money market rates is that all money market institutions should quote rates by the same method. Money market institutions should confer and select one single rate for quoting all varieties of money market instruments. The semiannual yield to maturity is the logical choice for a uniform rate because this rate is used for coupon-bearing bonds with maturities exceeding one-half year.[7]

Summary

Money market instruments have maturities of less than one year. Trading in money market instruments is very active, and the total volume of transactions is huge. A variety of money market instruments exist. Each meets a special need of borrowers and lenders.

Questions/Problems

1. Explain why each of the following money market instruments exists: commercial paper, bankers' acceptances, repurchase agreements, certificates of deposit, and federal funds. Why does each of these have an advantage over competing methods of financing?

2. Why did the market for Eurodeposits develop? What is the advantage of a Eurodeposit over a domestic deposit from a bank's viewpoint as well as a depositor's?

3. Find the prices of the following Treasury bills per dollar of par.
   (a) 40 days, discount rate of 6 percent
   (b) 90 days, discount rate of 12 percent
   (c) 80 days, discount rate of 8 percent
   (d) 92 days, discount rate of 7 percent

---

[7] In practice, coupon-bearing bonds with maturities of less than one-half year are quoted with yet another rate that approximates the bond equivalent yield. See Stigum and Mann (1981) for the details.

4. In problem 3, find the add-on interest rates, bond equivalent yields, and semiannual and annual yields to maturity.

5. Determine Treasury bill discount rates, assuming the following information. Assume $1 par values.
   (a) $P = .96$, $t = 91$ days
   (b) $P = .94$, $t = 91$ days
   (c) $P = .98$, $t = 91$ days
   (d) $P = .98$, $t = 90$ days

6. Assume a discount rate of 6 percent. Compute the add-on interest rate, the bond equivalent yield, and the semiannual and annual yield to maturity for 30, 60, 90, and 180 days. Graph these results.

7. Look in *The Wall Street Journal* for the column entitled "Money Rates." Compare the prime rate, the federal funds rate, the discount rate, the commercial paper rate, the bankers' acceptance rate, and the Treasury bill rate. For the federal funds rate, note the difference between the high and the low.

References

Cook, T. Q., and T. D. Rowe, eds., *Instruments of the Money Market,* 6e, Richmond, VA: Federal Reserve Bank of Richmond, 1986.

Grabbe, J. O., *International Financial Markets,* New York: Elsevier, 1986.

Lynch, J. J. and J. H. Mayle, *Standard Securities Calculations Methods: Fixed Income Formulas,* New York: Securities Industry Association, 1986.

Stigum, M., *The Money Market,* Homewood, IL: Dow Jones Books, 1990.

Stigum, M. and J. Mann, *Money Market Calculations,* Homewood, IL: Dow Jones Books, 1981.

17

International Financial Markets

Overview

The purpose of this chapter is to provide an understanding of the relationships between exchange rates and international investing. The factors determining currency exchange rates are discussed, as well as the impacts of exchange rates upon international trade and investment.

International Trade

Several theories have been proposed to explain why some countries import and others export particular items. Some countries have absolute advantages in trade. These countries are able to produce certain goods more cheaply than other countries because of resource availability or an expert work force. If one country has an absolute advantage over another country in the production of all items, international trade is still beneficial if one country has a comparative advantage in one item by being relatively more efficient in producing this item.

International trade may be restricted by quotas or tariffs. **Quotas** limit the number of units of a commodity imported or exported. **Tariffs** are a tax added to the price of a commodity. Quotas and tariffs protect domestic producers from foreign competition, either by limiting the number of units imported or by raising the price of imports. Tariffs also provide revenues for the government. The disadvantage of quotas and tariffs is high prices to consumers. For example, a 10 percent tariff on sugar imports allows domestic producers to charge more for sugar. The domestic producers are subsidized and the domestic consumers pay the subsidy. If imported goods are inputs for some domestic manufacturers, the costs of tariffs are passed on to other products. Thus, tariffs and quotas can have wide-ranging effects on the economy.

For more than 40 years, the **General Agreement on Tariffs and Trade** (GATT) has endeavored to reduce tariffs and quotas. The objective is cost reductions to consumers. GATT allows a framework for a large number of countries to agree to mutual reductions in trade restrictions. Over time, GATT has been able to significantly reduce trade restrictions and promote the expansion of international trade. The beneficiaries of trade are consumers, who pay lower prices. The cost of increased trade is disruptions in some industries. As trade restrictions are reduced, some inefficient producers are replaced with more efficient producers; some workers are displaced. In the long run, all consumers are better off, although displaced workers suffer in the short run.

International Investment

International investment has some advantages over domestic investment. First, portfolio risk is reduced whenever the investment returns in different countries are less than perfectly correlated. Internationally diversified portfolios have lower risk than purely domestic portfolios, if the economies in individual countries are affected by some factors unique to those countries.

Second, businesses make direct investments in other countries to achieve efficiencies in manufacturing and marketing. Some investments are made to ensure reliable sources of raw materials. U.S. firms also make foreign investments to take advantage of lower labor costs in foreign countries.

International investment has some disadvantages. Returns on international investments are affected by changes in exchange rates. The ensuing discussion examines the impact of exchange rates in detail. Besides the risk of changing exchange rates, investing in foreign securities has several special costs and risks.

First, acquiring information about investments in other countries is more difficult and expensive than obtaining information about domestic investments because of distance and language differences. Travel to foreign countries to acquire information can be quite expensive. Understanding foreign information requires fluency in a foreign language or ready access to a translator. Second, financial disclosure standards differ by country. In some foreign countries, firms are neither required nor expected to reveal nearly as much information to the public as in the United States. Third, accounting definitions are country-specific. As an example, earnings may mean quite different things in individual countries.

Fourth, international investors face political risks as governments and their policies change. In some countries the risk of radical political change is quite considerable. A recent example is South Africa, a country beset with major racial conflicts. The resolution of these conflicts will significantly alter the business environment. Clearly, international investors with funds committed to South African firms bear some of this risk.

Fifth, countries that have balance of payments problems may impose exchange controls in the future. These controls typically limit the transfer of funds out of the country. The chance of exchange controls introduces the possibility that funds invested in a particular country may be difficult or impossible to get out of that country.

Exchange Rates

Each country has its own currency, which is used domestically for purchases of goods and services. When someone wants to purchase a good or service from another country or transfer funds to another country, it may be necessary to exchange that country's currency for the currency of the foreign country.[1] The rate at which one currency is traded for another currency is called the **exchange rate**.

There are two ways of quoting exchange rates. First, the exchange rate can be expressed as the number of units of domestic currency per unit of foreign currency. If $1.50 of U.S. currency is required to buy one British pound, the exchange rate would be quoted as 1.50 dollars per pound. Second, the exchange rate can be expressed as the number of units of foreign currency per unit of domestic currency. Using the same numbers, the exchange rate could be quoted as .67 pounds per dollar. Either way of quoting exchange rates is conceptually acceptable. As a matter of custom, some exchange rates are quoted one way and some the other way. The U.S. dollar/British pound exchange rate is usually quoted as dollars per pound. The U.S. dollar/Japanese yen exchange rate is usually quoted as yen per dollar.

---

[1] Some transactions may be carried out in a foreign currency and currency exchange is unnecessary.

A currency declines in value (depreciates) if more units of that currency are required to buy the same number of units of the foreign currency. For example, if there are initially 1.5 U.S. dollars per British pound (i.e., .67 pounds per dollar), and if market conditions change the exchange rate to 2.0 U.S. dollars per British pound (i.e., .5 pounds per dollar), more dollars are required to buy the same number of pounds. The dollar has depreciated relative to the pound.[2]

A currency appreciates in value if fewer units of that currency are required to buy the same number of units of foreign currency. Suppose the exchange rate is initially 1.5 dollars per pound (i.e., .67 pounds per dollar). Suppose the dollar appreciates to 1.25 dollars per pound (i.e., .8 pounds per dollar). A dollar buys more pounds.

The dollar/yen exchange rate is usually quoted as yen per dollar. If the U.S. dollar depreciates, fewer yen are required to buy one dollar. For example, if the exchange rate is initially 125 yen per dollar, which then jumps to 100 yen per dollar, the dollar has depreciated. One dollar buys fewer yen; one yen buys more dollars.

The rest of this chapter quotes the exchange rate in terms of the number of units of foreign currency per dollar (i.e., yen per dollar, pounds per dollar, pesos per dollar). The exchange rate between two countries is denoted by X.

Cross Exchange Rates

If there is an exchange rate between the U.S. and country 2 and an exchange rate between the U.S. and country 3, the exchange rate between countries 2 and 3 is implied by the other two. This is called the **cross exchange rate**.

The relationships among the three exchange rates are shown in figure 17.1. Imagine three countries: the U.S. with dollars, Japan (country 2) with yen, and Mexico (country 3) with pesos. $1 can be exchanged for 120 yen. $1 can also be exchanged for 50 pesos. Therefore, 120 yen = 50 pesos, or one yen = 50/120 pesos.

To see the general case, define the following notation:

$X_{US,2}$ = the exchange rate between the U.S. and country 2.
$X_{US,3}$ = the exchange rate between the U.S. and country 3.
$X_{2,3}$ = the exchange rate between country 2 and country 3.

---

[2] Conversely, the pound has appreciated relative to the dollar.

Figure 17.1   Cross Exchange Rates

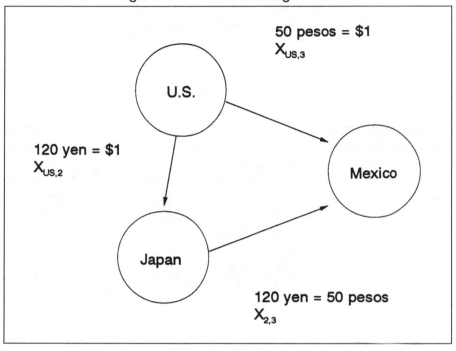

These three exchange rates are related as follows:

$$[X_{US,2}][X_{2,3}] = X_{US,3} \qquad (17.1)$$

To see why these relationships occur, start with one U.S. dollar in figure 17.1; exchange it for country 2's currency, i.e., $X_{US,2}$ units. Next exchange this currency for country 3's currency, i.e., $(X_{US,2})(X_{2,3})$ units. Alternatively, one U.S. dollar could be exchanged for country 3's currency directly. The amount of country 3's currency received in either case must be the same. Otherwise, there are arbitrage opportunities.

Solving for $X_{2,3}$:

$$X_{2,3} = [X_{US,3}]/[X_{US,2}] \qquad (17.2)$$

The cross exchange rate is the ratio of the other two exchange rates. If there are transactions costs for exchanging currencies, the cross exchange rate must lie in a band determined by the bid-asked spreads.

Balance of Payments

The **balance of payments** is a statement of the demand and supply of foreign currency (see table 17.1). The balance of payments is divided into current account items and capital account items. The current account includes imports, exports, services, and unilateral transfers. Unilateral transfers include interest, dividends, and profits. The capital account is composed of investment and changes in official reserves.

Long-term investment is divided into two types. *Direct investment* is the acquisition of plant and equipment. *Portfolio investment* is the purchase of stocks, bonds, and other securities.

Exports provide a source of funds, since goods produced domestically are sold to foreigners. Imports are a use of funds; domestic residents buy goods produced in foreign countries. The difference (exports − imports) is sometimes called the **balance of trade**.

Table 17.1 Balance of Payments

	Uses of Funds*	Sources of Funds†
Current Account		
1. Goods	Imports	Exports
2. Services	Purchased from foreign countries	Sold to foreign countries
3. Unilateral Transfers	Paid to foreign countries	Received from foreign countries
Capital Account		
1. Short-term investments	Assets purchased abroad	Domestic assets purchased by foreigners
2. Long-term investments	Assets purchased abroad	Domestic assets purchased by foreigners
Official Transactions		
1. Official reserve changes	Gained	Lost

*Debit
†Credit

If imports exceed exports, the balance of trade has a deficit. The other items in the balance of payments cover the deficit. Investments by foreigners in the U.S. has been a large source of financing for the U.S. deficit in the balance of trade.[3] Larger U.S. imports than exports have been financed by foreign investment in the U.S.

Total imports in the world must equal total exports. If imports exceed exports for the U.S., then exports must exceed imports for some other countries. Similarly, the total current account for the world must net to zero. Those countries with current account surpluses finance the U.S. current account deficit through investment or lending in the U.S.

Exchange Rate Policies

Fixed Exchange Rates

Under a fixed exchange rate system, the government sets the exchange rate. The exchange rate can be fixed in two ways. First, the government can require all currency exchange to go through the government at the government-determined rate of exchange. Second, the government can buy and sell in the open market in sufficient quantity to fix the price. If more people want to sell the domestic currency than buy it, the government has to buy the domestic currency and, therefore, sell the foreign currency. The foreign currency may come from government reserves, from sales of precious metals, or from borrowings. Conversely, if holders of foreign currency want to buy the domestic currency, the government has to sell the domestic currency and buy foreign currency. In this case, the government accumulates foreign currency reserves.

A completely fixed exchange rate reduces the uncertainty of importing and exporting goods and making foreign investments.[4] People involved in international transactions do not have to be concerned with exchange rate fluctuations. However, if the government sets the fixed exchange rate at the wrong level, some transactions are encouraged and some are discouraged.

---

[3] If the exchange rate is fixed, a change in official reserves may be required to achieve a balance.

[4] In practice, exchange rates are not completely fixed. There is always some risk of future exchange changes by the government.

Also, a severely mispriced exchange rate creates a balance of payments surplus or deficit and makes a later exchange rate adjustment likely. Market participants, incorporating information about the balance of payments into their business decisions, may be discouraged from committing themselves to international transactions if an exchange rate change appears likely.

Freely Floating Exchange Rates

Under a freely floating exchange rate, market forces set the exchange rate. If there is a big demand for imports, the demand for foreign currency increases and the exchange rate drops. Imagine an exchange rate of .7 British pounds equal to one U.S. dollar. Then, U.S. residents develop a sudden strong demand for British china plates. At this point there are many sellers of dollars and buyers of pounds. The U.S. dollar depreciates and the exchange rate changes to .50 pounds to one U.S. dollar.

Managed Float

A number of exchange rates have a managed float. For short periods of time government reserves are used to prop up the exchange rate at some level or push it down. If there is a deficit in the balance of payments, the government can adjust the exchange rate to a new level to restore a balance.

Current Situation

Since 1973, the U.S. has had a policy of a freely floating exchange rate and the dollar has fluctuated considerably. At times, the government does intercede in the foreign exchange markets.

A number of European (members of the European Economic Community) countries have a pegged exchange rate system. These currencies are relatively fixed compared to each other, but they float relative to the U.S. dollar. Within a small band, the currencies are tied to the German mark, which fluctuates relative to the U.S. dollar.

Impact of a Change in the Exchange Rate

Imports and Exports

If the U.S. dollar depreciates and the domestic currency prices of goods remain the same, goods imported into the U.S. from foreign countries become more expensive to U.S. buyers, and goods produced in the U.S. and exported to foreign countries become cheaper to the foreigners. For example, assume the following information: an initial exchange rate of $1 = 125 yen, a Japanese camera costing 12,500 yen ($100 U.S.), and a U.S. chair costing $50 (6,250 yen). Then, the dollar depreciates to $1 = 100 yen. If the yen price of the camera is fixed, the dollar price becomes $125; if the dollar price of the chair is fixed, the yen price becomes 5,000 yen. The camera imported into the U.S. is more expensive; the chair exported to Japan is cheaper to the Japanese.

In practice, domestic prices may be affected by exchange rate changes. In the preceding example of a depreciating U.S. dollar, the yen price of the camera may drop to 11,250 yen, resulting in a dollar price of $112.50. In addition, manufacturers can have a domestic currency price and a foreign currency price, and they can adjust the foreign currency price to changes in exchange rates.

Foreign Assets

Changes in exchange rates affect the realized rates of return on foreign asset holdings. Consider a simple case where interest rates in the U.S. and Japan are 10 percent. A U.S. investor has $1 and two ways to invest it (see figure 17.2).

1. Invest in U.S. dollar denominated assets. At the end of one year, the investor has $1.10.

Figure 17.2   Investing in U.S. versus Japan (1)

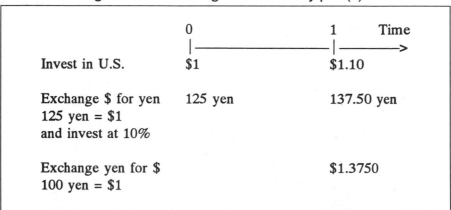

2. Exchange $1 for 125 yen at the exchange rate of 125 yen per dollar. Invest the yen at 10 percent for one year with a resulting value of 137.50 yen. Convert the yen to dollars. The dollar value of these yen depends upon the exchange rate in one year. If the dollar depreciates and the exchange rate jumps to 100 yen per dollar, the 137.50 yen can be exchanged for $1.3750 for a rate of return of 37.5 percent. The depreciation in the dollar has raised the rate of return in U.S. dollar terms.

Conversely, appreciation in the U.S. dollar lowers the return from foreign assets held by U.S. investors. If the dollar appreciates to 150 yen = $1, the investor exchanges 137.50 yen for $.9167. The total rate of return is negative.

This example can be generalized as follows. Let:

R_{US} = the spot interest rate for one period in the U.S.
R_J = the spot interest rate for one period in Japan
$_0X$ = the exchange rate at time 0 (yen per dollar)
$_1X$ = the exchange rate at time 1

The time 1 values from the two strategies (invest in U.S. or Japan) are shown in figure 17.3.

Invest in U.S.: $$1 + R_{US} \tag{17.3}$$

Invest in Japan: $$[1 + R_J][_0X/_1X] \tag{17.4}$$

Define ROR_J as the rate of return from investing in Japan. The $1 + ROR_J$ equals equation 17.4. Solving for ROR_J:

Figure 17.3   Investing in U.S. versus Japan (2)

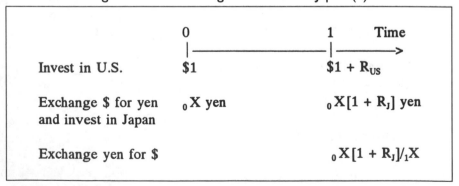

$$\text{ROR}_J = [_0X/_1X - 1] + [_0X/_1X]R_J \qquad (17.5)$$

The return from investing in Japan depends upon the change in the exchange rate. If the U.S. dollar depreciates, then $_0X/_1X > 1$, since $_1X < _0X$; the change in the exchange rate improves the return. If the U.S. dollar appreciates, then $_0X/_1X < 1$, since $_1X > _0X$; the change in the exchange rate reduces the return.

An international investor has to consider both the foreign currency return on an investment and the anticipated exchange rate change. A high foreign currency return may result in a low return after adjusting for the exchange rate effect. Countries with high domestic interest rates are likely to have an exchange rate anticipated to depreciate (i.e., the U.S. dollar appreciates).

Macroeconomic Factors and Exchange Rates

Inflation and Exchange Rates

The relative inflation rates in individual countries affect the exchange rate. Imagine a zero inflation rate in both the U.S. and Japan with a resulting equilibrium exchange rate. Then some shock causes the U.S. inflation rate to rise. The prices of U.S. exports become relatively high for foreign buyers and the amount of exports decreases; imports become relatively inexpensive to U.S. residents and total imports increase. Many more people are selling dollars and buying foreign currencies. The dollar depreciates. (The number of yen per dollar decreases.)

The precise impact of inflation upon the exchange rate depends upon the price sensitivities of imports and exports. For example, if the U.S. is the only supplier of a particular commodity for which there is no substitute, U.S. inflation increases the foreign exchange earned. In contrast, if a U.S. export has many competing sources, U.S. inflation raises export prices, inducing foreign buyers to buy elsewhere. In this case, U.S. inflation reduces foreign exchange earned. The impact on the exchange rate is markedly different.

Three theories of price levels and exchange rates have been discussed. First, according to the **law of one price**, the same transportable item should have the same price in different countries in the absence of transactions costs. If an ounce of gold sells for $350 in the U.S. and the exchange rate is 125 yen to one dollar, gold should sell for 43,750 yen (350 × 125) in Japan. If not, an arbitrager can buy in the lower priced country and sell in the higher priced location and continue to make profits until the prices converge.

Arbitrage is a powerful economic force insuring the validity of the law of one price for individual commodities without transactions costs. With transactions costs, the prices of transportable items may differ because of the costs of arbitrage. For nontransportable items, the transactions costs are effectively infinite and prices can be substantially different in individual countries. For example, the price of a haircut in Toronto, Canada, can be significantly different from the price of the same haircut in Orlando, Florida, 1,500 miles away.

Second, according to the hypothesis of **absolute purchasing power parity**, the basket of consumer goods should have the same price in different countries.[5] The basic argument in favor of this hypothesis is the ability of consumers in the high-priced market to switch their purchases to the low-priced market, tending to equalize the prices of the basket of consumer goods. In practice, absolute purchasing power does not hold because of transactions costs and differences in consumer preferences.

Third, according to **relative purchasing power parity**, the rate of inflation of consumer goods in individual countries affects the exchange. Comparing two countries, the currency of the country with the higher inflation rate depreciates by the difference in inflation rates. Let p_{US} = the U.S. inflation rate, p_J = the Japanese inflation rate, and x = the rate of depreciation in the U.S. dollar. According to relative purchasing power parity:

$$x = p_{US} - p_J \tag{17.6}$$

If the U.S. inflation rate is 8 percent and the Japanese inflation rate is 3 percent, the U.S. dollar depreciates by 5 percent according to relative purchasing power parity.

Empirically, countries with high inflation rates generally have depreciating currencies. But, relative purchasing power parity does not hold precisely. Countries with relatively high inflation rates do not always have depreciating currencies, and those with low inflation rates do not always have appreciating currencies.

---

[5] Absolute purchasing power parity is actually the law of one price applied to the basket of consumer goods.

Income and Exchange Rates

Changes in income levels affect exchange rates. Imagine some initial equilibrium with a given level of income in the U.S. and Japan and a given exchange rate. Because of a change in government policy, government spending increases income in the U.S. The demand for imports increases. More people want to sell dollars and buy yen, with a resulting depreciation in the U.S. dollar. Thus, a relatively high growth rate for a country puts downward pressure on the exchange rate. But the precise impact depends upon the nature of the demand for imports and the availability of domestic substitutes for imports.

Interest Rates and Exchange Rates

Interest rates affect exchange rates. Imagine an initial equilibrium with a given exchange rate and an interest rate of R_{US} for the U.S. and R_J for Japan. Because of a change in monetary policy, U.S. interest rates rise. The marginal investor who was content to invest in Japanese bonds finds it more attractive to invest in U.S. dollar-denominated bonds at the higher interest rate. Yen are sold and dollars bought. The U.S. dollar appreciates (more yen to the dollar).

Spot and Forward Exchange Rates

Spot exchange rates are time 0 transactions. Forward exchange rates are contracts signed at time 0 for an exchange to take place in the future. In a forward contract, both parties agree to set the price today for delivery at a future date (see figure 17.4).

Figure 17.4   Spot and Forward Exchange Rates

	0	1	Time
	|————————————|————————>	
Spot transaction	Exchange $ for yen		
Forward transaction	Sign contract	Exchange $ for yen	

Forward foreign exchange contracts allow investors and businesses to lock-in values in another currency. Imagine a firm expecting to receive $1,000,000 in 90 days and planning to invest this money in Japan. If the firm waits 90 days before exchanging dollars for yen, the exchange rate might change adversely. For example, the dollar may depreciate from 125 yen to one dollar to a new rate of 120 yen to one dollar. At this new rate, the firm receives fewer yen for each dollar and the investment has reduced profitability. Instead of waiting 90 days, the firm can buy yen in 90 days with a forward contract. A forward exchange contract allows the firm to lock-in immediately an exchange rate for 90 days hence. The forward contract allows the firm to avoid the risk of an adverse change in the exchange rate. The forward contract is a two-edged sword; the firm cannot benefit if the exchange rate changes favorably.

Forward contracts are actively traded by a number of banks that are dealers in the foreign exchange markets. These contracts can typically run up to 180 days. Thus, businesses can lock-in foreign exchange rates 180 days into the future.

Covered Interest Arbitrage

Interest rates in individual countries are closely linked by forward exchange rates. Assume some spot interest rates in the U.S. (R_{US}) and in Japan (R_J) and spot (X_S) and forward exchange rates (X_{f1}). A U.S. investor has two investment choices as shown in figure 17.5.

Figure 17.5   Covered Interest Arbitrage

	0	1	Time
	|————————————|————>	
Invest in U.S.	$1	$1(1 + R_{US})$	
Exchange \$ for yen X_S yen = \$1 and invest at R_J	X_S yen	$X_S (1 + R_J)$ yen	
Exchange yen for \$ using forward contract X_{f1} yen = \$1		$\dfrac{\$X_S (1 + R_J)}{X_{f1}}$	

1. **Strategy 1:** The investor invests in U.S. bonds for one period and earns the interest rate R_{US}.

2. **Strategy 2:** The investor exchanges U.S. dollars and receives X_S yen, which are invested for one period at the spot interest rate of R_J. At time 1, the yen are exchanged for dollars at the forward exchange rate X_{f1}. Note that the spot interest rates and the spot and forward exchange rates are known with complete certainty at time 0. The entire transaction is certain.

Since both strategies start with the same amount and there is no risk in either strategy, the values at time 1 must be equal. That is:

$$\$1(1 + R_{US}) = \frac{\$X_S(1 + R_J)}{X_{f1}} \tag{17.7}$$

Unless this condition holds, arbitragers will enter the market and make profits until this condition holds.

Covered interest arbitrage shows that interest rates in different countries are related. The relationship does not provide any information about the direction of causation. Does the U.S. interest rate determine the Japanese, or vice versa? As a practical matter, the interest rate in a very large economy has a significant impact upon the interest rate in a very small economy, but not vice versa. For two countries of the same size, the interest rates are probably determined by factors in both countries.

Solving the preceding equation for the forward exchange rate gives us:

$$X_{f1} = X_s(1 + R_J)/(1 + R_{US}) \tag{17.8}$$

This equation shows that the relationship between the forward exchange rate and the spot exchange rate depends upon the interest rates in the two countries. That is:

$$X_{f1} > X_s \text{ when } R_J > R_{US} \tag{17.9}$$

$$X_{f1} = X_s \text{ when } R_J = R_{US} \tag{17.10}$$

$$X_{f1} < X_s \text{ when } R_J < R_{US} \tag{17.11}$$

The forward exchange rate is greater (less) than the spot exchange rate when the spot interest rate in the foreign country is greater (less) than the domestic interest rate.

Covered interest rate arbitrage has a drawback as an explanation of the interest rates in different countries. Forward contracts are necessary for the arbitrage to hold. Since forward contracts exist only for relatively short maturities, covered interest arbitrage does not hold for long maturities. Thus, the long-term interest rates in two countries can diverge.

Time Series Properties of Exchange Rates

In an efficient market, investors seek out profit opportunities. Positions with abnormally high returns on a risk-adjusted basis attract many investors. The profit-seeking actions of these investors drive returns to a fair level, given the risk.

The foreign exchange markets are highly competitive. A sizable number of very sophisticated financial institutions continually monitor the markets for profit opportunities, making abnormal profits hard to achieve. If a significant future change in exchange rates is highly likely, competition for profits makes investors take action immediately. The impact of the future change is instantly reflected in the spot and forward exchange rates. Consequently, in a perfectly efficient market, exchange rates should be unbiased predictors of future exchange rates.

International Stock and Bond Markets

The markets for stocks in many foreign countries have expanded dramatically. Very large markets exist in Japan, Germany, the United Kingdom, France, and Canada. Many new markets in Europe, the Far East, and South America have developed. These markets allow investors to significantly increase their portfolio diversification.

A large market has developed for American Depository Receipts (ADRs). ADRs are claims on the stock of foreign companies. ADRs are traded in the U.S. and are denominated in U.S. dollars. In most cases the foreign company's stock is dual traded, i.e., traded in the foreign market in terms of the foreign currency and traded as ADRs in dollars in the U.S. In some cases, the foreign company is traded only in the U.S. The existence of ADRs increases the liquidity of the foreign companies' stocks and reduces transactions costs for buyers of the stocks. Buyers of ADRs do not have to exchange dollars for foreign currency, but the dollar value of the ADRs still reflects exchange rate fluctuations.

In recent years, the market for international bonds has become quite sizable. International bonds are of two varieties: foreign bonds and Eurobonds. Foreign bonds are issued by a foreign borrower in the currency where the bond is issued. For example, General Motors might issue foreign bonds in Switzerland denominated in Swiss currency. A foreign bond is subject to the regulations in the country of issue.

Eurobonds are denominated in a particular currency but sold in several countries. For example, IBM might issue Eurodollar bonds denominated in U.S. dollars but sold in many different countries. In general, Eurodollar bond issues are not subject to regulation. In contrast, a public offering of bonds by IBM in the U.S. would have to be registered with the SEC so registration costs and restrictions would be involved. Eurobonds are frequently bearer bonds, meaning that there is no formal record of the owners of these bonds. Owners receive interest by presenting coupons to the issuer. Anonymous ownership may have the advantage of avoiding taxes.

Investment in international bonds may have the advantage of allowing investors to diversify their portfolios. However, this advantage must be weighed against the disadvantages of international investments, including exchange rate risk and higher information and transactions costs.

For many investors, mutual funds represent the best choice for international investing. Mutual funds allow diversification and provide a professional investment manager to analyze the foreign markets.

Summary

Exchange rates are affected by international investment and international trade. International investment provides diversification benefits and production and marketing advantages. International trade occurs because of countries' absolute or relative advantages in production. Currency exchange rates are interrelated with inflation, economic growth, and monetary policy in different countries. The U.S. currently allows its exchange rate to fluctuate freely as market conditions change. Forward exchange rates are determined by domestic and foreign interest rates.

Questions/Problems

1. Explain the theory of comparative advantage.

2. Explain the terms **depreciation** and **appreciation** of the U.S. currency.

3. The exchange rate between U.S. dollars and British pounds is .6 pounds per dollar. The exchange rate between U.S. dollars and Japanese yen is 100 yen to the dollar. Determine the exchange rate of yen per pound and pounds per yen.

4. The U.S./Canadian exchange rate is $.90 Canadian equals $1 U.S. The U.S./UK exchange rate is $2 U.S. equals 1 pound. How many Canadian dollars are in 1 pound?

5. The exchange rate between U.S. dollars and British pounds is .6 pounds per dollar. You can invest in the U.S. for one year at the spot interest rate of 8 percent. Alternatively, you can exchange dollars for pounds and invest in Britain at 12 percent. After one year, you exchange the pounds for dollars at the prevailing exchange rate.
   (a) At what exchange rate would your total return on the British investment be 15 percent?
   (b) At what exchange rate would the returns on the U.S. and British investments be equal?
   (c) What should the forward exchange rate be?

6. Bobby Boyd is considering investing in U.S. one-year bonds at 8 percent or Canadian bonds at 12 percent. The current exchange rate is $.80 Canadian equals $1 U.S. If the Canadian bonds are chosen, Bobby intends to exchange U.S. dollars for Canadian today in the spot market; then in one year, Bobby would exchange the Canadian dollars for U.S. dollars at the spot exchange rate. At what spot exchange rate in one year would the two investments earn the same U.S. dollar returns?

7. The spot exchange rate is $.85 Canadian equals $1 U.S. The forward exchange rate for delivery in one year is $.90 Canadian equals $1. The one-year spot interest rate in the U.S. is 6 percent. What is the one-year spot interest rate in Canada?

8. Assume the U.S. interest rate is 6 percent, the U.S. inflation rate is 4 percent, the British inflation rate is 12 percent, and the current exchange rate is .60 pounds to one U.S. dollar. If relative purchasing power parity holds, what should happen to the exchange rate?

9. Assume that relative purchasing power parity holds. The current exchange rate is $1 U.S. = 300 Mexican pesos. The inflation rate in the U.S. over the next year will be 5 percent and the inflation rate in Mexico

will be 55 percent. If so, what should the exchange rate become in one year, other things held constant? $1 U.S. equals how many Mexican pesos?

10. Explain how a change in the domestic interest rate affects the spot and forward interest rates.

References

Abken, P. A., "Globalization of Stock, Futures, and Options Markets," Federal Reserve Bank of Atlanta, *Economic Review,* 76, July/August 1991, pp. 1–22.

Copeland, L. S., *Exchange Rates and International Finance,* Wokingham, England: Addison-Wesley, 1989.

Huang, R. D. and H. R. Stoll, "Major World Equity Markets: Current Structure and Prospects for Change," New York University Salomon Center, *Monograph Series in Finance and Economics,* Monograph 1991–3.

Madura, J., *International Financial Management,* 3e, St. Paul, MN: West Publishing Co., 1992.

Scarlata, J. G., "Institutional Developments in the Globalization of Securities and Futures Markets," Federal Reserve Bank of St. Louis *Review,* 74, January/February 1992, pp. 17–30.

Solnik, B., *International Investments,* 2e, Reading, MA: Addison-Wesley, 1991.

Urich, T. J., "U.K., German and Japanese Government Bond Markets," New York University Salomon Center, *Monograph Series in Finance and Economics,* Monograph 1991–2.

18

Taxation

Overview

This chapter covers the federal tax treatment of U.S. Treasury, corporate, and municipal bonds.[1] The coupons on municipal bonds are exempt from federal income taxes. Federal taxation of coupon payments and of any capital gain or loss can have a significant impact upon the price and the yield to maturity of bonds.[2]

Municipal Bonds

Municipal bonds are issued by state and local governments. The coupon interest on most municipal bonds is exempt from federal income taxation.[3]

---

[1] Our discussion covers tax treatments for individuals. Institutions have special tax treatments and are not covered. Dealers are taxed as corporations. Banks have usually enjoyed special tax rules. Pension funds are tax-exempt, although final distributions to pensioners are taxable to the pensioners as regular income.

[2] U.S. Treasury securities are exempt from taxation by the states. However, corporate bonds may be subject to state taxes. This chapter deals exclusively with federal taxation.

[3] See Peter Fortune (1991 and 1992) for a recent survey of municipal bonds.

However, there are capital gains taxes on a discount from par.[4] In addition, municipal bonds issued by another state may be subject to state income taxes. For example, a resident of New York state is subject to New York state income taxes on holdings of municipal bonds issued by another state. Because of the exemption from federal taxation, the interest rates on municipal bonds are relatively low compared to the rates on otherwise identical taxable securities.

A controversy exists concerning the tax-exempt feature of municipal bonds. A tax exemption for municipal bonds represents a subsidy to municipalities from the federal government, but it also represents a tax subsidy to (wealthy) individuals in high tax brackets. Why should wealthy individuals receive a large tax benefit from municipal bonds? A direct subsidy to the municipalities is more appropriate, since then all the benefit goes directly to the municipalities and none goes to individuals.

Many municipalities have issued industrial development bonds. Typically, these are bonds issued by a municipality to attract business to the municipality. For example, the municipality may issue bonds to build a new plant to attract a new business, which might then lease the plant from the municipality. The bonds can be issued at the lower (tax-free) municipal interest rate. This interest saving is then passed on to the new business in the form of low lease payments. Many observers feel that this form of subsidy to private businesses is inappropriate and that all industrial development bonds should be fully taxable.

Some municipal bonds are **revenue** bonds. These are sold to finance a particular project for public power, water and wastewater, housing, hospitals, education, transportation (including airports), bridges, tunnels, and pollution control. The revenues from the project are used to repay the interest and principal on the bonds. Municipal bonds may also be **general obligation bonds**, which are backed by the full taxing power of a municipality. The chance of default is much lower for general obligation bonds than for revenue bonds. General obligation bonds typically have lower yields than revenue bonds because of lower default risk.

---

[4] See Livingston (1982) for a detailed discussion of the tax treatment and coupon effects for municipal bonds. The asymmetric tax treatment of discounts and premiums from par can create unusual coupon effects for municipal bonds. Appendix C discusses the term structure and the tax treatment of municipal bonds.

The default risk on revenue bonds can be considerable, and the consequences of default can be disastrous for bondholders. As an example, sometimes municipalities have built toll roads in remote areas, with revenue bonds as the financing. When the toll revenues have been insufficient to pay interest, the bondholders are left with a claim on a worthless toll road and have suffered a near-total loss. Investors in municipal revenue bonds should diversify their holdings to avoid catastrophic losses.

Many municipal bonds are serial issues – the maturities of an issue are staggered. With staggered maturities, principal repayment is easier. The staggered maturities also provide more choices for bond investors. On the negative side, the staggered maturities make each issue smaller in size and reduce the marketability of the bonds.

The resale market for municipal bond issues is quite thin. Because of the relatively small size of most municipal bond issues and the staggering of maturities, trading in a particular maturity is infrequent. Dealers charge large bid-asked spreads to compensate for the risks of carrying infrequently traded bonds in their inventory. As the trading frequency decreases, the dealer bears a greater risk of a price decline.

Summary of Tax Rules for Bonds

1. The discount from par on a Treasury bill or other money market instrument is considered regular income.
2. Coupon interest payments on bonds are subject to taxation at the regular income tax rate (except for municipal bonds).
3. If coupon-bearing bonds are originally issued at par but subsequently sell at a discount or premium from par, the discount or premium is subject to special tax rules. The ensuing discussion summarizes these tax rules. Appendix A discusses equilibrium conditions.
4. Bonds originally issued at a discount from par require amortization of the discount by the constant yield method for both the issuer and the bondholder. Treasury STRIPS are considered original issue discount securities and require amortization of the discount as taxable income for the buyer.

Tax Rules for Bonds Originally Issued at Par

Discounts from Par

For the tax years 1987 and later, discounts from par are treated as capital gains taxed at the regular income tax rate at maturity or disposition. For tax years before 1987, discounts from par were taxed at a lower capital gains tax rate if the bond was issued at par before July 1984 and at the regular tax rate if the bond was issued after July 1984. For example, if a ten-year bond with $100 par value was purchased for $80, the individual who bought this bond was subject to a capital gains tax on the $20 gain if the bond was held to maturity. For the years 1987 and beyond, this $20 gain is taxed as regular income; for earlier years, the gain was taxed at a lower rate if the bond was issued before July 1984. The capital gains tax treatment is favorable because the tax is postponed until disposition of the bond. In addition, the gain was subject to a lower tax rate in earlier years.

The favorable tax treatment of discount bonds has allowed some investors to realize a tax arbitrage. The procedure was to buy a bond at a discount from par, resulting in deferred tax liabilities at low tax rates. The purchase of the bond was financed with a loan upon which interest was paid. The interest was deductible from regular income. In effect, the arbitrager borrowed at a low after-tax rate (because interest on the loan was deductible against regular income in the current period) and lent the proceeds at a high after-tax rate (because the capital gain was subject to a deferred tax at a low tax rate).

To reduce this tax loophole, the buyer of a discount bond is now taxed at the regular income tax rate on discounts from par. Since the bondholder has the option to defer the gain until bond maturity, there may have still been some opportunity for arbitrage. But equalization of the tax rates on capital gains and regular income reduces the size of any advantage.

Premiums Above Par

Issued before September 27, 1985   For a bond originally issued at par before September 27, 1985, but subsequently selling at a premium above par, the bondholder has a choice. The premium can be treated either as a capital loss at maturity or it can be amortized on a straight line basis and deducted from regular income over the bond's life.[5] When a bond premium is amortized, part of the premium is counted as a tax-deductible loss each year of the bond's life. For most people, amortization is preferable because the deductions are taken sooner and because the whole amount of the premium is deducted.

---

[5] An individual who elects to amortize one bond is required to amortize all premiums.

With a capital loss, only a percentage of the loss is deductible.[6] If the tax rate on capital gains is equal to the regular income tax rate, the advantage of linear amortization is reduced.

Consider the following example of straight line amortization of a premium. Assume that you buy a bond for $120, with a ten-year maturity and $100 par value. Then the annual amortization is $(120 - 100)/10 = 2$. There is a $2 deduction from regular income for each of the next ten years.

Issued after September 27, 1985 For a bond originally issued at par after September 27, 1985, but subsequently selling at a premium above par, the premium is amortized over the bond's remaining life by the constant yield method. This method is explained in detail in Appendix A. Compared to linear amortization, the constant yield method has smaller amortization in early years and bigger amortization in later years. Thus, the present value of the amortized tax deductions is smaller under the constant yield method and is less attractive from the taxpayer's viewpoint.

Equilibrium

All Investors in the Same Tax Bracket

If all investors are in the same tax bracket, the impact of taxation is as shown in figure 18.1. Appendix A shows the algebraic derivations of these results.

In figure 18.1, bond price is a linear function of bond coupon for discount bonds. For premium bonds, price is a linear function of coupon if linear amortization of bond premiums is used; if the constant yield method of amortization is used, the function is a straight line with a flat term structure, but it is nonlinear with other term structures. In this equilibrium, all bonds are fairly priced, and investors have no tax incentives to switch to other bonds.

---

[6] The percentage has varied as the tax law has changed.

Figure 18.1   Bond Price versus Coupon for Various Tax Treatments

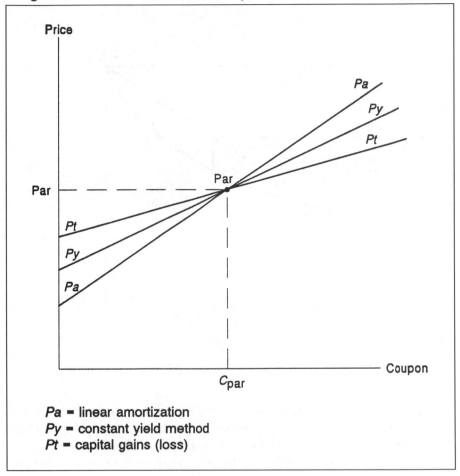

Pa = linear amortization
Py = constant yield method
Pt = capital gains (loss)

Different Tax Brackets

In a world with a progressive tax system, a clientele effect may develop. According to this viewpoint, investors in positive tax brackets hold the lowest coupon bonds for a given maturity, since these low coupon bonds have the most favorable capital gains tax treatment. Concentration of holdings in the lowest coupon bonds makes the relationship between price and coupon nonlinear, as shown in figure 18.2.

However, this clientele argument suffers from a major theoretical problem. Other things equal, lower coupon bonds are higher risk. While lower coupon bonds may have tax advantages, the greater risk of the bonds must

Figure 18.2   Price versus Coupon for the Clientele Effect

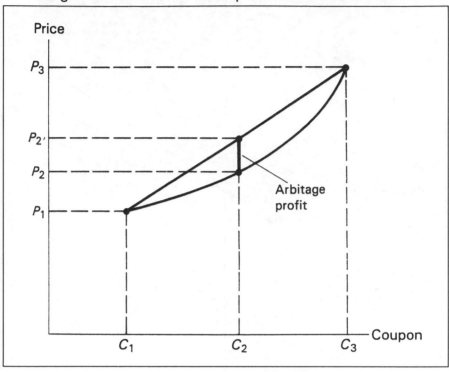

also be considered. Concentration of holdings in low coupon bonds does not dominate for all investors. Empirically, a linear relationship between price and coupon level exists, contradicting the clientele argument.[7]

The argument for a nonlinear relationship suffers from another theoretical problem. Arbitragers are able to profit if bond price is a convex function of coupon. The arbitrager can simultaneously buy an intermediate coupon level bond and shortsell a portfolio of high and low coupon bonds, such that the portfolio has the same coupon as the intermediate coupon bond.[8] As shown in figure 18.2, there is an immediate cash inflow, and all future cash flows cancel out. This arbitrage operation forces the price of the intermediate

---

[7] See Litzenberger and Rolfo (1984a).

[8] This is the same argument as that given in the nontax case in chapter 10 on coupon-bearing bonds.

coupon bond up and the prices of the high and low coupon bonds down until the relationship is a straight line.[9]

The Tax Timing Option

The preceding discussion assumes that bonds are held until maturity. In practice, bonds may be sold before maturity at the choice of the bondholder. In general, investors should realize losses to get tax deductions as soon as possible and allow gains to run to postpone tax payments. This choice is called the **tax timing option**. This tax timing option should have value to investors. The existence of tax timing options should have an impact on bond prices, but the size of the impact is hard to estimate concretely.

The Marginal Tax Rate

An extensive literature has developed on the implicit marginal tax rate in a world with progressive taxes. In one view, the marginal tax rate is the corporate tax rate. According to this position, if the marginal tax rate is less than the corporate tax rate, corporations borrow money until the marginal tax rate is driven up to the level of the corporate tax rate.

A second argument is that the marginal tax rate is determined by the tax rates faced by bond investors. Bond investors compare tax-free investments, such as municipal bonds, with taxable investments.[10] They switch to the investment with the highest after-tax return. In equilibrium, the after-tax returns are equal for both taxable and nontaxable investments for the marginal tax bracket. For example, if taxable par bonds have a 10 percent before-tax yield to maturity and if the marginal investor has a 50 percent tax rate, the tax-free rate should be 5 percent, the same as the after-tax return on the taxable bond.

If there is a progressive tax system, the marginal investor is not necessarily the investor with the highest tax rate. If the marginal tax rate is below

---

[9] This arbitrage argument requires the ability to shortsell without restriction, that is, the ability to use the proceeds of the shortsale to finance the purchase. If there are restrictions on shortsales, the arbitrage does not work.

[10] As described later, there are a number of differences between U.S. Treasury securities and municipal bonds.

the highest tax rate, then investors in tax brackets above the marginal tax rate find higher after-tax returns by investing in tax-free securities. For example, if the marginal tax rate is 40 percent, if taxable par bonds yield 10 percent,[11] and if tax-free par bonds yield 6 percent, someone in a 50 percent tax bracket would earn only 5 percent after tax [that is, (10 percent) (1 − .50)] on taxable bonds compared to 6 percent on tax-free bonds. Investors with the marginal tax bracket are indifferent between investing in taxable bonds or tax exempts. In our example, investors with a 40 percent tax rate would earn 6 percent after tax [that is, (10 percent)(1 − .40)] on taxable par bonds and 6 percent on tax-free bonds. Investors in brackets below the marginal tax rate find higher after-tax returns by investing in taxable bonds. For example, someone in a 20 percent bracket in our example could earn 8 percent after tax [that is, (10 percent)(1 − .20)] on taxable par bonds and only 6 percent on tax-free securities.

In a system with progressive income tax rates, a disequilibrium situation exists if individuals are allowed simultaneously to buy (shortsell) tax-free bonds and shortsell (buy) taxable securities. The U.S. tax law specifically prohibits these actions. If it did not, there would always be someone who could take a profitable arbitrage position.

Estimating the Marginal Tax Rate

Since the observed yields to maturity are not the true term structure, a considerable literature has developed on estimating the true term structure and the marginal tax rate. From a theoretical viewpoint, we would like to know the n after-tax discount rates (that is, $R_1, R_2, \ldots, R_n$) and the regular income tax rate and capital gains tax rate for each maturity – potentially three n variables. If the regular income tax rate and the capital gains tax rates are identical for every maturity, there are $n + 1$ variables to estimate. There is not enough information available to derive all of these variables from existing data for U.S. Treasury securities.[12]

Treasury STRIPS exist for a wide variety of maturities. As explained shortly, STRIPS are taxable, with the discount from par amortized by the

---

[11] A similar but much more complex argument can be presented for nonpar bonds. With nonpar bonds, the capital gains tax must be considered.

[12] See Livingston (1979a).

constant yield method. If there are n STRIPS and the tax rate is the same for all maturities, there are $n + 1$ unknowns. There is not enough information to deduce the tax-free term structure and the tax rate from data for n STRIPS.

The marginal tax rate has frequently been estimated by looking at the relationship between AAA municipal par bond yields and U.S. Treasury par bond yields. If y_t is the yield on a taxable Treasury par bond and y_m is the rate on a municipal par bond with the same maturity, it has been argued that:

$$y_t(1 - t) = y_m \qquad (18.1)$$

This condition equates the after-tax yields to maturity, but the approach has several drawbacks.

1. Since Treasury securities have no default risk, equation 18.1 assumes no default risk for municipal bonds. Even municipal bonds with the highest ratings have some default risk.
2. The tax status of U.S. Treasury securities is not the same as municipal bonds. Whereas Treasury securities are exempt from state income taxes, municipal bonds may be subject to state income taxes if held by someone who is not a resident of the state where the bond is issued. For example, someone living in New York state and owning a municipal bond issued by a municipality in Wisconsin is subject to New York state income taxes on this bond.
3. The condition in equation 18.1 is true only for par bonds. It is not true for discount or premium bonds. Since there are only a limited number of par bonds, the par bond yield needs to be extrapolated from yields on nonpar bonds. This introduces an element of error.
4. The liquidity of U.S. Treasury securities is substantially higher than the liquidity of municipals. Treasuries are issued in very large amounts and actively traded. In contrast, municipals are issued in relatively small amounts, often in serial issues, and are not actively traded. Because of this liquidity difference, municipals have higher yields, other things equal.

An interesting approach compares tax-free and taxable bonds issued for or on behalf of the same firm.[13] Since these bonds are essentially identical,

---

[13] See Ang, Peterson, and Peterson (1985).

the derived tax rate should be reasonably accurate. The estimated tax rate was in the range of 25–30 percent, considerably below the corporate tax rate and the highest individual tax rates. This approach suffers from the limited number of observations available.[14]

Flower Bonds

The U.S. Treasury has issued several bonds that are usually called **flower bonds**. If the owner of a flower bond is a wealthy individual with sizable potential federal estate tax liabilities, death of the bond's owner allows the deceased's estate to present flower bonds at par value to pay federal estate taxes. If the flower bond has a relatively low coupon and was purchased below par value, the estate of a wealthy individual is able to reap a considerable benefit from the individual's death.

Until fairly recently, individuals were able to purchase flower bonds up until the minute before they were pronounced legally dead. A recent legal case has forced the estate to hold the flower bonds for some time before death to show that the bonds were not purchased in anticipation of death. The case concerned Mr. Watson, who acquired a great deal of wealth and large potential federal estate tax liabilities as a founder of IBM. After retirement, Mr. Watson sustained a terminal accidental injury. In the several hours between the time of the injury and the time that Mr. Watson was pronounced legally dead, he made large purchases of flower bonds, even though he was unconscious in the hospital. The IRS refused to accept the flower bonds at par in payment of federal estate taxes, boldly claiming that the bonds were purchased in anticipation of death. Mr. Watson's estate disputed the IRS position. In the resulting legal battle, the IRS position was upheld in court.

Because of their attractive estate tax feature, flower bonds are priced differently from other U.S. Treasury securities. Low coupon flower bonds sell at unusually high prices and low yields to maturity. The unusually low yields on flower bonds make them easy to identify when reading the listings of U.S. Treasury bonds.

---

[14] Since reliable information on resale prices of bonds is not available, estimates from this approach are based upon prices on the date of original issue.

Nonpar Original Issue Price

Most bonds have been issued at par. This is not a chance event. The tax law provides for special tax treatment for any discounts or premiums from par at original issue. Note that bonds originally issued at par subsequently sell at nonpar prices as interest rates change. Bonds issued above par are very unusual and are not covered in this book, apart from noting that their tax treatment is symmetric and opposite to bonds issued at a discount.

Bonds originally issued at a discount are called **original issue discount bonds** (OIDs). Zero coupon bonds are by far the most common OIDs. To assist people in computing the taxes due on OIDs, the IRS annually issues Publication 1212, which has a listing of OIDs. For OIDs, the discount from par is amortized as an addition to taxable income for the bond buyer and as a deduction from taxable income for an issuing corporation. In effect, the amortized amount is treated as interest expense for the issuer and interest income for the buyer.

Before July 1982, OIDs were taxed by the linear amortization method, in which the discount from par was divided by the number of years until maturity. To illustrate linear amortization, assume a four-year zero coupon bond with $100 par value is sold for $68.30, implying a yield to maturity of 10 percent. The annual amortization is $(100 - 68.30)/4 = \$7.92$.

For some levels of interest rates, maturities, and taxes, linear amortization was very attractive to an issuing corporation because the firm was able to obtain sizable tax deductions in the early years of a bond issue. The present value of the resulting tax savings was quite large.

Since the additions to taxable income for the bond buyer are identical to the deductions from taxable income for the issuer, the present value of the taxes due on an OID can be very large relative to the present value of par. For the linear amortization method, the present value of the tax liabilities can exceed the present value of par, making the value of the OIDs negative. Since negative prices are impossible, the issuance of OIDs may be impossible for some interest rate levels and maturities under linear amortization.[15]

In July 1982, the tax law for both buyers and sellers of OIDs changed to the constant yield method. The constant yield method has smaller amortization in the early years and bigger amortization in the later years. This tax

---

[15] See Livingston (1979b).

treatment is far less favorable to the issuer than the linear amortization tax treatment. After the change in the law, corporations issued far fewer OIDs.

Suppose an OID is originally sold for a price of P. Its yield to maturity y is computed by finding the rate making the present value of the coupons and PAR value equal to the price.[16] The amortized amounts are shown in table 18.1. For a four-period example, if a zero coupon bond with $100 PAR value is sold for $68.30, the yield to maturity is 10 percent: that is, $68.30 = 100/(1.10)^4$. This is shown in table 18.2.

Linear amortization is a constant $7.92 per period for the same issue price of $68.30. The constant yield method has smaller amortization in the earlier years and larger amortization in the later years. For the buyer of the bond, the constant yield method is advantageous compared to linear amortization, since smaller amounts are added to taxable income in the early years; the tax liabilities are postponed to the later years. For the issuer of

Table 18.1   Amortization for the Constant Yield Method

Years	Amortization	
1	$P(1 + y) - P$	$= yP$
2	$P(1 + y)^2 - P(1 + y)$	$= yP(1 + y)$
3	$P(1 + y)^3 - P(1 + y)^2$	$= yP(1 + y)^2$
4	$P(1 + y)^4 - P(1 + y)^3$	$= yP(1 + y)^3$
.	.	.
.	.	.
.	.	.
n	$P(1 + y)^n - P(1 + y)^{n-1}$	$yP(1 + y)^{n-1}$

Table 18.2   Example of Amortization by the Constant Yield Method

Years	Amortization (dollars)	
1	$68.30(1.10) - 68.30$	$= 6.83$
2	$68.30(1.10)^2 - 68.30(1.10)$	$= 7.51$
3	$68.30(1.10)^3 - 68.30(1.10)^2$	$= 8.26$
4	$68.30(1.10)^4 - 68.30(1.10)^3$	$= 9.09$

---

[16] For a zero coupon OID bond, the following equation has to be solved for y: $P = PAR/(1 + y)^n$.

the bond, the constant yield method is disadvantageous compared to linear amortization because some of the tax deductions are postponed.

Chapter 9 on spot and forward interest rates discussed the stripping of U.S. Treasury securities, in which a coupon-bearing bond is broken into parts and claims on the coupons and par value are sold separately.[17] The stripped parts, which are called STRIPS, are taxed by the constant yield method. That is, each stripped part is taxed as if it were an OID at the time of stripping.

OIDs have an appeal to tax exempt buyers including pension funds, individual retirement accounts, and some foreign investors. For these investors, the tax considerations just described are not relevant. If taxable investors set the market prices, the tax exempt investors receive a windfall gain.

Summary

The federal taxation of coupons and capital gains or losses has a significant impact upon the prices and yields to maturity of bonds. Municipal bonds have coupons that are exempt from federal taxes. The coupons for other bonds are subject to taxation at the regular income tax rate.

Discounts from par are taxable at the regular income tax rate at maturity. Premiums above par can be amortized as deductions from taxable income. The amortization is straight line if the bonds were issued before September 27, 1985, and follows the constant yield method if the bonds were issued after this date.

Bonds that are originally issued at a discount from par require the discount to be amortized by the constant yield method as taxable income.

Questions/Problems

1. Describe the tax treatment for discount and premium bonds.

2. Describe the tax treatment for U.S. Treasury STRIPS, taxed as original issue zero coupon bonds. A four-period zero coupon bond is issued by

---

[17] For a detailed discussion of coupon stripping, see Livingston and Gregory (1989).

a corporation for $80 per $100 of par value. Determine the tax liabilities over the next four years for an investor in the 28 percent tax bracket.

3. What is the tax treatment of municipal bonds? What factors make municipal bonds riskier than Treasuries?

4. What is a flower bond? How can you identify a flower bond?

5. Theoretically, what should determine the tax rate of the marginal investor in the bond market? How can this marginal tax bracket be estimated empirically?

Appendix A: Equilibrium Conditions

In a world with individuals in the same tax bracket, the price of a bond is the present value of the after-tax cash flows discounted at after-tax discount rates. Let the after-tax discount rates be $R_1, R_2, \ldots, R_n$. Let P denote bond price. Let the regular income tax rate be denoted by t and the capital gains tax rate by tg.

Capital Gains Tax Treatment

Under the capital gains tax treatment, discounts (premiums) are taxed as gains (losses) at maturity at the lower capital gains tax rate tg. Although this tax treatment does not currently apply, the tax law might possibly be changed back to allow it once again. The price is the present value of the coupons after payment of regular income tax plus the present value of par minus the present value of the capital gains tax on the discount. If discounts (premiums) are taxed as capital gains (losses) at maturity, then let Pg equal the bond price:

$$Pg = \frac{c(1-t)}{(1+R_1)} + \frac{c(1-t)}{(1+R_2)^2} + \ldots + \frac{c(1-t)}{(1+R_n)^n} \quad \text{Present value of after-tax coupons}$$

$$+ \frac{PAR}{(1+R_n)^n} \quad \text{Present value of par} \quad (18A.1)$$

$$- \frac{(PAR - Pg)tg}{(1+R_n)^n} \quad \text{Present value capital gains tax liability}$$

Solving this equation for price Pg results in:

$$Pg = \frac{\dfrac{c(1-t)}{(1+R)} + \dfrac{c(1-t)}{(1+R_2)^2} + \cdots + \dfrac{c(1-t) + PAR(1-tg)}{(1+R_n)^n}}{1 - \dfrac{tg}{(1+R_n)^n}} \qquad (18A.2)$$

Let D_n be the present value of a tax-free dollar received n periods from now and let A_n be the present value of a tax-free annuity of \$1 per period for n periods:

$$D_n = \frac{1}{(1+R_n)^n} \qquad (18A.3)$$

$$A_n = \frac{1}{(1+R_1)} + \frac{1}{(1+R_2)^2} + \cdots + \frac{1}{(1+R_n)^n} \qquad (18A.4)$$

Writing equation 18A.2 in terms of a zero coupon bond D_n and an annuity A_n:

$$Pg = \frac{c(1-t)A_n + PAR(1-tg)D_n}{1 - tgD_n}$$

$$= \underbrace{\frac{c(1-t)A_n}{1-tgD_n}}_{\substack{\text{Present} \\ \text{value of} \\ \text{annuity}}} + \underbrace{\frac{PAR(1-tg)D_n}{1-tgD_n}}_{\substack{\text{Present value} \\ \text{of zero bond} \\ \text{taxed as capital} \\ \text{gain at maturity}}} \qquad (18A.5)$$

The first term on the right-hand side of equation 18A.5 is the present value of an annuity implicit in a coupon-bearing bond. The denominator of this annuity is somewhat peculiar, since it implies a capital loss at maturity if the annuity is purchased by itself. The second term on the right-hand side of equation 18A.5 is a zero coupon bond with a capital gain at maturity. The net capital gain or loss for a coupon-bearing bond depends upon the coupon level. For discount bonds, there is a net capital gain. For premium bonds, there is a net capital loss. For par bonds, there is no capital gain or loss, and equation 18A.5 simplifies to:

$$PAR = c(1-t)A_n + (PAR)D_n, \text{ for par bonds} \qquad (18A.6)$$

The yield to maturity, y, for a par bond is equal to c/PAR. Solving equation 18A.6 for c/PAR results in:

$$y = \frac{c}{\text{PAR}} = \frac{1 - D_n}{A_n(1 - t)} \qquad (18\text{A}.7)$$

This result is similar to the nontax case with the addition of the term $(1 - t)$ in the denominator. In the case of a flat after-tax term structure in which $R_1 = \ldots = R_n = R$, the yield to maturity on a par bond is $R/(1 - t)$. For example, if R equals 5 percent and the tax rate is 50 percent, the yield on a par bond is 10 percent [that is, $.05/(1 - .50)$].

Regular Tax Rate on Capital Gains

Under this tax treatment, discounts (premiums) from par are taxed as a gain (loss) at the regular income tax rate t at maturity. For tax years beginning in 1987, this method applies for discount bonds (originally issued at par). The price of a bond taxed by this method is the same as in equation 18A.5 with tg set equal to the regular income tax rate t.

$$Pt = \frac{c(1 - t)A_n + \text{PAR}(1 - t)D_n}{1 - tD_n} \qquad (18\text{A}.8)$$

Figure 18A.1 shows the relationship between coupon level and bond price for a given maturity of n periods for various tax treatments. From equation 18A.5 or 18A.8, it is clear that a linear relationship exists between bond price and coupon level for the capital gains tax treatment. For par bonds, equations 18A.5 and 18A.8 must intersect.[18] The slope of equation 18A.8 must be steeper than the slope of equation 18A.5.[19]

Linear Amortization Tax Treatment

Under linear amortization, the premium (discount) is amortized on a straight line basis as a deduction from (addition to) taxable income. Linear amortiza-

---

[18] For a par bond, $c/\text{PAR} = y = (1 - D_n)/A_n(1 - t)$.

[19] To see this, take the derivative of equation 18A.5 with respect to tg. For discount bonds, this derivative is negative; for premium bonds, the derivative is positive.

Figure 18A.1   Equilibrium with Differential Treatment of Premium and Discount Bonds

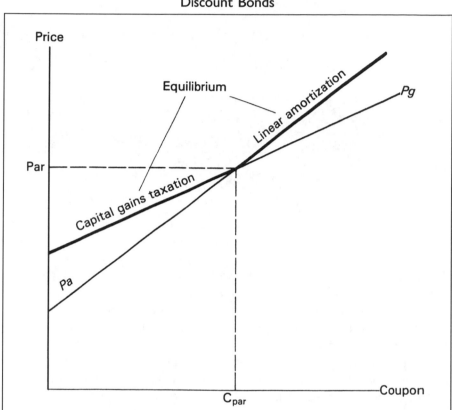

tion of premiums can be used for bonds issued before September 27, 1985. For linear amortization, the price is the present value of the after-tax cash flows discounted at the after-tax discount rates R_j. Let Pa equal the price of a bond with linear amortization:

$$Pa = \frac{c(1-t)}{(1+R_1)} + \frac{c(1-t)}{(1+R_2)^2} + \cdots + \frac{c(1-t)}{(1+R_n)^n} \quad \begin{array}{l}\text{Present value}\\ \text{of after-tax}\\ \text{coupons}\end{array}$$

$$+ \frac{\text{PAR}}{(1+R_n)^n} \quad \begin{array}{l}\text{Present value}\\ \text{of par value}\end{array} \quad (18A.9)$$

$$+ \frac{t[Pa - \text{PAR}]}{n}\left(\frac{1}{(1+R_1)} + \cdots + \frac{1}{(1+R_n)^n}\right) \quad \begin{array}{l}\text{Present value of}\\ \text{the amortized}\\ \text{deductions}\end{array}$$

Writing this in terms of an annuity, A_n, and zero coupon bond, D_n, leads to:

$$Pa = c(1 - t)A_n + (\text{PAR})D_n + tA_n(Pa - \text{PAR})/n \qquad (18\text{A}.10)$$

Simplifying this equation results in:

$$Pa = \frac{c(1 - t)A_n + \text{PAR}[D_n - (tA_n)/n]}{1 - (tA_n)/n} \qquad (18\text{A}.11)$$

$$= \frac{c(1 - t)A_n}{1 - (tA_n)/n} + \frac{\text{PAR}[D_n - (tA_n)/n]}{1 - (tA_n)/n} \qquad (18\text{A}.12)$$

Present value of annuity	Present value of a zero coupon bond with discount amortized on a straight line basis

The first term represents the present value of an annuity of coupon payments implicit in this type of bond. The second term represents the price of a zero coupon bond subject to linear amortization of the discount from par.

For a given maturity, figure 18A.1 shows the relationship between bond price and coupon level under the linear amortization assumption. The intercept is the price of the zero coupon bond in equation 18A.12. The slope is the price of the annuity in equation 18A.12; algebraic manipulations show that this slope is steeper than the slopes of equations 18A.5 or 18A.8.[20]

---

[20] The slope of equation 18A.12 > slope of equation 18A.5 if:

$$\frac{c(1 - t)A_n}{1 - tgD_n} < \frac{c(1 - t)A_n}{1 - (tA_n)/n}$$

The numerators cancel. By cross-multiplying and rearranging:

$$tA_n/n > tgD_n$$
$$A_n > nD_n(tg)/t$$

This must be true since tg/t is less than 1.0 and A_n is greater than nD_n. This last point follows from the fact that $D_1 \geq \ldots \geq D_n$, as discussed in chapter 9 on spot and forward interest rates.

Since the capital gains tax treatment is better for discount bonds and linear amortization is better for premium bonds, equilibrium should have two parts – one for discount bonds and one for premium bonds. This is shown in figure 18A.1.

The Constant Yield Method

If a bond is taxed by the constant yield method, the difference between par and bond price is amortized according to a precise formula shown shortly. Discounts from par are amortized as additions to regular income and premiums above par are amortized as deductions from regular income. The constant yield method of taxation applies for two cases: bonds originally issued at a nonpar price and premium bonds originally issued at par after September 27, 1985.

The **tax basis** is defined as the value of the bond for tax purposes. At the end of every tax period, the basis is computed. The change in the basis equals the amount amortized. For the constant yield method, the basis and amortization for a bond with price Py and yield to maturity y is shown in table 18A.1.

Table 18A.2 shows constant yield amortization for a four-period example of a bond with a par value of \$100, an annual coupon of \$12, and a yield to maturity of 10 percent. The price of this bond in the market is \$106.33973, that is, a premium of \$6.33973 above par. This premium is amortized as follows by the constant yield method.

The amortization increases each period. The total amount of amortization is the bond's premium above par. The price, Py, of a bond taxed by the constant yield method should be the present value of the coupons, par value, and amortization.

Table 18A.1   Constant Yield Method: Tax Basis and Amortization

Point in Time	Basis	Amortized Amount
0	Py	$(y)Py - c$
1	$Py(1 + y) - c$	$[(y)Py - c](1 + y)$
2	$Py(1 + y)^2 - c(1 + y) - c$	$[(y)Py - c](1 + y)^2$
3	$Py(1 + y)^3 - c(1 + y) - c(1 + y) - c$	$[(y)Py - c](1 + y)^3$
4	. . .	
etc.		

Table 18A.2   Four-Period Example of Constant Yield Method

Point in Time	Amortized Amount	Dollar Amount
0		
1	$(y)Py - c$	$1.36603
2	$[(y)Py - c](1 + y)$	$1.50263
3	$[(y)Py - c](1 + y)^2$	$4.65289
4	$[(y)Py - c](1 + y)^3$	$1.81817
Total	$Py - PAR$	$6.33973

$$Py = c(1 - t)A_n \qquad \text{Present value of after-tax coupons}$$

$$+ (PAR)D_n \qquad \text{Present value of par}$$

$$- t\{[(y)Py - c] + [(y)Py - c](1 + y) + \ldots\} \qquad \text{Present value of amortized tax liabilities}$$

$$(18A.13)$$

Solving for Py and simplifying:

$$Py = c(1 - t)A_n + (PAR)D_n \qquad (18A.14)$$

$$- t[(y)PAR - c] \sum_{j=1}^{n} \frac{D_j}{(1 + y)^j}$$

where Σ denotes the sum.

Appendix B: Coupon Effects

The coupon effect deals with the relationship between yield to maturity and coupon level for a given maturity. With a positive coupon effect, higher coupon bonds have higher yields to maturity. With a neutral coupon effect, bonds of all coupon levels have the same yield to maturity. For a negative coupon effect, higher coupon bonds have lower yields to maturity.

Chapter 10 on coupon-bearing bonds examined coupon effects in a nontax environment. The coupon effect was shown to depend upon the term structure of interest rates. In a tax world, the coupon effect also depends upon taxes. Because there are different tax treatments allowed for premium and discount bonds, there can be different coupon effects for discount and premium bonds. A complete treatment of coupon effects is quite intricate; therefore, some major results are presented.

For discount bonds subject to capital gains taxation, the coupon effect is always positive for declining and flat term structures. The coupon effect is frequently positive for rising term structures as well. Recall that in a nontax world, a rising term structure results in a negative coupon effect. In a capital gains tax world, the impact of taxes tends to overwhelm the pure term structure effect. In effect, the favorable capital gains taxation tends to bid up the relative price of low coupon bonds, making their yields relatively low.[21] This is illustrated by the examples[22] in tables 18B.1 and 18B.2, which are shown graphically in figure 18B.1.

Linear amortization is illustrated by table 18B.3, which is shown graphically in figure 18B.1. Tables 18B.1, 18B.2, and 18B.3 assume the same term structure. In table 18B.3, higher coupon bonds have lower yields to maturity – a negative coupon effect. The following reasoning explains this negative coupon effect. At par, the bonds in all three tables would have the same price of $100 and yield to maturity of 7.49 percent.[23] From a tax viewpoint, linear amortization is attractive for premium bonds, implying a

---

[21] This is illustrated in Figure 18A.1. With discount bonds of the same coupon level, the bond price is higher for a tax rate of tg than for a tax rate of t. The postponement of tax payment until maturity also raises the price for a given coupon level.

[22] The computations are done as follows. The tax rates are set. In table 18B.1, $t = 28$ percent and $tg = 14$ percent. Then the term structure of interest rates is set. In table 18B.1, $R_1 = .03$, $R_2 = .03(1.02)$, $R_3 = .03(1.02)^2$, ..., and so on. This is a rising term structure that increases geometrically at 2 percent per year. Using these tax rates, the term structure, and the relevant coupon level in table 18B.1, the bond price is computed for a 15-year bond by substituting into equation 18A.5. Given the price, coupon, and maturity, the yield to maturity is computed. For table 18B.2, the procedure is the same except that equation 18A.8 is used to compute the price. For table 18B.3, equation 18A.12 is used to compute the price.

[23] The coupon of a par bond would also be 7.49 percent. This is computed from the result that yield on a par bond is $(1 - D_n)/A_n(1 - t)$. In price, bond coupons are issued in eighth's. The nearest coupon in practice would be 7.50 percent, with a price slightly above par.

Table 18B.1   Capital Gains Tax, $tg = .5t$
Assumptions: t = 28%, tg = 14%, Maturity = 15, R_1 = 3%, Rate Increases
by 0.2% Per Year

Coupon (%)	Price per $100 Par	Before-Tax Yield to Maturity (%)
0	$39.28	6.43
2	$55.49	6.84
4	$71.70	7.13
6	$87.92	7.35
8	$104.13	7.53
10	$120.35	7.67

Table 18B.2   Capital Gains Tax, $t = tg$
Assumptions: t = 28%, tg = 28%, Maturity = 15, R_1 = 3%, Rate Increases
by 0.2% Per Year

Coupon (%)	Price per $100 Par	Before-Tax Yield to Maturity (%)
0	$35.13	7.22
2	$52.45	7.33
4	$69.77	7.40
6	$87.09	7.46
8	$104.42	7.50
10	$121.74	7.53

relatively high price. Notice that the bond with a 10 percent coupon has a higher price in table 18B.3 than in the other tables. This means a lower yield to maturity.

If discount bonds are priced by the capital gains tax treatment (either equation 18A.5 or 18A.8) and if premium bonds are priced by linear amortization (equation 18A.12), the relationship between price and coupon is two straight line segments. The coupon effect for discount bonds can be positive while the coupon effect for premium bonds is negative. Therefore, the yield to maturity can reach a maximum at par.[24] This possibility is illustrated in tables 18B.2 and 18B.3. From table 18B.2, a discount bond with a 6 percent

---

[24] See Livingston (1979c and 1979d).

Figure 18B.1   Coupon versus Yield for Three Tax Treatments

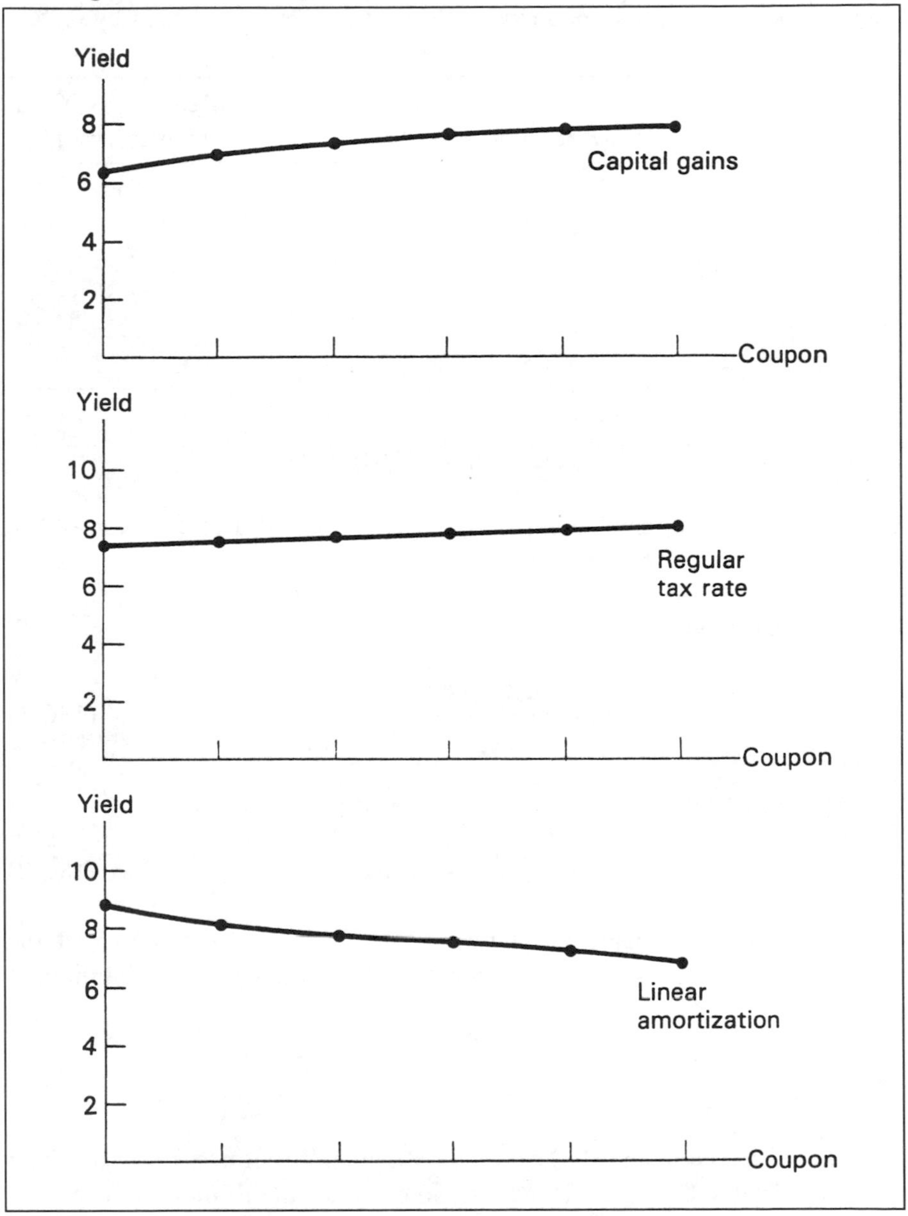

coupon has a yield to maturity of 7.46 percent; a par bond has a yield to maturity of 7.49 percent. From table 18B.3, a premium bond with an 8 percent coupon has a yield to maturity of 7.46 percent.

Table 18B.3   Linear Amortization
Assumptions: $t = 28\%$, Maturity = 15, $R_1 = 3\%$, Rate Increases by 0.2%
Per Year

Coupon (%)	Price per $100 Par	Before-Tax Yield to Maturity (%)
0	$28.87	8.63
2	$47.87	8.15
4	$66.86	7.83
6	$85.85	7.61
8	$104.84	7.46
10	$123.83	7.33

Appendix C: Municipal Bonds

The price of a municipal bond Pm can be expressed as a function of the term structure.[25]

For discount bonds:

$$Pm = \frac{cA_n + \text{PAR}(1 - t)D_n}{1 - tD_n} \tag{18C.1}$$

For par and premium bonds:

$$Pm = cA_n + (\text{PAR})D_n \tag{18C.2}$$

Discount bonds have a capital gains tax liability at maturity at the regular income tax rate t. Par and premium bonds have no tax liabilities.

References

Ang, J., D. Peterson, and P. Peterson, "Marginal Tax Rates: Evidence from Nontaxable Corporate Bonds: A Note," *Journal of Finance*, 40, March 1985, pp. 327–32.

---

[25] This discussion assumes no default risk on municipals.

Arditti, F. and M. Livingston, "The Relative Price Volatility of Taxable and Non-Taxable Bonds: A Note," *Journal of Finance,* 37, June 1982, pp. 877–81.

Brick, I. E. and O. Palmon, "Interest Rate Fluctuations and the Advantage of Long-term Debt Financing: A Note on the Effect of the Tax-Timing Option," *The Financial Review,* 27, August 1992, pp. 467–74.

Buser, S. A. and P. S. Hess, "Empirical Determinants of Relative Yields on Taxable and Tax-Exempt Securities," *Journal of Financial Economics,* 17, December 1986, pp. 335–55.

Constantinides, G. M. and J. E. Ingersoll, "Optimal Bond Trading Strategies with Personal Taxes," *Journal of Financial Economics,* 13, September 1984, pp. 299–335.

Dammon, R. M. and R. C. Green, "Tax Arbitrage and the Existence of Equilibrium Prices for Financial Assets," *Journal of Finance,* 42, December 1987, pp. 1143–66.

Dermody, J. C. and E. Z. Prisman, "Term Structure Multiplicity and Clientele in Markets with Transactions Costs and Taxes," *Journal of Finance,* 42, September 1987, pp. 893–911.

Dermody, J. C., and R. T. Rockafellar, "Mathematics of Debt Instruments Taxation," *Financial Markets, Institutions & Instruments,* 3:2, pp. 1–87.

Ehrhardt, M. C., "A New Linear Programming Approach to Bond Portfolio Management: A Comment," *Journal of Financial and Quantitative Analysis,* 24, December 1989, pp. 533–7.

Fortune, P., "The Municipal Bond Market, Parts I and II," Federal Reserve Bank of Boston, *New England Economic Review,* September/October 1991, pp. 13–36 and May/June 1992, pp. 47–64.

Green, Richard C., "A Simple Model of the Taxable and Tax-Exempt Yield Curve," *The Review of Financial Studies,* 6, 1993, pp. 233–264.

Heaton, H., "The Relative Yields on Taxable and Tax-Exempt Debt," *Journal of Money Credit and Banking,* 18, 1986, pp. 482–94.

Jordan, B. D. and S. D. Jordan, "Tax Timing Options and the Pricing of Treasury Bond Triplets," *Journal of Financial Economics,* 30, 1991, pp. 135–64.

Jordan, J. V., "Tax Effects in Term Structure Estimation," *Journal of Finance,* 39, June 1984, pp. 393–406.

Katz, E. and E. Z. Prisman, "Arbitrage, Clientele Effects, and the Term Structure of Interest Rates," *Journal of Financial and Quantitative Analysis,* 26, December 1991, pp. 435–43.

Lamb, R., and S. P. Rappaport, *Municipal Bonds,* 2e, New York: McGraw-Hill, 1987.

Litzenberger, R. and J. Rolfo, "An International Study of Tax Effects of Government Bonds," *Journal of Finance,* 39, March 1984a, pp. 1–22.

Litzenberger, R. and J. Rolfo, "Arbitrage Pricing, Transactions Costs and Taxation of Capital Gains: A Study of Government Bonds with the Same Maturity Date," *Journal of Financial Economics,* 13, September 1984b, pp. 337–51.

Livingston, M., "Bond Taxation and the Shape of the Yield to Maturity Curve," *Journal of Finance,* 34, March 1979a, pp. 189–96.

Livingston, M., "A Note on the Issuance of Long-term Pure Discount Notes," *Journal of Finance,* 34, March 1979b, pp. 241–46.

Livingston, M., "Taxation and Bond Market Equilibrium in a World of Uncertain Future Interest Rates," *Journal of Financial and Quantitative Analysis,* 14, March 1979c, pp. 11–27.

Livingston, M., "The Pricing of Premium Bonds," *Journal of Financial and Quantitative Analysis,* 14, September 1979d, pp. 517–27.

Livingston, M., "The Pricing of Municipal Bonds," *Journal of Financial and Quantitative Analysis,* 17, June 1982, pp. 179–93.

Livingston, M., "Comment on Expectations, Taxes, and Interest: The Search for the Darby Effect," *American Economic Review,* December 1991, pp. 1435–6.

Livingston, M. and D. W. Gregory, "Stripping of U.S. Treasury Securities," *NYU Salomon Bros. Monograph Series,* 1989.

Miller, M., "Debt and Taxes," *Journal of Finance,* 32, May 1977, pp. 261–75.

Mitchell, K. and M. D. McDade, "Preferred Habitat, Taxable/Tax-Exempt Yield Spreads, and Cycles in Property/Liability Insurance," *Journal of Money Credit and Banking,* 24, November 1992, pp. 528–52.

Prisman, E. Z., "A Unified Approach to Term Structure Estimation: A Methodology for Estimating the Term Structure in a Market with Frictions," *Journal of Financial and Quantitative Analysis,* 25, March 1990, pp. 127–42.

Pye, G., "On the Tax Structure of Interest Rates," *Quarterly Journal of Economics,* 83, November 1969, pp. 562–79.

Robichek, A. A. and W. D. Niebuhr, "Tax-Induced Bias in Reporting Treasury Yields," *Journal of Finance,* 25, December 1970, pp. 1081–90.

Ronn, E. I., "A New Linear Programming Approach to Bond Portfolio Management," *Journal of Financial and Quantitative Analysis,* 22, December 1987, pp. 439–66.

Schaefer, S. M., "Measuring a Tax-Specific Term Structure of Interest Rates in the Market for British Government Securities," *Economic Journal,* 91, June 1981, pp. 415–38.

Schaefer, S. M., "Tax Induced Clientele Effects in the Market for British Government Securities," *Journal of Financial Economics,* 10, July 1982, pp. 121–60.

Schaefer, S. M., "Taxes and Security Market Equilibrium," in William F. Sharpe and Cathryn M. Cootner, *Financial Economics: Essays in Honor of Paul Cootner,* pp. 159–78. Englewood Cliffs, NJ: Prentice Hall, 1982b.

19

Equities

Overview

Equity, or common stock, is an important source of financing for corporations. Equity represents a residual claim on the assets of the corporation after the obligations to creditors and bondholders have been satisfied. The stockholders have the right to choose the board of directors, which selects the managers of the firm. Thus, the power to control the firm ultimately rests with the common stockholders.[1]

Dividend payments by the firm to the stockholders are not fixed payments, as in the case of coupon interest paid to bondholders. The dividends paid to stockholders are set at the discretion of the board of directors. Although stockholders may be dissatisfied if dividends are not paid and may vote to remove the board of directors, nonpayment of dividends does not constitute default. In contrast, nonpayment of obligations to creditors or to bondholders constitutes default with probable legal consequences.

A number of methods for determining the current value of common stock will be discussed, including price/earnings ratios, asset values, dividends, and the capital asset pricing model. Each method provides some insights into common stock value, but none is entirely satisfactory. The basic problem in determining the value of common stock is that the current value depends upon expectations about future events. These expectations are not directly observable and, therefore, are hard to specify precisely.

---

[1] In practice, there may be a separation of ownership and control. Because the stockholders as owners are a widely dispersed group, the managers may effectively control the firm.

Price/Earnings Multiples

The price/earnings multiple is the ratio of current stock price to current earnings. A higher multiple indicates greater market price per dollar of earnings. Other things equal, a higher multiple is less desirable from the buyer's viewpoint because the buyer is paying more per dollar of earnings.

It is a true that:

$$\text{Price} = [\text{Multiple}][\text{Earnings}] \tag{19.1}$$

Since:

$$\text{Price} = \left[\frac{\text{Price}}{\text{Earnings}}\right][\text{Earnings}] \tag{19.2}$$

The multiple represents everything that affects price except earnings. These other factors include growth rates and risk. Other things equal, a firm with a higher growth rate has a higher multiple because current earnings are low relative to future earnings. Other things equal, a high-risk firm has a high multiple.

Many security analysts try to estimate the fair value of the multiple for securities, then estimate future earnings. Multiplying the two gives an estimate of intrinsic value of the security, that is:

$$\text{Intrinsic Value} = [\text{Estimated Multiple}][\text{Estimated Earnings}] \tag{19.3}$$

The intrinsic value is then compared with the current stock price. If intrinsic value is sizably above the current market price, the security is undervalued and is recommended for purchase. The analyst expects that the market will eventually realize the undervaluing of the security. When the market becomes aware of the true value, the price should jump up to the intrinsic value and generate high returns.

This intrinsic value approach implicitly believes that the market is temporarily inefficient. The analyst searches for the disparities between intrinsic value and market price. The approach is based upon the belief that inefficiencies are eventually eliminated as the market discovers true values.

The price/earnings multiple approach suffers from the difficulty that risk is not explicitly included. The risk is implicitly embedded in the multiple. In addition, multiples tend to change considerably over time, both for individual stocks and for the market as a whole. During periods of optimism, the multiple for the market can be over 20. During periods of widespread pessimism, the multiple for the market as a whole can be less than ten. These swings can affect returns considerably.

In discussing efficient markets, the random walk hypothesis was discussed for stock prices. The evidence was relatively consistent with the random walk. There is also considerable evidence that earnings follow a random walk to a fair degree of approximation. Since the multiple is price divided by earnings, the multiple must also follow a random pattern.

Asset Value

The asset value approach involves figuring the liquidating value of the individual assets of the firm. The liquidating value is essentially the value that the highest bidder is willing to pay for individual assets. This value can be estimated by finding comparable assets that have known market values.

The asset value approach is used in mergers and takeovers. Acquiring firms estimate the liquidating value of the assets of prospective acquisitions. The current market value of the stock is then compared with this liquidating value. If the current market value is sizably less than the liquidating value, an acquisition makes sense.

For example, Raider Corporation discovers that Gentle Lamb Enterprises has common stock valued at $50 million in the market. If Gentle Lamb is broken up and sold off as four individual businesses, the individual businesses have an estimated total value of $80 million, the liquidating value. If Raider can purchase Gentle Lamb for less than $80 million, it can liquidate the parts and make a profit.

Dividend Models

The price of a common stock should be equal to the present value of anticipated dividends. While the preceding statement is obvious, implementation is difficult because of two problems: the uncertainty about the value of future dividends and the uncertainty in choosing the correct discount rate required to find present value. We will proceed by considering several simplified cases.

Suppose the term structure of interest rates is flat at a discount of R and dividends are certain and equal to the stream shown in figure 19.1.

The stock price is P_0, the present value of dividends:

Figure 19.1 Stream of Dividends

Points in Time
0
1
2
3
4
5 . . .
D1
D2
D3
D4
D5 . . .

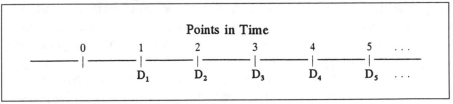

$$P_0 = \frac{D_1}{(1 + R)} + \frac{D_2}{(1 + R)^2} + \frac{D_3}{(1 + R)^3} + \frac{D_4}{(1 + R)^4} + \frac{D_5}{(1 + R)^5} + \ldots \tag{19.4}$$

If the future dividends are all the same and equal to D, then the price simplifies to:

$$P_0 = \frac{D}{R} \tag{19.5}$$

A widely considered situation is the case of dividends growing at a constant rate of growth g. Then, the pattern of dividends is shown in figure 19.2.

In the case of a constant growth rate, g, for dividends, the price is equal to:

$$P_0 = \frac{D_1}{(1 + R)} + \frac{(1 + g)D_1}{(1 + R)^2} + \frac{(1 + g)^2 D_1}{(1 + R)^3} + \frac{(1 + g)^3 D_1}{(1 + R)^4} + \ldots \tag{19.6}$$

This simplifies to:

$$P_0 = \frac{D_1}{R - g} \tag{19.7}$$

Figure 19.2 Dividends Growing at a Constant Growth Rate

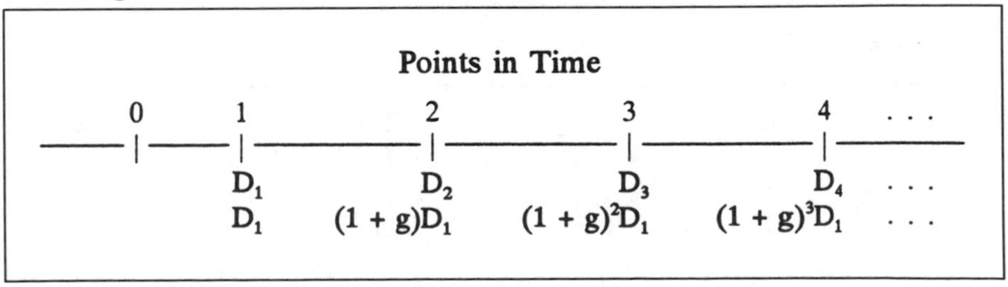

Points in Time
0
1
2
3
4 . . .
D1
D2
D3
D4 . . .
D1
(1 + g)D1
(1 + g)²D1
(1 + g)³D1 . . .

In order for price to be positive, the discount (or interest) rate R must be greater than the growth rate g. This constant growth rate case is highly restrictive because it assumes complete certainty and a constant growth indefinitely into the future. Nevertheless, the simplicity of the equation has made this model very popular.

Let's illustrate this constant growth rate model with a numerical example in which the discount rate R is 20 percent, the growth rate is 10 percent, and the dividend at time 1 is \$1. Then the cash flows to the owner of the stock are shown in figure 19.3. Price is the present value of these cash flows.

$$P_0 = \frac{1}{1.20} + \frac{(1.10)^1}{(1.20)^2} + \frac{(1.10)^2 1}{(1.20)^3} + \frac{(1.10)^3 1}{(1.20)^4} + \ldots \qquad (19.8)$$

$$P_0 = \frac{1}{.20 - .10} = \$10 \qquad (19.9)$$

The dividends in the constant growth rate model grow at the constant rate of g. This means that the price also increases by g percent. That is:

$$P_1 = P_0(1 + g) \qquad (19.10)$$

In terms of our numerical example, the price at time 1 is \$11 [i.e., 10(1.10)]. Consider the rate of return from holding this stock for one period. The stock is purchased for \$10 at time 0; it is sold for \$11 at time 1; and a dividend of \$1 is received at time 1. The rate of return (i.e., ROR) is computed as that discount rate equating the present value of the cash flows to the price. That is:

Figure 19.3   Illustration of the Constant Growth Rate Model

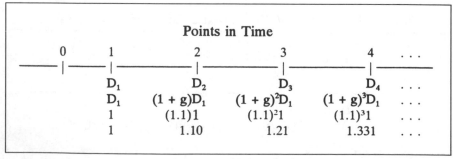

		Points in Time			
0	1	2	3	4	...
	D_1	D_2	D_3	D_4	...
	D_1	$(1 + g)D_1$	$(1 + g)^2 D_1$	$(1 + g)^3 D_1$	...
	1	$(1.1)1$	$(1.1)^2 1$	$(1.1)^3 1$	...
	1	1.10	1.21	1.331	...

$$10 = \frac{1 + 11}{(1 + \text{ROR})}$$

$$(1 + \text{ROR}) = 12/10 = 1.20 \qquad (19.11)$$

$$\text{ROR} = .20$$

Solving this equation indicates a rate of return of 20 percent, which is (and must be) the discount rate R. Given the future dividends and the appreciation in the stock price over time, the $10 price guarantees a ROR of 20 percent in every period.[2]

Utility companies are regulated. The regulatory authorities hold hearings to decide upon the prices charged utility customers, and the company and consumer advocates are allowed to present arguments about prices. An important aspect of the discussion is the allowed rate of return on stockholders' equity. Typically, the regulators decide upon a fair rate of return and then use some model to relate rate of return to prices. The constant growth model is frequently used by solving for R, the rate of return:

$$R = \frac{D_1}{P_0} + g \qquad (19.12)$$

In equation 19.12, the rate of return, R, equals the dividend yield, D_1/P_0, plus the growth rate, g.

Given the rate of return set by the regulators and the current stock price P_0, the prices charged to consumers are set to allow dividends to grow at the rate g. For example, assume a 20 percent allowable rate of return. The current stock price is $10 and the current dividend is $1. Given estimates of output, customer prices must be set to allow dividends to grow at 10 percent.

The constant dividend growth model has the advantage of simplicity, which probably explains its appeal and popularity. The model suffers from some deficiencies. First, it is technically correct only in the case of complete certainty. Some users adapt it for uncertainty by adding a risk premium. This adaptation has no firm theoretical basis. Second, the model assumes a constant growth rate of g from now until forever, a clearly unrealistic assumption. Very few firms have constant growth rates even for short periods of

---

[2] The reader can easily verify that the rate of return in the next period is also 20 percent.

time. Some investigators alter the model by allowing the growth rate to change in some regular way. For example, the growth rate is 10 percent for the next ten years; then it is 5 percent for the following ten years, and zero thereafter. This results in a model that is still relatively simple, but that captures more of reality.

A pragmatic question concerns the desirability of investing in firms with high growth rates. Do firms with high growth rates earn high rates of return? In the constant growth rate model, all stocks earn the same rate of return, R; this model does not provide an answer to the question, since the model assumes no risk.[3] Firms with high growth rates have their prices bid up until the rate of return is R. The total return on a stock is the dividend yield plus the growth rate. If the growth rate is high, the price is driven up and the dividend yield down so the rate of return is R.

Capital Asset Pricing Model

The **capital asset pricing model** (CAPM) is a single-period model relating a stock's expected rate of return to the risk-free interest rate and the risk of the individual stock. Its advantage is an explicit consideration of risk. Its disadvantages include the single-period assumption and the specific type of risk preferences assumed.

The most interesting thing about the CAPM is that it includes the advantage of diversification in equilibrium pricing. That is, the equilibrium required rate of return assumes optimally diversified portfolios. Second, the final risk measure for securities is their sensitivity to market returns. Firms with high sensitivity to macroeconomic events are very risky in the model. Firms that are not affected by macroeconomic events have low risk. Firms may have negative risk, if their performance moves counter to most other firms.

Rate of Return

The CAPM is a single-period model. An investor purchases a stock at time 0 for a price of P_0, receives a dividend of D_1 at time 1, and can sell the

---

[3] In practice, firms with high growth rates may have high risk because there is great uncertainty about the expanding parts of the business.

stock for a price of P_1 at time 1. The sequence of cash flows is shown in figure 19.4.

The rate of return on this investment, R, makes the present value of the cash flows at time 1 equal to the purchase price:

$$P_0 = \frac{D_1 + P_1}{(1 + R)} \tag{19.13}$$

Solving for the rate of return R:

$$R = \frac{P_1 - P_0 + D_1}{P_0} = \frac{P_1 - P_0}{P_0} + \frac{D_1}{P_0} \tag{19.14}$$

$$= \% \text{ capital gain (loss) + dividend yield}$$

Expected Return

The actual rate of return on an investment is not known for certain. Rather, there are several possible rates of return, each with a probability of occurrence. The expected rate of return is defined as the weighted average rate of return. Each possible return is weighted by its probability of occurrence. Its computation is shown in table 19.1. Consider a numerical example in which the returns and probabilities are shown in table 19.2.

The possible returns are 6 percent, 10 percent, and 14 percent; each is equally likely. The expected return is 10 percent, the weighted average return. If the returns are symmetric about the mean, the mean can often be computed by inspection. See figure 19.5 for examples.

Standard Deviation of Return

The standard deviation is a measure of the dispersion or spread of a distribution around the mean. The more spread out the distribution, the bigger the

Figure 19.4   Cash Flows in CAPM

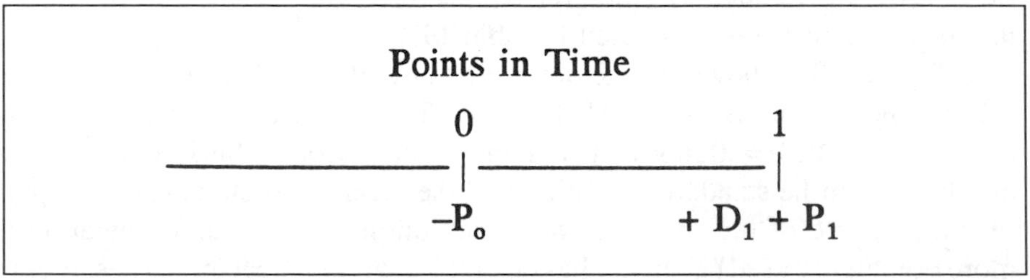

Points in Time

0   1
———————————|——————————|
$-P_0$ $+ D_1 + P_1$

Table 19.1   Returns, Probabilities, and Expected Value

Possible Returns R_i	Probability p_i	Product $(R_i)(p_i)$
R_1	p_1	$(R_1)(p_1)$ +
R_2	p_2	$(R_2)(p_2)$ +
.	.	⋮
.	.	+
.	.	
R_n	p_n	$(R_n)(p_n)$

$$\text{Expected Value} = \text{Sum} = \sum_{j=1}^{n} R_j p_j$$

Table 19.2   Computation of Expected Value

Possible Returns R_i	Probability p_i	Product $(R_i)(p_i)$
.06	1/3	(.06)(1/3) +
.10	1/3	(.10)(1/3) +
.14	1/3	(.14)(1/3)

Expected Value = .10

standard deviation, and the greater the risk. The standard deviation is the square root of the average squared deviation from the mean. Its computation is shown in table 19.3.

The reason for squaring the deviations from the mean in computing the standard deviation is simple. The mean is defined as the point for which the sum of the deviations from the mean is zero. If the deviations from the mean are simply added together, the sum is zero. The variance for the earlier numerical example is computed in table 19.4.

Figure 19.6 shows the actual deviations of this distribution from its mean. The deviations are −.04, 0.0, .04. The mean absolute deviation is (.04 + 0 + .04)/3 = .026667. The standard deviation is fairly close to this number. Both the standard deviation and the mean absolute deviation represent a measure of the spread of the distribution. The standard deviation is more commonly used because it has desirable mathematical properties. Figure

Figure 19.5   Examples of Symmetric Distributions

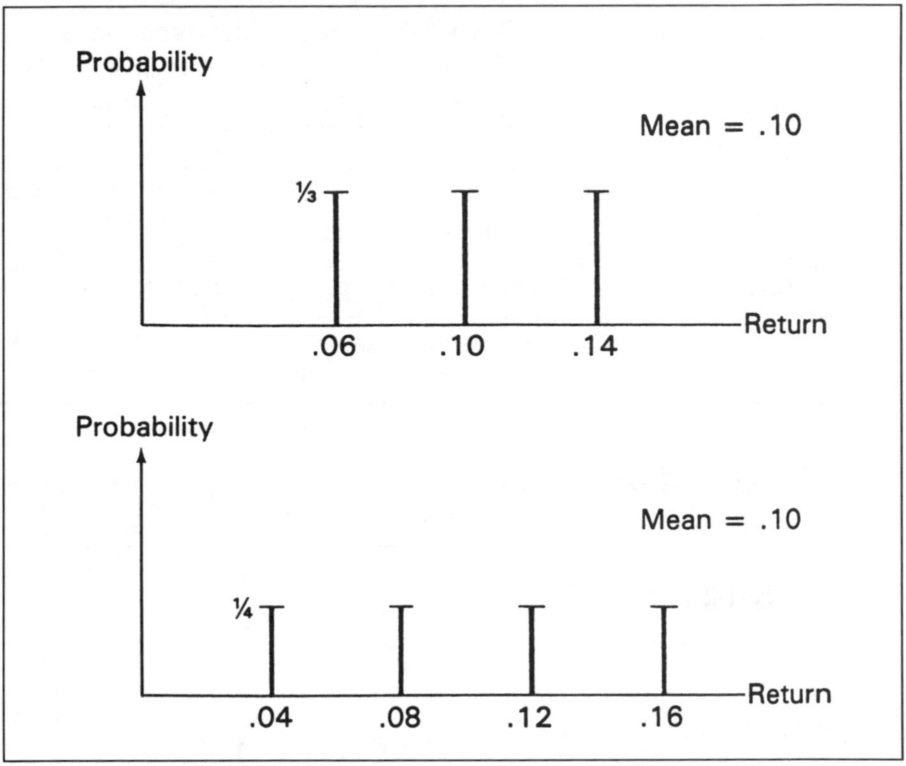

Table 19.3   Standard Deviation

Deviation from Mean $R_i - E$	Deviation Squared $(R_i - E)^2$	Deviation Times Probability $(R_i - E)^2 \, p_i$
$R_1 - E$	$(R_1 - E)^2$	$(R_1 - E)^2 \, p_1$ +
$R_2 - E$	$(R_2 - E)^2$	$(R_2 - E)^2 \, p_2$ +
.	.	⋮
.	.	+
$R_n - E$	$(R_n - E)^2$	$(R_n - E)^2 \, p_n$

$$\text{Variance} = \sum_{j=1}^{n} (R_j - E)^2 p_j$$

Standard deviation = Square root of sum

Table 19.4   Computation of Variance

Deviation from Mean $R_i - E$	Deviation Squared $(R_i - E)^2$	Deviation Times Probability $(R_i - E)^2 \, p_i$
.06 − .10	$(.06 − .10)^2$	$(.06 − .10)^2 \, (1/3)$ +
.10 − .10	$(.10 − .10)^2$	$(.10 − .10)^2 \, (1/3)$ +
.14 − .14	$(.14 − .10)^2$	$(.14 − .10)^2 \, (1/3)$

Variance = .001067
Standard deviation = .032659

Figure 19.6   Example of Distributions with Same Mean but Different Variables

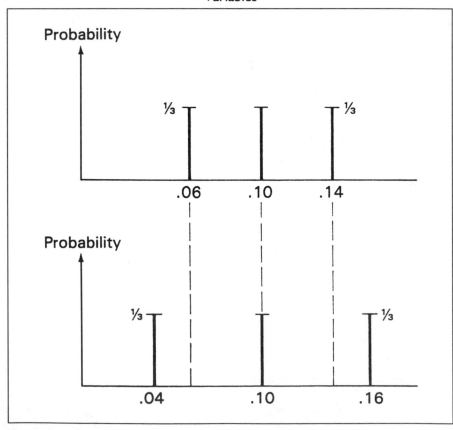

19.6 also shows another distribution with the same mean but with bigger deviations from the mean. This second distribution is obviously more spread out and it has a bigger standard deviation.

Correlation Coefficient

The relationship between variables is measured by the correlation coefficient, r. This a number between -1 and $+1$. Positive (negative) values of the correlation coefficient show that two variables move in the same (opposite) direction. If the correlation coefficient is $+1$ (-1), the two variables are perfectly, positively (negatively) related.[4] This is illustrated in figure 19.7. If the correlation coefficient is 0, there is no relationship between the variables.

In general, most stocks have returns that have positive correlation coefficients. A correlation coefficient of .50 is quite typical. This means that the returns frequently, but not always, move in the same direction. The calculation of the correlation coefficient is shown in table 19.5 for two stocks, A and B, with returns RA and RB. First, the expected values, E_A and E_B, and standard deviations, SD_A and SD_B, of each distribution must be computed.

Figure 19.7   Perfectly Correlated Variables

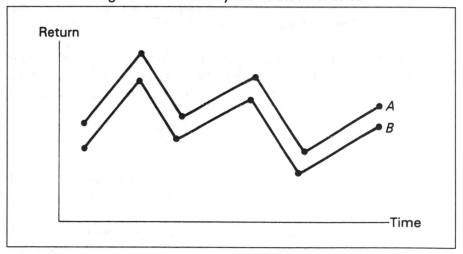

----

[4] Technically, the correlation coefficient measures the extent of linear relation between variables.

Table 19.5 Correlation Coefficient

Deviation from A's mean $RA_i - E_A$	Deviation from B's mean $RB_i - E_B$	Product of the Deviations $(RA_i - E_A)(RB_i - E_B)$	Product Times Probability $(RA_i - E_A)(RB_i - E_B)p_i$
$RA_1 - E_A$	$RB_1 - E_B$	$(RA_1 - E_A)(RB_1 - E_B)$	$(RA_1 - E_A)(RB_1 - E_B)p_1$
$RA_2 - E_A$	$RB_2 - E_B$	$(RA_2 - E_A)(RB_2 - E_B)$	$(RA_2 - E_A)(RB_2 - E_B)p_2$
.	.	.	+
.	.	.	⋮
.	.	.	+
$RA_n - E_A$	$RB_n - E_B$	$(RA_n - E_A)(RB_n - E_B)$	$(RA_n - E_A)(RB_n - E_B)p_n$

$$\text{Covariance} = \sum_{j=1}^{n} (RA_i - E_A)(RB_i - E_B)p_i$$

The covariance is the average of the product of the deviations from the means. It is a number that is hard to interpret. If the covariance is positive (negative), then the two variables move in the same (opposite) direction. If the covariance is zero, the variables are not (linearly) related. The covariance merely provides information about the direction of a relationship between two variables but does not provide insight into the extent of the relationship. For example, if the covariance is +.01, all that can be said with any conviction is that the two variables are positively related.

The correlation coefficient is used to provide a measure of the size of the relationship between two variables. The correlation coefficient is defined as the covariance divided by the product of the standard deviations, namely:

$$\frac{\text{Correlation}}{\text{coefficient}} = \frac{\text{Covariance}}{(SD_A)(SD_B)} \tag{19.15}$$

A correlation of +1 or −1 indicates a perfect (linear) relationship exists between two variables. As the correlation coefficient gets closer to zero, the relationship between the variables is weaker.

To illustrate the calculation of these statistics, consider the example in table 19.6 in which there are two investments, A and B. The means and standard deviations are computed in table 19.7. Next, the covariance and correlation coefficient are computed in table 19.8. The correlation coefficient between A and B is −1.0, meaning a perfect negative (linear) relationship exists between the two. The correlation coefficient measures the relationship between the deviations from the mean, weighted by the product of the

Table 19.6   An Example of Covariance Calculation

Period	Return A	Return B
1	.05	.15
2	.10	.10
3	.15	.05

Table 19.7   Computing Means and Standard Deviations

Period	(Return A)(frequency)	(Return B)(frequency)
1	.05(1/3)	.15(1/3)
2	.10(1/3)	.10(1/3)
3	.15(1/3)	.05(1/3)
Mean	.10	.10

Period	$(\text{Return A} - \text{Mean})^2$ (frequency)	$(\text{Return B} - \text{Mean})^2$ (frequency)
1	$(.05 - .10)^2(1/3)$	$(.15 - .10)^2(1/3)$
2	$(.10 - .10)^2(1/3)$	$(.10 - .10)^2(1/3)$
3	$(.15 - .10)^2(1/3)$	$(.05 - .10)^2(1/3)$
Standard Deviation	.040824	.040824

Table 19.8   Computing Covariance and Correlation Coefficient

Deviation from A's mean	Deviation from B's mean	Product of the Deviations	Product Times Probability
.05 − .1	.15 − .1	(.05 − .1)(.15 − .1)	(.05 − .1)(.15 − .1)(1/3)
.10 − .1	.10 − .1	(.1 − .1)(.1 − .1)	(.1 − .1)(.1 − .1)(1/3)
.15 − .1	.05 − .1	(.15 − .1)(.05 − .1)	(.15 − .1)(.05 − .1)(1/3)

$$\text{Covariance} = -.001667$$

$$\frac{\text{Correlation}}{\text{coefficient}} = \frac{\text{Covariance}}{(SD_A)(SD_B)} = \frac{-.001667}{(.040824)(.040824)} = -1$$

standard deviations. In figure 19.8, when A is above its mean by 5 percent, B is below its mean by 5 percent. Deviations from the mean are in opposite directions.

For most stocks, correlation coefficients are positive, meaning that returns above (below) the mean return tend to occur for most stocks at the same time. When economic times are good (poor), most companies perform unexpectedly well (poorly), and the returns on most stocks are above (below) the long-run average or mean return.

There are some stocks with returns that move counter to the overall economy, such as gold mining stocks. These stocks have negative correlation coefficients with most other stocks. When economic times are bad, gold prices tend to rise, and gold mining company stocks perform well. In good economic times, the demand for gold is relatively weak, gold prices fall, and gold mining stocks perform poorly. In bad (good) economic times, gold mining stocks have returns above (below) their long-run average, a pattern opposite most stocks.

Regression

To discover the best fitting relationship between two variables, regression analysis is used. Consider an example in which we are trying to find the

Figure 19.8   Example of Perfect Negative Correlation

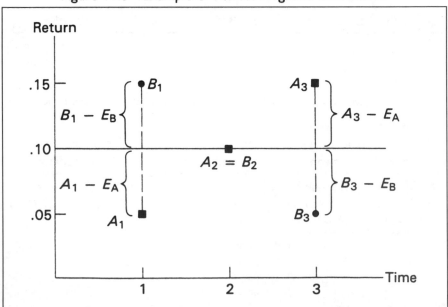

relationship between the returns on XYZ company's stock and a broad index of the stock market, such as the Standard & Poors (S&P) 500 Stock Index. In figure 19.9, the returns on XYZ and the S&P Index are plotted for recent periods. XYZ is on the vertical axis and the S&P Index is shown on the horizontal axis. We would like to fit a line to these observations to capture the nature of the relationship. Regression analysis provides a way of finding the best fitting line.[5] The slope of the fitted line is called β (i.e., **beta**). The slope measures the sensitivity of the returns on XYZ to the S&P Index.

Figure 19.9   Regression of the Return of XYZ Against the Return on the Market

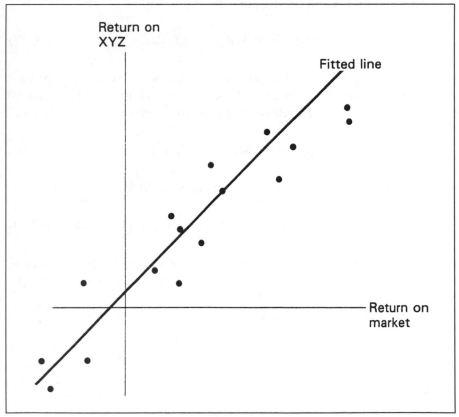

---

[5] Some criterion is required for picking the best fitting line. Regression analysis minimizes the sum of the squared vertical deviations from the fitted line.

Portfolios

Investors select portfolios of securities. We will consider the case of a two-security portfolio, A and B, and assume that distributions can be described by their means and standard deviations.[6] The investor holds W_A percent of the portfolio in security A and W_B percent in security B. The total percent of the portfolio invested in these securities is 100 percent. That is:

$$W_A + W_B = 1.00 \qquad (19.16)$$

The expected return on the portfolio is:

$$E(R_p) = W_A E(R_A) + W_B E(R_B) \qquad (19.17)$$

For example, if the expected returns on A and B are respectively 4 percent and 10 percent, and if 50 percent of the portfolio is invested in A and 50 percent in B, the expected return for the portfolio is 7 percent.

$$E(R_p) = .5(.04) + .5(.10) = .07 \qquad (19.18)$$

The variance of the portfolio returns is equal to V_p:

$$V_p = W_A^2(V_A) + W_B^2(V_B) + 2\ W_A(W_B)(SD_A)(SD_B)(r_{A,B}) \qquad (19.19)$$

In equation 19.19, the variance of a portfolio of two securities depends upon the percentage invested in each, the standard deviation of each, and the correlation coefficient between the two.

Consider the following numerical example:

$E(R_A) = .04$
$E(R_B) = .10$
$SD_A = .10$
$SD_B = .20$

---

[6] If the return distributions are normal (symmetric) and/or if utility functions are quadratic, investors choose portfolios on the basis of means and standard deviations.

The portfolio standard deviation depends upon the correlation coefficient between the securities. We will examine the case where one half of the portfolio is invested in each of the two securities, that is, $W_A = W_B = .50$.

If the correlation coefficient is 1.0, then:

$$V_p = W_A^2(V_A) + W_B^2(V_B) + 2\ W_A(W_B)(SD_A)(SD_B)(r_{A,B}) \quad (19.20)$$
$$V_p = .25(.01) + .25(.04) + 2(.5)(.5)(.1)(.2)(1)$$
$$= .0225$$

$$SD_p = .15 \qquad\qquad (19.21)$$

The expected return on the portfolio is equal to .07, as previously computed. The expected portfolio return depends upon the expected returns of each security and the percent of the portfolio invested in each. The correlation coefficient does not affect the expected portfolio return.

If the correlation coefficient is 1.0, the variance and standard deviation of the portfolio are computed as follows:

$$V_p = W_A^2(V_A) + W_B^2(V_B) + 2\ W_A(W_B)(SD_A)(SD_B) \qquad (19.22)$$
$$V_p = [W_A(SD_A) + W_B(SD_B)]^2 \qquad (19.23)$$
$$SD_p = W_A(SD_A) + W_B(SD_B) \qquad (19.24)$$

In this special case where the correlation coefficient is 1.0, the portfolio standard deviation is simply a weighted average of the individual standard deviations. There is a linear relationship between portfolio expected return and standard deviation of returns. Figure 19.10 shows this point.

If the correlation coefficient is .50, the portfolio standard deviation is:

$$V_p = W_A^2(V_A) + W_B^2(V_B) + 2\ W_A(W_B)(SD_A)(SD_B)(r_{A,B}) \quad (19.25)$$
$$V_p = .25(.01) + .25(.04) + 2(.5)(.5)(.1)(.2)(.5)$$
$$V_p = .0175$$

$$SD_p = .1323 \qquad\qquad (19.26)$$

The expected return on the portfolio remains at .07. The expected return and standard deviation are shown in figure 19.10. Notice that the portfolio standard deviation is lower for a correlation of .50 than for a correlation coefficient of 1.0. This reduction in portfolio standard deviation results from the less than perfect correlation between the two securities. In the portfolio, some of the deviations of A from its mean offset some of the deviations of B from its mean. Some of the variability of B about its mean cancels the

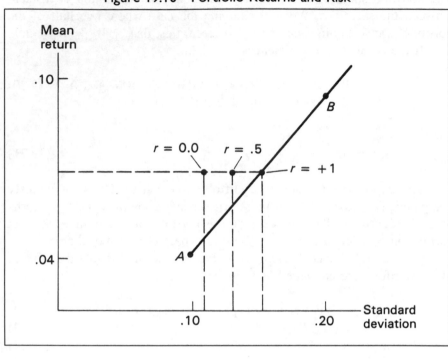

Figure 19.10   Portfolio Returns and Risk

variability of A around its mean. Because of these offsetting effects, the portfolio standard deviation is lower than a simple average of the standard deviations of the two securities.

Consider a correlation coefficient of zero. Then:

$$V_p = W_A^2(V_A) + W_B^2(V_B) + 2\ W_A(W_B)(SD_A)(SD_B)(r_{A,B}) \qquad (19.27)$$
$$V_p = .25(.01) + .25(.04) + 2(.5)(.5)(.1)(.2)(0)$$
$$V_p = .0125$$

$$SD_p = .1118 \qquad\qquad\qquad\qquad\qquad\qquad\qquad\qquad\qquad (19.28)$$

Figure 19.10 illustrates this case.

This example highlights a basic lesson. Diversification benefits occur from selecting a portfolio with securities having correlation coefficients less than +1.0. A lower correlation coefficient results in larger benefits. When the correlation coefficient is less than 1.0, some of the ups in one security tend to cancel some of the downs in the other. As the correlation coefficient falls, more of the ups cancel more of the downs, resulting in a steadier portfolio return.

The Efficient Frontier

For a pair of securities with given expected returns, standard deviations, and correlation coefficients, the expected returns and standard deviations of the possible portfolios depend upon the percent invested in each, W_A and W_B. If W_A is 1.0 (and W_B is 0.0), the entire portfolio is invested in A and the portfolio's expected return and standard deviation are A's expected return and standard deviation.

If W_A is less than 1.0 and W_B is $1 - W_A$, the portfolio is a combination of A and B. The set of possible portfolios is shown in figure 19.11. As the percent of the portfolio invested in B increases, we move along the line AB toward B.

Some of the points along the line AB are inferior to other points. For example, point A is inferior to point C because they have the same standard deviation, but C has a higher mean return. Points such as A are dominated portfolios and must be eliminated from the portfolios held by rational investors. The remaining points are called the **efficient frontier**.

Rational investors must select portfolios along this efficient frontier. The best portfolios depend upon the risk preferences of investors. Investors who would like to have low levels of risk in their portfolio pick portfolios such as point T. Investors willing to bear more risk select portfolios on the

Figure 19.11   The Efficient Frontier

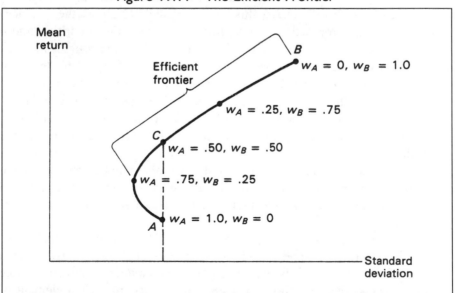

efficient frontier closer to the point B. These investors are willing to tolerate the higher variability of returns to earn higher returns on average.

n-*Security Portfolios*

The previous discussion can be extended to a case of n securities. With n securities, the expected rate of return on a portfolio is the expected return on each security weighted by the percentage of the portfolio invested in each, that is:

$$E(R_p) = (w_1)E(R_1) + (w_2)E(R_2) + \ldots + (w_n)E(R_n) \qquad (19.29)$$
$$= \sum_{i=1}^{n} (w_i)E(R_i)$$

The portfolio variance for n securities depends upon the variances of the n securities plus all the pairs of covariances and equals:

$$V_p = \sum_{i=1}^{n}\sum_{j=1}^{n} w_i(w_j)(SD_i)(SD_j)(r_{i,j}) \qquad (19.30)$$
$$V_p = \sum_{i=1}^{n}\sum_{j=1}^{n} w_i(w_j)(C_{i,j}) \qquad (19.31)$$

Where $C_{i,j}$ is the covariance between security i and security j. Note that $C_{i,j}$ equals $(SD_i)(SD_j)(r_{i,j})$. To clarify this formula, table 19.9 shows the variance-covariance matrix for two securities, three securities, four securities, and n securities. Since there are n rows and n columns, there are n times n, or n^2, elements in the matrix. For two securities, there are four elements – two variances along the main diagonal of the matrix and two covariances off the diagonal. For three securities, there are nine elements, with three variances along the main diagonal and six covariances off the diagonal. For n securities, there are n variances along the diagonal and $n(n-1)$ covariances off the main diagonal.

To compute the portfolio variance, the variances and covariances have to be multiplied by the products of the percent of the portfolio invested in each security as shown in table 19.10. The portfolio variance is the sum of all of the terms.

Consider a three-security example in which the standard deviations of the securities are .1, .2, and .3 and the correlation coefficient between each pair of securities is .80. The variance covariance matrix is shown in table 19.11. If 1/3 of the portfolio is invested in each security, each element of

Table 19.9   Variance-Covariance Matrices

2 Securities

V_1	$C_{1,2}$
$C_{2,1}$	V_2

3 Securities

V_1	$C_{1,2}$	$C_{1,3}$
$C_{2,1}$	V_2	$C_{2,3}$
$C_{3,1}$	$C_{3,2}$	V_3

4 Securities

V_1	$C_{1,2}$	$C_{1,3}$	$C_{1,4}$
$C_{2,1}$	V_2	$C_{2,3}$	$C_{2,4}$
$C_{3,1}$	$C_{3,2}$	V_3	$C_{3,4}$
$C_{4,1}$	$C_{4,2}$	$C_{4,3}$	V_4

n Securities

V_1	$C_{1,2}$	$C_{1,3}$	$C_{1,4}$	$\cdots$	$C_{1,n}$
$C_{2,1}$	V_2	$C_{2,3}$	$C_{2,4}$	$\cdots$	$C_{2,n}$
$C_{3,1}$	$C_{3,2}$	V_3	$C_{3,4}$		$C_{3,n}$
$C_{4,1}$	$C_{4,2}$	$C_{4,3}$	V_4		
.	.	.	.		.
.	.	.	.		.
.	.	.	.		.
$C_{n,1}$	$C_{n,2}$	$C_{n,3}$	$\cdots$		V_n

the matrix is multiplied by the product of the weights to compute the portfolio variance (see table 19.12). The sum of these terms is the portfolio variance and is equal to .035111. The portfolio's standard deviation is .1874.

The efficient frontier shows the portfolios with highest expected returns for each level of standard deviation of return. In the n-security case, mathematical programs have been developed to find the efficient frontier of portfolios.[7] An efficient frontier is shown in figure 19.12.

---

[7] See Markowitz (1959).

Table 19.10   Variances and Covariances Times the Weights

2 Securities	
$w_1 w_1 V_1$	$w_1 w_2 C_{1,2}$
$w_2 w_1 C_{2,1}$	$w_2 w_2 V_2$

3 Securities		
$w_1 w_1 V_1$	$w_1 w_2 C_{1,2}$	$w_1 w_3 C_{1,3}$
$w_2 w_1 C_{2,1}$	$w_2 w_2 V_2$	$w_2 w_3 C_{2,3}$
$w_3 w_1 C_{3,1}$	$w_3 w_2 C_{3,2}$	$w_3 w_3 V_3$

4 Securities			
$w_1 w_1 V_1$	$w_1 w_2 C_{1,2}$	$w_1 w_3 C_{1,3}$	$w_1 w_4 C_{1,4}$
$w_2 w_1 C_{2,1}$	$w_2 w_2 V_2$	$w_2 w_3 C_{2,3}$	$w_2 w_4 C_{2,4}$
$w_3 w_1 C_{3,1}$	$w_3 w_2 C_{3,2}$	$w_3 w_3 V_3$	$w_3 w_4 C_{3,4}$
$w_4 w_1 C_{4,1}$	$w_4 w_2 C_{4,2}$	$w_4 w_3 C_{4,3}$	$w_4 w_4 V_4$

Table 19.11   Example of Variance-Covariance Matrix

$.1^2$	$.1(.2)(.8)$	$.1(.3)(.8)$
$.2(.1)(.8)$	$.2^2$	$.2(.3)(.8)$
$.3(.1)(.8)$	$.3(.2)(.8)$	$.3^2$

Table 19.12   Example of Variance-Covariance Times Weights

$(1/3)^2 .1^2$	$(1/3)^2 .1(.2)(.8)$	$(1/3)^2 .1(.3)(.8)$
$(1/3)^2 .2(.1)(.8)$	$(1/3)^2 .2^2$	$(1/3)^2 .2(.3)(.8)$
$(1/3)^2 .3(.1)(.8)$	$(1/3)^2 .3(.2)(.8)$	$(1/3)^2 .3^2$

The best portfolio along the efficient frontier depends upon each individual investor's risk preferences. Investors with greater risk aversion will pick portfolios with lower risk and lower expected return. Investors willing to bear more risk pick higher risk and higher return portfolios.

The Capital Asset Pricing Model (CAPM)

The preceding discussion considered optimal portfolios of risky securities, i.e., securities for which the return is not certain. The capital asset pricing model adds a risk-free security and derives some interesting results.

Figure 19.12   Risk-Return Trade-off on the Efficient Frontier

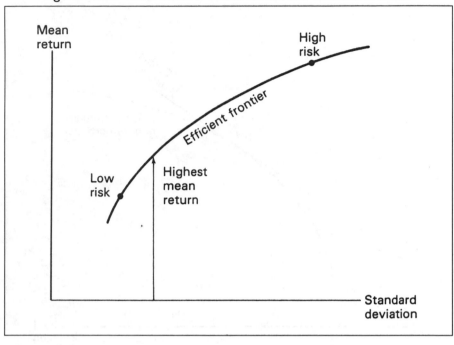

A risk-free security has a known and certain return over the one-period horizon. A risk-free security has a standard deviation return of zero. In addition, the risk-free security has a zero correlation coefficient with all portfolios along the efficient frontier. In practice, a Treasury bill that matures at the horizon date corresponds to a risk-free security. The buyer of a Treasury bill can lock in a certain return until maturity.

Consider an investor who picks a portfolio with w_f percent invested in the risk-free security and $1 - w_f$ invested in a portfolio G along the efficient frontier (see figure 19.13). Because the correlation coefficient between the risk-free security and portfolio G is zero, the portfolio variance is:

$$V_p = (1 - w_f)^2(V_G) \qquad (19.32)$$

$$SD_p = (1 - w_f)(SD_G) \qquad (19.33)$$

All the portfolios composed of the risk-free security and portfolio G lie along the straight line joining the two. The larger the percentage invested in the risk-free security, the closer toward the risk-free security. The more invested in G, the closer toward portfolio G.

Figure 19.13   Equilibrium with a Risk-Free Asset

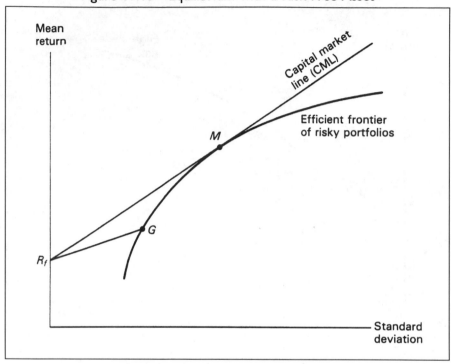

Investors choose portfolios that lie along the highest line showing combinations of the risk-free security and portfolios along the efficient frontier. The highest line is R_fM. Points along the line R_fM dominate points on lower lines, since for any level of standard deviation, points on the higher line have greater return.

The point M is usually called the market portfolio. It has a special significance. If investors hold risky securities, they hold the portfolio M. Consequently, M must include all risky securities. Each security in M carries a portfolio weight proportional to its total market value. Big companies carry a large weight; smaller companies have smaller weights.

The straight line R_fM has been called the **capital market line** (CML). All equilibrium portfolios lie along this line. Highly risk-averse investors hold portfolios close to the risk-free security. Investors willing to bear more risk hold portfolios higher up on the line.

In equilibrium, all investors hold a portfolio composed of the risk-free security and the market portfolio. The proportions of the portfolio invested in each depend upon the risk preferences of individual investors. This point has been called the **separation theorem**.

Portfolios above point M on the CML involve borrowing (see figure 19.14). The investor borrows at the risk-free rate and invests the original endowment plus the borrowings in the market portfolio, M. For example, an investor with an endowment of $1 might borrow another $1. The percentage of the portfolio invested in the risk-free security, w_f, is −1, and the percentage invested in the market portfolio, $1 - w_f$, is +2.

Individual securities lie below the capital market line (see figure 19.15). Their equilibrium position depends upon their correlation coefficient with the market portfolio. For a given level of standard deviation of return, a higher correlation coefficient with the market implies higher risk and higher expected return. A higher correlation coefficient with the market reduces the diversification benefit. A security with a correlation coefficient of +1 with the market portfolio M has no diversification benefit and, therefore, must lie on the CML. A security with a correlation with the market of .50 has a considerable diversification advantage, has a lower risk than securities on the CML, and, therefore, has lower expected returns. A security with a correlation coefficient of zero with the market has the same expected return as the risk-free security R_f.

The capital market line shows equilibrium for portfolios. For portfolios, risk is the standard deviation of return. Investors require higher returns as

Figure 19.14   Capital Market Line (CML)

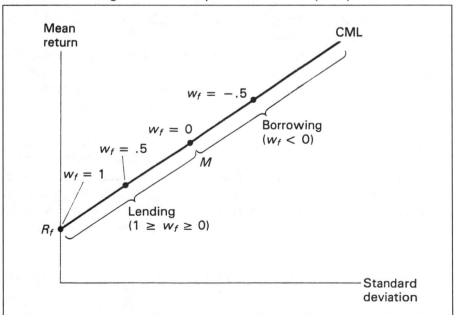

Figure 19.15   Impact of Correlation with the Market on Mean Return

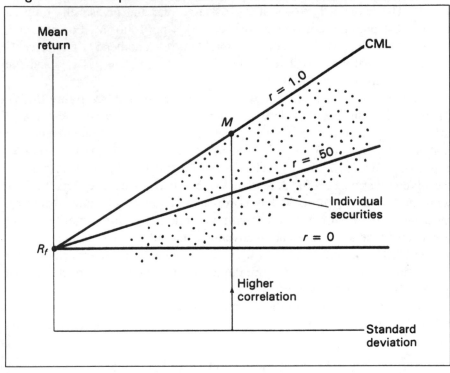

the portfolio standard deviation increases. The CML shows this risk-return trade-off for equilibrium portfolios.

In the CAPM, the risk for an individual security is not its standard deviation, since part of the standard deviation of returns can be diversified away in a large portfolio. The net risk, after diversifying fully, is the only risk that should matter to investors. The net risk is the security's beta coefficient.

The relationship between risk and expected return for individual securities is shown graphically in figure 19.16. The vertical axis shows the expected return of individual securities. The horizontal axis measures β, the beta coefficient, or risk measure for individual securities. The relationship between risk and return is the **security market line** (SML). As β increases, so do the risk and return required by investors for bearing this increased risk.

The equation of the SML is:

$$E(R_j) = R_f + [E(R_M) - R_f]\beta_j \qquad (19.34)$$

where:

Figure 19.16   Security Market Line (SML): Expected Return versus Beta
for Individual Securities

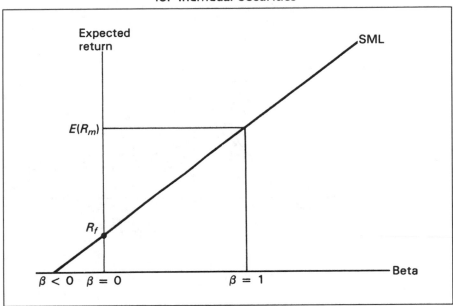

$E(R_j)$ = the expected return on security j
R_f = the return on the risk-free security
$E(R_M)$ = the expected return on the market

In equation 19.34, the required (or expected) return on a security is the risk-free return plus a premium for risk. The risk premium is the beta for the individual security times the slope of the SML line (i.e., $E(R_M) - R_f$).

Beta is the regression coefficient when an individual security's return is regressed against the market portfolio. It represents the sensitivity of the individual security to the market. So-called characteristic line diagrams are useful in understanding beta; characteristic line diagrams assume that the regressions of the individual security versus the market are perfect fits. Let's consider several possible values of beta shown in figure 19.17.

If beta is 1.0, the security tends to move with the market. Conglomerates, which are essentially a diversified portfolio of individual stocks, tend to have betas close to 1.0. If beta exceeds 1.0, the individual security tends to be more volatile than the market: when the market return is high, the high beta security has a very high return; when the market return is poor, the high beta security has a very poor return. Companies with operations highly sensitive to macroeconomic events have betas greater than 1.0. For example,

Figure 19.17   Characteristic Line Diagrams

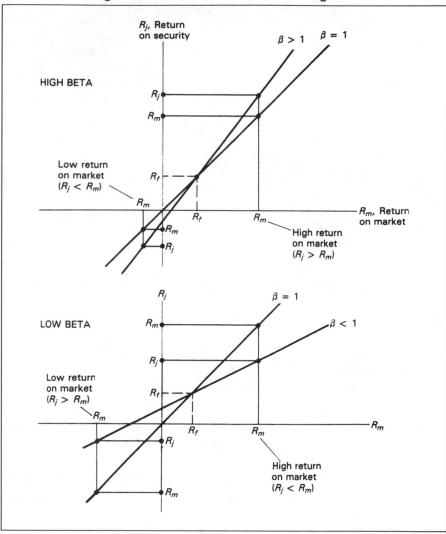

automobile companies sell many cars when economic times are good and make enormous profits. When economic times are poor, automobile companies have low sales and their financial performance is extremely poor.

If the beta coefficient is a small positive number such as .50, the security's return is less volatile than the market's. When the market's return is high (low), the low beta security has a return lower (higher) than the market's. Stocks with positive betas less than 1.0 tend to have operations only mildly sensitive to macroeconomic events. For example, an electrical

Figure 19.17 (Continued)   Characteristic Line Diagrams

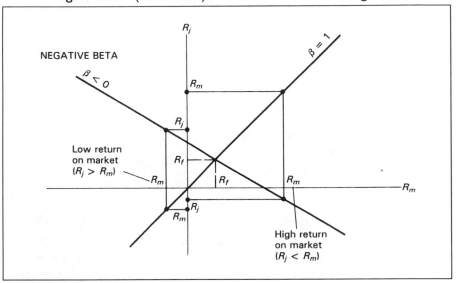

utility company serving residential customers is usually not very sensitive to changes in overall economic conditions. The residential customers tend to use largely the same amount of electricity although economic conditions change. During good economic times, customers may add more electric appliances, but the basic demand for electricity remains fairly steady. Consequently, the returns on the electric company's stock tend to be only mildly affected by economic conditions.

If beta is negative, the security tends to move counter to the rest of the market. As we showed earlier, the stocks of gold mining companies tend to have negative betas. When economic times are good (bad), the relative price of gold is low (high) and the returns on gold mining stocks are low (high). Stocks with negative betas should earn expected returns less than the risk-free rate, R_f. If the beta is sufficiently negative, the required return can be zero or even negative. Investors might be willing to hold negative beta securities at very low returns because these securities have considerable value in a portfolio. Negative beta securities can be used to offset the variability of the total portfolio. By mixing negative beta securities in a portfolio, the total portfolio risk can be reduced. This risk reduction may be so valuable that investors may hold negative beta securities with full knowledge that, on the average, the returns on the low beta securities are negative. Within the context of the entire portfolio, the negative expected returns on the low beta securities are compensated by the reduced portfolio variability.

The beta regression coefficient is defined statistically as:

$$\beta_j = \frac{(SD_j)(r_{j,M})}{SD_M} \tag{19.35}$$

where:

β_j = beta for security j
SD_j = the standard deviation of return for security j
$r_{j,M}$ = the correlation coefficient of security j with the market
SD_M = the standard deviation of return on the market

The slope of the regression, β_j, depends upon the standard deviation of returns on the individual stocks and the standard deviation of the market, as well as the correlation coefficient of the individual stocks with the market index. Other things equal, firms with large standard deviations of return tend to have high betas; other things equal, firms with high correlations with the market have high betas. The actual beta depends upon both the standard deviation and the correlation coefficient with the market.

Consider the case where the correlation coefficient with the market is 1.0. Then the beta coefficient is SD_j/SD_M, the ratio of the standard deviations. In this special case, high (low) standard deviation implies high (low) beta. If the correlation coefficient with the market is zero, the beta coefficient is zero also. The security's return is unrelated to the market's return. In this case, the standard deviation can be high or low.

In most cases, the correlation coefficient is a positive number. For example, if the correlation coefficient is .50, the beta coefficient is $.5(SD_j/SD_M)$. The sensitivity of the return to the market index is one half the ratio of the standard deviations.

Assumptions of CAPM

The CAPM makes a number of strong assumptions. Relaxation of these assumptions is discussed in Alexander and Francis (1986), Levy and Sarnat (1984), and Mossin (1973).

1. A single-period horizon. In practice, most investors probably look beyond one period. A more realistic model would include this possibility. Furthermore, the length of the holding period may vary from investor to investor.

Levy has shown that the model breaks down when investors have different holding periods.

2. Identical risk-free borrowing and lending rates. In practice, the borrowing rate is usually higher than the lending rate. There is always the possibility that borrowers may default, meaning that a more realistic model would include a risky borrowing rate. See Mossin (1973).

3. Quadratic utility functions and/or normal return distributions. Return distributions are close to normal distributions, but different from them, implying that normal distributions are not a realistic assumption. Probably utility functions are not quadratic for most investors. However, the evidence of Levy and Markowitz (1979) indicates that almost the same results would apply with many other types of utility functions.

4. Homogeneous beliefs about mean returns, standard deviations, and correlation coefficients between pairs of securities. Mossin (1973) has adapted the model for diverse beliefs about individual securities.

Summary

There are several methods for valuing common stock. To use the price/earnings multiple approach, the fair value of the multiple and anticipated earnings are estimated. The product of these provides an estimate of the intrinsic value of the stock. If the intrinsic value is substantially above the current price, the security should be purchased in anticipation of market price approaching intrinsic value in the future. This approach implicitly assumes temporary market inefficiency.

Some analysts estimate the liquidating value of company assets, trying to uncover situations in which the liquidating value exceeds the current market price of the firm's securities. Many mergers are motivated by the belief that liquidating value exceeds current market value of securities.

The value of common stock can also be viewed as the present value of all future dividends. A simple variant of this approach is the constant growth rate model in which the firm is assumed to grow at this constant growth rate.

The capital asset pricing model is a single-period model that explicitly incorporates risk. The model derives the required rate of return on individual securities, given that investors diversify their portfolios. The risk for individual securities is a security's beta coefficient, or sensitivity to the market.

Firms whose operations are highly sensitive to the overall economy are high beta and high risk. Since the variability of returns for a high beta firm is closely related to the overall economy, very little of its variability can be diversified away in a large portfolio; the net risk after diversifying is still large. Low beta firms have operations that are not closely related to the overall economy. A great deal of the variability of returns for these firms can be diversified away in a large portfolio; the net risk is small.

Each of these models has advantages and disadvantages. The price/earnings multiple approach has the advantage of simplicity. One disadvantage is the failure to explicitly consider risk; risk is somehow buried in the multiple. Another disadvantage is that multiples change over time in an unpredictable fashion.

The asset valuation model is relatively simple in concept but hard to implement. It is quite difficult to estimate liquidating values for parts of businesses.

The dividend models are multi-period models – a distinct advantage. They are hard to implement because of the difficulties of estimating future dividends and the appropriate discount rate for finding the present value of these dividends. The constant growth rate model makes the clearly unrealistic assumption of constant growth indefinitely into the future. Its advantage is a very simple formula.

The capital asset pricing model has the strong advantage of incorporating the benefits of diversification into the valuation of securities. Only nondiversifiable risk should matter in equilibrium. Its disadvantages include its very strong assumptions. The model is for a single period; extension to the case of multi-periods is not entirely clear. The model assumes risk-free borrowing and lending; if borrowing and lending rates differ and/or if default on loans is possible, the analysis is much more complicated. The model assumes a specific type of utility function (i.e., quadratic); the results with other utility functions have been shown to be quite similar. Finally, the CAPM makes the strong assumption of homogeneous beliefs about the mean returns, standard deviations, and correlation coefficients of all securities. Without this assumption, the model is much less precise.

Questions/Problems

1. Describe the price/earnings multiple approach to investing. What determines a company's multiple? Are multiples stable over time? What does this approach assume about market efficiency?

2. The asset valuation method assumes that the liquidating value of assets may be less than the market value of securities constituting a claim on those assets. How can such disparities exist in an efficient market?

3. Assume that the constant growth rate dividend valuation model applies. You estimate that a company has a growth rate of 8 percent, the return required by investors is 14 percent, and the current dividend is $1. Determine the price of the stock.

4. In the preceding problem, determine the price of the stock one period from now. What is the dividend yield, the percentage capital gain, and the total rate of return over this period?

5. In the CAPM, describe the CML and the SML. What is the difference between these lines?

6. Assume that the expected return on the market is 15 percent, the risk-free rate is 5 percent, and the standard deviation of the market is 10 percent. In the CAPM, determine the expected returns for stocks with the following betas:

    a. −.5   d. 1.0
    b. 0.0   e. 1.5
    c. .50

7. Using the same information as problem 6, determine the expected return on your portfolio if you invest w_f percent in the risk-free security and the rest in the market portfolio for the following values of w_f:

    a. 1.0   d. −.50
    b. .50   e. −1.0
    c. 0.0

Draw the CML line and plot these portfolios.

8. There are two securities, A and B, with expected returns of .02 and .14, respectively, and standard deviations of .05 and .25. The correlation coefficient between the two is .50. First, compute the expected return and standard deviation if portfolios have:

    a. .25 in A and .75 in B
    b. one-half in each
    c. .75 in A and .25 in B

Next, plot these portfolios.

9. Compute the covariance of return and correlation coefficient for the following information:

Period	Return A	Return B
I	−.05	−.0 I
2	+.05	+.04
3	+.20	+.I0

References

Alexander, G. J. and J. C. Francis, *Portfolio Analysis,* 3e, Englewood Cliffs, NJ: Prentice Hall, 1986.

Levy, H., "Portfolio Performance and the Investment Horizon," *Management Science,* 18, August 1972, pp. 645–53.

Levy, H., "Equilibrium in an Imperfect Market. A Constraint on the Number of Securities," *American Economic Review,* 68, September 1978, pp. 643–58.

Levy, H. and H. M. Markowitz, "Approximating Expected Utility by a Function of Mean and Variance," *American Economic Review,* 69, June 1979, pp. 308–17.

Levy, H. and M. Sarnat, *Portfolio and Investment Selection,* Englewood Cliffs, NJ: Prentice Hall, 1984.

Markowitz, H. M., *Portfolio Selection,* New York: Wiley, 1959.

Mossin, J., "Equilibrium in a Capital Asset Market," *Econometrica,* 34, October 1966, pp. 768–83.

Mossin, J., *Theory of Financial Markets,* Englewood Cliffs, NJ: Prentice Hall, 1973.

Sharpe, W. F., "Capital Asset Prices: A Theory of Market Equilibrium," *Journal of Finance,* 19, September 1964, pp. 425–42.

Sharpe, W. F., *Portfolio Theory and Capital Markets,* New York: McGraw-Hill, 1970.

20

Put and Call Options

Overview

Until the mid 1970s, puts and calls were traded over-the-counter. In 1975, the Chicago Board Options Exchange (CBOE) came into existence, and the organized trading of options has grown tremendously. Now options are traded on individual stocks, on stock indexes, on bonds, and on futures contracts.

The organized trading of options offers greater liquidity compared to over-the-counter trading. With organized trading, options are traded for a restricted set of maturity dates and for a restricted set of exercise prices. This results in a large volume of trading and high liquidity in each of the traded options. In addition, each organized exchange has a clearinghouse that guarantees performance by ensuring that market participants have sufficient collateral to cover likely losses. With a clearinghouse, the chance for default by either the buyer or the seller of the option is virtually eliminated.

There are two types of options: European and American. European options can be exercised only at expiration. American options can be exercised at any time. Most options traded in the United States are American options.

Call Options

A call option is the right to purchase the underlying asset for a specified exercise price until the expiration date.[1] The following notation is used:

---

[1] American options can be exercised at any time. European options can be exercised only at the expiration date.

C = market value of the call option
P = market value of underlying asset
E = exercise price (strike price)

If the price of the underlying asset (*P*) is less than the exercise price (*E*), the call is described as being out-of-the-money. If *P* equals *E*, the call option is described as being at-the-money. If the price of the underlying asset exceeds the exercise price (*P* > *E*), the call option is described as being in-the-money.

Value of Call Option at Expiration

At expiration, the value of the call must be zero if the market value of the underlying asset is less than or equal to the exercise price. No rational investor would exercise a call option if the underlying asset sells for the exercise price or less since buying the underlying security in the open market is cheaper than exercising the call option. For example, in table 20.1, if a bond sells for $90 in the open market, a call option with an exercise price of $100 is valueless at expiration. Instead of exercising the call and paying the $100 exercise price, it is preferable to buy the bond directly for $90.

In table 20.1, if the price of the underlying asset exceeds the exercise price, the call option is worth the price of the underlying asset minus the exercise price, that is, $P - E$.[2] If the call sells for less than $P - E$, an arbitrager would buy the call, exercise it, and make an arbitrage profit. At expiration, buying the call option for $*C* and exercising it is equivalent to buying the underlying security directly for $*P*. Thus, $P = C + E$, or $C = P - E$.

Table 20.1   Value of Call Option at Expiration, E = $100

P < E	P = E	P > E
e.g., P = 90	P = 100	P = 110
C = 0	C = 0	C = P − E
		e.g., C = 10
out-of-the-money	at-the-money	in-the-money

---

[2] The amount $P - E$ has been called the **intrinsic value** of a call option.

At expiration, the value of a call option is:

$C = 0$	if $P \leq E$	at- or out-of-the-money	(20.1)
$C = P - E$	if $P > E$	in-the-money	(20.2)

Value of Call Option Before Expiration

With time left until expiration, an American call option has a value greater than an otherwise identical expiring call option.[3] Table 20.2 illustrates the possibilities. Before expiration:

$C > 0$	if $P \leq E$	at- or out-of-the-money	(20.3)
$C > P - E$	if $P > E$	in-the-money	(20.4)

If these conditions do not hold, arbitrage opportunities are available to investors. For out-of-the-money call options, a zero price allows an arbitrager to buy the call for nothing. If the call expires worthless, the arbitrager loses nothing; if the call ends up in-the-money, the arbitrager has a net profit. For a zero investment, the arbitrager can never lose and may have a profit. To eliminate profitable arbitrage, the market value of the call option must be positive.

For in-the-money call options, a price less than the underlying asset price minus the exercise price $(P - E)$ allows an arbitrager to buy the call option for C and exercise it for E, for a total cost of $C + E$. The acquired security is then sold for its market value P, which, by assumption, is greater

Table 20.2   Value of Call Option Before Expiration, $E = \$100$

$P < E$	$P = E$	$P > E$
e.g., $P = 90$	$P = 100$	$P = 110$
$C > 0$	$C > 0$	$C > P - E$
		e.g., $C > 10$

---

[3] Recall that an American call option can be exercised at any time up to and including expiration. Merton's bound, discussed later, implies an even higher bound.

than $C + E$ for an arbitrage profit of $P - (C + E)$. To eliminate arbitrage profit opportunities, $C + E$ must be equal to or exceed P, meaning that C must be greater than or equal to $P - E$. For example, if a bond sells for $110 and if a call option with a $100 exercise price sells for $5, anyone could buy the call for $5, exercise it for $100, and sell the resulting bond for $110 for a sure profit of $5.

The greater than (>) symbol in equations 20.3 and 20.4 shows exercise of a call option before expiration to be an inferior choice. The possibility of a large value for the call option at some future date makes early exercise of an option a poor choice in most circumstances. For this reason, call options are generally described as being worth more "alive than dead," that is, worth more if not exercised immediately.

The price of the underlying security is a logical upper bound for the price of a call option. No one should logically pay more for an option to buy a security than the price to purchase the security outright. If a bond is selling for $100, a logical person would never pay more than $100 for a call option. The investor is better off buying the underlying asset itself. These bounds on the value of a call option are shown in figure 20.1, which relates the value of a call option to the value of the underlying security.

Figure 20.1   Call Option Bounds

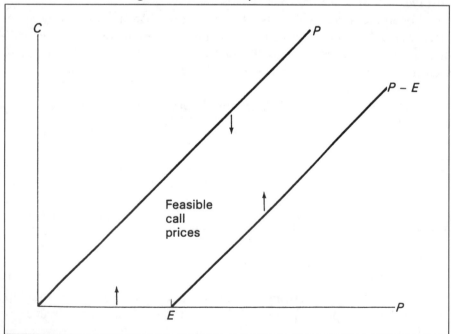

Profit Profile for a Call

The possible value of a call option can be seen from a profit profile. As a reference point, consider someone who buys a bond (for which options trade) currently selling at its exercise price of $100 and holds this bond for three months until the option expires. The possible profits and losses, overlooking coupon interest, are shown as a solid line in figure 20.2.

Consider the purchase of a call option for $4 with an exercise price of $100. The investor holds this call option for three months until expiration. The profit profile is shown as the dotted line in figure 20.2. The first step in drawing the profit profile is to compute the profit or loss on the position for several levels of the price of the underlying at expiration. These prices should include the option's exercise price and several points on either side of the exercise price. The procedure is illustrated in table 20.3.

The call buyer suffers a loss of $4, the entire purchase, if the bond price is below the exercise price of $100. This $4 is the maximum loss for the buyer of a call option. If the bond price at expiration is above the exercise, the profit equals $P - E - \$4$. A net loss is incurred if the bond price is

Figure 20.2   Profit Profiles for a Call Option

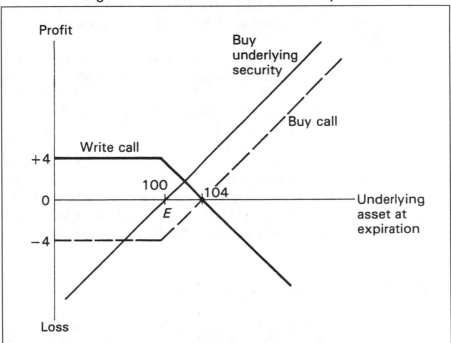

Table 20.3   Profits or Losses for a Call Buyer

	Price of Underlying at Expiration			
	98	100	102	104
Buy call	−4	−4	−4	−4
Exercise call at expiration			−100	−100
Sell underlying acquired from exercise			+102	+104
Net profit $= -C - E + P$	−4	−4	−2	0

below \$104 and a net profit if the bond price is above \$104. The profit profile indicates that call buyers are anticipating a rising price for the underlying asset.

If the bond price is at or below the exercise price, the profit profile shows the call buyer's maximum loss to be the purchase price, C. Since this call purchase price is a small percentage of the bond price, the loss from buying a call is small in absolute dollars compared to the loss from purchasing the bond outright. On the other hand, the call buyer gains substantially if the bond does well.

For everyone who buys a call option, someone sells or writes a call. The call writer agrees to sell the underlying asset at the exercise price if the option is exercised by the call buyer. Call options are a **zero sum game**, meaning that the call buyer's gains are the call writer's losses and vice versa. In effect, the buyer and the writer are betting against each other. The profits or losses for a call writer in the earlier example are shown in table 20.4.

The profit profile for the call writer is shown in figure 20.2. If the call is out-of-the-money at expiration, the call writer benefits by the original sale price of the call. For every dollar that the underlying asset rises above the exercise price, the call writer's profit is reduced by \$1. Because the potential loss is unlimited, the term **writing a naked call** is often used.

Writing a Covered Call Option

The previous section discussed writing a naked call option. This is a risky position because the potential for loss is unbounded. Notice in the profit

Table 20.4   Profits or Losses for a Call Writer

	Price of Underlying at Expiration			
	98	100	102	104
Write call	+4	+4	+4	+4
Sell underlying at call price at expiration			+100	+100
Buy underlying in the open market			−102	−104
Net profit = +C + E − P	+4	+4	+2	0

profile for writing a call in figure 20.2 that the losses become very large as the price of the underlying security increases.

Another, less risky, procedure is to write a covered call. This involves the purchase of the underlying security and the writing of a call option on that security. To illustrate the writing of a covered call option, assume that an investor buys the underlying security at its current price of $100 and simultaneously writes a three-month call option at an exercise price of $100. The profits and losses at expiration are shown in table 20.5.

Table 20.5   Profits or Losses from Writing a Covered Call

	Price of Underlying at Expiration			
	98	100	102	104
Buy underlying	−100	−100	−100	−100
Write call	+4	+4	+4	+4
Sell underlying at exercise price when call is exercised			+100	+100
Sell underlying at market price	+98	+100		
Net profit	+2	+4	+4	+4

The profit profile for writing a covered call option is shown in figure 20.3. If the call option is in-the-money, the option is exercised and the covered call writer must sell the underlying security at the exercise price of $100. The maximum gain is $4, the original sale price of the call option. If the call option is out-of-the-money, the covered call option writer receives $4 for writing the call, and this reduces the loss from owning the underlying security.

Put Options

A put option is a right to sell a security at a stated exercise price E during a stated time interval.

Value of Put Option at Expiration

To see the value of a put option, consider the possible payoffs at expiration for a buyer of a put (see table 20.6). The price of a put is denoted by Pp.

Figure 20.3   Profit Profile for Writing a Covered Call Option

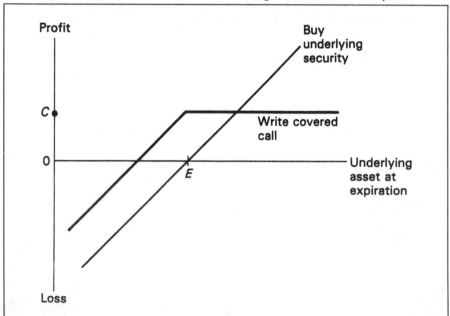

Table 20.6   Value of a Put Option at Expiration, E = $100

$P < E$	$P = E$	$P > E$
e.g., $P = 90$	$P = 100$	$P = 110$
$Pp = E - P$	$Pp = 0$	$Pp = 0$
e.g., $Pp = 10$		

At expiration, if the price of the underlying security equals or exceeds the exercise price $(P > E)$, the put has no value, since no investor would choose to sell the underlying asset at E when the higher market price of P is available. If a bond sells at $110 and if there is a put option with a $100 exercise price, exercising the put option involves selling the bond at the exercise price of $100. For any rational investor, selling the bond at its current market price of $110 is preferable. No one would exercise the put option. At expiration, the put option expires worthless.

At expiration, if the underlying asset price is less than the exercise price, the put has value, since it represents the right to sell the underlying asset at E, which is above the current market price. Clearly, the put is worth the difference $E - P$. For example, if a bond sells for $80, a put option with a $100 exercise price is worth $20 at expiration. If the put sells for $15, an arbitrager can buy the put for $15, buy the bond for $80, and sell the bond for $100 by exercising the put. There is a sure profit of $5.

At expiration, the value of a put, Pp, must be:

$$Pp = 0 \qquad \text{if } P \geq E \qquad \text{at- or out-of-the-money} \qquad (20.5)$$
$$Pp = E - P \qquad \text{if } P < E \qquad \text{in-the-money} \qquad (20.6)$$

Value of Put Option Before Expiration

Before expiration, the value of a put option is shown in table 20.7. Before expiration:

$$Pp > 0 \qquad \text{if } P \geq E \qquad \text{at- or out-of-the-money} \qquad (20.7)$$
$$Pp > E - P \qquad \text{if } P < E \qquad \text{in-the-money} \qquad (20.8)$$

Put Option Profit Profile

The example in table 20.8 illustrates a put option profit profile. Three months before expiration an investor buys a put option for a price (Pp) of $3 with exercise price (E) of $100.

Table 20.7   Value of a Put Option Before Expiration, $E = \$100$

$P < E$	$P = E$	$P > E$
e.g., $P = 90$	$P = 100$	$P = 110$
$Pp > E - P$	$Pp > 0$	$Pp > 0$
e.g., $Pp > 10$		
in-the-money	at-the-money	out-of-the-money

Table 20.8   Profits and Losses for Buying a Put Option

	Price of Underlying at Expiration			
	96	98	100	104
Buy put	−3	−3	−3	−3
Buy underlying at expiration	−96	−98		
Exercise put by selling underlying at $100	+100	+100		
Net profit $= -Pp + E - P$	+1	−1	−3	−3

The profit profile is shown in figure 20.4. The put buyer makes a net profit if the price of the underlying security is less than the exercise price minus the purchase price of the put (that is, if $P < E - Pp$). The profit profile clearly indicates that the put option purchaser expects falling prices for the underlying asset.

Figure 20.4 also shows the profits and losses from shortselling the asset. Buying the put is similar to shortselling, since for both positions profits are earned if the underlying asset declines. If the underlying asset rises, the results are quite different. Purchase of the put has a maximum loss of the original purchase price. In contrast, shortselling of the asset results in a loss of $1 for every dollar that the asset's price rises; the potential loss on shortselling is unlimited.

The put writer (seller) enters into a contract to buy the underlying asset at the exercise price if the buyer of the put option chooses to exercise. The put writer is playing directly against the put buyer. The cash inflows to one are cash outflows to the other.

Figure 20.4   Profit Profile for a Put Option

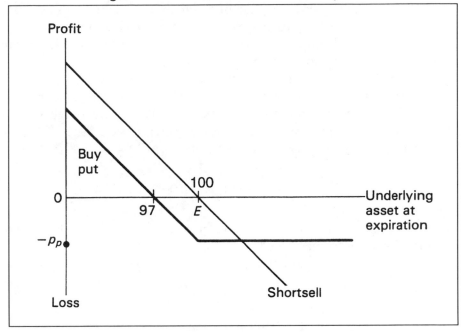

Put-Call Parity

There is a relationship between the price of a put option, the price of a call option with the same exercise price, the price of the underlying security, and the interest rate. This relationship is called **put-call parity**.

For European[4] options on nondividend-paying or noninterest-bearing assets, the put-call parity relationship is:

$$
\begin{array}{cccc}
\text{Price} & \text{Price} & \text{Price of} & \text{Borrowing the} \\
\text{of a} = & \text{of a} + & \text{underlying} + & \text{present value of} \\
\text{call} & \text{put} & \text{asset} & \text{the exercise price}
\end{array}
$$

---

[4] If the options are American, put-call parity may break down if the underlying security makes cash payments such as dividends. With cash dividends, there is a possibility that an American put option might have a higher value if exercised rather than held until expiration.

Table 20.9 shows that purchase of a European call option results in the same cash flows at expiration as purchase of a European put option plus purchase of the underlying asset plus borrowing the present value of the exercise price. Positions with the same value at expiration have the same value before expiration, assuming no intervening cash flows.

Put-call parity is illustrated by the example in table 20.10. An investor buys a call option with an exercise price of $100. Alternatively, the investor buys a put with an exercise price of $100, buys the underlying security for $100, and borrows the present value of the exercise price, $90.

This put-call parity result can be written as:

$$C = Pp + P - ED \qquad (20.9)$$

where D is the present value of $1 received at the expiration date of the options. This can be rearranged to:

$$P = C - Pp + ED \qquad (20.10)$$

Purchase of   Purchase   Sale   Lending PV
underlying = of call + of put + of exercise
asset   option   option   price

Table 20.9   Put-Call Parity

	Cash Flows at Expiration from Buying Call		
	$P < E$	$P = E$	$P > E$
Call	0	0	$P - E$

	Cash Flows at Expiration from Buying Put, Buying Underlying, and Borrowing Present Value of Exercise Price		
	$P < E$	$P = E$	$P > E$
Put	$E - P$	0	0
Underlying	$+P$	$+P$	$+P$
Loan	$-E$	$-E$	$-E$
Net	0	0	$P - E$

Table 20.10   Example of Put-Call Parity

	Cash Flows at Expiration from Buying Call		
	P = 90	P = 100	P = 110
Call	0	0	10

	Cash Flows at Expiration from Buying Put, Buying Underlying, and Borrowing Present Value of Exercise Price		
	P = 90	P = 100	P = 110
Put	10	0	0
Underlying	+90	+100	+110
Loan	−100	−100	−100
Net	0	0	+10

Similarly:

$$\begin{matrix} \text{Shortsale of} & \text{Sale} & \text{Purchase} & \text{Borrowing } PV \\ \text{underlying} = \text{of call} + & \text{of put} + & \text{of exercise} \\ \text{asset} & \text{option} & \text{option} & \text{price} \end{matrix}$$

The Volatility of a Call Option

From put-call parity, a call option has greater volatility than the underlying asset. That is, the percentage change in the price of a call option is greater than the percentage change in the price of the underlying asset.

Put-call parity provides an intuitive explanation for the greater volatility of the call option. The buyer of a call option has a position that is equivalent to buying a put, buying the underlying asset, and borrowing the present value of the exercise price. The call buyer effectively is able to borrow the present value of the exercise price and create the equivalent of a type of levered or margined position in the underlying security. Any levered position must have greater percentage price changes than the underlying asset because the holder of the levered position (that is, the call buyer) invests a smaller amount than an investor who buys the underlying asset for cash. For every dollar change in price of the underlying, the levered position has to change by a greater percent, because the levered investor has invested fewer dollars.

Merton's Bound

Since put-call parity implies $Pp = C - [P - ED]$, a nonnegative value for a put option implies that the following result must hold:

$$C \geq P - ED \qquad (20.11)$$

The value $P - ED$ has been called **Merton's lower bound**. The price of a European call option must be greater than or equal to the price of the underlying asset, P, minus the present value of the exercise price, ED. The cash flows from buying a call option can never be less than the cash flows from buying the underlying security and borrowing the present value of the exercise price. Table 20.11 shows the cash flows at expiration. If the call option is in-the-money or at-the-money, the cash flows from the two strategies are the same. If the call is out-of-the-money (i.e., $P < E$), the call has higher cash flows. Since the payoffs from buying the call are at least as good as buying the underlying security and borrowing the present value of the exercise, the call must have a larger value, which is equation 20.11.

If the price of a call option lies below Merton's bound, arbitrage opportunities are available to investors. Imagine that the exercise price on a call option is $100, that the underlying has a price of $100, and that the present value factor D is .9. Then Merton's bound is $10, that is, $100 - 100(.9)$, and the call option has a value of at least $10. If the call option sells at a price of $5 (in violation of Merton's bound), profitable arbitrage opportunities are available. The arbitrage is to buy the call option, simultaneously short

Table 20.11   Merton's Bound

	Cash Flows at Expiration from Buying Call		
	$P < E$	$P = E$	$P > E$
Call	0	0	$P - E$

	Cash Flows at Expiration from Buying Underlying and Borrowing Present Value of Exercise Price		
	$P < E$	$P = E$	$P > E$
Underlying	$+P$	$+P$	$+P$
Loan	$-E$	$-E$	$-E$
Net	$P - E$	$P - E = 0$	$P - E$

the underlying, lend the present value of the exercise price, and hold this position until expiration. The cash flows are shown in table 20.12. The arbitrage results in an immediate profit of $5 and a positive or zero cash flow in the future.

The vertical distance between Merton's bound $(P - ED)$ and the intrinsic value of a call option $(P - E)$ is equal to $E(1 - D)$, that is, $(P - ED) - (P - E) = E(1 - D)$. Since ED is the present value of the exercise price at expiration, $E(1 - D)$ is the interest earned by investing the present value of the exercise price over the life of the option. In the preceding arbitrage example, $E = \$100$, $P = \$100$, and $D = .9$. ED is $90 and the interest earned from investing $90 is $10.

As time elapses and the remaining life of a call option gets smaller, Merton's bound (that is, $P - ED$) falls and approaches the intrinsic value of a call option, or the value from exercising the call option immediately (that is, $P - ED$). The reason is that the interest, $E(1 - D)$, gets smaller as the remaining life of the options shortens.

Thus, Merton's bound can be decomposed into two parts: (1) the intrinsic value from exercising a call option immediately, that is, $P - E$; and (2) the interest earned from investing the present value of the exercise price, that is, $E(1 - D)$. As the remaining life of an option shortens, the interest earned gets smaller and Merton's bound approaches the intrinsic value of the option.

Since an American call option is worth at least as much as a European call option, Merton's bound also applies to American call options. Arbitrage ensures that the price of an American call option equals or exceeds $P - E$. Since $P - ED$ is greater than $P - E$, Merton's bound is higher. This is shown in figure 20.5.

Table 20.12   Arbitrage if Merton's Bound Is Violated

	Cash Flows at Time 0	Cash Flows at Expiration		
		$P < 100$	$P = 100$	$P > 100$
Buy call	−5	0	0	$P - 100$
Shortsell underlying	+100	−P	−P	−P
Lend PV	−90	+100	+100	+100
Net	+5	−P + 100 (Positive)	0	0

Figure 20.5   Merton's Bound

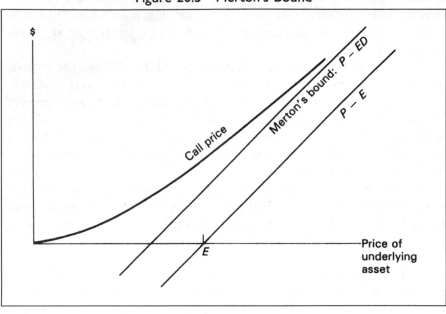

From put-call parity, C equals $P + Pp - ED$. Therefore, the price of a put is:

$$Pp = C - [P - ED] \qquad (20.12)$$

Since $P - ED$ is Merton's bound, the price of a put is the vertical distance between the price of a call and Merton's bound. This point is illustrated in figure 20.5. As the price of the underlying asset rises, the value of the call approaches Merton's bound, and, consequently, the value of a put gets very small. When the underlying asset's price is small, the value of a call option is small and the value of a put becomes large.

Determinants of the Value of a Call Option

The value of a call option is determined by the following six factors.

1. **The Price of the Underlying Asset**. The value of a call option is a positive function of the price of the underlying security. The higher the value of the underlying asset, the greater the value of the call option.

2. **The Exercise Price**. The value of a call option is inversely related to the exercise price. The lower the exercise price, the higher the value of the call option. Other things equal, a lower exercise price means that the call option is more in-the-money.

3. **The Time until Expiration**. The value of a call option is a positive function of time until expiration. The longer the time until expiration, the greater the value of the call option. Clearly, a longer-lived call option equals a shorter-lived option plus some additional value. For example, an option with six months to run is equal to a three-month option plus something additional. The impact of longer remaining life is shown graphically in figure 20.6.

These first three determinants of call option value are illustrated by table 20.13 on call option prices. Look across any row of the table; the value of the call option decreases as the exercise price increases. Look down any column; time to maturity increases and the value of the call option also increases.

4. **The Price Volatility of the Underlying Asset**. The greater the volatility of the underlying asset, the higher the value of the call option, since

Figure 20.6   Impact of Longer Remaining Life on the Value of a Call Option

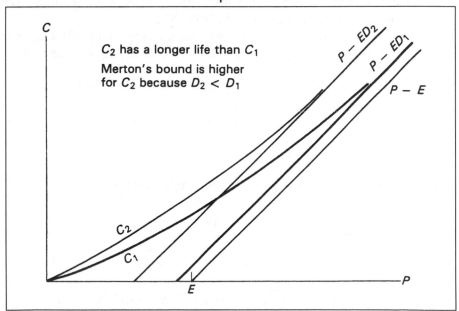

Table 20.13   The Impact of Maturity and Exercise Price upon Call Options

Maturity (months)	Price of Underlying = $110 Exercise Price		
	$90	$100	$110
3	$30	$16	$4
6	$34	$19	$6.50
9	$37	$21.50	$8.50

payoffs to a call buyer are asymmetric. If the underlying asset does poorly, the call buyer loses everything. If the underlying asset does well, the call buyer does very well. Greater dispersion in the possible value of the underlying asset implies bigger call option payoffs on the upside but the same payoff (loss of everything) on the downside, making a call option more valuable.

The impact of volatility upon call option value is illustrated by the two-security example in table 20.14. Assume two securities with the following possible prices at expiration. Each of these securities has the same mean of 100, but security 2 has greater dispersion of outcomes. An option on security 2 is more valuable because of this dispersion. To see the point, consider the case of call options with exercise prices of $100 on each security. The payoffs on these options are shown in table 20.15.

The call option on security 2 clearly has a greater value. If the options are out-of-the-money or at-the-money, both options expire worthless. If the

Table 20.14   Two-Security Example of Volatility

	Security 1		
Prices at expiration	90	100	110
Probability	1/3	1/3	1/3

Mean price = (90)(1/3) + (100)(1/3) + (110)(1/3) = 100

	Security 2		
Prices at expiration	80	100	120
Probability	1/3	1/3	1/3

Mean price = (80)(1/3) + (100)(1/3) + (120)(1/3) = 100

Table 20.15   Value of a Call

Call Option on Security 1

Prices of underlying	90	100	110
Value of call option	0	0	10
Probability	1/3	1/3	1/3

Mean value = (0)(1/3) + (0)(1/3) + (10)(1/3) = 3.33

Call Option on Security 2

Prices of underlying	80	100	120
Value of call option	0	0	20
Probability	1/3	1/3	1/3

Mean value = (0)(1/3) + (0)(1/3) + (20)(1/3) = 6.67

options are in-the-money, the second option has a higher payoff and, therefore, must be worth more. The impact of volatility upon the value of a call option is shown in figure 20.7.

5. **The Risk-Free Interest Rate**. The higher the interest rate, the greater the value of a call option, since Merton's bound rises as the interest rate increases.[5] This is illustrated in figure 20.8.

6. **Dividends or Interest on the Underlying Asset**. The higher the cash payments, the lower the value of a call option. The total return on an asset is the cash payment (dividends or coupon interest) plus price appreciation. For a given total rate of return, higher cash payments on an asset imply lower returns from price increases. Since the call buyer gains only if the price of the underlying asset increases, higher cash payments on the underlying asset tend to reduce the capital gains and the value of the call option.

From put-call parity, the price of a put can be shown to depend upon the call price, the price of the underlying asset, and the present value of the

---

[5] This overlooks the impact of the interest rate upon the value of the underlying security – clearly an important factor in the case of bonds.

Figure 20.7   Impact of the Volatility of the Underlying Asset on the Value of a Call Option

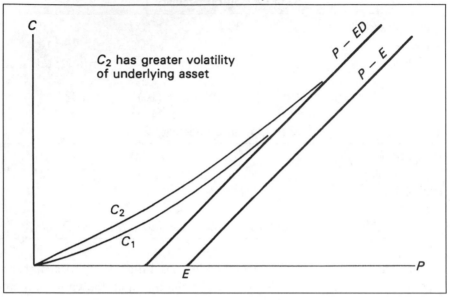

Figure 20.8   Impact of Higher Interest Rate on Value of Call Option

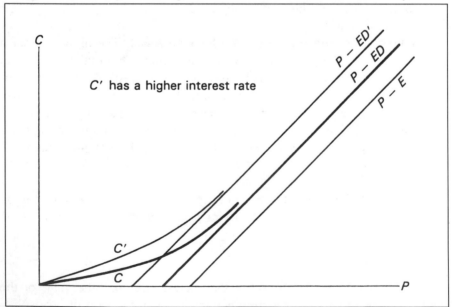

exercise price. It follows that the preceding six determinants of call prices also affect put prices. There are two major differences for puts. First, as the price of the underlying security increases, the value of the put goes down. That is, the value of a put is inversely related to the price of the underlying security. Second, higher exercise price increases the value of the put. The value of a put option is directly related to the exercise price.

Options versus Futures

Investors long in the underlying asset in the spot market may want to protect themselves against price declines. An example is an underwriter who has purchased an issue of bonds and is faced with the risk of reselling these to the public. The underwriter may find it desirable to reduce overall risk by shorting bond futures contracts. The net position has reduced price risk because changes in the value of the long spot market position are moderated by opposite changes in the short futures position. Consequently, the profit profile for a perfect futures hedge is shown in figure 20.9 as a flat line indicating no net profit or loss.

Someone hedging a long position in the spot market may be most concerned about protecting the position against price declines. The purchase of a put option provides the desired protection. If the value of the spot market position falls below the exercise price of the put, then the put can

Figure 20.9 Futures Short Hedge versus Purchase of a Put

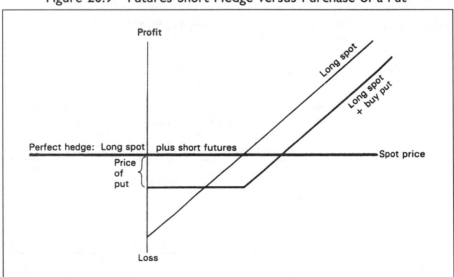

be exercised and the underlying security sold for the exercise price. If the spot market position has a value exceeding the exercise price, the put expires worthless.

A long position in the spot market combined with purchase of a put is illustrated by the example in table 20.16. The underlying asset is purchased for $90 and a put with an exercise price of $90 is purchased for $6. At the expiration date of the put, if the underlying security has a value less than $90, the put is exercised and the underlying is sold for the exercise price of $90. This results in a net loss of $6, whenever the underlying has a value less than $90. If the underlying sells at $90 or more, the put expires worthless and the underlying can be liquidated for its market value. At put expiration, if the underlying sells at $90, the net loss is $6, the purchase price of the put; if the underlying sells at $91, the net loss is $5 – a loss of $6 for purchasing the put minus a $1 profit on the underlying, and so on.

The profit profile for long in the spot market and purchase of a put is shown in figure 20.9. This position provides protection against price declines (in exchange for purchase of the put) and still has potential for price gains. Clearly, the existence of a separate market for put options increases the opportunities of a short hedger.

Options on Futures

Investors with long positions in the spot market may want to protect against downside risk (without surrendering upside potential) by purchasing put

Table 20.16   Profits and Losses for Buying Underlying and a Put Option

Original Purchase of Put				−6
Original Purchase of Underlying				−90
Total				−96

	Price of Underlying at Expiration			
	88	89	90	91
Sell underlying at expiration			+90	+91
Exercise put by selling underlying at $90	+90	+90		
Net Profit or Loss	−6	−6	−6	−5

options. The development of the market for put and call options on futures contracts has provided a new investment vehicle for achieving this goal. Trading in these options has become quite active as investors have sought to utilize the one-sided potential of options.

Options on futures contracts are somewhat different from options on underlying assets. First, if someone exercises an in-the-money option on a futures contract, the option writer pays the difference between the futures price and the option's exercise price. As an example, consider a call option with exercise price (E) of 90 and a futures price (F) of 95. If the call option is exercised, the call writer gives the call buyer a long futures position plus $5 ($95 - 90 = F - E$). A put is exercised only if the futures price is less than the exercise price (that is, $F < E$); the put writer would give the put buyer a short position plus $E - F$.

Second, for American options on futures contracts, Merton's lower bound does not apply. Consequently, the price of a call on a futures contract approaches $F - E$ for high futures prices. Figure 20.10 shows the relationship between the value of a call option on a futures contract and the price of the futures contract.

Black–Scholes Model

In the case of a European call option with no cash payments on the underlying asset and with a certain, continuously compounded interest rate, Black and

Figure 20.10   Call Option on Futures

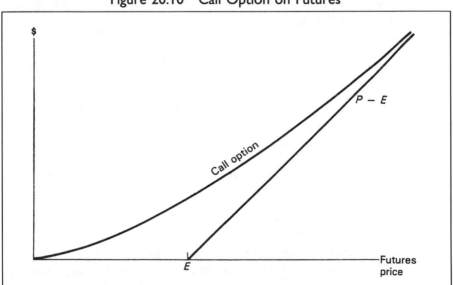

Scholes have shown that the value of a call option is an explicit function
of the first five factors mentioned previously. The Black-Scholes model is
the following:

$$C = PN(d_1) - Ee^{-rt}N(d_2) \qquad (20.13)$$

where:

C = the price of a call option
P = the current price of the underlying
E = the exercise price
e = the base of natural logarithms
r = the continuously compounded interest rate
t = the remaining life of the call option

$N(d_1)$ and $N(d_2)$ are the cumulative probabilities from the normal distribution
of getting the values d_1 and d_2, where d_1 and d_2 are as follows:

$$d_1 = \frac{\ln(P/E) + (r + .5\sigma^2)t}{\sigma\sqrt{t}}$$

$$d_2 = d_1 - \sigma\sqrt{t}$$

σ = the standard deviation of the continuously compounded rate of
    return on the underlying asset

The term e^{-rt} is the present value of \$1 received t periods from the
present. It is the continuously compounded equivalent of what we have
called D, the present value of \$1.[6]
To understand the Black-Scholes model better, consider the case where
$N(d_1)$ and $N(d_2)$ are both equal to 1. This is equivalent to assuming complete
certainty. Then, the model becomes:

$$C = P - Ee^{-rt} \qquad (20.14)$$

---

[6] We have previously discussed the cases where interest is compounded
annually and semiannually. Interest can be compounded quarterly, monthly,
daily, or in the limit instantaneously.

This expression is Merton's lower bound for continuously compounded interest rates. With complete certainty, the Black-Scholes model reduces to Merton's bound.

$N(d_1)$ and $N(d_2)$ represent cumulative probabilities from the normal distribution. Figure 20.11 illustrates these cumulative probabilities, which must be numbers between 0 and 1. If they are less than 1.0, there is some uncertainty about the level of the stock price at option expiration. From its definition, d_2 must be smaller than d_1. Assume that we know that $N(d_1)$ is .75 and $N(d_2)$ is .25. Then the Black-Scholes model becomes:

$$C = (.75)P - (.25)Ee^{-rt} \qquad (20.15)$$

The Black-Scholes function is shown in figure 20.12. As the figure shows, the call price approaches Merton's lower bound for high values of the underlying asset. The fact that $N(d_1)$ and $N(d_2)$ are less than 1.0 raises the value of the call option above Merton's bound. That is, uncertainty about the value of the underlying asset at option expiration raises the value of the call option.

Since the Black-Scholes model requires no cash payments and interest rate certainty, it cannot be applied to debt instruments. However, the Black-Scholes models can be applied to common stocks without dividends. The model can be adapted for common stocks that pay dividends.

One of the attractions of the Black-Scholes model is that most of the inputs are readily observable. The standard deviation of the return on the underlying asset is not directly observable. However, this can be estimated from past data, if the standard deviation is relatively stable over time.

Figure 20.11   Cumulative Normal Distribution

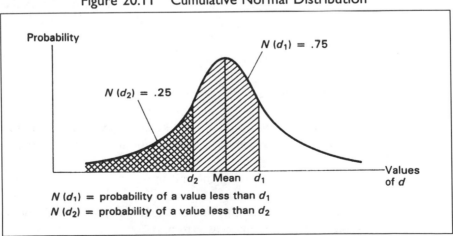

$N(d_1)$ = probability of a value less than d_1
$N(d_2)$ = probability of a value less than d_2

Figure 20.12   Black-Scholes Model

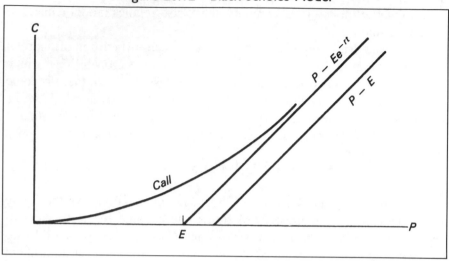

Summary

The market for put and call options has expanded greatly since 1975. Since these options are one-sided rights, they allow investors to protect themselves against one-sided risks. For example, the purchase of a put option allows the buyer to protect against the risk of a particular security dropping in price. The purchase of a call option allows the buyer to protect against the possibility that a security's price rises.

For every option buyer, there is an option writer who takes the exactly opposite position. The option buyer is playing a zero sum game against the option writer. Whatever one wins, the other loses. Put-call parity shows the relationship between the prices of a call option, a put option, the underlying security, and the present value of the exercise price.

Questions/Problems

1. A call option with an exercise price of $90 sells for $8. The call option has three months until expiration. The underlying asset sells for $90. A put with the same exercise price sells for $6.
   a. Draw a profit profile for buying the call option.
   b. Draw a profit profile for writing the call.
   c. Draw a profit profile for writing the call and buying the underlying security. Compare with your answer to part b.

d. Draw a profit profile for buying the put.
e. Draw a profit profile for writing the put.
f. Draw a profit profile for shortselling the underlying asset.
g. Draw a profit profile for shortselling the underlying asset and buying the call. Compare with your answer to part f.
h. Draw a profit profile for buying the underlying asset and buying a put option. Compare this with your answer to part a.
i. Draw a profit profile assuming you bought the underlying security at $80 and wrote a call (with exercise price of $90) for $8.
j. Draw a profit profile assuming you bought the underlying security at $95 and wrote a call (with exercise price of $90) for $8.
k. Draw a profit profile assuming you buy a call for $8 and buy a put for $6.
l. Draw a profit profile assuming you write a call for $8 and write a put for $6.

2. On the expiration date of a call option, the price of an underlying security is $115, the exercise price is $100, and the call sells for $5. What arbitrage opportunity is available?

3. A call option has an exercise price of $100, the underlying security sells for $150, and the call sells for $200. Is this consistent with equilibrium? Are there any arbitrage opportunities?

4. A one-year put with exercise price of $100 sells for $13, the underlying security sells for $90, and the interest rate is 10 percent. What is the price of a call with the same exercise price? Assume no premature exercise of the options.

5. A one-year call option has an exercise price of $100, the underlying security sells for $113, and the interest rate is 10 percent. From Merton's bound, what is the lowest possible price of the call option?

6. Explain why a call option has a larger percentage change than the underlying security.

7. Explain the impact of each of the following upon the value of a call option.
   a. price of the underlying
   b. exercise price
   c. time to expiration
   d. volatility of the underlying

References

Black, F. and M. Scholes, "The Pricing of Options and Corporate Liabilities," *Journal of Political Economy,* May/June 1973, pp. 637–59.

Kolb, R. W., *Futures, Options, and Swaps,* Miami: Kolb Publishing, 1994.

Merton, R. C., "Theory of Rational Option Pricing," *Bell Journal of Economics and Management Science,* Spring 1973, pp. 141–83.

Whaley, R. E., "Valuation of American Futures Options: Theory and Empirical Tests," *Journal of Finance,* 41, 1986, pp. 127–50.

21

Futures Contracts

Overview

Futures contracts on physical commodities have been traded for many years. In recent years, active markets have developed for financial futures contracts. This chapter describes futures contracts for physical commodities and the use of futures contracts in risk reduction and hedging. The next chapter examines several financial futures contracts and their uses.

A futures contract involves a contractual agreement to purchase or sell something at a future point in time, called the **delivery month**.[1] The buyer is called the **long** and the seller is called the **short**. Futures contracts are **zero sum games**; that is, the short and the long are playing against each other. The long's gains equals the short's losses and vice versa.

The actual purchase of the commodity is not scheduled to take place until the delivery month, as shown in figure 21.1. For example, suppose a contract is signed for the short to deliver one ounce of silver in one year for a price of $8.00. Figure 21.2 shows the futures obligations.

In fact, most futures contracts are closed out by an offsetting position before delivery occurs. A long offsets by going short; a short offsets by going long. Imagine an investor who has taken a short position in silver futures at $8.00 per ounce on March 15 as shown in figure 21.3. The scheduled delivery date is September 15. Any time before that delivery date, the short can offset the short position by going long. For example, suppose

---

[1] For futures contracts, the delivery date is actually a month. The seller has the option to pick the exact day during the month to make delivery of the contract and be paid.

Figure 21.1   Futures Contracts

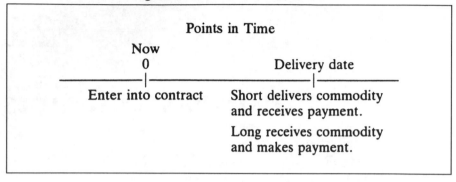

Figure 21.2   Short Position in Silver Futures

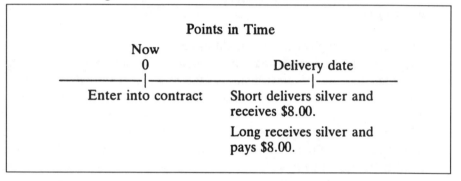

Figure 21.3   Offsetting a Short Futures Position

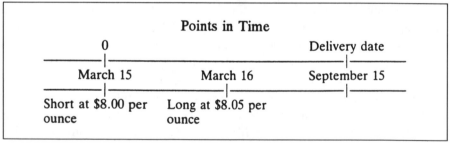

that on March 16 the short decides to close the position by offsetting, that is, going long at $8.05 per ounce. Going long one contract offsets the original short position for a loss of $.05 per ounce. There is a loss because the investor has sold (shorted) at $8.00 and bought (gone long) at $8.05. Had the position been closed at a price below $8.00, the short would have gained.

Offsetting does not involve any incremental brokerage fees because the fee to establish the initial short position includes the commission to take the offsetting long position – a so-called **round trip commission**. If actual delivery is made on the contract on September 15, silver has to be purchased and delivered to the location specified in the futures contract. Sizable transactions costs are incurred. Even with financial futures contracts in which the short has to deliver securities, the transactions costs involved in purchasing the securities in the spot market generally exceed the cost of an offsetting futures position.

A particular contract is traded in a designated **pit** at the exchange. A pit is a series of steps above the trading floor. The traders stand on the steps and engage in open outcry and hand signal trading. Because of the rapid ups and downs in futures prices, the pressures of being a trader are quite intense.

Open Interest

The total number of outstanding contracts is called the **open interest**. For every outstanding contract, one person is short and one is long. For the open interest to change, the number of shorts and longs must change. Consider the example in table 21.1. On March 15, the open interest is 30 contracts. In total, investors are long 30 contracts and short 30 contracts. For every contract long, there must be a contract short.

On March 16, Jones decides to offset one long contract by going short, reducing Jones' net position to 19 contracts long. When Jones goes short one contract, someone else must be going long. The identity of this long determines the change in the open interest.

The first possibility occurs if the long is one of the existing shorts. Then, a short is also offsetting at the same time as Jones. Suppose Peters decides to offset one contract. Then the new open interest is shown in table 21.2. In the second possibility, when Jones offsets one contract by shorting one contract, the long is another investor, Smith. Then, the open interest remains at 30 contracts (see table 21.3).

To summarize, if a particular transaction involves a new long *and* a new short, the open interest increases by one contract. If a transaction involves

Table 21.1   Open Interest – March 15

Longs		Shorts	
Jones	20	Smith	15
Roberts	10	Peters	15
Total	30	Total	30

Table 21.2   Open Interest – March 16

Longs		Shorts	
Jones	19	Smith	15
Roberts	10	Peters	14
Total	29	Total	29

Table 21.3   Open Interest – March 16

Longs		Shorts	
Jones	19	Smith	15
Roberts	10	Peters	15
Smiles	1		
Total	30	Total	30

offsetting by an existing long *and* offsetting by an existing short, the open interest declines by one contract. If a transaction entails offsetting by an existing short or long, and if the other side of the transaction is a new investor, the open interest remains unchanged. Each futures exchange has a **clearinghouse** to keep track of the short and long positions. The clearinghouse cancels the offsetting positions.

The amount of trading is different from the open interest. For example, if 50 longs decided to offset by going short and the other sides of the transactions were taken by 50 new long investors, we would have 50 trades and an unchanged open interest.

Margin and Marking-to-Market

Every long and short position is required to post a performance bond called **margin** with the clearinghouse. The margin allows the clearinghouse to guarantee the financial integrity of contracts. If one side defaults, the clearinghouse should have sufficient margin funds to ensure that the other side of the contract does not suffer financially.

Because an investor in futures markets must put down margin equal to only a small proportion of the market value of the underlying commodity, the investor's position is highly levered and quite risky. A small percentage change in the price of the futures contract brings about a much larger percentage change in the value of the margin. If the investor puts down m percent of the futures price, the margin will change $1/(m$ percent) for every

1 percent change in the futures price. For example, if an investor puts down 10 percent of the futures price, the margin will change 1/.10, or 10, times as fast as the futures price.

Each day the exchange computes a **settlement price**. The settlement price is not the closing price, the price from the very last trade of the day. Instead, the settlement price is an average of the prices near the end of trading.[2]

If the settlement price increases (decreases) from one day to the next, the long has a gain (loss) and the short has a loss (gain). Consider an example for silver futures as shown in figure 21.4. The settlement price on March 15 is $8.00 per ounce. At the end of trading on the next day, March 16, the settlement price is $8.20. This means that the long gains $.20 per ounce and the short loses $.20 per ounce. The clearinghouse transfers funds between the accounts of the short and the long in a process called **marking-to-market**. In the futures markets, every contract is marked-to-market every day. Every day, the longs and the shorts must "settle up."

The funds used to settle the accounts of the shorts and the longs come from the collateral deposited by investors with the clearinghouse. When prices increase, the collateral of the longs is increased and the shorts' collateral is reduced by the same amount. If an individual investor's collateral becomes too small as a result of market price changes, the investor is required to put up more margin or the position is closed. Thus, marking-to-market helps to guarantee performance on the contract.

Futures exchanges set **price limits** on individual futures contracts except during delivery months. Price limits restrict the change in price on a particular

Figure 21.4   Silver Futures

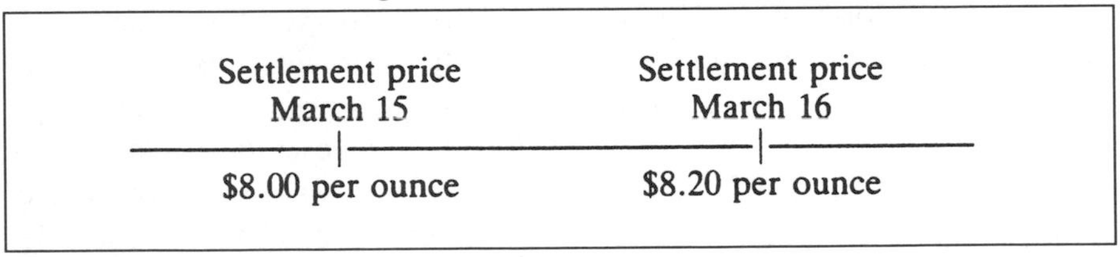

Settlement price March 15	Settlement price March 16
$8.00 per ounce	$8.20 per ounce

---

[2] Use of a settlement price instead of a closing price is motivated by the practice of marking-to-market, discussed here. The settlement price is used to figure the amount of cash transfer between shorts and longs after trading closes. If the closing price were used, some traders might be able to manipulate prices at the close to their advantage.

day to some maximum amount up or down. For example, if a futures contract settles on Monday at $8 and if a price limit of $1 is applicable, on Tuesday the contract is not allowed to trade at less than $7 or more than $9. The motivation for price limits is to restrict the price volatility of futures contracts. If a contract is up or down the limit, trading may stop until the following day, allowing the traders some time to cool down. The price limits also allow the clearinghouse time to collect more collateral from traders who have taken losses. Thus, price limits help maintain the financial integrity of traders' positions. Instead of having price limits, the clearinghouse could require greater amounts of collateral.[3]

In addition, limits are set on the total number of contracts in which a position can be taken. Position limits are motivated by the desire to keep markets competitive. There is fear that price manipulation might occur if one trader, or a syndicate of traders, controls too many contracts. These position limits, combined with price limits and margin requirements, guarantee the financial integrity of contract positions. Thus, one side of a contract can expect to suffer no financial harm if the other side defaults.

Forward versus Futures Contracts

In some markets, forward contracts are traded. Forward contracts have a number of similarities and differences with futures contracts, as summarized in table 21.4.

Forward markets exist in the foreign exchange markets. Typically, banks regularly dealing with each other write forward contracts on foreign currencies. The forward market is a small, private market. Since the banks dealing in these forward markets know each other quite well and have many interactions, default on a particular contractual agreement is unlikely. Consequently, these forward contracts do not involve collateral, although compensating balances may be expected. No cash flows occur between the initiation of the forward contract and the delivery date. The parties merely agree to exchange currencies at some future date. Delivery is usually made on forward contracts. Terms on particular contracts are tailor-made to meet the specific needs of the parties, making individual contracts unattractive to other parties and creating a thin resale market for forward contracts.

---

[3] See Brennan (1986).

Table 21.4   Forward versus Futures Contracts

	Forward	Futures
Collateral	None	Yes
Marking-to-Market	None	Daily
Compensating Balances	Usually	None
Resale	Limited	Active trading on organized exchanges
Contract Terms	Custom made	Standardized
Delivery	Usually delivered	Usually offset
Market Size	Small, private, participants know each other	Large, public, impersonal

Futures contracts are standardized and actively traded on impersonal exchanges. Since the short and long do not know each other, the risk of default is real. To reduce the likelihood of default, futures contracts require a performance bond and marking-to-market. As further protections, daily price limits and position limits are also used. With futures contracts, cash flows occur before the delivery date as the gains or losses from marking-to-market are settled daily.

In the theoretical forward contracts discussed in this book, default is impossible. In practice, the chance for default on a forward contract can be considerable. To illustrate, suppose a speculator enters into a forward contract to sell wheat at $2 per bushel for delivery next October 1. On the delivery date of October 1, the spot price of wheat is $4. Making delivery requires the speculator to buy wheat in the spot market and then sell it in the futures market to satisfy the short position, for a loss of $2 per bushel. Default on the forward contract is tempting.

The markets for forward foreign exchange attempt to solve the problem of default by having a small and private market in which the parties are unlikely to default because of their close ties. In contrast, futures markets attempt to solve the problem of possible default and contractual nonperformance by requiring margin and by marking-to-market.[4] In the example of the previous paragraph, if the speculator shorts futures (instead of a forward contract) at $2 and prices rise to $4, the short pays the long the amount of the price increase on a daily basis because of marking-to-market. If the speculator's margin on the futures contract is too low, more margin is posted or the speculator's position is closed out. Thus, the financial integrity of the futures contract is protected.

If all interest rates are certain,[5] futures and forward prices are identical, even though futures contracts have marking-to-market.[6] Since interest rates are uncertain in practice, a difference between futures and forward prices may exist. Azriel Levy has presented a powerful theoretical argument of the equivalence of futures and forward contracts even with uncertainty.[7] Empirically, any difference between futures and forwards appears to be a second order effect – perhaps a fraction of a percent.[8] The following discussion of futures markets overlooks the possible differences between futures and forward contracts created by collateral requirements and marking-to-market.

Determinants of Futures Prices

On the delivery date, a futures contract and a spot market contract are identical; therefore, the futures price equals the spot price of the deliverable commodity. If not, arbitrage opportunities are available from buying in the lower priced market and simultaneously selling in the higher priced market. If the futures price is higher than the spot price, an arbitrager can make a profit by shorting futures, buying the commodity, and delivering it into the futures contract for an immediate risk-free profit. If the futures price is below

---

[4] It has been suggested that daily price limits make default more difficult, since the margin is greater than the maximum daily price swing.

[5] There should also be a single delivery date, as opposed to delivery month, and no price and position limits.

[6] See Cox, Ingersoll, and Ross (December 1981) and Jarrow and Oldfield (1981).

[7] See Levy (1989).

[8] See Capozza and Cornell (1979) and Rendelman and Carabini (1979).

the spot price, an arbitrager can go long futures and shortsell the commodity; when delivery occurs on the futures contract, the delivered commodity can be used to close the short position.

Before the delivery date, there are two cases to consider. First, for a nonstorable commodity, the futures price is determined by the market's expectation of the future spot price on the delivery date. As an example, consider a futures market for tomatoes with a delivery date one year into the future. Since tomatoes are storable only for short periods, the futures price for delivery one year hence is set by the market's expectations of demand and supply for tomatoes on the delivery date. These expectations depend upon population trends, weather conditions, availability of substitutes, etc.

Second, the commodity may be storable. In practice, existing futures contracts are for storable commodities. Let the current futures price be F and the current spot price be P. Then, for storable commodities such as grains and metals, arbitrage will force the relationship:

$$F = P + \text{interest} + \text{storage until delivery} \qquad (21.1)$$

In other words, purchasing a futures contract is the equivalent of borrowing the purchase price of a commodity, buying the commodity, and storing it until the delivery date (see table 21.5). At the delivery date, the loan principal, interest charges, and storage costs must be paid. The total of these three costs equals the futures price.

Arbitrage forces equation 21.1 to hold. To prove equation 21.1, the cases where the futures price is above (below) its equilibrium value are shown shortly to provide arbitrage opportunities. This arbitrage forces the prices back to their equilibrium values in equation 21.1.

Equation 21.1 shows that the futures price is the spot price plus interest and storage until the delivery date. Expectations of market prices on the

Table 21.5   Creating a Forward Position from a Spot Position

Actions	Points in Time	
	0	Delivery Date
	Cash Flows	
Borrow	+P	Repay −[P + Interest + Storage]
Buy Commodity	−P	
Net Cash Flows	0	−[P + Interest + Storage]

delivery date do not appear directly in equation 21.1. However, expectations are implicitly incorporated in equation 21.1 because arbitrage forces expectations of the prices on the delivery date to affect both the futures price and the current spot price.

Futures Price Above Equilibrium Level

Table 21.6 shows the arbitrage if the futures price rises above its equilibrium price. The arbitrager can short futures, borrow money, purchase the commodity in the spot market, and store until the delivery date. On the delivery date, the arbitrager delivers the commodity, gets paid by the long, and repays the loan plus interest. There is a sure profit. To simplify the discussion, the storage cost is assumed to be zero, and R is defined as the total interest from time zero until delivery expressed as a percentage.[9]

If $F - P(1 + R)$ is positive, there is a sure arbitrage profit. The actions of arbitragers shorting futures and buying in the spot market drive the futures price F down and the spot market price P up until $F - P(1 + R)$ equals zero.

Consider the following numerical example of arbitrage. If the spot price of gold is \$400 and the one-year spot interest rate is 10 percent, the futures price for delivery in one year should be \$440 [i.e., 400(1.10)]. If the futures

Table 21.6 Arbitrage If Futures Price Is Above Equilibrium Level

Actions	Points in Time	
	0	Delivery Date
	Cash Flows	
Short Futures		$+F$
Borrow	$+P$	
Buy Commodity	$-P$	
Repay Loan + Interest		$-P(1 + R)$
Deliver Commodity in Futures Market		
Net Cash Flows	0	$F - P(1 + R)$

[9] For example, if \$100 is borrowed at time zero and \$101 is repaid in one month, R will be 1 percent. R is not an annualized rate.

price is actually $500, arbitrage profits are available from shorting futures, borrowing $400, buying gold, and storing it until the delivery date. The actions and cash flows are shown in table 21.7.

Futures Prices Below Equilibrium Level

Table 21.8 shows the arbitrage. The arbitrager goes long futures, shortsells the commodity, and invests the proceeds from the shortsale. On the delivery date, the arbitrager purchases the commodity through the futures contract, uses this to close the short position, and receives the amount lent plus interest for a sure profit.

Table 21.7   Arbitrage Example If Futures Price Is Above Equilibrium Level

	Points in Time	
	0	Delivery Date
Actions	Cash Flows	
Short Futures		+500
Borrow	+400	
Buy Commodity	−400	
Repay Loan + Interest		−400(1.10)
Deliver Commodity in		
Futures Market		
Net Cash Flows	0	500 − 400(1.10) = 60

Table 21.8   Arbitrage If Futures Price Is Below Equilibrium Level

	Points in Time	
	0	Delivery Date
Actions	Cash Flows	
Long futures		−F
Short commodity	+P	
Invest proceeds	−P	+P(1 + R)
Take delivery on futures		
and close short position		
Net Cash Flows	0	−[F − P(1 + R)]

If the futures price F is less than the spot price plus interest, $P(1 + R)$, the net cash flow from this arbitrage is positive with complete certainty. The actions of arbitragers repeatedly profiting from this arbitrage force the futures price up and the spot price down until the arbitrage profits are eliminated, i.e., until the futures price equals the spot price plus interest.

Consider the arbitrage opportunities for the following numerical example. The spot price of gold is $400 and the one-year interest rate is 10 percent, again implying a futures price of $440. If the futures price is actually $400, the arbitrage opportunity is shown in table 21.9.

The Length of Time Until Delivery

In equation 21.1, futures contracts for more distant delivery dates have higher price quotations because of higher interest and storage costs for carrying the commodity for a longer time period. To illustrate, consider the case where storage costs are zero. Then, the futures price for delivery in d periods is the spot price times 1 plus the spot interest rate to the power d [i.e., $(1 + R_d)^d$]. Figure 21.5 shows the futures prices for several delivery dates for a flat term structure of 10 percent and spot price of $400.

For precious metals such as gold, silver, and platinum, the storage costs are relatively small compared to the market price. For these precious metals, the differences in futures prices are largely determined by the term structure of interest rates. There is a close relationship between futures prices and the actual term structure of interest rates. Thus, the futures price for gold for delivery d periods from now (assuming zero storage costs) is:

Table 21.9 Example of Arbitrage If Futures Price Is Below Equilibrium Level

	Points in Time	
	0	Delivery Date
Actions	Cash Flows	
Long futures		−400
Short commodity	+400	
Invest proceeds	−400	+400(1.10)
Take delivery on futures and close short position		
Net Cash Flows	0	−[400 − 400(1.10)] = 40

Figure 21.5   Futures Prices for More Distant Delivery Dates

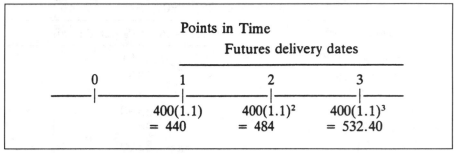

$$F_{GOLD} = P(1 + R_d)^d \qquad (21.2)$$

Convenience Yield

Possession of a particular commodity may have a convenience value to a firm. For example, for a bread manufacturer, an inventory of wheat and other raw materials is valuable. The convenience yield is subtracted from equation 21.1; convenience yield reduces the futures price relative to the spot price. The convenience yield increases in absolute value as the delivery date becomes more distant.

For most futures contracts, the futures price increases as the delivery date becomes more distant, and the total interest and storage costs increase as the delivery date becomes more distant. The case of oil futures prices during the war with Iraq in the fall of 1990 is a striking counterexample. Table 21.10 presents the futures price per barrel for light sweet crude oil observed on September 28, 1990, for various delivery dates. At the time, the spot price of oil was approximately $41 per barrel.

If equation 21.1 is correct, the futures price for distant delivery dates should exceed the spot price by the amount of interest and storage until the delivery date. With the spot price of oil at $41 in September 1990, the sum of the spot price plus interest and storage until April 1992 is considerably higher than $41. Yet, the futures price for April 1992 delivery was only $26.96. Consequently, the convenience yield exceeded $14.04 ($41 – 26.96).

The earlier discussion indicated an arbitrage opportunity if the futures price was less than the spot price plus interest and storage costs (see tables 21.8 and 21.9). The arbitrage was to (short)sell the commodity, invest the proceeds, go long futures, and use the oil purchased from the futures contract to cover the shortsale.

One version of the arbitrage is to shortsell the commodity. To shortsell, a lender of the commodity has to be found. Given fears about oil shortages

Table 21.10   Futures Price of Light Sweet Crude Oil Observed on September 28, 1990

Delivery Month	Futures Price ($ per Barrel)
November 1990	39.51
December 1990	38.31
January 1991	36.72
February 1991	35.40
March 1991	34.15
April 1991	33.00
May 1991	31.95
June 1991	31.00
July 1991	30.20
August 1991	29.55
September 1991	29.05
October 1991	28.62
November 1991	28.27
December 1991	27.98
January 1992	27.71
February 1992	27.45
March 1992	27.20
April 1992	26.96

resulting from the war, no lenders of oil were available. The potential lenders of oil were unwilling to lend because the convenience yield of oil was very high. A second version of the arbitrage is for holders of oil to sell their own oil, lend the proceeds, and buy back oil in the futures market. Again, the war uncertainties made holders of oil unwilling to give up the convenience yield of their inventories. In short, the war and the resulting high convenience yield made arbitrage impossible.

Speculative Futures Positions

Going short or long in futures without any offsetting position is often described as taking a **speculative position**. As an example, suppose you anticipate a sharp rise in the price of silver and go long in silver futures for

1,000 ounces at $5.00 per ounce. Happily, you are correct. The futures price goes to $6.00 and you make a profit of $1.00 per ounce, or $1,000.[10]

To set up your original futures position, margin is required in the form of marketable securities or cash. The broker will inform you of the exact amount of margin. For simplicity, assume that the initial margin is $500 (10 percent of the original value of the contract). If, in fact, the actual gain on your short position is $1,000, the percentage gain is 200 percent of the initial margin. The percentage gains and losses on futures can be very large. All your margin can be lost in a few days. For this reason, speculative positions (i.e., either short or long with no offsetting position) in futures contracts are very risky.

Hedging with Futures Contracts

In a futures **hedge**, an investor offsets a position in the spot market with a nearly opposite position in the futures market with the objective of reducing the overall risk of the position. The hedged position also has a lower expected return than an unhedged position. Hedges allow those unwilling or unable to bear the risk to transfer the risk to another party willing and able to take on the risks and possible rewards. This risk transfer function of futures markets is socially desirable.

In a **long hedge**, the investor takes a long position in futures. In a **short hedge**, the investor takes a short position in futures. A very important type of short hedge occurs when an investor with a long position in the spot market simultaneously shorts futures contracts. This variety of a short hedge is illustrated by the following example.

Suppose a farmer plants a wheat crop in the spring, expecting to harvest and sell the wheat in the fall. Effectively, the farmer has a long position in wheat. Because the price of wheat at the harvest time is uncertain, the farmer bears considerable risk about the eventual profits earned on the wheat.[11] To

---

[10] Because of daily price limits, this gain will not occur over one day but will be spread out over several days. Each day there will be marking-to-market, and some gains (or possibly losses) will be realized daily.

[11] Besides price uncertainty, the farmer also bears quantity risk. At planting time, the farmer does not know the exact number of bushels that will be harvested.

protect against this risk, the farmer shorts wheat futures (a short hedge) and locks-in the selling price of the wheat. If the futures price is $6.00 per bushel and production costs are $4 per bushel, the farmer's short position in wheat futures allows the wheat to be sold at $6.00 per bushel, locking-in a profit of $2.00 per bushel.

The short futures position is a two-edged sword. While the farmer can avoid losses if the wheat price at harvest is low, the farmer also gives up large profits if the wheat price is quite high at the harvest date. The farmer is willing to give up the chance for large profits in order to avoid possible catastrophic losses on the downside. The futures contract allows the farmer to transfer the risks to someone else better able to bear those risks.

As an example of a long hedge, consider a bread manufacturer in need of wheat to make the bread. To lock-in the purchase price of wheat on the harvest date and guarantee a profit from making bread, the bread manufacturer goes long wheat futures (a long hedge). The bread manufacturer foregoes windfall gains if the wheat price is low on the harvest date. In exchange, potentially large losses are avoided if wheat prices are high on the harvest date. The futures contract permits the bread manufacturer to pass on the price risks of wheat. Bread manufacturing becomes a more stable industry as a result.

Fine Tuning the Hedge

In short hedging, the hedger may be able to find a futures contract for a virtually identical item as the hedger's spot position. Then, the gains (losses) in the spot market are offset by the losses (gains) in the futures market. This offset is shown in figure 21.6, which shows profit profiles. The investor goes long in the spot market at $10. As the spot price increases (decreases), the investor gains (loses) dollar for dollar. The profit profile for a short futures position in the identical item is also shown. Gains (losses) in the spot position are offset dollar for dollar by the short futures position. The profit profile for the net position is a horizontal line, indicating no change in the value of the net position as the spot price changes. This flat profit profile represents a perfect hedge.[12]

---

[12] This profit profile assumes the futures price changes only because the spot price changes. Formally, since $F = P(1 + R_d)^d$, the profit profile assumes that the change in R_d and the change in d are zero.

Figure 21.6   Profit Profile For Perfect Hedge

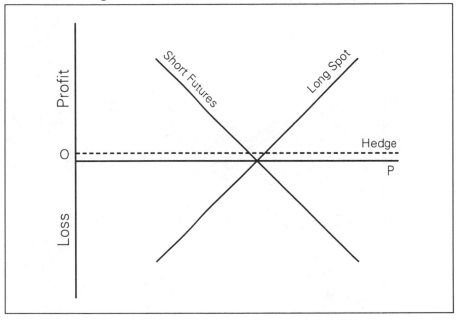

Many times, highly similar futures contracts do not exist. The hedger must utilize a short position in a similar, but different, item. This is called a cross hedge. Suppose a farmer is long in the spot market in grade A wheat, but futures trade for grade B wheat. Grades A and B are related, but different. Suppose the farmer engages in a one-for-one hedge. For every bushel of grade A wheat in the farmer's long spot position, the farmer shorts one bushel of grade A wheat. Figure 21.7 shows the profit profiles for long spot grade A wheat, short futures grade B, and the net position. Grade B wheat prices are assumed to move half as fast as grade A wheat. The slope of the profit profile for long spot grade A is 1.0; the slope of the profit profile for short grade B wheat is −.50. The net position has a slope on +.50. Thus, the gains and losses on the spot position in grade A wheat are cut in half by the short hedge.

The relationship between grade A wheat and grade B wheat is shown in figure 21.8. For every dollar change in grade B, grade A changes $2. Using this information, the farmer can construct a perfect hedge by shorting two bushels of grade B wheat for every bushel long of grade A wheat. For every dollar decrease in grade A wheat, grade B falls by $.50. But the total drop in the two short positions in grade B is $1.00 for a perfect offset.

In practice, the relationship between a spot position and a futures contract in a cross hedge is not a perfect straight line but the dots shown in figure

Figure 21.7   Profit Profile for a Cross Hedge

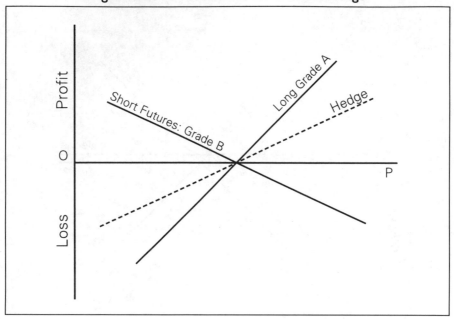

Figure 21.8   Relationship Between Grade A and Grade B

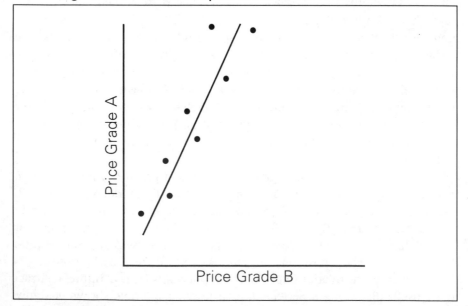

21.8. Using regression analysis, the hedger can estimate the slope of the best-fitting relationship, often called β. For every unit of the spot commodity, the hedger shorts β units of the futures. β is called the optimal hedge ratio. The optimal hedge is not a perfect hedge, since the link between the spot and futures is not perfect. The optimal hedge is the best hedge in the sense that the expected change in the hedged position is zero.

Summary

Futures contracts are obligations to buy and sell commodities at future delivery dates. These contracts allow businesses and individuals to transfer price risks to those who choose to bear the risks. The short is obligated to sell the commodity at a fixed price. The long is required to buy the commodity at the contractually agreed upon price.

The futures price of storable commodities equals the spot price plus interest and storage until the delivery date. Arbitrage guarantees this result in the absence of convenience yield.

In a hedge, a position in the spot market is offset with a futures position to reduce the overall risk. A short hedge involves a short futures position. A long hedge includes a long futures position.

Questions/Problems

1. The open interest includes:
   Longs

Bob	15 contracts
Lois	5 contracts

   Shorts

Bill	10 contracts
Helen	10 contracts

   Determine the new open interest under the following assumptions:
   a. Bill goes long 1 contract and Gene shorts 1 contract.
   b. Bill goes long 1 contract and Bob shorts 1 contract.

2. Explain the differences between forward and futures contracts.

3. What are price and position limits on futures contracts? What are the purposes of price and position limits?

4. Suppose you go long in gold futures at $400 per ounce. Your broker requires you to put up 5 percent of this price as collateral. The net day gold futures settle at $420. Compute the gain as a percent of your equity in the position. What is the general relationship between the percent change in the investor's equity and the percent change in the futures price?

5. Assume the following information about the futures price for gold.

	Delivery Dates (Number of Years into Future)		
	1	2	3
Current price of futures contract per ounce of gold	$300	$350	$400

If the current spot price of gold is $260, determine spot interest rates for periods 1, 2, and 3 and forward interest rates for periods 2 and 3, assuming no marking-to-market and no storage or transactions costs.

6. Assume no marking-to-market or storage costs. The spot price of gold is $300 and the futures price for delivery in one year is $360. The annual interest rate is 10 percent. Is the preceding information mutually consistent? If not, how can investors exploit the situation for their own profit?

7. Suppose that oil in the spot market is selling for $30 per barrel. Oil futures for delivery in two years are quoted at $20 per barrel. The two-year spot interest rate is 8 percent. Explain the perfect market arbitrage to profit from this situation. In practice what would prevent this arbitrage from occurring?

8. Investors can reduce their risk by using a futures market hedge to offset a spot market position. What happens to this risk? What are the consequences for the hedger?

9. A farmer plants enough wheat to harvest 10,000 bushels. The cost of planting the wheat is $2.50 per bushel. On the harvest date, the wheat price will be one of three prices with equal probability: $2.00, $4.00, or $6.00. Compute the farmer's profit for each of these possibilities.

The futures price for wheat is $3.80. Compute the farmer's profit for this price. When is hedging with futures the best choice for the farmer?

10. You buy gold in the spot market at $400 per ounce. You decide to hedge the gold position with a cross hedge in platinum futures. Suppose platinum futures are quoted at $600 per ounce. For every dollar that gold advances (or declines), platinum futures are likely to change by $1.25. Draw a profit profile for a one-to-one hedge – one ounce of short platinum futures for each ounce long spot gold. Then, derive the hedge ratio for a perfect hedge and draw the profit profile.

11. Look up *The Wall Street Journal* prices for gold futures. From the spot and futures prices for gold, determine the term structure of interest rates under the assumption of zero storage costs. Compare your answers with the yields on Treasury securities and explain the differences.

References

Brennan, M. J., "A Theory of Price Limits in Futures Markets," *Journal of Financial Economics,* 16, June 1986, pp. 213–33.

Capozza, D. R. and B. Cornell, "Treasury Bill Pricing in the Spot and Futures Markets," *Review of Economics and Statistics,* 61, November 1979, pp. 513–20.

Cox, J., J. E. Ingersoll, Jr., and S. A. Ross, "The Relationship Between Forward Prices and Futures Prices," *Journal of Financial Economics,* 9, December 1981, pp. 321–46.

Ederington, L. H., "The Hedging Performance of the New Futures Market," *Journal of Finance,* 34, March 1979, pp. 157–70.

Jarrow, R. A. and G. S. Oldfield, "Forward and Futures Contracts," *Journal of Financial Economics,* 9, December 1981, pp. 373–82.

Levy, A., "A Note on the Relationship Between Forward and Futures Prices," *Journal of Futures Markets,* 9, April 1989, pp. 171–4.

Rendleman, R. J. and C. E. Carabini, "The Efficiency of the Treasury Bill Futures Market," *Journal of Finance,* 34, September 1979, pp. 895–914.

Seidel, A. P. and P. M. Ginsberg, *Commodities Trading,* Englewood Cliffs, NJ: Prentice Hall, 1983.

22

Financial Futures Contracts

Overview

In the 1970s, futures contracts on financial instruments emerged. These new contracts have transformed the world of finance. This chapter explores several financial futures contracts and their uses. Zero transactions costs are assumed. The Appendix describes several technical aspects of the contracts.

A Hypothetical Contract: Treasury Strips

In order to clarify the link between futures contracts on physical commodities and financial futures, a discussion of a hypothetical contract on Treasury strips is useful. Treasury strips are zero coupon bonds, paying a par value at maturity, but having no intervening coupons.

The value of a futures contract depends upon the delivery date and the maturity of the deliverable security. The following discussion examines the possibilities.

Delivery Date in One Year

Consider a hypothetical futures contract with a delivery date in one year. A two-period strip is the only bond deliverable into the contract. The cash flows are shown in figure 22.1.

Figure 22.1   Delivery in 1 Year

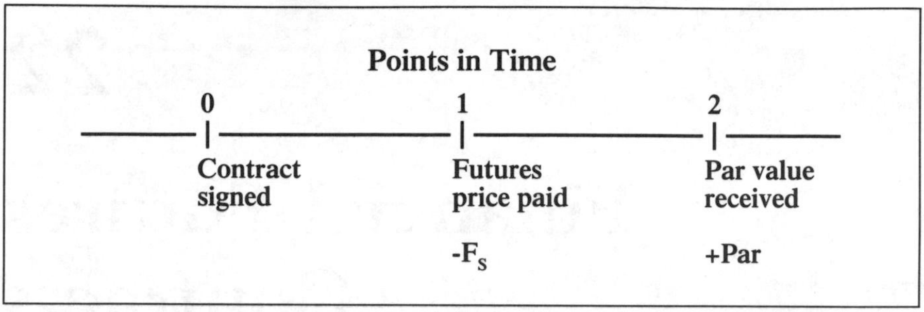

Points in Time

0	1	2
Contract signed	Futures price paid	Par value received
	$-F_s$	$+\text{Par}$

The futures price, F_s, should be the time 1 value of PAR discounted at the forward interest f_2, the interest rate from time 1 until time 2. This is mathematically equivalent to the spot price times one plus the interest rate.[1]

$$F_S = \frac{\text{PAR}}{1 + f_2} = P_2(1 + R_1) \qquad (22.1)$$

where:

P_2 = the spot price of a two-period strip
R_1 = the one-period spot interest rate

To illustrate, assume the following term structure:[2] $R_1 = .04$, $R_2 = .06$, and $f_2 = .0804$. For a \$100 par value, $P_2 = 100/(1.06)^2 = 89.00$. The futures price is:

$$F_S = \frac{100}{1.0804} = 89.00(1.04) = 92.56 \qquad (22.2)$$

---

[1] To prove the last part of the equation, note that:

$$P_2 = \frac{\text{PAR}}{(1 + R_1)(1 + f_2)}$$

Solve for PAR/$(1 + f_2)$ and substitute into equation 22.1.

[2] This same example is used in chapter 9 on spot interest rates.

Comparison with Gold Futures

For gold (metal) futures, the futures price is:

$$F_G = P_G(1 + R_1) \tag{22.3}$$

where

P_G = the spot price of gold

The formulas for Treasury strips and for gold are the same. The futures price equals the spot price times the future value factor $(1 + R_1)$. The futures price in each case equals the spot price plus interest until the delivery date.

Delivery in d Periods

Consider the case where the delivery date is in d periods and the deliverable strip has a maturity of n periods. Then, the cash flows are shown in figure 22.2.

In the d-period case, the futures price for strips is:[3]

$$F_S = \frac{PAR}{(1 + f_{d+1})(1 + f_{d+2}) \ldots (1 + f_n)} \tag{22.4}$$
$$= P_S(1 + R_d)^d$$

where:

R_d = the d-period spot interest rate

---

[3] To prove the last part of the equation, note the definition:

$$P_S = \frac{PAR}{(1 + R_d)^d(1 + f_{d+1}) \ldots (1 + f_n)}$$

Rearranging:

$$P_S(1 + R_d)^d = \frac{PAR}{(1 + f_{d+1}) \ldots (1 + f_n)}$$

Figure 22.2   Delivery in d Years

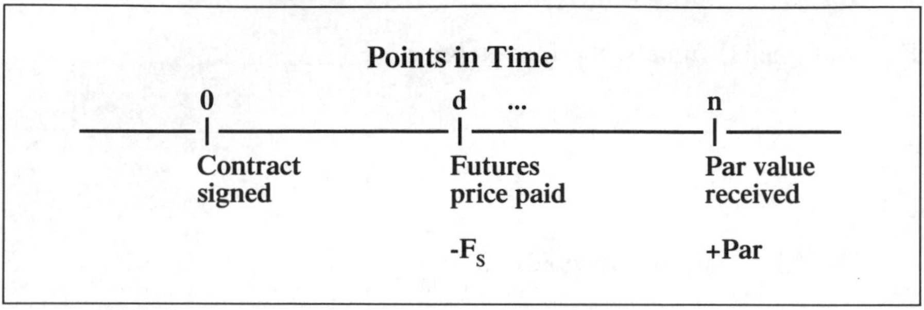

Points in Time

| 0 | d ... | n |

Contract signed | Futures price paid | Par value received

$-F_S$ | +Par

To illustrate, consider the term structure in table 22.1. Suppose the delivery date is in two periods and the deliverable strip matures in four periods. Then:

$$F_S = P_S(1 + R_d)^d = 68.30(1.06)^2 = 76.74 \qquad (22.5)$$

The formula with forward rates can also be used, but more computations are needed.

Comparison with Gold Futures in d Periods

For gold futures, the futures price for delivery in d periods is:

$$F_G = P_G(1 + R_d)^d \qquad (22.6)$$

The formulas for the futures prices for strips and for gold are the same. The futures price equals the spot price of the deliverable item plus interest until the delivery date.

Table 22.1   Strips Example

Maturity (Years)	Price per $100 of PAR	Spot Rate
1	$96.15	.04
2	$89.00	.06
3	$79.38	.08
4	$68.30	.10

Treasury Bill Futures

The Chicago Mercantile Exchange has a futures contract on U.S. Treasury bills. On the delivery date, the short must deliver a 90-day Treasury bill with a $1,000,000 par value. Figure 22.3 illustrates the contract.

A Treasury bill futures contract is similar to a contract on Treasury strips. Both are zero coupon securities. However, Treasury bills differ in two ways. Bills mature in one year or less. Bills are quoted in terms of discount rates. The Appendix shows the link between spot and forward interest rates on a discount basis.

Since there are 90 days from the delivery date to the maturity of the bill, the actual price is computed as follows:

$$F_{bill} = PAR\left[1 - f\left(\frac{90}{360}\right)\right] \qquad (22.7)$$

where:

F_{bill} = the futures price for Treasury bills
f = the forward discount rate

For example, if the forward rate is 8 percent, the price of a 90-day Treasury bill with a $1,000,000 par value is:

$$F_{bill} = 1,000,000\left[1 - .08\left(\frac{90}{360}\right)\right] = \$980,000 \qquad (22.8)$$

The price of this contract is quoted in a special way. Instead of quoting the price in terms of discount rates, the futures quotation is set equal to 100 minus the forward discount rate times 100. If f is the forward discount rate, then:

Figure 22.3 Treasury Bill Futures

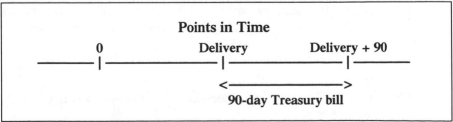

	Points in Time	
0	**Delivery**	**Delivery + 90**

<—————————————>
90-day Treasury bill

$$\text{Quote} = 100 - 100(f) \qquad (22.9)$$

This quotation is not a price, but an index of the forward interest rate. The Treasury bill futures quotation in our example is:

$$\text{Quote} = 100 - 100(.08) = 92.00 \qquad (22.10)$$

The Treasury bill futures quotation is expressed to two decimal places. The second decimal place is equivalent to .01 percent, which is frequently called one **basis point**. Each basis point is worth $25 for a 90-day Treasury bill with $1,000,000 par value. To see this point, suppose we start with a forward discount rate f and initial price of P. Then the discount rate changes to f^* and the price to P^*. Subtracting, the change in price is $P - P^*$:

$$P - P^* = \text{PAR}(f^* - f)\left[\frac{90}{360}\right] \qquad (22.11)$$

If the change in discount rate, $(f^* - f)$, is one basis point or .01 percent (or .0001), the change in price for a 90-day Treasury bill with $1,000,000 par value must be $25, that is:

$$P - P^* = \$1,000,000(.0001)\left[\frac{90}{360}\right] = \$25 \qquad (22.12)$$

If the Treasury bill futures quotation changes from 92.00 to 92.10, the price of the Treasury bill for future delivery has increased by $250. To check this result, compute the price of a $1,000,000 par value, 90-day Treasury bill at a discount rate of 8 percent; then compute the price if the discount rate changes to 7.90 percent. The change in price equals $250. Similarly, if the quote changes from 92.00 to 93.00, the change in price is $2,500.

Treasury Bond Futures

The Chicago Board of Trade (CBOT) has a U.S. Treasury bond futures contract calling for the delivery of $100,000 par value of Treasury bonds with at least 15 years to maturity or first call date, whichever is sooner.[4]

---

[4] For details of the delivery procedure, see Chicago Board of Trade Delivery Manual (1980).

For a number of years, this so-called T-bond futures contract has been one of the most actively traded futures contracts. This contract is extremely attractive as a hedging tool to bond dealers, underwriters, banks, and other financial institutions.

Treasury bond futures are quoted per $100 of par value in 32nds of a dollar. The quote is a percentage of the par value of $100,000 per contract. As an example, if the quotation is 81-10, the dollar amount is $81,000 plus 10/32 of $1,000, which is $312.25. Thus, a quote for Treasury bond futures of 81-10 translates into $81,312.50.

Futures Price on the Delivery Date

On the delivery date, the futures price must equal the spot price of the deliverable commodity. If a particular bond is deliverable into the T-bond futures contract, arbitrage forces the futures price to equal the spot market price. If the futures price is too high, the arbitrager shorts futures, buys the deliverable bond, and delivers the bond into the futures contract. If the futures price is too low, the arbitrager goes long futures and shorts the bond in the spot market; the bond acquired from the long futures position is used to cover the short position.

In practice, a sizable number of bonds are eligible for delivery into the T-bond futures contract. The large number of bonds makes it hard for anyone to manipulate prices. It also adds a number of complications covered in the Appendix to this chapter. In the text, one deliverable bond is assumed for simplicity.

Futures Price Before the Delivery Date

The CBOT Treasury bond futures contract is different from metals futures contracts because the underlying bond pays coupons. The coupon affects the futures price. Let's consider several cases. Initially, take the simple case of one deliverable bond and no marking-to-market (implying identical futures and forward prices).

Delivery in One Year and Deliverable Bond Matures in Two Years For this case, the futures cash flows are shown in figure 22.4.

The futures price, F_{BOND}, should be the time 1 value of the coupon and par values discounted at the forward interest rate f_2. That is:

Figure 22.4   Delivery in 1 Year

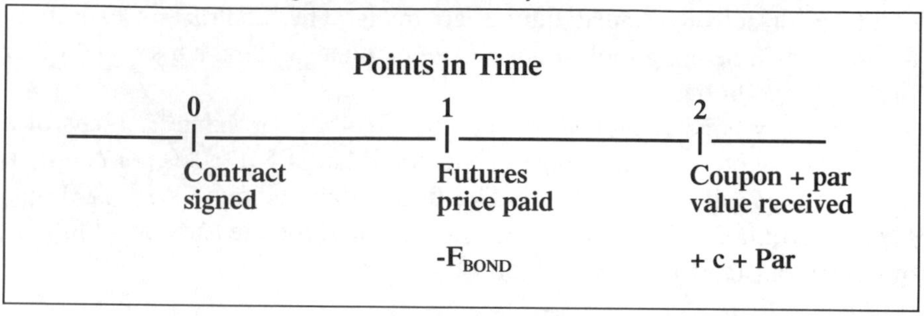

Points in Time		
0	1	2
Contract signed	Futures price paid	Coupon + par value received
	$-F_{BOND}$	$+c+$ Par

$$F_{BOND} = \frac{c + PAR}{1 + f_2} = P_2(1 + R_1) - c \qquad (22.13)$$

The futures price is mathematically equivalent to the time 1 value of the current bond price, P_2, minus the coupon paid at time 1. The time 1 coupon is subtracted since the buyer of futures is not entitled to this coupon. The buyer of the futures contract is entitled only to the time 2 coupon and the par value.

As an example, assume the term structure in table 22.1, an \$8 coupon, and \$100 par value.[5] The current or spot price of the bond is \$103.81. The forward interest rate, f_2, is .0804. Then:

$$F_{BOND} = \frac{108}{1.0804} = 103.81(1.04) - 8 \qquad (22.14)$$

$$= \$99.96$$

Delivery in One Year and Deliverable Bond Matures in n Years   The futures cash flows in this case are shown in figure 22.5.

The buyer of the futures contract receives the coupons from time 2 until time n and the par value at time n. The futures price is the time 1 value of these cash flows (see equation 22.15). The futures price is mathematically equivalent to $P_n(1 + R_1) - c$. The intuition is that the buyer of futures pays the time 1 value of the bond less the value of the time 1 coupon, which is not received.

---

[5] The same example is used in chapter 9.

Figure 22.5   Delivery in I Year; *n*-Period Bond

Points in Time

0	1	2 ...	n
Contract signed	Futures price paid	Coupon ...	Coupon + par value received
	$-F_{BOND}$	+c ...	+ c + Par

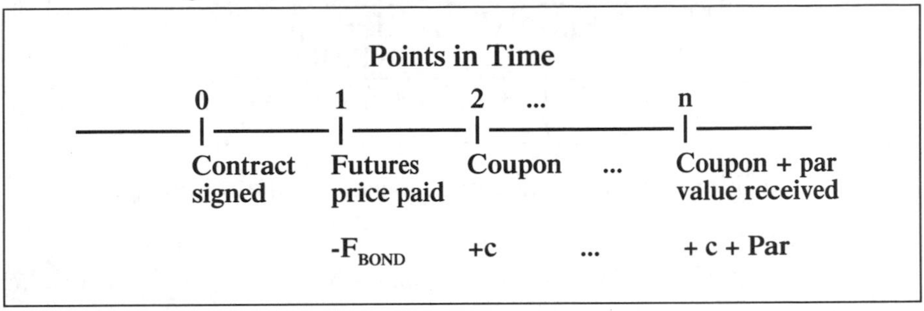

$$F_{BOND} = \frac{c}{1 + f_2} + \frac{c}{(1 + f_2)(1 + f_3)} + \cdots + \frac{c + PAR}{(1 + f_2)(1 + f_3) \ldots (1 + f_n)} \quad (22.15)$$

$$= P_n(1 + R_1) - c$$

where

P_n = the spot price of the *n*-period bond

Delivery in d Years and Deliverable Bond Matures in n Years   The futures cash flows in this case are shown in figure 22.6.

The buyer of the futures contract receives the coupons from time $d + 1$ until time n and par value at time n. The futures price is the time d value of these cash flows. The forward price can be derived by looking at the time d value of each individual cash flow. The coupon c received at time $d + 1$ must be discounted one period to time d at the forward rate f_{d+1} for a time d value of $c/(1 + f_{d+1})$. The coupon received at time $d + 2$ has a value at time d of $c/(1 + f_{d+1})(1 + f_{d+2})$. In general:

Figure 22.6   Delivery in *d* Periods; *n*-Period Bond

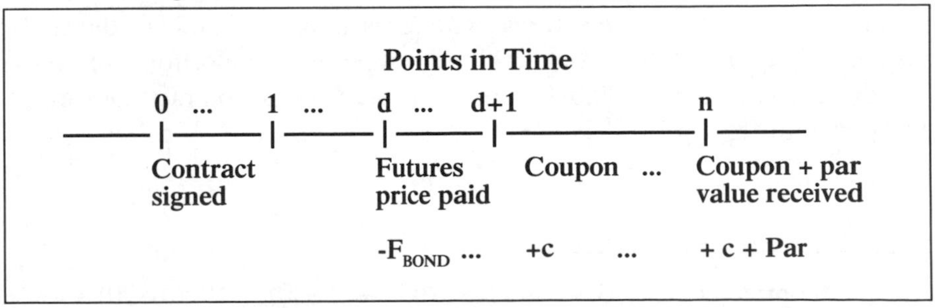

Points in Time

0 ...	1 ...	d ...	d+1	n
Contract signed		Futures price paid	Coupon ...	Coupon + par value received
		$-F_{BOND}$ ...	+c ...	+ c + Par

$$F_{\text{BOND}} = \frac{c}{1 + f_{d+1}} + \frac{c}{(1 + f_{d+1})(1 + f_{d+2})} + \ldots \qquad (22.16)$$
$$\ldots + \frac{c + \text{PAR}}{(1 + f_{d+1})(1 + f_{d+2}) \ldots (1 + f_n)}$$

This equation is mathematically equivalent to the following:

$$F_{\text{BOND}} = (P_n - cA_d)(1 + R_d)^d \qquad (22.17)$$

Thus, the forward price is equal to the current spot price P of a bond with coupon c and maturity n minus the annuity of \$$c$ of coupons from time 1 to time d (i.e., cA_d) times $[1 + R_d]^d$ to adjust for the fact that the cash flows are received at time d.

To illustrate, suppose the futures delivery date is in two years. The deliverable bond has a maturity of four years and a coupon rate of 8 percent. Assuming the term structure in table 22.1, the current price of the bond is 95.73.[6] The futures price is:

$$F_{\text{BOND}} = (95.73 - 8[.9615 + .89])(1.06)^2 \qquad (22.18)$$
$$= 90.92$$

Stock Index Futures

In some futures contracts, the deliverable commodity is a common stock index. The S&P Stock Index Futures is an actively traded contract on the Chicago Mercantile Exchange. This contract calls for delivery of the S&P 500 stock index. The dollar amounts involved are the futures quote times \$500. For example, if the futures contract is quoted at 600.00, the dollar amount is (600)(500), or \$300,000. A hedger with a portfolio of stocks worth approximately \$300,000 can short one futures contract and protect the portfolio from price declines.

---

[6] The price is 8(.9615 + .8900 + .7938 + .6830) + 100(.6830).

The stock index futures price depends upon the value of the stocks in the index, the dividends on these stocks, and the interest rate until the delivery date on the futures contract. The following symbols are used:

P = the current market value of the stocks in the index
DV = the dollar amount dividends on these stocks[7]
R_d = the spot interest rate from now until the delivery date
D_d = the present value of a dollar received on the delivery date

Table 22.2 shows how an investor can create the equivalent of a long futures position.

Arbitrage ensures that the futures contract should be the equivalent of buying the stocks in the index, borrowing the funds for this purchase, paying interest on the borrowed funds at the delivery date, and receiving any dividends. Algebraically:

$$F_{STOCK} = P_{STOCK}(1 + R_d)^d - DV \qquad (22.19)$$

Consider the following numerical example. Suppose that the S&P 500 Stock Index is quoted at 600. The one-year interest rate is 10 percent and

Table 22.2   Creating a Stock Index Futures Position

	Points in Time	
	0	Delivery Date
Actions	Cash Flows	
Borrow	$+P_{STOCK}$	
Buy Stocks	$-P_{STOCK}$	
Repay Loan + Interest		$-P_{STOCK}(1 + R_d)^d$
Receive Dividends		$+DV$
Deliver Commodity		
in Futures Market		
Net Cash Flows	0	$-[P_{STOCK}(1 + R_d)^d - DV]$

---

[7] The ensuing discussion requires dividends known with certainty and paid on the delivery date of the futures contract. Since there is some uncertainty about the dividends in practice, the derivation is only approximately correct.

the S&P 500 Stock Index pays a dividend in one year of $50. Then, the S&P Stock Index futures contract for delivery in one year should have a quotation of 610.

$$F_{STOCK} = 600(1.10) - 50 = 610 \qquad (22.20)$$

Unless the futures price is equal to $P_{STOCK}(1 + R_d)^d - DV$, arbitrage occurs.[8] This arbitrage has been called **program trading**. For example, figure 22.7 illustrates the case where the futures price is above $P(1 + R_d)^d$

Figure 22.7   Program Trading Arbitrage

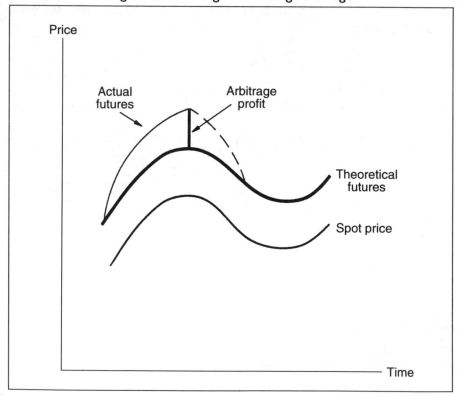

---

[8] The arbitrage is identical to that shown earlier for gold futures contracts.

$- DV.$[9] The arbitrage is to short futures and buy the stocks in the index. The arbitrage position is held until the futures and spot prices are once more in line; then, both positions are simultaneously closed for a profit. This type of arbitrage involves the purchase or sale of large numbers of stocks in the index. A computer program is required to initially uncover the arbitrage opportunity. Then, the buy or sell orders for a large number of stocks must be executed rapidly by computer program before the arbitrage profit opportunity disappears, hence, the name "program trading."

Currency Futures

A number of currency futures contracts are actively traded. These contracts allow businesses to hedge foreign exchange rate risk. In a world of floating exchange rates, foreign currency futures contracts allow businesses to transfer exchange risk and, therefore, encourage international trade.

Consider the contract for deutsche marks traded on the Chicago Mercantile Exchange. This contract calls for delivery of 125,000 marks. Suppose the spot exchange rate is .6250 dollars per mark and futures for delivery in 90 days trade at .6160 dollars per mark. The futures exchange rate is lower than the spot exchange rate. From covered interest arbitrage, we know that:

$$X_{f1} = X_s(1 + R_G)/(1 + R_{US}) \qquad (22.21)$$

where:

X_{f1} = the forward exchange rate ($ per deutsche mark)
X_s = the spot exchange rate ($ per deutsche mark)
R_G = the spot interest rate in Germany
R_{US} = the spot interest rate in the U.S.

From covered interest arbitrage, we know that a forward (futures) exchange rate lower than the spot exchange rate results from a higher interest rate in the U.S. than in Germany.

Foreign exchange futures contracts allow businesses to hedge to protect themselves against changes in the exchange rate. The following example

---

[9] If the futures price is below $P_{STOCK}(1 + R_d)^d - DV$, the arbitrage is to go long futures and shortsell the stocks in the index.

illustrates. Imagine a retail firm in the U.S. planning to purchase 125,000 deutsche marks of merchandise in Germany three months from now. At the current exchange rate of .6250 dollars per deutsche mark, the dollar cost is $78,125. This merchandise can be sold in the U.S. for $83,125. At the current exchange rate, the firm would make a profit of $5,000 on the merchandise.

The management is concerned about the prospect of a rise in the exchange rate to .70 dollars per deutsche mark when the merchandise is purchased in three months. At this exchange rate, the dollar cost of the merchandise is $87,500 and the firm would not make a profit. Suppose the importer goes long one futures contract at .6160 dollars per deutsche mark, locking-in the purchase of 125,000 marks for $77,000. Regardless of the value of the exchange rate in 90 days, the firm is guaranteed a profit.

Hedging with Financial Futures

In a futures hedge, a spot position is (partially) offset with hedging in a futures position. The net position has reduced risk. The futures market allows many types of investors to transfer risks to other investors more willing to bear these risks.

There are many types of hedges. The ensuing discussion concentrates on short hedges, in which a long position in the spot market is offset by a short position in futures. The previous chapter presented profit profile diagrams for short hedges. Short hedges may be used by any investor who has a long position in the spot market. Apart from small investors, many financial institutions might hedge, including underwriters, bond dealers, banks, insurance companies, and pension funds.

Short Hedge for Treasury Bond Futures

Suppose an underwriter has purchased a bond issue with a $100,000 par value for resale to the public. The underwriter purchases the bond expecting to be able to sell it for $100,000. Because the issue must be registered with the SEC, the underwriter anticipates a two-week period of owning the bond before selling it to the public. During this period, interest rates might rise considerably and the value of the underwriter's bond would decline. To protect against this risk, the underwriter shorts one contract of T-bond futures at 96-00.

At the end of the two-week period, interest rates have risen and the underwriter is forced to sell the bonds at $95,000 for a $5,000 loss. During the same period, the futures contract declines in value to 92-00, resulting in a gain of $4,000 on the short futures position. The net loss on the hedge position is $1,000. The underwriter has moderated the downside risk by having a partially offsetting position in futures. Figure 22.8 shows the gains and losses from a short hedge.

The net gain or loss on the hedge is

$$\text{Net Gain(Loss)} = -_0P +_1P +_0F -_1F \qquad (22.22)$$

where:

$-_0P$ = the value of the spot position purchased at time 0.
$+_1P$ = the value of the spot position sold at time 1.
$+_0F$ = the value of the futures position shorted at time 0.
$-_1F$ = the value of the long futures position at time 1.

In the numerical example:

$$\text{Net Gain(Loss)} = -100,000 + 95,000 + 96,000 - 92,000 \qquad (22.23)$$
$$= -1,000$$

Hedging is a two-edged sword. Losses are reduced by hedging, but so are gains. If interest rates drop, the underwriter makes a profit on the bonds, but suffers a loss on the short futures position. The net gain is smaller, or negligible. Hedgers are willing to forego both losses and gains because the hedger is risk averse. For a hedger, the penalties from losses are greater than the advantages of gains. Large losses from a sharp increase in interest rates might bankrupt an underwriter. To avoid this adverse possibility, the hedger is willing to forego large gains.

Figure 22.8   Gains and Losses from Short Hedging

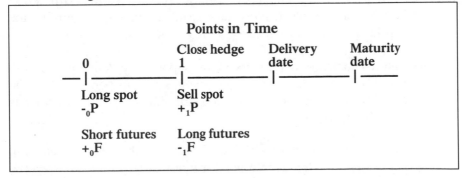

Hedges can be fine-tuned by changing the number of futures contracts in the hedge. In the underwriter hedge, the bond price changes $1.25 for every $1.00 change in the futures price. The hedge can be improved by shorting 1.25 futures contracts for every bond ($100,000 par) purchased.

The difference between the futures price and the spot price (i.e., $F - P$) has been called the basis (B). Note that the net gain (loss) on a hedge equals the change in the basis. That is:

$$\text{Net Gain(Loss)} = {}_{+0}F - {}_0P - [{}_{+1}F - {}_0F] \tag{22.24}$$
$$= {}_{+0}B - {}_1B$$

where:

$${}_0B = \text{the basis at time 0}$$
$${}_1B = \text{the basis at time 1}$$

Hedges are effective if the change in the basis is relatively small. The hedge is perfect if the change in the basis is zero, because then the change in the futures and spot prices exactly offset.

Summary

Financial futures contracts have transformed financial markets. Financial futures contracts allow individuals and businesses to transfer financial risks to other entities more willing and able to bear those risks.

Questions/Problems

1. Suppose that a futures contract is traded for Treasury strips. A two-period strip is deliverable. The delivery date is in one period. Determine the futures price per $100 of par if $R_1 = .04$ and $R_2 = .08$.

2. For a futures contract on Treasury strips, suppose the delivery date is in one period and the deliverable bond matures in two periods. $R_1 = .04$ and $R_2 = .08$. Describe the arbitrage opportunities if the futures price is $96 per $100 of par.

3. For a futures contract on Treasury strips, suppose the delivery date is in two periods and the deliverable bond matures in four periods. $R_1 = .04$,

$R_2 = R_3 = R_4 = .08$. Compute the futures price per $100 of par. Describe the arbitrage opportunities if the futures price is $80.

4. A Treasury bill futures contract requires the short to deliver in 45 days a bill with par of $1,000,000 and 90 days remaining until maturity. Suppose the futures quotation changes from 92.24 to 92.43. What are the gains and losses to the short and long positions? How would your answers change if the futures contract had 90 days until delivery?

5. Assume that the price quotation of the CBOT Treasury bond futures contract changes from 76-14 to 77-09. What are the gains and losses to the short and long as a result of marking-to-market for one contract with $100,000 par value?

6. An individual owns a 21-year maturity bond with an annual coupon of 10 percent, a face value of $100,000, and a price of $95,000. To protect against rising interest rates, this individual shorts one CBOT Treasury bond futures contract with a delivery date two years hence and a futures price of 92-16. In the course of the next year, interest rates change. The bond price drops to $88,000 and the futures price drops to 86-16.
   a. Overlooking bond coupon and marking-to-market, compute the gains or losses on the bond position, the futures position, and the net position.
   b. Suppose we knew the relationship between the futures and spot prices. For every dollar change in the futures, the spot price changed $1.10. Determine the optimal hedge ratio.

7. A bond dealer owns a 21-year maturity bond with an annual coupon of 5 percent, a face value of $100,000, and a price of $95,000. To hedge against rising interest rates, the dealer shorts one CBOT Treasury bond futures contract with a delivery date two years hence and a futures price of 92-16. In the course of the next year, interest rates drop. The futures price goes to 97-16. At what interest rate on the bond would the hedge just break even?

8. The S&P Stock Index is quoted at 650.00. The index pays a cash dividend of $18. The interest rate is 6 percent. S&P Stock Index Futures for delivery in one year are quoted at 668.00. Are these prices consistent with equilibrium? If not, what is the arbitrage opportunity?

9. Toy World is considering purchase of plastic building blocks from Germany for the Christmas season. It is now August 1 and Toy World would

like to purchase and receive the blocks on November 1. The order is for 12,500,000 marks. Currently, the spot exchange rate is .70 dollars per mark. The forward exchange rate for delivery on November 1 is .71 dollars per mark. The management feels that the exchange rate on November 1 will be one of three values with equal probabilities of .75, .70, and .65. The blocks can be sold in the U.S. for $9,500,000. Is it better to hedge with foreign exchange futures or wait until November and purchase at the spot exchange rate on that date? Explain. At what forward exchange rate would the firm just break even?

Appendix A: Forward Rates on a Discount Basis

The relationship between forward and spot interest rates on a discount basis differs slightly from the treatment in chapter 9 on spot and forward rates. Assume $1 par values. Let d_1 be the discount rate for a Treasury bill with a maturity of t_1 days and d_2 be the discount rate for a Treasury bill that matures on t_2 days, where $t_2 > t_1$. Let f be the forward discount rate from day t_1 to day t_2 (see figure 22A.1).

The present value of a dollar discounted at the rate d_2 for t_2 days must be the same as the present value of that dollar discounted at the rate f from t_2 to t_1 and at the rate d_1 from t_1 to the present. In equation form:

$$1 - \frac{d_2 t_2}{360} = \left[1 - \frac{f(t_2 - t_1)}{360} \right]\left[1 - \frac{d_1 t_1}{360} \right] \tag{22A.1}$$

Verbally, this represents:

$$\begin{pmatrix} \text{spot price of} \\ \$1 \text{ received} \\ \text{at time } t_2 \end{pmatrix} = \begin{pmatrix} \text{forward price} \\ \text{or value at } t_1 \\ \text{of } \$1 \text{ received} \\ \text{at time } t_2 \end{pmatrix} \times \begin{pmatrix} \text{spot price of} \\ \$1 \text{ received} \\ \text{at time } t_1 \end{pmatrix}$$

Figure 22A.1   Discount Rates

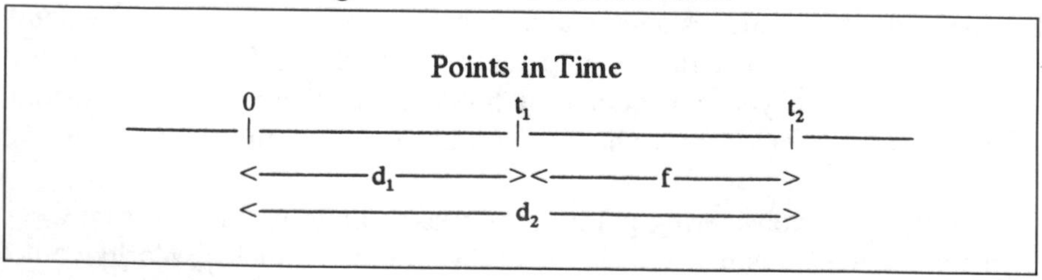

Thus, the present value of $1 received at time t_2 is the same if discounted at the rate d_2 for t_2 days or if discounted at the forward rate for $t_2 - t_1$ days and then discounted at the rate d_1 for t_1 days.

Solving for f results in:

$$f = \frac{\dfrac{d_2 t_2 - d_1 t_1}{t_2 - t_1}}{1 - \dfrac{d_1 t_1}{360}} \tag{22A.2}$$

In the special case where t_2 is twice t_1, this formula simplifies to:

$$f = \frac{2d_2 - d_1}{1 - \dfrac{d_1 t_1}{360}} \tag{22A.3}$$

As an example, assume that the discount rate on a 90-day (t_1) Treasury bill is 8 percent, while a 180-day (t_2) Treasury bill has a discount rate of 10 percent. Then the forward rate (f) from day 90 to day 180 is computed as follows:

$$f = \frac{\dfrac{(.10)(180) - (.08)(90)}{180 - 90}}{1 - \dfrac{(.08)(90)}{360}} = .1224 \tag{22A.4}$$

Thus, the forward rate on a discount basis is 12.24 percent when rounded to the nearest basis point.

Appendix B: Cheapest Deliverable Bond on CBOT Treasury Bond Futures

The investor who is short CBOT Treasury bond futures contracts is allowed to deliver any U.S. Treasury bond with $100,000 par value. A delivered bond must also have at least 15 years to the smaller of maturity or first call date.

Corners

The purpose of having many bonds deliverable is to reduce the likelihood of a corner by increasing the total supply of deliverable securities.[10] A **corner** occurs if one investor is able to purchase most of the deliverable supply of a commodity in the spot market and at the same time have large long positions in the futures markets. At the delivery date, the shorts are required to cover their positions either by purchasing the commodity in the spot market or by offsetting their futures market positions.[11] In either case, the shorts are at the mercy of the cornering investor, who is able to charge them a very high price to extricate themselves. Corners are illegal, and both the regulatory authorities (Commodity Futures Trading Commission) and the exchanges have the obligation and the power to break up corners.[12]

In 1979–80, the Hunt brothers attempted to corner the silver futures market. The first step in this corner was acquiring large amounts of silver in the spot market at low prices. The second step was taking very large long positions in the futures market at rising prices. During a relatively short period, the spot and futures prices more than quintupled, resulting in enormous paper profits. At this point, the exchanges stepped in and increased margin requirements on futures positions. A sharp decline in both spot and futures prices followed, as the alleged cornering group was forced to liquidate some of their positions to meet margin requirements. The corner was foiled.

Invoice Price

The long pays the short the invoice price for delivering a particular bond. The **invoice price** is equal to the settlement futures price times an **adjustment**

---

[10] Several authors suggest that having many deliverable varieties will result in a lower futures price than if the cheapest to deliver were the only deliverable variety. See Garbade and Silber (1983) and Gay and Manaster (1984). Livingston argues that in perfect markets the futures price will equal the price of the cheapest to deliver. See Livingston (1987a).

[11] To offset, the shorts would have to go long in futures.

[12] There are several things that an exchange can do to break a corner by the longs. First, the exchange can raise margin requirements. Second, the exchange can declare that there be trading for liquidation only. Then the longs cannot add to their positions and can only close out their positions with the shorts. Thirdly, the exchange can determine a price and close out all positions at this price.

factor. In trying to figure the best bond to deliver, the short has to do the following calculation for every bond:[13]

$$\text{Proceeds} = (F)(\text{adj}) - P \qquad\qquad (22\text{B}.1)$$

where F is the settlement futures price, adj is the adjustment factor, and P is the market price of the bond. The best or **cheapest bond to deliver** from the short's viewpoint is the bond for which the proceeds in the preceding expression are the largest. In general, the proceeds are negative for all bonds. If the proceeds are positive, there are arbitrage profits from shorting futures and delivering the bond with positive proceeds. In equilibrium, all arbitrage opportunities should be eliminated, resulting in the net proceeds being zero or negative. The short tries to find the bond for which the proceeds are closest to zero; this minimizes the cost to deliver.

On the delivery date, the cheapest bond to deliver is the bond for which the proceeds are zero in frictionless markets. Setting proceeds equal to zero in the preceding expression and solving for the futures price implies that:

$$F = P_k / \text{adj}_k \qquad\qquad (22\text{B}.2)$$

where P_k and adj_k are for the cheapest bond to deliver.

In practice, longer maturity bonds and/or low coupon bonds have been relatively cheap to deliver in the Treasury bond futures contract.[14] The price of these cheap-to-deliver bonds has set the price of the futures contract. Typically, there are several bonds that are relatively cheap to deliver. This makes corners very difficult.

The Adjustment Factor

To establish a relative value in delivery, the Chicago Board of Trade uses an adjustment factor (adj) for each security. The adjustment factor is computed from the following formula:

---

[13] This overlooks accrued interest. The long must pay the short the invoice price plus accrued interest. The short delivers a bond which entitles him to the accrued interest. Technically, the accrued interest should be added to the invoice price and added to the bond price. But, these two terms cancel.

[14] See Kilcollin (1982) and Livingston (1984 and 1987b).

$$\text{adj} = \frac{c/\text{PAR}}{(1.08)} = \frac{c/\text{PAR}}{(1.08)^2} + \ldots + \frac{c/\text{PAR} + 1.0}{(1.08)^n} \qquad (22\text{B}.3)$$

$$\text{adj} = \left(\frac{c}{\text{PAR}}\right)\left(\begin{array}{c}\text{Present value of} \\ \text{an annuity at } 8\% \\ \text{for } n \text{ periods}\end{array}\right) + \frac{1}{(1.08)^n}$$

To compute the adjustment factor, the coupon rate (i.e., coupon divided by par) and an assumed par value of 1.0 are discounted at an 8 percent discount rate.[15] The value of the adjustment factor adj depends upon the coupon rate. If the annual coupon rate is 8 percent of par, adj equals 1.0. If the annual coupon rate is greater (less) than 8 percent, adj is greater (less) than 1.0. Table 22B.1 illustrates the computation of the adjustment factor for 20-year bonds with coupon rates of 6 percent, 8 percent, and 10 percent and par values of $100. Note that the present value of a 20-period annuity at 8 percent is 9.818 and $1/(1.08)^{20}$ equals .215.

The short has the choice of bond to deliver. The adjustment factor attempts to adjust the invoice price for the relative worth of the bonds. Recall that the invoice price is the futures price times the adjustment factor. Consider the three preceding bonds. The 6 percent coupon bond has the lowest price. The amount that the short gets paid for delivering this bond (i.e., the invoice price) should reflect this lower value. If the highest coupon bond (10 percent) is delivered, the short should receive more money because this high coupon bond has a higher value. The invoice prices for the three bonds are computed in table 22B.2, assuming that the settlement futures price is $100.

Table 22B.1   The Adjustment Factor

Coupon	Price	Computation of Adjustment Factor			
6%	$80.41	(.06)(9.818)	+	.215	= .80408
8%	$100.00	(.08)(9.818)	+	.215	= 1.00
10%	$119.68	(.10)(9.818)	+	.215	= 1.1968

---

[15] In practice, n represents the number of quarters, rounded down to the nearest quarter from the futures delivery date, until the shorter of the bond's maturity or first call date. In addition, in practice the adjustment factor is computed using semiannual coupons discounted at 4 percent semiannually. We overlook these technicalities.

Table 22B.2　Invoice Price versus Market Price

Coupon	Invoice Price = (Futures Price)(Adjustment Factor)		Market Price
6%	(100)(.80408)	= 80.41	$80.41
8%	(100)(1.0)	= 100.00	$100.00
10%	(100)(1.1968)	= 119.68	$119.68

The preceding discussion can be clarified by the following example. From this table, the invoice prices equal the bonds' market prices. This shows the objective of the adjustment procedure – to adjust the invoice price for the relative value of the bond delivered. In this particular example, the invoice price equals the market price for every bond. In general, this is not true. Typically, bonds have invoice prices below their market prices. The shorts search for the best bond to deliver, the so-called cheapest to deliver. The cheapest bond to deliver has an invoice price very close to the market price of the bond. Frequently, the difference between the invoice price and the market is close to zero for many bonds. Then the deliverable supply of bonds is large and corners are hard to achieve.

Assume the bonds in table 22B.3 can be delivered by an investor who is short in Treasury bond futures. In perfect markets, the cheapest bond to deliver has the smallest ratio of bond price to adjustment factor. The computations in table 22B.4 use annual coupons discounted at 8 percent annually to compute the adjustment factors.

The lowest ratio of price/adjustment factor is for bond 4. The equilibrium futures price equals this ratio of 90.474566. Let's compute the invoice price and look at the proceeds from delivering each bond in table 22B.5. The invoice price for each bond equals the equilibrium futures price (90.474566) times the adjustment factor for each bond. For example, for bond 1 the invoice price is (90.474566)(.82881).

Table 22B.3　Example of Five Deliverable Bonds

Bond	Maturity (years)	Coupon (Annual)	Market Price
1	15	$6	$90.50
2	18	$7	$92.25
3	21	$8	$96.375
4	24	$9	$100.00
5	30	$8.50	$101.00

Table 22B.4   Computing Adjustment Factor

Bond	Adjustment Factor	Price/Adjustment	
1	.82881	109.19269	
2	.906283	101.78939	
3	1.00000	96.375	
4	1.105283	90.474566	←cheapest equilibrium price
5	1.05593	95.6503	

Table 22B.5   Net Proceeds

Bond	Invoice Price	Market Price	Proceeds from Delivery
1	$74.986025	$90.50	−$15.51
2	$81.995561	$92.25	−$10.25
3	$90.474566	$96.375	−$5.90
4	$100.00	$100.00	$0.0
5	$95.5348	$101.00	−$5.47

For the cheapest bond to deliver, bond 4, the invoice price exactly equals the market price of the bond. Therefore, the proceeds from delivering that bond are zero. Every other bond has a lower invoice price than market price. For these bonds, the proceeds from delivering the bond are negative, implying that these bonds are inferior to deliver.

Cash Settlement

Both Treasury bill futures and Treasury bond futures require delivery of securities on the delivery date, if both the short and long have not offset their positions. Most of the time positions are offset, and deliveries are not very common.

There is great concern in the futures markets about possible corners and their adverse consequences. Many contracts, such as CBOT Treasury bond futures, allow the delivery of different varieties of a particular commodity. As the previous discussion of Treasury bond futures indicates, having multiple deliverable varieties adds many complications to the futures contract.

An alternative approach is to allow cash settlement of a contract. This approach is now used with stock index futures, which are tied to an index of securities. On the delivery date, the settlement price is determined and all positions are marked-to-market. For settlement, the long position pays the short the invoice price, which is set equal to the settlement price. For cash settlement, the short delivers cash equal to the value of the index. After marking-to-market, the net cash flow is zero.

Arbitrage forces the settlement price to be equal to the value of the stock index at the time of settlement. This means that the invoice price (which the long pays to the short) is equal to the cash value delivered by the short to the long. In effect, the two cash payments exactly cancel. Settling the contract simplifies to marking-to-market.

For futures contracts for which physical or financial commodities have to be delivered, the delivery process is expensive. If the short delivers, the deliverable item is purchased and transactions costs are paid. It is usually cheaper to offset a short position by going long; for most futures contracts, deliveries are not common. For contracts with cash settlement, there are no costs for delivering, since delivery amounts to marking-to-market. Consequently, deliveries are quite common.

Cash settlement may possibly result in increased price swings in stock index futures. Arbitragers watch the futures quotation and the value of the underlying securities in the stock index. If there is a disparity, an arbitrager can profit by going long in the underpriced position and short in the overpriced position. In order to realize the arbitrage profit, the arbitrager must liquidate both positions simultaneously just before trading on the contract ends.[16] Liquidation of spot market positions can significantly alter spot prices if most arbitragers are taking the same action. For example, if futures contracts were above their equilibrium price in the last month of the futures contract, arbitragers would be short in futures and long in the stocks in the index. In closing all positions just before trading ends, the arbitragers would be selling stocks heavily, possibly causing considerable declines in stock prices.

With physical delivery of a commodity (as opposed to cash settlement), arbitragers would not have to close out all positions. An arbitrager could take delivery or make delivery and still realize an arbitrage profit. Consequently, cash settlement has a tendency to make wide price swings more likely.

Other Aspects of the Delivery Process

The delivery process for CBOT Treasury bond futures has some other interesting complications. As with most futures contracts, there is a delivery

---

[16] An arbitrage profit can also be realized before the end of trading, if the futures and spot markets converge.

month.[17] The short position has the option to deliver at any point during the month.

In the beginning of the month, the settlement price for that day is used for deliveries initiated on that day. On the seventh business day before the end of a delivery month, the settlement futures price is determined and this price is used for computing the invoice price for deliveries made in the rest of this delivery month. The fixing of the futures price gives the short an option to choose the day for delivery. This delivery option may turn out to be quite valuable. If the futures price is fixed at 90 seven days before the end of the month and spot prices subsequently decline, the short may be able to buy a deliverable bond for much less than its invoice price and deliver it for a profit. If bond prices subsequently rise during the last seven business days, the short would have to buy a bond at a high price and suffer a loss at delivery.

During most of the delivery month, the settlement futures price is set every day at 3 P.M. central time. The short has the option to deliver until 8 P.M. If the short chooses not to deliver, the same position is simply maintained until the next day, when the same choice is made. The option to initiate delivery between 3 P.M. and 8 P.M. has value to the short, since the trading of bonds continues after the futures markets close.[18] This option is called the **wildcard option**. If bond prices go down after 3 P.M. and the adjustment factor on the cheapest deliverable bond is greater than 1.0, the short's option has positive value, and delivery may be desirable. It has been suggested that this wildcard option tends to push the 3 P.M. futures price below the price that would prevail without the wildcard option.

References

Arak, M. and L. S. Goodman, ''Treasury Bond Futures: Valuing the Delivery Options,'' *Journal of Futures Markets,* 7, June 1987, pp. 269–86.

Barnhill, T. M., ''Quality Option Profits, Switching Option Profits, and Variation Margin Costs: An Evaluation of Their Size and Impact on

---

[17] Treasury bill futures have a single delivery date.

[18] The actual delivery process covers three business days. On day 1, the short position gives notice that delivery is being initiated. Actual delivery of the commodity and payment of the invoice price occurs on day 3.

Treasury Bond Futures," *Journal of Financial and Quantitative Analysis,* 25, 1990, pp. 65–86.

Boyle, P. P., "The Quality Option and Timing Option in Futures Contracts," *Journal of Finance,* 44, 1989, pp. 101–14.

Capozza, D. R. and B. Cornell, "Treasury Bill Pricing in the Spot and Futures Markets," *Review of Economics and Statistics,* 61, November 1979, pp. 513–20.

Chicago Board of Trade, *Delivery Manual,* Chicago: CBOT, 1980.

Ederington, L. H., "The Hedging Performance of the New Futures Markets," *Journal of Finance,* 34, March 1979, pp. 157–70.

Garbade, K. D. and D. L. Silber, "Futures Contracts on Commodities with Multiple Varieties: An Analysis of Premiums and Discounts," *Journal of Business,* 56, 1983, pp. 249–72.

Gay, G. D. and S. Manaster, "The Quality Option Implicit in Futures Contract," *Journal of Financial Economics,* 13, September 1984, pp. 353–70.

Hegde, S. P., "Coupon and Maturity Characteristics of the Cheapest-to-Deliver Bonds on the Treasury Bond Futures Contract," *Financial Analysts Journal,* 43, 1987, pp. 70–76.

Hegde, S. P., "On the Value of Implicit Delivery Options," *Journal of Futures Markets,* 9, 1989, pp. 421–38.

Hemler, M. L., "The Quality Option in Treasury Bond Futures Contracts," *Journal of Finance,* 45, 1990, pp. 1565–86.

Kilcollin, T. E., "Difference Systems in Financial Futures," *Journal of Finance,* 37, December 1982, pp. 1183–97.

Klemkosky, R. C. and D. J. Lasser, "An Efficiency Analysis of the T-Bond Futures Market," *Journal of Futures Markets,* 5, Winter 1985, pp. 607–20.

Labarge, K. P., "Daily Trading Estimates for Treasury Bond Futures Contract Prices," *Journal of Futures Markets,* 8, 1988, pp. 533–62.

Livingston, M., "The Cheapest Deliverable Bond for the CBT Treasury Bond Futures Contract," *Journal of Futures Markets,* 4, Summer 1984, pp. 161–72.

Livingston, M., "The Delivery Option on Forward Contracts," *Journal of Financial and Quantitative Analysis,* 22, March 1987a, pp. 79–87.

Livingston, M., "Treasury Bond Futures and Bond Coupon Level," *Journal of Futures Markets,* 7, Summer 1987b, pp. 303–9.

Livingston, M., "The Term Structure of Interest Rates and the Basis for Financial Futures," 6 (1993), pp. 117–135, *Advances in Futures and Options Research.*

Margrabe, W., "The Value of an Option to Exchange One Asset for Another," *Journal of Finance,* 33, March 1978, pp. 177–86.

Rendleman, R. J. and C. E. Carabini, "The Efficiency of the Treasury Bill Futures Market," *Journal of Finance,* 34, September 1979, pp. 895–914.

23

Financial Engineering: Specialized Financial Instruments

Overview

The term **financial engineering** refers to the creation of new financial instruments. In a sense, most of this book has been about financial engineering. We have analyzed short-term bonds, long-term bonds, futures, options, callable bonds, puttable bonds, mortgages and mortgage derivatives, and many other types of securities.

While many new types of securities have been introduced, only a portion have lasted. Lasting security types provide some significant and fundamental value to a sizable group of issuers or investors. The advantages of new instruments include one or more of the following.[1] First, innovations may reduce transactions costs. Second, innovations may allow investors to create a new type of security which divides the cash flows from one investment into a set of derivative securities. The resulting derivatives may appeal to a new group of investors. The total value of the derivatives may be greater than the value of the underlying components. An example is the decomposition of Treasury bonds into Treasury STRIPS. Third, new instruments (e.g., options) may allow the transfer or limiting of risks. Fourth, some products (e.g., futures contracts) allow investors to diversify more efficiently. Fifth, some

---

[1] See Finnerty (1988) and Van Horne (1985).

new financial instruments are responses to changes in tax laws and regulations.

This chapter briefly describes some of the more common types of specialized financial instruments including floating-rate notes, interest rate swaps, convertible bonds, and preferred stock. Index-linked bonds are also discussed. An index-linked bond has the coupon and principal payments tied to the realized inflation rate, thereby protecting the buyer from inflation. Although not issued in the U.S., index-linked bonds are widely discussed.

Floating-Rate Notes

A floating-rate note is a bond with a variable interest rate.[2] The coupon on the floating-rate note is tied to a particular short-term interest rate. Periodically, perhaps every six months, the coupon on the bond is reset to equal the short-term rate plus X percent.

As an example, suppose the bond's coupon is tied to the six-month Treasury bill rate plus 3 percent. When the bond is issued, the Treasury bill rate is 6 percent and the bond pays a coupon of 9 percent. Six months later, the Treasury bill rate is 4.5 percent; the bond's coupon is reset to 7.5 percent.

A floating-rate note is a long-term bond with a short-term interest rate. A floating-rate note is a substitute for repeated short-term loans. To the issuing firm, the advantage of a floating-rate note is avoidance of the transactions costs of repeatedly rolling over the short-term loan. To the bond buyer, the floating-rate note has low price risk. Since the coupon is reset periodically (for example, every six months) to bring the bond price close to par, the bond price is unlikely to depart markedly from par during the time between the reset dates.

The default premium for a long-term floating-rate loan differs from the default premium for a sequence of short-term loans. With repeated short-term loans, the default risk premium in the new loans is renegotiated at each rollover. If the firm becomes riskier, the default risk component of the interest rate rises. With a floating-rate instrument, the default risk premium is set initially and not changed. Thus, a floating-rate bond combines the default premium of a long-term bond with the sensitivity of a short-term bond to

---

[2] Chapter 15 on mortgages discusses adjustable rate mortgages, which are a variety of floating-rate debt.

changes in the default-free interest rate. At the issue date, rational lenders incorporate all available information concerning possible future changes in the issuer's default risk. These anticipations become part of the permanent default risk premium.

The periodic resetting of the bond's coupon brings the bond price to par if the default risk of the firm remains unchanged. If the market perceives new information about default risk, the bond price does not adjust to par. For example, consider again the floating-rate bond where the coupon equals the six-month Treasury bill rate plus a 3 percent default premium. If the default risk of the firm increases so that a new short-term note would have a 5 percent default premium, resetting of the floating rate's coupon does not bring the market price to par but instead somewhat below par to reflect the higher default premium. As you might expect, this discount increases as the bond's maturity gets longer.

Another way to engineer bond cash flows is through the use of reset notes, which are a special variety of variable-rate notes. With reset notes, the coupon is reset periodically (perhaps every two years) by an investment banker to bring the market price to par. Thus, if the default risk increases, the reset coupon reflects the higher default risk. After resetting, the bond sells at par. With a standard floating-rate note, the default premium is fixed; after resetting to reflect changes in the default-free interest rate, the bond price can deviate from par.

Interest-Rate Swaps

An interest-rate swap is an agreement to exchange the cash flows from debt obligations with different maturities.[3] In a typical interest-rate swap, one firm borrows long term. The second firm borrows at a floating (variable) rate. Then the two firms agree to swap the interest payments. This is a fixed/floating rate or **plain vanilla swap**. The interest payments are swapped but the principal payments are not. Thus, if one party defaults, the default involves the interest payments only. This reduces the risks to all parties.

In general, a commercial bank or an investment bank serves as an interest-rate swap dealer, as shown in figure 23.1. The term **counterparty**

---

[3] See Arak et al. (1988), Bicksler and Chen (1986), Brown and Smith (1990), Felgran (1987), Goodman (1990), Marshall and Kapner (1990), Turnbull (1987), and Wall and Pringle (1988).

Figure 23.1   Interest-Rate Swap

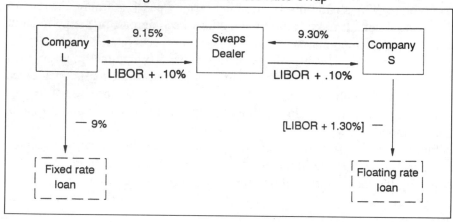

is used to describe the participants. Typically, the fixed-rate borrower swaps with a dealer as counterparty. In turn, the dealer swaps with the floating-rate borrower as counterparty. The dealer makes a commission for carrying out both ends of the swap.

Floating-rate loans are tied to a widely used interest rate index, for example, the London Interbank Offer Rate (LIBOR). LIBOR is the rate at which Eurocurrency deposits are exchanged between banks. The floating rate might be expressed as LIBOR plus .50 percent.

A simple (or plain vanilla) interest-rate swap is shown in figure 23.1. Assume that firms L and S can borrow on the terms shown in table 23.1. Firm L has a 2 percent advantage borrowing fixed rate and a 1 percent advantage borrowing floating rate. Suppose firm L borrows long term at the fixed rate of 9 percent and swaps with the swaps dealer. The swaps dealer pays firm L 9.15 percent and firm L pays the swaps dealer LIBOR plus .10 percent. The total interest payments paid and received by firm L are shown in table 23.2. As a result of the swap, firm L has a net position of a floating-rate loan at LIBOR minus .05 percent. Firm L saves .35 percent compared to borrowing directly at the floating rate of LIBOR + .30 percent.

In figure 23.1, firm S borrows floating rate at LIBOR plus 1.30 percent. Firm S swaps with the swaps dealer agreeing to pay 9.30 percent fixed rate

Table 23.1   Fixed and Floating Rates for Firms L and S

	Firm L	Firm S
Fixed Rate	9%	11%
Floating Rate	LIBOR + .30%	LIBOR + 1.30%

Table 23.2   Interest Paid and Received by Firm L in the Swap

Pays Interest on Long-Term Fixed-Rate Bond	−9%
Receives Fixed Rate from Swaps Dealer	9.15%
Pays Floating Rate to Swaps Dealer	−[LIBOR + .10%]
Net	−[LIBOR − .05]

and receive from the dealer LIBOR + .10 percent. The cash flows are shown in table 23.3. The swap results in a net fixed-rate loan for firm S at the interest rate of 10.50 percent, a saving of .50 percent compared to a direct fixed-rate interest rate of 11 percent.

The Swaps Dealer

The swaps dealer benefits by a commission of .15 percent. The commission compensates the dealer for the costs of matching the parties in the swap. In addition, the commission compensates the dealer for the risk of default by the counterparties. If there is a default, the dealer replaces the defaulting party with a new counterparty.[4]

The dealer's risk of default depends upon which counterparty defaults and the course of interest rates since the swap was originated. Suppose firm L defaults. Firm L is supposed to pay the dealer LIBOR + .10 percent (floating rate) and the dealer pays firm L 9.15 percent (fixed rate). If interest rates have not changed since the swap was originated, firm L is simply replaced by another firm; the dealer is unaffected except for transactions costs. If interest rates have gone down since the swap was issued, the dealer

Table 23.3   Interest Paid and Received by Firm S in the Swap

Pays Interest on Short-Term Floating-Rate Loan	−[LIBOR + 1.30%]
Pays Fixed Rate to the Swaps Dealer	−9.30%
Receives Floating Rate from the Swaps Dealer	+LIBOR + .10
Net	−10.50%

---

[4] The dealer can also sue the defaulting party and may recover part of any loss incurred.

gains since the dealer can pay less than 9.15 percent to the new counterparty.[5] If interest rates have risen, the dealer loses. For example, the new counterparty may be paid 9.50 percent by the dealer. The dealer loses .35 percent, the difference between 9.50 percent and 9.15 percent.

Suppose firm S defaults. The dealer is supposed to pay firm S LIBOR + .10 percent (floating rate) and receive 9.30 percent (fixed rate). If interest rates rise, firm S is replaced with a new counterparty paying more than 9.30 percent to the dealer; the dealer gains. If interest rates decline, a new counterparty paying less than 9.30 percent is found and the dealer loses.

Many swaps dealers are commercial banks. Bank regulators are concerned about the potential impact upon the entire bank's financial condition if widespread defaults occur in the swaps portfolio of a commercial bank. The swaps dealer loses if interest rates rise and companies such as L (which pay the dealer floating rate) default or if interest rates fall and companies such as S (which pay the dealer fixed rate) default. The dealer can reduce the risk by diversifying the swaps portfolio across many unrelated counterparties.

Reasons for Interest-Rate Swaps

The market for interest-rate swaps is huge. Over one trillion dollars of par value of bonds have been swapped in the U.S. alone. Several explanations are offered for the growing popularity of swaps.

Swaps are claimed to have a comparative advantage. Referring to the example in figure 23.1 and table 23.1, firm L has an absolute advantage in both long-term fixed-rate debt and in floating-rate debt. By borrowing fixed rate where firm L enjoys a comparative advantage, and by swapping, both firms enjoy lower borrowing costs.

Market imperfections are a possible cause of comparative advantage, allowing firm L to borrow at a favorable fixed rate. Although firm L really wants to borrow short term, it can reduce its costs by borrowing fixed rate and swapping. While the market imperfections-comparative advantage argument can explain some individual swaps, imperfections widespread enough to generate over one trillion dollars of swaps seem doubtful.

Low transactions costs of swaps may induce firms to swap rather than refinance their existing debt. Suppose a firm has an existing debt issue. Because of changed circumstances, the firm wants to retire this issue and

---

[5] Default by firm L is unlikely after a drop in interest rates.

replace it with a different issue. This procedure involves considerable transactions costs. A cheaper alternative is to swap the existing debt for a desired debt position. If the commission paid to the swap dealer is sufficiently small, swapping is cheaper.

Complicated swaps contracts allow some firms to significantly alter their capital structures. For example, many callable bonds have a period of call deferment. If interest rates fall during this call deferment period, the firm is unable to call the bond and realize refunding benefits. The firm can make a tender offer for the bonds. Tender offers have two drawbacks – the refunding benefits must be shared with the bondholders and transactions costs are incurred. A lower cost alternative may be to engage in a forward swap.[6] With a forward swap, the swapping of cash flows does not begin until some future date.

Convertible Bonds

A sizable number of corporate bonds are convertible into common stock at the option of the bondholder.[7] The bond indenture explains the conversion terms. In addition, the bonds are usually callable at par plus a call premium. A convertible bond is in-the-money if the stock value of the bond exceeds the call price. It is out-of-the-money if the stock value is less than the call price. The call feature is included to allow the firm to force conversion into common stock. Forced conversion works in the following way. Suppose a convertible bond has a call price of $110 for a $100 par value. If the value of the bond as stock is $150, calling in the bond at $110 gives the convertible bondholders the choice of $110 in cash or common stock which can be immediately sold for $150. Rational bondholders prefer to convert.

Conversion can be forced only if the bond is in-the-money. Call of an out-of-the-money convertible induces the bondholders to turn in their bonds at the call price. Sometimes voluntary conversion occurs if the convertible is in-the-money and the dividend yield on the stock exceeds the current yield on the convertible.

---

[6] See Brown and Smith (1990) and Goodman (1990).

[7] See Asquith and Mullins (1991), Brennan and Schwartz (1977, 1988), Campbell, Ederington, and Vankudre (1991), Dann and Mikkelson (1984), Green (1984), Harris and Raviv (1985), Jaffee and Shleifer (1990), Ofer and Natarajan (1987), and Singh, Nayar, and Cowan (1991).

Figure 23.2 shows the relationship between the stock value, the straight bond value, and the price of the convertible.[8] The stock value is initially below the par value and the stock value is assumed to grow over time. The straight bond value gradually approaches the par value as the bond gets closer to maturity. The call price declines over time to the par value. As the stock value rises above the call price, the premium of the convertible over the bond value declines and the market price of the convertible approaches the stock value.

The market price of the convertible must be higher than the higher of the straight bond value or the stock value. Otherwise, arbitrage occurs. For example, suppose the stock value is $115 and the present value of the coupons and par is $100. The convertible must sell for at least $115. If it sold for $110, an arbitrager could buy the convertible for $110, convert it, and sell the common stock for $115 – a risk-free profit of $5.

Figure 23.2   Convertible Bonds

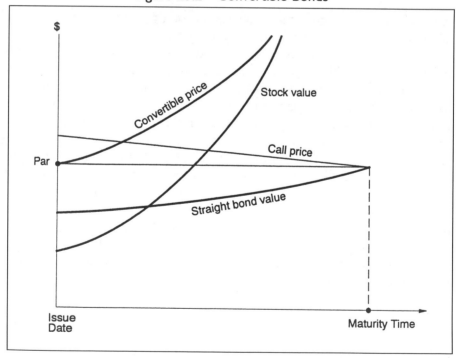

---

[8] See Brigham (1966).

Why Issue Convertibles?

In an efficient market, securities are fairly priced. At the margin, there is no advantage or disadvantage to issuing a convertible. Consequently, one argument for convertibles is that they have no disadvantage. Why not issue them?

Other arguments concerning convertibles focus on asymmetric information. The managers of the firm may have superior information compared to outside investors and find some advantage from convertibles. One possibility is that negative private information is available to the management. By issuing convertibles, the firm is able to sell common stock at an inflated price.

Another possible asymmetric information argument is that positive private information is available to the management.[9] Suppose the managers are aware of a great new product for which the firm has a competitive advantage. The new product will increase sales and earnings in the future; the firm will have a high growth rate. Since the security markets are unaware of these favorable prospects, the current stock price does not reflect the true value of the stock. Selling stock at the current price is unwise.

Since the typical convertible is issued when the stock value is substantially less than par, issuing a convertible allows the firm to effectively sell stock at a higher price. For example, suppose the value of the convertible as stock is only 60 percent of par when the bond is issued at par. With the growth opportunities incorporated, the value is actually double, 120 percent of par. Issuing the convertible allows the firm to effectively sell stock at a price above the current market value.

When convertible bonds are issued, the stock price tends to decline somewhat. This evidence is consistent with the view that issuing convertibles is a negative signal to the market. This evidence supports the position that convertibles are issued when the management has negative information.

A substantial literature examines the best time to call a convertible. In perfectly efficient markets, the convertible can be called as soon as the stock value reaches the call price. In practice, most convertibles are called long after this point. Several explanations have been offered. First, there may be no real disadvantage of leaving the convertible outstanding. In addition, the

---

[9] The arguments of positive and negative private information are contradictory. They could logically apply for different firms issuing convertibles, but not for the same firm.

firm has the advantage of the tax deductibility of the interest on the convertible. Second, the call of a convertible bond may force down the stock value below the call price. Then, bondholders will not convert but will instead redeem their bonds for the call price. To avoid this possibility, firms may wait until the stock value is well above the call price. When an issue of convertibles is called, the call is often backed by an underwriter who guarantees conversion to common stock.

Bonds with Detachable Warrants

Some bond issues include a straight bond with a detachable long-term call option, or warrant. When a warrant is exercised, the exercise price must be paid. For some warrants, exercise requires payment of the exercise price in cash. Many warrants allow the bond from which they were detached to be presented in lieu of a cash exercise price. If the warrant can be exercised by presenting the bond, the package of a bond with a detachable warrant is virtually the same as a convertible bond.

LYONs

A LYON (which stands for a Liquid Yield Option Note) is a corporate zero coupon, convertible, callable, and puttable bond. Since a LYON is a zero coupon bond, the interest accrues. Consequently, the call price and the put price must increase over time as the interest accrues. Each issue of a LYON has a schedule of call prices and a schedule of put prices. Since the LYON is a zero coupon bond, the minimum share price for which holders would convert to stock changes over time. LYONs appeal to a subset of investors who would like to have an option to convert to common stock if the common does well, who want to own a zero coupon bond without reinvestment risk, and who favor a put option as protection against a deterioration of the issuer's credit standing.

Preferred Stock

Preferred stock is a hybrid – somewhere between a bond and a stock. Preferred stock pays dividends instead of interest. The amount of the dividend is specified. If the dividend is not paid, the firm is not in default. The dividend is "in arrears," that is, owed with cumulative interest.[10] The firm cannot pay common stock dividends until all preferred dividends and arrearages are paid. If the dividend is not paid, the preferred stockholders may get voting rights for the board of directors.

In the event of a bankruptcy, preferred stockholders have a prior claim on the firm's assets ahead of common stockholders. The order of priorities is bondholders first, then preferred stockholders. Common stockholders have a residual claim on the firm's assets.

Preferred dividends are not tax deductible for corporate income tax purposes. In contrast, interest on bonds is deductible for corporate income tax purposes. Because of this difference in tax deductibility, preferred stock occurs largely in regulated industries, such as electrical utilities. Apparently, regulated firms are able to pass on the higher after-tax cost of preferred stock to their customers.

Convertible preferred stock is preferred stock that is convertible into common stock. Convertible preferred is very similar to convertible debt, except that preferred stock pays dividends and bonds pay interest.

Index-Linked Bonds

Index-linked bonds are inflation protected bonds. The coupons and par value are adjusted to reflect actual inflation experience.[11]

As an example, suppose the U.S. government issues a one-year bond with an annual coupon and par value increased by the realized inflation rate. If the real interest rate at the time of issue is 5 percent, the index-linked bond has a coupon rate of 5 percent. Suppose par and the issue price are $100, implying a coupon of $5. If the actual inflation rate is 10 percent over the bond's one-year life, the inflation-adjusted coupon is $5.50, that is, $100(.05)(1.10). The inflation-adjusted par value is $110, that is, $100(1.10). In real terms, the bond buyer receives a return of 5 percent.

In the case of a multi-period bond, the coupons and the par value are adjusted by the cumulative amount of inflation between the issue date of the bond and the payment date. If the actual inflation rates are i_1 for period

---

[10] The typical preferred is cumulative. Some preferred is noncumulative.

[11] See Arak and Kreicher (1985), Boschen (1986), de Kock (1991), and Woodward (1988, 1990).

1, i_2 for period 2, and so on, then the nominal payment for period n is the stated payment times $(1 + i_1)(1 + i_2) \ldots (1 + i_n)$. Suppose a 20-year bond with a 5 percent stated interest rate is issued; for a par value of $100, the coupon is $5. The actual inflation rates during the next three years are 10 percent, 8 percent, and 7 percent. Then, the coupon payment in year three is $5(1.10)(1.08)(1.07) = $6.3558.

Attractions of Index-Linked Bonds

Index-linked bonds have several attractions. First, for retired persons on a fixed income, index-linked bonds provide a low-risk investment with inflation protection. Standard bonds do not provide the same type of inflation protection. Suppose that the interest rate on a standard bond is set by the market to be the real interest rate plus the expected inflation rate plus a risk premium for the uncertainty surrounding inflation. If inflation expectations are realized on average, fixed income investors earn the real interest rate plus a fair risk premium on average.

Unfortunately, in individual periods, the returns to fixed-income investors can be markedly affected by changes in inflationary expectations. Suppose we have an initial real interest rate of 5 percent, an expected inflation rate of 5 percent, and an inflation risk premium of 2 percent. The nominal interest rate on nonindexed bonds is 12.25 percent (that is, the real rate of 5 percent plus the inflation rate of 5 percent plus the product of the two rates plus the 2 percent inflation risk premium).[12] If inflationary expectations change because of new information, the prices of nonindexed bonds adjust and the realized return is affected. As an example, suppose inflation expectations increase from 5 percent to 10 percent, interest rates increase from 12.25 percent to 17.50 percent, and the realized returns for bond investors are reduced for the period in which inflation expectations rose. In general, realized returns on long-term bonds are significantly affected by changes in interest rates; long-term bonds can have negative returns when interest rates rise.

Index-linked bonds protect investors from the risks of changing inflationary expectations. Although the holder of an index-linked bond is compensated for realized inflation, indexation of bonds does not protect investors from changes in real interest rates.

---

[12] See chapter 2 on the determinants of interest rates.

Second, the issuer of index-linked bonds is protected from inflation risk. An issuer of nonindexed bonds loses if inflationary expectations drop after the bond is issued. In our previous example, the initial interest rate for standard bonds was 12.25 percent because the real interest rate was 5 percent, expected inflation was 5 percent, and the inflation premium was 2 percent. Suppose the expected inflation rate drops to zero. The nominal interest rate on newly issued bonds drops to 7 percent, but the bond issuer is forced to pay the contractually binding 12.25 percent coupon. The real burden of the debt for the issuer has risen.

Interest rates declined considerably from 1982 to 1992 in the U.S. at least partially because of lower inflation expectations. During the earlier part of this period, the U.S. government issued a great deal of debt at relatively high interest rates. The real burden of paying this debt is considerable, since actual inflation rates are lower than earlier expectations. Some economists believe this debt burden to be a contributory cause of lower economic growth in the U.S. during the 1990s.

Third, nonindexed bonds contain a premium for inflation risk. Inflation risk premiums are unnecessary with index-linked bonds. By issuing index-linked bonds, the issuer reduces interest costs.

The Problems with Index-Linked Debt

Currently, index-linked bonds do not exist in the U.S. and most other countries. Issuance of index-linked bonds is largely confined to British and Israeli government bonds. The lack of index-linked bonds results from the following problems.

Taxation of the indexed part of the return presents one problem. In the U.S., coupon interest is fully taxable; bond principal repayment is tax-free. If the coupon is indexed, the investor earns the inflation rate times one minus the tax rate, which is necessarily less than the inflation rate. If consumption costs rise by the inflation rate, the investor has a shortfall because of taxes.[13] A similar problem occurs with indexation of the principal. If the indexed amount is a capital gain, the investor loses in real terms. A remedy is to make the indexation tax-free.

---

[13] Chapter 2 on determinants of interest rates discussed the Darby effect. Darby argued that the proper inflation adjustment is the inflation rate divided by one minus the tax rate if the coupon interest is fully taxable.

Tax exemption for the indexation of coupons presents a further problem. Coupons on standard bonds are taxed. If inflationary expectations are included in the coupon of standard bonds and are grossed-up as suggested by Darby, there is an inconsistency between standard and index-linked bonds. A possible solution is to make indexation of principal tax-free, but make indexation of coupon taxable.

In the U.S., index-linked bonds present legal problems. The U.S. congress prohibited index-linked bonds from 1933–1977. Although this law was changed, index-linked bonds may violate the uniform commercial code and state usury laws and thus may not be feasible under current law.

Individual firms are reluctant to issue inflation-linked debt because the firm's inflation rate can differ from the inflation rate for the overall economy. For example, consider a firm issuing a bond linked to the overall price index. If the overall inflation rate is 10 percent but the firm's inflation rate is only 5 percent, the firm loses; it is required to pay 10 percent more interest, but its assets increase by only 5 percent in value. Issuing bonds tied to a broad inflation index increases the firm's risk unless the firm's inflation rate is highly correlated with the overall inflation rate.

Corporations are able to issue floating-rate bonds tied to a short-term interest rate. If the short-term interest rate is highly correlated with realized inflation rates, the firm is able to inflation-index the coupon, although not the principal. Thus, floating-rate bonds provide partial indexation protection.

Summary

This chapter discusses several specialized financial instruments which have low transactions costs or allow the trading of risks. Floating-rate securities have coupon rates tied to a particular short-term interest rate. The borrower bears the risk of changes in the short-term default-free interest rate.

Interest-rate swaps allow borrowers to trade debt obligations of different maturities. They may allow some firms to take advantage of relatively low borrowing rates. In some cases, swapping of debt obligations is cheaper than refinancing.

Convertible bonds are, in essence, a combination of a straight bond and a call option. Growing firms may be able to effectively sell common stock above the current market price by issuing convertibles.

Index-linked bonds do not exist in the U.S. However, introduction of these bonds has been widely discussed. The coupon and principal are adjusted for the realized inflation rate, protecting the bondholder from inflation.

Questions/Problems

1. Describe a floating-rate note. There are two components of an interest rate – changes in the general level of interest rates and changes in the default risk of a particular issuer. How do each of these affect the interest rate on floating-rate debt? How does a reset note differ from a floating-rate note?

2. Explain the reasons why firms might swap their debt obligations.

3. Describe the impact of changing interest rates upon the default risk of a swaps dealer.

4. What are the possible motivations behind issuing convertible bonds?

5. Describe the differences between preferred stock and bonds.

6. Index-linked bonds have several attractions. What are they?

7. What are the disadvantages of index-linked bonds?

References

Arak, M., A. Estrella, L. Goodman, and A. Silver, "Interest Rate Swaps: An Alternative Explanation," *Financial Management,* 17, Summer 1988, pp. 12–18.

Arak, M. and L. Kreicher, "The Real Rate of Interest: Inferences from the New U.K. Indexed Gilts," *International Economic Review,* 26, June 1985, pp. 399–408.

Asquith, P. and D. Mullins, "Convertible Debt: Corporate Call Policy and Voluntary Conversion," *Journal of Finance,* 46, 1991, pp. 1273–89.

Asquith, P., "Convertible Bonds Are Not Called Late," *Journal of Finance,* 50, September 1995, pp. 1275–1289.

Bicksler, J. and A. H. Chen, "An Economic Analysis of Interest Rate Swaps," *Journal of Finance,* 41, July 1986, pp. 645–55.

Boschen, J. F., "The Information Content of Indexed Bonds," *Journal of Money, Credit and Banking,* 18, February 1986, pp. 76–87.

Brennan, M. and E. Schwartz, "Convertible Bonds: Valuation, and Optimal Strategies of Call and Conversion," *Journal of Finance,* 32, 1977, pp. 1699–715.

Brennan, M. and E. Schwartz, "The Case for Convertibles," *The Continental Bank's Journal of Applied Corporate Finance,* 1988.

Brigham, E. F., "An Analysis of Convertible Debentures: Theory and Some Empirical Evidence," *Journal of Finance,* 21, 1966, pp. 35–54.

Brown, K. C. and D. J. Smith, "Forward Swaps, Swap Options, and the Management of Callable Debt," *Journal of Applied Corporate Finance,* 2, Winter 1990, pp. 59–71.

Campbell, C., L. Ederington, and P. Vankudre, "Sample-Selection Bias, Tax Shields, and the Information Content of Conversion-Forcing Bond Calls," *Journal of Finance,* 46, 1991, pp. 1291–324.

Crabbe, L. E., and J. D. Argilagos, "Anatomy of the Structured Note Market," *Journal of Applied Corporate Finance,* 7, Fall 1994, pp. 85–98.

Dann, L. and W. Mikkelson, "Convertible Debt Issuance, Capital Structure Change, and Financial-Related Information: Some New Evidence," *Journal of Financial Economics,* 13, 1984, pp. 157–86.

de Kock, G., "Expected Inflation and Real Interest Rates Based on Index-Linked Bond Prices: The U.K. Experience," Federal Reserve Bank of New York, *Quarterly Review,* 16, Autumn 1991, pp. 47–60.

Felgran, S. D., "Interest Rate Swaps: Use, Risk, and Prices," Federal Reserve Bank of Boston, *New England Economic Review,* November/December 1987, pp. 22–32.

Finnerty, J. D., "Financial Engineering in Corporate Finance: An Overview," *Financial Management,* 17, Winter 1988, pp. 14–31.

Finnerty, J. D., "An Overview of Corporate Securities Innovation," *Journal of Applied Corporate Finance,* 4, Winter 1992, pp. 23–39.

Goodman, L. S., "The Uses of Interest Rate Swaps in Managing Corporate Liabilities," *Journal of Applied Corporate Finance,* 2, Winter 1990, pp. 35–47.

Green, R. C., "Investment Incentives, Debt, and Warrants," *Journal of Financial Economics,* 13, 1984, pp. 115–36.

Harris, M. and A. Raviv, "A Sequential Signalling Model of Convertible Debt Call Policy," *Journal of Finance,* 40, 1985, pp. 1263–81.

Ingersoll, J., "An Examination of Corporate Call Policies on Convertible Securities," *Journal of Finance,* 32, 1977, pp. 463–78.

Jaffee, D. and A. Shleifer, "Costs of Financial Distress, Delayed Calls of Convertible Bonds, and the Role of Investment Banks," *Journal of Business,* 63, 1990, pp. S107–S123.

Kolb, R. W., *Futures, Options, and Swaps,* Miami: Kolb Publishing, 1994.

Marshall, J. F. and K. R. Kapner, *Understanding Swap Finance,* Cincinnati, OH: South-Western Publishing, 1990.

McConnell, J. J., and E. S. Schwartz, "The Origin of LYONs: A Case Study in Financial Innovation," *Journal of Applied Corporate Finance,* 4, Winter 1992, pp. 40–47.

Ofer, A. and A. Natarajan, "Convertible Call Policies: An Empirical Analysis of an Information-Signalling Hypothesis," *Journal of Financial Economics,* 19, 1987, pp. 91–108.

Singh, A., N. Nayar, and A. Cowan, "Underwritten Calls of Convertible Bonds," *Journal of Financial Economics,* 29, 1991, pp. 173–96.

Turnbull, S. M., "Swaps: A Zero Sum Game?" *Financial Management,* 16, Spring 1987, pp. 15–21.

Van Horne, J. C., "Of Financial Innovations and Excesses," *Journal of Finance,* 40, July 1985, pp. 621–31.

Wall, L. D. and J. J. Pringle, "Interest Rate Swaps: A Review of the Issues," Federal Reserve Bank of Atlanta, *Economic Review,* 73, November/December 1988, pp. 22–40.

Woodward, G. T., "Comment: 'The Real Rate of Interest: Inferences from the New U.K. Indexed Gilts,' " *International Economic Review*, 29, August 1988, pp. 565–8.

Woodward, G. T., "A Dynamic Profile of the Term Structure of Real Interest Rates and Inflation Expectations in the United Kingdom 1982–89," *Journal of Business*, 63, July 1990, pp. 373–98.

PRESENT VALUE OF AN ANNUITY OF $1

	1%	2%	3%	4%	5%	6%	7%	8%	9%	10%	12%	14%
1	0.9901	0.9804	0.9709	0.9615	0.9524	0.9434	0.9346	0.9259	0.9174	0.9091	0.8929	0.8772
2	1.9704	1.9416	1.9135	1.8861	1.8594	1.8334	1.8080	1.7833	1.7591	1.7355	1.6901	1.6467
3	2.9410	2.8839	2.8286	2.7751	2.7232	2.6730	2.6243	2.5771	2.5313	2.4869	2.4018	2.3216
4	3.9020	3.8077	3.7171	3.6299	3.5460	3.4651	3.3872	3.3121	3.2397	3.1699	3.0373	2.9137
5	4.8534	4.7135	4.5797	4.4518	4.3295	4.2124	4.1002	3.9927	3.8897	3.7908	3.6048	3.4331
6	5.7955	5.6014	5.4172	5.2421	5.0757	4.9173	4.7665	4.6229	4.4859	4.3553	4.1114	3.8887
7	6.7282	6.4720	6.2303	6.0021	5.7864	5.5824	5.3893	5.2064	5.0330	4.8684	4.5638	4.2883
8	7.6517	7.3255	7.0197	6.7327	6.4632	6.2098	5.9713	5.7466	5.5348	5.3349	4.9676	4.6389
9	8.5660	8.1622	7.7861	7.4353	7.1078	6.8017	6.5152	6.2469	5.9952	5.7590	5.3282	4.9464
10	9.4713	8.9826	8.5302	8.1109	7.7217	7.3601	7.0236	6.7101	6.4177	6.1446	5.6502	5.2161
11	10.3676	9.7868	9.2526	8.7605	8.3064	7.8869	7.4987	7.1390	6.8052	6.4951	5.9377	5.4527
12	11.2551	10.5753	9.9540	9.3851	8.8633	8.3838	7.9427	7.5361	7.1607	6.8137	6.1944	5.6603
13	12.1337	11.3484	10.6350	9.9856	9.3936	8.8527	8.3577	7.9038	7.4869	7.1034	6.4235	5.8424
14	13.0037	12.1062	11.2961	10.5631	9.8986	9.2950	8.7455	8.2442	7.7862	7.3667	6.6282	6.0021
15	13.8651	12.8493	11.9379	11.1184	10.3797	9.7122	9.1079	8.5595	8.0607	7.6061	6.8109	6.1422
16	14.7179	13.5777	12.5611	11.6523	10.8378	10.1059	9.4466	8.8514	8.3126	7.8237	6.9740	6.2651
17	15.5623	14.2919	13.1661	12.1657	11.2741	10.4773	9.7632	9.1216	8.5436	8.0216	7.1196	6.3729
18	16.3983	14.9920	13.7535	12.6593	11.6896	10.8276	10.0591	9.3719	8.7556	8.2014	7.2497	6.4674
19	17.2260	15.6785	14.3238	13.1339	12.0853	11.1581	10.3356	9.6036	8.9501	8.3649	7.3658	6.5504
20	18.0456	16.3514	14.8775	13.5903	12.4622	11.4699	10.5940	9.8181	9.1285	8.5136	7.4694	6.6231
21	18.8570	17.0112	15.4150	14.0292	12.8212	11.7641	10.8355	10.0168	9.2922	8.6487	7.5620	6.6870
22	19.6604	17.6580	15.9369	14.4511	13.1630	12.0416	11.0612	10.2007	9.4424	8.7715	7.6446	6.7429
23	20.4558	18.2922	16.4436	14.8568	13.4886	12.3034	11.2722	10.3711	9.5802	8.8832	7.7184	6.7921
24	21.2434	18.9139	16.9355	15.2470	13.7986	12.5504	11.4693	10.5288	9.7066	8.9847	7.7843	6.8351
25	22.0232	19.5235	17.4131	15.6221	14.0939	12.7834	11.6536	10.6748	9.8226	9.0770	7.8431	6.8729
26	22.7952	20.1210	17.8768	15.9828	14.3752	13.0032	11.8258	10.8100	9.9290	9.1609	7.8957	6.9061
27	23.5596	20.7069	18.3270	16.3296	14.6430	13.2105	11.9867	10.9352	10.0266	9.2372	7.9426	6.9352
28	24.3164	21.2813	18.7641	16.6631	14.8981	13.4062	12.1371	11.0511	10.1161	9.3066	7.9844	6.9607
29	25.0658	21.8444	19.1885	16.9837	15.1411	13.5907	12.2777	11.1584	10.1983	9.3696	8.0218	6.9830
30	25.8077	22.3965	19.6004	17.2920	15.3725	13.7648	12.4090	11.2578	10.2737	9.4269	8.0552	7.0027

550

PRESENT VALUE OF $1

	1%	2%	3%	4%	5%	6%	7%	8%	9%	10%	12%	14%
1	0.9901	0.9804	0.9709	0.9615	0.9524	0.9434	0.9346	0.9259	0.9174	0.9091	0.8929	0.8772
2	0.9803	0.9612	0.9426	0.9246	0.9070	0.8900	0.8734	0.8573	0.8417	0.8264	0.7972	0.7695
3	0.9706	0.9423	0.9151	0.8890	0.8638	0.8396	0.8163	0.7938	0.7722	0.7513	0.7118	0.6750
4	0.9610	0.9238	0.8885	0.8548	0.8227	0.7921	0.7629	0.7350	0.7084	0.6830	0.6355	0.5921
5	0.9515	0.9057	0.8626	0.8219	0.7835	0.7473	0.7130	0.6806	0.6499	0.6209	0.5674	0.5194
6	0.9420	0.8880	0.8375	0.7903	0.7462	0.7050	0.6663	0.6302	0.5963	0.5645	0.5066	0.4556
7	0.9327	0.8706	0.8131	0.7599	0.7107	0.6651	0.6227	0.5835	0.5470	0.5132	0.4523	0.3996
8	0.9235	0.8535	0.7894	0.7307	0.6768	0.6274	0.5820	0.5403	0.5019	0.4665	0.4039	0.3506
9	0.9143	0.8368	0.7664	0.7026	0.6446	0.5919	0.5439	0.5002	0.4604	0.4241	0.3606	0.3075
10	0.9053	0.8203	0.7441	0.6756	0.6139	0.5584	0.5083	0.4632	0.4224	0.3855	0.3220	0.2697
11	0.8963	0.8043	0.7224	0.6496	0.5847	0.5268	0.4751	0.4289	0.3875	0.3505	0.2875	0.2366
12	0.8874	0.7885	0.7014	0.6246	0.5568	0.4970	0.4440	0.3971	0.3555	0.3186	0.2567	0.2076
13	0.8787	0.7730	0.6810	0.6006	0.5303	0.4688	0.4150	0.3677	0.3262	0.2897	0.2292	0.1821
14	0.8700	0.7579	0.6611	0.5775	0.5051	0.4423	0.3878	0.3405	0.2992	0.2633	0.2046	0.1597
15	0.8613	0.7430	0.6419	0.5553	0.4810	0.4173	0.3624	0.3152	0.2745	0.2394	0.1827	0.1401
16	0.8528	0.7284	0.6232	0.5339	0.4581	0.3936	0.3387	0.2919	0.2519	0.2176	0.1631	0.1229
17	0.8444	0.7142	0.6050	0.5134	0.4363	0.3714	0.3166	0.2703	0.2311	0.1978	0.1456	0.1078
18	0.8360	0.7002	0.5874	0.4936	0.4155	0.3503	0.2959	0.2502	0.2120	0.1799	0.1300	0.0946
19	0.8277	0.6864	0.5703	0.4746	0.3957	0.3305	0.2765	0.2317	0.1945	0.1635	0.1161	0.0829
20	0.8195	0.6730	0.5537	0.4564	0.3769	0.3118	0.2584	0.2145	0.1784	0.1486	0.1037	0.0728
21	0.8114	0.6598	0.5375	0.4388	0.3589	0.2942	0.2415	0.1987	0.1637	0.1351	0.0926	0.0638
22	0.8034	0.6468	0.5219	0.4220	0.3418	0.2775	0.2257	0.1839	0.1502	0.1228	0.0826	0.0560
23	0.7954	0.6342	0.5067	0.4057	0.3256	0.2618	0.2109	0.1703	0.1378	0.1117	0.0738	0.0491
24	0.7876	0.6217	0.4919	0.3901	0.3101	0.2470	0.1971	0.1577	0.1264	0.1015	0.0659	0.0431
25	0.7798	0.6095	0.4776	0.3751	0.2953	0.2330	0.1842	0.1460	0.1160	0.0923	0.0588	0.0378
26	0.7720	0.5976	0.4637	0.3607	0.2812	0.2198	0.1722	0.1352	0.1064	0.0839	0.0525	0.0331
27	0.7644	0.5859	0.4502	0.3468	0.2678	0.2074	0.1609	0.1252	0.0976	0.0763	0.0469	0.0291
28	0.7568	0.5744	0.4371	0.3335	0.2551	0.1956	0.1504	0.1159	0.0895	0.0693	0.0419	0.0255
29	0.7493	0.5631	0.4243	0.3207	0.2429	0.1846	0.1406	0.1073	0.0822	0.0630	0.0374	0.0224
30	0.7419	0.5521	0.4120	0.3083	0.2314	0.1741	0.1314	0.0994	0.0754	0.0573	0.0334	0.0196

Index